Norbert E. Fuchs (Ed.)

Logic Program Synthesis and Transformation

7th International Workshop, LOPSTR'97
Leuven, Belgium, July 10-12, 1997
Proceedings

Springer

Series Editors

Gerhard Goos, Karlsruhe University, Germany
Juris Hartmanis, Cornell University, NY, USA
Jan van Leeuwen, Utrecht University, The Netherlands

Volume Editor

Norbert E. Fuchs
University of Zurich, Department of Computer Science
CH-8057 Zurich, Switzerland
E-mail: fuchs@ifi.unizh.ch

Cataloging-in-Publication data applied for

Die Deutsche Bibliothek - CIP-Einheitsaufnahme

Logic program synthesis and transformation : 7th international
workshop ; proceedings / LOPSTR '97, Leuven, Belgium, July 10 -
12, 1997. Norbert E. Fuchs (ed.). - Berlin ; Heidelberg ; New York ;
Barcelona ; Budapest ; Hong Kong ; London ; Milan ; Paris ;
Singapore ; Tokyo : Springer, 1998
  (Lecture notes in computer science ; Vol. 1463)
  ISBN 3-540-65074-1

CR Subject Classification (1991): D.1.2, I.2.2, D.1.6, F.4.1, F.3.1

ISSN 0302-9743
ISBN 3-540-65074-1 Springer-Verlag Berlin Heidelberg New York

© Springer-Verlag Berlin Heidelberg 1998
Printed in Germany

Typesetting: Camera-ready by author
SPIN 10638423   06/3142 – 5 4 3 2 1 0   Printed on acid-free paper

Lecture Notes in Computer Science   1463

Edited by G. Goos, J. Hartmanis and J. van Leeuwen

Springer

Berlin
Heidelberg
New York
Barcelona
Budapest
Hong Kong
London
Milan
Paris
Singapore
Tokyo

Preface

This volume contains the papers from the Seventh International Workshop on Logic Program Synthesis and Transformation, LOPSTR '97, that took place in Leuven, Belgium, on July 10–12, 1997, 'back-to-back' with the Fourteenth International Conference on Logic Programming, ICLP '97. Both ICLP and LOPSTR were organised by the K.U. Leuven Department of Computer Science. LOPSTR '97 was sponsored by Compulog Net and by the Flanders Research Network on Declarative Methods in Computer Science. LOPSTR '97 had 39 participants from 13 countries.

There were two invited talks by Wolfgang Bibel (Darmstadt) on 'A multi-level approach to program synthesis', and by Henning Christiansen (Roskilde) on 'Implicit program synthesis by a reversible metainterpreter'. Extended versions of both talks appear in this volume.

There were 19 technical papers accepted for presentation at LOPSTR '97, out of 33 submissions. Of these, 15 appear in extended versions in this volume. Their topics range over the fields of program synthesis, program transformation, program analysis, tabling, metaprogramming, and inductive logic programming.

My thanks go to the workshop co-chairs and local organisers, Bart Demoen and Gerda Janssens, and to their team for efficiently organising the event and for preparing the preliminary proceedings. I wish to thank the members of the LOPSTR '97 program committee and the referees for their prompt and thorough work. I am grateful to the program chairman of LOPSTR'96, John Gallagher, for his helpful advice. LOPSTR '97 received sponsorship from Compulog Net and from the Flanders Research Network on Declarative Methods in Computer Science which is gratefully acknowledged. Furthermore, I would like to thank Maurice Bruynooghe and David Pearce for their help. Finally, thanks to Uta Schwertel who assisted in preparing these proceedings.

June 1998   Norbert E. Fuchs

Program Committee

Pierre Flener   (Bilkent, pf@cs.bilkent.edu.tr)
Norbert E. Fuchs (chair) (Zurich, fuchs@ifi.unizh.ch)
Tim Gegg-Harrison   (Winona, TSG@VAX2.Winona.MSUS.EDU)
Andreas Hamfelt   (Uppsala, hamfelt@csd.uu.se)
Pat Hill   (Leeds, hill@scs.leeds.ac.uk)
Christoph Kreitz   (Cornell, kreitz@cs.cornell.edu)
Kung-Kiu Lau   (Manchester, kung-kiu@cs.man.ac.uk)
Bern Martens   (Leuven, bern@cs.kuleuven.ac.be)
Ulf Nilsson   (Linkoeping, ulfni@ida.liu.se)
Alberto Pettorossi   (Roma, adp@iasi.rm.cnr.it)
Leon Sterling   (Melbourne,leon@cs.mu.oz.au)

Workshop Co-Chairs and Local Organizers

Bart Demoen   (Leuven, bmd@cs.kuleuven.ac.be)
Gerda Janssens   (Leuven, gerda@cs.kuleuven.ac.be)

Sponsors of LOPSTR'97

European Commission – Compulog Net
Flanders Research Network on Declarative Methods in Computer Science

List of Referees

The following people helped the Program Committee to referee the invited and submitted papers:
Roberto Bagnara, Hendrik Blockeel, Antony Bowers, Halime Büyükyildiz, Baudouin Le Charlier, Nicoletta Cocco, Stefaan Decorte, Dirk Dussart, Laurent Fribourg, Andrew Heaton, Andy King, Michael Leuschel, Jonathan Martin, Maurizio Proietti, Luc De Raedt, Sophie Renault, Jacques Riche, Konstantinos Sagonas, Aida Vitoria, Geraint Wiggins, Serap Yilmaz

Contents

X   Contents

A Multi-level Approach to Program Synthesis

W. Bibel[1], D. Korn[1], C. Kreitz[2], F. Kurucz[1], J. Otten[2], S. Schmitt[1], and
G. Stolpmann[1]

[1] Fachgebiet Intellektik, Fachbereich Informatik, Darmstadt University of Technology
Alexanderstr. 10, 64283 Darmstadt, Germany
[2] Department of Computer Science, Cornell University, Ithaca, NY 14853, USA

Abstract. We present an approach to a coherent program synthesis system which integrates a variety of interactively controlled and automated techniques from theorem proving and algorithm design at different levels of abstraction. Besides providing an overall view we summarize the individual research results achieved in the course of this development.

1 Introduction

The development of programs from formal specifications is an activity which requires logical reasoning on various levels of abstraction. The design of the program's overall structure involves reasoning about data and program structures. Inductive reasoning is necessary for determining a program's behavior on finite, but non-atomic data such as lists, arrays, queues, and sometimes even natural numbers. First-order reasoning is required to analyze the order of steps which are necessary to achieve a desired result. Propositional reasoning is used to make sure that all the formal details are correctly arranged.

Program synthesis and transformation is therefore strongly related to the concept of proofs. This has been particularly emphasized by the development of languages and tools for logic programming which use deductive techniques for the simulation of mathematical reasoning as their basic execution model.

In the field of Automated Theorem Proving (ATP) deductive systems have been developed for many of the above-mentioned areas. Each of these systems is tailored towards a particular style of reasoning but shows weaknesses outside its specific area. There is no single automated proof procedure which can handle all the reasoning problems occurring during program synthesis equally well and because of the very nature of the problem it is not very likely that there will ever be one. Instead, it is more meaningful to combine the strengths of the individual proof procedures by integrating them into a single reasoning system which can perform reasoning at all the above-mentioned levels of abstraction.

During the last few years the Intellectics Laboratory of Darmstadt Institute of Technology has been active in the development of such an integrated, application-oriented ATP-system which can serve as an inference engine of a coherent program synthesis system. For this purpose we have developed specialized proof procedures which deal with problem formalizations on the propositional, (constructive) first-order, inductive, and higher levels. On the other hand we

Norbert E. Fuchs (Ed.): LOPSTR'97, LNCS 1463, pp. 1–27, 1998.

have generated interfaces for each of these procedures which make it possible to present the generated proof in a common logical calculus. The resulting multi-level synthesis system, called MAPS, can extract individual proof tasks from a given programming problem, delegate them to specialized proof procedures, and combine the resulting proofs into a solution of the original problem. In addition to that it will be able to proceed interactively whenever none of the proof procedures can handle the task automatically.

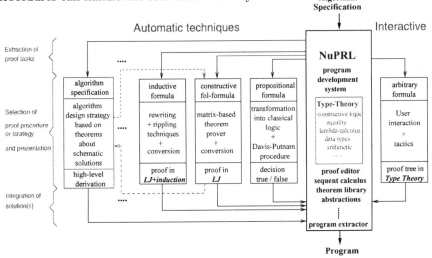

Fig. 1. Structure of the MAPS program synthesis system

The conceptual structure of MAPS is illustrated in Fig. 1. It shows on the left hand side automatic proof procedures for different levels of reasoning, viz. propositional, first-order, and inductive reasoning as well as high-level algorithm design strategies. Each of these procedures will receive proof tasks from a program development system, indicated by the horizontal arrows on top, which were extracted from a given synthesis problem. After solving their tasks the proof procedures will send their solution to a conversion module. This module will generate a representation of the solution in the common calculus and return it to the program development system (horizontal arrows on the bottom level). The dotted arrows indicate that the high-level strategies will ideally create subtasks which can be handled by the lower-level procedures immediately. If none of the available proof procedures suits the proof task to be solved the program development system will have to rely on user interaction (right hand side).

As common platform for our work we have chosen the NuPRL proof development system [10] since its underlying logical calculus can deal with a rich variety of problems from mathematics and programming and allows to formalize even high-level strategies in a natural way. Since it is based on the proofs-as-programs paradigm to program synthesis [2] it allows to treat algorithm design strategies as proof procedures and to integrate a great variety of reasoning techniques on all levels of abstraction. Finally it supports interaction with a human expert (programmer) whenever the automated strategies turn out to be too weak.

All our automated proof procedures were originally developed independently from the common platform and we had to provide techniques for integrating them into the top-down sequent proof style of NuPRL.

- Formulas from propositional intuitionistic logic will be decided by translating them into classical logic [17] and applying a non-normal form Davis-Putnam procedure [28]. This procedure will be embedded as trusted refiner which creates a sequent proof on demand.
- Matrix methods for constructive first-order logic use a non-clausal extension of the connection method [4,30]. They have been combined with an algorithm for translating matrix proofs into sequent proofs [36] and integrated into NuPRL as a proof tactic [22].
- Inductive proofs will be generated by proof planners involving rippling [9] and rewrite techniques. Sequences of rewrite steps will be transformed into applications of cut- and substitution rules while other techniques will determine the parameters of the general induction rule [25,23].
- High-level synthesis strategies will be integrated by verifying formal theorems about schematic program construction [18,19]. For each strategy a theorem describing the axioms for the correctness of a particular class of algorithms will serve as derived inference rule. It will be accompanied by specialized tactics for determining and validating values for its parameters [43]. This technique heavily relies on verified domain knowledge [42] but is very effective.

The MAPS enterprise may be seen as a milestone in the long tradition of program synthesis efforts of our group which started as early as 1974 eventually leading to the program system LOPS (see [6] for a detailed exposition of this development). In lack of powerful proof systems at that time the emphasis then was laid on high-level strategies guiding the synthesis (or search for a proof) while in MAPS it is laid more on the proof obligations resulting in the synthesis task. The present paper considerably extends the preliminary outline of the concepts underlying MAPS given in [8] and presents the results achieved in the meantime.

In the following we shall describe our proof methods and their integration into the NuPRL program development system. In Section 2 we shall discuss proof procedures for intuitionistic propositional and first-order logic while Section 3 describes the integration of rewriting techniques for inductive theorem proving. Section 4 deals with higher-level synthesis strategies, particularly with algorithm design strategies based on schematic solutions for certain classes of algorithms. We conclude with an outlook to future work.

2 Integrating Theorem Provers for First Order Logic

In this section we will give a survey on automated proof search procedures we have developed for the first-order and propositional fragment of intuitionistic logic. Furthermore we shall briefly discuss how to integrate the proofs constructed by these procedures into the NuPRL environment.

2.1   Decision Procedures for Intuitionistic Propositional Logic

The intuitionistic validity of propositional formulas could in principle be investigated by first-order proof procedures. Nevertheless there are good reasons to develop methods tailored to the specific properties of propositional logic:

1. first-order methods usually fail to detect the invalidity of a propositional formula
2. the technical overhead necessary to deal with quantifiers can be skipped if the formula under consideration is propositional only
3. in many cases all that is asked about a propositional formula can essentially be answered by "yes" or "no" instead of an actual proof construction

In classical logic these insights have led to decision procedures like the Davis-Putnam procedure which currently is about the most efficient complete proof method for propositional classical logic. Unfortunately, attempting to adopt this technique into intuitionistic propositional logic leads to serious difficulties:

- the existing Davis-Putnam procedures are defined for formulas in clausal form only whereas there is no clausal form for intuitionistic formulas
- the essential idea of the Davis-Putnam procedures is a successive application of the law of the excluded middle which does not hold in intuitionistic logic

In this section we present two techniques we have developed in order to overcome both difficulties: a translation method from intuitionistic into classical propositional logic as well as a non-clausal Davis-Putnam procedure.

Translating Intuitionistic into Classical Propositional Formulas.   A natural approach to deal with intuitionistic validity is to formalize the conditions for intuitionistic forcing within classical first-order logic. $A \Rightarrow B$, for instance, would be translated into $\forall v.(wRv \Rightarrow A(v) \Rightarrow B(v))$ where w denotes the current possible world. For the sake of completeness axioms encoding the properties of the accessibility relation R will be added which then must imply the translated formula. This technique is known as the *relational translation* [26,27,3].

A major difficulty of this approach is the potential undecidability of the resulting classical formula. On the other hand, any intuitionistic non-theorem has a *finite* countermodel. This means that only finitely many possible worlds need to be considered and that one could use finite conjunctions instead of having to quantify over all possible worlds. Our aim therefore was to find a sufficiently effective mechanism for constructing such finite potential countermodels. To this end we have investigated the reasons which lead to infinite countermodels as described in the following.

Essentially a potential countermodel can be extended by a new possible world in two cases which both yield important conditions for adding any further possible worlds. If these conditions are not considered then infinitely many worlds without "new" properties could successively be added to the countermodel:

The first case occurs when an implicative formula $A \Rightarrow B$ is assumed not to be forced at a given possible world w_0. In this case we have to assume an accessible

world w_1 where A is forced but B is not according to
the Kripke-semantics for intuitionistic logic. This countermodel is shown in the right figure. Note, however, that
A will remain forced at any world w_i accessible from w_1.

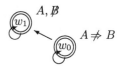

Thus if we encounter the case that $A \Rightarrow X$ is assumed not to be forced at such
a w_i then, in order to obtain a world accessible from w_i where A is forced but
X is not, we only need to ensure X not to be forced at w_i which is accessible from
itself by reflexivity. The respective situation is shown to the
right. Hence, once we have added a world to our countermodel refuting some $A \Rightarrow B$ it is not necessary anymore to
add another world accessible from there in order to refute $A \Rightarrow X$ for some X.

Likewise, the second case occurs when refuting a negated formula $\neg A$ at a
given world w_0. In this case we need to provide another accessible world w_1 where
A is forced. This situation is again shown in the right figure.
Once we have done so, however, there is no need to add *any*
other accessible world from there on. To see why, we need the
notion of *F-maximality* of a given world for a given proposi-
tional formula F. We consider a given possible world F-maximal iff no accessible
world forces some subformula of F which is yet unforced at the given world. One
can easily show that for any world w and any propositional formula F there
always is an accessible F-maximal world $\max_F(w)$ (cf. [17]). Once we have (potentially) added w_1 to our countermodel as shown above we know that there
must also be an F-maximal $\max_F(w_1)$ accessible from w_1, where F is the input
formula of our translation. But then A is also forced at $\max_F(w_1)$ and we can
well add $\max_F(w_1)$ to our countermodel instead of w_1. The main advantage of
doing so is that whenever we would have to add a new world to our countermodel
accessible from $\max_F(w_1)$ in order to force some subformula F' of F we know
that F' must already be forced at $\max_F(w_1)$. Thus instead of actually adding
this accessible world we can simply add its properties to $\max_F(w_1)$.

Obeying both restrictions for adding new worlds during the inductive construction of a potential countermodel for a propositional formula F will always
lead to a finite set of possible worlds within this countermodel since F has only
finitely many subformulas. To encode a potential intuitionistic countermodel for
a given input formula F we first associate a unique function symbol w_i with
each positive occurrence of an implicative or negated subformula in F. Then we
construct a set W of terms by applying a proper choice of concatenations of the
w_i to the root possible world w_0. The order of the w_i within these concatenations essentially reflects the possible refutation orderings between the associated
subformulas. No function symbol will occur more than once within a single concatenation and function symbols associated with negated subformulas will only
occur as the outermost symbol of a concatenation.

Given a term $t \in W$, which now denotes a particular possible world within
a potential countermodel, the finite set $R_F(t)$ of accessible worlds will then be
the set of those terms $t' \in W$ which contain t as a subterm. We can now essentially apply the usual relational translation approach to F. However, instead

of positive occurrences of universal quantifications over accessible worlds we use an appropriate such term as a representative for an arbitrary accessible world. Negatively occuring quantifications are replaced by finite conjunctions over all such terms denoting an accessible world. For any further details cf. [17].

To sum up we have achieved a morphism from intuitionistic to classical logic that maps propositional input formulas to propositional output formulas (note that no quantifiers or uninstantiated terms occur in the output formula).

A Non-clausal Davis-Putnam Proof Procedure. The Davis-Putnam procedure [11,12] is one of the most successful proof procedures for classical propositional logic. Its essential idea is to apply the following *splitting rule* to prove a formula F: assign the truth values *true* and *false* to a selected propositional variable X occurring in F and simplify the resulting formulas, yielding F_1 and F_2. This rule is applied recursively to the formulas F_1 and F_2 until the truth values *true* or *false* are reached. The investigated formula F is valid if all leaves of the resulting proof tree are marked with *true*, otherwise F is not valid.

Unfortunately the original formulation of the Davis-Putnam procedure and all existing implementations require the formula F in clausal form, i.e. in disjunctive normal form. The usual translation of a given formula into this form is based on the application of distributivity laws. In the worst case this will lead to an exponential increase of the resulting formula. The application of the so-called *definitional translation* [33] yields (at most) a quadratic increase of the resulting formula's size at the expense of introducing new propositional variables.

The translation of intuitionistic into classical propositional formulas described above leads to formulas which are strongly in non-normal form. Experimental results have shown that a translation to clausal form often yields formulas which are too large to obtain a proof, in particular if applying the standard translation techniques. To avoid any translation steps to clausal form we have developed a non-clausal proof procedure [29]. It is a generalization of the original clausal Davis-Putnam procedure and operates directly on arbitrary propositional formulas. To this end we represent formulas by nested matrices. A *matrix* is a very compact representation of a formula and the corresponding search space (see also section 2.2). In the clausal Davis-Putnam procedure we regard a matrix as a set of clauses where each clause is a set of literals. In our non-clausal approach a clause is a set of matrices and a matrix is either a literal or a set of clauses.

In the original Davis-Putnam procedure the above-mentioned splitting rule consists of a *clause elimination step* and a *literal deletion step*. Due to the more generalized treatment of arbitrary formulas the non-clausal splitting rule uses a *matrix elimination step* instead of the literal deletion step. In contrast to the latter it will delete a whole matrix, not only a single literal. Furthermore in the non-clausal approach an additional splitting rule, called *beta splitting rule*, is applicable. Our experimental results have shown three advantages of our non-clausal proof procedure: no translation to any clausal form is required, the application of a more general matrix elimination step is possible and an additional beta splitting rule is applicable which can shorten proofs considerably.

In practice, our translation from intuitionistic into classical logic combined with the Davis-Putnam procedure described above has turned out to be a very promising approach to deal with propositional intuitionistic logic. Already our prototypic implementations of both approaches in Prolog were able to decide the intuitionistic validity of a variety of propositional formulas with a performance competitive to any intuitionistic decision mechanism known to us.

2.2   Proof Construction in Intuitionistic First-Order Logic

The connection method is a well-known proof procedure for classical first-order logic and has successfully been realized in theorem provers like Setheo [24] or KoMeT [7]. It is based on a *matrix characterization* of logical validity: *A formula F is (classically) valid iff the matrix of F is (classically) complementary* [4,5].

In *propositional* classical logic the matrix of a formula F is *complementary* if there is a spanning set $\mathcal{C}$ of connections for F. A *connection* is a pair of atomic formulas with the same predicate symbol but different polarities.[1] A connection corresponds to an *axiom* in the sequent calculus. A set of connections $\mathcal{C}$ *spans* a formula F if every path through F contains at least one connection from $\mathcal{C}$. With regard to a sequent calculus this means that all branches are closed by an axiom. A *path* through F contains the atoms on a horizontal path through the matrix representation of F. A *matrix* of a formula F is a compact representation of F and the corresponding search space. This characterization also applies to classical *first-order* logic if each connection in $\mathcal{C}$ is complementary, i.e. the terms of each connection in $\mathcal{C}$ can be made identical by some *first-order substitution* σ_Q in which (quantifier-)variables are replaced by terms.

Certain rules in the intuitionistic sequent calculus $\mathcal{LJ}$ differ from the classical $\mathcal{LK}$ [14]. The arising non-permutabilities between these rules need a special treatment. In the matrix characterization for *intuitionistic* logic [44] this is done by an additional *intuitionistic substitution* σ_J. This substitution has to make the prefixes of each connection identical and therewith complementary. A *prefix* of an atom is a string consisting of variables and constants which essentially describes the position of it in the tree representation of the formula to be proved.

Example 1. Consider $F_1 \equiv (Pa \Rightarrow \neg\neg\exists x Px)$. The prefixes of the atomic formulas Pa and Px are $a_0 A_1$ and $a_0 a_2 A_3 a_4$, respectively, where capital letters refer to variables and small letters indicate constants. The set $\{Pa, Px\}$ is a connection. It is complementary under the first-order substitution $\sigma_Q = \{x \backslash a\}$ and the intuitionistic substitution $\sigma_J = \{A_1 \backslash a_2 A_3 a_4\}$. Since the set $\mathcal{C} = \{\{Pa, Px\}\}$ spans F_1, the formula F_1 is intuitionistically valid.

Example 2. Let $F_2 \equiv (\neg\neg P \Rightarrow P)$. The prefixes of the two atoms $a_0 A_1 a_2 A_3$ and $a_0 a_4$ are not unifiable. Therefore the formula F_2 is *not* intuitionistically valid.

According to the above matrix characterization the validity of a formula F can be proved by showing that all paths through the matrix representation

---

[1] The *polarity* of an atomic formula is either 0 or 1 and indicates whether it would occur negated (polarity 1) in the negational normal form or not (polarity 0).

of F contain a complementary connection. Therefore for an automated proof search procedure based on a matrix characterization we have to (1) search for a spanning set of connections and (2) test the connections for complementarity.

Developing a proof procedure for *intuitionistic* first-order logic based on Wallen's matrix characterization means extending Bibel's connection method accordingly. It consists of an algorithm which checks the complementarity of all paths and uses an additional string-unification procedure to unify the prefixes.

Searching for a Spanning Set of Connections. Proof search is done by a general path checking algorithm which is driven by connections instead of logical connectives [30,32]. Once a complementary connection has been identified all paths containing this connection are deleted. This is similar to Bibel's connection method for classical logic but without necessity for transforming the given formula to normal form. Dealing with arbitrary formulas is necessary since there is no clausal form in intuitionistic logic. The advantage of such a method is that the emphasis on *connections* drastically reduces the search space compared to calculi which are *connective*-driven such as the sequent calculus or tableau calculi. Furthermore it avoids the notational redundancy contained in these calculi.

Testing the Connections for Complementarity. In our path checking procedure we have to ensure that after adding a connection there are still first-order and intuitionistic substitutions which make all connections complementary. While the first-order substitution σ_Q can be computed by well-known *term*-unification algorithms we had to develop a specialized *prefix*-unification procedure for computing σ_J. This is done by a specialized algorithm for string-unification [31]. String-unification in general is quite complicated but unifying prefixes is much easier since there are certain restrictions on prefixes: prefixes are strings without duplicates and in two prefixes (corresponding to atoms of the same formula) equal characters can only occur within a common substring at the beginning of the two prefixes. This enabled us to develop a much simpler algorithm computing a *minimal* set of most general unifiers.

Our general proof procedure also allows a uniform treatment of other non-classical logics like various modal logics [32] or linear logic [21]. We only have to change the notion of complementarity (i.e. the prefix unification) while leaving the path checking algorithm unchanged.

Path checking can also be performed by using a semantic tableau [13]. The prover ileanTAP [28] is based on free-variable semantic tableaux extended by the above-mentioned prefix unification. It is a very compact Prolog implementation (about 4 kilobytes) and due to the modular treatment of the different connectives it can easily be adapted to other non-classical logics.

2.3   Embedding Matrix Methods into Program Development

As long as only the matter of truth is involved, NuPRL allows to use the above techniques as *trusted external refiners*. However, whenever a piece of code shall be extracted from the proof, it is necessary to convert the proofs generated by a search procedure back into a constructive sequent proof which, according to the *proofs-as-program paradigm* [2], can be turned into a program.

In [36,22] we have developed an embedding of connection based proof methods into NuPRL based on such conversions. The proof method described in [22] constructs a matrix proof closely related to a cut-free sequent proof in $\mathcal{LJ}_{mc}$, the multiply-conclusioned sequent calculus on which the matrix characterization for $\mathcal{J}$ is based [44]. Its integration into NuPRL basically consists of a transformation from $\mathcal{LJ}_{mc}$-proofs into sequent proofs in Gentzen's $\mathcal{LJ}$ [14], the first-order fragment of NuPRL's calculus. To allow a *structure preserving* transformation the *cut*-rule had to be used in a restricted and regular manner. For the sake of clarity we have hidden its application within an extended sequent calculus $\mathcal{LJ}^\star$.

Converting Matrix Proofs into Sequent Proofs. Improving the efficiency of proof search in the above procedures resulted in strategies which do not support a parallel construction of matrix proofs in $\mathcal{MJ}$ and $\mathcal{LJ}_{mc}$-proofs anymore. Proof strategies such as an *extension procedure* [32] or a *tableaux* prover [28] (see also section 2.2) make it necessary to transform matrix proofs into sequent proofs *after* the proof search has been finished. Hence, the above mapping $\mathcal{LJ}_{mc} \mapsto \mathcal{LJ}^\star$ has to be extended by an additional mapping $\mathcal{MJ} \mapsto \mathcal{LJ}_{mc}$.

This two-step conversion from intuitionistic matrix proofs into $\mathcal{LJ}^\star$-sequent proofs has first been presented in [36]. The first step $\mathcal{MJ} \mapsto \mathcal{LJ}_{mc}$ turns out to be non-trivial since the compact representation of $\mathcal{MJ}$-proofs, called *reduction ordering* $\propto^\star$, does not completely encode the non-permutabilities of sequent rules in an $\mathcal{LJ}_{mc}$-proof. In order to *complete* this representation in the above sense we have extracted some conditions, called *wait*-labels, which are dynamically added during the conversion process. These conditions prevent non-invertible $\mathcal{LJ}_{mc}$-rules from being applied too early such that no proof relevant sequent formulas will be deleted. We explain our approach by an example.

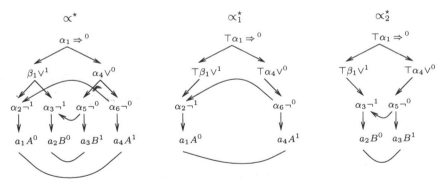

Fig. 2. Reduction ordering $\propto^\star$ of the matrix proof for F.

Consider the $\mathcal{J}$-formula $F \equiv \neg A \vee \neg B \Rightarrow \neg B \vee \neg A$ and its matrix proof $\mathcal{MJ}$ represented as a reduction ordering $\propto^\star$ (see Fig. 2, left hand side). $\propto^\star$ consists of the formula tree of F together with additional ordering constraints (curved arrows) which are extracted from the matrix proof and encode non-permutabilities of sequent rules wrt. $\mathcal{LJ}_{mc}$. Furthermore, the *connections* from the matrix proof are assigned to the atoms of F in $\propto^\star$. For unique reference to the subformulas of F each node in $\propto^\star$ contains a *position* x as well as the *main operator* $op(x)$ and *polarity* $pol(x)$ of the corresponding subformula F_x. Positions with a 'β' name denote subformulas which cause the sequent proof to split into two independent subproofs, e.g. β_1 in the example.

Proof reconstruction is based on a traversal of the reduction ordering $\propto^\star$ by visiting the positions of $\propto^\star$: (i) Select a position x from the *open position set* P_o which is not "blocked" by some arrow in $\propto^\star$, (ii) construct a unique sequent rule from $pol(x)$ and $op(x)$ of the subformula F_x and reduce the formula $F_x^{pol(x)}$ in the sequent, (iii) update P_o with the immediate successor positions $succ(x)$ of x in $\propto^\star$. The traversal process and the resulting sequent proof for F are depicted in Fig. 3. After reducing the β-position β_1 the reduction ordering is split into two suborderings $\propto_1^\star, \propto_2^\star$ and the conversion continues separately on each of the suborderings. For this we have developed an operation $split(\propto^\star, \beta_1)$ [37] which first splits the reduction ordering $\propto^\star$. Secondly non-normal form reductions are applied to each of the $\propto_i^\star$ in order to delete redundancies from $\propto_i^\star$ which are no longer relevant for the corresponding branch of the sequent proof. The result of the splitting process is shown in Fig. 2, right hand side, where the positions already visited are marked with '$\top$'.

$$\dfrac{\dfrac{\dfrac{\dfrac{\dfrac{\dfrac{A \vdash A}{\neg A, A \vdash} \neg l \quad \dfrac{B \vdash B}{\neg B, B \vdash} \neg l}{\neg B \vdash \neg B, \neg A} \neg r}{\neg A \vdash \neg B, \neg A} \neg r \quad }{\neg A \vee \neg B \vdash \neg B, \neg A} \vee l}{\neg A \vee \neg B \vdash \neg B \vee \neg A} \vee r}{\vdash \neg A \vee \neg B \Rightarrow \neg B \vee \neg A} \Rightarrow r$$

	P_o	select x	rule	applied on $F_x^{pol(x)}$
$\propto^\star$	$\{\alpha_1\}$	α_1	$\Rightarrow r$	$(\neg A \vee \neg B \Rightarrow \neg B \vee \neg A)^0$
	$\{\beta_1, \alpha_4\}$	α_4	$\vee r$	$(\neg B \vee \neg A)^0$
	$\{\beta_1, \alpha_5, \alpha_6\}$	β_1	$\vee l$	$(\neg A \vee \neg B)^1$
$\propto_1^\star$	$\{\alpha_2, \alpha_6\}$	α_6	$\neg r$	$\neg A^0$
	$\{\alpha_2, \alpha_4\}$	a_4	$-$	A^1
	$\{\alpha_2\}$	α_2	$\neg l$	$\neg A^1$
	$\{a_1\}$	a_1	$ax.$	A^0, A^1
$\propto_2^\star$	$\{\alpha_3, \alpha_5\}$	α_5	$\neg r$	$\neg B^0$
	$\{\alpha_3, a_3\}$	a_3	$-$	B^1
	$\{\alpha_3\}$	α_3	$\neg l$	$\neg B^1$
	$\{a_2\}$	a_2	$ax.$	B^0, B^1

Fig. 3. Sequent proof for F and the corresponding traversal steps of $\propto^\star$.

The problem of completing $\propto^\star$ occurs when starting the traversal with $\alpha_1, \alpha_4, \alpha_5$, which is not prevented by "blocking" arrows in $\propto^\star$. But such a selection ordering leads to a $\mathcal{LJ}_{mc}$-derivation which could not be completed to a proof since the reduction of α_5, i.e. applying $\neg r$ on $\neg B^0$, deletes the relevant formula $\neg A^0$ (position α_6). Adding two *wait*-labels dynamically to α_6 and α_5 completes $\propto^\star$ and avoids this deadlock during traversal. For a more detailed presentation of this approach as well as for an algorithmic realization we refer to [37].

Building Efficient Conversion Procedures. The basic problem for proof reconstruction in constructive logics lies in the deletion of redundancies after splitting at β-positions. The reason for this is that the reduction ordering together with dynamically assigned *wait*-labels could be totally blocked from further conversion steps although some of these labels are no longer needed. To avoid this kind of deadlocks and to ensure completeness of the reconstruction process we have to detect and delete these redundant subrelations from $\propto_i^\star$. One of the deletion concepts used in the operation *split* is based on a non-normal form purity reduction which is recursively applied to non-connected leaf positions in $\propto^\star$. Consider $\propto_1^\star$ in the example above. The atom a_3 is not connected after splitting at β_1. Application of the purity reduction deletes a_3 and α_5 from $\propto_1^\star$. Consequently, the *wait*-label could be removed from α_6 since α_5 does not exist any longer. If the purity reduction were not applied, both *wait*-labels would remain in $\propto_1^\star$ which would then be totally blocked for further reconstruction steps.

In [37,38] we have shown that complete redundancy deletion after splitting at β-positions cannot be performed *efficiently* when only the *spanning mating* is given from the matrix proof. Efficiency means that the selection of proof-relevant subrelations from the $\propto_i^\star$ should avoid any additional search. If only the spanning mating is given, backtracking may be required over this selection (i.e. converting irrelevant subrelations) in order to retain completeness.

For this purpose we have developed a concept of redundancy elimination from a reduction ordering during proof reconstruction [34,35]. The concept is based on the specification of additional *proof knowledge* from the search process in order to extract *reconstruction knowledge* for the conversion procedure. More precisely, the history of matrix proofs will be integrated into the conversion process rather than using only the spanning matings. This makes our procedure depend on a particular proof search strategy, i.e. an *extension procedure* [5,32]. But a compact encoding of this proof knowledge into the conversion process (which can be done in polynomial time in the size of the matrix proof) allows us to derive the reconstruction knowledge in terms of a few elegant conditions. Finally, the resulting *conversion strategy* integrates these conditions into the *split* operation which efficiently extends redundancy deletions after β-splits to a maximal level. We are able to show that *all* redundancies in the resulting subrelations $\propto_1^\star, \propto_2^\star$ will be eliminated after splitting $\propto^\star$ at a β-position. This guarantees that no decisions on selecting proof-relevant subrelations have to be made and hence, additional search wrt. these decisions will be avoided.

Our approach for reconstructing $\mathcal{LJ}_{mc}$-proofs from $\mathcal{MJ}$-proofs has been uniformly extended to various non-classical logics [37,21] for which matrix characterizations exist. A uniform representation of different logics and proofs within logical calculi as well as abstract descriptions for integrating special properties of these logics in a uniform way, e.g. the completion of reduction orderings $\propto^\star$, yields a general proof reconstruction method for all logics under consideration.

Furthermore, a technique for efficient redundancy elimination after splitting at β-positions has been developed for all of these logics [35]. The result can be seen as a general framework for building efficient and complete conversion procedures for non-classical logics when the basic proof search method is known.

The theoretical concept for extracting reconstruction knowledge form the corresponding proof knowledge is invariant wrt. a special logic and hence, extends the uniformity of the underlying conversion theory.

3   Induction Techniques

Pure first-order logic theorem proving can only generate programs without loops. For deriving recursive programs induction techniques are needed during the proof process. In [23] we have developed an induction prover for "simple" induction problems which is based on rippling [9,1]. The basic concept for integrating this external prover into the NuPRL system is similar to the first-order case: (i) separating a subgoal in the actual NuPRL sequent, (ii) searching an induction proof for the goal with the external prover, and (iii) converting the induction proof into a NuPRL sequent proof. This integration concept has been realized with tactics and extends an earlier approach presented in [25].

3.1   Introduction to Rippling

In order to prove a goal by induction an induction scheme of the form

$$A(base) \wedge (\forall x.A(x) \Rightarrow A(step(x))) \Rightarrow \forall x.A(x)$$

has to be applied to the goal which results in the following two subgoals: a *base case* $A(base)$, which for the most part can be proved directly, and a *step case* $\forall x.A(x) \Rightarrow A(step(x))$ which needs term rewriting to derive the conclusion $A(step(x))$ from the induction hypothesis $A(x)$. To perform rewriting in a goal oriented way, a special technique called *rippling* was introduced by Bundy [9]. A more refined and formalized version has later been developed by Basin and Walsh [1] from which we take the central ideas for our presentation.

Rippling uses *annotations* on subterms to mark the differences between the conclusion and the hypothesis. It first identifies additional function symbols in the conclusion, called *wave fronts*, which will be annotated by surrounding boxes. Subterms inside a wave front which are identical to the corresponding subterms in the hypothesis are called *wave holes* and will be underlined in the depictions. Consider for example the step case for the associativity of '+'

$$(x + y) + z = x + (y + z) \Rightarrow (s(x) + y) + z = s(x) + (y + z),$$

for which the annotated conclusion is given by

$$(\boxed{s(\underline{x})}^{\uparrow} + y) + z = \boxed{s(\underline{x})}^{\uparrow} + (y + z).$$

Arrows at boxes indicate the direction to which the wave fronts will be moved (or *rippled*) in the term tree. An '↑' means that a wave front has to be moved towards the root (*rippling-out*) whereas '↓' permits a wave front to be moved towards the leaves (*rippling-in*). For this purpose annotated rewrite rules called *wave rules* are used, e.g.

$$\boxed{s(\underline{U})}^{\uparrow} + V \overset{R}{\longmapsto} \boxed{s(\underline{U + V})}^{\uparrow} \qquad (1)$$

$$\boxed{s(\underline{U})}^{\uparrow} = \boxed{s(\underline{V})}^{\uparrow} \overset{R}{\longmapsto} U = V \qquad (2)$$

A proof using the rippling-out strategy is successfully finished, if all wave fronts have been eliminated by applying wave rules. If rippling-in is used instead each universally quantified variable of the hypothesis is marked with a special *sink* symbol '⌊*sink*⌋'. All wave fronts have to be rippled towards these sink positions, which requires the application of a rule for *switching* from '↑' to '↓' (there is no rule for the opposite direction) and of additional wave rules for rippling-in. Afterwards a substitution has to be found which matches the sink variables in the hypothesis with the corresponding terms in the wave fronts. Backtracking may be required in order to find instances for all sink variables.

The main difference between the two strategies is that rippling-out provides a goal-oriented proof search whereas rippling-in does not. For rippling-out each step moves a wave front towards the root of the term tree and the search cannot branch. In contrast to this, rippling-in guides a wave front only to be rippled towards the leaves without giving guarantee that there exists a sink under the actual wave front position. Backtracking is required to find a sequence of rules which ripples all wave fronts into sink positions. A *sink heuristic*, defined in [1], makes sure that rippling-in always ripples a wave front towards sink positions. The restriction on the class of provable problems caused by this heuristic is harmless compared with the gain one obtains by the reduced backtracking.

3.2   Rippling-Distance – A Uniform Rippling Strategy

Even with the sink heuristic rippling-in often has an untractable search space. In order to obtain an efficient induction strategy we have generalized rippling-out and rippling-in to a new uniform strategy, called *rippling-distance* [23]. The arrows '↑' and '↓' were removed from the wave fronts and each wave front is assigned to one *goal sink*. To guarantee termination a *distance measure* $\mathcal{MD}$ has been introduced which describes the distance between a wave front and its assigned goal sink in the term tree. Each application of a wave rule has to reduce this measure wrt. the selected wave front. This strategy splits the enormous search space into smaller subspaces which can be searched independently.

Rippling-distance provides a more goal-oriented proof search than rippling-in with sink heuristic since it implicitly contains the application of the switching-rule. No backtracking over the switching position in the term tree has to be done. In the worst case m^n assignments from wave fronts to goal sinks have to be tested for an annotated term with m wave fronts and n sinks. The number of possible assignments seems to be very large, but this heuristic allows us to divide the proof search into separate search tasks. Whereas a non-separated search has a complexity of about $m^{(\frac{1}{4}n \cdot m \cdot d^2)}$ steps for finding a rippling proof the divided search needs only about $m^{(n+m \cdot d)}$ steps, where d is the depth of the term. Furthermore, the assignment concept gives us control knowledge for avoiding assignments which most likely do not contribute to a successful search. An extension of dividing the proof search can be reached by separating the wave fronts into independent classes such that each class is assigned to a different goal sink. Then an independent proof search for each class reduces the complexity to about $m! \cdot d$ steps for $m = n$, and to $(m')^{(n+m' \cdot d)}$ steps for $m > n$, where $m' = m - (n - 1)$ (see [23] for details).

In order to uniformly integrate rippling-out into the rippling-distance strategy the definition of *sinks* has been generalized to arbitrary term positions. Then rippling-out can be seen as a special case of rippling-in by putting a sink around the whole term on which the wave rules will be applied, e.g.

$$\lfloor \boxed{s(\underline{x})} \rfloor \leq \boxed{s(\underline{x})} \cdot \boxed{s(\underline{x})} \rfloor$$

This approach can be optimized if the outermost relation of the term is equality. Then two sink positions are defined at the immediate subterms of '=', e.g.

$$\lfloor (\boxed{s(\underline{x})}^{\uparrow} + y) + z \rfloor = \lfloor \boxed{s(\underline{x})}^{\uparrow} + (y + z) \rfloor$$

The distance measure $\mathcal{MD}$ can be applied directly to this rippling-out simulation without any changes. For practical use within a rippling prover we have combined rippling-distance with *dynamically* annotated wave rules. This means that the annotations of wave rules are determined at runtime from a set of rewrite rules which do not have annotations. Since there are no direction marks '$\uparrow$', '$\downarrow$' at the wave fronts the number of possible annotations is decreased and the annotations are easier to compute [23].

The admissibility of annotated wave rules has to be tested using a well founded reduction ordering $\prec_x$ in order to avoid cyclic sequences of wave rules. From the measure $\mathcal{MD}$ we have developed a new reduction ordering $\prec_{dist}$ which can be computed more efficiently than the ordering $\prec_{comp}$, the compound reduction ordering for rippling-in presented in [1]. This advantage becomes remarkable if *multi-wave holes* are used where wave fronts may contain more then one wave hole. Furthermore, $\prec_{dist}$ has been extended with an additional weight-function, which allows the use of additional associativity and commutativity wave rules.

3.3 Integrating the Rippling-Distance Strategy into NuPRL

In [23] we have described the integration of an external rippling prover into the NuPRL system which uses rippling-distance with dynamic rule annotations for guiding a proof search. The prover is implemented in NuPRL-ML [15] and called during a NuPRL proof session via a tactic *Ripple*. This tactic prepares the proof goal for the prover by applying an appropriate induction scheme and extracting the induction step. After the prover has solved this step case the resulting rippling proof will be translated back into a NuPRL sequent.

An application of NuPRL's induction scheme for natural numbers $\mathbb{N}$ yields as step case a subgoal of the form $x - 1 \mapsto x$. This means that an additional function symbol '$-$' occurs in the hypothesis which cannot be handled directly by the rippling calculus. We have developed a simulation of the step case $x \mapsto x + 1$ in NuPRL which is admissible for rippling. Furthermore, NuPRL's induction scheme for list types $TList$ is also supported by our rippling prover.

Before applying an induction scheme the induction variable is moved in front of other universally quantified variables in order to maximize the number of sink

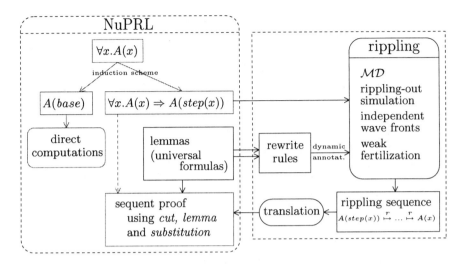

Fig. 4. Components and integration of the rippling module

variables. After the step case is proved the translation back into a sequent proof has to be done. In [25] a translation for rippling-out proofs was developed, which can be used for arbitrary sequences of rewrite rules. It is implemented as meta-tactic and uses the basic refinement rules *cut*, *substitution* and *lemma*. We have extended this approach with the following concepts [23]:

1. The (universally quantified) induction hypothesis can be instantiated.
2. Polymorphic types for integration of rewrite steps can be reconstructed.
3. Premises in a NuPRL-sequent can be used as rewrite rules.

The first improvement is necessary for completing rippling-in proofs. The hypothesis has to be instantiated with sink terms which have been rippled into the sink positions of the induction conclusion. To complete a rippling-out simulation with optimization for equality '=' (see Section 3.2) the generalized sink positions have to be unified by using the induction hypothesis as a rewrite rule.

The second extension determines the type and universe level for a substitution rule by analyzing the proof. This type reconstruction is necessary since the external rippling prover is untyped. A temporary proof goal will be generated in order to compute the type for a successful application of the substitution. Then the goal is forced to fail and the extracted type information will be used for the original proof.

The last improvement allows premises of the current proof goal to be used as wave rules if they are in NuPRL's *universal formula format* [16]. So second order proofs over universally quantified functions can be established by using the recursive definitions of these functions in the premises as wave rules.

Many additional improvements have been made for adapting the basic translation approach to the rippling-distance strategy. Furthermore, NuPRL's tactics *BackThruLemma* and *BackThruHyp* for backward chaining in universal formulas are applied to support a uniform translation of the rippling steps wrt. equality-, implication- and hypothesis-axioms. The components of the rippling module and its integration into the NuPRL system are summarized in Fig. 4.

In future work we will adapt NuPRL's induction scheme for integers $\mathbb{Z}$ to an admissible induction scheme for the rippling calculus. This can be realized by simply extending the presented adaption for natural numbers $\mathbb{IN}$ to $\mathbb{Z}$. Furthermore, a library of measures $\mathcal{MX}$ and corresponding reduction orderings $\prec_x$ will be built for realizing special extensions. In the current implementation there are two alternative measures, one for fast proofs in large terms and the other for more complicated proofs. The latter allows us to use additional associativity and commutativity rules for normalizing wave fronts which is necessary for unblocking proof search. In the current state of the system the user has to specify the measure which should be used but this can be done automatically as soon as syntactic and functional characterizations have been developed.

4   High-Level Synthesis Strategies

The theorem proving techniques described in the previous sections operate on a rather low level of abstraction and have only little to do with the way in which a programmer would reason when developing a program. The application of these methods is therefore restricted to programming problems which are conceptually simple and can be solved completely automatically.

Techniques which are to support the synthesis of larger programs, however, will depend on a cooperation between programmer and machine. A programmer will have to control and guide the derivation process while the system will fill in the formal details and ensure the correctness of the generated algorithms. The corresponding proof techniques have to operate on a higher level of abstraction and must be based on comprehensible formalizations of application domains and programming concepts rather than on low-level inferences of the logical calculus.

Algorithm design strategies based on schematic solutions for certain classes of algorithms [40] have proved to be suited best for this purpose since they can be formulated almost entirely in programmer's terminology. It has been demonstrated [41] that algorithm schemata do not only lead to a very efficient synthesis process but can also produce competitive algorithms if properly guided.

Formally verified theorems stating the requirements for the correctness of an abstract program scheme [19] are the key for an integration of these strategies into the general framework. Such theorems can be applied like high-level inference rules which decompose the synthesis task into the task of proving instances of the given axioms. The latter can then be solved by first-order theorem provers, simple inductions, applications of additional theorems, or knowledge-base queries. The conceptually difficult problem – generating the algorithm and proving it correct – has been solved once and for all while proving the formal theorem and requires only a single step in the synthesis process. In this section we shall illustrate how this methodology is used for integrating a strategy for the design of *global search algorithms* [39] into the uniform proof system.

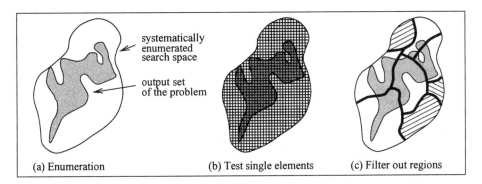

(a) Enumeration   (b) Test single elements   (c) Filter out regions

Fig. 5. Global Search as elimination process

4.1 Formalizing the Design of Global Search Algorithms

Solving a problem by enumerating candidate solutions is a well-known concept in computer science. *Global search* is a concept that generalizes binary search, back-tracking, branch-and-bound, and other methods which explore a search space by looking at whole sets of possible solutions at once.

The basic idea of global search, illustrated in Fig. 5, is to combine enumeration and elimination processes. Usually, global search has to compute the complete set of output values for a given input. Global search systematically enumerates a search space which must contain the set of all output values (a) and tests if certain elements of the search space satisfy the output-condition (b). The latter is necessary to guarantee correctness but is too fine-grained to achieve efficiency, particularly if the search space is much bigger than the set of solutions. Therefore whole regions of the search space are filtered out during the enumeration process if it can be determined that they cannot contain output values (c).

In order to synthesize global search algorithms from specifications, we have to formalize their general structure as an abstract program scheme and to describe techniques for automatically generating appropriate enumeration and filtering processes. We begin by fixing the notation for general programming concepts.

A programming problem is usually characterized by the domain D of the desired program, its range R, a condition I on acceptable input values x, and a condition O on the returned output values z. Formally, a *specification* can be described as 4-tuple $spec = (D, R, I, O)$ where D and R are data types, I is a predicate on D, and O is a predicate on $D \times R$. A specification and a (possibly partial) computable function $body : D \nrightarrow \mathtt{Set}(R)$ together form a *program*. A program is *correct* if it computes the complete set of output values for each acceptable input $(\forall x{:}D.\ I(x) \Rightarrow body(x) = \{z{:}R \mid O(x,z)\})$. A specification is *satisfiable* if it can be extended into a correct program. As in [40] we use a formal notation for programs which emphasizes that we are interested in computing the set of *all* solutions of a given problem (assuming that there are finitely many):

FUNCTION $f(\mathrm{x}{:}D){:}\,\mathtt{Set}(R)$ WHERE $I(\mathrm{x})$ RETURNS $\{\mathrm{z} \mid O(\mathrm{x},\mathrm{z})\} \equiv body(\mathrm{x})$.

```
FUNCTION f(x : D):Set(R) WHERE I(x)  RETURNS {z | O(x,z)}
≡ if Φ(x, s₀(x))  then f_gs(x, s₀(x))  else []

FUNCTION f_gs(x, s : D×S):Set(R)   WHERE I(x) ∧ J(x, s) ∧ Φ(x, s)
    RETURNS {z | O(x, z) ∧ sat(z, s)}
≡ let immediate_solutions =
        let extracted_candidates = ext(s) in
            filter (λz.O(x, z)) extracted_candidates
    and recursive_solutions =
        let filtered_subspaces = filter (λt.Φ(x, t)) (split(x, s)) in
            flatten (map (λt.f_gs(x, t)) filtered_subspaces)
    in append immediate_solutions recursive_solutions
```

Fig. 6. Structure of Global Search algorithms

The name f can be used in the body in order to describe recursive algorithms. Often we use only the left side to denote specifications in a more readable way.

All the above concepts, including an ML-like mathematical notation for computable functions, can be straightforwardly formalized in the logical language of NuPRL (see [19, section 2]) and are the formal foundation for the automated derivation of global search algorithms within the integrated synthesis system.

A careful analysis in [39] (later refined and formalized in [18,19]) has shown that the common structure of global search algorithms can be expressed by a pair of abstract programs which is presented in Fig. 6. These programs contain placeholders D, R, I, and O for a specification and seven additional components $S, J, s_0, sat, split, ext, \Phi$ which are specific for a global search algorithm. On input x this algorithm starts investigating an initial search space $s_0(x)$ and passes it through the filter Φ which globally checks whether a search region s contains solutions. Using the auxiliary function f_{gs} the algorithm then repeatedly extracts candidate solutions $(ext(s))$ for testing and splits a search space s into a set $split(x, s)$ of subspaces which are again passed through the filter Φ. Subspaces which survive the filter contain solutions and are investigated recursively.

For the sake of efficiency, search spaces are represented by *space descriptors* $s \in S$ instead of sets of values $z \in R$ and the fact that a value z belongs to the space described by s is denoted by a predicate $sat(z, s)$. The predicate $J(x, s)$ expresses that s is a *meaningful* search space descriptor for the input x. Formally S must be a data type. J and Φ must be predicates on $D×S$ and sat one on $R×S$. $s_0:D\nrightarrow S$, $split:D×S\nrightarrow S$, and $ext:S\nrightarrow Set(R)$ must be computable functions.

Six requirements, formalized in Fig. 7, must be satisfied to ensure the correctness of global search algorithms. The initial descriptor $s_0(x)$ must be meaningful (1) and splitting must preserve meaningfulness (2). All solutions must be contained in the initial search space (3) and be extractable after splitting finitely many times (4). Subspaces containing solutions must pass the filter (5) and filtered splitting, the combined enumeration/elimination process, must eventually terminate (6). In [39] (refined in [18,19]) the following theorem has been proved.

$\forall x: D. \ \forall z: R. \ \forall s: S.$

1. $I(x) \Rightarrow J(x, s_0(x))$
2. $I(x) \wedge J(x, s) \quad \Rightarrow \quad \forall t \in split(x, s). \ J(x, t)$
3. $I(x) \wedge O(x, z) \quad \Rightarrow \quad sat(z, s_0(x))$
4. $I(x) \wedge J(x, s) \wedge O(x, z) \quad \Rightarrow \quad sat(z, s) \iff \exists k. \ \exists t \in split^k(x, s). \ z \in ext(t)$
5. $I(x) \wedge J(x, s) \quad \Rightarrow \quad \Phi(x, s) \ \Leftarrow \ \exists z. \ sat(z, s) \wedge O(x, z)$
6. $I(x) \wedge J(x, s) \quad \Rightarrow \quad \exists k. \ split^k_\Phi(x, s) = \emptyset$

where $split_\Phi(x, s) = \{t \in split(x, s) \mid \Phi(x, t)\}$

and $\quad split^k_\Phi(x, s) = \begin{cases} s & \text{if } k = 0 \\ \bigcup_{t \in split^{k-1}_\Phi(x, s)} split_\Phi(x, t) & \text{if } k > 0 \end{cases}$

Fig. 7. Axioms of Global Search

Theorem 1. *If D, R, I, O, S, J, sat, s_0, split, ext, and Φ fulfill the axioms of global search then the pair of programs given in Fig. 6 is correct and satisfies the specification* FUNCTION $f(x: D)$: Set(R) WHERE $I(x)$ RETURNS $\{z \mid O(x, z)\}$.

Thus a global search algorithm can be synthesized for a given specification by deriving seven components S, J, sat, s_0, split, ext, and Φ which satisfy the axioms of global search and instantiating the abstract programs accordingly.

4.2   Knowledge Based Algorithm Construction

A direct derivation of global search algorithms on the basis of theorem 1 is obviously a difficult task. The theorem does not provide information how to *find* the seven additional components and the verification of the six axioms, particularly of axioms 4 and 6 which require induction, would put a heavy load on the proof process – even if the techniques mentioned in sections 2 and 3 were already integrated into the derivation strategy. Instead, it is much more meaningful to base the construction of global search algorithms on general knowledge about algorithmic structures. For a given range type R, for instance, there are usually only a few general techniques to enumerate search spaces and each global search algorithm will use a special case of such a technique. Therefore it makes sense to store information about generic enumeration processes in a knowledge base and to develop techniques for adapting them to a particular programming problem.

The investigations in [39] have shown that standard enumeration structures for some range type R can be stored in a knowledge base as objects of the form $G = ((D_G, R, I_G, O_G), S, J, s_0, sat, split, ext)$ which are proved to satisfy axioms 1 to 4. Such objects are called *GS-theories*. A *problem reduction* mechanism will make sure that the four axioms are preserved when the enumeration structure is specialized to a given specification which involves the same range.

Specializing a standard GS-theory G works as follows. Its specification $spec_G = (D_G, R_G, I_G, O_G)$ characterizes a general enumeration method f_G which explores the space R_G as far as possible. Specialization simply means to avoid enumerating elements which are not needed and results in a kind of "truncated" enumeration structure for the same type. Formally, $spec_G$ can be *specialized* to a given specification $spec = (D, R, I, O)$ if the the following condition is valid:

$$R = R_G \;\land\; \forall x{:}\, D. \; I(x) \Rightarrow \exists x_G{:}\, D_G.\, I_G(x_G) \;\land\; \forall z{:}\, R.\, O(x, z) \Rightarrow O_G(x_G, z)$$

Thus specialization also allows to adapt the *input* of a problem since the original input x is mapped to a value x_G which serves as input for the search performed by f_G. A proof of the above condition implicitly contains a substitution $\theta{:}\, D \rightarrow D_G$ which maps x to x_G. θ can be extracted from the proof and then be used for refining f_G into a search method with inputs from D instead of D_G. On the *output* side of the problem specialization restricts f_G to the computation of values which satisfy the stronger condition O. Technically, this can be done by checking O for each computed value. Altogether problem reduction allows us to create a global search algorithm f for the specification *spec* by defining

$$f(x) = \{z \in f_G(\theta(x)) \mid O(x, z)\}.$$

For the sake of efficiency, the modifications caused by θ and O will be moved directly into the components of the algorithm. By an index θ as in J_θ or $split_\theta$ we indicate that the transformation θ is applied to all arguments expecting a domain value from D, e.g. $split_\theta(x, s) = split(\theta(x), s)$.

Specializing predefined GS-theories allows us to derive six components of a global search algorithm which satisfy axioms 1 to 4 with comparably little effort. In a similar way, we can avoid having to prove the sixth axiom explicitly. For each enumeration structure there are only a few standard methods to ensure termination through an elimination process. In [18,19] it has been shown that these methods can be stored in the form of filters Φ for a GS-theory G which are proved to satisfy axiom 6. Such filters will be called *well-founded* wrt. G and this property will be preserved during specialization as well. Thus specialization reduces the proof burden to checking that, after specialization, the selected filter is *necessary* wrt. the GS-theory, i.e. that it satisfies axiom 5.

The process of adapting the search space to the specific problem can be completely formalized and expressed in a single reduction theorem.

Theorem 2. *Let $G = ((D_G, R, I_G, O_G), S, J, s_0, sat, split, ext)$ be a GS-theory. Let $spec = (D, R, I, O)$ be a specification such that $spec_G = (D_G, R, I_G, O_G)$ can be specialized to spec. Let θ be the substitution extracted from the specialization proof. Then $G_\theta = ((D, R, I, O), S, J_\theta, s_{0\theta}, sat, split_\theta, ext)$ is a GS-theory. Furthermore if Φ is a well-founded filter wrt. G then Φ_θ is well-founded wrt. G_θ*

Adapting standard algorithmic knowledge to a given problem moves most of the proof burden into the creation of the knowledge base and keeps the synthesis process itself comparatively easy. Information retrieved from the knowledge base will provide all the basic components and guarantee that axioms 1 to 4 and 6 are satisfied. Only the specialization condition and the necessity of the specialized filter – conditions whose proofs are much easier than those of axioms 4 and 6 – need to be checked explicitly. These insights led to the following strategy for synthesizing global search algorithms from formal specifications (see [19, Section 4.4] for an application example).

Strategy 3 *Given the specification*
    FUNCTION $f(|x|:D)$: $\mathrm{Set}(R)$ WHERE $I(|x|)$ RETURNS $\{|z| \mid O(|x|,|z|)\}$

1. *Select a GS-theory $G=((D_G, R, I_G, O_G), S, J, s_0, sat, split, ext)$ for R.*
2. *Prove that $spec_G=(D_G, R, I_G, O_G)$ can be specialized to the specification. Derive a substitution $\theta| : |D{\rightarrow}D_G$ from the proof and specialize G with θ.*
3. *Select a well-founded filter Φ for G and specialize it with θ.*
4. *Prove that the specialized filter is necessary for the specialized GS-theory.*
5. *Instantiate the program scheme given in Fig. 6.*

It should be noted that in step 4 the specialized filter could be refined by heuristically adding further conditions which do not destroy its necessity. In some case this can drastically improve the efficiency of the generated algorithm.

4.3 Integrating the Design Strategy into Deductive Systems

So far we have described the synthesis of global search algorithms only semi-formally in order to illustrate the fundamental ideas. Integrating the strategy into a proof based system now requires a more rigorous approach. Each step in a derivation must be completely formal such that it can be controlled by the proof system. On the other hand, each derivation step should remain on the high level of abstraction which we have used so far. In the following we will explain the techniques by which these two requirements could be achieved.

The *application of formally verified theorems* is one of the most important principles which make program synthesis within a formal proof system like NuPRL feasible (see [19, Section 3] for a detailed exposition). In such systems all derivations must eventually be based on primitive inference rules. Formal theorems, however, can serve as *derived inference rules* on a much higher level of abstraction. Their application corresponds to a single, conceptually large inference step which would require thousands of elementary proof steps if performed purely on the level of primitive inferences. In order to represent rule *schemes*, these theorems contain universally quantified variables which must be instantiated by concrete values *before* the theorem can be applied. Finding appropriate values is the only difficult aspect of this technique.

The kernel of our implementation of the global search strategy, for instance, is a single formal theorem which combines theorems 1 and 2. It quantifies over variables for GS-theories (gs), filters (Φ), transformations (θ), and specifications $(spec)$ which must be instantiated by a proof tactic for synthesizing global search algorithms. The instance for *spec* is obvious. G and Φ should be provided manually since their selection from a restricted set of alternatives is a design decision rather than a deductive task. The function θ, however, should be derived fully automatically, since it does not introduce any new algorithmic idea but is determined by the specialization conditions. The value for θ is only clear after these conditions have been investigated.

The different nature of these variables had be taken into consideration while developing a NuPRL-tactic for deriving global search algorithms. In general, the

⊢   *spec* is satisfiable
  BY InstLemma ⟨*name of global search theorem*⟩ [*gs*; *Φ*]

  ⊢   *gs* describes global search limited by *Φ*

  ⊢   R(*spec*) = R(specification(*gs*))

  1. PROGRAM SCHEME
     O SATISFIES ⟨*decidability of the output condition of spec*⟩
     θ SATISFIES ⟨*the specification for θ*⟩
    ⇒
      filtered_body(*gs* specialized to *spec* using *θ*; *Φ*; *O*)
      SATISFIES *spec*
    END
 ⊢   *spec* is satisfiable

Fig. 8. Principal structure of a proof generated by the Global Search tactic

design of proof tactics should correspond to the structure of the proofs they generate. As proofs are typically divided into subproofs for certain subgoals, the tactic should be organized in the same manner and provide subtactics for the different tasks. The handling of variables representing design decisions has to be moved to the beginning of the proof, since they pre-structure the rest of it. Almost all tactics have to reflect the structure of the terms to which they are applied, since the primitive rules only allow a *structural* analysis or synthesis of terms.

This leads to a fixed anatomy on the top-level of a proof, as illustrated in Fig. 8. A typical synthesis proof begins by stating that an algorithm for a specification *spec* shall be found. It then instantiates the global search theorem by invoking the tactic InstLemma which requires the 'design parameters' *gs* and *Φ*, denoting the concrete GS-theory and the filter, to be provided manually. This results in three preconditions for the initial formula (NuPRL proceeds top-down). The first says that *gs* is valid, i.e. fulfills the axioms 1 to 4, and that *Φ* makes the search space well-founded. These assumptions are usually shown by referring to lemmas, since *gs* and *Φ* are selected from a few alternatives whose properties are stored as lemmas in the NuPRL library. The second subgoal states that the range types of the specification and the GS-theory are identical. The third expresses that the algorithmic scheme introduced by *gs* and *Φ* can be adapted to *spec*. Here the specialization to be performed is described in terms of so-called *program schemes*. By this we emphasize that *θ* is the missing *algorithmic* link between the schematic search space and the final program for *spec*.

Program schemes express that a complex problem can directly be reduced to simpler problems. The part after the implication symbol in Fig. 8 describes how the algorithm for the complex problem is formed by algorithms for the simpler ones. The latter may occur as variables which have to be declared before the implication symbol. The SATISFIES clause specifies the problem associated with the variable to be solved. Thus the final program filtered_body(...) can be constructed as soon as the two auxiliary algorithms O and θ are given.[2] The *specification for θ* as algorithm contains all conditions in which θ finally occurs, i.e. the conditions for specialization and necessity. Necessity is usually viewed as property of the filter Φ but, since specialization prunes the search space, we have to check whether the *combination* of Φ and θ results in a necessary filter.

The overall effect of the concept of *program schemes* is that we can formulate the final program although two auxiliary algorithms are yet unknown. Applying the basic theorem therefore corresponds to a macro reduction step transforming a complicated initial specification into one or more simpler subproblems. This results in improved comprehensibility of both the proof and the tactic.

Automatic proof methods are especially valuable for solving the third subgoal. We have already pointed out that θ can be only derived *together* with the proof showing that θ satisfies its specification. This means that we need a separate proof search phase, in which we find out how to successfully solve the goal, before we can actually construct the proof. The methods discussed in sections 2 and 3 have these capabilities, and we will investigate to what extent they can be applied to subgoals of the discussed kind. In the KIDS system, term rewriting is successfully used to prove these conditions. Term rewriting can again be realized by theorem application. But in this case the theorems have a much simpler structure and instances for the quantified variables can almost always be found by first-order matching.

One should now be able to imagine what had to be done to fully implement the global search strategy on a platform like NuPRL. As logical calculi provide only primitive concepts, we first had to increase their level of abstraction by representing standard data types like lists, finite sets, etc. as well as the corresponding operations and their laws. This allows us to formulate simple programs and to prove their properties. Next, in order to reason about programs as such, we had to implement concepts like *program*, *specification* and related notions which were formalized in [18, chapter 2]. The conditions for specialization and filtering reside on a similar level. They are used in the axioms of the GS-theories which had to be implemented on the basis of the specific data structure containing the different components. Furthermore, we need the fundamental global search theorem and its proof. Finally, relevant GS-theories together with the associated well-foundedness filters had to be represented. In both cases, lemmas have to guarantee that the required properties are fulfilled. Together, these definitions and lemmas describe the formal knowledge about global search.

All the rest is tactic development. The global search strategy, as explained above, had to be built from the top-level tactic and many subtactics solving specific subtasks. Moreover, tactics had to be written for proving the laws of the data types, the global search theorem, the properties of different GS-theories and filters. Although these proofs have to be constructed only once, it does not make sense to create them without automatic support. We expect that integrating the

---

[2] When presenting the global search method on paper one easily overlooks the fact that the predicate O must be transformed into a computable function.

techniques discussed in sections 2 and 3, especially induction, into our tactics will be very helpful for this purpose.

Once the global search tactic has found a proof, we can extract a correct algorithm from it using NuPRL's standard extraction mechanism. The KIDS system has shown that the efficiency of this algorithm can dramatically be improved by postprocessing steps. It needs to be investigated where to place such a step in a system which relies of derivations in a formal logic.

In our current implementation we have completed only the essential parts of the global search strategy in NuPRL. Especially, only the proofs for the relevant library theorems have been implemented, because the necessary proof methods were not yet integrated. Instead, while formalizing the various concepts, we have focused on the question whether type theory, despite the many formal details, is suitable for practical program synthesis. As it turned out, the strict semantics of type theory led to deeper insights into some of the concepts: it forced us to change their formulation since the obvious one often meant something different or was not even well-formed. Our work also led to improvements of some standard tactics of NuPRL: in the term rewriting tactic we can often infer type information automatically. By this the chances for success have been dramatically increased; an automatic invocation of such a tactic is now imaginable. This allows handling many difficulties resulting from the peculiarities of the calculus. We believe that the formal complications can be further limited by integrating additional proof methods which will make program synthesis feasible even within the strict framework of proof systems.

5   Conclusion

We have presented the design of the program synthesis system MAPS which integrates a variety of techniques from automated theorem proving and algorithm design at different levels of abstraction. We have demonstrated how proof procedures for (constructive) propositional, first-order logic, and induction as well as schema-based algorithm design strategies can be embedded into a single framework for automated proof and program development.

Because of the rigorous formal framework into which all these methods are embedded, executing the individual techniques is somewhat less efficient than separate implementations. We believe however that the integrated approach is the safest way of combining them into an automated reasoning system which can deal with many of the problems occurring during a formal program derivation.

Future work will involve a more efficient implementation of the individual techniques and support for a stronger cooperation *between* the high- and low-level methods. We are currently elaborating a method for extracting programs *directly* from matrix and induction proofs. We also intend to deepen our studies on induction techniques and to integrate additional algorithm design strategies using the same methodology. We will also work on supporting several existing functional, logical, and imperative programming languages as a target language of our derivations. Recent work on embedding the Objective Caml programming language into NuPRL's formal language [20] has shown that the practical usefulness of systems for program synthesis and transformation can be drastically increased by such efforts.

References

1. D. Basin & T. Walsh. A calculus for and termination of rippling. *Journal of Automated Reasoning*, 16(1-2), pp. 147-180, 1996.
2. J. L. Bates & R. L. Constable. Proofs as programs. *ACM Transactions on Programming Languages and Systems*, 7(1):113–136, 1985.
3. J. Van Benthem Correspondence Theory In D. Gabbay & F. Guenther, eds., *Handbook of Philosophical Logic*, II, pp. 167–247, Reidel, 1984.
4. W. Bibel. On matrices with connections. *Journal of the ACM*, 28(633–645), 1981.
5. W. Bibel. *Automated Theorem Proving*. Vieweg Verlag, 1987.
6. W. Bibel. Toward predicative programming. In M. R. Lowry & R. McCartney, eds., *Automating Software Design*, pp. 405–424, AAAI Press / The MIT Press, 1991.
7. W. Bibel, S. Brüning, U. Egly, T. Rath. Komet. In *12th Conference on Automated Deduction*, LNAI 814, pp. 783–787. Springer Verlag, 1994.
8. W. Bibel, D. Korn, C. Kreitz, S. Schmitt. Problem-oriented applications of automated theorem proving. In J. Calmet & C. Limongelli, eds., *Design and Implementation of Symbolic Computation Systems*, LNCS 1126, Springer Verlag, pp. 1–21, 1996.
9. A. Bundy, F. van Harmelen, A. Ireland, A. Smaill. Rippling: a heuristic for guiding inductive proofs. *Artificial Intelligence*, 1992.
10. R. L. Constable, et. al. *Implementing Mathematics with the NuPRL proof development system*. Prentice Hall, 1986.
11. M. Davis & H. Putnam. A computing procedure for quantification theory. *Journal of the ACM*, 7:201–215, 1960.
12. M. Davis, G. Logemann, D. Loveland. A machine program for theorem-proving. *Communications of the ACM*, 5:394–397, 1962.
13. M. C. Fitting. *First-Order Logic and Automated Theorem Proving*. Springer Verlag, 1990.
14. G. Gentzen. Untersuchungen über das logische Schließen. *Mathematische Zeitschrift*, 39:176–210, 405–431, 1935.
15. P. Jackson. NuPRL's Metalanguage ML. Reference Manual and User's Guide, Cornell University, 1994.
16. P. Jackson. The NuPRL Proof Development System, Version 4.1. Reference Manual and User's Guide, Cornell University, 1994.
17. D. Korn & C. Kreitz. Deciding intuitionistic propositional logic via translation into classical logic. In W. McCune, ed., *14th Conference on Automated Deduction*, LNAI 1249, pp. 131–145, Springer Verlag, 1997.
18. C. Kreitz. *METASYNTHESIS: Deriving Programs that Develop Programs*. Thesis for Habilitation, TH Darmstadt, 1992. Forschungsbericht AIDA–93–03.
19. C. Kreitz. Formal mathematics for verifiably correct program synthesis. *Journal of the IGPL*, 4(1):75–94, 1996.
20. C. Kreitz. Formal reasoning about communication systems I: Embedding ML into type theory. Technical Report TR 97-1637, Cornell University, 1997.

21. C. Kreitz, H. Mantel, J. Otten, S. Schmitt. Connection-Based Proof Construction in Linear Logic. In W. McCune, ed., 14th Conference on Automated Deduction, LNAI 1249, pp. 207–221, Springer Verlag, 1997.

22. C. Kreitz, J. Otten, S. Schmitt. Guiding Program Development Systems by a Connection Based Proof Strategy. In M. Proietti, ed., 5th International Workshop on Logic Program Synthesis and Transformation, LNCS 1048, pp. 137–151. Springer Verlag, 1996.

23. F. Kurucz. Realisierung verschiedender Induktionsstrategien basierend auf dem Rippling-Kalkül. Diplomarbeit, TH Darmstadt, 1997.

24. R. Letz, J. Schumann, S. Bayerl, W. Bibel. Setheo: A high-performance theorem prover. Journal of Automated Reasoning, 8:183–212, 1992.

25. T. van thanh Liem. Induktion im NuPRL System. Diplomarbeit, TH Darmstadt, 1996.

26. R. C. Moore. Reasoning about Knowledge and Action IJCAI-77, pp 223–227, 1977.

27. H. J. Ohlbach. Semantics–Based Translation Methods for Modal Logics Journal of Logic and Computation, 1(6), pp 691–746, 1991.

28. J. Otten. ileanTAP: An intuitionistic theorem prover. In Didier Galmiche, ed., International Conference TABLEAUX '97. LNAI 1227, pp. 307–312, Springer Verlag, 1997.

29. J. Otten. On the advantage of a non-clausal Davis-Putnam procedure. Forschungsbericht AIDA–97–01, TH Darmstadt, 1997.

30. J. Otten & C. Kreitz. A connection based proof method for intuitionistic logic. In P. Baumgartner, R. Hähnle, J. Posegga, eds., 4th Workshop on Theorem Proving with Analytic Tableaux and Related Methods, LNAI 918, pp. 122–137, Springer Verlag, 1995.

31. J. Otten & C. Kreitz. T-String-Unification: Unifying Prefixes in Non-Classical Proof Methods. In U. Moscato, ed., 5th Workshop on Theorem Proving with Analytic Tableaux and Related Methods, LNAI 1071, pp. 244–260, Springer Verlag, 1996.

32. J. Otten & C. Kreitz. A Uniform Proof Procedure for Classical and Non-classical Logics. In G. Görz & S. Hölldobler, eds., KI-96: Advances in Artificial Intelligence, LNAI 1137, pp. 307–319. Springer Verlag, 1996.

33. D. Plaisted & S. Greenbaum. A structure-preserving clause form translation. Journal of Symbolic Computation, 2:293–304, 1986.

34. S. Schmitt. Avoiding redundancy in proof reconstruction 1st International Workshop on Proof Transformation and Presentation, Schloß Dagstuhl, Germany, 1997.

35. S. Schmitt. Building Efficient Conversion Procedures using Proof Knowledge. Technical Report, TH Darmstadt, 1997.

36. S. Schmitt & C. Kreitz. On transforming intuitionistic matrix proofs into standard-sequent proofs. In P. Baumgartner, R. Hähnle, J. Posegga, eds., 4th Workshop on Theorem Proving with Analytic Tableaux and Related Methods, LNAI 918, pp. 106–121. Springer Verlag, 1995.

37. S. Schmitt & C. Kreitz. Converting non-classical matrix proofs into sequent-style systems. In M. McRobbie & J. Slaney, eds., 13th Conference on Automated Deduction, LNAI 1104, pp. 418–432. Springer Verlag, 1996.

38. S. Schmitt & C. Kreitz. A uniform procedure for converting non-classical matrix proofs into sequent-style systems. Technical Report AIDA-96-01, TH Darmstadt 1996.

39. D. R. Smith. Structure and design of global search algorithms. Technical Report KES.U.87.12, Kestrel Institute, 1987.

40. D. R. Smith & M. R. Lowry. Algorithm theories and design tactics. *Science of Computer Programming*, 14(2-3):305–321, 1990.
41. D. R. Smith & E. A. Parra. Transformational approach to transportation scheduling. *8th Knowledge-Based Software Engineering Conference*, pp. 60–68, 1993.
42. G. Stolpmann. Datentypen und Programmsynthese. Studienarbeit, TH Darmstadt, 1996.
43. G. Stolpmann. Schematische Konstruktion von Globalsuchalgorithmen. Diplomarbeit, TH Darmstadt, 1997.
44. L. Wallen. *Automated deduction in nonclassical logic*. MIT Press, 1990.

Programs Without Failures

Annalisa Bossi and Nicoletta Cocco

Dip. di Matematica Applicata e Informatica
Università di Venezia-Ca' Foscari - Italy
`bossi, cocco@dsi.unive.it`

Abstract. We try to formalize the intuitive reasoning which we normally use to get convinced that a query has successful LD-derivations in a program. To this purpose we define the class of *programs and queries without failures* which have the property of not having finitely failing derivations. Such property is simple to verify, it is preserved through leftmost unfolding and it can be useful both in verifying properties of logic programs and in program transformation. The class of programs without failures is very restricted but in program transformations it is sufficient that only some predicates in the program are in the class.
Keywords and Phrases: finitely failing derivations, program transformation, program verification

1 Introduction

Logic programming is a declarative paradigm. This pleasant characteristic allows one to ignore the computation and simply define which are its desired results. But, when queried through a Prolog interpreter, logic definitions are performed with backtracking: some fail and some succeed. Finitely failing LD-derivations (FDs) are not relevant from the logical point of view, unless the entire LD-tree is finitely failing. Thus FDs are ignored in the formal description of the program which is concerned only with successes and computed answer substitutions (c.a.s.) or with the total absence of successes for a given query. Also formal techniques for verifying program properties focus only on successful computations. Nevertheless FDs are relevant from the efficiency point of view; in correctness verification absence of successes can be hidden; in Prolog program transformations, where the size of the LD-tree for a query is relevant, the presence of FDs can make difficult to check applicability conditions for transformation operations, such as unfold, replacements or switching of two atoms.

On the other hand when we write a logic program, we have some intuitive confidence that it will produce the desired computed answer substitutions for some sets of queries. In some intuitive way we are able to distinguish failing computations from successful ones.
We try to formalize this intuitive feeling, by giving a sufficient condition which ensures that a given program and query are without failures, namely they cannot have finitely failing derivations (noFD). Then we discuss the use of this condition both in verifying program correctness and in program transformation.

Norbert E. Fuchs (Ed.): LOPSTR'97, LNCS 1463, pp. 28–48, 1998.

Our condition is very restrictive since we want it to be verifiable from the text of the program and failures are difficult to be syntactically characterized. Nevertheless we believe that it can be useful, since in general it is necessary to verify the condition only on some parts of the program.

In Section 2 we set some notation, then in Section 3 the *class of programs and queries without failures (noFD programs and queries)* is introduced and exemplified. We prove that a noFD query in a noFD program cannot finitely fail. In Section 4 we discuss how to use these concepts for verifying program correctness and for program transformation. Conclusions follow in Section 5. In the Appendix some useful definitions and proofs are given.

2 Basic Notions

Given a substitution η and a set of variables X, we denote by $\eta_{|X}$ the substitution obtained from η by restricting its domain to X. Given an expression (term, atom, query,...) E, we denote the set of variables occurring in it by $Var(E)$. We often write $\eta_{|E}$ to denote $\eta_{|Var(E)}$. A *renaming* is a substitution which is a permutation of its domain. We write $E \sim E'$ to denote that E and E' are *variant expressions*, that is there exists a renaming ρ such that $E = E'\rho$. When a renaming of E maps $Var(E)$ in "new" variables we call it a *new renaming of E* and we speak of $E\rho$ as a *new variant of E*.

We consider definite logic programs executed by means of the *LD-resolution*, which consists of the usual *SLD*-resolution combined with the leftmost selection rule as Prolog interpreters do. Throughout the paper we use queries instead of goals. A *query* is a sequence of atoms or **fail**. **fail** stands for the query associated to a failure and $\Box$ for the *empty query*. An *LD*-derivation ending with $\Box$ is a *successful LD-derivation*, one ending with **fail** is a *failing one (FD)*.
We denote sequences by bold characters and we use identifiers to label clauses and derivations. Then $l : \mathbf{Q} \vdash\!\!\!\xrightarrow{*\sigma}_P \mathbf{R}$ stands for "there exists an *LD*-derivation, l, of the query $\mathbf{Q}$ in P ending in the query $\mathbf{R}$ and σ is the composition of the relevant and idempotent $mgu's$ applied during the derivation". Similarly $\mathbf{Q} \vdash\!\!\!\xrightarrow{*\sigma}_P \Box$ denotes a successful *LD*-derivation of $\mathbf{Q}$ in P with c.a.s. $\sigma_{|\mathbf{Q}}$. $\mathbf{Q} \vdash\!\!\!\xrightarrow{\sigma}_P \mathbf{R}$ denotes one derivation step and we say that it is *non-trivial* if $\mathbf{R}$ is not **fail**. The *length* of an *LD*-derivation l is denoted by $\mid l \mid$.

The rest of the notation is more or less standard and essentially follows [18,1].

In the paper we make use of the notion of modes and types introduced in [12,4,2]. We consider a combination of modes and types and adopt the following assumption: *every considered relation has a fixed mode and a fixed type associated with it*. This assumption allows us to talk about types of *input positions* and of *output positions of an atom*. For example, $app(+ : List, + : List, - : List)$ denotes a ternary relation app with the first two positions moded as input and typed as *List* and the third position moded as output and typed as *List*. A similar denotation is called *a directional type* in [11].

From [2,4] we take also the notion of *well-typed query and program*. A complete treatment of this topic can be found in [2,4]. In the Appendix we recall only the main definition.

Definition 1. *Let P be a well-typed program and $\mathbf{B}$ a well-typed query in P.*
The terms of $\mathbf{B}$ are denoted by $Term(\mathbf{B})$.
The input (output) terms of $\mathbf{B}$, denoted by $In(\mathbf{B})(Out(\mathbf{B}))$, are the terms in input (output) positions in $\mathbf{B}$. □

3   Programs and Queries Without Failures (noFD)

In this section we give a sufficient condition for absence of failing derivations (FDs). We assume to have directional types information and to deal only with well-typed programs and queries. Intuitively in an LD-derivation, FDs may happen when some term is instantiated in an "incorrect" way, namely it forbids unification with further input clauses. This intuitively means that *for avoiding FDs, inputs must be correctly given, while outputs should be correctly instantiated by the evaluation.*

We define an interesting class of programs: *programs without failures (noFD programs)*. These programs have a clear functionality from input to output and they can be non-deterministic. They satisfy the strong property that, in an LD-Derivation, for any selected atom correctly typed in input positions and with uninstantiated variables in output positions, there exists a unifying clause in P.

Definition 2. *Let P be a well-typed program.*
A clause $c : H \leftarrow A_1, \ldots, A_i, \ldots, A_n.$ in P is without failures (noFD clause) *iff for $i \in [1, n]$*

1. *(Output positions in the body are filled in with distinct variables:)*
   $Out(A_i) = Var(Out(A_i))$ *and if* $X_1, \ldots, X_k$ *are the output terms in* A_i, *then*
   $X_j \neq X_h$, *for* $j \neq h$, $j, h \in [1, k]$,
   (which do not appear in input terms in the head and leftmost in the body:)
   and $Out(A_i) \cap (Var(In(H)) \cup Var(A_1, \ldots, A_{i-1}) \cup Var(In(A_i))) = \emptyset$;
2. *for all substitutions α such that*
   $A_i\alpha$ *is correctly typed in input and* $Out(A_i\alpha)$ *is a new variant of* $Out(A_i)$,
   there exists a variant of a clause $K \leftarrow C_1, \ldots, C_r.$ *in P, standardized apart wrt* $A_i\alpha$, *and an mgu* σ *such that* $\sigma = mgu(K, A_i\alpha)$.

A predicate p in P is without failures (noFD predicate) *iff all the clauses in (the deductive closure of) its definition in P are noFD ones.*
The program defining p is then a program without failures (noFD program). □

Definition 3. *Let $\mathbf{Q} = B_1, \ldots, B_j, \ldots, B_m$ be a well-typed query.*
$\mathbf{Q}$ *is without failures (noFD query) in a program P iff for $j \in [1, m]$,*

1. *(Output positions are filled in with distinct variables:)*
   $Out(B_j) = Var(Out(B_j))$ *and if* $X_1, \ldots, X_k$ *are the output terms in* B_j, *then*
   $X_i \neq X_h$, *for* $i \neq h$, $i, h \in [1, k]$,
   (which do not appear leftmost:)
   and $Out(B_j) \cap (Var(B_1, \ldots, B_{j-1}) \cup Var(In(B_j))) = \emptyset$;
2. *for all substitutions* α *such that*
   $B_j\alpha$ *is correctly typed in input and* $Out(B_j\alpha)$ *is a new variant of* $Out(B_j)$,
   there exists a clause $K \leftarrow C_1, \ldots, C_r$. *in* P, *standardized apart wrt* $B_j\alpha$, *and*
   an mgu σ *such that* $\sigma = mgu(K, B_j\alpha)$.   □

The condition for being noFD is local, namely each clause can be considered separately. Only atoms in the clause bodies and in the queries have to satisfy the restrictions, on the head atoms no restriction is required. Hence *a well-typed program containing only facts is trivially noFD*. Note also that the first condition is syntactic and then very simple to verify. The second condition is more complex since it is semantic and relates the clause to its context, but, if a type definition is available, it can be statically verified as shown in the following simple examples.

Example 1. 1) Let us consider the *append* program

```
app([], Ys, Ys).
app([X |Xs], Ys, [X |Zs])  ←  app(Xs, Ys, Zs).
```

with the directional type $app(+ : List, + : List, - : List)$.
This program is noFD. In order to verify this, we observe that it is well-typed wrt its directional type.
The first clause is a fact. Then we consider only the second clause.
The clause has only one atom in the body: $A_1 = app(Xs, Ys, Zs)$, where
   $Out(A_1) = \{Zs\}$, which is a variable and
   $Out(A_1) \cap (Var(In(H) \cup Var(In(A_1)))) = \{Zs\} \cap (\{X, Xs, Ys\} \cup \{Xs, Ys\}) = \emptyset$.
The first condition of Definition 2 is then satisfied.
Moreover for any substitution α such that $Xs\alpha, Ys\alpha \in List$ and $Zs\alpha$ is a new variant of Zs, we have a unifying clause in the program. In fact $Ys\alpha$ unifies with a variable in both the clauses. By definition of $List$, $Xs\alpha$ is either an empty list or a non-empty one, the two cases are respectively captured by the first and the second clause in the program.

2) Let us consider now the query $\mathbf{Q} = app([1], [2], Zs), app(Zs, [3], Ys)$.
It is a noFD query in the previous program *app*. In fact it is well-typed and it satisfies the first condition in Definition 3. Namely $Out(B_1) = \{Zs\}$, $Out(B_2) = \{Ys\}$ and $Out(B_2) \cap (Var(B_1) \cup Var(In(B_2))) = \emptyset$. It also satisfies the second condition in Definition 3. For $B_1\alpha$, with α a new renaming of Zs, the second clause of *append* unifies. For $B_2\alpha$, with $Zs\alpha \in List$ and $Ys\alpha$ new variant of Ys, one of the two clauses of *append* unifies since $Zs\alpha$ is either an empty or a non-empty list.

3) Let us consider now the two queries: $app([1], [2], a)$ and $app([1], [2], [3])$.
They both are well-typed but they do not satisfy the first condition for noFD queries. In fact $Out(B_1)$ is not a variable in both of them.

4) Let us consider the two queries $\mathbf{Q_1} = app([1], [2], Zs), app(Zs, [3], Zs)$ and $\mathbf{Q_2} = app([1], [2], Zs), app([2], [3], Zs)$.

These queries are well-typed but they do not satisfy the first condition for noFD queries too. In this case the problem is that $Out(B_2) \cap (Var(B_1) \cup Var(In(B_2))) \neq \emptyset$.

5) Let us consider now *append* with the reverse directional type $app(- : List, - : List, + : List)$.

Also in this case the program is noFD.

Let us consider the query $app(X, X, [1, 2, 3])$ wrt the same directional type. This query is not noFD since $Out(B_1)$ does not contain distinct variables.   □

noFD programs and queries form a rather restricted class since output terms in the query and body atoms must always be uninstantiated variables. But this is also a very interesting class since we can prove that a noFD query in a noFD program cannot have FDs.

First we state an important property of programs and queries, namely that *LD*-resolution preserves the property of being noFD.

Lemma 1. *Let P be a noFD program and $\mathbf{Q}$ a noFD query in P. Let us consider one non-trivial LD-derivation step $\mathbf{Q} \overset{\sigma}{\longmapsto}_P \mathbf{Q}'$. The query $\mathbf{Q}'$ is also noFD.*

The proof can be found in the Appendix.

Theorem 1. *Let P be a noFD program and $\mathbf{Q}$ a noFD query in P. Then $\mathbf{Q}$ cannot have finitely failing derivations.*

Proof. We prove that for any noFD query $\mathbf{Q}$ and any natural number n, if $\mathbf{Q}$ has a finite *LD*-derivation of length n then it is a successful derivation.

The proof can be given by induction on n.

$n = 1$. $\mathbf{Q} \overset{\sigma}{\longmapsto}_P \mathbf{R}$.

By contradiction let us assume $\mathbf{R} = \mathbf{fail}$. Hence the first atom of $\mathbf{Q}$ can unify with no clause in P.

But $\mathbf{Q}$ is noFD in P, hence well-typed, and its first atom, B_1, is then correctly typed in input positions. By the second property in Definition 2, we have a contradiction for $\alpha = \epsilon$.

Hence finite derivations of one step can only be successful ones.

$n > 1$.   Let us distinguish the first step in the derivation: $\mathbf{Q} \overset{\sigma_1}{\longmapsto}_P \mathbf{Q}' \overset{*\sigma_2}{\longmapsto}_P \mathbf{R}$.

By Lemma 1 we know that the first resolvent $\mathbf{Q}'$ is still a noFD query. Then, by inductive hypothesis applied to $\mathbf{Q}' \overset{*\sigma_2}{\longmapsto}_P \mathbf{R}$, we have the thesis.   □

Note that *our conditions for being noFD are only sufficient to guarantee absence of FDs*. They are clearly not necessary, in fact the query $\mathbf{Q} = app([1], [2], Zs), app([1], [2], Zs)$ is not noFD, since it does not satisfy the first condition in Definition 3, but it does not have FDs.

On the other hand the fact of being noFD clearly does not imply anything on termination. Let us consider the query $p(a, Y)$ and the trivial program

```
p(X,Y) ← p(X,Y).
p(X,b).
```

with directional type $p(+ : Const, - : Const)$. Both the query and the program are noFD but the query has an infinite LD-tree. What we can safely claim is that all finite LD-derivations in such a tree are successful.

The class of noFD programs and queries is very restrictive, in fact outputs cannot be compound terms. For example the queries $\mathbf{Q_1} = app([0, 1, 2], [3], [0|Xs])$ and $\mathbf{Q_2} = app([0, 1, 2], [3], [X|Xs])$, which do not have FDs, are not noFD. Another case which is not captured is exemplified by the query $app([X, 1, 2], [3], [X|Xs])$ which is not in the noFD class since $Var(In(B_1)) \cap Var(Out(B_1)) = \{X\}$ and then the first condition in Definition 3 is not satisfied. But this query clearly does not have FDs!

In order to capture also the previous examples, it would be nice to weaken the first syntactic conditions in Definition 2 and 3. Unluckily there seems to be no easy way to do it. Let us consider for example the finitely failing query $app([1, 1, 2], [3], [a|Xs])$. As soon as we allow for compound terms in output, we have to face these cases. The well-typing condition is no more sufficient to ensure absence of FDs, we would need to impose semantic conditions such as the ones given in [3]. Namely we should require that *for all substitutions α such that $B_i\alpha$ is correctly typed in input and $Out(B_i\alpha)$ is a new variant of $Out(B_i)$, there exist γ such that $B_i\alpha\gamma \in M_P$, where M_P is the least Herbrand model of P.*

Since our goal is to define a static analysis technique for determining absence of FDs, we do not want to have "semantic" conditions.

Moreover, and more seriously, *test queries cannot be in the noFD class.* In fact for a test query the last condition in Definition 3 cannot be satisfied for all type-correct inputs since the purpose of a test is just to act as a filter. As a simple example let us consider the noFD program:

```
test(a,a).
test(a,b).
test(c,c).
```

with directional type $test(+ : Const, - : Const)$ and the query $test(b, Y)$. Clearly such a query cannot satisfy the second condition!

As another example consider the simple query $\mathbf{Q} = app([1], Ys, Zs), Ys \neq [2, 3]$. Clearly the second atom in this query cannot satisfy the second condition.

For this reason, all generate-and-test programs are automatically excluded from the class of noFD programs, as well as all the programs which use tests.

Example 2. 1) Let us consider the following program

```
sumlist([], 0).
sumlist([X |Xs], SX) ← sumlist(Xs, S), sum(S, X, SX).
sum(0, X, X).
sum(s(X), Y, s(Z)) ← sum(X, Y, Z).
```

The predicate $sumlist(x_1, x_2)$ defines the relation between a list of natural numbers, x_1, and a natural number, x_2, which is the sum of the elements of the list. The directional types are $sumlist(+ : ListNat, - : Nat)$ and $sum(+ : Nat, + : Nat, - : Nat)$.

The predicate $sumlist$ is noFD. In order to prove it we observe that it is well-typed and then we consider the two recursive clauses in the definition of $sumlist$ and sum.

Let us consider the clause $sumlist([X|Xs], SX) \leftarrow sumlist(Xs, S), sum(S, X, SX)$.

The first syntactic condition in Definition 2 is trivially satisfied.

For the second one: let us consider α_1 such that $sumlist(Xs, S)\alpha_1$ is correctly typed in input and with $S\alpha_1$ new variant of S. Then $Xs\alpha_1 \in List$, namely either it is an empty list or it is non-empty one. In the first case $sumlist(Xs, S)\alpha_1$ unifies with the first clause in the definition of $sumlist$, in the second case with the second clause.

Let us consider the clause $sum(s(X), Y, s(Z)) \leftarrow sum(X, Y, Z)$.

The first condition in Definition 2 is trivially satisfied.

For the second one we have to consider α_2 such that $sum(X, Y, Z)\alpha_2$ is correctly typed in input and with $Z\alpha_2$ new variant of Z. Then $X\alpha_2, Y\alpha_2 \in Nat$. $Y\alpha_2$ can unify with any clause in the definition of sum, since the second term in both the clauses is a variable. $X\alpha_2$ is either 0 or $s(N)$, with $N \in Nat$. In the first case it can unify with the first clause in the definition of sum, in the second case with the second clause.

2) Let us consider a few programs taken from [25]. Wrt the specified directional types, they are all noFD.

```
prefix([], Ys).
prefix([X |Xs], [X |Ys]) ← prefix(Xs, Ys).
```

with directional type $prefix(- : List, + : List)$;

```
suffix(Xs, Xs).
suffix(Xs, [Y |Ys]) ← suffix(Xs, Ys).
```

with directional type $suffix(- : List, + : List)$;

```
length([], 0).
length([X |Xs], s(N)) ← length(Xs, N).
```

with directional type $length(+ : List, - : Nat)$;

```
reverse([], []).
reverse([X |Xs], Zs) ← reverse(Xs, Ys), append(Ys, [X], Zs).
```

with directional types $reverse(+ : List, - : List)$ and $app(+ : List, + : List, - : List)$;

```
preorder(void, []).
preorder(tree(X, L ,R), Xs) ← preorder(L, Ls),
    preorder(R, Rs),
    append([X |Ls], Rs, Xs).
```

with directional types $preorder(+ : Btree, - : List)$ and $app(+ : List, + : List, - : List)$.

```
hanoi(s(0), A, B, C, [A to B]).
hanoi(s(N), A, B, C, Moves) ← hanoi(N, A, C, B, Ms1),
    hanoi(N, C, B, A, Ms2),
    append(Ms1, [A to B |Ms2], Moves).
```

with directional type $preorder(+ : Nat, + : Pegs, + : Pegs, + : Pegs, - : List)$, where $Pegs = \{a, b, c\}$. □

4   Applications

4.1   Program Correctness

Many techniques have been developed for proving properties of logic programs. Among the properties we usually want to prove are termination wrt a given query [5,10,24], partial correctness of the program wrt a given specification [16,6,13,15,4,3,20] and program completeness wrt a specification [6,15,3].

A difference with imperative programmming is that in logic programming partial correctness of a program wrt a given specification and universal termination of a query do not imply that the query has correct computed answers. In fact, as pointed out in [3], partial correctness and termination do not imply that there are actually correct results, because finite failures are ignored in the verification. For example we can prove the partial correctness of the *app* program wrt the Pre/Post specification $\{x1, x2 \in List\}app(x1, x2, x3)\{x1, x2, x3 \in List\}$. This is exactly the same as proving well-typing of *app* wrt the directional type $app(+ : List, + : List, - : List)$. It means that if *app* is invoked with the first two terms $x1, x2$ which are lists and *if it successfully terminates*, then the c.a.s. will be such that also the third term, $x3$, is a list. We can also prove that the query $app([1], [1, 2], [1, 2])$ universally terminates in *app* since such a proof basically depends on the groundness of the first list. We can prove that it is partially correct wrt an appropriate instance of the same Pre/post specification, namely $\{[1], [1, 2] \in List\}app([1], [1, 2], [1, 2])\{[1], [1, 2], [1, 2] \in List\}$. But nevertheless the query has only a finitely failing *LD*-derivation. This cannot be seen in the verification process and it is due to the fact that correctness proofs are inductive and they ignore failures. *When the Pre-condition is satisfied for an atom in a clause body or in a query, if the atom succeeds then the proof method assumes that the Post-condition holds.* In order to state that there are correct solutions to our query, we need to know also that there are actually successful derivations. To this purpose the following Corollary can be used.

Corollary 1. *Let P be a noFD program and* **Q** *a noFD query in P. If* **Q** *universally terminates, then it has at least a successful derivation.* □

Hence in order to be sure that there are correct c.a.s. we can verify: universal termination of the query + partial correctness of the program and the query + the noFD property of both.

Clearly proving the noFD property is stronger than what we actually need. In fact being noFD and universally terminating implies absence of finite failures, while it would be enough to know that there is at least one successful *LD*-derivation. But this is in general more difficult to prove, while the noFD property is rather easy to prove statically and the proof can be automatized.

Example 3. 1) Let us consider the *app* program with the usual directional type $app(+ : ListNat, + : ListNat, - : ListNat)$ and the query $\mathbf{Q} = app([1, 2], [3, 5], Zs), app(Zs, [6, 8], Ys)$.
We can prove, with one of the existing techniques, that $app(l1, l2, l3)$ is partially correct wrt the Pre/Post specification $\{l1, l2 \in List\}/\{l3 = l1 \cdot l2\}$ and that the query universally terminates and it is partially correct wrt the same Pre/Post specification. But since we know that both *app* and $\mathbf{Q}$ are noFD, we can state also that $l3$ *is actually correctly computed*. Moreover we can claim also that *the computation of the correct result $l3$ is efficient, namely it contains no failing sub-computation.*

2) Let us consider again the program for computing the sum of the elements of a list:

```
sumlist([], 0).
sumlist([X |Xs], SX) ← sumlist(Xs, S), sum(S, X, SX).
sum(0, X, X).
sum(s(X), Y, s(Z)) ← sum(X, Y, Z).
```

with directional types $sumlist(+ : ListNat, - : Nat)$ and $sum(+ : Nat, + : Nat, - : Nat)$.
Let us consider the well-typed query $sumlist([1, 2, 3, 4, 5, 6], N)$. We can prove that the program $sumlist(ls, s)$ is partially correct wrt the Pre/Post specification: $\{ls \in List\}/\{s = \sum e_i, \text{ with } e_i \in ls\}$. We can also prove that the query is universally terminating and partially correct wrt the Pre/Post specification. But since the program and the query are noFD, we can actually state that there is a c.a.s. $(N = 21)$.
As in the previous example we can also state that the computation of N is efficient, since it contains no failing sub-computation.   □

4.2   Program Transformation

When dealing with Prolog programs the order of atoms in the clauses is relevant, as a consequence program transformation techniques become much more restrictive in order to preserve the semantics.
In [7] we define a *safe transformation sequence*, based on new-definition, unfolding and folding, which preserves c.a.s. and universal termination of Prolog programs. Such safe transformation sequence is similar to the one defined by Tamaki and Sato for logic programs [26], but it is more restrictive. The order of the atoms in the bodies is taken into account and moreover the transformation operations have to be applied in the following fixed order:

i)   extend the program with a new, non-recursive, definition;
this extension is the only part of the program which is manipulated in the following three steps (ii, iii, iv);
ii)   apply a decreasing unfold;
iii)   apply unfold or any other non-increasing and complete transformation operation;
iv)   apply fold to introduce recursion;
v)   apply fold to the rest of the program.
Note that the transformation sequence includes a *decreasing unfolding* step (ii) which is necessary in order to prevent folding in step (iv) from introducing loops. For characterizing decreasing unfolding in [7] we state the following Lemma which requires to verify absence of FDs.

Lemma 2 ([7]). *Let $c : N \leftarrow \mathbf{A}, B, \mathbf{C}$. be the only clause in P defining the predicate symbol of N. Let α be a substitution such that $Var(\alpha) \cap Var(c) \subseteq Var(N)$ and $\mathbf{A}\alpha$ has no failing derivation in P.*
Then, unfolding B in c in P is decreasing wrt $\mathbf{G} = \{N\alpha\}$.   □

Clearly unfolding the leftmost atom in the definition is decreasing. But we can now ensure the requirement of the Lemma also on a non-trivial $\mathbf{A}\alpha$ by verifying that $\mathbf{A}\alpha$ is a noFD query in a noFD program. Hence *the noFD property gives the possibility of unfolding also atoms which are not leftmost while preserving universal termination.*

In [8] we extend the safe transformation sequence by adding the possibility to apply a replacement operation in step (iii). *Replacement* is a very powerful transformation operation used to replace a sequence of atoms in a clause body with another (equivalent) sequence [26,19,23,17,9,21]. The *switching* operation, which switches two adjacent atoms in a body, is just a special case of replacement. It is often necessary to reorder the atoms in the body of clauses for applying other transformations such as folding. In the Appendix we recall Definition 5 from [8]. It gives an applicability condition for *safe replacement* such that it is both non-increasing and complete. This guarantees that it preserves both c.a.s. and universal termination when used in a safe transformation sequence. If the two sequences of atoms involved in the replacement are noFD queries, the verification of such applicability condition can be greatly simplified.

Here is a concrete example of transforming a program by a safe transformation sequence which uses two kinds of replacement: associativity of a predicate and switch.

Example 4. Let us consider again $sumlist(x_1, x_2)$:

```
sumlist([], 0).
sumlist([X |Xs], SX) ← sumlist(Xs, S), sum(S, X, SX).
sum(0, X, X).
sum(s(X), Y, s(Z)) ← sum(X, Y, Z).
```

with directional types $sumlist(+ : ListNat, - : Nat)$ and $sum(+ : Nat, + : Nat, - : Nat)$.

We can prove, with one of the known techniques [5,10,24], that *both the well-typed queries $sumlist(x,y)$ and $sum(x1,x2,x3)$ universally terminate*. Moreover we have already verified that, wrt the specified directional types, *the program is noFD*. We apply now the extended safe transformation sequence defined in [7,8] in order to linearize *sumlist* with the accumulation technique.

i)   add a new definition for introducing the accumulator:

```
d: sacc(L, Tot, Acc) ← sumlist(L, SX), sum(SX, Acc, Tot).
```

with the induced directional type $sacc(+ : ListNat, - : Nat, + : Nat)$.
sacc is well-typed and it universally terminates.
Note that *the new clause is noFD*.
In order to optimize *sacc* we apply the following transformations:

ii)   unfold the first atom *sumlist* in *d* (decreasing unfold):

```
sacc([], Tot, Acc) ← sum(0, Acc, Tot).
sacc([X |Xs], Tot, Acc) ← sumlist(Xs, S), sum(S, X, SX),
     sum(SX, Acc, Tot).
```

iii)   unfold the first clause and *apply the associative property of sum to the second clause*, namely replace $\mathbf{B} = sum(S, X, SX), sum(SX, Acc, Tot)$ with $\mathbf{B'} = sum(X, Acc, T), sum(S, T, Tot)$.

This is a safe replacement wrt its directional type by Definition 5 (see the Appendix). In fact it is easy to verify that such replacement is syntactically safe and it preserves the well-typing. Moreover in the following two Lemmas we prove the validity of the other two conditions required by Definition 5

Lemma 3. $\mathbf{B}$ *and* $\mathbf{B'}$ *are equivalent in the second clause, c, wrt the program.*

Proof We have to prove that:
for all substitutions θ such that $Var(\theta) \cap Var(c) \subseteq Var(H, \mathbf{A})$, $Var(\theta) \cap Y = \emptyset$ and $c\theta$ is well-typed,

$$\mathcal{M}[\![P]\!](\mathbf{B}\theta)_{|X\theta} = \mathcal{M}[\![P]\!](\mathbf{B'}\theta)_{|X\theta}.$$

This can be proved by transformation [22,21] as follows.
Since θ in Definition 5 cannot modify $\{SX, T\}$, we can apply to $\mathbf{B}$ our safe transformation sequence.

i)   We define

```
d: p1(S, X, Acc, Tot) ← sum(S, X, SX), sum(SX, Acc, Tot).
```

with directional type $p1(+ : Nat, + : Nat, + : Nat, - : Nat)$, *d* is well-typed and the well-typed instances of *d* exactly correspond to the instances $\mathbf{B}\theta$ of Definition 5.

ii)   We unfold the leftmost atom in *d*. It is a decreasing unfold.

```
1: p1(0, X, Acc, Tot) ← sum(X, Acc, Tot).
2: p1(s(X'), X, Acc, Tot) ← sum(X',X,SX'), sum(s(SX'),Acc,Tot).
```

iii)   We unfold clause 1 and the second atom in clause 2.

```
3: p1(0, 0, Acc, Acc).
4: p1(0, s(X'), Acc, s(Tot')) ← sum(X', Acc, Tot').
5: p1(s(X'), X, Acc, s(Tot')) ← sum(X', X, SX'),
                                 sum(SX', Acc, Tot').
```

iv)   We apply fold to clause 5, thus obtaining the final program:

```
3: p1(0, 0, Acc, Acc).
4: p1(0, s(X'), Acc, s(Tot')) ← sum(X', Acc, Tot').
5: p1(s(X'), X, Acc, s(Tot')) ← p1(X', X, Acc, Tot').
```

We now apply the safe transformation sequence to $\mathbf{B}'$.
i)   We define

```
d: p2(S, X, Acc, Tot) ← sum(X, Acc, T), sum(S, T, Tot).
```

with directional type $p2(+ : Nat, + : Nat, + : Nat, - : Nat)$, d is well-typed
and the well-typed instances of d exactly correspond to the instances $\mathbf{B}'\theta$ of
Definition 5.
ii)   We unfold the second atom in d.
By Lemma 2, this is a decreasing unfold wrt $\mathbf{G} = \{p2(S, X, Acc, Tot)\alpha\}$ *for all*
α *which can be applied in an LD-derivation to d, when used as input clause.* In
fact for all substitutions α such that $Var(\alpha) \cap Var(d) \subseteq \{S, X, Acc, Tot\}$ and $d\alpha$
well-typed, we have that $T\alpha = T$ and then $sum(X, Acc, T)\alpha$ cannot fail. *This*
can be obtained as a consequence of the fact that $sum(X, Acc, T)\alpha$ is universally
terminating and noFD.

```
1: p2(0, X, Acc, Tot) ← sum(X, Acc, Tot).
2: p2(s(X'), X, Acc, s(Tot')) ← sum(X,Acc,T), sum(X',T,Tot').
```

iii-iv)   We unfold clause 1 and then fold clause 2 thus obtaining the final
program:

```
3: p2(0, 0, Acc, Acc).
4: p2(0, s(X'), Acc, s(Tot')) ← sum(X', Acc, Tot').
5: p2(s(X'), X, Acc, s(Tot')) ← p2(X', X, Acc, Tot').
```

The two programs obtained by $\mathbf{B}$ and $\mathbf{B}'$ through a safe transformation sequence
are identical modulo predicate renaming. In this way we proved that $\mathbf{B}\theta$ and $\mathbf{B}'\theta$
are equivalent wrt our semantics and wrt their common variables for all instances
θ as required in Definition 5.   □

We should now verify the last condition in Definition 5.

Lemma 4. $\mathbf{B}'$ *is non-increasing in c wrt $\mathbf{B}$ in P.*

Proof We have to prove that:
for all substitutions θ such that $Var(\theta) \cap Var(c) \subseteq Var(H, \mathbf{A})$, $Var(\theta) \cap Y = \emptyset$
and $c\theta$ is well-typed,

for any finite LD-derivation $l' : \mathbf{B'}\theta \overset{\delta'}{\longmapsto}_P \mathbf{R}$, *where either* $\mathbf{R} = \square$ *or* $\mathbf{R} = \mathbf{fail}$, *there exists a corresponding finite LD-derivation* $l : \mathbf{B}\theta \overset{\delta}{\longmapsto}_P \mathbf{R}$, *with* $X\theta\delta' \sim$ $X\theta\delta$, *which is not shorter:* $|\, l \,| \geq |\, l' \,|$.

We should then analyze both successful and failing *LD*-derivations of $\mathbf{B'}$ and $\mathbf{B}$. But *the original program defining sum is noFD and the tranformation steps performed until now did not modify the definition of sum. We can then easily prove that the queries* $\mathbf{B}$ *and* $\mathbf{B'}$ *are noFD. Hence by Theorem 1 we know that* $\mathbf{B}$ *and* $\mathbf{B'}$ *have no finitely failing LD-derivations, which allows us to cosider only successful LD-derivations of* $\mathbf{B}$ *and* $\mathbf{B'}$.

Successful derivations of a well-typed query $sum(X, Y, Z)\theta$ *have length* $|\, X\theta \,| +1$. This can be easily proved by induction on $|\, X\theta \,|$.

Then successful derivations of $\mathbf{B'}\theta$ have length
$$|\, X\theta \,| +1+ |\, S\theta \,| +1 = |\, X\theta \,| + |\, S\theta \,| +2$$
and successful derivations of $\mathbf{B}\theta$ have length
$$|\, S\theta \,| +1+ |\, SX\theta \,| +1 = |\, S\theta \,| +1 + (|\, S\theta \,| + |\, X\theta \,|) + 1 = 2\,|\, S\theta \,| + |\, X\theta \,| +2.$$

Hence the non-increasing property of Definition 5 is satisfied. $\square$

Note also that the program resulting from this transformation step is still noFD:

```
sacc([], Acc, Acc).
sacc([X |Xs], Tot, Acc) ←  sumlist(Xs, S), sum(X, Acc, T),
      sum(S, T, Tot).
```

- *switch* $sumlist(Xs, S)$ *and* $sum(X, Acc, T)$. It is a safe replacement wrt its directional type by Definition 5. In fact the replacement is syntactically safe and it preserves the well-typing.

Moreover θ in Definition 5 cannot modify $\{S, T\}$, then we can prove that $\mathbf{B}\theta$ and $\mathbf{B'}\theta$ are universally terminating, noFD queries. This allows us to prove, in a rather simple way, both that $\mathbf{B}, \mathbf{B'}$ are equivalent in the second clause wrt the program and that $\mathbf{B'}$ is non-increasing in the clause wrt $\mathbf{B}$. In fact the two atoms in $\mathbf{B}\theta$ cannot share variables since they are both ground in the input terms and $S\theta = S, T\theta = T$. Hence *the two atoms in* $\mathbf{B}\theta$ *are independent, universally terminating and noFD. Clearly switching them has no effect on the length and the c.a.s. of their LD-derivations.*

Note that *the resulting program is still noFD*:

```
sacc([], Acc, Acc).
sacc([X |Xs], Tot, Acc) ←  sum(X, Acc, T), sumlist(Xs, S),
      sum(S, T, Tot).
```

iv)   fold with *d* in *sacc* definition:

```
sacc([], Acc, Acc).
sacc([X |Xs], Tot, Acc) ←  sum(X, Acc, T), sacc(Xs, Tot, T).
```

The resulting program is still noFD.

v)   fold with *d* in the original definition of *sumlist*:

```
sumlist([], 0).
sumlist([X |Xs], SX) ← sacc(Xs, SX, X).
sacc([], Acc, Acc).
sacc([X |Xs], Tot, Acc) ← sum(X, Acc, T), sacc(Xs, Tot, T).
```

This is the final program, optimized through the accumulation technique.   □

This example shows that, *if we know that the sequences of atoms we deal with in a replacement are noFD, we can greatly simplify the verification of the replacement applicability condition.* Furthermore, as exemplified in the equivalence proof, *the noFD property gives the possibility of unfolding also atoms which are not leftmost while preserving universal termination.*

Even if the noFD condition is very restrictive, we generally need to verify it only on some predicates, namely the ones to which we want to apply a specific transformation operation.

On the other hand sometimes we could be interested in preserving the noFD property through the various transformation operations. Let us briefly consider them.

When we introduce a *new definition* which refers to noFD predicates, we have to impose on it the further requirements given by our Definition 2, so that the extended program is also noFD. In our example we define *sacc* which refers to *sumlist* and *sum*, which are both noFD predicates. The new definition *d* is also noFD.

Leftmost unfold unconditionally preserves the noFD property. This is a consequence of Lemma 1. On the contrary general unfold preserves neither the noFD property nor absence of FDs, as shown by the following example.

Example 5. Let us consider the trivial program:

```
1: p(X, Z) ← q(X, Y), r(Y, Z).
   q(b, a).
   r(b, T).
   r(a, T).
```

with directional types:
$p(+ : \{b\}, - : Any), q(+ : \{b\}, - : \{a\}), r(+ : \{a, b\}, - : Any)$.
The program is well-typed and noFD.
By unfolding the second atom in clause 1 we obtain the following program.

```
2: p(X, Z) ← q(X, b).
3: p(X, Z) ← q(X, a).
   q(b, a).
   r(b, T).
   r(a, T).
```

This program is no more noFD since clause 2 does not satisfy the first syntactic condition.

Moreover clause 2, when used as input clause in an LD-derivation, produces a finitely failing derivation. □

Let us now consider *replacement*. In general we need to require that also the resulting clause is noFD. But for some special cases of replacement it is sufficient to require only part of the conditions in Definition 2, as shown in the following discussion.

Fold is a special case of replacement. Let us assume that *we fold a noFD clause* $c : H \leftarrow \mathbf{A}, \mathbf{B}, \mathbf{C}$. *by using a new definition d which is also noFD and let $d\theta$:* $K \leftarrow \mathbf{B}$. Then by definition of fold [7], the replacement of $\mathbf{B}$ with K in c is syntactically safe and preserves well-typing. *The only property we need to require is that the first condition of Definition 3 holds for K.* In fact it is sufficient that
$Out(K) = Var(Out(K))$;
if $X_1, \ldots, X_k$ are the output terms in K, then $X_i \neq X_h$, for $i \neq h$, $i, h \in [1, k]$;
$Out(K) \cap Var(In(K)) = \emptyset$;
in order to be able to prove that
$(c : H \leftarrow \mathbf{A}, \mathbf{B}, \mathbf{C}$. is noFD) implies $(c' : H \leftarrow \mathbf{A}, K, \mathbf{C}$. is noFD).
Note that in our example both d and *fold with d* clearly satisfy the condition.

The *associativity of a predicate* is also a special case of replacement. *This replacement naturally preserves the property of being noFD.* In fact let $\mathbf{B} = (p(X1, X2, T), p(T, X3, Z))\theta$ and $\mathbf{B}' = (p(X2, X3, V), p(X1, V, Z))\theta$, where p is an associative predicate, such as *sum* or *app*, with moding $(+, +, -)$ and θ is a well-typed input substitution with $Dom(\theta_{|\mathbf{B}}) = Dom(\theta_{|\mathbf{B}'}) = \{X1, X2, X3\}$. By definition of replacement, when the associativity is applicable it must be syntactically safe and preserve well-typing. Hence it is easy to prove that
($\mathbf{B}$ is a noFD query) iff ($\mathbf{B}'$ is a noFD query)
and then also
$(c : H \leftarrow \mathbf{A}, \mathbf{B}, \mathbf{C}$. is noFD) iff $(c' : H \leftarrow \mathbf{A}, \mathbf{B}', \mathbf{C}$. is noFD).

Switch is also a special case of replacement. Let $c : H \leftarrow \mathbf{C}, A, B, \mathbf{D}$. Switching A and B in c is clearly syntactically safe and, in order to be applicable, it has to preserve well-typing. Hence we need to impose only the further condition
$Out(A) \cap Var(B) = \emptyset$.
In fact if this is verified, we have that
$(c : H \leftarrow \mathbf{C}, A, B, \mathbf{D}$. is noFD) implies $(c' : H \leftarrow \mathbf{C}, B, A, \mathbf{D}$. is noFD).
Note that *when the two atoms A and B do not share variables*, as in our example, such condition is already verified and then *the noFD property is naturally preserved through switching.*

5   Conclusion

We have defined the class of programs and queries without failures which have the property of not having finitely failing derivations. Such property is easy to check, it is preserved through leftmost unfolding and it is useful both for verifying program properties and for program transformation. The class of noFD programs is very restricted but usually it is sufficient that only some of the predicates in the program are in the class. One of the most serious restrictions is that programs containing tests cannot be in the class. We could extend the noFD class by following two directions: one consists in finding new weaker syntactic conditions for absence of FDs, the other, on which we are presently working, consists in defining the wider class of *successful programs* which includes also programs with tests. noFD queries for successful programs have the property of having at least one successful derivation, if they are universally terminating. This property is more complex to verify but it is less restrictive and still useful both for verifying program properties and for program transformation.

Finitely failing *LD*-derivations, even if relevant in practice, are difficult to study and characterize. Previous studies have focused on the set of atoms which finitely fail. This can be used to characterize properties of negation-as-failures. In program verification and transformation we are actually interested in identifying both the queries which have some successful *LD*-derivations and those which have some finitely failing *LD*-derivations.

Non-failure analysis is interesting also for parallel execution optimization. In [14] a method is given for detecting programs and queries which produce at least one solution or do not terminate. The method is based on a different notion of mode and type information and deals also with programs containing tests. Our proposal is clearly more restrictive, but also simpler to verify.

Acknowledgements

We are grateful to the anonymous referee for their useful remarks.

This work was supported partly by the Italian MURST with the National Research Project on "Modelli della Computazione e dei Linguaggi di programmazione" (40% funding) and partly by the Italian C.N.R. with the "Progetto Coordinato - Programmazione Logica: Strumenti per Analisi e Trasformazione di Programmi; Tecniche di Ingegneria del Software; Estensioni con Vincoli, Concorrenza, Oggetti".

References

1. K. R. Apt. Introduction to Logic Programming. In J. van Leeuwen, editor, *Handbook of Theoretical Computer Science*, volume B: Formal Models and Semantics. Elsevier, Amsterdam and The MIT Press, Cambridge, 1990.
2. K. R. Apt. Declarative programming in Prolog. In D. Miller, editor, *Proceedings of the 1993 International Symposium on Logic Programming*, pages 12–35. The MIT Press, 1993.
3. K. R. Apt. *From Logic Programming to Prolog*. Prentice Hall International Series in Computer Science, 1997.
4. K. R. Apt and E. Marchiori. Reasoning about Prolog programs: from modes through types to assertions. *Formal Aspects of Computing*, 6(6A):743–765, 1994.
5. K. R. Apt and D. Pedreschi. Reasoning about termination of pure Prolog programs. *Information and Computation*, 106(1):109–157, 1993.

6. A. Bossi and N. Cocco. Verifying correctness of logic programs. In J. Diaz and F. Orejas, editors, *TAPSOFT '89, Barcelona, Spain, March 1989, (Lecture Notes in Computer Science, vol. 352)*, pages 96–110. Springer-Verlag, 1989.

7. A. Bossi and N. Cocco. Preserving Universal Termination through Unfold/Fold. In G. Levi and M.Rodriguez-Artalejo, editors, *Algebraic and Logic Programming - Proceedings ALP'94*, volume 850 of *Lecture Notes in Computer Science*, pages 269–286. Springer-Verlag, Berlin, 1994.

8. A. Bossi and N. Cocco. Replacement Can Preserve Termination. In J. Gallagher, editor, *Proceedings LOPSTR'96*, volume 1207 of *Lecture Notes in Computer Science*, pages 104–129. Springer-Verlag, Berlin, 1997.

9. A. Bossi, N. Cocco, and S. Etalle. Transforming Normal Programs by Replacement. In A. Pettorossi, editor, *Meta Programming in Logic - Proceedings META'92*, volume 649 of *Lecture Notes in Computer Science*, pages 265–279. Springer-Verlag, Berlin, 1992.

10. A. Bossi, N. Cocco, and M. Fabris. Norms on terms and their use in proving universal termination of a logic program. *Theoretical Computer Science*, 124:297–328, 1994.

11. J. Boye and J. Maluszynski. Two Aspects of Directional Types. In Sterling, editor, *Proc. Int'l Conf. on Logic Programming*, pages 747–761. MIT Press, 1995.

12. F. Bronsard, T. K. Lakshman, and U. S. Reddy. A framework of directionalities for proving termination of logic programs. In K. R. Apt, editor, *Proceedings of the Joint International Conference and Symposium on Logic Programming*, pages 321–335. The MIT Press, 1992.

13. L. Colussi and E. Marchiori. Proving Correctness of Logic Programs using axiomatic semantics. In *Proc. Eighth Int'l Conf. on Logic Programming*, pages 629–644. MIT Press, 1991.

14. S. Debray, P. Lopez-Garcia, and M.Hermenegildo. Non-Failure Analysis for Logic Programs. In *Proceedings of the International Symposium on Logic Programming*, pages 48–62, 1997.

15. P. Deransart. Proof Methods of Declarative Properties of Definite Programs. *Theoretical Computer Science*, 118:99–166, 1993.

16. W. Drabent and J. Maluszynski. Inductive assertion method for logic programs. *Theoretical Computer Science*, 59:133–155, 1988.

17. P.A. Gardner and J.C. Shepherdson. Unfold/fold Transformations of Logic Programs. In J-L Lassez and editor G. Plotkin, editors, *Computational Logic: Essays in Honor of Alan Robinson*. 1991.

18. J. W. Lloyd. *Foundations of Logic Programming*. Springer-Verlag, Berlin, 1987. Second edition.

19. M.J. Maher. Correctness of a Logic Program Transformation System. IBM Research Report RC13496, T.J. Watson Research Center, 1987.

20. D. Pedreschi and S. Ruggeri. Verification of Metainterpreters. *Journal of Logic and Computation*, 7(2), 1997.

21. A. Pettorossi and M. Proietti. Transformation of Logic Programs: Foundations and Techniques. *Journal of Logic Programming*, 19(20):261–320, 1994.

22. M. Proietti and A. Pettorossi. Synthesis of Programs from Unfold/Fold Proofs. In Y. Deville, editor, *LOPSTR'93*, pages 141–158, 1994.

23. T. Sato. An equivalence preserving first order unfold/fold transformation system. In *Second Int. Conference on Algebraic and Logic Programming, Nancy, France, October 1990, (Lecture Notes in Computer Science, Vol. 463)*, pages 175–188. Springer-Verlag, 1990.

24. D. De Schreye and S. Decorte. Termination of Logic Programs: the never-ending story. *Journal of Logic Programming*, 19-20:199–260, 1994.

25. L. Sterling and E. Shapiro. *The Art of Prolog.* The MIT Press, 1986.

26. H. Tamaki and T. Sato. Unfold/Fold Transformations of Logic Programs. In Sten-Åke Tärnlund, editor, *Proc. Second Int'l Conf. on Logic Programming*, pages 127–139, 1984.

6 Appendix

6.1 Well-Typed Queries and Programs

We recall the definiton of well-typed query and program from [2,4].

To simplify the notation, when writing an atom as $p(\mathbf{u} : \mathbf{S}, \mathbf{v} : \mathbf{T})$, we assume that $\mathbf{u} : \mathbf{S}$ is a sequence of typed terms filling in the input positions of p and $\mathbf{v} : \mathbf{T}$ is a sequence of typed terms filling in the output positions of p.

Definition 4 ([2]).

- *A query $p_1(\mathbf{i_1} : \mathbf{I_1}, \mathbf{o_1} : \mathbf{O_1}), \ldots, p_n(\mathbf{i_n} : \mathbf{I_n}, \mathbf{o_n} : \mathbf{O_n})$ is* well-typed *iff for $j \in [1, n]$*

$$\models \mathbf{o_1} : \mathbf{O_1}, \ldots, \mathbf{o_{j-1}} : \mathbf{O_{j-1}} \;\Rightarrow\; \mathbf{i_j} : \mathbf{I_j}.$$

- *A clause $p_0(\mathbf{o_0} : \mathbf{O_0}, \mathbf{i_{n+1}} : \mathbf{I_{n+1}})$*
  $\leftarrow p_1(\mathbf{i_1} : \mathbf{I_1}, \mathbf{o_1} : \mathbf{O_1}), \ldots, p_n(\mathbf{i_n} : \mathbf{I_n}, \mathbf{o_n} : \mathbf{O_n}).$ *is* well-typed *iff for $j \in [1, n+1]$*

$$\models \mathbf{o_0} : \mathbf{O_0}, \ldots, \mathbf{o_{j-1}} : \mathbf{O_{j-1}} \;\Rightarrow\; \mathbf{i_j} : \mathbf{I_j}.$$

- *A program is* well-typed *iff every clause of it is.*   □

Thus, a query is well-typed if

- the types of the terms filling in the *input* positions of an atom can be deduced from the types of the terms filling in the *output* positions of the previous atoms.

And a clause is well-typed if

- ($j \in [1, n]$) the types of the terms filling the *input* positions of a body atom can be deduced from the types of the terms filling in the *input* positions of the head and the *output* positions of the previous body atoms,
- ($j = n + 1$) the types of the terms filling in the *output* positions of the head can be deduced from the types of the terms filling in the *input* positions of the head and the types of the terms filling in the *output* positions of the body atoms.

Note that a query with only one atom is well-typed iff this atom is correctly typed in its input positions.

6.2   Safe Replacement Wrt Directional Types

In [8] we extend the safe transformation sequence by adding the replacement operation and state the following applicability condition in order to ensure that it preserves both c.a.s. and universal termination.

Definition 5 ([8]). *Let* **B** *and* **B**′ *be sequences of atoms,* P *a well-typed program and* $c : H \leftarrow \mathbf{A}, \mathbf{B}, \mathbf{C}$. *a clause in* P. *Let* X *be the set of* common variables *and* Y *the set of* private variables in **B** and **B**′.
Replacing **B** with **B**′ in c is safe wrt P and its directional types *iff*

- it is syntactically safe, *that is*
  the variables in Y *are local wrt* c *and* c':

$$Var(H, \mathbf{A}, \mathbf{C}) \cap Y = \emptyset;$$

for all substitutions θ *such that* $Var(\theta) \cap Var(c) \subseteq Var(H, \mathbf{A})$, $Var(\theta) \cap Y = \emptyset$ *and* $c\theta$ *is well-typed,*

- the well-typing is preserved, *namely*
  $c'\theta$ *is also well-typed;*
- **B** *and* **B**′ *are equivalent in* c *wrt* P:

$$\mathcal{M}[\![P]\!](\mathbf{B}\theta)_{|X\theta} = \mathcal{M}[\![P]\!](\mathbf{B}'\theta)_{|X\theta};$$

- **B**′ *is non-increasing in* c *wrt* **B** *in* P:
  for any finite LD-derivation $l' : \mathbf{B}'\theta \overset{\delta'}{\longmapsto}_P \mathbf{R}$, *where either* $\mathbf{R} = \square$ *or* $\mathbf{R} = \mathbf{fail}$, *there exists a corresponding finite LD-derivation* $l : \mathbf{B}\theta \overset{\delta}{\longmapsto}_P \mathbf{R}$, *with* $X\theta\delta' \sim X\theta\delta$, *which is not shorter:* $|l| \geq |l'|$. □

The last two conditions are in general not computable and often difficult to verify. For the third one it is possible to use program transformation techniques, while the last one usually requires inductive proofs which can be difficult in presence of FDs.

6.3   Proof of Lemma 1

Lemma *Let* P *be a noFD program and* **Q** *a noFD query in* P. *Let us consider one non-trivial LD-derivation step* $\mathbf{Q} \overset{\sigma}{\longmapsto}_P \mathbf{Q}'$. *The query* **Q**′ *is also noFD.*

Proof. **Q**′ is well-typed by a Lemma in [4].
Let $\mathbf{Q} = B_1, \ldots, B_m$, then $\mathbf{Q}' = (C_1, \ldots, C_r, B_2, \ldots, B_m)\sigma$, where $c : K \leftarrow C_1, \ldots, C_r$. is the input clause used in the derivation step, $\sigma = mgu(K, B_1)$ and c is standardized apart wrt **Q**.
First we prove that the first condition of noFD queries in Definition 3 holds for **Q**′, namely:
  $Out(C_j\sigma)$, for $j \in [1, r]$ and $Out(B_i\sigma)$, for $i \in [2, m]$ are all distinct variables and they do not appear leftmost:

(a) $Out(C_j\sigma) = Var(Out(C_j\sigma))$,

if $X_1, \ldots, X_k$ are the output terms in $C_j\sigma$, then $X_i \neq X_h$, for $i \neq h$, $i, h \in [1, k]$ and

$Out(C_j\sigma) \cap (Var(C_1\sigma, \ldots, C_{j-1}\sigma) \cup Var(In(C_j\sigma))) = \emptyset$, for $j \in [1, r]$;

(b) $Out(B_i\sigma) = Var(Out(B_i\sigma))$,

if $X_1, \ldots, X_k$ are the output terms in $B_i\sigma$, then $X_i \neq X_h$, for $i \neq h$, $i, h \in [1, k]$ and

$Out(B_i\sigma) \cap (Var(C_1\sigma, \ldots, C_r\sigma, B_2\sigma, \ldots, B_{i-1}\sigma) \cup Var(In(B_i\sigma))) = \emptyset$, for $i \in [2, m]$.

c is standardized apart wrt $\mathbf{Q}$ and σ is idempotent and relevant hence $Var(\mathbf{Q}) \cap Var(c) = \emptyset$ and $\sigma = \sigma_{|B_1} \cdot \sigma_{|K}$.

$\mathbf{Q}$ is noFD in P, then by the first property of noFD queries, we know that:

- $Out(B_1)$ are all distinct variables and $Out(B_1) \cap Var(In(B_1)) = \emptyset$; then σ is the identity on $Var(Out(K)) - Var(In(K))$.
- $Out(B_i)$, for $i \in [1, m]$, are all distinct variables and they do not appear leftmost:
  $Out(B_i) \cap (Var(B_1, \ldots, B_{i-1}) \cup Var(In(B_i))) = \emptyset$, for $i \in [2, m]$; then σ is the identity on $Out(B_i)$, for $i \in [2, m]$.

On the other hand c is noFD then

- $Out(C_j)$, for $j \in [1, r]$, are all distinct variables and they do not appear in input terms in the head and leftmost in the body:
  $Out(C_j) \cap (Var(In(K)) \cup Var(C_1, \ldots, C_{j-1}) \cup Var(In(C_j))) = \emptyset$, for $j \in [1, r]$;

then σ is the identity also on $Out(C_j)$, for $j \in [1, r]$.

Hence we can omit some σ in (a), thus it remains to prove:

(a) $Out(C_j) \cap (Var(C_1\sigma, \ldots, C_{j-1}\sigma) \cup Var(In(C_j\sigma))) = \emptyset$, for $j \in [1, r]$.

Since σ is the identity on $Out(C_1, \ldots, C_r)$ and c is noFD, we can reduce it to

(a) $Out(C_j) \cap (Var(In(C_1\sigma, \ldots, C_j\sigma)) = \emptyset$, for $j \in [1, r]$.

Then it is sufficient to prove that $Out(C_j)$ has no variable in common with the ones introduced by σ in $In(K)$, for $j \in [1, r]$.

But $Var(\sigma_{|In(K)}) = Var(In(K)) \cup Var(In(B_1))$ and we already observed that σ is the identity on the terms which are only in output in K, then

$Out(C_j) \cap Var(B_1) = \emptyset$, because c is standardized apart;

$Out(C_j) \cap Var(In(K)) = \emptyset$, since the first property in Definition 2 holds for c.

This concludes the proof of (a).

Let us consider (b). Since σ is the identity on $Out(C_j)$ and on $Out(B_i)$, for $j \in [1, r]$ and $i \in [2, m]$, and since c and $\mathbf{Q}$ are noFD, we can reduce (b) to:

(b) $Out(B_i) \cap (Var(In(C_1\sigma, \ldots, C_r\sigma, B_2\sigma, \ldots, B_i\sigma))) = \emptyset$, for $i \in [2, m]$.

But c and $\mathbf{Q}$ are standardized apart and $\mathbf{Q}$ is noFD, hence it sufficient to prove that $Out(B_i)$ has no variable in common with the ones introduced by σ, for $i \in [2, m]$:

$Out(B_i) \cap Var(\sigma) = \emptyset$, for $i \in [2, m]$, where $Var(\sigma) = Var(K) \cup Var(B_1)$.
As before

$Out(B_i) \cap Var(B_1) = \emptyset$, because **Q** is noFD;

$Out(B_i) \cap Var(K) = \emptyset$, because of the standardization apart.

This concludes the proof of (b). Hence the first condition of Definition 3 is proved for **Q′**.

Let us consider now the second condition of noFD queries.

Such condition holds for **Q** and c and then for the atoms $C_1, \ldots, C_r, B_2, \ldots, B_m$. As we already noticed, σ is the identity on $Out(C_j)$ and on $Out(B_i)$, for $j \in [1, r]$ and $i \in [2, m]$, and the property of being well-typed is preserved through resolution [2,4].

Hence the second condition of Definition 3 is satisfied also for the well-typed query $\mathbf{Q'} = (C_1, \ldots, C_r, B_2, \ldots, B_m)\sigma$.   □

Generalised Logic Program Transformation Schemas

Halime Büyükyıldız and Pierre Flener

Department of Computer Engineering and Information Science
Faculty of Engineering, Bilkent University, 06533, Bilkent, Ankara, Turkey
pf@cs.bilkent.edu.tr

Abstract. Schema-based logic program transformation has proven to be an effective technique for the optimisation of programs. This paper results from the research that began by investigating the suggestions in [11] to construct a more general database of transformation schemas for optimising logic programs at the declarative level. The proposed transformation schemas fully automate accumulator introduction (also known as descending computational generalisation), tupling generalisation (a special case of structural generalisation), and duality laws (which are extensions to relational programming of the first duality law of the fold operators in functional programming). The schemas are proven correct. A prototype schema-based transformation system is evaluated.

1 Introduction

Schema-based program *construction* and *synthesis* were studied in logic programming [9,10,16,14,23] and in functional programming [20,21]. Using schemas for logic program *transformation* was first studied in [13] and then extended in [25,18]. Schema-based logic program transformation was also studied in [11,15]. This paper results from the research that began by investigating the suggestions in [11] and extending the ideas in [1] to construct a database of more general transformation schemas for optimising logic programs at the declarative level. For full details of this research, the reader is invited to consult [5].

Throughout this paper, the word program (resp. procedure) is used to mean typed definite program (resp. procedure). An *open program* is a program where some of the relations appearing in the clause bodies are not appearing in any heads of clauses, and these relations are called *undefined* (or *open*) relations. If all the relations appearing in the program are *defined*, then the program is a *closed program*. The format of a *specification* S_r of a relation r is:

$$\forall X : \mathcal{X}. \ \forall Y : \mathcal{Y}. \ \mathcal{I}_r(X) \Rightarrow [r(X,Y) \Leftrightarrow \mathcal{O}_r(X,Y)]$$

where $\mathcal{I}_r(X)$ denotes the *input condition* that must be fulfilled before the execution of the procedure, and $\mathcal{O}_r(X,Y)$ denotes the *output condition* that will be fulfilled after the execution.

We now give the definitions of the notions that will be used throughout the paper. All the definitions are given for programs in closed *frameworks* [12]. A

Norbert E. Fuchs (Ed.): LOPSTR'97, LNCS 1463, pp. 49–68, 1998.
© Springer-Verlag Berlin Heidelberg 1998

framework can be defined simply as a full first-order theory (with identity) with intended model. A closed framework has no parameters and open symbols. Thus, it completely defines an abstract data type (ADT).

Correctness and Equivalence Criteria. We first give correctness and equivalence criteria for programs.

Definition 1 ((Correctness of a Closed Program)).
Let P be a closed program for a relation r in a closed framework $\mathcal{F}$. We say that P is *(totally) correct* wrt its specification S_r iff, for any ground term t of $\mathcal{X}$ such that $\mathcal{I}_r(t)$ holds, we have $P \vdash r(t, u)$ iff $\mathcal{F} \models \mathcal{O}_r(t, u)$, for every ground term u of $\mathcal{Y}$. If we replace 'iff' by 'implies' in the condition above, then P is said to be *partially correct* wrt S_r, and if we replace 'iff' by 'if', then P is said to be *complete* wrt S_r.

This kind of correctness is not entirely satisfactory, for two reasons. First, it defines the correctness of P in terms of the procedures for the relations in its clause bodies, rather than in terms of their specifications. Second, P must be a closed program, even though it might be desirable to discuss the correctness of P without having to fully implement it. So, the abstraction achieved through the introduction (and specification) of the relations in its clause bodies is wasted. This leads us to the notion of steadfastness (also known as parametric correctness) [12,9].

Definition 2 ((Steadfastness of an Open Program)).
In a closed framework $\mathcal{F}$, let:

- P be an open program for a relation r
- $q_1, \ldots, q_m$ be all the undefined relation names appearing in P
- $S_1, \ldots, S_m$ be the specifications of $q_1, \ldots, q_m$.

We say that P is *steadfast* wrt its specification S_r in $\{S_1, \ldots, S_m\}$ iff the (closed) program $P \cup P_S$ is correct wrt S_r, where P_S is any closed program such that:

- P_S is correct wrt each specification S_j $(1 \leq j \leq m)$
- P_S contains no occurrences of the relations defined in P.

For program equivalence, now, we do not require the two programs to have the same models, because this would not make much sense in some program transformation settings, where the transformed program features relations that are not in the initially given program. That is why our program equivalence criterion establishes equivalence wrt the specification of a common relation (usually the root of their call-hierarchies).

Definition 3 ((Equivalence of Two Open Programs)).
In a closed framework $\mathcal{F}$, let P and Q be two open programs for a relation r. Let $S_1, \ldots, S_m$ be the specifications of $p_1, \ldots, p_m$, which are all the undefined relation names appearing in P, and let $S'_1, \ldots, S'_t$ be the specifications of

$q_1, \ldots, q_t$, which are all the undefined relation names appearing in Q. We say that $\langle P, \{S_1, \ldots, S_m\}\rangle$ is *equivalent to* $\langle Q, \{S'_1, \ldots, S'_t\}\rangle$ wrt the specification S_r (or simply that P is equivalent to Q wrt S_r) when P is steadfast wrt S_r in $\{S_1, \ldots, S_m\}$ and Q is steadfast wrt S_r in $\{S'_1, \ldots, S'_t\}$. Since the 'is equivalent to' relation is symmetric, we also say that P and Q are *equivalent* wrt S_r.

In program transformation settings, there sometimes are conditions that have to be satisfied by some parts of the initial and/or transformed program in order to have a transformed program that is equivalent to the initially given program wrt the specification of the top-level relation. Hence the following definition.

Definition 4 ((Conditional Equivalence of Two Open Programs)).

In a closed framework $\mathcal{F}$, let P and Q be two open programs for a relation r. We say that P is *equivalent to* Q wrt the specification S_r *under* conditions C iff P is *equivalent to* Q wrt S_r whenever C holds.

Program Schemas and Schema Patterns. The notion of program schema was also used in [9,10,11,13,16,14,15,6,25], but here we have an additional component, which makes our definition [12] of program schemas different.

Definition 5 ((Program Schemas)).
In a closed framework $\mathcal{F}$, a *program schema* for a relation r is a pair $\langle T, C\rangle$, where T is an open program for r, called the *template*, and C is a set of specifications of the open relations of T, in terms of each other and in terms of the input/output conditions of the closed relations of T. The specifications in C, called the *steadfastness constraints*, are such that, in $\mathcal{F}$, T is steadfast wrt its specification S_r in C.

Sometimes, a series of schemas are quite similar, in the sense that they only differ in the number of arguments of some relation, or in the number of calls to some relation, etc. For this purpose, rather than having a proliferation of similar schemas, we introduce the notion of *schema pattern* (compare with [6]).

Definition 6 ((Schema Patterns)).
A *schema pattern* is a program schema where term, conjunct, and disjunct ellipses are allowed in the template and in the steadfastness constraints.

For instance, $TX_1, \ldots, TX_t$ is a term ellipsis, and $\bigwedge_{i=1}^{t} r(TX_i, TY_i)$ is a conjunct ellipsis. Our schemas are more general than those in [11] in the sense that we now allow such ellipses.

Schema-based Program Transformation. In schema-based transformation, transformation techniques are pre-compiled at the schema-level.

Definition 7 ((Transformation Schemas)).
A *transformation schema* is a 5-tuple $\langle S_1, S_2, A, O_{12}, O_{21}\rangle$, where S_1 and S_2 are program schemas (or schema patterns), A is a set of *applicability conditions*,

which ensure the equivalence of the templates of S_1 and S_2 wrt the specification of the top-level relation, and O_{12} (resp. O_{21}) is a set of *optimisability conditions*, which ensure further optimisability of the output program schema (or schema pattern) S_2 (resp. S_1).

If a transformation schema embodies some generalisation technique, then it is called a *generalisation schema*. The problem generalisation techniques that are used in this paper are explained in detail in [9]. Using these techniques for synthesising and/or transforming a program in a schema-based fashion was first proposed in [9,10], and then extended in [11]. The generalisation methods that we pre-compile in our transformation schemas are *tupling generalisation*, which is a special case of *structural generalisation* where the structure of some parameter is generalised, and *descending generalisation*, which is a special case of *computational generalisation* where the general state of computation is generalised in terms of what remains to be done. If a transformation schema embodies a duality law, then it is called a *duality schema*.

In the remainder of this paper, we first give two divide-and-conquer schema patterns in Section 2. We then explain in detail how automation of program transformation is achieved by tupling and descending generalisation, in Sections 3 and 4. In Section 5, we explain the duality schemas. In Section 6, we discuss, by using the results of performance tests, the effects of the optimisability conditions in the transformation schemas. Before we conclude, the prototype transformation system, which was developed to test the practicality of the ideas explained in this paper, is presented in Section 7.

2   Divide-and-Conquer Programs

The schema patterns in this section abstract sub-families of divide-and-conquer (DC) programs. They are here restricted to binary relations with X as the induction parameter and Y as the result parameter, to reflect the schema patterns that can be handled by the prototype transformation system explained in Section 7. Another restriction in the schema patterns is that when X is non-minimal, then X is decomposed into $h = 1$ head HX and $t > 0$ tails $TX_1, \ldots, TX_t$, so that Y is composed from 1 head HY (which is the result of processing HX) and t tails $TY_1, \ldots, TY_t$ (which are the results of recursively calling the relation with $TX_1, \ldots, TX_t$, respectively) by p-fix composition (i.e., Y is composed by putting its head HY between its tails TY_{p-1} and TY_p).

These schema patterns are called $DCLR$ and $DCRL$ (the reason for these names will be explained soon). Template $DCLR$ (resp. $DCRL$) below is the template of the $DCLR$ (resp. $DCRL$) schema pattern. In these patterns, *minimal*, *solve*, etc., denote place-holders for relation symbols. During the particularisation of a schema pattern to a schema, all these place-holders are *renamed*, because otherwise all divide-and-conquer programs would have the same relation symbols. Indeed, since a template is an open program, the idea is to obtain concrete programs from the template by *adding* programs for the open relations, such that these programs satisfy the steadfastness constraints. The steadfastness constraints corresponding to these DC templates (i.e., the specifications of their open relations) are the same, since these templates have the same open relations. Such constraints are shown in [12] in this volume.

$$r(X,Y) \leftarrow$$
$$minimal(X),$$
$$solve(X,Y)$$
$$r(X,Y) \leftarrow$$
$$nonMinimal(X),$$
$$decompose(X,HX,TX_1,\ldots,TX_t),$$
$$r(TX_1,TY_1),\ldots,r(TX_t,TY_t),$$
$$init(I_0),$$
$$compose(I_0,TY_1,I_1),\ldots,compose(I_{p-2},TY_{p-1},I_{p-1}),$$
$$process(HX,HY),compose(I_{p-1},HY,I_p),$$
$$compose(I_p,TY_p,I_{p+1}),\ldots,compose(I_t,TY_t,I_{t+1}),$$
$$Y = I_{t+1}$$

Template $DCLR$

$$r(X,Y) \leftarrow$$
$$minimal(X),$$
$$solve(X,Y)$$
$$r(X,Y) \leftarrow$$
$$nonMinimal(X),$$
$$decompose(X,HX,TX_1,\ldots,TX_t),$$
$$r(TX_1,TY_1),\ldots,r(TX_t,TY_t),$$
$$init(I_{t+1}),$$
$$compose(TY_t,I_{t+1},I_t),\ldots,compose(TY_p,I_{p+1},I_p),$$
$$process(HX,HY),compose(HY,I_p,I_{p-1}),$$
$$compose(TY_{p-1},I_{p-1},I_{p-2}),\ldots,compose(TY_1,I_1,I_0),$$
$$Y = I_0$$

Template $DCRL$

We can now explain the underlying idea why we have two different schema patterns for DC, and why we call them $DCLR$ and $DCRL$. If we denote the functional version of the *compose* relation with $\oplus$, then the composition of Y in template $DCLR$ by *left-to-right (LR) composition ordering* can be written as:

$$Y = ((((((e \oplus TY_1) \oplus \ldots) \oplus TY_{p-1}) \oplus HY) \oplus TY_p) \oplus \ldots) \oplus TY_t \quad (1)$$

where e is the (unique) term for which *init* holds. Similarly, the composition of Y in $DCRL$ by *right-to-left (RL) composition ordering* can be written as:

$$Y = TY_1 \oplus (\ldots \oplus (TY_{p-1} \oplus (HY \oplus (TY_p \oplus (\ldots \oplus (TY_t \oplus e)))))) \qquad (2)$$

Throughout the paper, we use the *infix_flat* problem, whose DC programs are given in the example below.

Example 1. The specification of *infix_flat* is:

infix_flat(B, F) iff list F is the infix representation of binary tree B

where *infix representation* means the list representation of the infix traversal of the tree. Program 1 (resp. Program 2) below is the program for the *infix_flat*/2 problem that is a (partially evaluated) instance of the $DCLR$ (resp. $DCRL$) schema pattern, for $t = p = 2$. Note the line-by-line correspondence between the program computations and the templates.

$infix\_flat(B, F) \leftarrow$	$infix\_flat(B, F) \leftarrow$
$\quad B = void,$	$\quad B = void,$
$\quad F = []$	$\quad F = []$
$infix\_flat(B, F) \leftarrow$	$infix\_flat(B, F) \leftarrow$
$\quad B = bt(\_, \_, \_),$	$\quad B = bt(\_, \_, \_),$
$\quad B = bt(L, E, R),$	$\quad B = bt(L, E, R),$
$\quad infix\_flat(L, FL),$	$\quad infix\_flat(L, FL),$
$\qquad infix\_flat(R, FR),$	$\qquad infix\_flat(R, FR),$
$\quad I_0 = [],$	$\quad I_3 = [],$
$\quad append(I_0, FL, I_1),$	$\quad append(FR, I_3, I_2),$
$\quad HF = [E], append(I_1, HF, I_2),$	$\quad HF = [E], append(HF, I_2, I_1),$
$\quad append(I_2, FR, I_3),$	$\quad append(FL, I_1, I_0),$
$\quad F = I_3$	$\quad F = I_0$

Program 1	**Program 2**

3   Program Transformation by Tupling Generalisation

If a program for a relation r, which has the specification S_r of Section 1, is given as an instance of $DCLR$ (or $DCRL$), then the specification of the tupling-generalised problem of r, namely $S_{r\_tupling}$, is:

$$\forall Xs : list \text{ of } \mathcal{X}. \ \forall Y : \mathcal{Y}. \ (\forall X : \mathcal{X}. \ X \in Xs \Rightarrow \mathcal{I}_r(X)) \Rightarrow$$
$$(r\_tupling(Xs, Y) \Leftrightarrow (Xs = [] \wedge Y = e) \vee (Xs = [X_1, X_2, \ldots, X_n]$$
$$\wedge \bigwedge_{i=1}^{n} \mathcal{O}_r(X_i, Y_i) \ \wedge I_1 = Y_1 \wedge \bigwedge_{i=2}^{n} \mathcal{O}_c(I_{i-1}, Y_i, I_i) \ \wedge Y = I_n))$$

where $\mathcal{O}_c$ is the output condition of *compose*, and e is the (unique) term for which *init* holds.

The tupling generalisation schemas (one for each DC schema pattern) are:

TG_1 : $\langle$ $DCLR$, TG, A_{t_1}, $O_{t_1}12$, $O_{t_1}21$ $\rangle$ where

$\quad A_{t_1}$: - $compose$ is associative

$\qquad$ - $compose$ has e as the left and right identity element

$\qquad$ - $\forall X : \mathcal{X}.\ \ \mathcal{I}_r(X) \wedge minimal(X) \Rightarrow \mathcal{O}_r(X, e)$

$\qquad$ - $\forall X : \mathcal{X}.\ \ \mathcal{I}_r(X) \Rightarrow [\neg minimal(X) \Leftrightarrow nonMinimal(X)]$

$\quad O_{t_1}12$: partial evaluation of the conjunction

$\qquad process(HX, HY), compose(HY, TY, Y)$

$\qquad$ results in the introduction of a non-recursively defined relation

$\quad O_{t_1}21$: partial evaluation of the conjunction

$\qquad process(HX, HY), compose(I_{p-1}, HY, I_p)$

$\qquad$ results in the introduction of a non-recursively defined relation

TG_2 : $\langle$ $DCRL$, TG, A_{t_2}, $O_{t_2}12$, $O_{t_2}21$ $\rangle$ where

$\quad A_{t_2}$: - $compose$ is associative

$\qquad$ - $compose$ has e as the left and right identity element

$\qquad$ - $\forall X : \mathcal{X}.\ \ \mathcal{I}_r(X) \wedge minimal(X) \Rightarrow \mathcal{O}_r(X, e)$

$\qquad$ - $\forall X : \mathcal{X}.\ \ \mathcal{I}_r(X) \Rightarrow [\neg minimal(X) \Leftrightarrow nonMinimal(X)]$

$\quad O_{t_2}12$: partial evaluation of the conjunction

$\qquad process(HX, HY), compose(HY, TY, Y)$

$\qquad$ results in the introduction of a non-recursively defined relation

$\quad O_{t_2}21$: partial evaluation of the conjunction

$\qquad process(HX, HY), compose(HY, I_p, I_{p-1})$

$\qquad$ results in the introduction of a non-recursively defined relation

where the template of the common schema pattern TG is given on the next page.

Note that, in the TG template, *all* the open relations of $DCLR$ (or $DCRL$) appear, but *no* new relations. This crucial observation enables the once-and-for-all verification of the conditional equivalence of the two templates in the TG_i transformation schemas wrt S_r under A_{t_i}, which verification is thus independent of the actual specifications of the open relations (i.e., the steadfastness constraints) [4].

The applicability conditions of TG_1 (resp. TG_2) ensure the equivalence of the $DCLR$ (resp. $DCRL$) and TG programs for a given problem. The optimisability conditions ensure that the output programs of these generalisation schemas can be made more efficient than the input programs. Indeed, the optimisability conditions, together with some of the applicability conditions, check whether the $compose$ calls in the TG template can be eliminated. For instance, the conjunction $solve(X, HY), compose(HY, TY, Y)$ in the second clause of $r\_tupling$ can be simplified to $Y = A$, if relation r maps the minimal form of X into e, and if e is also the right identity element of $compose$. This is already checked by the second and third applicability conditions of TG_1 and TG_2. Also, in the third and fourth clauses of $r\_tupling$, the conjunction $process(HX, HY), compose(HY, TY, Y)$ can be partially evaluated, resulting in the disappearance of that call to $compose$, and thus in a merging of the $compose$ loop into the r loop in the $DCLR$ (or $DCRL$) template, if the optimisability condition $O_{t_1}12$ (or $O_{t_2}12$) holds.

Let us illustrate tupling generalisation by applying the TG_i generalisation schemas on the $infix\_flat$ problem.

$r(X, Y) \leftarrow$
  $r\_tupling([X], Y)$
$r\_tupling(Xs, Y) \leftarrow$
  $Xs = [\,],$
  $init(Y)$
$r\_tupling(Xs, Y) \leftarrow$
  $Xs = [X|TXs],$
  $minimal(X),$
  $r\_tupling(TXs, TY),$
  $solve(X, HY),$
  $compose(HY, TY, Y),$
$r\_tupling(Xs, Y) \leftarrow$
  $Xs = [X|TXs],$
  $nonMinimal(X),$
  $decompose(X, HX, TX_1, \ldots, TX_t),$
  $minimal(TX_1), \ldots, minimal(TX_t),$
  $r\_tupling(TXs, TY),$
  $process(HX, HY),$
  $compose(HY, TY, Y)$
$r\_tupling(Xs, Y) \leftarrow$
  $Xs = [X|TXs],$
  $nonMinimal(X),$
  $decompose(X, HX, TX_1, \ldots, TX_t),$
  $minimal(TX_1), \ldots, minimal(TX_{p-1}),$
  $(nonMinimal(TX_p); \ldots; nonMinimal(TX_t)),$
  $r\_tupling([TX_p, \ldots, TX_t|TXs], TY),$
  $process(HX, HY),$
  $compose(HY, TY, Y)$
$r\_tupling(Xs, Y) \leftarrow$
  $Xs = [X|TXs],$
  $nonMinimal(X),$
  $decompose(X, HX, TX_1, \ldots, TX_t),$
  $(nonMinimal(TX_1); \ldots; nonMinimal(TX_{p-1})),$
  $minimal(TX_p), \ldots, minimal(TX_t),$
  $minimal(U_1), \ldots, minimal(U_{p-1}),$
  $decompose(N, HX, U_1, \ldots, U_{p-1}, TX_p, \ldots, TX_t),$
  $r\_tupling([TX_1, \ldots, TX_{p-1}, N|TXs], Y)$
$r\_tupling(Xs, Y) \leftarrow$
  $Xs = [X|TXs],$
  $nonMinimal(X),$
  $decompose(X, HX, TX_1, \ldots, TX_t),$
  $(nonMinimal(TX_1); \ldots; nonMinimal(TX_{p-1})),$
  $(nonMinimal(TX_p); \ldots; nonMinimal(TX_t)),$
  $minimal(U_1), \ldots, minimal(U_t),$
  $decompose(N, HX, U_1, \ldots, U_t),$
  $r\_tupling([TX_1, \ldots, TX_{p-1},$
       $N, TX_p, \ldots, TX_t|TXs], Y)$

$infix\_flat(B, F) \leftarrow$
  $infix\_flat\_t([B], F)$
$infix\_flat\_t(Bs, F) \leftarrow$
  $Bs = [\,],$
  $F = [\,]$
$infix\_flat\_t(Bs, F) \leftarrow$
  $Bs = [B|TBs],$
  $B = void,$
  $infix\_flat\_t(TBs, TF),$
  $HF = [\,],$
  $append(HF, TF, F)$
$infix\_flat\_t(Bs, F) \leftarrow$
  $Bs = [B|TBs],$
  $B = bt(\_, \_, \_),$
  $B = bt(L, E, R),$
  $L = void, R = void,$
  $infix\_flat\_t(TBs, TF),$
  $HF = [E],$
  $append(HF, TF, F)$
$infix\_flat\_t(Bs, F) \leftarrow$
  $Bs = [B|TBs],$
  $B = bt(\_, \_, \_),$
  $B = bt(L, E, R),$
  $L = void,$
  $R = bt(\_, \_, \_),$
  $infix\_flat\_t([R|TBs], TF),$
  $HF = [E],$
  $append(HF, TF, F)$
$infix\_flat\_t(Bs, F) \leftarrow$
  $Bs = [B|TBs],$
  $B = bt(\_, \_, \_),$
  $B = bt(L, E, R),$
  $L = bt(\_, \_, \_),$
  $R = void,$
  $U_L = void,$
  $N = bt(U_L, E, R),$
  $infix\_flat\_t([L, N|TBs], TF),$
$infix\_flat\_t(Bs, F) \leftarrow$
  $Bs = [B|TBs],$
  $B = bt(\_, \_, \_),$
  $B = bt(L, E, R),$
  $L = bt(\_, \_, \_),$
  $R = bt(\_, \_, \_),$
  $U_L = void, U_R = void,$
  $N = bt(U_L, E, U_R),$
  $infix\_flat\_t([L, N, R|TBs], F)$

Template TG and Program 3

Example 2. The specification of the *infix_flat* problem, and its *DCLR* and *DCRL* programs, are in Example 1 in Section 2. The *infix_flat* problem can be tupling-generalised using the TG_i transformation schemas above, since the *infix_flat* programs have open relations that satisfy the applicability and optimisability conditions of these schemas. So, the specification of the tupling-generalised problem of *infix_flat* is:

infix_flat_t(Bs, F) iff F is the concatenation of the infix representations of the elements in the binary tree list Bs.

Program 3 on the previous page is the tupling-generalised program for *infix_flat* as an instance of TG, for $t = p = 2$.

Although the tupling generalisation schemas are constructed to tupling-generalise DC programs (i.e., to transform DC programs into TG programs), these schemas can also be used in the reverse direction, such that they transform TG programs into DC programs, provided the optimisability conditions for the corresponding *DC* schema pattern are satisfied; note that applicability conditions work in both directions.

4 Program Transformation by Descending Generalisation

Descending generalisation [9] can also be called the *accumulation strategy* (as in functional programming [2], and in logic programming [17]), since it introduces an accumulator parameter and progressively extends it to the final result. Descending generalisation can also be seen as transformation towards *difference structure* manipulation, since any form of difference structures can be created by descending generalisation, and not just difference-lists.

Four descending generalisation schemas (two for each DC schema pattern) are given. Since the applicability conditions of each descending generalisation schema are different, the process of choosing the appropriate generalisation schema for the input DC program is done only by checking the applicability and optimisability conditions, and the eureka (i.e., the specification of the generalised problem) then comes for free.

The reason why we call the descendingly generalised (DG) schema patterns '*DGLR*' and '*DGRL*' is similar to the reason why we call the divide-and-conquer schema patterns *DCLR* and *DCRL*, respectively. In descending generalisation, the composition ordering for extending the accumulator parameter in the template *DGLR* (resp. *DGRL*) is from *left-to-right* (LR) (resp. *right-to-left* (RL)).

The first two descending generalisation schemas are:

$DG_1 : \langle\ DCLR,\ DGLR,\ A_{dg_1},\ O_{dg_1 12},\ O_{dg_1 21}\ \rangle$ where
    A_{dg_1} : - *compose* is associative
           - *compose* has e as the left identity element
    $O_{dg_1 12}$: - *compose* has e as the right identity element
            and $\mathcal{I}_r(X) \wedge minimal(X) \Rightarrow \mathcal{O}_r(X, e)$
           - partial evaluation of the conjunction

$$process(HX, HY), compose(A_{p-1}, HY, A_p)$$
results in the introduction of a non-recursively defined relation
$O_{dg_1 21}$: - partial evaluation of the conjunction
$$process(HX, HY), compose(I_{p-1}, HY, I_p)$$
results in the introduction of a non-recursively defined relation

DG_4 : $\langle$ $DCRL$, $DGLR$, A_{dg_4}, $O_{dg_4 12}$, $O_{dg_4 21} \rangle$ where
  A_{dg_4} : - $compose$ is associative
      - $compose$ has e as the left and right identity element
  $O_{dg_4 12}$: - $\mathcal{I}_r(X) \land minimal(X) \Rightarrow \mathcal{O}_r(X, e)$
      - partial evaluation of the conjunction
      $$process(HX, HY), compose(A_{p-1}, HY, A_p)$$
      results in the introduction of a non-recursively defined relation
  $O_{dg_4 21}$: - partial evaluation of the conjunction
      $$process(HX, HY), compose(HY, I_p, I_{p-1})$$
      results in the introduction of a non-recursively defined relation

where e is the (unique) term for which $init$ holds. These schemas have the *same* formal specification (i.e., eureka) for the relation $r\_descending_1$ of the schema pattern $DGLR$, namely:

$$\forall X : \mathcal{X}. \ \forall Y, A : \mathcal{Y}. \ \ \mathcal{I}_r(X) \Rightarrow$$
$$[r\_descending_1(X, Y, A) \ \Leftrightarrow \ \exists S : \mathcal{Y}. \ \mathcal{O}_r(X, S) \land \mathcal{O}_c(A, S, Y)]$$

where $\mathcal{O}_c$ is the output condition of *compose*. The template of the common schema pattern $DGLR$ of DG_1 and DG_4 is:

$r(X, Y) \leftarrow$
  $init(A), r\_descending_1(X, Y, A)$
$r\_descending_1(X, Y, A) \leftarrow$
  $minimal(X),$
  $solve(X, S), compose(A, S, Y)$
$r\_descending_1(X, Y, A) \leftarrow$
  $nonMinimal(X),$
  $decompose(X, HX, TX_1, \ldots, TX_t),$
  $init(E), compose(A, E, A_0),$
  $r\_descending_1(TX_1, A_1, A_0), \ldots, r\_descending_1(TX_{p-1}, A_{p-1}, A_{p-2}),$
  $process(HX, HY), compose(A_{p-1}, HY, A_p),$
  $r\_descending_1(TX_p, A_{p+1}, A_p), \ldots, r\_descending_1(TX_t, A_{t+1}, A_t),$
  $Y = A_{t+1}$

Template $DGLR$

Note that, in the $DGLR$ template, *all* the open relations of $DCLR$ (or $DCRL$) appear, but *no* new relations. The applicability and optimisability conditions of these two generalisation schemas differ, since the composition ordering is changed from RL to LR in DG_4.

We now illustrate descending generalisation on our $infix\_flat$ problem.

Example 3. The specification of a program for the LR descendingly generalised version of $infix\_flat$ is:

$infix\_flat\_descending_1(B, F, A)$ iff list F is the concatenation of list A and the infix representation of binary tree B.

Program 4 is the program for $infix\_flat$ as an instance of $DGLR$, for $t = p = 2$.

$$infix\_flat(B, F) \leftarrow$$
$$infix\_flat\_descending_1(B, F, [\,])$$
$$infix\_flat\_descending_1(B, F, A) \leftarrow$$
$$B = void,$$
$$S = [\,], append(A, S, F)$$
$$infix\_flat\_descending_1(B, F, A) \leftarrow$$
$$B = bt(\_,\_,\_),$$
$$B = bt(L, E, R),$$
$$append(A, [\,], A_0),$$
$$infix\_flat\_descending_1(L, A_1, A_0),$$
$$HF = [E], append(A_1, HF, A_2),$$
$$infix\_flat\_descending_1(R, A_3, A_2),$$
$$F = A_3$$

Program 4

Since the applicability conditions of DG_1 (resp. DG_4) are satisfied for the input $DCLR$ (resp. $DCRL$) $infix\_flat$ program, the descendingly generalised $infix\_flat$ program can be Program 4. However, for this problem, descending generalisation of the $infix\_flat$ programs with the DG transformation schemas above should *not* be done, since the optimisability conditions of DG_1 (resp. DG_4) are not satisfied by the open relations of $infix\_flat$. Indeed, in the non-minimal case of $infix\_flat\_descending_1$, partial evaluation of the conjunction $HF = [E], append(A_1, HF, A_2)$ does not result in the introduction of a non-recursively defined relation, because of properties of $append$ (actually, due to the inductive definition of lists). Moreover, the induction parameter of $append$, which is here the accumulator parameter, increases in length each time $append$ is called in the non-minimal case, which shows that this program is not a good choice as a descendingly generalised program for this problem. So, the optimisability conditions are really useful to prevent non-optimising transformations.

The other two descending generalisation schemas are:

$DG_2 : \langle\ DCLR,\ DGRL,\ A_{dg_2},\ O_{dg_212},\ O_{dg_221}\ \rangle$ where
$\quad A_{dg_2}\ :$ - *compose* is associative
$\qquad$ - *compose* has e as the left and right identity element
$\quad O_{dg_212} :$ - $\mathcal{I}_r(X) \wedge minimal(X) \Rightarrow \mathcal{O}_r(X, e)$
$\qquad$ - partial evaluation of the conjunction

$$process(HX, HY), compose(HY, A_p, A_{p-1})$$
results in the introduction of a non-recursively defined relation
$O_{dg_2 21}$: - partial evaluation of the conjunction
$$process(HX, HY), compose(I_{p-1}, HY, I_p)$$
results in the introduction of a non-recursively defined relation

DG_3 : $\langle$ $DCRL$, $DGRL$, A_{dg_3}, $O_{dg_3 12}$, $O_{dg_3 21}\rangle$ where
$\quad A_{dg_3}$: - $compose$ is associative
$\qquad$ - $compose$ has e as the right identity element
$\quad O_{dg_3 12}$: - $compose$ has e as the left identity element
$\qquad$ and $\mathcal{I}_r(X) \wedge minimal(X) \Rightarrow \mathcal{O}_r(X, e)$
$\qquad$ - partial evaluation of the conjunction
$\qquad process(HX, HY), compose(HY, A_p, A_{p-1})$
$\qquad$ results in the introduction of a non-recursively defined relation
$\quad O_{dg_3 21}$: - partial evaluation of the conjunction
$\qquad process(HX, HY), compose(HY, I_p, I_{p-1})$
$\qquad$ results in the introduction of a non-recursively defined relation

where e is the (unique) term for which $init$ holds. These schemas have the *same* formal specification (i.e., eureka) for the relation $r\_descending_2$ of the schema pattern $DGRL$, namely:

$$\forall X : \mathcal{X}. \ \forall Y, A : \mathcal{Y}. \ \mathcal{I}_r(X) \Rightarrow$$
$$[r\_descending_2(X, Y, A) \ \Leftrightarrow \ \exists S : \mathcal{Y}. \ \mathcal{O}_r(X, S) \wedge \mathcal{O}_c(S, A, Y)]$$

where $\mathcal{O}_c$ is the output condition of *compose*. Note the reversal of the roles of A and S compared to the specification of $r\_descending_1$ above. The template of the common schema pattern $DGRL$ of DG_2 and DG_3 is:

$r(X, Y) \leftarrow$
$\quad init(A), r\_descending_2(X, Y, A)$
$r\_descending_2(X, Y, A) \leftarrow$
$\quad minimal(X),$
$\quad solve(X, S), compose(S, A, Y)$
$r\_descending_2(X, Y, A) \leftarrow$
$\quad nonMinimal(X),$
$\quad decompose(X, HX, TX_1, \ldots, TX_t),$
$\quad init(E), compose(E, A, A_{t+1}),$
$\quad r\_descending_2(TX_t, A_t, A_{t+1}), \ldots, r\_descending_2(TX_p, A_p, A_{p+1}),$
$\quad process(HX, HY), compose(HY, A_p, A_{p-1}),$
$\quad r\_descending_2(TX_{p-1}, A_{p-2}, A_{p-1}), \ldots, r\_descending_2(TX_1, A_0, A_1),$
$\quad Y = A_0$

Template $DGRL$

Note that, in the $DGRL$ template, *all* the open relations of $DCLR$ (or $DCRL$) appear, but *no* new relations. The applicability and optimisability conditions of these two generalisation schemas differ, since the composition ordering is changed from LR to RL in DG_2.

Example 4. The specification of a program for the RL descendingly generalised version of *infix_flat* is:

infix_flat_descending₂(B, F, A) iff list F is the concatenation of the infix representation of binary tree B and list A.

Program 5 is the program for *infix_flat* as an instance of $DGRL$, for $t = p = 2$.

$$infix\_flat(B, F) \leftarrow$$
$$infix\_flat\_descending_2(B, F, [\,])$$
$$infix\_flat\_descending_2(B, F, A) \leftarrow$$
$$B = void,$$
$$S = [\,], append(S, A, F)$$
$$infix\_flat\_descending_2(B, F, A) \leftarrow$$
$$B = bt(\_, \_, \_),$$
$$B = bt(L, E, R),$$
$$append([\,], A, A_3),$$
$$infix\_flat\_descending_2(R, A_2, A_3),$$
$$HF = [E], append(HF, A_2, A_1),$$
$$infix\_flat\_descending_2(L, A_0, A_1),$$
$$F = A_0$$

Program 5

Since both the applicability conditions and the optimisability conditions of DG_2 (resp. DG_3) are satisfied for the input $DCLR$ (resp. $DCRL$) *infix_flat* program, descending generalisation of the *infix_flat* programs results in Program 5. Partial evaluation of the conjunction $HF = [E], append(HF, A_2, A_1)$ in the non-minimal case of *infix_flat_descending₂* then results in $A_1 = [E|A_2]$. Similarly, partial evaluation of the conjunction $S = [\,], append(S, A, F)$ in the minimal case results in $F = A$. Altogether, this amounts to the elimination of *append*.

Although the descending generalisation schemas are constructed to descendingly generalise DC programs, these schemas can also be used to transform DG programs into DC programs, provided the optimisability conditions for the corresponding DC schema pattern are satisfied. It is thus possible that we have Program 4 for the *infix_flat* problem, and that we want to transform it into a more efficient program; then the DC programs are good candidates, if we have the descending generalisation schemas above.

5   Program Transformation Using Duality Laws

In Section 2, while we discussed the composition ordering in the DC program schemas, the reader who is familiar with functional programming has noticed the similarities with the *fold* operators in functional programming. A detailed explanation of the fold operators and their laws can be found in [3]. Here, we only give the definitions of the *fold* operators, and their first law. The *foldr* operator can be defined as follows:

$$foldr\ (\oplus)\ a\ [x_1, x_2, \ldots, x_n] = x_1 \oplus (x_2 \oplus (\ldots (x_n \oplus a) \ldots))$$

where $\oplus$ is a variable that is bound to a function of two arguments. Similarly, the *foldl* operator can be defined as follows:

$$foldl\ (\oplus)\ a\ [x_1, x_2, \ldots, x_n] = (\ldots ((a \oplus x_1) \oplus x_2) \ldots) \oplus x_n$$

Thus, equation (1) in Section 2, which illustrates the composition of Y in the $DCLR$ template, can be rewritten using *foldl*:

$$Y = foldl\ (\oplus)\ e\ [TY_1, \ldots, TY_{p-1}, HY, TY_p, \ldots, TY_t]$$

Similarly, the *foldr* operator can be used to rewrite equation (2), which illustrates the composition of Y in the $DCRL$ template:

$$Y = foldr\ (\oplus)\ e\ [TY_1, \ldots, TY_{p-1}, HY, TY_p, \ldots, TY_t]$$

The first three laws of the fold operators are called *duality theorems*. The *first duality theorem* states that:

$$foldr\ (\oplus)\ a\ xs = foldl\ (\oplus)\ a\ xs$$

if $\oplus$ is associative and has (left/right) identity element a, and xs is a finite list.

By adding optimisability conditions, we can now devise a transformation schema based on this first duality theorem (compare with [16]):

$D_{dc} : \langle\ DCLR, DCRL, A_{ddc}, O_{ddc12}, O_{ddc21} \rangle$ where
    A_{ddc} : - *compose* is associative
            - *compose* has e as the left and right identity element
    O_{ddc12} : - partial evaluation of the conjunction
            $process(HX, HY), compose(HY, I_p, I_{p-1})$
            results in the introduction of a non-recursively defined relation
    O_{ddc21} : - partial evaluation of the conjunction
            $process(HX, HY), compose(I_{p-1}, HY, I_p)$
            results in the introduction of a non-recursively defined relation

where e is the (unique) term for which *init* holds, where the schema patterns $DCLR$ and $DCRL$ are given in Section 2, and where A_{ddc} comes from the constraints of the first duality theorem. The optimisability conditions check whether the *compose* operator can be eliminated in the output program.

Similarly, it is possible to give a duality schema between the DG schema patterns:

$D_{dg} : \langle\ DGLR, DGRL, A_{ddg}, O_{ddg12}, O_{ddg21} \rangle$ where
    A_{ddg} : - *compose* is associative
            - *compose* has e as the left and right identity element

O_{ddg12}: - $\forall X : \mathcal{X}.\ \mathcal{I}_r(X) \wedge minimal(X) \Rightarrow \mathcal{O}_r(X, e)$
    - partial evaluation of the conjunction
    $process(HX, HY), compose(HY, A_p, A_{p-1})$
    results in the introduction of a non-recursively defined relation
O_{ddg21}: - $\forall X : \mathcal{X}.\ \mathcal{I}_r(X) \wedge minimal(X) \Rightarrow \mathcal{O}_r(X, e)$
    - partial evaluation of the conjunction
    $process(HX, HY), compose(A_{p-1}, HY, A_p)$
    results in the introduction of a non-recursively defined relation

where e is the (unique) term for which *init* holds, and where the schema patterns *DGLR* and *DGRL* are given in Section 4.

6   Evaluation of the Transformation Schemas

We evaluate the transformation schemas using performance tests done on partially evaluated input and output programs of each transformation schema. However, the reader may find this evaluation a little bit dubious, since the transformation schemas in this paper are only dealing with the declarative features of programs. This evaluation is made because we think that these performance tests will help us see what our theoretical results amount to when tested practically, although in an environment with procedural side-effects. The programs are executed using Mercury 0.6 (for an overview of Mercury, please refer to [22]) on a SPARCstation 4. Since the programs are really short, the procedures were called 500 or 1000 times to achieve meaningful timing results. In Table 1, the results of the performance tests for five selected relations are shown, where each column heading represents the schema pattern to which the program written for the relation of that row belongs. (Of course, *quicksort* is not really a relation: we just mean to indicate that some partitioning is used as *decompose* for the *sort* relation.) The timing results are normalised wrt the DCLR column.

relations	DCLR	DCRL	TG	DGLR	DGRL
Prefix *flat*	1.00	0.92	0.23	11.88	0.15
Infix *flat*	1.00	0.49	0.02	7.78	0.05
Postfix *flat*	1.00	0.69	0.14	5.48	0.09
reverse	1.00	1.00	0.04	1.01	0.01
quicksort	1.00	0.85	0.72	6.02	0.56

Table 1. Performance test results

The reason why we chose the relations above is that for all the five considered schema patterns programs can be written for these relations.

Let us first compare the *DCLR* and *DCRL* schema patterns. For *reverse*, the *DCLR* and *DCRL* programs are the same, since they are singly recursive, and their *compose* relation is *append*, which is associative. For the binary tree *flat* relations and for *quicksort*, the *DCRL* programs are much better than the

$DCLR$ programs, because of properties of relations like *append* (which is the *compose* relation in all these programs), which are the main reason for achieving the optimisations of the $DCRL$ programs for the relations above. Hence, if the input programs for the binary tree *flat* relations and for the *quicksort* problem to the duality schema are instances of the $DCLR$ schema pattern, then a duality transformation will be performed, resulting in $DCRL$ programs for these relations, since both the applicability and the optimisability conditions are satisfied by these programs. If the $DCRL$ programs for the relations above are input to the duality schema, then the duality transformation will *not* be performed, since the optimisability conditions are not satisfied by *append*, which is the *compose* relation of the $DCRL$ programs. Of course, there may exist some other relations where the duality transformation of their $DCRL$ programs into the $DCLR$ programs will provide an efficiency gain. Unfortunately, we could not find a meaningful relation of this category.

The next step in evaluating the transformation schemas is to compare the generalised programs of these example relations. If we look at Table 1, the most obvious observation is that the $DGRL$ programs for all these relations are very efficient programs. However, tupling generalisation seems to be the second best as a generalisation choice, and it must even be the first choice for relations like infix *flat*, where the composition place of the head in the result parameter is in the middle, and where the *minimal* and *nonMinimal* checks can be performed in minimum time. Although a similar situation occurs for *quicksort*, its TG program is not quite as efficient as its $DGRL$ program. This is mainly because of *partition*, which is the *decompose* relation of *quicksort*, being a costly operation, although we eliminated most of the *partition* calls by putting extra minimality checks into the TG template. Since *append*, which is the *compose* relation in all the programs, cannot be eliminated in the resulting $DGLR$ programs, the $DGLR$ programs for these relations have the worst timing results. The reason for their bad performance is that the percentages of the total running times of the $DGLR$ programs used by *append* are much higher than the percentages of the total running times of the $DCLR$ and $DCRL$ programs used by *append* for these relations. The reason for the increase in the percentages is that the length of the accumulator, which is the input parameter to *append* in the $DGLR$ programs, is larger than the length of the input parameter of *append* in the $DCLR$ and $DCRL$ programs, since the partial result has to be repeatedly input to the *compose* relation in descending generalisation.

A transformation should be performed only if it really results in a program that is more efficient than the input program. So, for instance, the descending generalisation of the input $DCLR$ program for infix *flat* resulting in the $DGLR$ program must not be done, even though the applicability conditions are satisfied. This is the main reason for the existence of the optimisability conditions in the schemas.

In some of the cases, using generalisation schemas to transform input programs that are already generalised programs into DC programs can produce an efficiency gain. For example, if the $DGLR$ program for any of the *flat* relations is the input program to descending generalisation (namely DG_1 or DG_4), then a de-generalisation will be performed resulting in the $DCLR$ (or $DCRL$) program, which is more efficient than the input $DGLR$ program. However, with the current optimisability conditions, if the input program for any of the relations above to generalisation is a $DGRL$ program, then the generalisation schemas are still applied in the reverse direction, resulting in a $DCRL$ program, which means that the de-generalisation will result in a program that is less efficient than the input program. This makes us think of even more accurate ways of defining the optimis*ability* conditions, namely as actual optimis*ation* conditions, such that the transformation will always result in a better program than the input program. However, more performance analyses and complexity analyses are needed to derive such conditions.

7   A Prototype Transformation System

TRANSYS is a prototypical implementation of the schema-based program transformation approach summarised in this paper. TRANSYS is a fully automatic program transformation system and was developed to be integrated with a schema-guided program development environment. Therefore, the input program to TRANSYS is assumed to be developed by a synthesiser using the database of schema patterns known to TRANSYS. The schema pattern of which the input program is an instance is thus a priori known, and so are the renamings of the open relation symbols, the particularisations of the schema variables such as t and p, as well as the "closing" programs defining these open relations of the template. In other words, no matching between the input program and the templates of the transformation schemas has to be performed, unlike in [6,25]. Given an input program, TRANSYS outputs (what it believes to be) the best programs that are more efficient than the input program: this is done by collecting the leaves of the tree rooted in that input program and where child nodes are developed when both the applicability and the optimisability conditions of a transformation schema hold. All the transformation schemas and the schema patterns, which are the input (or output) schema patterns of these transformation schemas, given in [5] (i.e., a superset of the schemas given in this paper), are available in the database of the system.

TRANSYS has been developed in SICStus Prolog 3. Since TRANSYS is a prototype system, for some parts of the system, instead of implementing them ourselves, we reused and integrated other systems:

- For verifying the applicability conditions and some of the optimisability conditions, PTTP is integrated into the system. The *Prolog Technology Theorem Prover* (PTTP) was developed by M. Stickel (for a detailed explanation of PTTP, the reader can refer to [24]). PTTP is an implementation of the model elimination theorem proving procedure for the full first-order predicate calculus. TRANSYS uses the version of PTTP that is written in Prolog and that compiles clauses into Prolog.

- For verifying the other optimisability conditions, and for applying these optimisations to the output programs of the transformation schemas, we integrated Mixtus 0.3.6. Mixtus was developed by D. Sahlin (for a detailed explanation of Mixtus, the reader can refer to [19]). Mixtus is an automatic partial evaluator for full Prolog. Given a Prolog program and a query, it will produce a new program specialised for all instances of that query. The partial evaluator is guaranteed to terminate for all input programs and queries.

For a detailed explanation of the TRANSYS system, the reader is invited to consult [5].

8 Conclusions and Future Work

This paper results from the research that began by investigating the suggestions in [11]. The contributions of this research are:

- pre-compilation of more general generalisation schemas (tupling and descending) than those in [11], which were restricted to sub-families of divide-and-conquer programs;
- discovery of the duality schemas;
- discovery of the optimisability conditions;
- validation of the correctness of the transformation schemas, based on the notions of correctness of a program, steadfastness of a program in a set of specifications, and equivalence of two programs (the correctness proofs of the transformation schemas given in this paper and in [5] can be found in [4]; another approach to validation of transformation schemas can be found in [18]);
- development of a prototype transformation system;
- validation of the effectiveness of the transformation schemas by performance tests.

This research opens future work directions, such as:

- extension to normal programs and open frameworks;
- consideration of other program schemas (or schema patterns);
- extension of the schema pattern language so as to express even more general program families;
- representation of the loop merging strategy as a transformation schema;
- search for other transformation schemas;
- identification of optimis*ation* conditions that *always* ensure improved performance (or complexity) of the output program wrt the input program;
- validation of the effectiveness of the transformation schemas by automated complexity analysis (using GAIA [7] and/or CASLOG [8]).

Acknowledgments. We wish to thank the anonymous reviewers of the previous versions of this paper as well as the participants of the LOPSTR'97 workshop for their valuable comments and suggestions, especially Yves Deville (UC Louvain, Belgium). We also gratefully acknowledge the feedback of the students of the second author's Automated Software Engineering course at Bilkent, especially Necip Fazıl Ayan, Brahim Hnich, Ayşe Pınar Saygın, Tuba Yavuz, and Cemal Yılmaz.

References

1. T. Batu. *Schema-Guided Transformations of Logic Algorithms.* Senior Project Report, Bilkent University, Department of Computer Science, 1996.
2. R.S. Bird. The promotion and accumulation strategies in transformational programming. *ACM Transactions on Programming Languages and Systems* 6(4):487–504, 1984.
3. R.S. Bird and P. Wadler. *Introduction to Functional Programming.* Prentice Hall, 1988.
4. H. Büyükyıldız and P. Flener. *Correctness Proofs of Transformation Schemas.* Technical Report BU-CEIS-9713. Bilkent University, Department of Computer Science, 1997.
5. H. Büyükyıldız. *Schema-based Logic Program Transformation.* M.Sc. Thesis, Technical Report BU-CEIS-9714. Bilkent University, Department of Computer Science, 1997.
6. E. Chasseur and Y. Deville. Logic program schemas, semi-unification, and constraints. In: N.E. Fuchs (ed), *Proc. of LOPSTR'97* (this volume).
7. A. Cortesi, B. Le Charlier, and S. Rossi. Specification-based automatic verification of Prolog programs. In: J. Gallagher (ed), *Proc. of LOPSTR'96*, pp. 38–57. LNCS 1207. Springer-Verlag, 1997.
8. S.K. Debray and N.W. Lin. Cost analysis of logic programs. *ACM TOPLAS* 15(5):826–875, 1993.
9. Y. Deville. *Logic Programming: Systematic Program Development.* Addison-Wesley, 1990.
10. Y. Deville and J. Burnay. Generalization and program schemata: A step towards computer-aided construction of logic programs. In: E.L. Lusk and R.A. Overbeek (eds), *Proc. of NACLP'89*, pp. 409–425. The MIT Press, 1989.
11. P. Flener and Y. Deville. Logic program transformation through generalization schemata. In: M. Proietti (ed), *Proc. of LOPSTR'95*, pp. 171–173. LNCS 1048. Springer-Verlag, 1996.
12. P. Flener, K.-K. Lau, and M. Ornaghi. On correct program schemas. In: N.E. Fuchs (ed), *Proc. of LOPSTR'97* (this volume).
13. N.E. Fuchs and M.P.J. Fromherz. Schema-based transformation of logic programs. In: T. Clement and K.-K. Lau (eds), *Proc. of LOPSTR'91*, pp. 111–125. Springer Verlag, 1992.
14. T.S. Gegg-Harrison. Representing logic program schemata in λProlog. In: L. Sterling (ed), *Proc. of ICLP'95*, pp. 467–481. The MIT Press, 1995.
15. T.S. Gegg-Harrison. Extensible logic program schemata. In: J. Gallagher (ed), *Proc. of LOPSTR'96*, pp. 256–274. LNCS 1207. Springer-Verlag, 1997.
16. A. Hamfelt and J. Fischer Nilsson. Declarative logic programming with primitive recursion relations on lists. In: L. Sterling (ed), *Proc of JICSLP'96*. The MIT Press.

17. A. Pettorossi and M. Proietti. Transformation of logic programs: foundations and techniques. *Journal of Logic Programming* 19(20):261–320, 1994.
18. J. Richardson and N.E. Fuchs. Development of correct transformation schemata for Prolog programs. In: N.E. Fuchs (ed), *Proc. of LOPSTR'97* (this volume).
19. D. Sahlin. *An Automatic Partial Evaluator of Full Prolog*. Ph.D. Thesis, Swedish Institute of Computer Science, 1991.
20. D.R. Smith. Top-down synthesis of divide-and-conquer algorithms. *Artificial Intelligence* 27(1):43–96, 1985.
21. D.R. Smith. KIDS: A semiautomatic program development system. *IEEE Transactions on Software Engineering* 16(9):1024–1043, 1990.
22. Z. Somogyi, F. Henderson, and T. Conway. Mercury: An efficient purely declarative logic programming language. In: *Proc. of the Australian Computer Science Conference*, pp. 499–512, 1995.
23. L.S. Sterling and M. Kirschenbaum. Applying techniques to skeletons. In: J.-M. Jacquet (ed), *Constructing Logic Programs*, pp. 127–140, John Wiley, 1993.
24. M.E. Stickel. A Prolog technology theorem prover: A new exposition and implementation in Prolog. *Theoretical Computer Science* 104:109–128, 1992.
25. W.W. Vasconcelos and N.E. Fuchs. An opportunistic approach for logic program analysis and optimisation using enhanced schema-based transformations. In: M. Proietti (ed), *Proc. of LOPSTR'95*, pp. 174–188. LNCS 1048. Springer-Verlag, 1996.

Logic Program Schemas, Constraints, and Semi-unification

Eric Chasseur and Yves Deville

Université catholique de Louvain,
Department of Computing Science and Engineering,
Place Sainte-Barbe,
1348 Louvain-la-Neuve, Belgium
{ec,yde}@info.ucl.ac.be

Abstract. Program schemas are known to be useful in different applications such as program synthesis, transformation, analysis, debugging, teaching ... This paper tackles two complementary aspects of program schemas. We first propose a language for the description of program schemas. It is based on a subset of second-order logic, enhanced with constraints and specific features of program schemas. One of the basic operations on schemas is the semi-unification of a schema with a program. We then express the semi-unification process over schemas as rewriting and reduction rules, using CLP techniques, where constraints are used to guide the semi-unification process.

1 Introduction

In logic programming, the use of program schemas is a very promising technique. In program *synthesis*, program schemas can formalize particular resolution methods (divide-and-conquer, generate-and-test approaches...), as investigated by Flener [3]. Program *transformations* can advantageously be performed on *schemas* rather than on their instances (i.e. programs). See Fuchs, Fromherz [6], Vasconcelos, Fuchs [22,23], Flener, Deville [4], Richardson, Fuchs [20], Büyükyıldız, Flener [1]. In fact, the distinction between transformation and synthesis is not definitive, as said in Deville, Lau [2].

In this introduction, we first describe the different ways of representing program schemas. We justify our choice of second-order objects for schema representation. Related works are then presented. We finally make precise the objectives and contributions of this paper.

1.1 Representing Schemas

A schema is an object representing a set of programs. Various representations can be used for the description of a schema. We do not aim at presenting here an exhaustive survey.

Norbert E. Fuchs (Ed.): LOPSTR'97, LNCS 1463, pp. 69–89, 1998.

First-Order Representation. First-order representations of schemas use first-order place-holders. In the following example (schema S):

Example 1. Schema S:

r(X,Y) ← *minimal*(X),
        solve(X,Y).
r(X,Y) ← *nonminimal*(X),
        decompose(X,Head,Tail),
        r(Tail,Transf),
        compose(Head,Transf,Compl),
        Y=Compl.

the first-order template predicates of the schema S (in *italic* in the schema) must be replaced by instance (non-place holders) predicates. For example, we obtain the program P from S by replacing the corresponding place-holders by "reverse", "emptylist", "declist" and "addatend" (and switching some of their parameters):

Example 2. Program P:

reverse(X,Y) ← emptylist(X),
        emptylist(Y).
reverse(X,Y) ← nonempty(X),
        declist(X,H,T),
        reverse(T,T2),
        addatend(T2,H,Y2),
        Y=Y2.

The main characteristics of this approach are the following :

1. There is no clear distinction between place-holder and non place-holder predicates.
2. It is not easy to introduce place-holders for constants (e.g. empty list). For this purpose, extra predicates could be added.
3. Considering our semi-unification objective, there is no easy formalization of the matching process between schemas and programs.

Other first-order representations are possible, such as the representation advocated by Flener *et al.* [1,5] where the concept of *open program* is used. In this framework, a schema can be seen as a program where some of its predicates are *open* (their implementation is not known, but they fulfill some given axiomatic properties).

Second-Order Representation. Higher-order terms are normally difficult to deal with, since higher-order unification is undecidable [11] and there is no most general unifier. To handle these difficulties we can either use "standard" or "specific" second-order logic.

Using "Standard" Second-Order Logic. One can accept the previous difficulties and use, for instance, the pre-unification procedure of Huet [13]. This procedure performs a systematic search for determining the existence of unifiers.

Using "standard" second-order logic has a major drawback: the lack of expressiveness if one generalizes too much, for instance, by allowing second-order variables to represent entire clauses.

Using "Specific" Second-Order Logic. One can also restrict oneself to a subset of higher-order terms which is tractable. Higher-order patterns form such a subset of higher-order terms which was investigated among others by Nipkow [19]. Higher-order patterns unification is decidable and there exists a most general unifier of unifiable terms. Another alternative is to use decidable subcases of higher-order unification without changing the language (for instance second-order matching [14]) if the problem permits it.

Using "specific" second-order logic does not necessarily mean using a subset of second-order logic. One can also *extend* second-order logic by introducing new features.

Our choice. In this paper, schemas are formalized using a second-order logic. The basis of the language is a subset of classical second-order logic. We also extend the language by first introducing specific features of program schemas, and by introducing constraints in the language.

The resulting language, described in the next sections, offers a powerful formalization of program schemas. The introduction of constraints enhances the expressiveness of the language and guides the semi-unification process.

In this language, the schema S of example 1 would be written as schema S':

Example 3. Schema S':

$$R(\_E,Y) \leftarrow Min(\_E),$$
$$\qquad\qquad Solve(Y).$$
$$R(\_N,Y) \leftarrow NMin(\_N),$$
$$\qquad\qquad Decompose(\_N,\_Head,\_Tail),$$
$$\qquad\qquad R(\_Tail,\_Tail2),$$
$$\qquad\qquad Compose(\_Tail2,\_Head,\_Res),$$
$$\qquad\qquad Y=\_Res.$$

The substitution θ, solution of $S'\theta = P$, is:
{ R/reverse, Solve/emptylist, _E/X, _N/X, Min/emptylist, NMin/nonempty, Decompose/declist, _Head/H, _Tail/T, _Tail2/T2, Compose/concat, _Res/Y2 }. See Sects. 2 and 3 for details.

We now give a more elaborated example illustrating various aspects of such schemas.

Example 4.

$$P([], \&_1) \leftarrow G_1.$$
$$P([\_H|\_T], \&_2) \leftarrow \ll Q(\_H) \gg, P(\_T, \&_3), G_2.$$

In this schema, $\&_1$, $\&_2$ and $\&_3$ denote three sequences of terms, G_1 and G_2 denote an atom and the annotation $\ll \gg$ means that $Q(\_H)$ is optional. Possible global constraints on this schema are:

1. length_eq($\&_1, L$) $\wedge$ length_eq($\&_2, L$) $\wedge$ length_eq($\&_3, L$), which means that the instances of $\&_1$, $\&_2$ and $\&_3$ must have the same length,
2. variable($\_H$) $\wedge$ variable($\_T$): $\_H$ and $\_T$ instances are first-order variables.

1.2   Related Work

Miller, Nadathur [17] present λProlog which is a higher-order extension of Prolog manipulating objects such as function and predicate variables, formulas and programs. Unification in λProlog is based on second-order unification. The *pre-unification procedure* of Huet is used to handle the second-order unification undecidability.

There is a major difference between λProlog and our schema language. Their goals are different. λProlog is a logic programming language in the same way Prolog is. It is aimed at computing some results from some program. Our purpose is not to execute program schemas, but to provide a powerful and expressive representation language for program schemas.

Kraan et al. [16] synthesize logic programs as a by-product of the planning of their verification proofs. This is achieved by using higher-order meta-variables at the proof planning level, which become instantiated in the course of planning. These higher-order variables can represent functions and predicates applied to bound variables. The formulas containing them are *higher-order patterns*.

Hannan, Miller [12] present source-to-source program transformers as meta-programs that manipulate programs as objects. They show how simple transformers can be used to specify more sophisticated transformers. They use the *pre-unification algorithm* of Huet.

Gegg-Harrison [8] proposes a hierarchy of fourteen logic program schemas which are second-order logic expressions and generalize classes of programs in the most specific generalization (*msg*) sense. In [9], he defines logic program schemas with the help of λProlog to avoid using any meta-language. In [10], he extends these λProlog program schemas by applying standard programming techniques, introducing additional arguments and combining existing schemas.

Flener, Deville [4] show that some logic program generalization techniques can be pre-compiled at the program schema level so that the corresponding transformation can be fully automated. They also use *second-order matching* implicitly.

Flener [3] defines a logic algorithm schema as: $\forall X_1...\forall X_n \; R(X_1...X_n) \Leftrightarrow F$. This is a second-order form of Kraan's specification [16]: $\forall \overline{args}.prog(\overline{args}) \leftrightarrow$

spec($\overline{args}$). The author presents semantic constraints on instances of place-holders. In particular, he details constraints on the divide-and-conquer schema. For the instantiation of the latter to result in valid divide-and-conquer logic algorithms, constraints are expressed on the induction parameter, for example.

Huet, Lang [15] describe a program transformation method based on rewriting rules composed of second-order schemas. Fuchs, Fromherz [6] and Vasconcelos, Fuchs [22,23] present schema-based transformation formalisms and techniques. Implicit *second-order matching* is used in these papers [15,6,22,23].

The formalism of schemas, as defined in Vasconcelos, Fuchs [22,23], allows one schema to describe a class of logic programs in a suitable Horn-clause notation. Vasconcelos, Fuchs introduce features adding expressiveness to schemas: predicate and function symbol variables, possibly empty sequences of goals or terms. They also introduce constraints over schemas: argument positions, argument optionality, recursive or non-recursive predicates. In [22], constraints are part of schemas and take part of the expressiveness augmentation.

In the paper, the formalism describing schemas is a variant of that of Vasconcelos, Fuchs [22,23]. But here constraints are separated from first- and second-order objects.

1.3   Objectives

Due to the extensive use of program schemas in various domains, there is a need for a powerful language for the description of schemas, and for operations (such as semi-unification) manipulating such schemas. The objective of the paper is first to provide a description language for schemas, where constraints are integrated, then to propose a semi-unification process over schemas.

Coming from Vasconcelos, Fuchs' work, this paper obviously stands in the field of program transformation, where semi-unification is useful to match second-order schemas and programs. That is the reason why we focus ourselves onto the semi-unification problem.

Let S be a schema, and c be the initial constraint set associated to S. Let P be the program with which S has to be semi-unified.

The starting pair $\langle S = P, c \rangle$ is transformed via successive rewriting rules to $\langle \emptyset, c' \rangle$. During the whole process, the successive versions of the constraint set remain consistent. At the end, there is a substitution $\theta \in c'$ such that θ satisfies c in S and $S\theta = P$.

1.4   Contributions

The main contributions of the paper are the following:

1. Definition of a description language for program schemas, where constraints are explicitly integrated. The introduction of constraints increases the expressive power of the language. It allows schemas to contain more knowledge. It also offers a guided search in the semi-unification process.
2. Definition of an extensible first-order constraint language over schemas,

3. Expression of the semi-unification process over schemas as rewriting and reduction rules,
4. Presentation of two semantics: one based on program instances, and the other on rewriting rules.

1.5   Structure of the Paper

Section 2 gives the syntax of schemas. It defines first- and second-order objects. Section 3 presents needed features of schemas and the first-order language of constraints. We make the distinction between global and local constraints. The fourth section gives the meaning of schemas relating to their instances (semantics 1). It also defines substitution pairs. Section 5 presents the general form and spirit of the rewriting rules. It also presents the rewriting semantics of schemas (semantics 2). Finally, we conclude in Section 6 and give further research steps. Appendix A presents a subset of rewriting rules. Appendix B gives an example.

2   Syntax of Schemas

A schema contains second-order and first-order objects. In order to simplify the presentation, the number of clauses in a schema will be fixed, although some interesting schemas have a variable number of clauses. The technical results can easily be extended to remove this restriction.

In our framework, no variable can represent an entire clause, but only atoms and sequences of atoms in a clause. This is a compromise between expressiveness and efficiency of the semi-unification process. We thus choose a subset of full second-order logic.

2.1   Basic Components

Basic components of programs and of schemas are first-order and second-order objects. *First-order objects* are present in schemas and in programs. *Second-order objects* only appear in schemas.

Definition 1. *A first-order object (FObject) is either a term (term), in particular constant or variable, an atom (atom), a function symbol (fs), a predicate symbol (ps), a sequence of terms (seqterm) or a sequence of atoms (seqatom).*

Constants are denoted by a, b, c ..., variables by X, Y, Z ..., function symbols by f, g, h ... or particular symbols like $\bullet$ (list function symbol) and predicate symbols by p, q, r ...

Definition 2. *A second-order variable (SObject), also called* place-holder, *is either a term variable (Vterm), an atom variable (Vatom), a function symbol variable (Vfs), a predicate symbol variable (Vps), a sequence of terms variable (Vseqterm) or a sequence of atoms variable (Vseqatom).*

In next sections, two other place-holders, length variable (Vlength) and position variable (Vpos), will be introduced and their meanings explained.

In the following, term variables are denoted by $\_X$, $\_Y$, $\_Z$ ... (note the *under-score*), atom variables by P_1, P_2, P_3 ..., function symbol variables by F, G, H ..., predicate symbol variables by P, Q, R ..., sequence of terms variables by $\&_1$, $\&_2$, $\&_3$ ... and sequence of atoms variables by G_1, G_2, G_3 ... Vlength are denoted by L, L_1, L_2, L_3 ... and Vpos by p, p_1, p_2, p_3 ...

2.2   Grammar of Schema

All place-holders are implicitly universally quantified. It means that all second-order variables are global to the schema. Thus there is a difference between schemas and programs in which first-order variables are local to clauses.

Definition 3. *A second-order schema is defined by the grammar:*

$$
\begin{array}{ll}
Schema & ::= SOrdCl \mid SOrdCl\ Schema \\
SOrdCl & ::= SOrdP \mid SOrdP \leftarrow SOrdBody \\
SOrdBody & ::= SOrdP \mid SOrdP,\ SOrdBody \\
SOrdP & ::= Vseqatom \mid Vatom \mid Vps \mid Vps(SOrdArg) \mid atom \mid ps(SOrdArg) \\
SOrdArg & ::= SOrdT \mid SOrdT,\ SOrdArg \\
SOrdT & ::= Vseqterm \mid Vterm \mid Vfs \mid Vfs(SOrdArg) \mid term \mid fs(SOrdArg)
\end{array}
$$

All terminal symbols have been defined in Section 2.1. In the remaining of the paper, SOrdP is called *second-order predicate* and SOrdT *second-order term*. Characteristics of the syntax are described next.

In a program schema (and in a logic program), a comma separating two atoms has the same meaning as the logic *and* ($\wedge$) but constrains the order of atoms. A comma separating two terms is an argument separator which also constrains the order of the parameters.

In a schema, first-order objects may co-exist with second-order objects. This is viewed as a partially instantiated schema. For instance: in the one-clause schema

$$p(\_X) \leftarrow Q(Y).$$

p is a predicate symbol, Q a predicate symbol variable, Y a first-order term (a first-order variable) and $\_X$ a second-order term variable.

Definition 4. *A* program *is a schema without second-order variables. More precisely, we define Program (resp. FOrdBody, FOrdCl, FOrdP and FOrdT) as being Schema (resp. SOrdBody, SOrdCl, SOrdP and SOrdT) without second-order variables.*

Programs are thus classical Horn clause programs (without extra logical features such as cuts). Schemas and programs do not contain negations in the body of clauses. This syntactical restriction can easily be removed without affecting the complexity of our results.

Example 5. Complete example.
Let the schema S be:

$$P([], \&_1) \leftarrow G_1.$$
$$P([\_H|\_T], \&_2) \leftarrow G_2, P(\_T, \&_3), G_3.$$

where

1. P is a predicate symbol variable (Vps)
2. $\&_1$, $\&_2$ and $\&_3$ are variables of sequence of terms (Vseqterm)
3. G_1, G_2 and G_3 are variables of sequence of atoms (Vseqatom)
4. $\_H$ and $\_T$ are term variables (Vterm)

Let the program *Prog* be:

$$\text{sum}([], 0).$$
$$\text{sum}([X|X_s], S) \leftarrow \text{sum}(X_s, SX_s), S \text{ is } X + SX_s.$$

S is semi-unified with *Prog* ($S.\theta = Prog$) if $\theta = \{ P/\text{sum}, \&_1/0, \&_2/S, \&_3/SX_s,$
$\_H/X, \_T/X_s, G_1/\emptyset, G_2/\emptyset, G_3/S \text{ is } X + SX_s \}$

3   Constraints Language

In our framework, a schema is not a classical second-order object. It needs incorporating features essential to the objectives of program representation and manipulation.

1. Term positions among arguments of predicates and functions,
2. Representation of possibly empty sequences of atoms,
3. Representation of possibly empty sequences of terms,
4. Argument length constraints,
5. Instantiation form constraints (constant, ground, var ...),
6. Optional atoms and terms,
7. Interchangeability of predicate and function parameters.

Most of these features are already present in [22,23].

Restrictions.

1. Although the above characteristics are syntactical, semantic constraints on place-holders, such as defined in [3], could also be considered. Such constraints are useful to instantiate schemas into valid programs. However we do not consider such constraints in this paper. These could easily be included in the framework.
2. Interchangeability of clauses and predicates in bodies of clauses is not considered here. Such a reordering can be performed at the program level, as in the Mercury language [21].

In order to express such constraints on program schema, a first-order constraint language is now defined. It is necessary and useful in the context of program schema and program synthesis/transformation. Constraints are defined on schema place-holders. Some are global to the whole schema and others are local to occurrences of place-holders. Constraints on a schema will restrict the possible instantiations of the schemas to instances satisfying the constraints. The following set of constraints are extensible.

3.1 Global Constraints

Global constraints handle forms and lengths of instances of second-order variables. In our framework, an instantiation of a second-order variable is also a global constraint.

1. *Form Constraints.* Term variable instances can be constrained to be *constant*, *variable* or *ground*, and atom variable instances to be *ground*. Possible form constraint predicates are: $constant(\_X)$, $ground(\_X)$ and $var(\_X)$ for terms and $ground(P_k)$ for atoms.
2. *Length Constraints.* Global constraints can also apply on the length of the instances of sequence of terms (resp. atoms) variables, i.e. on the number of terms (resp. atoms) in Vseqterm (resp. Vseqatom) instances. Length constraint predicates are: $length\_eq\,(X, L)$, $length\_geq\,(X, L)$ and $length\_leq\,(X, L)$. Length constraints include *hard* constraints (length is compared to an integer) and *soft* constraints (length is compared to a variable). Variables constraining the lengths of sequence of terms and atoms variable instances are called Vlength variables and will have to be instantiated to integers.
3. *Global Constraint Combinators.* Form and length constraints can be linked by constraint combinators: $\wedge$ (logic and), $\vee$ (logic or) and $\neg$ (logic not).

   Example 6. Term variable instance constrained to be either a constant or a variable: $constant(\_X) \vee var(\_X)$; two Vseqterm variables instances constrained to have equal lengths: $length\_eq(\&_1, L) \wedge length\_eq(\&_2, L)$.

We choose an untyped second-order representation. Notice that types could be introduced at the constraint level (global constraints).

3.2 Local Constraints

Local constraints relate to positions of parameters, interchangeability of groups of parameters, and locally empty place-holder instances.

1. *Position Constraint.* The position constraint applies to second-order predicates and terms, except sequence variables (Vseqatom and Vseqterm). A position constraint is denoted by # followed by an integer (hard constraint) or a position variable (soft constraint) which will have to be instantiated to integers.

Example 7. In the partial schema "$P(\&_1, \_X \# p), Q(\&_2, \_Y, \&_3, \_Z \# p, \&_4)$", the instances of $\_X$ and $\_Z$ must have the same positions among the parameters of P and Q predicate instances.

2. *Interchangeability of Parameters.* Interchangeability constraints are defined via unordered groups, denoted by $\odot(\dots)$. This introduces the commutativity of predicate and function parameters in schemas. Inside unordered groups, only second-order terms may appear. In such groups, second-order terms order is not fixed. It is only at the instance level that the parameters have fixed positions.

Example 8. According to the schema part "$P(\odot(\&_1, \_X, \&_2))$", any instance of $\odot(\&_1, \_X, \&_2)$ in P will be a permutation of instances of $\&_1, \_X$ and $\&_2$.

3. *Optional Objects.* Optional arguments and atoms are denoted by: $\ll X \gg$. Option constraints apply to second-order predicates and terms.

Example 9. According to the schema part "$P(\&_1, \ll \_X \gg, \&_2)$", the instance of $\ll \_X \gg$ in P is either the instance of $\_X$ itself or $\emptyset$.

Example 10. Complete example.
Over the following schema:

$$
\begin{array}{l}
P([], \&_1) \leftarrow G_1. \\
P([\_H | \_T], \&_2) \leftarrow \ll Q(\_H) \gg, P(\_T, \&_3), G_2.
\end{array}
$$

a local constraint (optional object) is defined: $\ll Q(\_H) \gg$. Other global constraints could be defined:

1. length_eq$(\&_1, L) \wedge$ length_eq$(\&_2, L) \wedge$ length_eq$(\&_3, L)$ which means that all $\&_i$ $(1 \leq i \leq 3)$ instances must be of same length,
2. variable$(\_H) \wedge$ variable$(\_T)$: $\_H$ and $\_T$ instances are first-order variables,
3. length_eq$(G_1, 0)$ which means that G_1 instance must be of length equal to 0.

We can easily extend the set of constraints by adding new constraint predicates. For example, we could use the following predicate to mean that G_2 does not contain predicate P: not_in(G_2, P).

From the examples of this section, one can easily see the expressiveness of the proposed constraint language. It allows the description of schemas to contain knowledge. It also allows a single schema to represent what would require several schemas using other representation schemes. The extensibility of the constraint part of the language is an advantage. One can add new constraints depending of the specific use of the schemas (program transformation, program synthesis ...).

4   Meaning of Schemas

In this section, we introduce the semantics of schemas. The semantics of program schemas can be defined in different ways. The first semantics defines the meaning of a schema as the set of all its possible instances which respect the constraints. This is close to the idea that a schema "represents" a class of programs. With this representational semantics of schemas, one can then choose any semantics at the program level. A second, constructive, semantics will be presented in Section 5.5.

Definition 5. *A* schema *is a pair* $\langle S, c \rangle$, *where S is a program schema annotated with local constraints, and c is a set of global constraints.*

4.1   Substitutions

Definition 6. *A* substitution pair *(SP) is a pair SObject/FObject of type: Vterm/term, Vfs/fs, Vseqterm/seqterm, Vatom/atom, Vps/ps, Vseqatom/ seqatom, Vlength/integer or Vpos/integer. Since sequence of terms and atom variables may instantiate to the empty sequence (denoted $\emptyset$), the pairs Vseqterm/$\emptyset$ and Vseqatom/$\emptyset$ are allowed.*

In our approach, substitution pairs themselves are viewed as global constraints on schema place-holders.

Definition 7. *A* substitution *is a finite set of substitution pairs s_i/p_i, i.e. $\sigma = \{ s_i/p_i \mid 1 \leq i \leq n \}$ with the property that $\forall i, j \leq n : s_i = s_j \Rightarrow i = j$.*

Example 11.
Vterm/term: $\_X/sum(X, Y, Z)$,
Vseqterm/seqterm: $\&_1/f(X), g(Y)$,
Vfs/fs: F/sum,
Vseqatom/seqatom: $G_1/father(X, Y), husband(X, Z)$,
Vps/ps: $P/father$.

Definition 8. *The* application *of a substitution $\sigma = \{ s_i/p_i \mid 1 \leq i \leq n \}$ to a schema S, denoted $S\sigma$, is obtained by the simultaneous replacement of all occurrences of s_i by p_i in S.*

4.2   Satisfaction of Constraints

Let us first make precise the concept of a substitution θ satisfying a global constraint c. We consider the different form of the constraint c :

1. $constant(\_X)$ is true iff $\_X\theta$ is a constant,
2. $ground(\_X)$ is true iff $\_X\theta$ is ground,
3. $var(\_X)$ is true iff $\_X\theta$ is a variable,

4. *length_eq*(X, L) (*length_geq*(X, L), *length_leq*(X, L)) is true iff $X\theta$ has length equal (greater than or equal, less than or equal) to L.

This extends easily to constraint combinators.

The satisfaction of the local position constraint is now defined. Let $\_X\#p$ be a position constraint occurring in a subformula $F(\ldots\_X\#p\ldots)$ of a schema S. A substitution θ satisfies this position constraint in S iff, in $S\theta$, the above subformula is instantiated to $f(e_1,\ldots,e_{k-1},t\#k,e_{k+1},\ldots,e_n)$ for some terms $e_1,\ldots,e_n$, and some predicate or function symbol f ($\_X$ is instantiated to some term t, and p to the integer k).

The definitions of satisfaction for the other local constraints can be defined similarly.

Definition 9. *Let* $\langle S, c \rangle$ *be a schema and* θ *a substitution.* θ *satisfies the constraints of* $\langle S, c \rangle$ *iff* θ *satisfies* c, *and* θ *satisfies the local constraints in* S.

4.3   Schema Instances

We are now in position to define the first semantics. The semantics of the schema $\langle S, c \rangle$, denoted by $[\![S, c]\!]_1$, is defined by means of all its possible program instances.

Definition 10. P *is an* instance *of schema* $\langle S, c \rangle$, *denoted by* $P \in [\![S, c]\!]_1$, *iff there exists a substitution* θ *such that* $P \simeq S\theta$, *and* θ *satisfies the constraints of* $\langle S, c \rangle$.

$P \simeq S\theta$ means $P = S\theta$ after elimination in $S\theta$ of the syntactic constructs attached to schemas by the local constraints ($\odot(\ )$, $\#$ and $\ll\gg$).

Example 12. Schema S: $Q(\_X\#1, \ll \_Y \gg)$ with $c = \emptyset$; program P: $q(X,Y)$. Then the substitution θ is: $\theta=\{\ Q/q,\ \_X/X,\ \_Y/Y\ \}$. We have $P = q(X,Y) \simeq q(X\#1, \ll Y \gg) = S\theta$.

The semi-unification process is not deterministic. If $P \in [\![S, c]\!]_1$, there could exist different substitutions θ_1 and θ_2 such that $P \simeq S\theta_1$ and $P \simeq S\theta_2$.

Example 13.

Schema S: $P(\_X) \leftarrow G_1, Q(\_X), G_2$ with $c = \emptyset$
Program P: $p(X) \leftarrow q_1(X), q_2(X)$
The two substitutions $\theta_1=\{\ P/p,\ \_X/X, G_1/q_1(X), Q/q_2, G_2/\emptyset\ \}$ and $\theta_2=\{\ P/p, \_X/X,\ G_1/\emptyset,\ Q/q_1, G_2/q_2(X)\ \}$ are such that $P \simeq S\theta_1$ and $P \simeq S\theta_2$.

5   Rewriting Rules

We present here a more constructive semantics, based on rewriting rules. This semantics will allow an implementation of a semi-unification algorithm.

5.1 Form of Equations

An equation Eq appearing in a rewriting rule is an equation (or a set of equations) of type $\alpha=\beta$ where:

1. α and β are respectively second-order (Schema, SOrdBody, SOrCl, SOrdP, SOrdT) and first-order (Program, FOrdBody, FOrCl, FOrdP, FOrdT) expressions: for example, $P([\_H|\_T]), \&_2) = islist([T|Q])$,
2. *or* α is a [sequence of atoms] variable (Vseqatom) and β is a sequence of second-order predicates without Vseqatom: for example, $G_1 = P_1, P_2, P_3$,
3. *or* α is a [sequence of terms] variable (Vseqterm) and β is a sequence of second-order terms without Vseqterm: for example, $\&_1 = \_T_1, \_T_2, \_T_3$.

5.2 Starting Point

Let $\langle S, c\rangle$ be a schema to semi-unify with a program P. The associated constraint set is c. It is composed of global constraints and substitutions considered as global constraints in this framework.

The starting point is: $\langle Eq, c\rangle$ with equation $Eq \equiv S = P$.

5.3 Form of Rewriting Rules

Rewriting rules handle the semi-unification process as well as constraint satisfaction. During the process, global constraints can be deleted from and added to the constraint set c. Substitutions, considered as global constraints, are also added to c.

Rewriting rules are of two different forms:

$$\frac{\text{Applicability condition}}{\langle Eq, c\rangle \longmapsto \textbf{failure}}$$

$$\frac{\text{Applicability condition}}{\langle Eq, c\rangle \longmapsto \langle Eq', c'\rangle}$$

We also keep the invariant that, in a pair $\langle Eq, c\rangle$, c is satisfiable in Eq. Otherwise, this leads to failure. We thus have the rewriting rule:

$$\frac{\text{unsatisfiable}(Eq, c)}{\langle Eq, c\rangle \longmapsto \textbf{failure}}$$

In addition to the applicability condition of each rewriting rule, it is assumed that the following invariant holds:

$$\frac{\text{satisfiable}(Eq, c)}{\langle Eq, c\rangle \longmapsto \langle Eq', c'\rangle}$$

Finally, in the following, "$[eq_1], [eq_2] \ldots [eq_i] \bullet Eq$" means "the set of equations composed of $Eq \cup \{ eq_1, eq_2 \ldots eq_i \}$".

Appendix A presents some representative rewriting rules.

5.4   Final Point

The process can fail or succeed:

1. failure: $\langle S = P \, , \, c \rangle \longmapsto^* \textbf{failure}$
2. success: $\langle S = P \, , \, c \rangle \longmapsto^* \langle \emptyset \, , \, c' \rangle$

where $\longmapsto^*$ is the transitive closure of $\longmapsto$, the rewriting symbol.

5.5   Rewriting Semantics

Now we define the semantics of a schema according to the rewriting rules. The semantics of a schema $\langle S, c \rangle$, denoted by $[\![S, c]\!]_2$, is defined as follows.

Definition 11. *P is an* instance of schema $\langle S, c \rangle$, *denoted by* $P \in [\![S, c]\!]_2$, *iff there exists a constraint set c' such that* $\langle S = P \, , \, c \rangle \longmapsto^* \langle \emptyset \, , \, c' \rangle$.

Obviously, the semantics $[\![S, c]\!]_1$ and $[\![S, c]\!]_2$ should be equivalent. The formal proof will not be developed in this paper. Let S be a schema, P a program.

Definition 12. *Existence of substitution:*
if $\langle S = P \, , \, c \rangle \longmapsto^* \langle \emptyset \, , \, c' \rangle$
and θ is *the set of all substitution pairs of c'*
then θ is a substitution.
θ is called the complete substitution *of c'.*

Conjecture 1 Soundness of $[\![\textbf{S, c}]\!]_2$ wrt. $[\![\textbf{S, c}]\!]_1$:
if $\langle S = P \, , \, c \rangle \longmapsto^* \langle \emptyset \, , \, c' \rangle$
and θ is **the complete substitution** of c'
then $S\theta \simeq P$ and θ **satisfies** $\langle S, c \rangle$.

Conjecture 2 Completeness of $[\![\textbf{S, c}]\!]_2$ wrt. $[\![\textbf{S, c}]\!]_1$:
if $\textbf{P} \in [\![\textbf{S, c}]\!]_1$
then $\textbf{P} \in [\![\textbf{S, c}]\!]_2$.

As the semi-unification process is not deterministic, some of the rewriting rules are non-deterministic (see Appendix A). In general, the semi-unification process in second-order logic is known to be decidable, but NP-complete [7]. Although our language is a subset of second-order logic (with some extensions), the potential exponential complexity is still present. However, the active use of constraints in the semi-unification offers a more efficient search for a correct solution.

6   Conclusion

In this paper, we proposed a language for the description of program schemas. This language is based on a subset of second-order logic enhanced with constraints and specific features of program schemas. The constraint language is extensible and permits the possible introduction of domain knowledge for the schemas. We then expressed the semi-unification process over schemas as rewriting and reduction rules, using CLP techniques, where constraints are used to guide the semi-unification process. Appendix A shows some of these rewriting and reduction rules. Two semantics were also presented. The first semantics is based on program instances and the second on the rewriting rules.

Further Research Steps. A first step will be the theoretical and practical analysis of the complexity of the semi-unification algorithm. We are also interested in the use of schemas in program synthesis. Starting from a schema and a set of constraints on its schema place-holders, the objective is the synthesis of a program. The synthesis is guided by successive additions of constraints. The initial schema becomes more and more instantiated until the program level is reached. The constraints used to instantiate the successive schema versions come from heuristics, specifications and user demands. This will require the extension of syntactical constraints to semantic constraints.

This problem does not handle equations as defined in the paper, but only partially instantiated schemas (left-side of current equations). Let S be the initial schema, c the associated constraint set. We construct the program P by means of a derivation:

$$\langle S \,,\, c \rangle \longmapsto \langle S_1 \,,\, c_1 \rangle \longmapsto \langle S_2 \,,\, c_2 \rangle \longmapsto \ldots \longmapsto \langle P \,,\, c_n \rangle.$$

At each step i of this derivation, new constraints can be added to the resulting set of constraints c_i $(0 < i < n)$ to guide the synthesis process.

Acknowledgements

This research is supported by the subvention *Actions de recherche concertées* of the Direction générale de la Recherche Scientifique - Communauté Franaise de Belgique. We also acknowledge the reviewers for helping us to improve this paper. Special thanks to Pierre Flener for our fruitful and constructive discussions.

References

1. H. Büyükyıldız and P. Flener, *Generalized logic program transformation schemas*, In: N.E. Fuchs (ed.), Proc. of LOPSTR'97 (this volume)
2. Y. Deville and K.-K. Lau, *Logic program synthesis: A survey*, Journal of Logic Programming, 19-20:321-350, May/July 1994
3. P. Flener, *Logic Program Synthesis From Incomplete Information*, Kluwer Academic Publishers, 1995
4. P. Flener and Y. Deville, *Logic program transformation through generalization schemata*, In: M. Proietti (ed.), Proc. of LOPSTR'95, Springer-Verlag, 1996

5. P. Flener, K.-K. Lau and M. Ornaghi, *On Correct Program Schemas*, In: N.E. Fuchs (ed.), Proc. of LOPSTR'97 (this volume)

6. N.E. Fuchs and M.P.J. Fromherz, *Schema-Based Transformations of Logic Programs*, In: T.P. Clement, K.-K. Lau (eds.), Proc. of LOPSTR'91, Springer-Verlag, 1992

7. M.R. Garey and D.S. Johnson, *Computers and Intractability. A Guide to the Theory of NP-completeness*, W.H. Freeman and Company, 1979

8. T.S. Gegg-Harrison, *Learning Prolog in a Schema-Based Environment*, Instructional Science, 20:173-192, 1991

9. T.S. Gegg-Harrison, *Representing Logic Program Schemata in λProlog*, In: L. Sterling (ed.), Proc. of the 12th International Conference on Logic Programming, Japan, pp. 467-481, The MIT Press, 1995

10. T.S. Gegg-Harrison, *Extensible Logic Program Schemata*, In: J. Gallagher (ed.), Proc. of the 6th International Workshop on Logic Program Synthesis and Transformation, Stockholm, Sweden, pp. 256-274, Springer-Verlag, 1996

11. W.D. Goldfarb, *The Undecidability of the second-order unification problem*, Theoretical Computer Science, 13:225-230, 1981

12. J. Hannan and D. Miller, *Uses Of Higher-Order Unification For Implementing Program Transformers*, In: A. Kowalski, K.A. Bowen (eds.), Proc. of ICLP'88, The MIT Press, 1988

13. G. Huet, *A unification algorithm for lambda calculus*, Theoretical Computer Science, 1:27-57, 1975

14. G. Huet, *Résolution d'Équations dans les langages d'ordre 1, 2... ω*, PhD thesis, Université Paris VII, 1976

15. G. Huet and B. Lang, *Proving and Applying Program Transformations Expressed with Second-Order Patterns*, Acta Informatica 11 (1978), 31-55

16. I. Kraan, D. Basin and A. Bundy, *Middle-Out Reasoning for Logic Program Synthesis*, In: D.S. Warren (ed.), Proc. of ICLP'93, The MIT Press, 1993

17. D. Miller and G. Nadathur, *A logic programming approach to manipulating formulas and programs*, Proc. of the IEEE Fourth Symposium on Logic Programming, IEEE Press, 1987

18. A. Martelli and U. Montanari, *An Efficient Unification Algorithm*, ACM Transactions on Programming Languages and Systems, Vol. 4, No. 2, April 1982, pp.258-282

19. T. Nipkow, *Higher-order critical pairs*, In: Proc. 6th IEEE Symp. Logic in Computer Science, pp. 342-349, 1991

20. J. Richardson and N.E. Fuchs, *Development of correct transformation schemata for Prolog programs*, In: N.E. Fuchs (e.), Proc. of LOPSTR'97 (this volume).

21. Z. Somogyi, F. Henderson and T. Conway, *The execution algorithm of Mercury: an efficient purely declarative logic programming language*, Journal of Logic Programming, 29(1-3):17-64, October-December 1996

22. W.W. Vasconcelos and N.E. Fuchs, *Enhanced Schema-Based Transformations for Logic Programs and their Opportunistic Usage in Program Analysis and Optimisation*, technical report, Institut für Informatik, Universität Zürich, 1995

23. W.W. Vasconcelos and N.E. Fuchs, *An Opportunistic Approach for Logic Program Analysis and Optimisation Using Enhanced Schema-Based Transformations*, In: M. Proietti (ed.), Proc. of LOPSTR'95, Springer-Verlag, 1996

A   Rewriting Rules Examples

We only present here a subset of the rewriting rules. We focus on the most significant ones. The set of rewriting rules contains the classical rules for first-order unification [18].

A.1   Constraints

Interchangeability of Parameters Rule (Non-deterministic).

$X_1 \ldots X_n \in$ SOrdT, $\overline{X}$ is one of the $n!$ permutations of $X_1 \ldots X_n$, $t \in$ seqterm, A and B are sequences of SOrdT

$$\langle [A, \odot(X_1 \ldots X_n)], B = t] \bullet Eq \, , \, \sigma \rangle \longmapsto \langle [A, \overline{X}, B = t] \bullet Eq \, , \, \sigma \rangle$$

Length Constraints Rules.

Hard Length Constraints Rule. Hard length constraint rewriting rules are presented for the *length_eq* predicate constraint. The first rule is about constraint on Vseqatom , and the second, on Vseqterm.

$G_k \in$ Vseqatom, $i \in I\!N$

$$\langle Eq \, , \, \sigma \cup \{length\_eq(G_k, i)\} \rangle \longmapsto \langle [G_k = P_1 \ldots P_i] \bullet Eq\{G_k/P_1 \ldots P_i\} \, , \, \sigma \rangle$$
where $P_1 \ldots P_i$ are brand-new Vatom variables

$\&_k \in$ Vseqterm, $i \in I\!N$

$$\langle Eq \, , \, \sigma \cup \{length\_eq(\&_k, i)\} \rangle \longmapsto \langle [\&_k = \_T_1 \ldots \_T_i] \bullet Eq\{\&_k/\_T_1 \ldots \_T_i\} \, , \, \sigma \rangle$$
where $\_T_1 \ldots \_T_i$ are brand-new Vterm variables

Soft Length Constraints Rule (Non-Deterministic). Soft length constraint rewriting rules are presented for the *length_eq* predicate constraint on Vseqatom. The Vseqterm case is similarly expressed. The rule is non-deterministic because j can be chosen between 0 and n (if $j = 0$, $G_k = \emptyset$).

$G_k \in$ Vseqatom, $p_1 \ldots p_n \in$ atom, $L \in$ Vlength, $0 \le j \le n$, A and B are sequences of SOrdP

$$\langle [A, G_k, B = p_1 \ldots p_n] \bullet Eq \, , \, \sigma \cup \{length\_eq(G_k, L)\} \rangle$$
$$\longmapsto \langle [G_k = P_1 \ldots P_j], [A, P_1 \ldots P_j, B = p_1 \ldots p_n] \bullet Eq\{G_k/P_1 \ldots P_j\} \, ,$$
$$\sigma\{L/j\} \rangle$$
where $P_1 \ldots P_j$ are brand-new Vatom variables

Hard Position Constraint Rules.

$X \in$ SOrdP, $X_1 \ldots X_j, Y_1 \ldots Y_k \in$ SOrdP, $p_1 \ldots p_n \in$ atom, $1 \le i \le n$

$$\langle [X_1 \ldots X_j, X \# i, Y_1 \ldots Y_k = p_1 \ldots p_n] \bullet Eq \, , \, \sigma \rangle$$
$$\longmapsto \langle [X_1 \ldots X_j = p_1 \ldots p_{i-1}], [X = p_i], [Y_1 \ldots Y_k = p_{i+1} \ldots p_n] \bullet Eq \, , \, \sigma \rangle$$

$$\frac{X \in \text{SOrdP}, \ X_1 \ldots X_j, Y_1 \ldots Y_k \in \text{SOrdP}, \ p_1 \ldots p_n \in \text{atom}, \ i \leq 0 \text{ or } i > n}{\langle [X_1 \ldots X_j, X \# i, Y_1 \ldots Y_k = p_1 \ldots p_n] \bullet Eq, \sigma \rangle \longmapsto \textbf{failure}}$$

Similar rules are for SOrdT.

Optional Objects Rule (Non-deterministic).

$$\frac{X \in \text{SOrdP (resp. SOrdT)}, \ x \in \text{seqatom (resp. seqterm)}, \ A \text{ and } B \text{ are sequences of SOrdP (resp. SOrdT)}}{\langle [A, \ll X \gg, B = x] \bullet Eq, \sigma \rangle \longmapsto \langle [A, X, B = x] \bullet Eq, \sigma \rangle}$$

$$\frac{X \in \text{SOrdP (resp. SOrdT)}, \ x \in \text{seqatom (resp. seqterm)}, \ A \text{ and } B \text{ are sequences of SOrdP (resp. SOrdT)}}{\langle [A, \ll X \gg, B = x] \bullet Eq, \sigma \rangle \longmapsto \langle [A, B = x] \bullet Eq, \sigma \rangle}$$

A.2   Others

Vseqatom Rewriting Rule (Non-deterministic).
Here we show the rewriting rules for the case of unconstrained Vseqatom.

$$\frac{G_k \in \text{Vseqatom}, p_1 \ldots p_n \in \text{atom}, 0 \leq j \leq n, A \text{ and } B \text{ are sequences of SOrdP}}{\langle [A, G_k, B = p_1 \ldots p_n] \bullet Eq, \sigma \rangle}$$
$$\longmapsto \langle [G_k = P_1 \ldots P_j], [A, P_1 \ldots P_j, B = p_1 \ldots p_n] \bullet Eq\{G_k/P_1 \ldots P_j\}, \sigma \rangle$$
where $P_1 \ldots P_j$ are brand-new Vatom variables

A Decomposition Rule.
Here is an example of a decomposition rule applying on terms. Another similar rule applies on atoms. Failure rules are also needed if the numbers of the left-side and right-side arguments are not the same.

$$\frac{T_1 \ldots T_n \in \text{SOrdT and } T_1 \text{ without option and position constraint}, \ t_1 \ldots t_m \in \text{term},}{\langle [T_1 \ldots T_n = t_1 \ldots t_m] \bullet Eq, \sigma \rangle}$$
$$\longmapsto \langle [T_1 = t_1], [T_2 \ldots T_n = t_2 \ldots t_m] \bullet Eq, \sigma \rangle$$

$$\frac{T_1 \ldots T_n \in \text{SOrdT and } T_1 \text{ without option and position constraint}}{\langle [T_1 \ldots T_n = \emptyset] \bullet Eq, \sigma \rangle \longmapsto \textbf{failure}}$$

$$\frac{t_1 \ldots t_m \in \text{term}}{\langle [\emptyset = t_1 \ldots t_m] \bullet Eq, \sigma \rangle \longmapsto \textbf{failure}}$$

Second-Order Substitution Rule.

$$\frac{X \in \text{SObject}, x \in \text{FObject} \cup \{\emptyset\}}{\langle [X = x] \bullet Eq, \sigma \rangle \longmapsto \langle Eq\{X/x\}, \sigma \cup \{X/x\} \rangle}$$

First-Order Checking Rules.

$$\frac{x \in \text{FObject} \cup \{\, \emptyset \,\}}{\langle [x = x] \bullet Eq \,,\, \sigma \rangle \longmapsto \langle Eq \,,\, \sigma \rangle}$$

$$\frac{x_1,\, x_2 \in \text{FObject} \cup \{\, \emptyset \,\},\ x_1 \neq x_2}{\langle [x_1 = x_2] \bullet Eq \,,\, \sigma \rangle \longmapsto \textbf{failure}}$$

B Working Example

Let the following schema $\langle S, c \rangle$, with

> Schema S: $P([\,], \&_1) \leftarrow G_1$.
> $\qquad\quad P([\_H|\_T], \&_2) \leftarrow G_2,\, P(\_T, \&_3),\, G_3$.

and global constraints

> $c = \{$ length_eq$(\&_1, L)$, length_eq$(\&_2, L)$, length_eq$(\&_3, L)$ $\}$

be semi-unified with the program P:

> Program P: islist($[\,]$).
> $\qquad\qquad$ islist($[\,T|Q\,]$) $\leftarrow$ islist(Q).

As a first step, starting from $\langle S = P,\ c \rangle$, a previously undescribed rewriting rule derives the following set of equations:
$\langle\ P([\,], \&_1) = $ islist($[\,]$),
$\quad G_1 = \emptyset$,
$\quad P([_H|_T], \&_2) = $ islist($[\,T|Q\,]$),
$\quad G_2,\, P(_T, \&_3),\, G_3 = $ islist(Q),
$\quad c$
$\rangle$

For clarity, we will handle the four equations separately now:

1. **First equation:** $P([\,], \&_1) = $ islist($[\,]$)

   $\rightarrow$ by an undescribed rewriting rule instantiating predicate symbol variable P to predicate symbol islist:
   $\langle\ [\,], \&_1 = [\,]$,
   $\quad \{\ P/$islist, length_eq$(\&_1, L)$, length_eq$(\&_2, L)$, length_eq$(\&_3, L)\ \}\ \rangle$
   $\rightarrow$ by the non-deterministic rule A.1 (soft length constraint rule):
   $\langle\ \&_1 = \emptyset$,
   $\quad [\,], \emptyset = [\,]$,
   $\quad \{\ P/$islist, length_eq$(\&_2, 0)$, length_eq$(\&_3, 0)\ \}\ \rangle$
   Remark: if another branch of this non-deterministic rule is followed, the process fails. For example: $\langle\ \&_1 = \_T_1\ ;\ [\,],\, \_T_1 = [\,]\ ;\ \{\ P/$islist, length_eq$(\&_2, 1)$, length_eq$(\&_3, 1)\ \}\ \rangle \rightarrow$ by rule A.2 (decomposition rule): $\langle\ \&_1 = \_T_1,\, [\,] = [\,],\, \_T_1 = \emptyset,\ \{\ P/$islist, length_eq$(\&_2, 1)$, length_eq$(\&_3, 1)\ \}\ \rangle \rightarrow$ by rule A.2

again: **failure** due to $\_T_1 = \emptyset$. In the remaining of the example, we shall follow success branches only.
$\rightarrow$ by rule A.2 (second-order substitution):
$\langle\,[\,], \emptyset = [\,],$
  $\{\ P/\text{islist}, \text{length\_eq}(\&_2,0), \text{length\_eq}(\&_3,0), \&_1/\emptyset\ \}\ \rangle$
$\rightarrow$ by rule A.2 (decomposition rule):
$\langle\,[\,] = [\,],$
  $\emptyset = \emptyset,$
  $\{\ P/\text{islist}, \text{length\_eq}(\&_2,0), \text{length\_eq}(\&_3,0), \&_1/\emptyset\ \}\ \rangle$
$\rightarrow$ by rule A.2 (first-order checking): **success**
$\langle\,\emptyset,$
  $\{\ P/\text{islist}, \text{length\_eq}(\&_2,0), \text{length\_eq}(\&_3,0), \&_1/\emptyset\ \}\ \rangle$

2. **Second equation:** $G_1 = \emptyset$

   $\rightarrow$ from the result of the first equation and by rule A.2 (second-order substitution): **success**
   $\langle\,\emptyset,$
     $\{\ P/\text{islist}, \text{length\_eq}(\&_2,0), \text{length\_eq}(\&_3,0), \&_1/\emptyset, G_1/\emptyset\ \}\ \rangle$

3. **Third equation:** $P([\_H|\_T], \&_2) = \text{islist}([\ T|Q\ ])$

   $\rightarrow$ from the result of the previous equations:
   $\langle\,\text{islist}([\ \_H|\_T\ ], \&_2\ ) = \text{islist}([\ T|Q\ ]),$
     $\{\ P/\text{islist}, \text{length\_eq}(\&_2,0), \text{length\_eq}(\&_3,0), \&_1/\emptyset, G_1/\emptyset\ \}\ \rangle$
   $\rightarrow$ by an undescribed rewriting rule checking predicate symbols (islist):
   $\langle\,[\ \_H|\_T\ ], \&_2 = [\ T|Q\ ],$
     $\{\ P/\text{islist}, \text{length\_eq}(\&_2,0), \text{length\_eq}(\&_3,0), \&_1/\emptyset, G_1/\emptyset\ \}\ \rangle$
   $\rightarrow$ by the rule A.1 (hard length constraint rule):
   $\langle\,\&_2=\emptyset,$
     $[\ \_H|\_T\ ] = [\ T|Q\ ],$
     $\{\ P/\text{islist}, \text{length\_eq}(\&_3,0), \&_1/\emptyset, G_1/\emptyset\ \}\ \rangle$
   $\rightarrow$ by a variant of rule A.2 (second-order substitution): **success**
   $\langle\,\emptyset,$
     $\{\ P/\text{islist}, \text{length\_eq}(\&_3,0), \&_1/\emptyset, G_1/\emptyset, \&_2/\emptyset, \_H/T, \_T/Q\ \}\ \rangle$

4. **Fourth equation:** $G_2, P(\_T, \&_3), G_3 = \text{islist}(Q)$

   $\rightarrow$ from the result of the previous equations:
   $\langle\,G_2, \text{islist}(Q, \&_3), G_3 = \text{islist}(Q),$
     $\{\ P/\text{islist}, \text{length\_eq}(\&_3,0), \&_1/\emptyset, G_1/\emptyset, \&_2/\emptyset, \_H/T, \_T/Q\ \}\ \rangle$
   $\rightarrow$ by the non-deterministic rule A.2 (Vseqatom rewriting rule):
   $\langle\,G_2 = \emptyset,$
     $G_3 = \emptyset,$
     $\text{islist}(Q, \&_3) = \text{islist}(Q),$
     $\{\ P/\text{islist}, \text{length\_eq}(\&_3,0), \&_1/\emptyset, G_1/\emptyset, \&_2/\emptyset, \_H/T, \_T/Q\ \}\ \rangle$

$\rightarrow$ by rule A.2 (second-order substitution):

$\langle$ islist$(Q, \&_3)$ = islist(Q),

  { P/islist, length_eq($\&_3$,0), $\&_1/\emptyset$, $G_1/\emptyset$, $\&_2/\emptyset$, _H/T, _T/Q,

  $G_2/\emptyset$, $G_3/\emptyset$ } $\rangle$

$\rightarrow$ by an undescribed rule checking predicate symbols:

$\langle Q, \&_3 = Q$,

  { P/islist, length_eq($\&_3$,0), $\&_1/\emptyset$, $G_1/\emptyset$, $\&_2/\emptyset$, _H/T, _T/Q,

  $G_2/\emptyset$, $G_3/\emptyset$ } $\rangle$

$\rightarrow$ by same rewriting rules as before: **success**

$\langle \emptyset$,

  { P/islist, $\&_1/\emptyset$, $G_1/\emptyset$, $\&_2/\emptyset$, $\&_3/\emptyset$, _H/T, _T/Q, $G_2/\emptyset$, $G_3/\emptyset$ } $\rangle$

At the end of the resolution we have: $\langle\emptyset; \sigma\rangle$, with $\sigma=$ { P/islist, $\&_1/\emptyset$, $\&_2/\emptyset$, $\&_3/\emptyset$, _H/T, _T/Q, $G_1/\emptyset$, $G_2/\emptyset$, $G_3/\emptyset$ }. From this constraint set, we derive the complete substitution which is σ itself. We have that $S\ \sigma \simeq P$.

In this complete example, 14 rewriting rules have been applied to find the substitution. For failure branches of the non-deterministic rules to be explored until failure, 10 extra rewriting rules have also to be applied.

Implicit Program Synthesis by a Reversible Metainterpreter

Henning Christiansen

Department of Computer Science, Roskilde University,
P.O.Box 260, DK-4000 Roskilde, Denmark
E-mail: henning@ruc.dk

Abstract. Synthesis of logic programs is considered as a special instance of logic programming. We describe experience made within a logical metaprogramming environment whose central component is a reversible metainterpreter, in the sense that it is equally well suited for generating object programs as well as for executing them. Requirements telling that certain goals should be provable in a program sought can be integrated with additional sideconditions expressed by the developer at the metalevel, and the resulting specifications tend to be quite concise and declarative. For problems up to a certain degree of complexity, this provides a mode of working characterized by experimentation and an ability to combine different methods which is uncommon in most other systems for program synthesis. Reversibility in the metainterpreter is obtained using constraint logic techniques.

1   Introduction

The synthesis of a logic program is usually understood as a constructive process starting from a more or less complete logical specification and/or examples of what belongs (or not belongs) to the desired relation. This may be guided by the developer's growing understanding of the task or by heuristics built in to automatic or semiautomatic tools. This process can be performed on logic specifications, gradually being transformed into the subset consisting of efficient logic programs, or on other mathematical structures such as proofs from which programs can be extracted.

In this paper, we propose a slight shift which is more along the line of logic programming in general. The logic programmer tends to state requirements to the result he wants rather than concentrating on the procedure or process that leads to this result. In program synthesis, the desired result is a program — as opposed to, say, a sorted or reversed list.

We describe a metaprogramming environment whose central component is a reversible 'demo' predicate. This is a binary proof predicate parameterized by representations of object program and query, reversibility means that it can be used, not only for executing object programs, but also for generating them. By means of 'demo', the program developer (i.e., the metaprogrammer) can state semantic requirements to the program sought of the form "this and this must

Norbert E. Fuchs (Ed.): LOPSTR'97, LNCS 1463, pp. 90–110, 1998.

be provable" or "... not provable". This can be combined with syntactic requirements concerning which predicates, control patterns, etc. that are allowed, and
perhaps other calls to demo that express integrity constraints or similar things.
As in logic programming in general, we expect the underlying interpreter to
come up with solutions (here: programs) that satisfy the different requirements.

The possible success of such an approach depends on to what extent the
available linguistic means make it possible to express "in a natural way" requirements that effectively delineate a class of interesting programs. We will
show examples developed in our system and especially for simple abduction and
induction tasks the approach looks promising, the definitions of such tasks being
surprisingly concise and readable. The most interesting observation is, perhaps,
to see how declarative specifications can be re-used in order to express different
ways of reasoning. It appears also that the experimental mode of working, for
which logic programming is appreciated (by some developers, at least) is preserved, by continually enhancing and testing a specification. For the synthesis
of recursive programs, we cannot present similar experience and we will discuss
possible extensions of our approach in the final section.

It is obvious to us that the sort of technology we present only can develop into
a complement to "explicit" techniques based on program transformations. There
are knowledge and heuristics needed for complex and realistic programming tasks
which best can be described — if it can be described at all — by means of
transformation techniques. This is quite analogous to the fact that declarative
programming never completely can rule out procedural programming.

In the rest of this introduction we give an overview of the approach and a comparison with related work. Section 2 describes the principles behind our constraint-
based implementation of 'demo' and section 3 sketches the features of the implemented system that we will refer to as the Demo system. Section 4 shows
examples of program synthesis developed in this system, one giving a combination of default reasoning with abduction and induction, and a natural language
analysis based on abduction in a way that would be difficult to fit into other
systems for abduction. Section 5 discusses possible improvements to make it possible to approach more complex problems. The Demo system is available on the
World Wide Web at the address http://www.dat.ruc.dk/software/demo.html.

1.1   A Brief Overview

An approach to program synthesis has an object language in which the resulting
programs appear, in our case positive Horn clause programs. We represent object
programs and fragments thereof as ground terms in a metalanguage which basically is Prolog extended with various metaprogramming facilities, most notably
the 'demo' predicate. For any phrase P of the object language, the notation $\lceil P \rceil$
will stand for the term in the metalanguage designated as the name of P. The
'demo' predicate is a formalization of the usual notion of provability embedded
in a logic program interpreter; we can specify it as follows.

demo($\lceil P \rceil, \lceil Q \rceil$)   iff P and Q are object program and query such that there exists substitution σ with

$$P \vdash Q\sigma$$

A metavariable, say X, placed in the first argument will thus stand for a piece of program text, and a logically satisfactory implementation will produce program fragments which make Q provable. By means of additional side-conditions, 'demo' can be instructed to produce programs within a certain class as illustrated by the following pattern.

useful(X) $\wedge$ demo($\cdots X \cdots, \cdots$)

The 'useful' predicate may specify syntactic requirements perhaps extended with additional calls to 'demo'. In this way, a choice of 'useful' can define a reasoning method, e.g., abduction or a class of inductive problems, and the remaining parts of the arguments to demo set up the specific problem to be solved.

1.2   The Need for Constraints and Delays

It can be argued that a direct implementation of in "classical" Prolog, with its top-down computation rule, is insufficient in order to provide the reversibility in the 'demo' predicate that we have assumed. The problem is that the space of solutions to a call to 'demo' — or the subgoals we can expect inside 'demo' — typically is infinite in such a way that no finite set of terms will cover it by subsumption. This implies that a failure in the computation easily can provoke a generate-and-test-forever loop. In addition, all known implementations in Prolog of 'demo' (i.e., those parameterized by a detailed representation of the object program) include tests which, depending on the underlying interpreter, will lead to either floundering or unsound behaviour in case of an uninstantiated metavariable standing for a part of the program being interpreted. An obvious way to get around this problem is to use constraint logic. We have used a well known program structure for implementing 'demo', but with the primitive operations implemented as constraints — which means that these operations typically delay when called with partly instantiated arguments, and the constraint solver makes sure that the set of delayed constraints always is satisfiable. In section 2 we describe our constraint-based implementation; the constraint solver can be found in the appendix.

A similar argument can be made for the additional sideconditions depicted as the 'useful' predicate above. However, it is a quite difficult task to write a constraint solver and luckily, as it will appear in our examples, it turns out to be sufficient to use the sort of delay mechanisms that are available in current implementations of Prolog [36].

The 'demo' predicate was initially suggested by Kowalski in his book from 1979 [28], however, with no attention to the possibility of using it in reverse for program synthesis. In 1992, T. Sato [35] and Christiansen [7] published independently different methods for obtaining this kind of reversibility in 'demo' although these results were mostly of a theoretical interest. Apart from our own constraint-based implementation, we are not aware of any practically relevant, fully reversible versions; for more background in this topic, see [8].

1.3   Related Work

For a general overview of the area of logic program synthesis, we refer to the present and previous proceedings of the LOPSTR workshops, and to comprehensive reviews contained in two recent books [9,10].

In order to compare our approach with other work, we emphasize the notion of program schemas. A program schema is a template which represents a certain class of programs, e.g., the class of divide-and-conquer programs, having placeholders which can be instantiated as to produce concrete programs. Such schemas are used in "manual" approaches to program construction, e.g., [1,17], and in (semi-) automatic transformation-based approaches, e.g., [14,12,5,13,33]. A transformation can be specified in such a way that a program matching one schema is transformed into another, intendedly improved, program described by another schema. Program schemas can be understood as second-order objects [6,18,22]. Other authors [5,13] represent program schemas by means of so-called open first-order programs, open in the sense that some of the predicates used are unspecified.

In our framework, the ground representation combined with metalevel predicates supplied by the user serves the purpose of program schemas. Programs are given by first order terms, and ordinary logical variables take the role of placeholders, referred to here as metavariables as they are part of a metalanguage and in general stand for representations of object program fragments. In [6] a suggestion is given for a general framework for program schemas integrated with constraints, quite similar to what we obtain in a logic metaprogramming setting.

Most approaches to program synthesis, including those mentioned above, incorporate some kind of strategy for controlling the application of transformation steps in order to provide a convergence towards an improved program. In our approach, which is an application of logic programming, 'demo' becomes a blind robot, which will produce in principle any program satisfying the different requirements set up by the developer. As in logic programming in general, it is difficult to point out a *best* solution to a problem, which is relevant when we are searching not only for a correct program but also for an efficient one. On the other hand, this is partly compensated by the ease with which new criteria can be set up.

We also mention the work by Numao and Shimura from 1990 [34] which seems to be the first suggestion for using a reversible 'demo' predicate for program synthesis. They propose a quite interesting approach, using explanation based learning [30] for analyzing existing programs in order to re-use their inherent strategy for the synthesis of new programs. This can be seen as an automatic way to extract "program schemas" that otherwise may be difficult to formalize by hand. It could be interesting to take up this idea with a capable implementation of 'demo' such as our constraint-based version.

Inductive logic programming (ILP) is another area concerned with problems similar to those that we approach, namely the synthesis of programs from samples of their intended behaviour and additional conditions about the sort of programs that are preferred (in ILP called "bias"); we refer to [2,31,32] for an overview and introduction to the most common methods. The ILP systems described in the literature are typically directed towards specific kinds of applications and the techniques used are often related to those used in transformation-based program synthesis. Within specific areas, ILP has reported impressive results that we cannot match in our declarative and highly generic approach. On the other hand, it appears to be fairly easy in our system to adapt and combine different methods, e.g. integrating abduction in induction which also have been introduced in ILP methods recently [11,29].

Hamfelt and Nilsson [19] have proposed to use 'demo' together with a higher-order 'fold' operator and least-general-generalization techniques for producing recursive programs. The authors apply a multilayered structure ('demo' interpreting 'demo') as a means to get around the mentioned generate-and-test problems which we avoid using constraints. The advantage of using recursion operators such as 'fold' is that 'demo' only needs to invent non-recursive plug-in's in order to define, say, the 'append' predicate. It is difficult to judge the generality of this proposal but it seems worthwhile to combine our 'demo' with more recent and thorough work by the authors [20,21] on recursion operators.

Finally, we contrast our approach with the large-scale project presented by Bibel *et al* [3] in these proceedings, clearly heading at a methodology for programming in the large. We consider our Demo system as a light-weight and easy-to-use environment, primarily intended for experimentation and illustrative purposes in research and teaching, perhaps useful as a prototyping tool in larger contexts.

2   A Constraint-Based Metainterpreter

In this section we describe the theoretical background for our constraint-based implementation of 'demo'. In a first reading of this paper, it may be recommended only to take a brief look at the first subsection and then go directly to the examples in section 3. For the full account on the technical matters, including proofs, we refer to [8].

2.1   Syntax and Semantics of Object and Metalanguage

The presence of a naming relation induces a natural classification of metalevel terms into different types, namely those that stand for programs, those that stand for clauses, etc., We consider a class of constraint logic languages $\mathrm{CLP}(\mathcal{X})$ similarly to [25], but here adapted for typed languages. In our case, the parameter $\mathcal{X}$ refers to some domain of constraints over terms with no interpreted function symbols. Each such constraint logic language is characterized by a finite set of types,[1] collections of predicate, constraint and function symbols, and variables, each with fixed ranks/types.

Capital letters such as X and Y are used for variables; the underline character '_' is used as an anonymous variable in the sense that each occurrence of it stands for a variable that does not occur elsewhere.

A *program* is a finite set of *clauses* of the form $h \leftarrow b_1 \wedge \ldots \wedge b_n$ with h being an atom, each b_i an atom or a constraint, composed in the usual way respecting the ranks of each symbol; a *query* is similar to the body of a clause. Queries and bodies of clauses are collectively called *formulas* and we assume two inclusion operators, both denoted ↑, from atoms and from constraints into formulas; to simplify the notation, we leave out these operators except in a few, essential cases. Finally, the truth constant *true* is used to indicate the empty body of a fact.

The meaning of the constraints in a given language is assumed given by a set of ground constraints referred to as *satisfied* constraints. We assume, for each type τ, constraint symbols '=: $\tau * \tau$' and '$\neq$: $\tau * \tau$' with the usual meanings of syntactic identity and non-identity. To cope with the semantics of $\neq$ constraints, we require, for each type τ, that there exist infinitely many constant symbols (not necessarily of rank $\rightarrow \tau$) which can occur in a term of type τ.

We assume any substitution to be idempotent similarly to the sort of answers generated by Prolog and for reasons of technical simplicity, we define satisfiers and answer substitutions to be ground substitutions. The logical semantics is given in terms a proof relation defined for ground queries as follows.

Definition 1. *The* proof relation *for a constraint language* $\mathcal{L} = \mathrm{CLP}(\mathcal{X})$, *denoted* $\vdash_{\mathcal{L}}$, *between programs and ground queries is defined inductively as follows.*

- $P \vdash_{\mathcal{L}} true$ *for any program P.*
- *Whenever P has a clause with a ground instance* $H \leftarrow B$ *such that* $P \vdash_{\mathcal{L}} B$, *we have* $P \vdash_{\mathcal{L}} H$.
- *Whenever* $P \vdash_{\mathcal{L}} A$ *and* $P \vdash_{\mathcal{L}} B$, *we have* $P \vdash_{\mathcal{L}} A \wedge B$.
- $P \vdash_{\mathcal{L}} C$ *whenever C is a satisfied constraint of* $\mathcal{X}$.

A correct answer *for a query Q with respect to a program P is a substitution* σ *for the variables of Q such that* $P \vdash_{\mathcal{L}} Q\sigma$. □

The object language for 'demo' is called $\mathcal{HCL}$ and consists of untyped, positive Horn clauses with equality and inequality constraints allowed in the body of clauses. The precise syntax and semantics are given by considering $\mathcal{HCL}$ as a constraint logic language (as defined above) with only one type and no additional constraints.

2.2   The Metalanguage $\mathrm{CLP}(\mathcal{HCL})$

The 'demo' predicate is programmed in a language $\mathrm{CLP}(\mathcal{HCL})$ having function symbols that reflect the syntax of $\mathcal{HCL}$ and constraints that make it possible to express its proof relation. $\mathrm{CLP}(\mathcal{HCL})$ has the following types:

---

[1] We consider only simple types with no notion of parameterization or subtypes.

program, clause, formula, atom, constraint, term, substitution, substitution-pair.

For each symbol f of $\mathcal{HCL}$, $\mathrm{CLP}(\mathcal{HCL})$ includes a function symbol $'f$ of arity and rank corresponding to the syntax of $\mathcal{HCL}$, e.g.,

$'\leftarrow$: *atom* $*$ *formula* $\rightarrow$ *clause*,

and for each $\mathcal{HCL}$ variable, say X, a constant $'X$: $\rightarrow$ *term*. For any phrase P of $\mathcal{HCL}$, the notation $\lceil P \rceil$ refers to the ground term that arises when each symbol f occurring in P is replaced by $'f$ and we call $\lceil P \rceil$ a *name* for P. Formally, these brackets are not part of the metalanguage but will be used as syntactic sugar. The reverse brackets $\lfloor \cdots \rfloor$ are used inside $\lceil \cdots \rceil$ to indicate the presence of a metavariable. If, for example, Z is a metavariable of type *atom*, we have

$$\lceil \lfloor Z \rfloor \leftarrow q(f(X,b)) \rceil \;=\; Z \, '\!\leftarrow '\!\uparrow \, 'q('f('X,'b)).$$

In addition, there are functions to build representations of object programs and substitutions, we will use Prolog's list notation for those, and substitution pairs will be written (x,t) where x names an object variable and t an object term.

For each type $\tau \in \{clause, formula, atom, constraint, term\}$, $\mathrm{CLP}(\mathcal{HCL})$ has a constraint symbol

instance$_\tau$: $\tau * \tau *$ *substitution*.

The type subscript will be left out when obvious from the context or when a distinction is unnecessary. Additionally, we have the following constraint symbols.

no-duplicates: *program*,
member: *clause* $*$ *program*
not-member: *clause* $*$ *program*

Constraint satisfaction is defined by exactly the following ground constraints recognized as satisfied:

- any constraint instance($\lceil P_1 \rceil$, $\lceil P_2 \rceil$, $\lceil \sigma \rceil$) where P_1, P_2 are phrases of $\mathcal{HCL}$, σ a $\mathcal{HCL}$ substitution with $P_1\sigma = P_2$,
- any constraint of the form member($c, [\ldots, c, \ldots]$),
- any constraint of the form not-member($c, [c_1, \ldots, c_n]$), $n \geq 0$ where c is different from all $c_1, \ldots, c_n$, and
- any constraint of the form no-duplicates($[c_1, \ldots, c_n]$), $n \geq 0$ where all $c_1, \ldots, c_n$ are different.

The 'member' constraints, used for selecting clauses out of an object program, could in principle have been specified as an ordinary predicate, but in order to suppress the generation of different representations of the same object program, we need to have a detailed procedural control, which is only possible by explicit derivation rules. The 'no-duplicates' constraints are used to ensure that terms of type *program* really are names of programs; 'not-member' and $\neq$ constraints are used here as auxiliaries. A constraint solver for $\mathrm{CLP}(\mathcal{HCL})$ is described in the appendix.

2.3   The Metainterpreter

Using $\mathrm{CLP}(\mathcal{HCL})$, we can give our constraint-based version of the so-called 'instance-demo' predicate, which has been studied by several other authors recently [15,16,23,4].

$$\mathrm{demo(P, Q)} \leftarrow$$
$$\quad \mathrm{no\text{-}duplicates(P)} \land$$
$$\quad \mathrm{instance(Q, Q_1, \_)} \land$$
$$\quad \mathrm{demo_1(P, Q_1)}.$$

$$\mathrm{demo_1(P, \lceil true \rceil)} \leftarrow \quad true.$$
$$\mathrm{demo_1(P, \lceil \uparrow \lfloor A \rfloor \rceil)} \leftarrow$$
$$\quad \mathrm{member(C, P)} \land \mathrm{instance(C, \lceil \lfloor A \rfloor \leftarrow \lfloor B \rfloor \rceil, \_)} \land$$
$$\quad \mathrm{demo_1(P, B)}.$$
$$\mathrm{demo_1(P, \lceil \lfloor T_1 \rfloor = \lfloor T_2 \rfloor \rceil)} \leftarrow \quad T_1 = T_2.$$
$$\mathrm{demo_1(P, \lceil \lfloor T_1 \rfloor \neq \lfloor T_2 \rfloor \rceil)} \leftarrow \quad T_1 \neq T_2.$$
$$\mathrm{demo_1(P, \lceil \lfloor A \rfloor \land \lfloor B \rfloor \rceil)} \leftarrow$$
$$\quad \mathrm{demo_1(P, A)} \land$$
$$\quad \mathrm{demo_1(P, B)}.$$

The $\uparrow$ symbol is the inclusion operator of atoms into formulas that is left implicit in most other cases; the purpose of the 'no-duplicates' constraint is to impose our convention of programs being sets and not lists of clauses, a property which cannot be expressed directly with the sort of types normally used in logic programming. This, together with the rules of the constraint solver (see appendix) for 'member' constraints, prevents the generation of alternative presentations of the same program due to permutation and duplication of clauses.

Precise statements and proofs of soundness and completeness can be found in [8]. We will mention here that satisfiability of instance constraints in general may be expected to be undecidable. More precisely, if we had used general substitutions in our framework — and not idempotent ones, as we prefer — the satisfiability problem becomes equivalent to the multiple semi-unification problem known to be undecidable [27]. Whether this disappears in the idempotent case is not known at present. However, the way the constraints are used in the 'demo' program implies a number of invariant properties that ensure termination in constraint solving. The most important invariant is that of *safeness* which means that the sets of metavariables occurring in first arguments to instance constraints and those occurring in second arguments are disjoint.

3   Outline of the Implemented Demo System

The metalanguage $\mathrm{CLP}(\mathcal{HCL})$ has been implemented in Sicstus Prolog [36] using its attributed variables' library. Soundness and completeness results are preserved for the constraint solver but the 'demo' program is interpreted directly by Prolog and inherits, thus, Prolog's overall termination behaviour.

In the implemented system, we use actually a more detailed naming relation which makes it possible to implement a subtype relation, so that, e.g., *constant* is a subtype of *term* and *atom* a subtype of *formula* (which means that the inclusion operator ↑ becomes unnecessary). Types are implemented in Sicstus Prolog also as constraints, so for each type τ of $\mathrm{CLP}(\mathcal{HCL})$, there is a constraint $\tau(t)$ satisfied for exactly all terms t of type τ. These constraints are represented as predicates program_(-), clause_(-), atom_(-), etc., the underline character consistently used to distinguish constraints from a few Prolog built-in's.

An extended notation is provided to facilitate the use of the naming relation. A Prolog-like syntax is used for the object language with three different operators representing the naming brackets $\lceil \cdots \rceil$ in order to resolve ambiguity, \ is used for object programs and clauses, \\ for formulas, atoms and constraints, and \\\ for terms. So, e.g., \\p(a,X) is a way of writing the *ground* term which names the $\mathcal{HCL}$ atom $p(a, X)$. A '?' operator represents $\lfloor \cdots \rfloor$, so the expression \\p(a,?Z) stands for the name of an $\mathcal{HCL}$ atom whose predicate is p, whose first argument is a and whose second argument is unspecified, indicated by the metavariable Z.

The naming relation and the 'member' constraints have been extended to support a concatenation operator '&' for programs and a notion of object program modules. In the following,

```
demo( \ ( m1 & m2 & ?P), ...)
```

m1 and m2 are expected be defined as object program modules.

We can illustrate the use of the extended syntax and program modules by a very simple example of abduction inspired by [26]. The following source file defines an object module called garden together with an auxiliary predicate called abducible.

```
:- object_module( garden,
     \[ (grass_is_wet:- rained_last_night),
        (grass_is_wet:- sprinkler_was_on)
     ]).

:- block abducible(-).

abducible( \ (rained_last_night:- true) ).
abducible( \ (sprinkler_was_on:- true) ).
abducible( \ (full_moon:- true) ).
```

The block directive is a Sicstus Prolog primitive which causes the abducible predicate to delay until its argument gets instantiated. In less trivial examples, the use of delays may become essential in order to prevent such auxiliary conditions from enumerating under backtracking the perhaps infinite space of their solutions. It should be emphasized that although the block directive is a procedural device, it does not destroy the declarative semantics as do other control facilities in Prolog.

We can now express the abductive problem of finding a cause why `grass_is_wet` holds in the following dialogue with the system.[2]

```
?- abducible(WHY), demo(\ (garden & [?WHY]), \\grass_is_wet).

WHY = \ (rained_last_night:-true) ? ;
WHY = \ (sprinkler_was_on:-true) ? ;

no
```

The program argument to `demo` describes a conjunction of the `garden` module and a program consisting of one unknown clause, indicated by the metavariable `WHY` and the the system returns the possible, abducible explanations.

Other facilities of the implemented system will be explained as they appear in the examples.

4 Examples, Program Synthesis by Means of 'Demo'

Here we will show two examples developed in the Demo system, the first showing an integration of different modes of reasoning, the second a variant of abduction applied for a simplified natural language analysis problem. These and other application of Demo concerning view update, abduction in a fragment of linear logic, and diagnosis are described in [8] and available together with the implemented system (see WWW address in the introduction).

We do not consider, here, synthesis of recursive programs as we cannot present any convincing examples; we discuss this issue in the concluding section.

4.1 Default Reasoning Combined with Abduction and Induction

This is intended as a "working example" and we do not care about the formal relation to other work on default reasoning. We consider only monadic predicates and constants. The current system cannot handle negation so we represent a negative literal $\neg p(a)$ as `p(a,no)` and correspondingly $p(a)$ as `p(a,yes)`. We consider a default theory to be a triplet $\langle F, D, E \rangle$ where, informally,

- F is a set of facts,
- D is a set of default rules of the form `p(X,yes):- q(X,yes)`; only ground instances of default rules that do not violate the overall consistency can be used in a proof,
- E is a set of exception of the form `p(X,no):- q(X,yes)`.

---

[2] All examples are authentically produced in our implemented system except that we have retouched away explicit calls to an alternative reader that recognizes the extended syntax; by a more careful coding of the user interface, this could have been avoided anyhow.

The notion of consistency of a program with encoded **yes**/**no** values can be formalized at the metalevel in the following way; the notation \\ ··· ?Q-[?C,?YN1] displays an alternative syntax for atoms which makes it possible to parameterize over the predicate symbol, so here Q is a metavariable ranging over predicate names.

```
consistent(P):-
    for_all( (constant_(C), constant_(YN1), constant_(YN2),
            demo(P, \\ (?Q-[?C,?YN1], ?Q-[?C,?YN2]))),
        YN1=YN2 ).
```

The `for_all` construct is control device using a negation-as-failure principle[3] to generate all solutions given by the first argument and the whole construct succeeds if the second argument succeeds in all cases. So the definition reads:

> A program is consistent whenever, for any predicate q and constant a, we do not have $q(a,\text{yes})$ and $q(a,\text{no})$ at the same time.

We should be aware, however, that this implementation of the consistency check only works correctly when the program argument does not contain uninstantiated metavariables.

A first sketch of a formalization in our system of provability in a default theory may look as follows, where D1 stands for some set of ground instances of the default rules D, and F, E for the other components of the default theory, Q represents the query or "observations" to be proved.

```
demo(\ (?F & ?D1 & ?E), Q),
consistent(\ (?F & ?D1 & ?E ).
```

The following proof predicate will be sufficient for deductive reasoning within a default theory. In this case, the default theory is completely given in advance, i.e., given by a ground term at the metalevel.

```
demo_default(F,D,E, Q):-
    default_instances(D, D1),
    demo(\ (?F & ?D1 & ?E), Q),
    close_constraints(D1),
    consistent(\ (?F & ?D1 & ?E) ).
```

We will not show definitions for all auxiliary metapredicates, but `default_instances` can give a good illustration of the general pattern.

```
% default_instances(Defaults,Instances).
:- block default_instances(?,-).

default_instances(_,\[]).

default_instances(D, \[(?P-[?C,yes]:- ?Q-[?C,yes] ) | ?E]):-
    member_(\ (?P-[?_,yes]:- ?Q-[?_,yes]), D),
    constant_(C),
    default_instances(D, E).
```

---

[3] Implemented as follows, `for_all(P,T):- \+ (P, (T -> fail ; true))`.

This implements, quite directly, that the second argument is a program of clauses created from members of the first by replacing the object variable by some constant. The `block` directive makes the predicate delay until its second argument gets instantiated (here by an event inside 'demo' when it attempts to grab a clause in the yet uninstantiated program component D1). The tail recursion means that the predicate will iterate in a lazy fashion through D1 as more and more elements may be needed. The `member_` predicate is the system's standard constraint for selecting clauses in object programs.

Finally, we should explain the `close_constraints` predicate used in the definition of `demo_default`. It is a device built into the system that investigates the possibly uninstantiated metavariables in its argument and, according to certain heuristics, instantiates to prototypical values that will satisfy the pending constraints. In the particular case above, it will close the open program tail of D1, which is necessary in order to have the naively implemented consistency check to execute correctly.

To test our proof predicate for default theories, we define the following object modules.

```
:- object_module( facts,
      \[  penguin(tweety,yes),
          bird(john,yes)                    ]).

:- object_module( defs,
      \[  (bird(X,yes):- penguin(X,yes)),
          (fly(X,yes):- bird(X,yes))    ]).

:- object_module( excs,
      \[  (fly(X,no):- penguin(X,yes))    ]).
```

The following queries and answers show the overall behaviour of the `demo_default` predicate defined above.

```
?- demo_default(\facts,\defs,\excs,
                  \\ (fly(john,yes), fly(tweety,no))).

yes
?- constant_(X),
      demo_default(\facts,\def,\excs, \\fly(?X,yes)).

X = \\\john
```

When moving from deduction to abduction and induction we have to formalize the assumptions we have made implicitly about what constitutes a default theory, otherwise the `demo` predicate will be free to invent any strange program that makes the given query provable. As a first approach, we can write predicates `facts(-)`, `defaults(-)`, and `exceptions(-)` which in a straightforward way formalize the syntactic assumptions mentioned in the introduction to this example, e.g.,

```
:- block exceptions(-).

exceptions(\[]).

exceptions(\[(?P-[X,no]:- ?Q-[X,yes]) | ?More]):-
    exceptions(More).
```

We can now improve the definition of the `demo_default` predicate in such a way that it may be able to answer in a reasonable way queries with partly specified theory.

```
demo_default(Facts,Defaults,Excs,Obs):-
    facts(Facts),
    defaults(Defaults),
    exceptions(Excs),
    default_instances(Defaults, DefIs),
    demo(\ (?Facts & ?Excs & ?DefIs), Obs),
    close_constraints(\ (?Facts & ?Excs & ?DefIs) ),
    consistent(\ (?Facts & ?Excs & ?DefIs) ).
```

The following queries and answers illustrate abduction and induction of defaults-with-exceptions from examples.

```
?- demo_default(F,\defs,\excs, \\fly(tweety,no)).

F = \[(penguin(tweety,yes):-true)]

?- demo_default(\facts,\[?D],\[?E],
                \\ (fly(tweety,no), fly(john,yes))).

D = \ (fly(X,yes):-bird(X,yes))
E = \ (fly(X,no):-penguin(X,yes))
```

In the first query we abduce, from the background knowledge given by modules `defs` and `excs`, the fact that `tweety` is a `penguin` from the observation that `tweety` does not `fly`. In the second, the background knowledge `facts` together with the observations about the two individuals' (lacking) ability to `fly` makes the system conclude the expected pair of default and exception rules.

While `demo_default` works quite well in these examples, where some background knowledge is given in each case, it will not work as a general concept learner that produces from scratch a class of "intuitively correct" default theories that can explain or systematize a larger sample of observations. This will require a further refinement of the metalevel conditions that takes into account a suitable stratification among the different predicates.

This example showed the Demo system "at work" for small problems of automated reasoning and it is worth noticing the very little amount of code that the developer had to supply in order to implement different reasoning methods. Another important point is displayed, namely the learning process went through by the developer in this test-refine-and-extend cycle which is characteristic for logic programming. If someone elaborated the example above further into a general concept learner as indicated, we will claim that he or she would have learned some essential points about logic and machine learning — although not so much about the algorithmic concerns that need to be considered for solving complex problems.

4.2   A Natural Language Example

Here we show a variation of abduction which seems difficult to implement in a similar direct way in those systems for abduction, we have seen described in the literature, see [26] for an overview. Our example is concerned with the relation between simple still-life scenes and sentences about them.

Let T be a $\mathcal{HCL}$ program describing a number of things in the world together with some of their properties, e.g., thing(the_flower), thing(the_vase), thing(the_table), container(the_vase). An actual scene is described by another program of facts about the immediate physical relation between the objects of T, e.g., in(the_flower, the_vase), on(the_vase, the_table). Utterances about a scene are defined by an $\mathcal{HCL}$ program, declared as a module grammar in the following way.

```
:- object_module( grammar,

       \   [ (sentence(S):- simple(S)),
             (sentence(S):- folded(S)),
             (simple([X, is, on, Y]):-
                 thing(X), thing(Y),
                 on(X,Y)   ),
             (simple([X, is, in, Y]):-
                 thing(X), thing(Y),
                 in(X,Y)   ),
             (folded([X, is, PREP, Y]):-
                 simple([X, is, _, Z]),
                 simple([Z, is, PREP, Y])  )
          ]).
```

The folded sentence allows us to say 'the flower is on the table' instead of the longer 'the flower is in the vase, the vase is on the table'. Assuming also modules things and scene defining a particular scene as above, we can use the metainterpreter to execute queries in the normal deductive way, e.g., for testing the correctness of a given sentence.

```
?- demo( \   (grammar & things & scene),
            \\ sentence([the_flower, is, on, the_table]).
```

This model can be extended with abduction so that the program component scene can be generated "backwards" from sentences about it. In other words, the problem to be solved is to construct explanations in terms of 'in' and 'on' facts which can explain the stated sentences. Any such explanation must satisfy some integrity constraints with respect to the actual things theory; an in fact, for example, must satisfy the following metalevel predicate.

```
scene_fact(T, \ (in(?A,?B) :- true)):-
    constant_(A),
    constant_(B),
    demo(T, \\ (thing(?A), container(?B))),
    dif(A,B).
```

The dif(A,B) condition serves, together with other conditions, to preserve a sensible, physical interpretation of the programs generated. We can write a similar rule for 'on' and then pack the whole thing together as a predicate scene_description($\lceil T \rceil$, $\lceil S \rceil$) satisfied whenever S is a sensible scene built from the objects defined by T. An example of the abductive problem can now be stated by the following query.

```
?- scene_description( \things, X),
   demo( \ (grammar & things & ?X),
         \\sentence([the_flower, is, on, the_table])).
```

The system produces the following three answers.

```
X = \[(on(the_flower,the_table):-true)]

X = \[(on(the_flower,the_vase):-true),
      (on(the_vase,the_table):-true)]

X = \[(in(the_flower,the_vase):-true),
      (on(the_vase,the_table):-true)]
```

We can also extend the example by abducing a things program T in parallel with the scene. In case a fact, say, in(the_dog, the_house) is abduced, the integrity constraint will abduce in turn as part of T the facts thing(the_dog), container(the_house). Furthermore, the integrity constraint concerned with T (not shown) will trigger the abduction of thing(the_house). This recursive triggering of new abductions via integrity constraints, that appears quite natural in our metaprogramming setting, does not appear to be possible in other implementations of abduction that we are aware of.

As in the previous example, we could continue to refine and extend the metalevel conditions, for example for inducing grammars from sample sentences. This would require a formalization at the metalevel of, firstly, what sort of object programs that can be conceived as grammars and, secondly, what it means for a grammar to be a good grammar.

5   Conclusions, Possible Extensions of the Demo System

We have presented an approach to program synthesis based on metaprogramming in logic, using a ground representation of object programs and a reversible 'demo' predicate. The ground representation (when supported by a proper notation!) together with metalevel predicates provided by the user, appears to be a quite flexible tool for describing different classes of not-too-complex programs, thus serving the purpose program schemas used in other approaches. For the sort of problems that we have illustrated in our examples, the Demo system appears as a highly generic environment in which different modes of reasoning can be developed and combined with each other in a straightforward way which seems quite uncommon in those other systems for program synthesis and automated reasoning that we are aware of.

When it comes to the specification of more complicated patterns, say, defining a class of divide-and-conquer programs, the direct and isomorphic representation that we have used tends to be insufficient. In order to complete our approach for handling more complex program synthesis tasks, it seems relevant to suggest alternative representation forms together with specialized constraints that give a certain bias towards particular program structures. If, for example, we are interested in synthesizing recursive programs, a representation based on the recursion operators of [20,21] may seem appropriate (see also discussion in section 1.3). In a forthcoming re-implementation of the Demo system, we will support the development of such representations, by making the naming relation extensible by the user and by providing a layer for constraint programming, which makes it possible for users to write constraint solvers in terms of derivation rules similar to those appearing in the appendix. We will also refer to [6] which can be seen as a starting point for the systematic development of such representations.

Another striking shortage in the present Demo system is its lack of ability to handle negative examples in a proper way. We suggest here, to add an additional proof predicate, demo_fails($\lceil P \rceil$, $\lceil Q \rceil$) with the meaning that the query Q fails in the program P. This predicate should be implemented in such a way that, whenever in a standard negation-as-failure search, it runs into an open program part (i.e., an uninstantiated metavariable), it delays. In general, this will result in several delayed or-branches and if one of them reports that Q can succeed, the call to demo_fails should fail immediately. In this way, negative examples can be set up as conditions before the usual demo predicate is set to work, and when some action triggered inside demo adds something to the object program that makes one negative example succeed, demo (or the 'responsible' side-conditions) will be forced to take another choice. With such an extension, it should be possible to approximate some of the results gained in the ILP area. With similar techniques it may also be possible to have integrity constraints in, say, view update problems to execute in a truly incremental way.

Appendix: A Constraint Solver for CLP($\mathcal{HCL}$)

Constraint solving for CLP($\mathcal{HCL}$) is described by means of top-down derivations in the sense of [25], however here adapted for typed languages. As we have in mind implementations using Prolog-like technology, we assume an indivisible (and efficiently implemented) unification operation in the underlying interpreter.

In general, we define a *derivation system* to consist of *transition rules* $S \rightsquigarrow S'$ over *states* of the form

$$\langle C, \alpha \rangle$$

where C is a finite set of atoms and constraints and α an *accumulated substitution*, which represents the explicit variable bindings made so far.

States are assumed to be *idempotent* in the sense that no variable $x \in \mathrm{dom}(\alpha)$ occurs in C, i.e., α is mapped consistently over the constraint set C. We assume a special state called FAILURE with empty set of satisfiers.

We use also $\leadsto$ to denote the *derivation relation* induced in the natural way by a set of derivation rules $\{\leadsto\}$; $\leadsto^*$ is the reflexive, transitive closure of $\leadsto$. Whenever, for some query Q, that $\langle Q, \emptyset \rangle \leadsto^* S$, where S does not contain atoms and no derivation step is possible from S, any satisfier for S restricted to the variables of Q is called a *computed answer* for Q.

The following transition rules, labeled (Unif), (Res), (Dif1), (Dif2), and (True), constitute the core of any transition system. The unification rule (Unif) is the only one that changes the accumulated substitution.

(Unif) $\langle C \cup \{s = t\}, \alpha \rangle \leadsto \langle C, \alpha \rangle \mu$
— where μ is a most general unifier of s and t chosen so that the new state becomes idempotent; however, if s and t have no unifier, the result is FAILURE.

In any other rule, we will leave out the accumulated substitution assuming it to be copied unchanged. Other rules can of course affect it indirectly by setting up one or more equations as is the case in the following resolution rule. Resolution is only meaningful in the context of some program P.

(Res) $C \cup \{A\} \leadsto C \cup \{B_1, \ldots, B_n, A = H\}$
— whenever A is an atom, $H \leftarrow B_1 \wedge \ldots \wedge B_n$ a variant with new variables of a clause in P.

Occurrences of the truth constant *true* are removed by the following rule.

(True) $C \cup \{true\} \leadsto C$

We need the following characterization in order to handle inequality constraints.

Definition 2. *Two terms t_1 and t_2 are said to be* distinguishable *if they have no unifier, i.e., for any substitution σ, $t_1\sigma$ and $t_2\sigma$ are different.*
□

The following two rules define a behaviour of inequalities quite similarly to the `dif` predicate of Sicstus Prolog [36].

(Dif1) $C \cup \{t_1 \neq t_2\} \leadsto C$
— whenever t_1 and t_2 are distinguishable.

(Dif2) $C \cup \{t_1 \neq t_2\} \leadsto$ FAILURE
— whenever t_1 and t_2 are identical.

The constraint solver for $\text{CLP}(\mathcal{HCL})$ assumes a computation rule which is

fast-solving: the resolution rule (Res) cannot be applied if another rule is applicable, and

fast-unifying: the rules (Unif), (Dif1), and (Dif2) take precedence over all other rules.

The following derivations rules are specific for $\text{CLP}(\mathcal{HCL})$. We start with the rules concerned with instance constraints. The rule (I) expresses that a given variable can have one and only one instance under a given substitution.

(I) $C \cup \{\text{instance}(v, t, s), \text{instance}(v, t', s)\} \rightsquigarrow C \cup \{t = t', \text{instance}(v, t', s)\}$
— when v is variable.

The following two rules (It1–2) reduce instance constraints that express bindings to object variables; the first one applies when a binding has been recorded already for the given variable, the second one installs an initial binding in the substitution.

(It1) $C \cup \{\text{instance}_{term}('x, t, s)\} \rightsquigarrow C \cup \{t = t'\}$
— when $'x$ is the name of an $\mathcal{HCL}$ variable and $s = [\cdots ('x, t') \cdots]$

(It2) $C \cup \{\text{instance}_{term}('x, t, s)\} \rightsquigarrow C \cup \{w = [('x, t)|w']\}$
— when $'x$ is the name of an $\mathcal{HCL}$ variable, (It1) does not apply,
   and $s = [\cdots |w]$; w' is a new variable.

Notice that a fast-unifying computation rule is relevant for (It2) in order to avoid different and incompatible expansions of the substitution tail w. — An invariant property can be shown, that these substitution argument always have open tails so that rule (It2) always can apply when relevant.

Instance constraints with names of structured object language terms in the first argument are reduced as follows.

(It3) $C \cup \{\text{instance}_{term}('f(t_1, \ldots, t_n), t', s)\}$
   $\rightsquigarrow C \cup \{t' = {'f}(v_1, \ldots, v_n),$
         $\text{instance}_{term}(t_1, v_1, s), \ldots, \text{instance}_{term}(t_n, v_n, s)\}$
— when $'f$ is the name of a function symbol of $\mathcal{HCL}$, $n \geq 0$;
   $v_1, \ldots, v_n$ are new variables.

The reduction of a term instance constraint is, thus, triggered by its first argument being non-variable. Rules for all other syntactic constructs in $\mathcal{HCL}$ of categories *clause*, *formula*, *atom*, and *constraint* are defined similarly to (It3) except that they are triggered also by the second argument being non-variable. As an example, we show the rule (Ic) for reduction of instance constraints on clauses.

(Ic) $C \cup \{\text{instance}_{clause}(t_1, t_2, s)\}$
   $\rightsquigarrow C \cup \{t_1 = (u_1' \leftarrow u_2), t_2 = (v_1' \leftarrow v_2),$
         $\text{instance}_{atom}(u_1, v_1, s), \text{instance}_{formula}(u_2, v_2, s)\}$
— when t_1 or t_2 is of the form $(\cdots ' \leftarrow \cdots)$; u_1, u_2, v_1, v_2 are new variables.

Member constraints and its companions are reduced by the following rules.

(M1) $C \cup \{\text{member}(c, v)\} \rightsquigarrow C \cup \{v = [c|v']\}$
— when v is a variable; v' is a new variable.

(M2) $C \cup \{\text{member}(c, [c'|p])\} \rightsquigarrow C \cup \{m\}$
— where m is either $c = c'$ or member(c, p).

(M3) $C \cup \{\text{member}(c, [\,])\} \rightsquigarrow \text{FAILURE}$.

(ND1) $C \cup \{\text{no-duplicates}([c|p])\} \rightsquigarrow C \cup \{\text{not-member}(c, p), \text{no-duplicates}(p)\}$.

(ND2) $C \cup \{\text{no-duplicates}([\,])\} \rightsquigarrow C$.

(NM1) $C \cup \{\text{not-member}(c, [c'|p])\} \rightsquigarrow C \cup \{c \neq c', \text{not-member}(c, p)\}$.

(NM2) $C \cup \{\text{not-member}(c, [\,])\} \rightsquigarrow C$.

Termination and soundness conditions are formulated and proved in [8].

References

1. Barker-Plummer, D. Cliche programming in Prolog. Bruynooghe, M. (ed.), *Proc. of the Second Workshop on Meta-programming in Logic.* April 4–6, 1990, Leuven, Belgium. pp. 247–256, 1990.
2. Bergadano, F., Gunetti, D., *Inductive logic programming, From machine learning to software engineering.* MIT Press, 1996.
3. Bibel, W., Korn, D., Kreitz, C., Kuruc, F., Otten, J., Schmitt, S., Stopmann, G., A multilevel approach to program synthesis. In: Fuchs, N.E. (ed), *Proc. of LOPSTR'97* (this volume).
4. Bowers, A.F., Gurr, C.A., Towards fast and declarative meta-programming, In: Apt, K.A., Turini, F. (eds), *Meta-Logics and Logic Programming*, MIT Press, pp. 137–166, 1995.
5. Büyükyıldız, H., Flener, P., Generalized logic program transformation schemas. In: Fuchs, N.E. (ed), *Proc. of LOPSTR'97* (this volume).
6. Chasseur, E., Deville, Y. Logic program schemas, constraints and semi-unification. In: Fuchs, N.E. (ed), *Proc. of LOPSTR'97* (this volume).
7. Christiansen, H., A complete resolution method for logical meta-programming languages. In: Pettorossi, A. (ed.), Meta-Programming in Logic, *Lecture Notes in Computer Science* 649, pp. 205–219, 1992.
8. Christiansen, H., Automated reasoning with a constraint-based metainterpreter. To appear in: *Journal of Logic Programming*, 1998.
9. Flach, P. *Simply logical, Intelligent reasoning by example.* Wiley, 1994.
10. Flener, P. *Logic program synthesis from incomplete information.* Kluwer, 1995.
11. Flener, P. Inductive logic program synthesis with DIALOGS. In: Muggleton, S. (ed), Proc. of ILP'96. *Lecture Notes in Artificial Intelligence* 1314, Springer-Verlag, pp. 175–198, 1997.
12. Flener, P., Deville, Y. Logic program transformation through generalization schemata. In: Proietti, M. (ed), Proc. of LOPSTR'95. *Lecture Notes in Computer Science* 1048, Springer-Verlag, pp. 171–173, 1996.

13. Flener, P., Lau, K.-K., Ornaghi, M. On correct program schemas. In: Fuchs, N.E. (ed), *Proc. of LOPSTR'97* (this volume).
14. Fuchs, N.E., Fromherz, M.P.J, Schema-based transformation of logic programs. In: Clement, P., Lau, K.-K. (eds.), *Proc. of LOPSTR'91*, Springer-Verlag, pp. 111–125, 1992.
15. Gallagher, J.P., *A system for specialising logic programs*. Technical Report TR-91-32, University of Bristol, Department of Computer Science, 1991.
16. Gallagher, J.P., Tutorial on specialisation of logic programs. *Proc. of the ACM SIGPLAN Symposium on Partial Evaluation and Semantics-Based Program Manipulation (PEPM'93), Copenhagen*, pp. 88–98, 1993.
17. Gegg-Harrison, T.S. Learning Prolog in a schema-based environment. *Instructional Science* 20, pp. 173–192, 1991.
18. Gegg-Harrison, T.S. Representing logic program schemata in λProlog. Sterling, L. (ed.). *Proc. of ICLP'95*, MIT Press, pp. 467–481, 1995.
19. Hamfelt, A., Nilsson, J.F. Inductive metalogic programming. In: S. Wrobel (ed), *Proc. of ILP'94*, pp. 85–96. *GMD-Studien* Nr. 237, Sankt Augustin (Germany), 1994.
20. Hamfelt, A., Nilsson, J.F. Declarative logic programming with primitive recursive relations on lists. Maher, M. (ed.). *Proc. of JISCLP'96*, MIT Press, pp. 230–243, 1996.
21. Hamfelt, A., Nilsson, J.F. Towards a logic programming methodology based on higher-order predicates. *New generation Computing* 15, pp. 421–228, 1997.
22. Hannan, J., Miller, D. Uses of higher-order unification for implementing program transformers. Kowalski, R.A., Bowen, K.A. (eds). *Proc. of ICLP'88*, MIT Press, pp. 942–959, 1988.
23. Hill, P.M., Gallagher, J.P., Meta-programming in Logic Programming. To be published in Volume V of *Handbook of Logic in Artificial Intelligence and Logic Programming*, Oxford University Press.
    Currently available as *Research Report Series* 94.22, University of Leeds, School of Computer Studies, 1994.
24. Hill, P.M. and Lloyd, J.W., Analysis of meta-programs. *Meta-programming in Logic Programming*. Abramson, H., and Rogers, M.H. (eds.), MIT Press, pp. 23–51, 1989.
25. Jaffar, J., Maher, M.J., Constraint logic programming: A survey. *Journal of logic programming*, vol. 19,20, pp. 503–581, 1994.
26. Kakas, A.A., Kowalski, R.A., Toni, F., Abductive logic programming. *Journal of Logic and Computation* 2, pp. 719–770, 1993.
27. Kfoury, A.J., Tiuryn, J., and Urcyczyn, P., The undecidability of the semi-unification problem. *Proc. 22nd Annual ACM Symposium on Theory of Computing*, pp. 468–476, 1990.
28. Kowalski, R., *Logic for problem solving*. North-Holland, 1979.
29. Lamma, E., Mello, P., Milano, M., Riguzzi, F. A hybrid extensional/intensional system for learning multiple predicates and normal logic programs. In: Fuchs, N.E. (ed.), *Proc. of LOPSTR'97*, (this volume).
30. Mitchell, T.M., Keller, R.M., Kedar-Cabelli, S.T. Explanation-based generalization: A unifying view. *Machine Learning* 1, pp. 47–80, 1986.
31. Muggleton, S., de Raedt, L. Inductive logic programming: Theory and methods. *Journal of Logic Programming* 19/20, pp. 669–679, 1994.
32. Nienhuys-Cheng, S.-H., de Wolf, R., Foundations of Inductive Logic Programming. *Lecture Notes in Artificial Intelligence* 1228, Springer-Verlag, 1997.
33. Richardson, J., Fuchs, N.E., Development of correct transformation schemata for Prolog programs. In: Fuchs, N.E. (ed.), *Proc. of LOPSTR'97*, (this volume).

34. Numao, M., Shimura, M. Inductive program synthesis using a reversible meta-interpreter. In: Bruynooghe, M. (ed.), *Proc. of the Second Workshop on Meta-programming in Logic.* April 4–6, 1990, Leuven, Belgium. pp. 123–136, 1991.

35. Sato, T., Meta-programming through a truth predicate. *Logic Programming, Proc. of the Joint International Conference and Symposium on Logic Programming*, ed. Apt, K., pp. 526–540, MIT Press, 1992.

36. *SICStus Prolog user's manual.* Version 3#5, SICS, Swedish Institute of Computer Science, 1996.
    See also `http://www.sics.se/isl/sicstus/sicstus_toc.html`.

Termination Analysis for Tabled Logic Programming

Stefaan Decorte, Danny De Schreye, Michael Leuschel, Bern Martens, and
Konstantinos Sagonas

Department of Computer Science
Katholieke Universiteit Leuven
Celestijnenlaan 200A, B-3001 Heverlee, Belgium
{stefaan,dannyd,michael,bern,kostis}@cs.kuleuven.ac.be

Abstract. We provide a theoretical basis for studying the termination
of tabled logic programs executed under SLG-resolution using a left-
to-right computation rule. To this end, we study the classes of *quasi-
terminating* and *LG-terminating* programs (for a set of atomic goals S).
These are tabled logic programs where execution of each call from S
leads to only a finite number of different (i.e., non-variant) calls, and a
finite number of different calls and computed answer substitutions for
them, respectively. We then relate these two classes through a program
transformation, and present a characterisation of quasi-termination by
means of the notion of *quasi-acceptability* of tabled programs. The latter provides us with a practical method of proving termination and the
method is illustrated on non-trivial examples of tabled logic programs.

1 Introduction

The relative novelty of tabled-based logic programming implementations has
given rise to a number of both theoretical and practical questions related to
the study of the characteristics of such programs and to improving their performance. This work has been motivated by an initial study on how to adapt
advanced program specialisation techniques, originally developed for standard
logic programming, to the context of tabled logic programming. In a companion
paper [12], we describe how left-propagation of bindings in a program executed
under SLG-resolution [4] using a fixed left-to-right computation rule (as SLG
is usually implemented in practical tabled-based systems such as XSB [15]) can
seriously endanger the termination characteristics of that program. A simple
example from [12] is the program:

$$p(X) \leftarrow p(Y), Y = f(X)$$
$$X = X \leftarrow$$

For the query $\leftarrow p(X)$, the program finitely fails in SLG since its left-to-right
evaluation encounters (a variant of) an existing call for which no answers can be
produced. By performing one unfolding step with respect to the atom $Y = f(X)$,
giving rise to the clause $p(X) \leftarrow p(f(X))$, the same query $\leftarrow p(X)$ will now result
in an infinite computation under SLG.

Norbert E. Fuchs (Ed.): LOPSTR'97, LNCS 1463, pp. 111–127, 1998.

In [12], preconditions for safe (i.e. termination preserving) program specialisation through unfolding are proposed. In the present paper we study the *universal* termination of tabled programs (where we are interested in the termination of the computation after all solutions have been generated), executed under SLG using a fixed left-to-right computation rule, in its own right. We adapt existing results on acceptability of programs with respect to sets of atoms from [6]. We show how this provides a natural necessary and sufficient condition for the termination of tabled logic programs. We also briefly discuss automatic verification of the proposed termination conditions, and present a non-trivial example (Appendix B).

The rest of the paper is structured as follows. In the next section we introduce some preliminaries and present a brief formalisation of SLG-resolution restricted to definite programs. In Section 3 we present the notions of quasi-termination and quasi-acceptability with respect to sets of atoms and prove that they are equivalent. In Section 4 we discuss the stronger notion of LG-termination and, again, characterise it in terms of quasi-termination. We end with a discussion.

2   Preliminaries

Throughout the paper, P will denote a definite tabled logic program. We also assume that in all programs all predicates are tabled (i.e. executed under SLG-resolution). The extended Herbrand Universe, U_P^E, and the extended Herbrand Base, B_P^E, associated with a program P, were introduced in [7]. They are defined as follows. Let $Term_P$ and $Atom_P$ denote the sets of respectively all terms and atoms that can be constructed from the alphabet underlying P. The variant relation, denoted $\approx$, defines an equivalence. U_P^E and B_P^E are respectively the quotient sets $Term_P/\approx$ and $Atom_P/\approx$. For any term t (or atom A), we denote its class in U_P^E (B_P^E) as $\tilde{t}$ (or $\tilde{A}$). However, when no confusion is possible, we omit the tildes. Finally, by $Pred_P$ and Fun_P we denote the sets of predicate and function symbols of P, respectively.

In this paper, we consider termination of SLG-resolution (see [4]), using a fixed left-to-right computation rule, for a *given set of atomic* (top level) *queries* with atoms in $S \subseteq B_P^E$. We will abbreviate SLG-resolution under the left-to-right computation rule by LG-resolution (which for definite programs is similar to OLDT-resolution [16,11], modulo the fact that OLDT specifies a more fixed control strategy and uses subsumption checking and term-depth abstraction instead of variant checking to determine existence of subgoals and answers in the tables). Below, we formalise these notions. While doing so, we also introduce some example programs that are used throughout the paper to illustrate various aspects of (non)-termination of tabled logic programs.

2.1   SLG-Resolution for Definite Programs

We present a non-constructive definition of SLG-resolution that is sufficient for our purposes, and refer the reader to [2,4,16,17] for more constructive formulations of (variants of) tabled resolution.

Definition 1.   (pseudo SLG-tree, pseudo LG-tree) *Let P be a definite program, $\mathcal{R}$ be a computation rule, and A an atom. A* pseudo SLG-tree *for $P \cup \{\leftarrow A\}$ under $\mathcal{R}$ is a tree τ_A such that:*

1. *the nodes of τ_A are labeled by goals along with an indication of the selected atom,*
2. *the arcs are labeled by sets of substitutions (either most general unifiers or computed answer substitutions),*
3. *the root of τ_A is $\leftarrow A$,*
4. *the children of the root $\leftarrow A$ are obtained by resolution against all matching (program) clauses in P,*
5. *the (possibly infinitely many) children of non-root nodes can only be obtained by resolving the selected (using $\mathcal{R}$) atom B of the node with clauses of the form $B\theta \leftarrow$ (not necessarily in P).*

If $\mathcal{R}$ is the leftmost literal selection rule, τ_A is called a pseudo LG-tree *for $P \cup \{\leftarrow A\}$.*

We say that a pseudo SLG-tree τ_A for $P \cup \{\leftarrow A\}$ is smaller *than another pseudo SLG-tree τ'_A for $P \cup \{\leftarrow A\}$ iff τ'_A can be obtained from τ_A by attaching new sub-branches to nodes in τ_A.*

*A (*computed*) answer clause of a pseudo SLG-tree τ_A for $P \cup \{\leftarrow A\}$ is a clause of the form $A\theta \leftarrow$ where θ is the composition of the answer substitutions found on a branch of τ_A whose leaf is labeled by the empty goal.*

Intuitively, a pseudo SLG-tree (in an SLG-forest, see Definition 2 below) represents the tabled computation of all answers for a given subgoal labeling the root node of the tree. The trees in the above definition are called *pseudo SLG-trees* because there is no condition yet on which clauses $B\theta \leftarrow$ exactly are to be used for resolution in point 5. These clauses represent the answers found — possibly in another tree of the forest — for the selected atom. This interaction between the trees of an SLG-forest is captured in the following definition.

Definition 2.   (SLG-forest, LG-forest) *Let P be a program, $\mathcal{R}$ be a computation rule, and S be a (possibly infinite) set of atoms such that no two different atoms in S are variants of each other. $\mathcal{F}$ is an* SLG-forest *for P and S under $\mathcal{R}$ iff $\mathcal{F}$ is a set of minimal pseudo SLG-trees $\{\tau_A \mid A \in S\}$ where*

1. *τ_A is a pseudo SLG-tree for $P \cup \{\leftarrow A\}$ under $\mathcal{R}$,*
2. *every selected atom B of each node in some $\tau_A \in \mathcal{F}$ is a variant of an element B' of S, such that every clause resolved with B is a variant of an answer clause of $\tau_{B'}$ and vice versa.*

Let $Q =\leftarrow A$ be an atomic query. An SLG-forest *for $P \cup \{Q\}$ is an SLG-forest for a minimal set S with $A \in S$. An* LG-forest *is an SLG-forest containing only pseudo LG-trees.*

Point 2 of Definition 2, together with the imposed minimality of trees in a forest, now uniquely determines these trees. So we can drop the designation "pseudo" and refer to (S)LG-trees in an (S)LG-forest. The notion of an (S)LG-forest introduces explicitly the relation between selected atoms and their computed answers. Also note that (S)LG-trees always have a finite depth.

Example 1 (NAT). Let NAT be the program below:

$$nat(0) \leftarrow$$
$$nat(s(X)) \leftarrow nat(X)$$

The (unique) (S)LG-forest for NAT and $\{nat(X)\}$, shown in Figure 1, consists of a single (S)LG-tree. Note that this tree has an infinitely branching node.

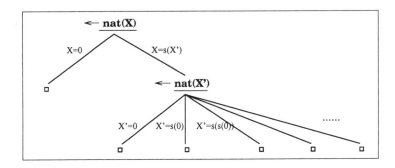

Fig. 1. SLG-forest for $NAT \cup \{\leftarrow nat(X)\}$.

Example 2. (NAT_{sol}) Let NAT_{sol} be the following program:

$$nat(0) \leftarrow$$
$$nat(s(X)) \leftarrow nat(X), sol(nat(X))$$
$$nat_{sol}(X) \leftarrow nat(X), sol(nat(X))$$
$$sol(X) \leftarrow$$

The LG-forest for $NAT_{sol} \cup \{\leftarrow nat(X)\}$ contains an infinite number of LG-trees; see Figure 2.

Finally, given $S \subseteq B_P^E$, by $Call(P, S)$ we denote the subset of B_P^E such that $\tilde{B} \in Call(P, S)$ whenever an element of $\tilde{B}$ is a selected literal in an LD-derivation for some $P \cup \{\leftarrow A\}$, with $\tilde{A} \in S$. We note that we can use the notions of LD-derivation and LD-computation even in the context of SLG-resolution, as the set of call patterns and the set of computed answer substitutions are not influenced by tabling; see e.g. Theorem 2.1 in [11].

3   Quasi-Termination and Quasi-Acceptability

As the examples in the previous section show, an LG-forest can be infinite. In particular, whenever LD-computation from an initial goal leads to infinitely many

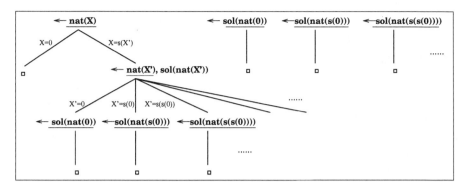

Fig. 2. The (infinite) LG-forest for Example 2.

different, non-variant calls, the corresponding LG-forest under tabled execution will be infinite. Obviously, such a phenomenon is undesirable, and therefore a first basic notion of termination studied in this paper is *quasi-termination* (a term borrowed from [9], defining a similar notion in the context of termination of off-line partial evaluation of functional programs). It is defined as follows.

Definition 3. (quasi-termination) *Let P be a program and $S \subseteq B_P^E$. P quasi-terminates with respect to S iff for every $A \in S$, $Call(P, \{A\})$ is finite. Also, P quasi-terminates iff it quasi-terminates wrt B_P^E.*

Lemma 1. *Let P be a program, $A \in B_P^E$, and let $\mathcal{F}$ be the LG-forest for $P \cup \{\leftarrow A\}$. Then P quasi-terminates wrt $\{A\}$ iff $\mathcal{F}$ consists of a finite number of LG-trees.*

This is the termination notion that also forms the heart of the study in [12].

Example 3. Consider the programs NAT and NAT_{sol} of Examples 1 and 2 respectively. With respect to $\{nat(X)\}$, NAT quasi-terminates, but NAT_{sol} does not.

In order to characterise the notion of quasi-termination, we adopt the following concept from [6].

Definition 4. (level mapping) *A level mapping for a program P is a function $l : B_P^E \to I\!N$.*

Definition 5. (finitely partitioning) *A level mapping l is finitely partition-ing iff for all $n \in I\!N : \#l^{-1}(n) < \infty$.*

In other words, only finitely many atoms are mapped to any $n \in I\!N$.

We now introduce the notion of *quasi-acceptability*. It is adapted from the acceptability notion defined in [6] and not from the more "standard" definition of acceptability by Apt and Pedreschi in [1]. The reason for this choice is that the quasi-termination property of a tabled program and (set of) goal(s) is *not* invariant under substitution. Consider the following example from [12]:

Example 4. Let $p/2$ be a tabled predicate defined by the following clause.

$$p(f(X), Y) \leftarrow p(X, Y)$$

Then, the query $\leftarrow p(X, Y)$ quasi-terminates while $\leftarrow p(X, X)$ does not!

The acceptability notion in [1] is expressed in terms of ground instances of clauses and its associated notion of left-termination is expressed in terms of the set of all goals that are *bounded* under the given level mapping. Such sets are closed under substitution. Because quasi-termination lacks invariance under substitution, we need a stronger notion of acceptability, capable of treating *any* set of interest S.

Definition 6. (quasi-acceptability) *Let l be a finitely partitioning level mapping on B_P^E. We say that P is* quasi-acceptable *with respect to l and S iff*
- *for every atom A such that $\tilde{A} \in Call(P, S)$,*
- *for every clause $H \leftarrow B_1, \ldots, B_n$ in P, such that $mgu(A, H) = \theta$ exists,*
- *for every initial subsequence $B_1, \ldots, B_{i-1}$ of $B_1, \ldots, B_n$ and every LD-computed answer substitution θ_{i-1} for $\leftarrow (B_1, \ldots, B_{i-1})\theta$:*

$$l(A) \geq l(B_i \theta \theta_{i-1})$$

In brief, the main differences with the acceptability notion of [6] are that:

1. level mappings are assumed to be finitely partitioning the extended Herband Base, and
2. decreases of the level mapping are not assumed to be strict.

Intuitively, the reasons for these differences can be understood as follows. Contrary to SLD, computations in which a call has a variant of itself as its (immediate) recursive descendant do not lead to non-termination under tabled evaluation. As we want to allow such computations, requiring a strict decrease of the level mapping is too strong. On the other hand, we do not want to allow that infinitely many different calls within a same level occur (due to the non-strict decrease). To exclude this, we impose the finite partitioning requirement.

More directly, it should be intuitively clear that the combination of the non-strict decrease with finitely partitioning level mappings implies that only a finite number of different calls are allowed to descend from a given call. This corresponds to quasi-termination.

Given these definitions, we can now prove one of the main results of this paper.

Theorem 1. (termination condition) *Let P be a program and $S \subseteq B_P^E$. P is quasi-acceptable wrt some finitely partitioning level mapping l and S iff P is quasi-terminating with respect to S.*

For a proof, we refer to Appendix A.

Quasi-termination captures the property that, under LD-computation, a given atomic goal leads to only finitely many different calls. It is exactly in such cases that tabling aims at achieving actual termination of top-down logic program execution. Hence the importance of quasi-termination as a key property for tabled programs.

Also, in a broader context, techniques for proving quasi-termination can be of great value to ensure termination of off-line specialisation of logic programs (whether tabled or not). Currently, in all off-line partial evaluation methods for logic programs (e.g. [13,10]) termination has to be ensured manually. In the context of off-line partial evaluation, quasi-termination is actually *identical* to termination of the partial evaluator. Thus, given a technique to establish quasi-termination, one can also establish whether a given binding time annotation will ensure termination or whether further abstraction is called for. This idea has already been successfully applied in the context of functional programming (cf. [8]), using the termination criterion of [9].

4   LG-Termination

Even when tabling, quasi-termination as in Definition 3 and Lemma 1 only partially corresponds to our intuitive notion of a 'terminating computation'.

Example 5. Consider the program of Example 1. Given the set $S = \{nat(X)\}$, NAT quasi-terminates with respect to S. This is obvious since $Call(NAT, S) = \{nat(X)\}$, which is finite. The program is also quasi-acceptable with respect to S and *any* finitely partitioning level mapping $B_{NAT}^E \to I\!N$.

Nevertheless, this example does not correspond to our intuitive notion of a terminating program. Although the LG-forest is finite, its unique LG-tree is infinitely branching (see Figure 1) and the computation does not terminate. Notice however that the computed answers do not lead to new calls. Therefore, quasi-termination does hold. Also note that the same program is not LD-terminating either: there exists an infinite LD-derivation. To capture this, we define the following stronger termination notion.

Definition 7.   (LG-termination) *Let P be a program and $S \subseteq B_P^E$. P is LG-terminating with respect to S iff for every $A \in S$, the LG-forest for $P \cup \{\leftarrow A\}$ is a finite set of finite LG-trees.*
Also, P is LG-terminating iff it is LG-terminating wrt B_P^E.

Let us now study how quasi-termination and LG-termination relate to each other. According to Lemma 1, quasi-termination only corresponds to part of the LG-termination notion; it does not capture infinitely branching LG-trees. But a simple program transformation can remedy this.

Definition 8.   (sol(ution) transformation) *The* sol *transformation is defined as follows:*

- *For a clause $C = H \leftarrow B_1, \ldots, B_n$ we define*
  $C_{sol} = H \leftarrow B_1, sol(B_1), \ldots, B_n, sol(B_n)$
  Here, $sol(B_i)$ is the syntactic application of the predicate $sol/1$ on B_i.

- *For a program P, we define:*

$$P_{sol} = \{C_{sol} \mid C \in P\} \cup$$
$$\{p_{sol}(X_1,\ldots,X_n) \leftarrow p(X_1,\ldots,X_n),$$
$$sol(p(X_1,\ldots,X_n)) \mid p/n \in Pred_P\} \cup$$
$$\{sol(X) \leftarrow\}$$

where each p_{sol}/n is a new predicate symbol.
- *For a set of atoms $S \subseteq B_P^E$, we define*
$$S_{sol} = \{\tilde{p}_{sol}(t_1,\ldots,t_n) \mid \tilde{p}(t_1,\ldots,t_n) \in S\}$$

The goal of the construction is that P LG-terminates wrt S iff P_{sol} quasi-terminates wrt S_{sol}. Note that P_{sol} is finite provided that P is also finite.

Example 6. The programs NAT of Example 1, and NAT_{sol} of Example 2 are related through the sol transformation.

Example 7. Let P be the following extension of the NAT program.
$$t(X) \leftarrow nat(X), fail$$
$$nat(0) \leftarrow$$
$$nat(s(X)) \leftarrow nat(X)$$
Then $Call(P, \{t(X)\}) = \{t(X), nat(X), fail\}$, so P quasi-terminates wrt $\{t(X)\}$. However, note that the query $\leftarrow t(X)$ does not terminate but fails infinitely in tabled evaluation under a left-to-right computation rule. Using the sol transformation, we have that $\{t(X)\}_{sol} = \{t_{sol}(X)\}$, and P_{sol} is the following program:
$$t(X) \leftarrow nat(X), sol(nat(X)), fail, sol(fail)$$
$$nat(0) \leftarrow$$
$$nat(s(X)) \leftarrow nat(X), sol(nat(X))$$
$$t_{sol}(X) \leftarrow t(X), sol(t(X))$$
$$nat_{sol}(X) \leftarrow nat(X), sol(nat(X))$$
$$sol(X) \leftarrow$$
Now, we have that

$$Call(P_{sol}, \{t_{sol}(X)\}) =$$
$$\{t_{sol}(X), t(X), nat(X), fail, sol(nat(0)), sol(nat(s(0))), \ldots\}$$

and as expected P_{sol} does not quasi-terminate wrt $\{t(X)\}_{sol}$.

Theorem 2. *Let P be a program and $S \subseteq B_P^E$. Then P LG-terminates wrt S iff P_{sol} quasi-terminates wrt S_{sol}.*

Proof. (Sketch) As can be seen in Figure 3 for a node in an LG-tree labeled by a compound goal $\leftarrow \underline{B}, \overline{Q}$, where B is the selected atom, every answer clause resolution for B in P (with the answer clause $B\theta$) translates into two answer clause resolutions (for B and $sol(B\theta)$) and one new LG-tree (for $sol(B\theta)$) in

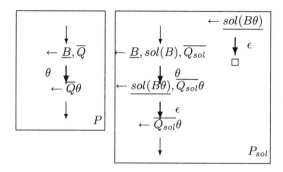

Fig. 3. Relating answer clause resolution in P and P_{sol}.

P_{sol}. Note that in the same figure, $\overline{Q_{sol}}$ is the sol-translation of $\overline{Q}$. Let $A \in S$.
($\Rightarrow$) If $\leftarrow A$ LG-terminates in P, then we can build a finite set of finite LG-trees.
Thus in P_{sol} only finitely many answer clause resolutions and finitely many LG-trees are added and, by Lemma 1, P_{sol} quasi-terminates wrt $\{A\}_{sol}$.
($\Leftarrow$) If $\leftarrow A$ does not LG-terminate in P, then we either have an infinite set of LG-trees, and thus also an infinite set of LG-trees for P_{sol}. Or we have an infinite branching in some tree, which translates into an infinite set of LG-trees for P_{sol}.
So, by Lemma 1, in both cases P_{sol} does not quasi-terminate wrt $\{A\}_{sol}$.

A fully worked out example of a termination proof using the level mappings of Section 3 can be found in Appendix B.

5   Discussion

Tabled logic programming is receiving increasing attention in our community. It avoids many of the shortcomings of SLD(NF) execution and provides a more flexible and often extremely efficient execution mechanism for logic programs. In particular, tabled execution of logic programs terminates more often than execution based on LD-resolution. Nevertheless, termination can still not be guaranteed. Our motivation for the reported work is that we want to port program specialisation techniques for "standard" logic programs to tabled ones. In this attempt, we noticed that simple transformations, which are termination-preserving in the standard logic programming setting, can distort the termination behaviour in the setting of tabled logic programs. This motivated us to start a deeper study of termination of tabled logic programs, in the hope of using the results as tools in the further development and study of optimisation of tabled logic programs through transformations.

There are only relatively few works (in disguise) studying termination under tabled execution. [14], within the context of well-moded programs, gives a sufficient (but not necessary) condition for the bounded term-size property, which implies LG-termination. [9] provides another sufficient (but not necessary) condition for quasi-termination in the context of functional programming.

A specific concern that one might raise with respect to the termination conditions we propose is to what extent existing (automated) termination analyses can be adapted to verify the quasi-acceptability condition. Before addressing this question, we note that all programs that terminate under LD-resolution, are LG-terminating as well. Thus, verification of termination under LD-resolution (i.e., ignoring the designation of predicates as tabled) using an existing automated termination analysis (such as those surveyed in e.g. [5]) is a sufficient proof of the program's quasi-acceptability. Naturally this is not a necessary condition, since there are LG-terminating programs which do not terminate under LD-resolution (from trivial ones as the program in the introduction to more interesting ones as that presented in Appendix B). In such cases, existing termination analyses may require modifications or extensions. The most important issue in this context is to what extent the focus on *finitely partitioning* level mappings becomes a bottleneck in providing level mappings in practice. Or, more specifically, which of the level mappings used in practice in (automated) termination analysis are finitely partitioning?

In most automatic approaches to termination analysis, level mappings are defined in terms of positive linear combinations of *norms*. A norm is a function $n : U_P^E \rightarrow I\!N$. Given such a norm n, a level mapping is induced by selecting a number of argument positions, I_p, for each predicate symbol p/k, and by defining: $l(p(t_1, \ldots, t_k)) = \sum_{i \in I_p} p_i n(t_i)$, where all p_i are natural numbers.

Note that if the selected norm n is 'finitely partitioning', meaning that for every $m \in I\!N : \#n^{-1}(m) < \infty$, and $I_p = [1, k]$ as well as $p_i > 0$, then the level mapping l is finitely partitioning as well (assuming that the language underlying P only contains a finite number of predicate symbols). So, the question is: which norms are finitely partitioning ?

Let us first assume that the language underlying P contains only a finite number of constants and functions symbols. In that case, consider any semi-linear norm [3], which are norms that can be defined as:

$$n(f(t_1, \ldots, t_k)) = c_f + \sum_{i \in I_f} n(t_i)$$

where $c_f \in I\!N$, $I_f \subseteq [1, k]$ and depend on f/k only.

Given the restriction on the language underlying P, any semi-linear norm which has $c_f > 0$ and $I_f = [1, k]$, for all f/k in Fun_P, (in other words no part of the term can be ignored) is finitely partitioning. In particular, the well-known *termsize* norm is finitely partitioning (but e.g. the list-length norm is not).

If the underlying language contains an infinite number of constants (e.g. the natural numbers), we can still design very natural finitely partitioning norms by exploiting any existing well-founded ordering on the infinite data set and incorporating that in the norm.

Therefore, automated termination analysis can be quite easily adapted to the case of quasi-termination and in fact requires nothing more than moving from a strict inequality check to verifying the weaker inequality expressed in quasi-acceptability.

However, the requirement that $c_f > 0$ can in some cases complicate the task of finding appropriate norms and level mappings, as the following example illustrates.

Example 8. Let P just consist of the following clause C:

$p([H_1, H_2|T]) \leftarrow p([[H_1, H_1, H_2]|T])$

Let us restrict our attention to calls $p(t)$ where t is a ground list. Then P quasi-terminates (failing finitely) and it even terminates under ordinary, un-tabled evaluation. For the un-tabled case we can simply use the level mapping $l(p(t)) = list\_length(t)$ and we have that the level mapping of the head of a ground instance of C is strictly larger than the level mapping of the corresponding body atom. As previously mentioned, a termination proof under un-tabled execution implies LG-termination. However, such an indirect proof of LG-termination could not be used if the program also contained the clause $p(X) \leftarrow p(X)$. In such a case, the list length norm could not be used to directly prove quasi-acceptability as it is not finitely partitioning (there are infinitely many different terms up to variable renaming with the same list length) and we would have to search for another candidate. Unfortunately, we could not simply use the termsize norm either, because it will lead to the heads of ground instances of C being strictly smaller than the corresponding body atoms. Thus, using the termsize norm we are not able to prove quasi-acceptability and one has to resort to more powerful level mappings. The following, slightly involved, level mapping, where we denote the termsize by $\|.\|$, will fortunately be sufficient:

$l(p([t_1, \ldots, t_n])) = 2^n(n + \sum_{i \in [1,n]} \|t_i\|)$

Now let $p([t_1, t_2|t]) \leftarrow p([[t_1, t_1, t_2]|t])$ be any ground instance of C, where $list\_length([t_1, t_2|t]) = n$, $t = [s_1, \ldots, s_{n-2}]$ and $s = \sum_{i \in [1,n-2]} \|s_i\|$. We have that $l(p([t_1, t_2|t])) = 2^n(n + \|t_1\| + \|t_2\| + s)$ which is (strictly) larger than $l(p([[t_1, t_1, t_2]|t])) = 2^{n-1}(n - 1 + 1 + 2\|t_1\| + \|t_2\| + s)$.

Acknowledgements

Stefaan Decorte and Michael Leuschel are supported by the Belgian GOA "Non-Standard Applications of Abstract Interpretation". Danny De Schreye is a senior research associate of the Belgian National Fund for Scientific Research. Bern Martens is a post-doctoral fellow of the K.U.Leuven Research Council. Konstantinos Sagonas is a post-doctoral fellow of the Fund for Scientific Research — Flanders Belgium (FWO).

References

1. K.R. Apt and D. Pedreschi. Reasoning about Termination of Pure Prolog Programs. *Information and Computation*, 106(1):109–157, 1993.
2. R. Bol and L. Degerstedt. The Underlying Search for Magic Templates and Tabulation. In D. S. Warren, editor, *Proceedings of the Tenth International Conference on Logic Programming*, pages 793–811, Budapest, Hungary, June 1993. The MIT Press.

122   Stefaan Decorte et al.

3. A. Bossi, N. Cocco, and M. Fabris. Norms on Terms and their use in Proving Universal Termination of a Logic Program. *Theoretical Computer Science*, 124(2):297–328, February 1994.
4. W. Chen and D. S. Warren. Tabled Evaluation with Delaying for General Logic Programs. *Journal of the ACM*, 43(1):20–74, January 1996.
5. D. De Schreye, S. Decorte. Termination of Logic Programs: The never-ending story. *Journal of Logic Programming*, 19/20:199–260, May/July 1994.
6. D. De Schreye, K. Verschaetse, and M. Bruynooghe. A Framework for Analysing the Termination of Definite Logic Programs with respect to Call Patterns. In *Proceedings of the International Conference on Fifth Generation Computer Systems (FGCS'92)*, pages 481–488, ICOT Tokyo, 1992. ICOT.
7. M. Falaschi, G. Levi, M. Martelli, and C. Palamidessi. Declarative Modeling of the Operational Behaviour of Logic Languages. *Theoretical Computer Science*, 69(3):289–318, 1989.
8. A. J. Glenstrup and N. D. Jones. BTA algorithms to ensure Termination of off-line Partial Evaluation. In *Perspectives of System Informatics: Proceedings of the Andrei Ershov Second International Memorial Conference*, LNCS, pages 25–28. Springer-Verlag, June 1996.
9. C. K. Holst. Finiteness Analysis. In J. Hughes, editor, *Proceedings of the 5th ACM Conference on Functional Programming Languages and Computer Architecture (FPCA)*, number 523 in LNCS, pages 473–495. Springer-Verlag, August 1991.
10. J. Jørgensen and M. Leuschel. Efficiently Generating Efficient Generating Extensions in Prolog. In O. Danvy, R. Glück, and P. Thiemann, editors, *Proceedings of the 1996 Dagstuhl Seminar on Partial Evaluation*, number 1110 in LNCS, pages 238–262, Schloß Dagstuhl, 1996. Springer-Verlag.
11. T. Kanamori and T. Kawamura. OLDT-based Abstract Interpretation. *Journal of Logic Programming*, 15(1&2):1–30, January 1993.
12. M. Leuschel, B. Martens, and K. Sagonas. Preserving Termination of Tabled Logic Programs While Unfolding. In N. Fuchs, editor, *Proceedings of Logic Program Synthesis and Transformation (LOPSTR'97)*, Leuven, Belgium, July 1997.
13. T. Mogensen and A. Bondorf. Logimix: A self-applicable Partial Evaluator for Prolog. In K.-K. Lau and T. Clement, editors, *Proceedings of Logic Program Synthesis and Transformation (LOPSTR'92)*, pages 214–227. Springer-Verlag, 1992.
14. L. Plümer. *Termination Proofs for Logic Programs*, number 446 in LNCS. Springer-Verlag, 1990.
15. K. Sagonas, T. Swift, and D. S. Warren. XSB as an Efficient Deductive Database Engine. In *Proceedings of the ACM SIGMOD International Conference on the Management of Data*, pages 442–453, Minneapolis, Minnesota, May 1994. ACM Press.
16. H. Tamaki and T. Sato. OLD Resolution with Tabulation. In E. Shapiro, editor, *Proceedings of the Third International Conference on Logic Programming*, number 225 in LNCS, pages 84–98, London, July 1986. Springer-Verlag.
17. L. Vieille. Recursive Query Processing: The Power of Logic. *Theoretical Computer Science*, 69(1):1–53, 1989.

A   Termination Condition

The following concept will be useful for proving our termination condition. To any fixed P and S, we can associate a call graph as follows.

Definition 9.   (call graph associated to S) *Let P be a program and $S \subseteq B_P^E$. The* call graph $Call\text{-}Gr(P, S)$ *associated to P and S is a graph such that:*
- *its set of nodes is $Call(P, S)$,*
- *there exists a directed arc from $\tilde{A}$ to $\tilde{B}$ iff*
  - *there exists a clause $H \leftarrow B_1, \ldots, B_n$ in P, such that $mgu(A, H) = \theta$ exists,[1] and*
  - *there exists $i \in [1, n]$, such that there is an LD-refutation for*

$$\leftarrow (B_1, \ldots, B_{i-1})\theta$$

with computed answer substitution θ_{i-1}, and $B \approx B_i \theta \theta_{i-1}$.

The notion of a call graph has a particularly interesting property, which will be useful in the study of termination.

Proposition 1.   (paths and selected atoms) *Let P be a program, $S \subseteq B_P^E$, $Call(P, S)$ and $Call\text{-}Gr(P, S)$ be defined as above. Let p be any directed path in $Call\text{-}Gr(P, S)$. Then there exists an LG-derivation for some element of $Call(P, S)$, such that all the nodes in p occur as selected atoms in the derivation.*

Proof. By definition of $Call\text{-}Gr(P, S)$, for every arc from $\tilde{A}$ to $\tilde{B}$ in $Call\text{-}Gr(P, S)$, there exists a sequence of consecutive LG-derivation steps, starting from $\leftarrow A$ and having a variant of B as its selected atom at the end. Because (a variant of) B is selected at the end-point, any two such derivation-step sequences, corresponding to consecutive arcs in $Call\text{-}Gr(P, S)$, can be composed to form a new sequence of LG-derivation steps. In this sequence, all 3 nodes of the consecutive arcs remain selected atoms in the new sequence of derivation steps. Transitively exploiting the above argument yields the result.

Note that by definition of $Call\text{-}Gr(P, S)$ and $Call(P, S)$, this also implies that there is a sequence of derivation steps starting from $P \cup \{\leftarrow A\}$, with $\tilde{A} \in S$, such that all nodes in the given path p are selected atoms in the derivation sequence.

Theorem 1 (termination condition) *Let P be a program and $S \subseteq B_P^E$. P is quasi-acceptable with respect to some finitely partitioning level mapping l and S iff P is quasi-terminating with respect to S.*

Proof. The "only-if" part of the proof is fairly straightforward. We have that P is quasi-acceptable with respect to l and S. Take any atom A with $\tilde{A} \in S$. Due to the acceptability condition, any call in $Call(P, S)$ directly descending from A, say B, is such that $l(A) \geq l(B)$. The same holds recursively for the atoms descending from B. Thus, the level mapping of any call, recursively descending from A, is smaller than or equal to $l(A) \in \mathbb{N}$. Since l is finitely partitioning, we have that: $\cup_{n \leq l(A)} l^{-1}(n)) < \infty$. Hence, $\#Call(P, \{\tilde{A}\}) < \infty$ and the program is quasi-terminating for $\leftarrow A$.

---

[1] Throughout the paper we assume that representatives of equivalence classes are systematically provided with fresh variables, to avoid the necessity of renaming apart.

The "if"-part of the proof is slightly more complicated. Given is that P quasi-terminates for all atomic queries $\leftarrow A$, with $\tilde{A} \in S$. We need to design a finitely partitioning level mapping, l, such that the quasi-acceptability condition with respect to l and s holds.

First of all, we will only define l on the elements of $Call(P,S)$. On elements of the complement of $Call(P,S)$ in B_P^E, l can be assigned any value (as long as we don't group infinitely many in one layer), as these elements do not turn up in the inequality condition of quasi-acceptability. In order to define l on $Call(P,S)$, consider the $Call\text{-}Gr(P,S)$-graph.

A first crucial point in this part of the proof is that the strongly connected components of $Call\text{-}Gr(P,S)$ are necessarily all finite. To see this, assume that $Call\text{-}Gr(P,S)$ contains an infinite strongly connected component. Then, there exists an infinitely long path p, starting from an element in S, through elements of this infinite strongly connected component. By Proposition 1, this means that there exists a derivation for that element in S, such that an infinite number of different atoms from $Call(P,S)$ are selected within this derivation. Obviously, this contradicts quasi-termination.

So, all strongly connected components of $Call\text{-}Gr(P,S)$ are finite. Define $Call\text{-}Gr(P,S)/reduced$ as the graph obtained from $Call\text{-}Gr(P,S)$ by replacing any strongly connected component by a single contracting node and replacing any arc from $Call\text{-}Gr(P,S)$ pointing to (resp. from) any node in that strongly connected component by an arc to (resp. from) the contracting node.

$Call\text{-}Gr(P,S)/reduced$ does not have any (non-trivial) strongly connected components. Moreover, any strongly connected component from $Call\text{-}Gr(P,S)$ that was collapsed into a contracting node of $Call\text{-}Gr(P,S)/reduced$ necessarily consists of only a finite number of nodes.

We now define l as follows.

Let layer-0 be the set of leaves in $Call\text{-}Gr(P,S)/reduced$. We will order these nodes and assign to them an odd number within $I\!\!N$. For every atom in a strongly connected component represented by one of the nodes in layer-0, we will assign the level mapping of that atom to be equal to the assigned value of the corresponding contracting node.

Then, we move up to the next layer in $Call\text{-}Gr(P,S)/reduced$. This layer, layer-1, consists of all nodes N, such that:

$$max(\{length(p) \mid p \text{ is a path starting from } N \text{ in } Call\text{-}Gr(P,S)/reduced\}) = 1$$

To any element of layer-1, we assign a natural number n, such that n is larger than all the natural numbers assigned to descendants of this node in layer-0 (note that the graph is finitely branching), but such that there is at least 1 natural number larger than the ones assigned to its descendants which remains unassigned.

We continue this process layer by layer. In each step we make sure that an infinite number of natural numbers remain "unassigned" to nodes, but also that numbers assigned to nodes in higher levels of $Call\text{-}Gr(P,S)$ are strictly larger than the numbers assigned to their descendants. The value of the level mapping on elements of $Call(P, S)$ is as defined for layer-0 above: all calls in a same strongly connected component of $Call(P, S)$ receive the number assigned to their representative in $Call\text{-}Gr(P, S)/reduced$.

Due to this construction, l is finitely partitioning on $Call(P, S)$. Also, by construction again, the quasi-acceptability condition of P with respect to l and S holds.

B   An Extended Termination Proof

In this appendix, the approach is illustrated on a non-trivial example. Systems like the one in [6], after the slight adaptations discussed in Section 5, are able to automatically derive this proof. Consider the following context-free grammar, defining well-built numerical expressions, built up from integers and the operators $+$ and $*$.

$Expr \Rightarrow Term \mid Expr + Term$
$Term \Rightarrow Primary \mid Term * Primary$
$Primary \Rightarrow \textbf{integer} \mid (\ Expr \ )$

If we encode expressions as ground lists of tokens, we can use the following program $Parse$ to parse such expressions in all possible ways.

$expr(A, B) \leftarrow term(A, B)$
$expr(A, B) \leftarrow expr(A, C), C = [+|D], term(D, B)$

$term(A, B) \leftarrow primary(A, B)$
$term(A, B) \leftarrow term(A, C), C = [*|D], primary(D, B)$

$primary(A, B) \leftarrow A = [C|B], integer(C)$
$primary(A, B) \leftarrow A = ['('|C], expr(C, D), D = [')'|B]$

It is not difficult to see that the program is *not* LD-terminating wrt the following set of atoms:

$$S = \{expr(l, t) \mid l \text{ is a list of atoms and } t \text{ is any term }\}$$

For example, the query $\leftarrow expr([1], B)$ generates the answer $B = []$ and then gets stuck in an infinite loop.

The program is however LG-terminating. To see this, consider $Parse_{sol}$ which corresponds to the following program.

$expr(A, B) \leftarrow term(A, B), sol(term(A, B))$
$expr(A, B) \leftarrow expr(A, C), sol(expr(A, C)), C = [+|D], sol(C = [+|D]),$
$\qquad\qquad term(D, B), sol(term(D, B))$

$term(A, B) \leftarrow primary(A, B), sol(primary(A, B))$
$term(A, B) \leftarrow term(A, C), sol(term(A, C)), C = [*|D], sol(C = [*|D]),$
$\qquad\qquad primary(D, B), sol(primary(D, B))$

$primary(A, B) \leftarrow A = [C|B], sol(A = [C|B]), integer(C), sol(integer(C))$
$primary(A, B) \leftarrow A = ['('|C], sol(A = ['('|C]), expr(C, D),$
$\qquad\qquad sol(expr(C, D)), D = [')'|B], sol(D = [')'|B])$

$$expr_{sol}(A, B) \leftarrow expr(A, B), sol(expr(A, B))$$
$$term_{sol}(A, B) \leftarrow term(A, B), sol(term(A, B))$$
$$primary_{sol}(A, B) \leftarrow primary(A, B), sol(primary(A, B))$$
$$sol(X) \leftarrow$$

The following level mapping can then be used to prove quasi-acceptability of $Parse_{sol}$ wrt S_{sol}, which according to Theorem 2 establishes LG-termination of $Parse$ with respect to S.

$$\|term(t_1, t_2)\| \equiv \|expr(t_1, t_2)\| \equiv \|primary(t_1, t_2)\|$$
$$= 2 \times termsize(t_1) + termsize(t_2) + 1$$
$$\|t_1 = t_2\| = termsize(t_1) + termsize(t_2)$$
$$\|integer(n)\| = abs(n), \text{ if } n \text{ is an integer}$$
$$\|integer(t)\| = termsize(t), \text{ if } t \text{ is not an integer}$$
$$\|sol(t)\| = \begin{cases} termsize(t_1) + termsize(t_2) \\ \quad \text{if } t \text{ is of the form } p(t_1, t_2) \text{ and} \\ \quad p/2 \in \{expr/2, term/2, primary/2, =/2\} \\ termsize(t) \quad \text{otherwise} \end{cases}$$
$$\|p_{sol}(\bar{t})\| = \|p(\bar{t})\|, \forall p/n \in Pred_P$$

The following set is a superset of $Call(Parse_{sol}, S_{sol})$:

$$\{expr(l,t), term(l,t), primary(l,t),$$
$$integer(g), sol(t), expr_{sol}(l,t),$$
$$term_{sol}(l,t), primary_{sol}(l,t) \mid l \text{ is a ground list of atoms,}$$
$$t \text{ is any term and } g \text{ is a ground term}\}$$

As $Fun_{Parse_{sol}}$ is a finite set and $\|A\|$ is defined in terms of the termsize of all arguments of A, $\|.\|$ is finitely partitioning. We can then prove quasi-acceptability of $Parse_{sol}$ wrt S_{sol}. Consider the first clause defining $expr/2$ and take any atom $expr(l,t) \in Call(Parse_{sol}, S_{sol})$ such that $mgu(expr(l,t), expr(A,B)) = \theta$ exists. Obviously, $\|expr(l,t)\| \geq \|term(A,B)\theta\|$ as $expr(l,t) = expr(A,B)\theta$.

To prove that $\|expr(l,t)\| \geq \|sol(term(A,B))\theta\theta_2\|$ for any θ_2 such that θ_2 is a computed answer substitution for $\leftarrow term(A,B)\theta$, we need the following observation. In the following, let $t_1, t_2 \in Term_{Parse_{sol}}$. The set:

$$\{expr(t_1,t_2), term(t_1,t_2), primary(t_1,t_2) \mid termsize(t_1) \geq termsize(t_2)\} \cup$$
$$\{expr_{sol}(t_1,t_2), term_{sol}(t_1,t_2), primary_{sol}(t_1,t_2) \mid termsize(t_1) \geq termsize(t_2)\}$$
$$\cup \{t_1 = t_2 \mid termsize(t_1) = termsize(t_2)\} \cup \{integer(n) \mid n \text{ is an integer}\}$$

is a model of $Parse_{sol}$.

Now, whenever θ_2 is a computed answer substitution for $\leftarrow term(A,B)\theta$, $\theta\theta_2$ is a grounding substitution. Consequently, for $term(A,B)\theta\theta_2$, $termsize(A\theta\theta_2) \geq termsize(B\theta\theta_2)$. Therefore and because $A\theta$ is ground, we have that

$$\|expr(l,t)\| = \|expr(A,B)\theta\| = 2 \times termsize(A\theta) + termsize(B\theta) + 1$$
$$\geq 2 \times termsize(A\theta\theta_2)$$
$$\geq termsize(A\theta\theta_2) + termsize(B\theta\theta_2)$$
$$= \|sol(term(A,B))\theta\theta_2\|$$

Consider now the second clause of $expr/2$. Again, take any atom $expr(l,t) \in Call(Parse_{sol}, S_{sol})$ such that $mgu(expr(l,t), expr(A,B)) = \theta$ exists. We can apply the same arguments as above to infer that $\|expr(l,t)\| \geq \|expr(A,C)\theta\|$ and that $\|expr(l,t)\| \geq \|sol(expr(A,C))\theta\theta_2\|$, θ_2 being as above. To prove that $\|expr(l,t)\| \geq \|C = [+|D]\theta\theta_3\|$ for any θ_3 such that θ_3 is a computed answer substitution for $\leftarrow (expr(A,C), sol(expr(A,C)))\theta$, we need the observation that $expr(A,C)\theta\theta_3$ is ground and thus $termsize(A\theta\theta_3) \geq termsize(C\theta\theta_3)$. Therefore and because $A\theta$ is ground, we have that:

$$\|expr(l,t)\| = 2 \times termsize(A\theta\theta_3) + termsize(B\theta) + 1$$
$$\geq termsize(C\theta\theta_3) + 1 \geq \|C = [+|D]\theta\theta_3\|$$

We can use similar arguments on all remaining atoms and clauses.

On Correct Program Schemas

Pierre Flener[1], Kung-Kiu Lau[2], and Mario Ornaghi[3]

[1] Department of Computer Science
Bilkent University, 06533 Bilkent, Ankara, Turkey
pf@cs.bilkent.edu.tr
[2] Department of Computer Science
University of Manchester, Manchester M13 9PL, United Kingdom
kung-kiu@cs.man.ac.uk
[3] Dipartimento di Scienze dell'Informazione
Universita' degli studi di Milano, Via Comelico 39/41, Milano, Italy
ornaghi@dsi.unimi.it

Abstract. We present our work on the representation and correctness of program schemas, in the context of logic program synthesis. Whereas most researchers represent schemas purely syntactically as higher-order expressions, we shall express a schema as an open first-order theory that axiomatises a problem domain, called a *specification framework*, containing an open program that represents the template of the schema. We will show that using our approach we can define a meaningful notion of correctness for schemas, viz. that correct program schemas can be expressed as *parametric* specification frameworks containing templates that are *steadfast*, i.e. programs that are always correct provided their open relations are computed correctly.

1 Introduction

A program schema is an abstraction of a class of actual programs, in the sense that it represents their data-flow and control-flow, but does not contain (all) their actual computations or (all) their actual data structures. Program schemas have been shown to be useful in a variety of applications, such as proving properties of programs, teaching programming to novices, guiding both manual and (semi-)automatic synthesis of programs, debugging programs, transforming programs, and so on, both within and without logic programming. An overview of schemas and their applications can be found in [6].

In this paper, we present our work on two aspects of schemas: representation and correctness, in the context of logic program synthesis. In logic programming, most researchers represent their schemas as higher-order expressions, sometimes augmented by extra-logical annotations and features, so that actual (first-order) programs are obtained by applying higher-order substitutions to the schema. We shall take a different approach and show that a schema S can also be expressed as an *open* first-order theory $\mathcal{F}$ containing an *open* (first-order) program T, viz. a program in which some of the relations are left undefined. One advantage of this approach is that it simplifies the semantics of schemas and of their manipulations.

Norbert E. Fuchs (Ed.): LOPSTR'97, LNCS 1463, pp. 128–147, 1998.

We shall endow a schema S with a formal (model-theoretic) semantics by defining $\mathcal{F}$ as a *specification framework*, i.e. an axiomatisation of the (possibly open) problem domain, and call T the *template* of S. This allows us to define a meaningful notion of correctness for schemas. Indeed, we show that *correct* program schemas can be expressed as *parametric* specification frameworks containing templates that are *steadfast* open programs, i.e. programs that are always correct provided their open relations, i.e. their *parameters*, are computed correctly. Steadfastness is *a priori* correctness, and therefore correct schemas are *a priori* correctly reusable.

We shall also briefly indicate how to use correct schemas in practice. Using any kind of schemas requires suitable strategies, and we shall touch on some ideas for such strategies for correct schemas.

2   Program Schemas as Open Frameworks

Our approach to schemas (and program synthesis) is set in the context of a (fully) first-order axiomatisation $\mathcal{F}$ of the problem domain in question, which we call a *specification framework* $\mathcal{F}$. Specifications are given in $\mathcal{F}$, i.e. written in the language of $\mathcal{F}$. This approach enables us to define program correctness wrt specifications not only for closed programs but also for open programs, i.e. programs with parameters (open relations), in both closed and open frameworks. In this section, we briefly define specification frameworks, specifications, open programs.

2.1   Specification Frameworks

A specification framework is a full first-order logical theory (with identity) with an intended model:

Definition 1. (Specification Frameworks)
A *specification framework* $\mathcal{F}(\Pi)$ with parameters Π consists of:

- A (many-sorted) signature Σ of *sort, function* and *relation* symbols (together with their declarations).
  We distinguish between symbols of Σ that are *closed* (i.e. *defined* symbols) and those that are *open* (i.e. *parameters*). The latter are indicated by Π.
- A set of first-order axioms for the (declared) closed and open function and relation symbols of Σ.
  Axioms for the closed symbols may contain first-order *induction schemas*.
  Axioms for the open symbols, or parameters, are called *p-axioms*.

$\mathcal{F}(\Pi)$ is *open* if the set Π of parameters is not empty; it is *closed* otherwise.

A closed framework $\mathcal{F}$ axiomatises one problem domain, as an intended model (unique up to isomorphism). In our approach, intended models are *reachable isoinitial* models:

Definition 2. (Reachable Isoinitial Models)

A *reachable isoinitial model* i of $\mathcal{F}$ is a model such that i is reachable (i.e. the elements of its domain can be represented by ground terms) and, for any relation r defined in $\mathcal{F}$, ground instances $r(t)$ or $\neg r(t)$ are true in i iff they are true in all models of $\mathcal{F}$.

Example 1. (Closed Frameworks)

A typical closed framework is (first-order) Peano arithmetic $\mathcal{NAT}$ (we will omit the most external $\forall$ quantifiers):

Specification Framework $\mathcal{NAT}$;

SORTS:	Nat;
FUNCTIONS:	$0 \ : \to Nat$;
	$s \ : Nat \to Nat$;
	$+, * : (Nat, Nat) \to Nat$;
AXIOMS:	C-AXS$(0, s)$;
	$x + 0 = x$;
	$x + s(y) = s(x + y)$;
	$x * 0 = 0$;
	$x * s(y) = x + x * y$;

C-AXS$(0, s)$ contains Clark's Equality Theory (see [20]) for the constructors 0 and s, and the related (first-order) *induction schema* $H(0) \wedge (\forall i . \ H(i) \to H(s(i)) \to \forall x . \ H(x)$, where H stands for any formula of the language, i.e. the schema represents an infinite set of first-order axioms.

An isoinitial model of $\mathcal{NAT}$ is the term model generated by the constructors, equipped with the usual *sum* $(+)$ and *product* $(*)$.

The induction schema is useful for reasoning about properties of $+$ and $*$ that cannot be derived from the other axioms, e.g. associativity and commutativity. This illustrates the fact that in a framework we may have more than just an abstract data type definition, as we will see again later.

In general, a closed framework $\mathcal{F}$ is constructed incrementally from existing closed frameworks, and the new abstract data type axiomatised by $\mathcal{F}$ is completely defined thus. For example, a new sort T (possibly) depending on other pre-defined sorts is constructed from *constructors* declared as functions. The freeness axioms for the pre-defined sorts are imported and new axioms are added to define the (new) functions and relations on T.

The syntax of a framework $\mathcal{F}$ is thus similar to that used in algebraic abstract data types (e.g. [13,29,24]). However, whilst an algebraic abstract data type is an *initial* model ([12,15]) of its specification, the intended model of $\mathcal{F}$ is an *isoinitial* model. Of course, a framework may have no intended (i.e. reachable isoinitial) model. We will only ever use frameworks with such models, i.e. adequate frameworks:

Definition 3. (Adequate Closed Frameworks)

A closed framework $\mathcal{F}$ is *adequate* if it has a reachable isoinitial model.

Now a framework $\mathcal{F}$ may also contain other forms of formulas, such as:

- *induction schemas* (as we saw in Example 1);
- *theorems*, i.e. proven properties of the problem domain (we will not encounter these in this paper);
- *specifications*, i.e. definitions of new symbols in terms of Σ symbols;
- (and even (*steadfast*)) *programs*.

However, such formulas are only admissible in $\mathcal{F}$ if their inclusion preserves $\mathcal{F}$'s adequacy (we will return to this in Section 2.2).

An open framework $\mathcal{F}(\Pi)$ has a non-empty set Π of parameters, that can be *instantiated* by closed frameworks as follows:

Definition 4. (Framework Instantiation)
Let $\mathcal{F}(\Pi)$ be an open framework with signature Σ, and $\mathcal{G}$ be a closed framework with signature Δ. If Π is the intersection of Σ and Δ, and $\mathcal{G}$ proves the p-axioms of $\mathcal{F}$, then the $\mathcal{G}$-*instance* of $\mathcal{F}$, denoted by $\mathcal{F}[\mathcal{G}]$, is the union of $\mathcal{F}$ and $\mathcal{G}$.

Instantiation may be defined in a more general way, involving renamings. Since renamings preserve adequacy and steadfastness, we can use this simpler definition without loss of generality.

Now we can define adequate open frameworks:

Definition 5. (Adequate Open Frameworks)
An open framework $\mathcal{F}(\Pi)$ is *adequate* if, for every adequate closed framework $\mathcal{G}$, the instance $\mathcal{F}(\Pi)[\mathcal{G}]$ is an adequate closed framework.

Adequacy means that parameter instantiation works properly, so we will also refer to adequate open frameworks as *parametric* frameworks.

Example 2. (Open Frameworks)
The following open framework axiomatises the (kernel of the) theory of lists with parametric element sort *Elem* and parametric total ordering relation $\lhd$ (we use lower and upper case for elements and lists respectively):

> **Specification Framework** $\mathcal{LIST}(Elem, \lhd)$;
> IMPORT: $\mathcal{NAT}$;
> SORTS: $Nat, Elem, List$;
>
> FUNCTIONS: $nil : \rightarrow List$;
> $\quad\quad\quad\quad\quad\ \cdot\ : (Elem, List) \rightarrow List$;
> $\quad\quad\quad\ nocc : (Elem, List) \rightarrow Nat$;
> RELATIONS: $elemi : (List, Nat, Elem)$;
> $\quad\quad\quad\quad \lhd\ \ : (Elem, Elem)$;

AXIOMS: C-AXS$(nil, \cdot)$;
$elemi(L, i, a) \leftrightarrow \exists h, T, j . L = h \cdot T \wedge$
$(i = 0 \wedge a = h \vee i = s(j) \wedge elemi(T, j, a))$;
$nocc(x, nil) = 0$;
$a = b \rightarrow nocc(a, b \cdot L) = nocc(a, L) + 1$;
$\neg a = b \rightarrow nocc(a, b \cdot L) = nocc(a, L)$;

P-AXIOMS: $x \triangleleft y \wedge y \triangleleft x \leftrightarrow x = y$;
$x \triangleleft y \wedge y \triangleleft z \rightarrow x \triangleleft z$;
$x \triangleleft y \vee y \triangleleft x$.

where C-AXS$(nil, \cdot)$ contains Clark's Equality Theory (see [20]) for the list constructors $\cdot$ and nil, and the first-order induction schema $H(nil) \wedge (\forall a, J . H(J) \rightarrow H(a \cdot J)) \rightarrow \forall L . H(L)$; the function $nocc(a, L)$ gives the number of occurrences of a in L, and $elemi(L, i, a)$ means a occurs at position i in L. The p-axioms are the parameter axioms for $\triangleleft$. In this case, they state that $\triangleleft$ must be a (non-strict) total ordering.

The parameters $Elem$ and $\triangleleft$ can be instantiated (after a possible renaming) by a closed framework proving the p-axioms. For example, suppose $\mathcal{INT}$ is a closed framework axiomatising the set Int of integers with total ordering $<$. Then $\mathcal{LIST}(Int, <)[\mathcal{INT}]$ becomes a closed framework with an isoinitial model where Int is the set of integers, Nat contains the natural numbers, and $List$ finite lists of integers. Note that $\mathcal{LIST}(Int, <)[\mathcal{INT}]$ contains the renaming of $Elem$ by Int and $\triangleleft$ by $<$. Note also that defined symbols can be renamed, when convenient. For example, we could rename $List$ by $ListInt$.

Whilst an adequate closed framework has *one* intended (isoinitial) model, an adequate open framework has a *class* of intended models.

2.2 Specifications

A framework is the context where a specification must be written, where it receives its proper meaning, and where we can reason about it and derive correct programs from it.

More formally, a specification S_δ in a framework is an axiom that defines a new relation δ in terms of the symbols Σ of the framework. Thus S_δ is a formula containing symbols from Σ and the new relation symbols δ:

Definition 6. (Specifications)
In a specification framework $\mathcal{F}(\Pi)$, a *specification* S_δ is a set of sentences that define new function or relation symbols δ in terms of the symbols Σ of $\mathcal{F}$. If S_δ contains symbols of Π, then it is called a *p-specification*.

S_δ can be interpreted as an *expansion operator* that associates with the isoinitial model i of $\mathcal{F}$ one or more classes of $(\Sigma + \delta)$-interpretations, that are the expansions of i defined by S_δ.

Definition 7. (Expansion)
Let j be a Σ-interpretation, and i be an expansion of j to $\Sigma + \delta$. We say that i
is an *expansion* of j determined by a specification S (of δ) iff i $\models S$.

We say that S_δ is *strict* if it defines just one expansion; it is *non-strict* if it
defines more than one expansion. A more detailed discussion and classification
of specifications can be found in [17].

For uniformity, in this paper, we shall use only *conditional specifications*, that
is specifications of the form

$$\forall x : \mathsf{X}, \forall y : \mathsf{Y} . \, Q(x) \rightarrow (r(x, y) \leftrightarrow R(x, y))$$

where Q and R are formulas in the language of $\mathcal{F}$, and x:X, y:Y are (possibly
empty) lists of sorted variables, with sorts in $\mathcal{F}$. Q is called the *input condition*,
and R the *output condition* of the specification.

When Q is *true*, we drop it and speak of an *iff specification*. *Iff* specifications
are strict, while in general a conditional specification is not.

In our approach, we maintain a clear distinction between frameworks and
specifications. The latter introduce new symbols and assume their proper meaning only in the context of the framework. To distinguish the specified symbols
from the signature of the framework, we will call them *s-symbols*. We also distinguish clearly between specifications and axioms.

Example 3. (Specifications)
In the open framework $\mathcal{LIST}(Elem, \lhd)$, we can specify the following functions
and relations:

S-FUNCTIONS: $l : List \rightarrow Nat;$
$\qquad\qquad\qquad | : (List, List) \rightarrow List;$

S-RELATIONS: $mem \quad : (Elem, List);$
$\qquad\qquad\quad len \quad : (List, Nat);$
$\qquad\qquad\quad append : (List, List, List);$
$\qquad\qquad\quad perm \quad : (List, List);$
$\qquad\qquad\quad ord \quad : (List);$
$\qquad\qquad\quad sort \quad : (List, List);$

SPECS: $\quad mem(e, L) \leftrightarrow \exists i . \, elemi(L, i, e);$
$\qquad\quad len(L, n) \leftrightarrow \forall i . \, i < n \leftrightarrow \exists a . \, elemi(L, i, a);$
$\qquad\quad n = l(L) \leftrightarrow len(L, n);$
$\qquad\quad append(A, B, L) \leftrightarrow (\forall i, a . \, i < l(A) \rightarrow$
$\qquad\qquad\qquad\qquad\qquad\qquad (elemi(A, i, a) \leftrightarrow elemi(L, i, a))) \wedge$
$\qquad\qquad\qquad\qquad\qquad\qquad (\forall j, b . \, elemi(B, j, b) \leftrightarrow$
$\qquad\qquad\qquad\qquad\qquad\qquad elemi(L, j + l(A), b));$
$\qquad\quad perm(A, B) \leftrightarrow \forall e . \, nocc(e, A) = nocc(e, B);$
$\qquad\quad C = A|B \leftrightarrow append(A, B, C);$

P-SPECS: $\quad ord(L) \leftrightarrow \forall i . \, elemi(L, i, e_1) \wedge elemi(L, s(i), e_2) \rightarrow e_1 \lhd e_2;$
$\qquad\qquad sort(L, S) \leftrightarrow perm(L, S) \wedge ord(S)$

As we will see in the next section, program predicates must be s-symbols. However, the specification of a program predicate may be non-strict and, in this case there may be many correct implementations, one for each expansion.

An s-symbol δ can be used also to expand the signature of the framework, in order to get a more expressive specification language. In this case, the specification S_δ is added to the axioms of the framework and δ is added to its signature. This operation will be called *framework expansion*.

We must use adequate framework expansions, i.e. expansions that preserve the adequacy of the framework. For example, the expansions of $\mathcal{LIST}(Elem, \lhd)$ by l, $|$, *mem*, *append*, *perm*, *ord* and *sort* in Example 3 can be shown to be adequate. In the following we will consider $\mathcal{F}$ thus expanded.

2.3   Closed and Open Programs

Open programs arise in both closed and open frameworks.

An *open program* may contain open relations, or parameters. The parameters of a program P are relations to be computed by other programs. They are not defined by P.

A relation in P is *defined* (by P) if and only if it occurs in the head of at least one clause of P. It is *open* if it is not defined (by P). An open relation in P is also called a *parameter* of P.

A program is *closed* if it does not contain open relations. We consider closed programs a special case of open ones.

Open programs are always given in the context of an (open or closed) framework $\mathcal{F}(\Pi)$. In $\mathcal{F}(\Pi)$, we will distinguish program sorts, i.e. sorts that can be used by programs. A closed program sort must have constructors (see axioms C-AXS($\ldots$)), and an open program sort may only be instantiated by program sorts. In programs, constant and function symbols may only be constructors. A program relation must be an s-symbol, i.e. it must have a specification.

Example 4. (Open Programs)
A possible open program for $sort(L, S)$ in $\mathcal{LIST}(Elem, \lhd)$ is the following:

$$\begin{aligned}
sort(L, S) &\leftarrow L = nil, S = nil \\
sort(L, S) &\leftarrow L = h.T, part(T, h, TL_1, TL_2), \\
&\quad sort(TL_1, TS_1), sort(TL_2, TS_2), append(TS_1, h.TS_2, S) \\
part(L, p, S, B) &\leftarrow L = nil, S = nil, B = nil \\
part(L, p, S, B) &\leftarrow L = h.T, h \lhd p, part(T, p, TS, TB), \\
&\quad S = h.TS \wedge B = TB \\
part(L, p, S, B) &\leftarrow L = h.T, \neg h \lhd p, part(T, p, TS, TB), \\
&\quad S = TS \wedge B = h.TB
\end{aligned}$$

The s-symbols *sort* and *append* are specified in Example 3. The conditional specification of *part* can be found in Example 7.

2.4 Program Schemas

For representing schemas [1,2,3,4,5,6,10,14,16,21,22,23,25,26,27,28], there are essentially two approaches, depending on the intended schema manipulations.

First, most researchers represent their schemas as higher-order expressions, sometimes augmented by extra-logical annotations and features, so that actual programs are obtained by applying higher-order substitutions to the schema. Such schemas could also be seen as first-order schemas, in the mathematical sense, namely designating an infinite set of programs that have the form of the schema. The reason why some declare them as higher-order is that they have applications in mind, such as schema-guided program transformation [7,28,11], where some form of higher-order matching between actual programs and schemas is convenient to establish applicability of the starting schema of a schematic transformation.

Second, Manna [21] advocates first-order schemas, where actual programs are obtained via an interpretation of the (relations and functions of the) schema. This is related to the approach we advocate here, namely that a schema S can also be represented as a (first-order) framework $\mathcal{F}$ containing an open program T, so that actual programs can be obtained by adding programs for some (but not necessarily all) of T's open relations. So there is no need to invent a new (or higher-order) schema language, at least in a first approximation (but see [6]).

Formally we define a program schema as follows:

Definition 8. (Program Schemas)
A *(program) schema* for a relation r is an open framework $S(\Pi)$ containing a program P_r for r.
P_r is called the *template* of $S(\Pi)$.
The p-axioms and the p-specifications are called the *constraints* of $S(\Pi)$. Moreover, relation symbols of Π used only in specifications and (possibly) in p-axioms are called *s-parameters*.
A schema S *covers* a program P if (S and) its template can be instantiated to P.

We distinguish *s-parameters* from other parameters because in an instantiation by a closed framework $\mathcal{G}$ they can be replaced by *formulas* of the language of $\mathcal{G}$.[1] This does not hold for other parameters, since they must be instantiated by symbols of $\mathcal{G}$, in order to get a closed instance of the framework with a reachable isoinitial model.

Most definitions of schemas, with the laudable exception of the one by Smith [25,26], reduce this concept to what we here call the template. Such definitions are thus merely syntactic, providing only a pattern of place-holders, with no concern about the semantics of the template, the semantics of the programs it covers, or the interactions between these place-holders. So a template by itself has no guiding power for teaching, programming, or synthesis, and the additional knowledge (corresponding to our constraints) somehow has to be hardwired into

---

[1] Of course, after the replacement, the p-axioms must be satisfied.

the system or person using the template. Despite the similarity, our definition is an enhancement of even Smith's definition, because we consider relational schemas (rather than "just" functional ones), open schemas (rather than just closed ones), and set up everything in the explicit, user-definable background theory of a framework (rather than in an implicit, predefined theory). The notion of constraint even follows naturally from, or fits naturally into, our view of correct schemas as (adequate) frameworks containing steadfast programs (see later), rather than as entities different from programs.

Example 5. (Program Schemas)
The schema in Figure 1 is our way of defining the divide-and-conquer schema. Note that the schema contains only p-axioms, and that $I_r, O_r, \ldots$ are s-parameters, i.e. they can be replaced by formulas in framework instantiations.

Schema $\mathcal{DC}(\mathsf{X}, \mathsf{Y}, \mathsf{H}, \prec, I_r, O_r, I_{dec}, O_{dec})$;

SORTS: $\mathsf{X}, \mathsf{Y}, \mathsf{H}$;

RELATIONS: $I_r, I_{dec} : (\mathsf{X})$;
                    $O_r \quad : (\mathsf{X}, \mathsf{Y})$;
                    $O_{dec} \quad : (\mathsf{X}, \mathsf{H}, \mathsf{X}, \mathsf{X})$;

P-AXIOMS: $I_{dec}(x) \wedge O_{dec}(x, hx, tx_1, tx_2) \rightarrow I_r(tx_1) \wedge tx_1 \prec x$ (c_1)
                                  $\wedge I_r(tx_2) \wedge tx_2 \prec x$;
           $I_{dec}(x) \rightarrow \exists h, x_1, x_2 . O_{dec}(x, h, x_1, x_2)$; (c_2)

P-SPECS: $I_r(x, y) \rightarrow (r(x, y) \leftrightarrow O_r(x, y))$ (S_r)
            $I_r(x) \rightarrow (primitive(x) \leftrightarrow \neg I_{dec}(x))$ (S_{prim})
            $I_{dec}(x) \rightarrow (decompose(x, hx, tx_1, tx_2) \leftrightarrow$ (S_{dec})
                                     $O_{dec}(x, hx, tx_1, tx_2))$
            $I_r(x) \wedge \neg I_{dec}(x) \rightarrow (solve(x, y) \leftrightarrow O_r(x, y))$ (S_{solve})
            $O_{dec}(x, hx, tx_1, tx_2) \wedge O_r(tx_1, ty_1) \wedge O_r(tx_2, ty_2) \rightarrow$ (S_{comp})
                            $(compose(hx, ty_1, ty_2, y) \leftrightarrow O_r(x, y))$

TEMPLATE: $r(x, y) \leftarrow primitive(x), solve(x, y)$
             $r(x, y) \leftarrow \neg primitive(x), decompose(x, hx, tx_1, tx_2),$ (T_r)
                        $r(tx_1, ty_1), r(tx_2, ty_2), compose(hx, ty_1, ty_2, y)$

Fig. 1. A divide-and-conquer schema.

3   Correct Schemas

A model-theoretic definition of correctness of open programs in a framework, called *steadfastness*, is given in [19]. Here, we give a less abstract, but more conventional definition. In this paper, for simplicity, we only give definitions and results that work for definite programs. Nevertheless they extend to normal programs, under suitable termination assumptions.

For closed programs in closed frameworks, we have the classical notion of (total) correctness:

Definition 9. (Total Correctness)

In a closed framework $\mathcal{F}$ with isoinitial model i, a closed program P_r for relation r is *totally correct* wrt its specification S_r

$$\forall x : X, \forall y : Y.\ I_r(x) \to (r(x,y) \leftrightarrow O_r(x,y)) \qquad (S_r)$$

iff for all $t : X$ and $u : Y$ such that $i \models I_r(t)$ we have:

$$i \models O_r(t,u) \text{ iff } P_r \vdash r(t,u) \qquad (1)$$

If P_r satisfies the if-part of (1), it is *partially correct* (wrt S_r). If it satisfies the only-if part, then it is *total*.

Total correctness as defined here is unsatisfactory for logic programs, since it cannot deal with different cases of termination. In particular, we consider the following two cases:

(i) P_r is totally correct wrt to S_r, and terminates with either success or finite failure, for every ground goal $\leftarrow r(t,u)$ such that $i \models I_r(t)$.
    In this case, P_r correctly decides r, and we say that P_r is *correct* wrt $TC(r, S_r)$.

(ii) P_r is partially correct wrt S_r, and, for every ground $t : X$ such that $i \models I_r(t)$, the computation with open goal $\leftarrow r(t,y)$ terminates with at least one answer $y = u$.
    In this case, P_r correctly computes a *selector* of r (i.e. a function or relation that, for every input x such that $I_r(x)$, selects at least one output y such that $O_r(x,y)$), and we say that P_r is *correct* wrt $PC(r, S_r)$.

$TC(r, S_r)$ and $PC(r, S_r)$ are called *termination requirements*.

It is easy to see that total correctness is too weak for case (i), since a totally correct P_r could fail to terminate for a false $r(t,u)$, and too strong for case (ii), since for computing a selector, we do not need success for every true $r(t,u)$. Therefore, a *specification of a program relation* r will be of the form $(S_r, S_1, \ldots, S_n, T_r \Leftarrow T_1, \ldots, T_n)$, i.e. it will include a termination requirement. Moreover, in the definition of steadfastness, we will consider correctness wrt (S_i, T_i) and (S_r, T_r), instead of total correctness.

Termination and termination requirements are an important issue. For lack of space, however, we will not further deal with them here.

The definition of correctness wrt (S_r, T_r) is still unsatisfactory. First, it defines the correctness of P_r in terms of the programs for the relations other than r, rather than in terms of their specifications. Second, all the programs for these relations need to be included in P_r (this follows from P_r being closed), even though it might be desirable to discuss the correctness of P_r without having to fully solve it (i.e. we may want to have an open P_r). So, the abstraction achieved through the introduction (and specification) of the new relations is wasted.

This leads us to the following notion of steadfastness of an open program in a closed framework.

Definition 10. (Steadfastness in a Closed Framework)
In a closed framework $\mathcal{F}$, let P_r be an open program for r, with parameters p_1, ..., p_n, specifications $S_r, S_1, \ldots, S_n$, and termination requirements $T_r, T_1, \ldots, T_n$.
P_r is *steadfast* in $\mathcal{F}$ if, for any closed programs $P_1, \ldots, P_n$ that compute $p_1, \ldots, p_n$ such that P_i is correct wrt (S_i, T_i), the (closed) program $P_r \cup P_1 \cup \ldots \cup P_n$ is correct wrt (S_r, T_r).

Now we can define steadfastness in an open framework:

Definition 11. (Steadfastness in an Open Framework)
In an open framework $\mathcal{F}(\Pi)$, let P_r be an open program for r, with parameters $p_1, \ldots, p_n$, specifications $S_r, S_1, \ldots, S_n$, and termination requirements $T_r, T_1, \ldots, T_n$.
P_r is *steadfast* in $\mathcal{F}(\Pi)$ if it is steadfast in every instance $\mathcal{F}[\mathcal{G}]$ for a closed framework $\mathcal{G}$.

This is similar to Deville's notion of 'correctness in a set of specifications' [5, p.76], except that his specifications and programs are not set within frameworks. Moreover, we also (but not in this paper, hence the simplified definition above) consider other cases of steadfastness, namely where *several* (but not necessarily all) defined relations of a program are known by their specifications, the other defined relations being known by their clauses only.
Now we can formally define correctness for program schemas:

Definition 12. (Correct Program Schemas)
A (program) schema for a relation r, i.e. an (adequate) open framework $\mathcal{S}(\Pi)$ containing a template P_r for r, is *correct* iff P_r is steadfast in $\mathcal{S}(\Pi)$.

Example 6. (Correct Program Schemas)
We will now show that the schema $\mathcal{S}$ in Example 5 is correct because ($\mathcal{S}$ is an adequate framework and) its template T_r:

$$r(x,y) \leftarrow primitive(x), solve(x,y)$$
$$r(x,y) \leftarrow \neg primitive(x), decompose(x, hx, tx_1, tx_2), \qquad (T_r)$$
$$r(tx_1, ty_1), r(tx_2, ty_2), compose(hx, ty_1, ty_2, y)$$

is steadfast, if we add to it the following termination requirement:

T-REQS: $PC(r, S_r) \Leftarrow TC(primitive, S_{primitive}), PC(solve, S_{solve}),$
$PC(decompose, S_{decompose}), PC(compose, S_{compose})$

In fact we can derive the whole schema (including these termination requirements) from our attempt to prove that T_r is steadfast. Thus this example also serves to illustrate how we might derive correct schemas.
In the absence of constraints, an open program such as T_r has no fixed meaning, since it covers *every* program, which is obviously nonsensical. Indeed, it would suffice to instantiate *primitive* by *true*, and *solve* by the given program!

However, we can give this template an informal intended semantics, as follows. For an arbitrary relation r over formal parameters x and y, the program is to determine the value(s) of y corresponding to a given value of x. Two cases arise: either x has a value (when $primitive(x)$ holds) for which y can be easily directly computed (through $solve$), or x has a value (when $\neg primitive(x)$ holds) for which y cannot be so easily directly computed; the divide-and-conquer principle is then applied by:

1. *dividing* (through *decompose*) x into a term hx and two terms tx_1 and tx_2 that are both of the same sort as x but smaller than x according to some well-founded order,
2. *conquering* (through r) to determine values of ty_1 and ty_2 corresponding to tx_1 and tx_2, respectively,
3. *combining* (through *compose*) terms hx, ty_1, ty_2 to build y.

Just as the semantics of open programs is defined parametrically, we can do the same for this template, and whilst so doing, we can enforce the informal semantics and supply the corresponding axioms of the open relations (i.e. the constraints of the schema). We can do so by introducing an open framework $\mathcal{S}(I_r, O_r, \ldots)$ with a signature containing the sorts of the template and the open relation symbols $I_r, O_r, \ldots$ We can abduce the constraints of the schema by proving at an abstract level that T_r is steadfast in $\mathcal{S}$, wrt the specifications of r and the unknown axioms of the open relations the template introduces, and enforcing the informal semantics of the template during this proof. The proof itself must of course fail due to the lack of knowledge about r and the introduced open relations, but the reasons of this failure can be used to abduce the necessary relationships between r and these open relations. These relationships are of course the *constraints* on the open relations of the template!

Program T_r is steadfast in $\mathcal{S}$ if it is steadfast in every instance of $\mathcal{S}$. So let $\mathcal{F}$ be a *generic* instance $\mathcal{S}[\mathcal{G}]$, where $\mathcal{G}$ is a closed framework. Suppose the specification of r in $\mathcal{F}$ is:

$$\forall x : \mathsf{X}, \forall y : \mathsf{Y} . \ I_r(x) \to (r(x, y) \leftrightarrow O_r(x, y)) \qquad (S_r)$$

We have to find (at least) the p-specifications (in $\mathcal{F}$) $S_{prim}, S_{solve}, S_{dec}, S_{comp}$ of *primitive*, *solve*, *decompose*, *compose*, respectively, such that T_r is a steadfast program for r in $\mathcal{F}$. For each S_i, let the input and output conditions be I_i and O_i respectively.

Suppose also that we only require that instances of the template T_r be partially correct and terminating (i.e. $PC(r, S_r)$ holds for each instance). Let t be a ground term such that $I_r(t)$, and consider the open goal $\leftarrow r(t, Y)$. We have to prove that T_r terminates with some answer $Y = u$. We have the following possibilities:

1. The next goal is $\leftarrow primitive(t), solve(t, Y)$, and $primitive(t)$ succeeds. We are blocked, but we can unblock the situation by abducing that $PC(solve, S_{solve})$ holds and that:

$$I_r(t) \wedge O_{prim}(t) \to I_{solve}(t) \qquad (2)$$

2. The next goal is $\leftarrow primitive(t), \ldots$ or $\leftarrow \neg primitive(t), \ldots$, and the call to $primitive(t)$ does not terminate. We have to exclude this case, so we assume $TC(primitive, S_{primitive})$ and:

$$I_r(t) \rightarrow I_{prim}(t) \tag{3}$$

3. The next goal is $\leftarrow \neg primitive(t), \ldots$ and $primitive(t)$ finitely fails. Then we get the goal $\leftarrow decompose(t, HX, TX_1, TX_2), r(TX_1, TY_1), r(TX_2, TY_2), compose(HX, TY_1, TY_2, Y)$. Again, we are blocked, but we can unblock the situation by assuming:

$$I_{dec}(t) \wedge O_{dec}(t, HX, TX_1, TX_2) \rightarrow I_r(TX_1) \wedge TX_1 \prec t \wedge \\ I_r(TX_2) \wedge TX_2 \prec t \tag{4}$$

where $\prec$ is a well-founded relation.[2] By structural induction, we can see that, if $PC(decompose, S_{decompose})$, $PC(compose, S_{compose})$, and

$$I_r(t) \wedge \neg O_{prim}(t) \rightarrow I_{dec}(t) \tag{5}$$

$$I_{dec}(t) \wedge O_{dec}(t, HX, TX_1, TX_2) \wedge O_r(TX_1, TY_1) \wedge O_r(TX_2, TY_2) \\ \rightarrow I_{comp}(HX, TY_1, TY_2, Y) \tag{6}$$

then the computation terminates with an answer for Y. Indeed, by the induction hypothesis, we can assume that, for $TX_1 \prec t$ and $TX_2 \prec t$, program T_r computes TY_1 and TY_2 such that $O_r(TX_1, TY_1) \wedge O_r(TX_2, TY_2)$ holds.

Thus, we have abduced:

$$PC(r, S_r) \Leftarrow TC(primitive, S_{primitive}), PC(solve, S_{solve}), \\ PC(decompose, S_{decompose}), PC(compose, S_{compose}) \tag{7}$$

$PC(solve, S_{solve})$, $PC(decompose, S_{decompose})$, and $PC(compose, S_{compose})$ admit correct programs only if their specifications S_{solve}, S_{dec}, and S_{comp} are such that

$$\begin{aligned} I_{dec}(t) &\rightarrow \exists HX, TX_1, TX_2 . O_{dec}(t, HX, TX_1, TX_2) \\ I_{comp}(HX, TY_1, TY_2) &\rightarrow \exists Y . O_{comp}(HX, TY_1, TY_2, Y) \\ I_{solve}(t) &\rightarrow \exists Y . O_{solve}(t, Y) \end{aligned} \tag{8}$$

Now we have to prove that T_r is partially correct. For this, we assume:[3]

$$\begin{aligned} r(x, y) &\leftrightarrow \neg I_r(x) \vee O_r(x, y) \\ primitive(x) &\leftrightarrow \neg I_{prim}(x) \vee O_{prim}(x) \\ solve(x, y) &\leftrightarrow \neg I_{solve}(x) \vee O_{solve}(x, y) \\ decompose(x, hx, tx_1, tx_2) &\leftrightarrow \neg I_{dec}(x) \vee O_{dec}(x, hx, tx_1, tx_2) \\ compose(hx, ty_1, ty_2, y) &\leftrightarrow \neg I_{comp}(hx, ty_1, ty_2, y) \vee \\ & \quad O_{comp}(hx, ty_1, ty_2, y) \end{aligned} \tag{9}$$

---

[2] In the isoinitial model and, hence, in the Herbrand base of the closed version T_r' of T_r.

[3] Here we make use of the fact that if $\mathcal{F} \cup \{\forall x : \mathsf{X}, \forall y : \mathsf{Y} . r(x, y) \leftrightarrow \neg I_r(x) \vee O_r(x, y)\} \vdash T_r$, then T_r is partially correct wrt S_r. See [19].

We have to prove that $\mathcal{F} \cup (9) \vdash T_r$. Let us try to prove the first clause. We abduce:

$$\neg I_r(x) \vee O_r(x,y) \leftarrow (\neg I_{prim}(x) \vee O_{prim}(x)) \wedge (\neg I_{solve}(x) \vee O_{solve}(x,y))$$

This is logically equivalent to

$$O_r(x,y) \leftarrow I_r(x) \wedge (\neg I_{prim}(x) \vee O_{prim}(x)) \wedge (\neg I_{solve}(x) \vee O_{solve}(x,y))$$

Since any instance $\mathcal{F}$ must prove the p-axioms of $\mathcal{S}$ and since we have already abduced (2) and (3), we can simplify this to:

$$O_r(x,y) \leftarrow I_r(x) \wedge O_{prim}(x) \wedge O_{solve}(x,y) \tag{10}$$

By an analogous reasoning, from the attempt of proving the second clause, we obtain the simplified p-axiom:

$$\begin{aligned} O_r(x,y) \leftarrow I_r(x) \wedge \neg O_{prim}(x) \wedge O_{dec}(x,hx,tx_1,tx_2) \wedge \\ O_r(tx_1,ty_1) \wedge O_r(tx_2,ty_2) \wedge O_{comp}(hx,ty_1,ty_2,y) \end{aligned} \tag{11}$$

As before, the simplification of the input conditions is due to the p-axioms already abduced.

By the above proof, we have abduced a schema containing a suitable signature, our template, the termination requirements (7), and the p-axioms (2) ... (11).

This schema is correct, but it contains redundancies, due to constraints that make some parameters depend on others. We can try to simplify it as follows:

1. When we use the schema, we know the actual specification, which specifies in $\mathcal{F}$ a program P'_r such that $PC(r, S_r)$ holds, so we can instantiate I_r, O_r, X, and Y.
2. Then we instantiate $\prec$ by a well-founded relation on X.
3. Now the two constraints (10) and (11) contain four unknown output conditions. If we fix some of them, we can hope to deduce the other ones, and to simplify some constraints. In a divide-and-conquer strategy, it is reasonable to assume that we first choose the decomposition, i.e. I_{dec} and O_{dec}. We now have to infer I_{prim} and O_{prim} such that they satisfy the constraints (3) and (5). A possible reduction is based on the observation that (5) is logically equivalent to $I_r(x) \rightarrow (O_{prim}(x) \leftarrow \neg I_{dec}(x))$. We replace $\leftarrow$ by $\leftrightarrow$. By identifying I_{prim} and I_r, we satisfy (3) and can thus reduce S_{prim} to:

$$I_r(x) \rightarrow (primitive(x) \leftrightarrow \neg I_{dec}(X))$$

hence setting O_{prim} to $\neg I_{dec}$.
4. Now, by substitution and a simple logical manipulation, we transform (10) and (11) into:

$$I_r(x) \wedge \neg I_{dec}(x) \rightarrow (O_r(x,y) \leftarrow O_{solve}(x,y))$$
$$I_r(x) \wedge I_{dec}(x) \wedge O_{dec}(x,hx,tx_1,tx_2) \wedge O_r(tx_1,ty_1) \wedge O_r(tx_2,ty_2) \rightarrow$$
$$(O_r(x,y) \leftarrow O_{comp}(hx,ty_1,ty_2,y))$$

where the unknown predicates O_{comp} and O_{solve} are defined, on the right-hand side of $\rightarrow$, by $\leftarrow$ instead of $\leftrightarrow$. We can assume stronger[4] constraints, by replacing $\leftarrow$ by $\leftrightarrow$. We get a conditional definition of O_{solve} and O_{comp}. Moreover, S_{solve} and S_{comp} can be reduced to:

$$I_r(x) \wedge \neg I_{dec}(x) \rightarrow (solve(x,y) \leftrightarrow O_r(x,y))$$
$$O_{dec}(x, hx, tx_1, tx_2) \wedge O_r(tx_1, ty_1) \wedge O_r(tx_2, ty_2) \rightarrow (compose(hx, ty_1, ty_2, y)$$
$$\leftrightarrow O_r(x, y))$$

Using the reduced specifications, we see that the constraints (2), (6), and the second and third constraints of (8) become proved.

Therefore we obtain the schema $\mathcal{DC}$ as defined in Example 5.

The above abduction process proves the following theorem:

Theorem 1. (Correctness of the divide-and-conquer schema)
The schema $\mathcal{DC}$ in Example 5, with the addition of the termination requirement (7), is correct, i.e. it contains a steadfast template.

This theorem is related to the one given by Smith [25] for a divide-and-conquer schema in functional programming. The innovations here are that we use specification frameworks and that we can thus also consider open programs. Moreover, we could also prove total correctness (and not just partial correctness as we have done here), because we are in a relational setting. Finally, we eliminated Smith's *Strong Problem Reduction Principle* by endeavouring to achieve these objectives.

Finally, we can specialise a schema to a data type. For example, we can incorporate the data type of lists with generic elements, by incorporating in S the framework $\mathcal{LIST}(\mathsf{X}, \lhd)$, or part of it. All the properties of S are inherited, and we can add further properties. For example, we can already know at the schema level that the relation defined by $A \prec B \leftrightarrow l(A) < l(B)$ is a well-founded relation in every instance of the schema, and therefore that it is one of the candidates to be used when instantiating the template.

4   Using Correct Schemas in Practice

Our characterisation of correct program schemas allows us to synthesise steadfast open programs. This is a significant step forwards in the field of synthesis, because the synthesised programs are then not only correct, but also *a priori* correctly reusable. This is achieved by means of steadfast templates together with their constraints. However, since we have identified correct templates with steadfast programs, there seems to be some circularity in our argument: how can we guide the synthesis of steadfast programs by steadfast programs? The answer is that some open programs are "more open" than others, and that such

---

[4] This reduces the search space, but, in general, it could cut some solutions. We do not discuss this issue here.

"more open" programs thus have more "guiding power," especially considering the specifications for their open relations. In [9], we discuss the synthesis of steadfast programs guided by correct schemas. To conclude this paper, in this section we briefly outline the main ideas.

Much of the program synthesis process can be pre-computed at the level of "completely open" schemas. The key to pre-computation is such a schema, especially its constraints. These specifications can be seen as an "overdetermined system of equations (in a number of unknowns)", which may be unsolvable as it stands (for instance, this is the case for the divide-and-conquer schema in Example 5). An arbitrary instantiation (through program extension), according to the informal semantics of the template, of one (or several) of its open relations may then provide a "jump-start", as the set of equations may then become solvable.

This leads us to the notion of *synthesis strategy* (cf. Smith's work [25]), as a pre-computed (finite) sequence of synthesis steps, for a given schema. A strategy has two phases, stating (*i*) which parameter(s) to arbitrarily instantiate first (by re-use), and (*ii*) which specifications to "set up" next, based on a pre-computed propagation of these instantiation(s). Once correct programs have been synthesised from these new specifications (using the synthesiser all over again, of course), they can be composed into a correct program for the original specified relation, according to the template. There can be several strategies for a given schema (e.g., Smith [25] gives three strategies for a divide-and-conquer schema), depending on which parameter(s) are instantiated first (e.g., *decompose* first, or *compose* first, or both at the same time).

Synthesis is thus a recursive problem reduction process followed by a recursive solution composition process, where the problems are specifications and the solutions are programs. Problem reduction stops when a "sufficiently simple" problem is reached, i.e. a specification that "reduces to" another specification for which a program is known and can thus be re-used. This is thus the "base case" of synthesis, and requires a formalisation of the process of re-use (see [9] for details).

Let us illustrate these ideas on the divide-and-conquer schema. In [8], we design the following strategy for it:

1. **Select an induction parameter** among x and y (such that it is of an inductively defined sort). Suppose, without loss of generality, that x is selected.
2. **Select (or construct) a well-founded order** over the sort of the induction parameter. Suppose that $\prec$ is selected (from a "knowledge base").
3. **Select (or construct) a decomposition operator** *decompose*. Suppose that the following specification is selected (from a "knowledge base"):

$$\forall x, t_1, t_2 : \mathsf{X}, \forall h : \mathsf{H}\,.$$
$$I_{dec}(x) \rightarrow (decompose(x, h, t_1, t_2) \leftrightarrow Dec(x, h, t_1, t_2)). \qquad (S'_{dec})$$

4. **Set up the specification of the discriminating operator** *primitive.*
This amounts to first deriving a formula G such that

$$\mathcal{F} \models \forall x, tx_1, tx_2 : X, \forall hx : H . G(x) \wedge$$
$$Dec(x, hx, tx_1, tx_2) \leftrightarrow I_r(tx_1) \wedge I_r(tx_2) \wedge tx_1 \prec x \wedge tx_2 \prec x,$$

and then setting up the following specification:

$$\forall x : X . \ primitive(x) \leftrightarrow \neg(I_{dec}(x) \wedge G(x)). \qquad (S'_{prim})$$

5. **Set up the specification of the solving operator** *solve.* All place-holders of S_{solve} are known now, so we can set up a specification S'_{solve} by instantiating inside S_{solve}.

6. **Set up the specification of the composition operator** *compose.* Similarly, all place-holders of S_{comp} are known now, so we can set up a specification S'_{comp} by instantiating inside S_{comp}.

Four specifications (S'_{dec}, S'_{prim}, S'_{solve}, and S'_{comp}) have been set up now, so four auxiliary syntheses can be started from them, using the same overall synthesiser again, but not necessarily the (same) strategy for the (same) divide-and-conquer schema. The programs P_{dec}, P_{prim}, P_{solve}, and P_{comp} resulting from these auxiliary syntheses are then added to the open program P_r of the schema, which extension of P_r is guaranteed, by Theorem 1, to be steadfast.

Example 7. (A Sample Synthesis)
Suppose in $\mathcal{LIST}(Elem, \lhd)$ we want a steadfast sorting program with termination requirement $PC(sort, S_{sort})$.

First, we select the specification of a decomposition operator *part*, partitioning a list L into its first element h, the list A of its remaining elements that are smaller (according to $\lhd$) than h, and the list B of its remaining elements that are not smaller (according to $\lhd$) than h:

$$\neg L = nil \rightarrow (part(L, h, A, B) \leftrightarrow$$
$$L = h.T \wedge perm(A|B, T) \wedge A \sqsubseteq h \wedge B \sqsupseteq h) \qquad (S_{part})$$

where the following axioms:

$$L \sqsubseteq e \leftrightarrow \forall x . \ mem(x, L) \rightarrow x \lhd e$$
$$L \sqsupseteq e \leftrightarrow \forall x . \ mem(x, L) \rightarrow \neg x \lhd e$$

are added to $\mathcal{LIST}(Elem, \lhd)$.

In [9], we synthesise the following extension of the divide-and-conquer template by using the strategy outlined above:

$$sort(L, S) \leftarrow primitive(L), solve(L, S)$$
$$sort(L, S) \leftarrow \neg primitive(L), part(L, h, A, B),$$
$$sort(A, C), sort(B, D), compose(h, C, D, S)$$
$$primitive(L) \leftarrow L = nil$$
$$solve(L, S) \leftarrow S = nil$$
$$part(L, h, A, B) \leftarrow L = h.T, part(T, h, A, B)$$
$$part(L, p, A, B) \leftarrow L = nil, A = nil, B = nil$$
$$part(L, p, A, B) \leftarrow L = h.T, h \lhd p, part(T, p, TA, TB), A = h.TA, B = TB$$
$$part(L, p, A, B) \leftarrow L = h.T, \neg h \lhd p, part(T, p, TA, TB), A = TA, B = h.TB$$
$$compose(e, C, D, S) \leftarrow append(C, e.D, S)$$

This is the classical Quicksort program. After a series of unfolding steps, this program can easily be transformed into the program of Example 4. Note that this is an open program, as there are no clauses yet for *append*, nor for $\lhd$.

5 Conclusion

We have shown that program schemas can be expressed as open (first-order) specification frameworks containing steadfast open programs, and we have outlined how correct and *a priori* correctly reusable (divide-and-conquer) programs can be synthesised, in a schema-guided way, from formal specifications expressed in the first-order language of a framework. These aspects of schema-guided synthesis are our new contribution.

Our work is very strongly influenced by Smith's pioneering work [25] in functional programming in the early 1980s. This is, in our opinion, inevitable, as this approach seems to be the only structured approach to synthesis. Our work is however *not* limited to simply transposing Smith's achievements to the logic programming paradigm: indeed, we have also enhanced the theoretical foundations by adding frameworks, enlarged the scope of synthesis by allowing the synthesis of a larger class of non-deterministic programs, and simplified (the formulation and proof of) the theorem on the correctness of the divide-and-conquer schema (Theorem 1).

Future work includes redoing the constraint abduction process for a more general (divide-and-conquer) template, namely where $nonPrimitive(x)$ is not necessarily $\neg primitive(x)$, and developing the corresponding strategies, in order to allow the synthesis of a larger class of non-deterministic programs.

Other strategies for the divide-and-conquer schema need to be elaborated, and other design methodologies need to be captured in program schemas and strategies.

Another important objective is the development of a proof system for deriving antecedents (as needed at Step 4 of the given strategy) and for obtaining simplifications of output conditions (the specifications S'_{solve} and S'_{comp} are often amenable to considerable simplifications). Eventually, a proof-of-concept implementation of the outlined synthesiser (and the adjunct proof system) is planned.

Acknowledgements

We wish to thank Doug Smith for his pioneering work that inspired us, John Gallagher for pointing out a technical error in our presentation at the workshop, and Yves Deville for his insightful comments which will help us in our future work. This work was partially supported by the European Union HCM Project on Logic Program Synthesis and Transformation, contract no. 93/414.

References

1. D. Barker-Plummer. Cliche Programming in Prolog. In M. Bruynooghe, editor, *Proc. META 90*, pages 246-256, 1992.
2. E. Chasseur and Y. Deville. Logic program schemas, semi-unification and constraints. This volume.
3. N. Dershowitz. *The Evolution of Programs*. Birkhäuser, 1983.
4. Y. Deville and J. Burnay. Generalization and program schemata: A step towards computer-aided construction of logic programs. In E.L. Lusk and R.A. Overbeek, editors, *Proc. NACLP'89*, pages 409–425. MIT Press, 1989.
5. Y. Deville. *Logic Programming: Systematic Program Development*. Addison-Wesley, 1990.
6. P. Flener. *Logic Program Synthesis from Incomplete Information*. Kluwer, 1995.
7. P. Flener and Y. Deville. Logic program transformation through generalization schemata. In M. Proietti, editor, *Proc. LOPSTR'95*, pages 171–173. *LNCS* 1048, Springer-Verlag, 1996.
8. P. Flener and K.-K. Lau. Program Schemas as Steadfast Programs and their Usage in Deductive Synthesis. Tech Rep BU-CEIS-9705, Bilkent University, Ankara, Turkey, 1997.
9. P. Flener, K.-K. Lau, and M. Ornaghi, Correct-schema-guided Synthesis of Steadfast Programs, *Proc. 12th IEEE International Automated Software Engineering Conference*, pages 153-160, IEEE Computer Society, 1997.
10. T.S. Gegg-Harrison. Representing logic program schemata in λ-Prolog. In L. Sterling, editor, *Proc. ICLP'95*, pages 467–481. MIT Press, 1995.
11. T.S. Gegg-Harrison. Extensible Logic Program Schemata. In J. Gallagher, editor, *Proc. LOPSTR'96*, *LNCS* 1207, pages 256-274, Springer-Verlag, 1997.
12. J.A. Goguen, J.W. Thatcher, and E. Wagner. An initial algebra approach to specification, correctness and implementation. In R. Yeh, editor, *Current Trends in Programming Methodology, IV*, pages 80–149. Prentice-Hall, 1978.
13. J.A. Goguen and J. Meseguer. Unifying functional, object-oriented and relational programming with logical semantics. In B. Shriver and P. Wegner, editors, *Research Directions in Object-Oriented Programming*, pages 417–477. MIT Press, 1987.
14. A. Hamfelt and J. Fischer-Nilsson. Inductive metalogic programming. In S. Wrobel, editor, *Proc. ILP'94*, pages 85–96. *GMD-Studien* Nr. 237, Sankt Augustin, Germany, 1994.
15. W. Hodges. Logical features of Horn clauses. In D.M. Gabbay, C.J. Hogger, and J.A. Robinson, editors, *Handbook of Logic in Artificial Intelligence and Logic Programming, Volume 1: Logical Foundations*, pages 449-503, Oxford University Press, 1993.
16. A.-L. Johansson. Interactive program derivation using program schemata and incrementally generated strategies. In Y. Deville, editor, *Proc. LOPSTR'93*, pages 100–112. Springer-Verlag, 1994.

17. K.-K. Lau and M. Ornaghi. Forms of logic specifications: A preliminary study. In J. Gallagher, editor, *Proc. LOPSTR'96*, pages 295–312, *LNCS* 1207, Springer-Verlag, 1997.
18. K.-K. Lau, M. Ornaghi, and S.-Å. Tärnlund. The halting problem for deductive synthesis of logic programs. In P. van Hentenryck, editor, *Proc. ICLP'94*, pages 665–683. MIT Press, 1994.
19. K.-K. Lau, M. Ornaghi, and S.-Å. Tärnlund. Steadfast logic programs. *J. Logic Programming*, submitted.
20. J.W. Lloyd. *Foundations of Logic Programming*. Springer-Verlag, 2nd edition, 1987.
21. Z. Manna. *Mathematical Theory of Computation*. McGraw-Hill, 1974.
22. E. Marakakis and J.P. Gallagher. Schema-based top-down design of logic programs using abstract data types. In L. Fribourg and F. Turini, editors, *Proc. LOPSTR/META'94*, pages 138–153, *LNCS* 883, Springer-Verlag, 1994.
23. J. Richardson and N. Fuchs. Development of correct transformational schemata for Prolog programs. This volume.
24. D. Sannella and A. Tarlecki. Essential concepts of algebraic specification and program development. *Formal Aspects of Computer Science*, forthcoming.
25. D.R. Smith. Top-down synthesis of divide-and-conquer algorithms. *Artificial Intelligence* 27(1):43–96, 1985.
26. D.R. Smith. KIDS: A semiautomatic program development system. *IEEE Trans. Software Engineering* 16(9):1024–1043, 1990.
27. L.S. Sterling and M. Kirschenbaum. Applying techniques to skeletons. In J.-M. Jacquet, editor, *Constructing Logic Programs*, pages 127–140. John Wiley, 1993.
28. W.W. Vasconcelos and N.E. Fuchs. An opportunistic approach for logic program analysis and optimisation using enhanced schema-based transformations. In M. Proietti, editor, *Proc. LOPSTR'95*, pages 174–188. *LNCS* 1048, Springer-Verlag, 1996.
29. M. Wirsing. Algebraic specification. In J. Van Leeuwen, editor, *Handbook of Theoretical Computer Science*, pages 675–788. Elsevier, 1990.

Analysis of Logic Programs with Delay

Andrew Heaton[1], Pat Hill[1], and Andy King[2]

[1] School of Computer Studies, University of Leeds, LS2 9JT, UK
[2] Computing Laboratory, University of Kent at Canterbury, CT2 7NF, UK

Abstract. The paper focuses on practical analyses for logic programs with delay. The method described is for downward-closed program properties and, in particular, groundness. A program transformation is defined which eliminates the delay statements but still enables an accurate approximation of the behaviour of delayed goals to be traced by the analyser. An implementation has been built which shows that the analysis can be both accurate and efficient.

1 Introduction

Second-generation logic programming languages, such as Gödel, IF/Prolog, SIC-Stus Prolog provide flexible computation rules in which goals delay if their arguments are insufficiently instantiated. Goals are reawoken, later on, if their arguments become further instantiated. In these languages the default computation rule is left to right. Flexible computation rules can provide a sound treatment of negation, underpin constrained search, improve termination behaviour of programs and allow co-routining. The program permute illustrates the use of the block declaration of SICStus Prolog.

```
permute([ ],[ ]).                    ordered([ ]).
permute([u|x1],y) :-                 ordered([x]).
    remove(u,y,z), permute(x1,z).    ordered([x,y|z]) :-
                                         new_ordered(x,y,z).
remove(x,[u|u1],z) :-
    new_remove(u,u1,x,z).            :- block new_ordered(−,?,?), new_ordered(?,−,?).
                                     new_ordered(x,y,ys) :-
:- block new_remove(?,?,−,−).           x ≤ y, ordered([y|ys]).
new_remove(x,x,z,z).
new_remove(x,u,y1,[u|z1]) :-
    remove(x,y1,z1).
```

Declaratively, the predicate permute/2 is true iff the first argument is a permutation of the second. remove/3 holds iff the second and third arguments are lists and the third can be obtained from the second by removing an element which corresponds to the first argument. The block declarations ensure that permute

Norbert E. Fuchs (Ed.): LOPSTR'97, LNCS 1463, pp. 148–167, 1998.

terminates for all queries. In the declaration :- block new_remove$(?, ?, -, -)$, the "-" in the third and fourth argument positions means that in a call to new_remove/4, if the third and fourth arguments are both uninstantiated then the call will delay until one of these arguments becomes instantiated. Without the new_remove block declaration, the query ?- permute$([1, 2], x)$. would backtrack into an infinite loop after producing the single solution $x = [1, 2]$[3].

The query ?-ordered(y), permute$([2, 1], y)$. is an example of the generate-and-test paradigm and illustrates how block declarations can be used to improve efficiency. The block declaration for new_ordered/3 delays goals until *both* the first and second arguments are non-variable. This causes the ordered/1 goals to co-routine (interleave) with permute/2 goals constraining the search and reducing backtracking.

Groundness analysis detects which program variables are bound to ground terms and is important in detecting determinacy, simplifying unification, *etc.* In [18] it is also shown that groundness information can be used to simplify delay conditions, thus enabling transformations which give significant improvements in performance. In particular this allows the elimination of redundant delay declarations. Consider a groundness analysis for the query ?- ⓐpermute$([1, 2], y)$ⓑ. where ⓐ and ⓑ denote program points. Groundness analysis should infer that y is ground at ⓑ but may be either ground or non-ground at ⓐ. Frameworks capable of tracing groundness in the context of co-routining, however, tend to be either imprecise or inefficient. This is reviewed in the related work section at the end of the paper. One of the major problems is in tracing the behaviour of delayed goals. Our method deals with this problem by transforming programs into abstract programs which have no delay statements but which can still trace the effects of the delaying goals. This enables potentially very efficient analyses.

In [4] a highly efficient groundness analysis using the *Pos* domain is given based on abstract compilation techniques. Following these techniques, we show that the *Pos* domain gives an accurate analysis for the special case of groundness. For example, with the above query to permute, our method will detect that y will be ground at program point ⓑ. The method is simple to implement, and the results for the programs tested so far indicate an efficient analysis for small and medium-sized programs.

The rest of the paper is organised as follows. In the next section a worked example demonstrating our approach is given. Section 3 gives the standard definitions and notation used. Section 4 defines the *Pos* domain whilst section 5 formalizes the program transformation central to the analysis and describes the abstract semantics. Section 6 outlines the implementation method whilst sections 7 and 8 summarise related and future work respectively.

---

[3] Note that an additional block permute$(-, -)$ declaration might also be useful since the query ?- permute(x, y) enumerates its solutions in the following order: $x = [\ ], y = [\ ]; x = [z_1], y = [z_1]; x = [z_1, z_2], y = [z_1, z_2]; x = [z_1, z_2, z_3], y = [z_1, z_2, z_3]$ *etc*, missing solutions such as $x = [z_1, z_2], y = [z_2, z_1]$. Unfairness can be avoided by delaying the call permute(x, y) until either of its arguments are instantiated.

2   Worked Example

To illustrate our approach to groundness analysis, consider the following query program below with initial goal :- query(x, y) annotated with program points ⓐ, ⓑ, ©, ⓓ and ⓔ.

$$\text{query}(x, y) \text{ :- } ⓐ\text{delay}(x, y), ⓑ x = [\,] ©\,.$$
$$\text{:- block delay}(-, ?).$$
$$\text{delay}(x, y) \text{ :- } ⓓ x = y \ ⓔ\,.$$

The equations $\phi_a = \phi_b = \varepsilon$, $\phi_c = \{x = [\,], y = [\,]\}$ represent the actual bindings on x and y at ⓐ, ⓑ and © respectively.

Our method basically transforms the program to a Datalog program which, although free from delay statements, can still trace synchronisation behaviour. The abstract program for query is listed below. Let $gr(x)$ denote that x is a ground term. The unification $x = [\,]$ has been abstracted by the propositional formula $gr(x)$. The block declaration is modelled by the formula $gr(x) \rightarrow ((gr(x) \leftrightarrow gr(x')) \wedge (gr(y) \leftrightarrow gr(y')))$. The unification $x = y$ has been abstracted by the propositional formula $gr(x') \leftrightarrow gr(y')$. The intention is that x' and y' will be unified with x and y whenever x is a ground term.

$$\text{query}(x, y) \text{ :- } ⓐ\text{delay}(x, y), ⓑ\{gr(x)\} ©$$
$$\text{delay}(x, y) \text{ :- } ⓓ\{gr(x) \rightarrow ((gr(x) \leftrightarrow gr(x')) \wedge (gr(y) \leftrightarrow gr(y')))$$
$$\wedge(gr(x') \leftrightarrow gr(y'))\} ⓔ$$

Restricting the formula on the right hand side of delay(x, y) to just the variables x, y we get the formula $gr(x) \rightarrow (gr(x) \leftrightarrow gr(y))$. At the program points ⓓ and ⓔ, $gr(x)$ holds and so at ⓔ the abstract description will be $gr(x) \wedge (gr(x) \leftrightarrow gr(y))$. This is logically equivalent to $gr(x) \wedge gr(y)$. Hence it has been deduced that x and y are both ground at ⓔ and so this is the answer pattern for delay.

With the block statements removed, the call and answer patterns can now be computed automatically by transforming the abstract program with a query-answer transformation and then calculating the minimal model. Implementation is thus straightforward even though synchronisation behaviour is accurately traced. Note that, in the case of the permute program, the analysis is powerful enough to infer that if the call pattern for permute(x,y) has x ground, then the answer pattern will have both x and y ground.

3   Preliminaries

3.1   Syntax of Logic Programs

Var denotes the set of variables, $Term$ the set of terms, $Pred$ the set of predicate symbols, $Atom$ the set of atoms of the form $p(\boldsymbol{x})$ where p is a predicate symbol and $\boldsymbol{x}$ are distinct variables. Eqn denotes the set of finite sets of equations of the form $a = b$ where either $a, b \in Term$ or $a, b \in Atom$. A literal is either an atom or an equation whereas a goal is a finite sequence of literals. The sets of literals and goals are denoted by Lit and $Goal$ respectively. A clause is a syntactic object of the form $h \leftarrow b$ where h, the head, is an atom and b, the body, is a finite sequence of literals. *Prog* is the set of programs, that is, the set of finite sets of clauses. *Var*, *Term*, *Atom*, *Eqn*, *Lit*, *Goal* and *Prog* respectively have typical members v, w, x, y, z; t; a, b; e; l; G and P. P_G denotes a program P with initial goal G. Initial goals are restricted to be single atoms. Also var(obj) denotes the set of variables in a syntactic object *obj*, :: denotes concatenation of sequences, and ϵ denotes the empty sequence.

The set of idempotent substitutions from *Var* to *Term* is denoted *Sub* and the set of renamings (which are bijective mappings from *Var* to *Var*) is denoted *Ren*. *Sub* and *Ren* extend in the usual way from functions from variables to terms, to functions from terms to terms, to functions from substitutions to substitutions, to functions from atoms to atoms and to functions from clauses to clauses. The restriction of a substitution θ to a set of variables U is denoted by $\theta \upharpoonright U$ and the composition of two substitutions θ and ϑ is denoted by $\theta \circ \vartheta$ and defined such that $(\theta \circ \vartheta)(u) = \theta(\vartheta(u))$. ε denotes the empty substitution and sets of substitutions will usually be denoted by Φ and Ψ. There is a natural mapping from substitutions to equations, that is, $eqn(\theta) = \{u = t \,|\, u \mapsto t \in \theta\}$, and mgu(E) denotes the set of most general unifiers for an equation set E.

Let $\leq$ denote the instance ordering, that is, $\theta \leq \theta'$ iff there exists a substitution $\sigma \in Sub$ such that $\theta = \sigma \circ \theta'$. Similarly, a syntactic object o is an instance of another o', denoted $o \leq o'$, iff there exists a substitution σ such that $o = \sigma(o')$. Instance lifts to $\wp(Atom)$ by $I \leq I'$ iff for all $a \in I$ there exists $a' \in I'$ such that $a \leq a'$. This, in turn, defines the equivalence relation $\sim$, that is $I \sim I'$ iff $I \leq I'$ and $I' \leq I$. Finally, the (quotiented) set of interpretations $Int = \wp(Atom)/\sim$ is ordered by $[I]_\sim \leq [I']_\sim$ iff $I \leq I'$.

3.2 Operational Semantics of Logic Programs with Delay

The operational semantics is described in terms of reductions between states. The set of states is defined by $State = Goal \times Sub \times Goal$. A state $\langle G, \theta, D \rangle$ records a sequence of literals G, the current substitution θ, and a sequence of delayed atoms D. For a given state s and a program P, the relation $\ll_s$ is defined such that $h \leftarrow b \ll_s P$ iff there exists $\rho \in Ren$ such that $\rho(h \leftarrow b) \in P$ and var(h $\leftarrow b$) $\cap$ var(s) $= \emptyset$. Similar to [16], to abstract away from particular language considerations, the operational semantics is defined in terms of two parametric functions *reduce* and *woken*. (In [16], a *delay* truth function is used instead with $delay \equiv \neg reduce$.) We say the atom a reduces with the substitution θ whenever $reduce(a, \theta)$ holds, whereas $woken(D, \theta)$ denotes the subset of atoms in D (ordered as a sequence) that are woken with the substitution θ. These functions are assumed to satisfy four conditions:

1. $a \in woken(D, \theta)$ iff $a \in D$ and $reduce(a, \theta)$.
2. $reduce(a, \theta)$ iff $reduce(\rho(a), \rho(\theta))$ for all $\rho \in Ren$.
3. $reduce(a, \theta)$ iff $reduce(a, \theta \upharpoonright var(a))$.
4. if $\theta \leq \vartheta$ and $reduce(a, \vartheta)$ then $reduce(a, \theta)$.

Definition 1 (reduction). The relation $s \rightarrow_P s'$ where $s, s' \in State$ is defined as follows:

- if $s = \langle x = t :: G, \theta, D \rangle$ then $s' = \langle D' :: G, \theta', D \setminus D' \rangle$ where
  $\theta' \in \text{mgu}(\{x = t\} \cup \text{eqn}(\theta))$ and $D' = woken(D, \theta')$;
- if $s = \langle a :: G, \theta, D \rangle$ and $reduce(a, \theta)$ holds then $s' = \langle b :: G, \theta', D \rangle$ where
  $h \leftarrow b \ll_s P$ and $\theta' \in \text{mgu}(\{h = a\} \cup \text{eqn}(\theta))$;
- if $s = \langle a :: G, \theta, D \rangle$ and $reduce(a, \theta)$ fails then $s' = \langle G, \theta, a :: D \rangle$.

Note that when an atom a has no defining clause, $reduce(a, \theta)$ fails and it is added to the delay sequence. In practise such an atom will usually cause an error. These atoms are reduced, however, to avoid the need for an error state and thus provide a simple basis for analysis. Also the relative execution order of simultaneously reawoken goals is left undefined to reflect the scheduling behaviour of implementations like SICStus [2] and IF/Prolog [19]. Our analysis defined in this paper is not dependent on any particular scheduling order for these atoms.

Definition 2 (derivation). A derivation from a state s for a program P is a (finite or infinite) sequence of reductions $s_1 \to_P s_2 \to_P \ldots$ where $s = s_1$.

The operational semantics of a program is in terms of its qualified answers. Given a derivation from a state s and a program P with last state $\langle \epsilon, \theta, D \rangle$ we say the tuple $\langle \theta, D \rangle$ is a qualified answer to s. It is successful if $D = \epsilon$ and it flounders otherwise. Call patterns can now be defined in terms of the operational semantics.

Definition 3 (call patterns). For a given program P and initial goal G,

$$\text{call}(P_G) = [\{\langle 1, \theta \upharpoonright \text{var}(1) \rangle \mid \langle G, \epsilon, \epsilon \rangle \to_P^* \langle 1 :: G', \theta, D \rangle\}]_{\sim}$$

3.3 Galois Connections

A Galois connection between $D^{\mathcal{A}}$ and D is a 4-tuple $\langle D (\sqsubseteq), \alpha, D^{\mathcal{A}} (\sqsubseteq^{\mathcal{A}}), \gamma \rangle$ where $D (\sqsubseteq)$ and $D^{\mathcal{A}} (\sqsubseteq^{\mathcal{A}})$ are posets; $\alpha : D \to D^{\mathcal{A}}$ and $\gamma : D^{\mathcal{A}} \to D$; α and γ are monotonic; $d \sqsubseteq \gamma(\alpha(d))$ for all $d \in D$ and $\alpha(\gamma(d^{\mathcal{A}})) \sqsubseteq^{\mathcal{A}} d^{\mathcal{A}}$ for all $d^{\mathcal{A}} \in D^{\mathcal{A}}$.

We next formalise the notion of a downward-closed property, following a similar approach to [5].

Definition 4 (downward-closure).

- Given a poset $D (\sqsubseteq)$, the downward-closure of $S \subseteq D$ is defined by $down(S)$ $= \{d \in D \mid \exists s \in S.d \sqsubseteq s\}$. S is downward-closed iff $down(S) = S$;
- A Galois connection $\langle D (\sqsubseteq), \alpha, D^{\mathcal{A}} (\sqsubseteq^{\mathcal{A}}), \gamma \rangle$ is downward-closed iff for all $d^{\mathcal{A}} \in D^{\mathcal{A}}$ $\gamma(d^{\mathcal{A}})$ is downward-closed.

A predicate p on a poset $D (\sqsubseteq)$ is a subset of D and therefore is downward-closed iff the set p is downward-closed. A truth-function is downward-closed iff the predicate it defines is downward-closed.

Example 1. Given the standard instance ordering on terms, the unary predicates gr and nv are downward-closed where gr and nv are defined such that $gr(t)$ holds iff t is ground, and $nv(t)$ holds iff t is non-variable.   □

4   Abstract Domains

Abstract substitutions A *Pos* domain is used to capture positive information about downward-closed predicates. Following [7], we let $\Omega_S(\{\wedge, \vee, \leftrightarrow, \neg\})$ denote the set of propositional formulae formed from the set of connectives $\{\wedge, \vee, \leftrightarrow, \neg\}$ and a set of propositional symbols S. A truth assignment is a function $r : S \rightarrow \{0, 1\}$. Given $f, f' \in \Omega_S(\{\wedge, \vee, \leftrightarrow, \neg\})$, $r \models f$ denotes that r satisfies f and the notation $f \models f'$ abbreviates $r \models f$ implies $r \models f'$. Two formulae are logically equivalent, $f \equiv f'$, iff $f \models f'$ and $f' \models f$.

To enable an analysis to simultaneously trace and relate multiple downward-closed properties, like groundness and non-variable (denoted from here on by *gr* and *nv* respectively), on a set of program variables V, *Pos* is defined in terms of a set of propositional symbols $\{gr(v), nv(v) | v \in V\}$. More generally, given n properties, $p_1, \ldots, p_n$, the set of propositional symbols is $\{p_i(v) | v \in V \wedge 1 \leq i \leq n\}$. As notation, we will usually add the $\sharp$ annotation to denote abstract substitutions, that is, to indicate propositional formulae.

Definition 5. $Pos_V = \{f \in \Omega_S(\{\wedge, \vee, \leftrightarrow, \neg\}) | u \models f\}$ where $S = \{p_i(v) | v \in V\}$ and $u : S \rightarrow \{1\}$ denotes the unit truth assignment.

Note that if Pos_V is defined for a single predicate p_1 then the definition can be simplified so that just the variables themselves represent the property. This special case coincides with the groundness analysis of [4, 7, 17]. $Pos_V / \equiv (\models)$ is a complete lattice with lub $\vee$ and glb $\wedge$ and the least and greatest elements *false* and *true* [7].

Abstraction and concretisation of substitutions To formalise the relationship between a substitution and a formula an auxiliary function $assign_V$ is introduced. Because $p_i(v)$ can be used both as a propositional symbol and to assert that p_i holds for v, for clarity, in what follows a truth-function f_i is used to test for a property in the concrete whereas p_i is used for a symbol in abstract formulae.

Definition 6. $assign_V(\phi) = \bigwedge_{i=1}^{n} \bigwedge_{v \in V} q_i(v)$ where $q_i(v) = \begin{cases} p_i(v) & \text{if } f_i(v) \\ \neg p_i(v) & \text{if } \neg f_i(v) \end{cases}$

Note that $assign_V(\phi)$ is not necessarily positive.

Example 2. Suppose $V = \{x, y, z\}$, $p_1 = gr$, $p_2 = nv$, $\phi = \{x \mapsto f(y)\}$ and $\phi' = \{x \mapsto f(1), y \mapsto 1\}$ (note that $\phi' \leq \phi$). Then
$assign_V(\phi) = \neg gr(x) \wedge nv(x) \wedge \neg gr(y) \wedge \neg nv(y) \wedge \neg gr(z) \wedge \neg nv(z)$ and
$assign_V(\phi') = gr(x) \wedge nv(x) \wedge gr(y) \wedge nv(y) \wedge \neg gr(z) \wedge \neg nv(z)$. □

We can now define the concretisation and abstraction functions γ and α.

Definition 7.

$$\gamma_V : Pos_V \rightarrow \wp(Sub), \qquad\qquad \alpha_V : \wp(Sub) \rightarrow Pos_V$$
$$\gamma_V(\phi^\sharp) = \{\phi | \forall \varphi \leq \phi . assign_V(\varphi) \models \phi^\sharp\}, \; \alpha_V(\Phi) = \bigwedge_{\Phi \subseteq \gamma_V(\phi^\sharp)} \phi^\sharp$$

Note that defining γ_V on Pos_V ensures that $\alpha_V(\Phi) \in Pos_V$.

Example 3. Suppose $V = \{x, y, z\}$, $p_1 = gr$, $p_2 = nv$ and $\phi = \{x \mapsto f(y)\}$. Let $\phi^\sharp = (gr(x) \leftrightarrow gr(y)) \wedge nv(x)$. Then $\phi \in \gamma_V(\phi^\sharp)$ since $assign_V(\phi') \models \phi^\sharp$ for all $\phi' \leq \phi$. $\qquad\square$

We now have a Galois connection between the abstract and concrete domains as stated below.

Proposition 1. $\langle \wp(Sub) \ (\subseteq), \alpha_V, Pos_V \ (\models), \gamma_V \rangle$ is a Galois connection.

We also want to abstract concrete interpretations, which we shall use to define abstract call patterns. This is done by pairing atoms with formulae as follows:

Definition 8.

$$Atom^\sharp = \{\langle p(\boldsymbol{x}), \phi^\sharp \rangle \mid p \in Pred \wedge \phi^\sharp \in Pos_{\mathrm{var}(\boldsymbol{x})}\}$$

The concretisation and abstraction functions can be naturally extended to interpretations as follows:

Definition 9.

$$\gamma : \wp(Atom^\sharp) \to Int$$
$$\gamma(I^\sharp) = [\{\langle p(\boldsymbol{x}), \phi \upharpoonright \mathrm{var}(\boldsymbol{x}) \rangle \mid \langle p(\boldsymbol{x}), \phi^\sharp \rangle \in I^\sharp \wedge \phi \in \gamma_{\mathrm{var}(\boldsymbol{x})}(\phi^\sharp)\}]_\sim$$

γ induces a natural equivalence relation on $\wp(Atom^\sharp)$, that is $I^\sharp \approx I^{\sharp'}$ iff $\gamma(I^\sharp) = \gamma(I^{\sharp'})$. This in turn is used to define $Int^\sharp = \wp(Atom^\sharp)/\approx$, the abstract analogue of Int. An ordering for $Int^\sharp$ is given by $[I^\sharp]_\approx \sqsubseteq [I^{\sharp'}]_\approx$ iff $\gamma([I^\sharp]_\approx) \subseteq \gamma([I^{\sharp'}]_\approx)$ and the lub is defined by $\sqcup_i [I_i^\sharp]_\approx = [\cup_i I_i^\sharp]_\approx$.

Definition 10.

$$\gamma : Int^\sharp \to Int \quad \alpha : Int \to Int^\sharp$$

$$\gamma(I^\sharp) = [\gamma(I^\sharp)]_\approx \quad \alpha(I) = \bigsqcup_{I \subseteq \gamma([I^\sharp]_\approx)} [I^\sharp]_\approx$$

We can thus prove:

Proposition 2. $\langle Int^\sharp \ (\sqsubseteq), \alpha, Int \ (\leq), \gamma \rangle$ is a Galois connection.

5   Abstract Compilation

First we define the set of monotonic formulae, Mon_V.

Definition 11. $Mon_V = \Omega_S(\{\wedge, \vee\})$ where $S = \{p_i(v) \mid v \in V\}$.

For technical reasons apparent in the proof for safety, we define the abstract reduce function in terms of monotonic formulae. We will use certain properties of monotonic formulae in the proof. Here it suffices just to note that $Mon_V \subseteq Pos_V$. See, e.g. [7], for details.

Definition 12.

$$reduce^\sharp(p(\boldsymbol{x}), \phi^\sharp) \leftrightarrow (\phi^\sharp \in Mon_{var(\boldsymbol{x})} \wedge \forall \phi \in \gamma_{var(\boldsymbol{x})}(\phi^\sharp) \,.reduce(p(\boldsymbol{x}), \phi)).$$

The intention is that an abstract goal will never reduce if its corresponding concrete goal never reduces.

Example 4. Let us define $reduce^\sharp(p(\boldsymbol{x}), \phi^\sharp) \leftrightarrow \forall \phi \in \gamma_{var(\boldsymbol{x})}(\phi^\sharp) \,.reduce(p(\boldsymbol{x}), \phi)$. In SICStus Prolog, given the declaration :- block $p(d_1, ..., d_n)$ for the n-ary predicate p, where $d_i \in \{-, ?\}$ for $1 \le i \le n$, then an abstract reduce function is:

$$reduce^\sharp(\mathrm{p}(\boldsymbol{x}), \phi^\sharp) \leftrightarrow \phi^\sharp \models \bigvee_{d_i = -} nv(x_i)$$

□

Next we define the program transformation central to the analysis. For clarity, we introduce a notation for writing propositional formulae in terms of their variables rather than the properties of the variables (which strictly speaking are the propositional symbols), e.g. given the propositional formula $q(p_1(x), ..., p_n(x))$ we denote this by $q(x)$.

Definition 13 (abstract compilation α).

$$\alpha[\![c_1, \ldots, c_n]\!] = \alpha_{\text{clause}}[\![c_1]\!], \alpha_{\text{bot}}[\![c_1]\!] \ldots, \alpha_{\text{clause}}[\![c_n]\!], \alpha_{\text{bot}}[\![c_n]\!]$$
$$\alpha_{\text{clause}}[\![p(\boldsymbol{x}) \leftarrow \boldsymbol{b}]\!] = p(\boldsymbol{x}') \leftarrow (\phi_r^\sharp \rightarrow \phi_s^\sharp), \alpha_{\text{goal}}[\![\boldsymbol{b}]\!]$$
$$\alpha_{\text{bot}}[\![p(\boldsymbol{x}) \leftarrow \boldsymbol{b}]\!] = p(\boldsymbol{x}) \leftarrow \phi_b^\sharp$$
$$\alpha_{\text{goal}}[\![l_1, \ldots, l_n]\!] = \alpha_{\text{literal}}[\![l_1]\!], \ldots, \alpha_{\text{literal}}[\![l_n]\!]$$
$$\alpha_{\text{literal}}[\![p(\boldsymbol{x})]\!] = p(\boldsymbol{x})$$
$$\alpha_{\text{literal}}[\![t = t']\!] = \phi_t^\sharp$$

where

$$\begin{cases} \phi_b^\sharp = \bigwedge_i \bigwedge_{v \in \boldsymbol{x}} p_i(v) \\ \phi_r^\sharp = \bigvee_{reduce^\sharp(p(\boldsymbol{x}'), \phi^\sharp)} \phi^\sharp \\ \phi_s^\sharp = \alpha_{var(\boldsymbol{x} = \boldsymbol{x}')}^\sharp(\text{mgu}(\{\boldsymbol{x} = \boldsymbol{x}'\})) \\ \phi_t^\sharp = \alpha_{var(t = t')}^\sharp(\text{mgu}(\{t = t'\})) \end{cases}$$

and $\boldsymbol{x}'$ are fresh variables, that is, $var(\boldsymbol{x}') \cap var(\mathrm{p}(\boldsymbol{x}) \leftarrow \boldsymbol{b}) = \emptyset$.

Example 5. The abstract program for the program permute listed in section 1 is below. First note we have written new to denote the predicate new_remove. The first (normalised) clause for permute is

permute(u, v):- $u = [\,]$, $v = [\,]$.

This is abstracted by the propositional formula $nv(u) \wedge gr(u) \wedge nv(v) \wedge gr(v)$. When α_{bot} is applied to this same clause the propositional formula $\phi_b^\sharp$ obtained is again $nv(u) \wedge gr(u) \wedge nv(v) \wedge gr(v)$.

Next we turn to how the block declaration

:- block new_remove$(?, ?, -, -)$.

has been abstracted. Following Example 4, the abstract reduce condition is modelled as follows:

$reduce^{\sharp}(\text{new\_remove}(u, v, w, x), \phi^{\sharp}) \leftrightarrow \phi^{\sharp} \models nv(w) \lor nv(x)$.

For convenience, a separate predicate reduce is defined. This essentially consists of the propositional formula $(\phi_r^{\sharp} \to \phi_s^{\sharp})$ as given in the formal definition above.

permute(u, v) :-
$\quad \{\, nv(u) \land gr(u) \land nv(v) \land gr(v) \,\}$.
permute(u, v) :-
$\quad \{\, nv(u) \land gr(u) \leftrightarrow (gr(w) \land gr(x)) \,\}$,
$\quad$ remove(w, v, y),
$\quad$ permute(x, y).

remove(u, v, w) :-
$\quad \{\, nv(v) \land (gr(v) \leftrightarrow (gr(x) \land gr(y))) \,\}$,
$\quad$ new(u, x, y, w).
remove(u, v, w) :-
$\quad \left\{ \begin{array}{l} nv(v) \land nv(v) \land nv(x) \land \\ gr(v) \land gr(v) \land gr(x) \end{array} \right\}$.

new(u, v, w, x) :-
$\quad$ reduce(new(u, v, w, x), new(u', v', w', x')),
$\quad \left\{ \begin{array}{l} nv(u') \leftrightarrow nv(v') \land gr(u') \leftrightarrow gr(v') \land \\ nv(w') \leftrightarrow nv(x') \land gr(w') \leftrightarrow gr(x') \end{array} \right\}$.
new(u, v, w, x) :-
$\quad$ reduce(new(u, v, w, x), new(u', v', w', x')),
$\quad \{\, nv(x') \land (gr(x') \leftrightarrow (gr(v') \land gr(y))) \,\}$,
$\quad$ remove(u', w', y).
new(u, v, w, x) :-
$\quad \left\{ \begin{array}{l} nv(u) \land nv(v) \land nv(w) \land nv(x) \land \\ gr(u) \land gr(v) \land gr(w) \land gr(x) \end{array} \right\}$.

reduce(new(u, v, w, x), new(u', v', w', x')) :-
$\quad \left\{ \begin{array}{l} (nv(w) \lor nv(x)) \to \\ \quad nv(u) \leftrightarrow nv(u') \land gr(u) \leftrightarrow gr(u') \land \\ \quad nv(v) \leftrightarrow nv(v') \land gr(v) \leftrightarrow gr(v') \land \\ \quad nv(w) \leftrightarrow nv(w') \land gr(w) \leftrightarrow gr(w') \land \\ \quad nv(x) \leftrightarrow nv(x') \land gr(x) \leftrightarrow gr(x') \end{array} \right\}$. $\qquad \square$

Note that having α_{bot} as part of the definition will lose no precision in the analysis. This is because it merely adds the possibility that all properties might hold at (almost!) any point in the program. But since only downward-closed properties are considered, this is already implicitly assumed. We are, however, making sure that all the abstract programs will terminate. If termination is not ensured then information may be lost in the case when delayed goals remain unexecuted in the concrete program.

Example 6. Suppose we had defined $\alpha[\![c_1, \ldots, c_n]\!] = \alpha_{\text{clause}}[\![c_1]\!], \ldots, \alpha_{\text{clause}}[\![c_n]\!]$. Consider the call and answer patterns of the loop program (listed below on the left) with an initial goal go, and the corresponding abstract program (listed on the right) defined by $loop^{\sharp} = \alpha[\![loop]\!]$ for a *Pos* domain that just traces groundness, that is, $p_1 = gr$.

go :- $p(v), r(v)$.
:- block $p(-)$.
$p(w)$:- $q(w)$.
$q(y)$:- $q(y)$.
$r(z)$.

go :- $p(v), r(v)$.
$p(w)$:- $(gr(w) \to (gr(w) \leftrightarrow gr(x))), q(x)$.
$q(y)$:- $q(y)$.
$r(z)$.

The only derivation for loop flounders and is finite

$$\langle \text{go}; \varepsilon; \epsilon \rangle \rightarrow_{loop} \langle p(w), r(w); \varepsilon; \epsilon \rangle \rightarrow_{loop} \langle r(w); \varepsilon; p(w) \rangle \rightarrow_{loop} \langle \epsilon; \{w \mapsto z\}; p(w) \rangle$$

whereas the only derivation for $loop^\sharp$ is infinite since $q(y)$ will be executed. One consequence of this behaviour is that the control fails to reach the goal $r(v)$ so that the abstract call patterns of $loop^\sharp$ do not safely abstract the concrete call patterns of loop, that is,

$$\text{call}(loop_{\text{go}}) = [\{\langle \text{go}, \varepsilon \rangle, \langle p(x), \varepsilon \rangle, \langle r(x), \varepsilon \rangle\}]_\sim$$

$$\text{call}^\sharp(loop^\sharp_{\text{go}}) = [\{\langle \text{go}, true \rangle, \langle p(x), true \rangle, \langle q(x), true \rangle\}]_\approx.$$

so that $\text{call}(loop_{\text{go}}) \not\subseteq \gamma(\text{call}^\sharp(loop^\sharp_{\text{go}}))$.
Defining $\alpha[\![c_1, \ldots, c_n]\!] = \alpha_{\text{clause}}[\![c_1]\!], \alpha_{\text{bot}}[\![c_1]\!] \ldots, \alpha_{\text{clause}}[\![c_n]\!], \alpha_{\text{bot}}[\![c_n]\!]$ however, we instead get

go :- $p(v), r(v)$.	$q(y)$:- $q(y)$.
go :- $gr(v)$.	$q(y)$:- $gr(y)$.
$p(w)$:- $(gr(w) \rightarrow (gr(w) \leftrightarrow gr(x)))$, $q(x)$.	$r(z)$.
$p(w)$:- $gr(w)$.	$r(z)$:- $gr(z)$.

The infinite loop caused by executing $q(x)$ is now avoidable and so we get $\langle \text{r(x)}, \varepsilon \rangle \in \text{call}^\sharp(loop^\sharp_{\text{go}})$.   □

Finally, we introduce an operation to relax the propositional formulae obtained in the call patterns. The relax operation is required for technical reasons which are apparent in the proof for the safety of the analysis. For the case where only the property of groundness is analysed, the *relax* operator weakens a propositional formula to a (monotonic) conjunction of ground variables.

Definition 14.

$$relax_V(\phi^\sharp) = \bigwedge \{p_i(v) \mid v \in V \wedge \phi^\sharp \models p_i(v) \text{ for } 1 \le i \le n \}$$

$$relax([I^\sharp]_\approx) = \left[\{ \langle p(\boldsymbol{x}), relax_{\text{var}(\boldsymbol{x})}(\phi^\sharp) \rangle \mid \langle p(\boldsymbol{x}), \phi^\sharp \rangle \in I^\sharp \}\right]_\approx$$

The following example illustrates the problems that can arise without this weakening of the formulae.

Example 7. Consider the program P listed below on the left together with its corresponding abstract program $P^\sharp$ on the right.

go :- $p(x, y), q(x, y)$.	go :- $p(x, y), q(x, y)$.
:- block $p(-, ?)$.	$p(x, y)$:- $(gr(x) \rightarrow gr(y))$.
$p(x, y)$:- $x = y$.	$q(x, y)$.
$q(x, y)$.	

With the initial goal go, the atom $p(x, y)$ will be delayed and the call pattern for $q(x, y)$ is $\langle q(x, y), \varepsilon \rangle$. The abstract call pattern is $\langle q(x, y), gr(x) \rightarrow gr(y) \rangle$. Note that even though $assign_{\text{var}(\text{q(x,y)})}(\varepsilon) \models gr(x) \rightarrow gr(y)$, due to the downward-closure condition imposed on γ we have $\varepsilon \notin \gamma_{\text{var}(\text{q(x,y)})}(gr(x) \rightarrow gr(y))$. Applying the *relax* operation, however, we instead get the abstract call pattern $\langle q(x, y), true \rangle$ and we now have $\varepsilon \in \gamma_{\text{var}(\text{q(x,y)})}(true)$.   □

We now formally describe an abstract semantics. Like the concrete semantics, this is described in terms of reductions between states. The set of abstract states $State^\sharp$ is defined by $State^\sharp = Goal \times Pos_{Var}$.

Definition 15. For an abstract program $P^\sharp$, the abstract reduction relation $s \rightarrow_{P^\sharp} s'$, where $s, s' \in State^\sharp$ and $s = \langle l :: \mathbf{l}, \phi^\sharp \rangle$, is defined as follows:

- if $l \in Pos_{var(s)}$ then $s' = \langle \mathbf{l}, \phi^\sharp \wedge l \rangle$;
- if l is $p(\mathbf{x})$ and $h \leftarrow \mathbf{b} \ll_s P^\sharp$ then $s' = \langle \mathbf{b} :: \mathbf{l}, \phi^\sharp \wedge \varphi^\sharp \rangle$ where $\varphi^\sharp = \alpha_{var(h=l)}(mgu(\{h = l\}))$.

Thus an abstract derivation from an abstract state $s^\sharp$ for an abstract program $P^\sharp$ is an (finite or infinite) sequence of abstract reductions $s_1^\sharp \rightarrow_{P^\sharp} s_2^\sharp \rightarrow_{P^\sharp} \ldots$ where $s^\sharp = s_1^\sharp$. Abstract call patterns can now be defined in terms of the abstract semantics.

Definition 16. $\mathrm{call}^\sharp(\mathrm{P}^\sharp_{\mathrm{G}^\sharp}) = [\{\langle l, \theta^\sharp \upharpoonright var(l) \rangle \mid \langle \mathrm{G}^\sharp, true \rangle \rightarrow_{P^\sharp}^* \langle l :: \mathrm{G}^{\sharp'}, \theta^\sharp \rangle\}]_\approx$

The theorem below ensures the safety of the analysis. The proof is given in the appendix.

Theorem 1 (Safety). If $P^\sharp = \alpha[\![P]\!]$, and $G^\sharp = \alpha_{goal}[\![G]\!]$ then

$$\mathrm{call}(\mathrm{P}_\mathrm{G}) \le \gamma(relax(\mathrm{call}(\mathrm{P}^\sharp_{\mathrm{G}^\sharp})))$$

6   Implementation

An analyser has been implemented in SICStus Prolog which takes, as input, SICStus Prolog programs with block and freeze declarations and produces, as output, call patterns for each predicate in the program. The analyser is largely based on [4] and essentially infers which program variables are bound to ground and non-variable terms. Following [4], Pos formulae are represented as their models and n-ary predicates iff$(x, x_1, \ldots, x_{n-1})$ are used to express formulae of the form $x \leftrightarrow x_1 \wedge \ldots \wedge x_{n-1}$.

Example 8. Consider again the abstract **permute** program and, in particular, the **new** and **reduce** predicates of example 5. In the case of **new**, each of its clauses are translated into a clause by expressing Pos formulae, like $gr(x') \leftrightarrow (gr(v') \wedge gr(y))$ and $nv(x')$, in terms of iff predicates, like iff(nv(x')) and iff(gr(x'), gr(v'), gr(y)). The single **reduce** clause, on the other hand, is expanded into three clauses, the formulae $(x_1 \vee x_2) \rightarrow x_3$ being logically equivalent to $(x_1 \wedge x_3) \vee (x_2 \wedge x_3) \vee (\neg x_1 \wedge \neg x_2)$. The **neg**($x$) predicate expresses $\neg x$. Note that although $\neg x$ is not positive, the model represented by the disjunction of the three clauses is positive. Expressing implications as non-positive formulae merely simplifies the translation of block declarations.

new(u, v, w, x) :-
    reduce(new(u,v,w,x), new(u',v',w',x')),
    iff(nv(u'), nv(v')), iff(gr(u'), gr(v')),
    iff(nv(w'), gr(x')), iff(gr(w'), gr(x')).
new(u, v, w, x) :-
    reduce(new(u,v,w,x), new(u',v',w',x')),
    iff(nv(x')),
    iff(gr(x'), gr(v'), gr(y)),
    remove(u', w', y).
new(u, v, w, x) :-
    iff(nv(u)), iff(nv(v)), iff(nv(w)), iff(nv(x)),
    iff(gr(u)), iff(gr(v)), iff(gr(w)), iff(gr(x)).

reduce(new(u,v,w,x), new(u',v',w',x')) :-
    iff(nv(w)),
    iff(nv(u), nv(u')), iff(gr(u), gr(u')),
    iff(nv(v), nv(v')), iff(gr(v), gr(v')),
    iff(nv(w), nv(w')),iff(gr(w), gr(w')),
    iff(nv(x), nv(x')), iff(gr(x), gr(x')).
reduce(new(u,v,w,x), new(u',v',w',x')) :-
    iff(nv(x)),
    iff(nv(u), nv(u')), iff(gr(u), gr(u')),
    iff(nv(v), nv(v')), iff(gr(v), gr(v')),
    iff(nv(w), nv(w')),iff(gr(w), gr(w')),
    iff(nv(x), nv(x')), iff(gr(x), gr(x')).
reduce(new(u,v,w,x), new(u',v',w',x')) :-
    neg(nv(w)),
    neg(nv(x)).

Finally, a magic transform (see, e.g. [4]) coupled with bottom-up evaluation is used to calculate the call patterns of the predicates.   □

The benchmarks below are arranged in order according to size. The first program permute.pl is defined earlier in the paper. slowsort.pl (a generate and test algorithm) and interl.pl (simple interpreter for co-routining programs) are NU-Prolog programs with dynamic scheduling written by L. Naish which have been translated into SICStus. nand.pl (a nand-gate circuit designer written by E. Tick) and transp.pl (a matrix transposer written by V. Saraswat) are programs with dynamic scheduling resulting from the automatic translation of concurrent logic programs by the QD-Janus system [9]. Dynamic scheduling is used to emulate the concurrency present in the original programs. The programs send.pl (a cryptoarithmetic problem) and queens.pl (a coroutining n-queens) were provided by M. Carlsson. Finally primes.pl (a lazy primes sieve) and permcon.pl (a monotonic permutation generator) have been written by ourselves.

Program	Cl	Lit	DL	Analysis Time (Secs)
permute.pl	5	4	1	0.00
send.pl	6	13	4	0.01
slowsort.pl	9	8	8	0.01
primes.pl	10	12	8	0.01
interpl.pl	11	10	3	0.01
queens.pl	12	17	1	0.01
permcon.pl	21	28	7	0.03
nand.pl.pl	90	157	13	0.41
transp.pl	112	180	20	1.10

Cl is the number of clauses analysed, Lit is the number of literals and DL is the number of delaying literals. The analysis times are based on a Pentium 200MHz PC machine with 64M of memory running SICStus prolog version 3.5 under Linux where the analyser is compiled into compact code (byte code).

Our times indicate an efficient analysis for small and medium-sized programs. This is in contrast for the times reported in [18] for a groundness and non-variable analysis based on the more general closure framework of [13]. Although the results given in [18] were mostly acceptable, there were some anomalous times. In particular the time quoted for transp.pl was 168.5 seconds compared to 1.10 seconds using our analyser. (Note that this is not an exact comparison since the times are based on different machines.)

7 Related Work

Suspension-analysis framework The simple and practical framework of [8], though adequate for inferring suspension-freeness – its primary objective – it does not provide a suitable basis for accurately tracing properties like groundness since it abstracts the behaviour of possibly delaying goals in a very conservative way. Even when equipped with a *Pos* domain (rather than a traditional mode domain [8]) the analysis cannot infer modes to the precision of our framework.

Multiset framework The multiset framework of [16] uses a multiset to record which atoms are definitely delayed and which atoms are possibly delayed. However, in [13] (which builds on and improves the method) it is reported that "the analysis is imprecise and rather inefficient in practice".

Closure framework In an attempt to alleviate some of the problems with the multiset framework, a closure based semantics is proposed in [13]. The semantics improves the precision but efficient implementation is still difficult. For example, for the approach to be practical, the implementation described in [13] makes "observational equivalence" of closures, represents closures in a special way, and uses a number of techniques, including the differential approach [12], to improve the handling of cases when no atoms are delayed. Furthermore, this framework is more complicated than necessary for applications like determinacy analysis since the framework is aimed at tracing properties such as definite freeness that are not downward closed. Our work adapts and simplifies this work for applications like determinacy analysis. In [18], the closure framework is used to underpin two program transformations: one that simplifies delay conditions, and another that reorders delayed literals.

Abstracting synchronisation framework Our transform, which *encodes* synchronisation, is not to be confused with the *NoSynch* transform of [20] which *removes* synchronisation from a concurrent constraint program. The work of [20] shows how analyses developed for constraint programs can be used to reason about non-suspending concurrent constraint programs.

Abstract compilation frameworks Our analysis blends the closure framework of [13] with the abstract compilation work of [4] and [10]. Abstract compilation and abstract programs have been proposed for deriving modes [4, 6], encoding regular approximations [11], inferring directional types [3] and deducing inter-argument relationships [14]. In addition, [4, 15], [14] and [6] present abstract compilation schemes in which analysis is realised as the bottom-up and top-down evaluation of constraint logic programs. None of these approaches, however, traces synchronisation behaviour.

8 Future Work

Future work will focus on generalising the technique to other downwards-closed domains and then later to non downwards-closed domains. Another direction would be to investigate how demand-driven analysis can be used to infer the modes that suspending goals are reawoken with. We also plan to adapt widening techniques from [1] and investigate their effect on our method.

Acknowledgments

This work was supported by EPSRC Grant GR/K79635 and partly by the Nuffield Grant SCI/180/94/417/G. We gratefully acknowledge Brandon Bennett, Mats Carlsson, Jan Smaus and Andy Verden for their helpful discussions. Also we thank Roberto Bagnara, Mike Codish and Germán Puebla for help with the implementation and benchmarking.

References

[1] F. Benoy, M. Codish, A. Heaton, and A. King. Widening Pos for Efficient and Scalable Groundness Analysis of Logic Programs. Submitted for Publication.

[2] M. Carlsson. Personal communication on the `freeze/2` and `block` declaration awakening order in SICStus Prolog 3. April 1996.

[3] M. Codish and B. Demoen. Deriving polymorphic type dependencies for logic programs using multiple incarnations of prop. In *SAS'94*, pages 281–297. Springer-Verlag, 1994.

[4] M. Codish and B. Demoen. Analysing Logic Programs using "prop"-ositional Logic Programs and a Magic Wand. *Journal of Logic Programming*, 25(3):249–274, 1995.

[5] M. Codish, M. Falaschi, and K. Marriott. Suspension analyses for concurrent logic programs. *ACM Transactions on Programming Languages and Systems*, 16(3):649–686, 1994.

[6] P. Codognet and G. Filé. Computations, Abstractions and Constraints. Technical report, Dipartimento di Matematica Pura e Applicata, Università di Padova, 1991.

[7] A. Cortesi, G. Filé, and W. Winsborough. Optimal Groundness Analysis using Propositional Logic. *Journal of Logic Programming*, 27(1, 2 and 3):137–169, 1996.

[8] S. Debray, D. Gudeman, and P. Bigot. Detection and Optimization of Suspension-free Logic Programs. In *ILPS'94*, pages 487–504. MIT Press, 1994.

[9] S.K. Debray. QD-Janus: A Sequential Implementation of Janus in Prolog. *Software- Practice and Experience*, 23(12):1337–1360, 1993.

[10] J. Gallagher, D. Boulanger, and H. Saglam. Practical Model-Based Static Analysis for Definite Logic Programs. Technical Report CSTR-95-011, University of Bristol, 1995.

[11] J. Gallagher and A. de Waal. Fast and precise regular approximations of logic programs. In *ICLP'94*, pages 599–613. MIT Press, 1994.

[12] M. García de la Banda, K. Marriott, H. Søndergaard, and P. Stuckey. Improved Analysis of Logic Programs using a Differential Approach. Technical Report 95/20, Computer Science Department, Melbourne University, May 1995.

[13] M. García de la Banda, K. Marriott, and P. Stuckey. Efficient Analysis of Logic Programs with Dynamic Scheduling. In *ILPS'95*, pages 417–431. MIT Press, 1995.

[14] R. Giacobazzi, S. K. Debray, and G. Levi. A generalised semantics for constraint logic programs. In *FGCS'92*, pages 581–591. ACM Press, 1992.

[15] M. Hermenegildo, R. Warren, and S. K. Debray. Global flow analysis as a practical compilation tool. *J. Logic Programming*, 13(1, 2, 3 and 4):349–366, 1992.

[16] K. Marriott, M. García de la Banda, and M. Hermenegildo. Analyzing Logic Programs with Dynamic Scheduling. In *POPL'94*, pages 240–253. ACM Press, 1994.

[17] K. Marriott and H. Søndergaard. Precise and efficient groundness analysis. *ACM Lett. Program. Lang. Syst.*, 13(2–3):181–196, 1993.

[18] G. Puebla, M. García de la Banda, K. Marriott, and P. Stuckey. Optimization of Logic Programs with Dynamic Scheduling. In *ICLP'97*. MIT Press, 1997.

[19] A. Verden. Personal communication on `freeze/2` and the `const_delay` module of IF/Prolog V5.0. April 1996.

[20] E. Zaffanella, R. Giacobazzi, and G. Levi. Abstracting Synchronisation in Concurrent Constraint Programming. In *PLILP'94*, pages 57–72. Springer-Verlag, 1994.

A   Proof for Safety

The first stage of the proof is to define semi-abstract reduction sequences. These are sequences where the selection rule of the concrete derivation is preserved. Hence each abstract state for a semi-abstract reduction sequence requires a set to store delayed atoms (as in the concrete case). The next stage is to define a reordering procedure for the semi-abstract reduction sequences. This allows us to obtain the "full" abstract reduction sequences.

Note that for $\alpha_{\text{clause}}[\![c_1]\!]$, $\alpha_{\text{goal}}[\![b]\!]$, ... we omit the subscript to instead write $\alpha(c_1)$, $\alpha(b)$, ...

Definition 17 (labelled reductions). Reductions are labelled $s \rightarrow_P{}^q s'$ as follows:

- if $s = \langle l :: G, \theta, D \rangle$, l is $x = t$ and $s' = \langle D' :: G, \theta', D \setminus D' \rangle$ then $s \rightarrow_P{}^{(r(l), D')} s'$;
- if $s = \langle l :: G, \theta, D \rangle$ and l is an atom such that $reduce(l, \theta)$ holds and $s' = \langle b :: G, \theta', D \rangle$ then $s \rightarrow_P{}^{(r(l), b)} s'$;
- if $s = \langle l :: G, \theta, D \rangle$ and l is an atom such that $reduce(l, \theta)$ fails then $s \rightarrow_P{}^{(d(l), \epsilon)} s'$;

Definition 18 (derived selection rule for a sequence of reductions). Given a sequence of reductions $s_1 \rightarrow_P \ldots \rightarrow_P s_n$, the derived selection rule is $q_1, \ldots, q_{n-1}$ where for each $1 \leq i \leq n-1$, $s_i \rightarrow_P{}^{q_i} s_{i+1}$.

Definition 19 (semi-abstract reduction sequences).
Suppose $s_1 \to_P \ldots \to_P s_n$ is a sequence of reductions with the derived selection rule $q_1, \ldots q_{n-1}$. Then the semi-abstract sequence of reductions $s'_1 \Rightarrow_{P^\sharp} \ldots \Rightarrow_{P^\sharp} s'_n$ is defined such that $s'_1 = \langle \alpha(G_1), true, \epsilon \rangle$, and for each $1 \le i \le n-1$, letting $s_i = \langle \alpha(G_i), \phi^\sharp_i, \alpha(D_i) \rangle$ then
$s_{i+1} = \langle \alpha(G_{i+1}), \phi^\sharp_{i+1}, \alpha(D_{i+1}) \rangle$ where:

- if $q_i = (r(l), D)$, $\alpha(G_i) = \alpha(l) :: \alpha(G'_i)$ and $\alpha(l) \in Pos_{\text{var(s)}}$ then $\alpha(G_{i+1}) = \alpha(D) :: \alpha(G'_i)$, $\phi^\sharp_{i+1} = \phi^\sharp_i \wedge \alpha(l)$, and $\alpha(D_{i+1}) = \alpha(D_i) \setminus \alpha(D)$;

- if $q_i = (r(l), \boldsymbol{b})$, $\alpha(G_i) = \alpha(l) :: \alpha(G'_i)$, $\alpha(l)$ is $p(\boldsymbol{x})$ and $p(\boldsymbol{y}) \leftarrow (\phi^\sharp_r \to \phi^\sharp_s), \alpha(\boldsymbol{b}) \ll_s P^\sharp$ then $\alpha(G_{i+1}) = \alpha(\boldsymbol{b}) :: \alpha(G'_i)$, $\phi^\sharp_{i+1} = \phi^\sharp \wedge \varphi^{\sharp'} \wedge (\phi^\sharp_r \to \phi^\sharp_s)$ and $\alpha(D_{i+1}) = \alpha(D_i)$ where $\varphi^{\sharp'} = \alpha_{\text{var}(p(\boldsymbol{x})=p(\boldsymbol{x}'))}(mgu(\{p(\boldsymbol{x}) = p(\boldsymbol{x}')\}))$, $\phi^\sharp_r = \bigvee_{reduce^\sharp(p(\boldsymbol{x}'), \phi^\sharp)} \phi^\sharp$, $\phi^\sharp_s = \alpha^\sharp_{\text{var}(\boldsymbol{x}'=\boldsymbol{y})}(mgu(\{\boldsymbol{x}' = \boldsymbol{y}\}))$, and also var(s_i), var($\boldsymbol{x}'$) and var($p(\boldsymbol{y}) \leftarrow \boldsymbol{b}$) are all distinct from each other.

- if $q_i = (d(l), \epsilon)$, $\alpha(G_i) = \alpha(l) :: \alpha(G'_i)$ and $\alpha(l)$ is $p(\boldsymbol{x})$ then $\alpha(G_{i+1}) = \alpha(G'_i)$, $\phi^\sharp_{i+1} = \phi^\sharp_i$ and $\alpha(D_{i+1}) = \alpha(D_i) \cup \{\alpha(l)\}$.

Lemma 1. Let $s_1 \to_P \ldots \to_P s_n$ be a sequence of concrete reductions such that $s_i = \langle G_i, \theta_i, D_i \rangle$ for each $1 \le i \le n$. Then in the sequence of semi-abstract reductions $s'_1 \Rightarrow_P \ldots \Rightarrow_P s'_n$ we have $s'_i = \langle \alpha(G_i), \phi^\sharp_i, \alpha(D_i) \rangle$ and also for every $1 \le i \le n$
$assign_{\text{var}(s_i)}(\theta_i) \models \phi^\sharp_i \upharpoonright \text{var}(s_i)$.

Proof. The proof is by induction on i.

For the base case we have $i = 1$ and $s_1 = \langle G_1, \varepsilon, \epsilon \rangle$, $s'_1 = \langle \alpha(G_1), true, \epsilon \rangle$. But $assign_{\text{var}(s_1)}(\varepsilon) \models true$ and so the result holds.

Next consider the induction step. First suppose that $G_i = l_i :: G'_i$ where l_i is an equation $x = t$. Here we have $s_i = \langle x = t :: G'_i, \theta_i, D_i \rangle \to_P \langle D :: G'_i, \theta', D_i \setminus D \rangle$ where $\theta' \in mgu(\{x = t\} \cup eqn(\theta_i))$. Using the induction hypothesis there is a state $s'_i = \langle \alpha(x = t :: G_i), \phi^\sharp_i, \alpha(D_i) \rangle$ with $assign_{\text{var}(s_i)}(\theta_i) \models \phi^\sharp_i \upharpoonright \text{var}(s_i)$. Now $s'_i \Rightarrow_{P^\sharp} \langle \alpha(D :: G_i), \phi^\sharp_i \wedge \alpha(l_i), \alpha(D_i) \setminus \alpha(D) \rangle$, and also we have $\alpha(l_i) = \alpha_{\text{var}(x=t)}(mgu(\{x = t\}))$. But

$$mgu(\{x = t\}) \subseteq \gamma_{\text{var}(x=t)}(\alpha_{\text{var}(x=t)}(mgu(\{x = t\})))$$

and so for $\varphi \in mgu(\{x = t\})$ we get $assign_{\text{var}(x=t)}(\varphi) \models \alpha_{\text{var}(x=t)}(mgu(\{x = t\}))$. Now var(s_i) = var(s_{i+1}), and so it follows that for $\theta' \in mgu(\{x = t\} \cup eqn(\theta_i))$ we get $assign_{\text{var}(s_{i+1})}(\theta') \models \phi^\sharp_i \wedge \alpha_{\text{var}(x=t)}(mgu(\{x = t\})) \upharpoonright \text{var}(s_i)$, as required. (This last step corresponds to the safety of abstract unification for the *Pos* domain. See, e.g. [7] for details).

Next suppose that l_i is an atom $p(\boldsymbol{x})$ and l_i suspends, i.e. $s_i = \langle l_i :: G'_i, \theta_i, D_i \rangle \to_{P^\sharp} s_{i+1} = \langle G'_i, \theta_i, D_i \cup \{l_i\} \rangle$. By the induction hypothesis, $s'_i = \langle \alpha(l_i :: G_i), \phi^\sharp_i, \alpha(D_i) \rangle$ with $assign_{\text{var}(s_i)}(\theta_i) \models \phi^\sharp_i \upharpoonright \text{var}(s_i)$. But $s'_i \Rightarrow_{P^\sharp} \langle \alpha(G_i), \phi^\sharp_i, \alpha(D_i) \cup \{\alpha(l_i)\} \rangle$, and since var(s_i) = var(s_{i+1}) the result follows.

Finally, suppose that l_i is an atom $p(\boldsymbol{x})$ and reduces, i.e. $s_i = \langle l_i :: G_i', \theta_i, D_i \rangle$ $\rightarrow_{P^\sharp} \langle \boldsymbol{b} :: G_i', \theta', D_i \rangle$ where $\theta' \in \text{mgu}(\{\text{h} = 1\} \cup \text{eqn}(\theta_i))$, $h = p(\boldsymbol{y})$ and $p(\boldsymbol{y}) \leftarrow \boldsymbol{b} \ll_s P^\sharp$. Now $s_i' \Rightarrow_{P^\sharp} \langle \alpha(\boldsymbol{b} :: G_i'), \phi_i^\sharp \wedge \varphi^\sharp \wedge (\phi_r^\sharp \rightarrow \phi_s^\sharp), \alpha(D_i) \rangle$, where $\varphi^\sharp = \alpha_{\text{var}(p(\boldsymbol{x}) = p(\boldsymbol{x}'))}(mgu(\{p(\boldsymbol{x}) = p(\boldsymbol{x}')\}))$ and $\phi_r^\sharp = \bigvee_{reduce^\sharp(p(\boldsymbol{x}'), \phi^\sharp)} \phi^\sharp$ and $\phi_s^\sharp = \alpha_{\text{var}(\boldsymbol{x}' = \boldsymbol{y})}^\sharp(mgu(\{\boldsymbol{x}' = \boldsymbol{y}\}))$, and also $\text{var}(\boldsymbol{x}')$, $\text{var}(s_i')$ and $\text{var}(p(\boldsymbol{y}) \leftarrow \boldsymbol{b})$ are all distinct variables. We have $assign_{\text{var}(s_i)}(\theta_i) \models \phi_i^\sharp$ by the induction hypothesis. Can show that $\text{mgu}(\{\text{h} = 1\}) \subseteq \gamma_{\text{var}(s_i)}((\varphi^\sharp \wedge \phi_s^\sharp) \upharpoonright \text{var}(s_i))$ and hence $assign_{\text{var}(s_i)}(\psi) \models (\varphi^\sharp \wedge \phi_s^\sharp) \upharpoonright \text{var}(s_i)$ for $\psi \in \text{mgu}(\{\text{h} = 1\})$. Hence from the induction hypothesis, $assign_{\text{var}(s_i)}(\theta') \models (\phi_i^\sharp \wedge \varphi^\sharp \wedge \phi_s^\sharp) \upharpoonright \text{var}(s_i)$ since $\theta' \in \text{mgu}(\{\text{h} = 1\}) \cup \text{eqn}(\theta_i))$. Noting that $a \rightarrow b \equiv \neg a \vee b$, it follows that $assign_{\text{var}(s_i)}(\theta') \models (\phi_i^\sharp \wedge \varphi^\sharp \wedge (\phi_r^\sharp \rightarrow \phi_s^\sharp)) \upharpoonright \text{var}(s_i)$ as required.

Definition 20 (reawoken goals). *Suppose* $s_1 \rightarrow_{P^\sharp} \ldots \rightarrow_{P^\sharp} s_n$ *is a sequence of semi-abstract reductions with selection rule* $q_1, \ldots, q_{n-1}$. *An atom* a *is reawoken if there exists* $1 \leq i < j \leq n$ *such that* $q_i = (d(a), \epsilon)$ *and* $q_j = (r(a), A)$ *for some* A.

Lemma 2. *Let* $s = \langle G :: G', \phi^\sharp, D \rangle$ *be an abstract state. Then there is a sequence of abstract reductions such that* $s \rightarrow_{P^\sharp} \ldots \rightarrow_{P^\sharp} s' = \langle G', \phi^{\sharp'}, D \rangle$ *for some* $\phi^{\sharp'}$.

Proof. Follows easily since every abstract atom $p(\boldsymbol{x})$ has a rule $p(\boldsymbol{x}) \leftarrow \phi_b^\sharp$ defining it.

Definition 21 (procedure for reordering reductions).

Let $s_1 \Rightarrow_{P^\sharp} \ldots \Rightarrow_{P^\sharp} s_n$ *be a sequence of semi-abstract reductions labelled by* $q_1, \ldots, q_{n-1}$, *and suppose there are* m *reawoken goals. The procedure* $R(m)$ *is defined inductively according to the number of reawoken goals* m *as follows:*

- *If there are no reawoken goals then the sequence remains the same.*
- *If there are* $m + 1$ *reawoken goals then suppose the procedure* $R(m)$ *for* m *reawoken goals is already defined. Let* $s_j = \langle l :: G, \phi^\sharp, D \rangle$ *be the state such that* $q_j = (r(l), A)$ *where* l *is the last reawoken goal in* $s_1 \Rightarrow_{P^\sharp} \ldots \Rightarrow_{P^\sharp} s_n$, *and suppose* $\exists j_0 \leq n$ *such that* $s_j \Rightarrow_{P^\sharp} \ldots \Rightarrow_{P^\sharp} s_{j_0} = \langle G, \phi^{\sharp'}, D \rangle$. *Let* $q_1^m, \ldots, q_{n_0}^m$ *be the selection rule obtained by applying* $R(m)$ *to* $s_1' \Rightarrow_{P^\sharp} \ldots \Rightarrow_{P^\sharp} s_j'$, *where the selection rule giving this sequence is the same as* $q_1, \ldots, q_{n-1}$ *except that it does not reawake* l. *Letting* $q_k^m = (d(l), \epsilon)$, *replace the selection rule* $q_1^m, \ldots, q_{n_0}^m$ *with the new selection rule*

$$q_1^m, \ldots, q_{k-1}^m, q_j, \ldots, q_{j_0-1}, q_{k+1}^m, \ldots, q_{n_0}^m, q_{j_0}, \ldots, q_{n-1}.$$

- *For the case above suppose there is no* $j_0 \leq n$ *such that* $s_j \Rightarrow_{P^\sharp} \ldots \Rightarrow_{P^\sharp} s_{j_0} = \langle G, \phi^{\sharp'}, D' \rangle$. *As above, let* $q_1^m, \ldots, q_{n_0}^m$ *be the selection rule obtained by applying* $P(m)$ *to* $s_1' \Rightarrow_{P^\sharp} \ldots \Rightarrow_{P^\sharp} s_j'$. *Let* $s_n \rightarrow_{P^\sharp} \ldots \rightarrow_{P^\sharp} s_{j_1+1}$ *be a sequence of* reductions (obtained using the α_{bot} clauses) such that $s_{j_1+1} = \langle G, \phi^{\sharp\prime}, D'\rangle$, and also let $q_n, \ldots, q_{j_1}$ be the derived selection rule for this sequence. Letting $q_k^m = (d(l), \epsilon)$, replace the selection rule $q_1^m, \ldots, q_{n_0}^m$ with the new selection rule

$$q_1^m, \ldots, q_{k-1}^m, q_j, \ldots, q_{j_1}, q_{k+1}^m, \ldots, q_{n_0}^m.$$

Proposition 3. The process above terminates with the new selection rule containing no reawoken goals.

Definition 22. Let $s_1 \to_P \ldots \to_P s_n$ be a sequence of concrete reductions with $s_n = \langle l_n :: G_n, \theta_n, D_n \rangle$. Also suppose there is a state $s_i = \langle l_i :: G_i, \theta_i, D_i \rangle$ such that $s_i \to_P \langle \boldsymbol{b} :: G', \theta', D' \rangle$ and $l_n \in \boldsymbol{b}$. Then for any literal l, l is a parent atom of l_n if either $l = l_i$ or l is a parent atom of l_i.

Definition 23. Let $s_1 \to_P \ldots \to_P s_n$ be a sequence of concrete reductions with $s_n = \langle l_n :: G_n, \theta_n, D_n \rangle$. Then s_n is in a reawoken part of $s_1 \to_P \ldots \to_P s_n$ iff l_n has a parent atom which is reawoken. Otherwise we say that s_n is in a non-reawoken part of $s_1 \to_P \ldots \to_P s_n$.

Lemma 3. Suppose $\phi^{\sharp}$ is a monotonic formula. Then $assign_V(\theta) \models \phi^{\sharp} \Rightarrow \theta \in \gamma_V(\phi^{\sharp})$.

Proof. In [7] it is shown that $assign_V(\theta) \models \phi^{\sharp} \Rightarrow assign_V(\theta') \models \phi^{\sharp}$ for all $\theta' \leq \theta$ when $\phi^{\sharp}$ is monotonic. Hence result follows from the definition of $\gamma_V(\phi^{\sharp})$.

Lemma 4. Let $s_1 \to_P \ldots \to_P s_n$ be a sequence of concrete reductions with m reawoken goals, and suppose that $s_i = \langle l_i :: G_i, \theta_i, D_i \rangle$ is a state in a non-reawoken part. Then there is a state $s'_{i_0} = \langle \alpha(l_i) :: G'_i, \phi^{\sharp}_{i_0}, D'_{i_0} \rangle$ in the sequence of semi-abstract reductions $s'_1 \Rightarrow_{P^{\sharp}} \ldots \Rightarrow_{P^{\sharp}} s'_{n_0}$ given by $R(m)$, $assign_{\mathrm{var}(l_i)}(\theta_i) \models relax_{\mathrm{var}(l_i)}(\phi^{\sharp}_{i_0})$.

Proof. By lemma 1 there is a semi-abstract sequence of reductions with the same selection rule as the concrete sequence of reductions and also with $assign_{\mathrm{var}(s_i)}(\theta_i) \models \phi^{\sharp}_i \restriction \mathrm{var}(s_i)$ for each i. By induction on the number of reawoken goals m, we show that $assign_{\mathrm{var}(s_i)}(\theta_i) \models \phi^{\sharp}_{i_0} \restriction \mathrm{var}(s_i)$ in the semi-abstract sequence given by $R(m)$. Since $\phi^{\sharp}_{i_0} \restriction \mathrm{var}(s_i) \models relax_{\mathrm{var}(l_i)}(\phi^{\sharp}_{i_0})$, the result then follows.

If the are no reawoken goals then the semi-abstract sequence remains unchanged and so the result holds.

Suppose there are $m+1$ reawoken goals. Let $s_j = \langle l :: G, \phi^{\sharp}, D \rangle$ be the state such that $q_j = (r(l), A)$ where l is the last reawoken goal in $s_1 \Rightarrow_{P^{\sharp}} \ldots \Rightarrow_{P^{\sharp}} s_n$, and suppose $\exists j_0 \leq n$ such that $s_j \Rightarrow_{P^{\sharp}} \ldots \Rightarrow_{P^{\sharp}} s_{j_0} = \langle G, \phi^{\sharp\prime}, D' \rangle$. Let $q_1^m, \ldots, q_{n_0}^m$ be the selection rule obtained by applying $R(m)$ to $s'_1 \Rightarrow_{P^{\sharp}} \ldots \Rightarrow_{P^{\sharp}} s'_j$. Letting $q_k^m = (d(l), \epsilon)$, the new selection rule is $q_1^m, \ldots, q_{k-1}^m, q_j, \ldots, q_{j_0-1}, q_{k+1}^m, \ldots, q_{n_0}^m, q_{j_0}, \ldots, q_{n-1}$. Let s_i be a concrete state in a non-reawoken part. First suppose $i \leq j$. By the induction hypothesis there is a corresponding state $s'_{i_0} = \langle \alpha(l_i) ::$

$G', \phi^{\sharp}_{i_0}, D'\rangle$ in the semi-abstract sequence of reductions $s^m_1 \Rightarrow_{P^{\sharp}} \ldots \Rightarrow_{P^{\sharp}} s^m_{n_0}$ given by $R(m)$ with $assign_{var(s_i)}(\theta_i) \models \phi^{\sharp}_{i_0}$. Consider the selection rule given by $R(m+1)$. For every $1 \le i' \le k$, we have $s^{m+1}_{i'} = s^m_{i'}$. Hence the result holds for this case by the induction hypothesis. Let $l = p(\boldsymbol{x})$. We have

$$s^{m+1}_k = \langle \alpha(l) :: G', \phi^{\sharp}_k, D'\rangle \Rightarrow_{P^{\sharp}} \ldots \Rightarrow_{P^{\sharp}}$$

$$s^{m+1}_{k+j_0-j} = \langle G', \phi^{\sharp}_k \wedge \varphi^{\sharp'} \wedge (\phi^{\sharp}_r \to \phi^{\sharp}_s) \wedge \phi^{\sharp}_b, D''\rangle$$

for some $\phi^{\sharp}_b$, where $\varphi^{\sharp} = \alpha_{var(p(\boldsymbol{x})=p(\boldsymbol{x}'))}(mgu(\{p(\boldsymbol{x}) = p(\boldsymbol{x}')\}))$ and $\phi^{\sharp}_r = \bigvee_{reduce^{\sharp}(p(\boldsymbol{x}'),\phi^{\sharp})} \phi^{\sharp}$ and $\phi^{\sharp}_s = \alpha_{var(\boldsymbol{x}'=\boldsymbol{y})}(mgu(\{\boldsymbol{x}' = \boldsymbol{y}\}))$, and also $var(\boldsymbol{x}')$, $var(s'_j)$ and $var(p(\boldsymbol{y}) \leftarrow \boldsymbol{b})$ are all distinct variables. It follows that for all $k < i' \le i$ we have

$$s^{m+1}_{i'+j_0-j} = \langle l_{i'} :: G_{i'}, \phi^{\sharp}_{i'} \wedge \varphi^{\sharp'} \wedge (\phi^{\sharp}_r \to \phi^{\sharp}_s) \wedge \phi^{\sharp}_b, D_{i'}\rangle$$

where $s^m_{i'} = \langle l_{i'} :: G_{i'}, \phi^{\sharp}_{i'}, D'_{i'}\rangle$ for some $D'_{i'}$. Now for every concrete state s_i in a non-reawoken part, $reduce(l_i, \theta_i)$ fails. Hence it is sufficient to show that

$$assign_{var(s_i)}(\theta_i) \models \phi^{\sharp} \Rightarrow assign_{var(s_i)}(\theta_i) \models \phi^{\sharp} \wedge \varphi^{\sharp'} \wedge (\phi^{\sharp}_r \to \phi^{\sharp}_s) \wedge \phi^{\sharp}_b$$

whenever $reduce(l_i, \theta_i)$ fails.

Let $\varphi^{\sharp}_r = \bigvee_{reduce^{\sharp}(p(\boldsymbol{x}),\phi^{\sharp})} \phi^{\sharp}$, and suppose that $assign_{var(s_i)}(\theta_i) \models \varphi^{\sharp}_r$. Then $assign_{var(l_i)}(\theta_i) \models \varphi^{\sharp}_r$ also. Since $\varphi^{\sharp}_r$ is monotonic, we get $\theta_i \in \gamma_{var(l_i)}(\phi^{\sharp})$. But $reduce^{\sharp}(l_i, \varphi^{\sharp}_r)$ holds and so we must have $reduce(l_i, \theta_i)$ holds. This is a contradiction, and so we cannot have $assign_{var(s_i)}(\theta_i) \models \varphi^{\sharp}_r$. Since $var(\varphi^{\sharp}_r) \subseteq var(s_i)$ it follows that $assign_{var(s_i)}(\theta_i) \models \neg\varphi^{\sharp}_r$. Hence we also get $assign_{var(s_i)}(\theta_i) \models (\neg\phi^{\sharp}_r \wedge \varphi^{\sharp}) \restriction var(s_i)$. Therefore we have $assign_{var(s_i)}(\theta_i) \models (\phi^{\sharp} \wedge \neg\phi^{\sharp}_r \wedge \varphi^{\sharp}) \restriction var(s_i)$. Now since $var(\phi^{\sharp}_b)$ are distinct from both $var(s_i)$ and $var(\varphi^{\sharp})$, it also follows that $assign_{var(s_i)}(\theta_i) \models (\phi^{\sharp} \wedge \neg\phi^{\sharp}_r \wedge \varphi^{\sharp} \wedge \phi^{\sharp}_b) \restriction var(s_i)$. Hence noting that $a \to b \equiv \neg a \vee b$, we obtain $assign_{var(s_i)}(\theta_i) \models (\phi^{\sharp} \wedge (\phi^{\sharp}_r \to \phi^{\sharp}_s) \wedge \varphi^{\sharp} \wedge \phi^{\sharp}_b) \restriction var(s_i)$ as required.

Next suppose that $i > j$. Since s_i is in a non-reawoken part we must have $i > j_0$. Consider the corresponding state $s^{m+1}_{i_1}$ for s_i in the sequence of reductions given by $R(m+1)$, i.e. the state with $q^{m+1}_{i_1} = q(i)$. The goals reduced in the sequence $s^{m+1}_1 \Rightarrow_{P^{\sharp}} \ldots \Rightarrow_{P^{\sharp}} s^{m+1}_{i_1}$ will be the same as those reduced in the semi-abstract sequence of reductions with the selection rule $q_1, \ldots, q_{n-1}$. Hence this corresponding state will be the same as the corresponding state in the semi-abstract sequence of reductions with the same selection rule as the concrete sequence of reductions. Hence the result follows from lemma 1.

For the third case (of definition 21), the proof follows similarly to the above.

Lemma 5. Let $s_1 \to_P \ldots \to_P s_n$ be a sequence of concrete reductions such that $s_n = \langle l :: G, \theta, D\rangle$ with s_n in a non-reawoken part. Then there is a sequence of abstract reductions $s'_1 \to_{P^{\sharp}} \ldots \to_{P^{\sharp}} s'_m$ such that $s'_m = \langle \alpha(l) :: G', \phi^{\sharp}\rangle$ and $assign_{var(l)}(\theta) \models relax_{var(l)}(\phi^{\sharp})$.

Proof. Suppose $l' \in D$. Hence for all $1 \le i \le n$, $reduce(l', \theta_i)$ fails where $s_i = \langle G_i, \theta_i, D_i\rangle$. Let s_j be the state such that $q_j = (d(l'), \epsilon)$. In the semi-abstract sequence of reductions obtained using lemma 4 replace q_j with q'_j, q''_j where $q'_j = (r(l'), \phi^\sharp_b)$ (where $l' \leftarrow \phi^\sharp_b \ll_s P^\sharp$), and $q''_j = (r(\phi^\sharp_b), \epsilon)$. We can now show that $assign_{\text{var}(1)}(\theta) \models relax_{\text{var}(1)}(\phi^\sharp)$ with the new semi-abstract sequence of reductions using a similar argument to that found in the proof of lemma 4. Repeating this process, we end up with a semi-abstract sequence of reductions without any atoms being delayed. This is equivalent to having a sequence of "full" abstract reductions.

Lemma 6. Let $s_1 \rightarrow_P \ldots \rightarrow_P s_n$ be a sequence of concrete reductions such that $s_n = \langle l :: G, \theta, D \rangle$ where s_n is in a reawoken part. Then there is a sequence of semi-abstract reductions $s'_1 \rightarrow_{P^\sharp} \ldots \rightarrow_{P^\sharp} s'_m$ such that $s'_m = \langle \alpha(l) :: G', \phi^\sharp \rangle$ and $assign_{\text{var}(1)}(\theta) \models relax_{\text{var}(1)}(\phi^\sharp)$.

The proof (omitted here) essentially involves defining a procedure giving a reordering of the concrete sequence of reductions similar to that given by the procedure $R(m)$ for the semi-abstract reduction sequences. This allows us to obtain a new concrete substitution θ' such that θ is an instance of θ' and $assign_{\text{var}(1)}(\theta') \models \phi^\sharp$. Given this, it then follows that $assign_{\text{var}(1)}(\theta) \models relax_{\text{var}(1)}(\phi^\sharp)$ as required.

Theorem 2 (Safety). If $P^\sharp = \alpha[\![P]\!]$, and $G^\sharp = \alpha_{\text{goal}}[\![G]\!]$ then

$$\text{call}(P_G) \leq \gamma(relax(\text{call}(P^\sharp_{G^\sharp})))$$

Proof. If $\langle l, \theta \upharpoonright \text{var}(1) \rangle \in \gamma(relax(\text{call}(P^\sharp_{G^\sharp})))$ then exists $\langle \alpha(l), \phi^\sharp \upharpoonright \text{var}(1) \rangle \in \text{call}(P^\sharp_{G^\sharp})$ such that $\theta \in \gamma_{\text{var}(1)}(relax_{\text{var}(1)}(\phi^\sharp))$. Since $relax_{\text{var}(1)}(\phi^\sharp)$ is monotonic this is equivalent to having $assign_{\text{var}(1)}(\theta) \models relax_{\text{var}(1)}(\phi^\sharp)$. Hence the result follows from lemmas 4 and 6.

Constraint-Based Partial Evaluation of Rewriting-Based Functional Logic Programs

L. Lafave and J.P. Gallagher

Department of Computer Science, University of Bristol, Bristol BS8 1UB, U.K.
{lafave, john}@cs.bris.ac.uk

Abstract. The aim of this work is to describe a procedure for the partial evaluation of functional logic programs in rewriting-based languages using constraint-based information propagation. The constraint-based partial evaluation algorithm incorporated with local and global control describes a KMP partial evaluator. Results from the implementation of the partial evaluator in the functional logic language Escher show that the algorithm is also able to perform intermediate list elimination. Renaming operations and termination and correctness properties are presented. Finally, extensions of the constraint-based procedure which may lead to greater specialisation are discussed.

1 Introduction

Partial evaluation is a program transformation technique which optimises programs by performing some of the computation at compile-time. A partial evaluator, given a program and some of the input to that program, will generate a *residual program*, which is the original program specialised with respect to that partial input. Given the rest of the input data, the residual program computes the same answers as the original program run with the entire set of input data.

The algorithm described in this work transforms rewriting-based functional logic programs by partial evaluation. An example of a such a language is the Escher language [Llo95]. Generally, in these functional logic languages, terms are rewritten by matching a term to an instance of a statement in the program. In Escher, the concept of substitution is not defined. This differs from narrowing-based functional logic languages, in which unification propagates answers to a term, computing answer substitutions for variables in the term.

This partial evaluation procedure uses constraint-based information propagation to improve the specialisation of the transformation. There are several different methods for propagating information during program specialisation. Table 1, from [GS96], shows the effect of transforming a conditional statement in each case.

Traditional partial evaluation of functional programs [JGS93] uses constant propagation; this was shown to be less powerful than partial evaluation in logic programming (called partial deduction [LS91]), which is a unification-based program transformer [SGJ94]. Positive supercompilation has adopted the

Norbert E. Fuchs (Ed.): LOPSTR'97, LNCS 1463, pp. 168–188, 1998.

$T[\![$ if $u = v$ then t else $s]\!] =$	information propagation
(a) if $u = v$ then $T[\![t]\!]$ else $T[\![s]\!]$	constant propagation
(b) if $u = v$ then $T[\![t\{u := v\}]\!]$ else $T[\![s]\!]$	unification-based
(c) if $u = v$ then $T[\![t\{u = v\}]\!]$ else $T[\![s\{u \neq v\}]\!]$	constraint-based

Table 1. The types of information propagation, from Glück and Sørensen, LNCS 1110.

unification-based information propagation procedure for the partial evaluation of functional programs [SGJ96, GS96]. The technique resembles that of partial deduction [GS94]: a partial process tree is generated using driving and generalisation from which a program is extracted. In addition, the partial evaluation of narrowing-based functional logic programs also uses unification-based propagation [AFV96, AFJV97].

Both positive supercompilation and partial deduction pass the KMP test, which checks that the residual program generated from a naive pattern matcher has the efficiency of a Knuth-Morris-Pratt pattern matcher. However, the pattern matching programs generated using unification-based partial evaluation usually contain one or more unnecessary tests in the residual program; this is due to the lack of negative information in the transformation. Program transformation techniques that do propagate negative information during program specialisation include Turchin's perfect supercompilation [GK93] and Futamura's generalized partial computation [FN88]. Furthermore, the partial deduction procedure of [LS95, LS97] uses negative (binding) constraints, a subset of CLP($\mathcal{FT}$), in order to improve precision of the specialisation.

Constraint solving involves a group of well-established algorithms for determining whether a set of constraints is satisfiable. Constraint solvers have been developed for various constraint domains, including linear, non-linear, Boolean, and Herbrand domains. We use the generality of constraint solving to propagate information from tests in conditional statements; this is not only limited to equality/disequality tests, but tests that can be represented as constraints in the domain(s) employed in the partial evaluator. Therefore, the partial evaluation procedure may be more precise, approaching levels of specialisation obtained by generalized partial computation without a general automated theorem prover.

In this work, an algorithm for the partial evaluation of Escher programs will be presented which incorporates constraint-based information propagation. Local control is achieved by imposing an ordering on terms in Escher computations and the global control is an extension of recent work in generalisation of partial deduction and positive supercompilation [SG95, LS95]. We will show that the implemented partial evaluator passes the KMP test and removes all unnecessary tests. We present the correctness results for the procedure, and compare the technique to other program transformation techniques. Finally, we discuss possible extensions to the procedure.

2   The Language

The syntax of the rewriting-based functional logic language used in this paper will be that described in [Llo95]. This choice of syntax should not restrict this algorithm to the partial evaluation of Escher programs. Any (higher-order) functional logic language using a similar computational model will be able to be transformed using this procedure.

The function ITE(c, t, e) will be used in this paper as shorthand notation for the conditional statement IF c THEN t ELSE e. The quantifiers in the syntax are of the form Q[x_1,...x_n] T, where Q is either SOME, ALL, or LAMBDA, and the list of variables [x_1,...x_n] are bound in T. A program is a set of rewrite rules, in the form of statements $H \Rightarrow B$, where the term H is the head of the statement, and the term B is the body. Given a set of equations, $\mathbf{A}$, $rhs(\mathbf{A})$ is the set of terms in the bodies of the equations: $rhs(\mathbf{A}) = \{R_j \mid L_j \Rightarrow R_j \in \mathbf{A}\}$. The free variables of a term T is $\mathcal{FV}(T)$. The *definition* Def_P^G of a k-ary function G in a program P is the set of statements in P with head $G(t_1,\ldots,t_k)$. For a program P, a term T is a *standard term* if $T = F(s_1,\ldots,s_n)$ and F is an n-ary user-defined function, i.e. $\exists \mathrm{Def}_P^F$. Let $\mathcal{S}_P(T)$ be the set containing all the standard subterms of T (may contain T if it is a standard term) wrt to the program P. We will use ϵ in this paper to denote the empty term.

Rewriting of a term T is performed by matching the head of an instance of a statement[1] with a redex of T. Formally, a term S is obtained from a term T_j by a *computation step* if the following are satisfied:

1. The set of redexes of T_j, $L_j = \{R_\alpha\}$, is a non-empty set.
2. For each α, the redex $R_\alpha \in L_j$ is identical to the head H_α of some instance $H_\alpha \Rightarrow B_\alpha$ of a statement schema (rule).
3. S is the term obtained from T_j by replacing, for each α, the redex R_α by B_α.

The partial evaluation algorithm described in this paper does not place restrictions on the reduction strategy. We will refrain from specifying a reduction strategy.

A *computation* is a sequence of terms $\{T_i\}_{i=1}^n$ such that T_{i+1} is obtained by a computation step from T_i and T_n contains no rewritable subterms. A *partial computation* does not require the term T_n to be in normal form. We define a shorthand notation for describing the result of a partial computation.

Definition 1. $\Rightarrow^\phi$: *Let $T_1 \Rightarrow^\phi T_n$ represent the equation resulting from the partial computation $\{T_i\}_{i=1}^n$.*

3   The Algorithm

We have designed a constraint-based algorithm for the partial evaluation of functional logic languages based on rewriting. The algorithm combines computations

---

[1] Actually, the statements of an Escher program are statement *schemas*, metaexpressions which represent a collection of the instances of that statement.

together with a "restart step", which either performs unification or splits a term when the term is not instantiated enough for the computation to continue. We start by giving some preliminary definitions.

The following function, $specialise((T, C), P)$, returns a specialised definition for a term T with constraints C wrt a program P.

Definition 2. $specialise((T, C), P)$: *Let T be an arbitrary term, C be a set of constraints, and P be a program. Let $select(T, P) = S$ be a subterm in T. Let F be the outermost function of S. Then, $specialise((T, C), P)$ is the set of adorned equations:*

$$specialise((T, C), P) = \{(T\theta_i \Rightarrow T_j, C\theta_i, S\theta_i) \mid L_i \Rightarrow R_i \in \mathrm{Def}_P^F \ \&$$
$$\theta_i = \lceil S, L_i \rceil \neq fail \ \& \ C\theta_i \text{ is satisfiable} \ \& \ T\theta_i \Rightarrow^\phi T_j\}$$

If $select(T, P)$ is undefined, $specialise((T, C), P) = \emptyset$.

The expression $\lceil a, b \rceil$ denotes the idempotent most general unifier of a and b if it exists; otherwise, it equals *fail*. The function $proj(T, C)$ is a projection of the constraints C onto free variables of the term T.

In the above definition, the function $select(T, P)$ is used to find a standard subterm to restart the partial evaluation; the definition of this function depends on the reduction strategy of the language being specialised. Without choosing a particular reduction strategy, we can define a property that must be satisfied by the *select* function.

Definition 3. Select Property
Given a program P, term T, let $\mathbf{U}$ be the set of standard subterms of T which unify with at least one head of a statement in the program. Then, $S = select(T, P) \in \mathbf{U}$, the subterm of T selected for restarting the computation, contains the first demanded argument of T.

An argument of a function F is *demanded* if there is a non-variable term in that argument position in the head of at least one of the statements in the definition of F in a program P [Han97]. For example, for a simple leftmost outermost reduction strategy, the *select* function may be defined as follows. Given a term T and a program P, $select(T, P) = F(t_1, \ldots, t_n)$ is the leftmost outermost *standard subterm* of T such that there is at least one L_i in Def_P^F such that $\lceil S, L_i \rceil \neq fail$.

Example 1. Consider the following definition of `Inv`, included in program P:

```
Inv(True)  => False.
Inv(False) => True.
```

In order to generate a specialised definition for the term `Inv(Inv(x))` with respect to the above definition, $specialise((\texttt{Inv(Inv(x))}, \emptyset), P)$ is called. Assuming a leftmost outermost reduction rule, the selected subterm of the term is `Inv(x)` (the innermost occurrence of `Inv`). Then, $specialise((\texttt{Inv(Inv(x))}, \emptyset), P)$ is the set of adorned equations:
$\{(\texttt{Inv(Inv(True))} \Rightarrow \texttt{True}, \emptyset, \texttt{Inv(True)}),$
$(\texttt{Inv(Inv(False))} \Rightarrow \texttt{False}, \emptyset, \texttt{Inv(False)})\}$

We combine the notation of [GJMS96] and [MG95] to define m-trees, a data structure for recording computation paths during partial evaluation.

Definition 4. *An* m-tree μ *is a labelled tree where nodes can either be marked or unmarked. A node N is labelled with a tuple of terms (T_N, C_N, S_N), where T_N is the term of the computation, C_N is the set of constraints, and S_N is the term used to restart the computation. For a branch β of the tree, $\mathcal{N}_\beta$ is the set of labels of β and for a leaf L of a tree, β_L is the unique branch containing L.*

The *extend* function adds leaves to the m-tree as they are generated during the partial evaluation. An example of adding leaves to an m-tree via *extend* can be found in Example 3 below.

Definition 5. $extend(\mu, P)$ *Let μ be an m-tree and P a program.*

$extend(\mu, P) = $ *for all unmarked leaf nodes $L \in \mu$:*

> *mark L in μ;*
> $\mathbf{A} = specialise((T_L, C_L), P)$;
> *if $\mathbf{A} \neq \emptyset$,*
> > *for all $(T, C, S) \in \mathbf{A}$(add leaf L' to branch β_L with label $(rhs(T), C, S)$);*
> *otherwise, if $\mathbf{A} = \emptyset$,*
> > $\mathbf{A}' = covered(T_L, C_L)$;
> > *for all $B \in \mathbf{A}'$(add leaf L' to branch β_L with label B);*

That is, if a specialised definition is created for the term, then the different reductions of the term are added to the tree as leaves. In the case where no specialised definition is generated (i.e. there is no available selectable subterm), all standard subterms must be extracted from the term, and a specialised definition must be generated for each. Splitting the term ensures that all of the standard subterms that might be nested in the term are eventually covered in the residual program. We add a minor optimisation to this rule for conditional statements; in the case that the condition is a constraint of one of the domains of the partial evaluator, the satisfiability of the current set of constraints, with the new condition added, is tested. If it is found to be unsatisfiable, we can safely omit the appropriate branch of the conditional statement from the m-tree. Formally, this step is described in the first part of the definition of *covered*.

Definition 6. $covered(T, C)$: *Let T be a term, and C a set of constraints.*

> *if $T = $ IF_THEN_ELSE(c, t, e), and c is a constraint in one of the domains, then $covered(T, C) = $*
> > $\{(t, proj(t, C \cup c), \epsilon)\}$, *if $C \cup \neg c$ is unsatisfiable, or*
> > $\{(e, proj(e, C \cup \neg c), \epsilon)\}$, *if $C \cup c$ is unsatisfiable, or*
> > $\{(t, proj(t, C \cup c)), (e, proj(e, C \cup \neg c), \epsilon)\}$, *otherwise;*
> *else, for $T = F(t_1, \ldots, t_m)$, $covered(T, C) = split(T, C)$.*

Definition 7. split(T, C): *Let* $T = F(t_1, \ldots, t_m)$ *be a term, and* C *a set of constraints. Then,* split$(T, C) = \{(F(y_1, \ldots, y_m), True, \epsilon), (t_1, proj(t_1, C), \epsilon), \ldots,$ $(t_m, proj(t_m, C), \epsilon)\}$ *where* $y_1, \ldots, y_m$ *do not occur in* T.

As an example of the use of the *split* function, in the following example, no selectable subterm can be found, and splitting the term is necessary for the program specialisation to continue. This case typically arises when system (built-in) functions are in the term.

Example 2. Suppose we are specialising the following program wrt `Inv(x & y)`:

```
Inv(True)  => False.
Inv(False) => True.
```

According to the definition of *select*, there are no selectable subterms in `Inv(x & y)`, as the term does not unify with either of the heads of the statements in the definition of `Inv`. However, the definition of `Inv` must be included in the residual program. The solution lies in splitting the term. After adding the terms `Inv(w)` and `x & y` to the m-tree, on the next iteration of the algorithm, *specialise* will return the definition of `Inv`.

The "double append" example (where "append" is called `Concat` here) is popular in the presentation of partial evaluation procedures; it is not only a simple example that will help the discussion of our techniques, it also shows the degree of specialisation available from the program transformation. The repeated use of `Concat` results in an intermediate list being constructed. In some cases, transformation eliminates this intermediate list; deforestation, conjunctive partial deduction, and the partial evaluation of narrowing-based functional logic programs all perform this optimisation.

Example 3. Given the following program P:

```
Concat([], y)      => y.
Concat([h | t], y) => [h | Concat(t, y)].
```

Consider the specialisation of P wrt `Concat(Concat(x, y),z)`. Assume the initial m-tree is a tree with one node, the root node:

$$(\texttt{Concat(Concat(x, y), z)}, True, \epsilon).$$

specialise$((\texttt{Concat(Concat(x, y), z)}, True), P)$ is the non-empty set containing the following elements:

```
(Concat(Concat([], y), z) => Concat(y, z), True, Concat([], y)), and
(Concat(Concat([h | t], y), z) => [h | Concat(Concat(t, y), z)], True,
Concat([h | t], y)).
```

The labels corresponding to these terms are added as children to the m-tree (Figure 1).

Finally, we present the constraint-based partial evaluation algorithm.

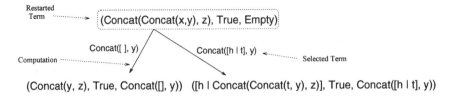

Fig. 1. The m-tree during partial evaluation of double append.

Definition 8. Algorithm Input: *a program* P *and an arbitrary term* T.

Output: *a program* P' *which is the partial evaluation of* P *wrt* T, *and an m-tree of terms* μ.
Initialisation:
$\quad P_0 := P \cup \{Ans(x_1 \ldots x_n) \Rightarrow T\}$, *where* $FV(T) = (x_1 \ldots x_n)$;
$\quad \mu_0 :=$ *the tree containing one node labelled* $(Ans(x_1, \ldots, x_n), True, \epsilon)$;
$\quad i := 0$;
repeat
$\quad \mu_{i+1} = \alpha(extend(\mu_i, P_0))$;
$\quad i = i + 1$;
until $\mu_i = \mu_{i-1}$
return μ_i
$P' := \mathcal{R}_\sigma(\mu_i)$.

The α operator generalises the m-tree; this operator is described in the next section. The $\mathcal{R}_\sigma$ function extracts the program from the m-tree; σ is a renaming function for the m-tree. We discuss extraction and renaming in Section 5.

4   Local and Global Control

Local Control: Termination of $\Rightarrow^\phi$

The operator $\Rightarrow^\phi$ as it is defined is not guaranteed to terminate. However, with the addition of an ordering on terms, we can define $\Rightarrow^\phi$ to ensure finite computations. Ordering the terms of a computation has been used for local control before, for example, in conjunctive partial deduction [GJMS96]. The strict homeomorphic embedding relation, $\trianglelefteq$, is a well-quasi ordering [Leu97]. For two terms S_1 and S_2, $S_1 \prec S_2$ indicates that S_2 is a strict instance of S_1.

Definition 9. *strict homeomorphic embedding*

- *For variables* x, y, $x \trianglelefteq y$.
- *For terms* $S, F(t_1, \ldots, t_n)$, $S \trianglelefteq F(t_1, \ldots, t_n)$ *if* $S \trianglelefteq t_i$ *for some* i.
- *For terms* $F(s_1, \ldots, s_n), F(t_1, \ldots, t_n)$, $F(s_1, \ldots, s_n) \trianglelefteq F(t_1, \ldots, t_n)$ *if* $s_i \trianglelefteq t_i$ *for all* i *and* $F(t_1, \ldots, t_n) \not\prec F(s_1, \ldots, s_n)$.

Definition 10. *Given a partial computation $\{T_i\}_{i=1}^m$, the set of selectable re-dexes, L_m^S, is defined inductively as follows.*

- *For $m = 1$, $L_1^S = L_1$, the set of redexes of T_1.*
- *For $m > 1$, if $\exists R \in L_m, \exists R' \in L_j^S$ such that $R' \unlhd R$ for some $1 \le j < m$, then $L_m^S = \emptyset$; else, $L_m^S = L_m$.*

There are several other methods that can be used for ensuring termination of these computations. In fact, this definition just describes the basic idea of this technique; in some cases, such as if T_i is a tuple of terms, partitioning of the set R based on the position of the redex is necessary to increase precision. A selectable computation step incorporates the selectable redexes into the computation.

Definition 11. *A term S is obtained from a term T_j by a selectable computation step if the following are satisfied:*

1. *The set of selectable redexes of T_j, $L_j^S = \{R_\alpha^S\}$, is a non-empty set.*
2. *For each α, the selectable redex $R_\alpha^S \in L_j^S$ is identical to the head H_α of some instance $H_\alpha \Rightarrow B_\alpha$ of a statement schema.*
3. *S is the term obtained from T_j by replacing, for each α, the selectable redex R_α^S by B_α.*

We can now redefine our $\Rightarrow^\phi$ operator. A selectable computation $\{T\}_{i=1}^n$ is a sequence of terms obtained using the selectable computation steps where $L_n^S = \emptyset$.

Definition 12. $\Rightarrow^\phi$: *Given a selectable computation $\{T\}_{i=1}^n$, $T_1 \Rightarrow^\phi T_n$.*

Proposition 1. *For every term T, the selectable computation of T will be finite.*

By Kruskal's Theorem, this is a finite sequence. Therefore, the computation sequences will be finite.

The local precision of the algorithm may benefit from the use of a refined well-quasi ordering. A version of the homeomorphic embedding relation which imposes a well-quasi ordering on functors is described in [Leu97].

Global Control: The Abstraction Operator, α

In order to guarantee the specialised definitions cover possible future calls to the functions, yet ensuring termination of the partial evaluation procedure, the abstraction operator α of the m-tree of the algorithm occasionally must gener-alise the bodies of the specialised definitions. The abstraction operator removes a leaf L with label (T_L, C_L, S_L) from a tree μ if there exists a label (T, C, S) in $\mathcal{N}_{\beta_L}$, $T \unlhd T_L$ and C_L entails C. The basis for this method has been previously described in [SG95, MG95]. The most specific generalisation $\lfloor T, T_L \rfloor$ guaran-tees termination of this generalisation step, since there exists the well-founded ordering $>$ such that $T, T_L > \lfloor T, T_L \rfloor$.

The definitions of generalisation and msg are included for completeness here; the original definitions can be found in [SG95, GS96].

Definition 13. *A generalisation of T_1 and T_2 is a triple (T, θ_1, θ_2) where θ_1, θ_2 are substitutions and $T\theta_1 = T_1$ and $T\theta_2 = T_2$. A most specific generalisation (msg) of T_1 and T_2 is a generalisation (T, θ_1, θ_2) of T_1 and T_2 such that for every generalisation $(T', \theta_1', \theta_2')$ of T_1 and T_2, T is an instance of T'.*

Now, we can define the α abstraction operator. It has two main functions: folding and generalisation. We use *folding* and *generalisation* nodes [SG95] in the m-tree to indicate where the operations occurred. These nodes are represented using the functions *Fold* and *Gen* for folding and generalisation nodes respectively. It is assumed that these functions are not defined in any program.

Folding occurs when the leaf of a branch is an instance of an ancestor in that branch. The specialised definition generated at the ancestor node is not repeated in the new leaf. We designate this by a dotted line to the earlier node, although, as in [SGJ96], by ignoring these dotted lines, we can still consider the m-tree to be an acyclic graph. The leaf node is replaced with a fold node (using the *Fold* function) and the terms in the substitution become the new leaves of this branch.

Generalisation occurs when the embedding relation is satisfied; this indicates that the term is growing and there is danger of an infinite branch being constructed. Therefore, we impose several conditions that have to be satisfied before generalisation can occur. If all of these conditions are satisfied, an infinite branch of the m-tree is almost guaranteed if partial evaluation is allowed to proceed. Firstly, the selected subterm which was used to restart the computation must embed a selected subterm of an ancestor. Using this check reduces the occurrences of generalising when there is no danger of a growing term. Then, we test if the term of the ancestor node is embedded in the term of the leaf node. We can safely generalise in this case. In the definition below, the operator $\mathcal{W}$ is a widening operator; given two tuples $(T_1, C_1), (T_2, C_2)$ where T is a term and C is a set of constraints, the operator $\mathcal{W}$ computes a widening of C_1 and C_2 [CC77].

Definition 14. $\alpha(\mu)$: *For a m-tree μ containing branch β with added leaf L with label (T_L, C_L, S_L), $\alpha(\mu)$ is:*

- *if there exists $(T_{L'}, C_{L'}, S_{L'}) \in \mathcal{N}_\beta$ on node $L'(\neq L)$ such that $T_{L'}\theta = T_L$, $\theta = \{x_1 = t_1, \ldots, x_m = t_m\}$ and C_L entails $C_{L'}$, then fold the tree as follows. Replace the label of L with $Fold(x_1, \ldots, x_m)$, draw a dashed line to L', and add leaves with labels $(t_1, proj(t_1, C_L), \epsilon), \ldots, (t_m, proj(t_m, C_L), \epsilon)$ to branch β.*
- *if there exists $(T_{L'}, C_{L'}, S_{L'}) \in \mathcal{N}_\beta$ on node $L'(\neq L)$ such that $S_{L'} \trianglelefteq S_L$ and $T_{L'} \trianglelefteq T_L$, then let $\lfloor T_L, T_{L'} \rfloor = (T, \theta_1, \theta_2)$ where $\theta_2 = \{x_1 = t_1, \ldots, x_m = t_m\}$ and generalise the tree in the following manner:*
    if T is not a variable, then:
    * *delete the branch β from after L' to L;*
    * *replace the label of L' with $Gen(x_1, \ldots, x_m)$;*
    * **Lb** $= genLeaves(T, \mathcal{W}((T_{L'}, C_{L'}), (T_L, C_L)), \theta_2)$;
    * *for all $G \in$ **Lb**(add a leaf to branch $\beta_{L'}$ with label G);*

else, if T is a variable:
   * *replace the label of L with $Gen(y_1, \ldots, y_n)$;*
   * $\mathbf{Lb} = \text{split}(T_L, C_L)$;
   * *for all $G \in \mathbf{Lb}(add\ a\ leaf\ to\ branch\ \beta_L\ with\ label\ G)$;*
- μ *otherwise.*

Definition 15. genLeaves(M, C, θ): *Let M be a term, C a set of constraints, and θ a substitution. Let $(M', \{x_1 = t_1, \ldots, x_m = t_m\}) = \text{generalise}(M, \theta)$.*

$$\text{genLeaves}(M, C, \theta) = \{(M', proj(M', C), \epsilon), (t_1, proj(t_1, C), \epsilon), \ldots, (t_m, proj(t_m, C), \epsilon)\}.$$

The *generalise* function, defined below, handles the generalisation of quantified expressions. Because the partial evaluation algorithm depends on computation in the functional logic language, complications can arise as a result of variable elimination. For example, the following is an Escher rule, eliminating bound variable xi in the term:

```
SOME [x1,...,xn] (x & (xi = u) & y)  =>
    SOME [x1,...,xi-1,xi+1,...,xn] (x{xi/u} & y{xi/u})
```

where xi is not free in u, and u is free for xi in x and y. The following is an example of bound variables being replaced by free variables in the msg, and the problems this can cause.

Example 4. Consider the following definition of Split.

```
Split([], x, y) => x = [] & y = [].
Split([h | t], x, y) =>
    (x = [] & y = [h | t]) \/
    (SOME[z](x = [h | z] & Split(t, z, y))).
```

In the partial evaluation of Split([1 | t], x, y), the following terms must be generalised:
SOME[z](x = [1 | z] & Split(t, z, y)), and
SOME[z1](x = [1, h1 | z1] & Split(t1, z1, y))
The msg of these terms is:

SOME[u1](u2 = [u3 | u4] & Split(u5, u1, u7))

The variable u1 remains bound in the msg. However, the bound variables z and z1 of the growing lists in the original terms are now generalised with a free variable u4.

If a value for u1 is computed during a later Escher computation, all occurrences of variable u1 will be eliminated, and the value will be lost. This will cause the computation of an incorrect residual program, since there is no way to propagate this computed value of u1 to u4.

Therefore, the *generalise* function must remove all possibility of variable elimination in subsequent computations during the partial evaluation, so that no computed values are lost. This is accomplished by computing a generalisation which is more general than the msg. In this paper, we elect to rename all bound variables in the msg with new variables. However, depending on the functional logic language, more specific generalisations are possible of these terms in order to achieve the most variable elimination, while preserving the correctness of the partial evaluation.

Definition 16. generalise(M, θ): *Let M be a term and θ a substitution. Assume the variables of M are renamed apart. Let* generalise$(M, \theta) = (M', \theta')$, *where $M' = M$, $\theta' = \theta$. Then, for each subterm in M, S, such that $S = Q[x](T)$, rename $Q[x]$ in M' with $Q[y]$, where y is a variable not occurring in M or M', and add $(y = x)$ to θ'.*

The actions of the generalise operation are shown graphically in Figure 2. In both cases shown in Figure 2, the branch of the original m-tree is deleted up to the ancestor, the label of the ancestor is replaced with one containing the *Gen* function, and the children are added to that leaf.

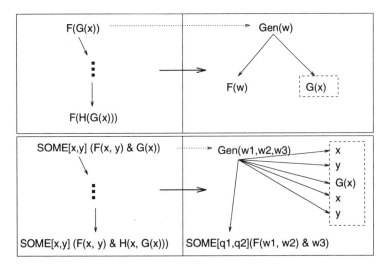

Fig. 2. Representations of the generalisation operations.

The following proposition the termination of this global control technique. Similar propositions have been proved in [Sør, GJMS96, MG95].

Proposition 2. *For all programs P and terms T, the m-tree generated during the partial evaluation of P wrt T is finite. For all leaves in $\alpha(\mu)$, the terms in the leaves either do not embed any of the earlier terms in the tree or are variants of earlier terms.*

5   Extraction and Renaming

The $\mathcal{R}_\sigma$ function extracts the residual program from μ. The function is based on a renaming operator; conditions for the renaming operator in conjunctive partial deduction are adapted for the renaming of terms in the m-tree [LSdW96].

Definition 17. *A renaming function for a given partial evaluation of P wrt T with m-tree μ is a mapping σ which maps from terms in μ to terms such that for any term T in a node of μ:*

- *$\mathcal{FV}(\sigma(T)) \subseteq \mathcal{FV}(T)$*
- *For all T, T' in distinct nodes of $\mu, T \neq T'$, the outermost functions of $\sigma(T)$ and $\sigma(T')$ are different from each other and from any other function in P^2.*

The function $\mathcal{R}_\sigma$ extracts the program from the m-tree by looking at each node and all of its immediate children. For each node that is not a folding or generalisation node, the term is renamed using σ. Examples of the behaviour of $\mathcal{R}_\sigma$ in four cases are shown in Figure 3. The formal definition of $\mathcal{R}_\sigma$ is beyond the scope of this paper.

Example 5. Given the program P and term $T = \text{Concat}(\text{Concat}(x, y), z)$ from Example 3, the following m-tree (Figure 4) is constructed as a result of the partial evaluation of P wrt T. In the m-tree of Figure 4, the constraints have been omitted, since they are all True, and leaves with variable terms have been removed for simplicity.

The following program is extracted from the m-tree (where the residual program has been post-unfolded).

```
FN_SP1([], y, z) => FN_SP2(y, z).
FN_SP1([x_3 | y_4], y, z) =>
    [x_3 | FN_SP1(y_4, y, z)].

FN_SP2([], x_5) => x_5.
FN_SP2([x_5 | y_6], z_7) =>
    [x_5 | FN_SP2(y_6, z_7)].
```

The intermediate list of the original program has been eliminated in the residual program.

6   Specialisation of a Pattern Matcher

We have implemented the partial evaluator for Escher in Gödel, using Escher as the constraint solver by means of constraint handling rules [Frü94] for subsets of finite tree and linear constraint domains. As an example of the performance of the partial evaluator with constraint-based information propagation, we partially

---

[2] In the case of system modules, the new outermost function name must not be in any system module.

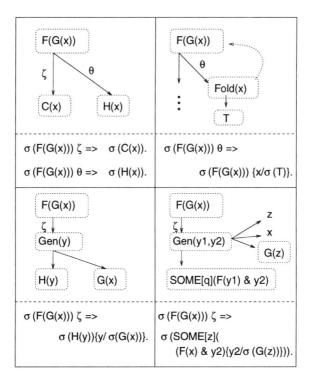

Fig. 3. The extraction of a program from an m-tree.

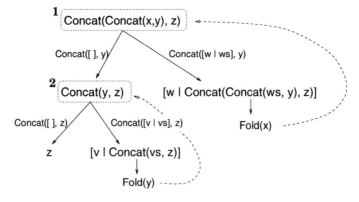

Fig. 4. M-tree from the partial evaluation of double append.

evaluate the naive pattern matching program below, with the aim of generating a KMP-pattern matcher[3] for the string of integers "112".

```
FUNCTION  Match : List(a) * List(a) -> Boolean.
Match(p, s) => Loop(p, s, p, s).

FUNCTION  Loop : List(a) * List(a) * List(a) * List(a) -> Boolean.
MODE      Loop(?, ?, _, _).
Loop([], [], op, os) =>  True.
Loop([], [s | ss], op, os) =>  True.
Loop([p | pp], [], op, os) =>  False.
Loop([p | pp], [s | ss], op, os) =>
    IF   p = s
    THEN Loop(pp, ss, op, os)
    ELSE Next(op, os).

FUNCTION  Next : List(a) * List(a) -> Boolean.
MODE      Next(_, ?).
Next(op, []) =>  False.
Next(op, [s | ss]) =>
    Loop(op, ss, op, ss).
```

With the constraint-based information propagation, partially evaluating the above program with respect to the term Match([1,1,2], u) generated the following statements (types are omitted and post-processing unfolding is assumed). The function names automatically generated by the partial evaluator have been replaced with descriptive identifiers.

```
Match([1, 1, 2], u) =>
    Loop_112(u).
```

```
Loop_112([]) => False.            Loop_12([], s_9) => False.
Loop_112([s_9 | ss_10]) =>        Loop_12([s_16 | ss_17], s_9) =>
    IF s_9 = 1                        IF s_16 = 1
    THEN Loop_12(ss_10, s_9)          THEN Loop_2(ss_17, s_9, s_16)
    ELSE Loop_112(ss_10).             ELSE Loop_112(ss_17).
```

```
Loop_2([], s_9, s_16) => False.
Loop_2([s_24 | ss_25], s_9, s_16) =>
    IF s_24 = 2
    THEN End(ss_25, s_9, s_16, s_24)
    ELSE Loop_12([s_24 | ss_25], s_16).
```

```
End([], s_9, s_16, s_24) => True.
End([s_33 | ss_34], s_9, s_16, s_24) => True.
```

It can be shown that this is a KMP pattern matching program; the specialised pattern matcher never has to go "backwards" to test elements of the list previous

---

[3] The Knuth Morris Pratt pattern matching algorithm runs in time $O(|p| + |s|)$ for a pattern and string, p and s, respectively.

to the one currently being tested. The program transformation has removed some unnecessary tests; for example, in the statement Loop_12, if the test s_16 = 1 fails, the program starts the matching with the next element of the list, since the constraint $s\_16 \neq 1$ is propagated. A section of the m-tree generated during partial evaluation is shown in Figure 5. For the KMP test, the partial evaluator achieves specialisation similar to that obtained by perfect supercompilation and generalized partial computation.

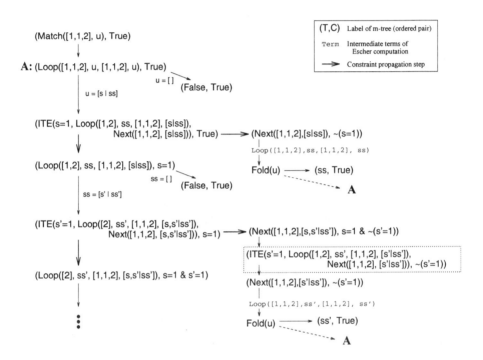

Fig. 5. Section of the m-tree for the specialisation of the naive pattern matching program wrt Match([1,1,2], u). Note the use of negative information propagation at the IF-THEN-ELSE term in the dotted box; this leads to the removal of the unnecessary test in Loop_12, as described in Section 4. The definition of Loop_112 in the residual program is extracted from the node marked "A".

7   Elimination of Intermediate Data Structures

Deforestation is a program transformation for optimising away intermediate data structures [Wad90]. In some cases, our partial evaluation procedure also performs this optimisation. An example of this optimisation is the specialisation of the following program, which uses an intermediate list for the computation of the sum of squares of a sequence of numbers. We partially evaluate the program wrt SumSqUpTo(n).

```
FUNCTION    SumSqUpTo : Integer -> Integer.
SumSqUpTo(n) =>
    Sum(Squares(UpTo(1, n))).

FUNCTION    Sum : Integer -> Integer.
Sum([]) => 0.
Sum([n | ns]) => n +  Sum(ns).

FUNCTION    Sq : Integer -> Integer.
Sq(n) => n * n.

FUNCTION    Squares : List(Integer) -> List(Integer).
Squares([]) => [].
Squares([n | ns]) => [Sq(n) |  Squares(ns)].

FUNCTION    UpTo : Integer -> List(Integer).
UpTo(m, n) =>
    IF    m > n
    THEN []
    ELSE [m | UpTo(m+1, n)].
```

The following program is the result of the partial evaluation. The intermediate lists have been optimised away.

```
SumSqUpTo(n) =>
    IF 1 > n
    THEN 0
    ELSE FN_SP12(1, n).

FN_SP12(x_7, n) =>
    IF (x_7 + 1) > n
    THEN (x_7 * x_7) + 0
    ELSE (x_7 * x_7) + FN_SP12((x_7 + 1), n).
```

Simple post-processing of this program can improve the efficiency by introducing local definitions in the definition of FN_SP12 for the expressions that are repeated (e.g. x_7 * x_7). Similar results have been obtained for the flip example of [Wad90].

In some examples which have been successfully transformed by deforestation, the generalisation operator α is too restrictive to allow the elimination of the intermediate data structures. Growing terms are generalised before the intermediate data structure can be identified. Wadler's Deforestation transformation is only guaranteed to terminate for a class of functional programs called treeless programs. Static analysis can guarantee termination of deforestation for general functional programs. A related static analysis for specialisation of functional logic programs is presented in [CK96].

8   Correctness

In order to prove the correctness of this algorithm, we must first give an amended closedness condition.

Definition 18. subs*(P)*: *Let* **S** *be a finite set of terms, P a program.*
$$subs(\mathbf{S}) = \bigcup\{\mathcal{S}_P(T) \mid T \in \mathbf{P}\}$$

Definition 19. **W**-closed: *Let* **W**, **P** *be finite sets of terms. Then,* **P** *is* **W**-*closed if, for all terms* $T \in subs(\mathbf{P})$, $\exists W \in \mathbf{W}$ *such that* $W\theta = T$.

For a program $P = \{L_1 \Rightarrow R_1, \dots, L_n \Rightarrow R_n\}$, P is **W**-closed if the set of terms of P, $\{L_1, R_1, \dots, L_n, R_n\}$, is **W**-closed. The definition of *translation function* is also adapted from [LSdW96].

Definition 20. *A* translation function *based on a* renaming function σ *is a mapping* ρ_σ *from terms to terms such that for any term S:*

- *if S is an instance of a term in* μ, M, *then* $\rho_\sigma(S) = \sigma(M)\rho_\sigma(\theta)$ *where* $M\theta = S$.
- *if S is not an instance of a term in* μ, *then* $\rho_\sigma(S) = S$.

In the above definition, $\rho_\sigma(\theta)$ is the application of the translation function to all terms in the substitution θ. We state the correctness proposition for our partial evaluation procedure and note the key properties that are needed to establish it.

Proposition 3. *Let P be a program, T a term. Let P' be the partial evaluation of P wrt T with m-tree* μ. *Let* **M** *be the terms of* μ. *Let* $\{T\theta\}$ *be* **M**-*closed. Let* T_n^P, $T_n^{P'}$ *be the results of the computations of* $T\theta$ *and* $\rho_\sigma(T\theta)$ *in P and P', respectively. Then, the following are true.*

- *If* $\mathcal{S}_P(T_n^P) = \emptyset$, T_n^P *is equal to* $T_n^{P'}$ *(modulo variable renaming).*
- *if* $\mathcal{S}_{P'}(T_n^{P'}) = \emptyset$, $T_n^{P'}$ *is equal to* T_n^P *(modulo variable renaming).*

The formal proof has yet to be completed, but the reasoning behind the proposition is based on the correspondence between the computation of $T\theta$ in P, and paths in the graph (m-tree with folds considered). The Select Property is key in stating this soundness result; since the evaluation order is not affected by the partial evaluation, the result is the same in both P and P'. In some cases, when quantified terms are generalised during partial evaluation, the terms of the m-tree will have subterms of the form x = a which are eliminated earlier in the computation of $T\theta$ in P. However, in the computation of $\rho_\sigma(T\theta)$ in P', these extra binding terms are eliminated at equivalent points in the computation. The completeness result is a direct consequence of how the residual program is constructed by our procedure.

9 Discussion

The algorithm for specialisation of a lazy higher-order functional logic language based on rewriting draws on and extends techniques developed in the specialisation of other languages. This is not surprising, considering that the language itself integrates several aspects of different computational models. In this section, we will both compare our technique with existing work, and note the techniques extracted from each.

The global control described in this paper may be viewed as a version of the global control described by Martens and Gallagher in [MG95]. In this work, the m-tree is used for collecting the atoms for which specialised definitions have been constructed, in order to increase the specialisation. Less generalisation is necessary to ensure independence. Similarly, the terms for which we have constructed a specialised definition are stored in the m-tree in this work. The concepts from [MG95] have been extended to allow for nested functions and constraints.

Conjunctive partial deduction [LSdW96], a refinement of partial deduction, allows partial evaluation of logic programs wrt *conjunctions* of literals, (instead of sets of literals). Handling the conjunction of literals allows for greater specialisation, since dependencies between literals are exploited. The results approach those available by unfold/fold transformation, with the advantages of lower complexity and easier control. This transformation procedure can be compared quite closely with the technique described in this paper; the functional counterpart of conjunctions of literals are nested terms, particularly nested terms containing the Boolean function &. In particular, we have adapted the correctness of renaming schemes from conjunctive partial deduction. In addition, an embedding relation ensures finite SLD-trees for the local control in this procedure. In a similar way, we impose an ordering on the redexes of a term in the computations between nodes of the m-tree.

Supercompilation [TNT82, Tur86] and positive supercompilation [SGJ96, GS96] transform functional programs, in the former, a strict first-order language named Refal, in the latter, a simpler lazy first-order functional language[4].

Past work has noted similarities in the information propagation between the unfolding operation in partial deduction and the driving step in positive supercompilation [GS94]. In positive supercompilation, partial process trees are constructed via driving. These trees are comparable to the m-trees in this work; indeed, in [SG95], Glück and Sørensen note that this generalisation algorithm for positive supercompilation can be viewed as an instance of Martens' and Gallagher's technique for the global termination of partial deduction [MG95]. In partial process trees, transient ancestors (terms in the tree that are deterministically unfolded) are not checked in the generalisation of the partial process tree. In our procedure, these terms are elements of the computations in *specialise* and are not added to the m-tree.

We have adapted the *Whistle* function of positive supercompilation for the generalisation of nested functions [GS96]. Changes were necessary to reflect the

---

[4] In later work [GK93], Glück and Klimov present supercompilation of a tail-recursive functional language.

unique problem of handling bound variables during generalisation. Furthermore, in supercompilation, Turchin was restricted only to representing negative binding constraints (bindings that failed) in the environments. As stated earlier, general constraints can represent information beyond bindings of variables, depending on the choice of constraint domains implemented in the partial evaluator. Neither positive supercompilation nor supercompilation have been defined for higher-order functional languages. However, deforestation [Wad90] is able to transform both first-order and higher-order functional programs [Mar96].

Recent work in the partial evaluation of narrowing-based functional-logic programs has been described in [AFV96, AFJV97]. Alpuente et al. describe a partial evaluation procedure for narrowing-based functional logic programs which is based on partial deduction; incomplete narrowing trees are generated for the terms and subterms, and resultants are extracted from these trees.

Clearly, since the narrowing-based and rewriting-based languages share common features, the algorithms also show signs of similarity. Both techniques defined a closedness for the procedure which involves recursively searching the terms for user-defined functions. In our technique, this closedness condition is implicit in the correctness result. In addition, the local control of the partial evaluation for narrowing-based functional logic programs also uses the homeomorphic embedding relation on the selected redexes to identify possibly infinite branches of narrowing trees. Furthermore, a renaming step is described as the second phase of the algorithm in [AFJV97] to guarantee that lazy narrowing can execute a goal in the residual program; this is also necessary in our procedure.

Finally, in the introduction, we presented a comparison of the information propagation techniques of different program transformers. As mentioned earlier, both partial deduction [LS97] and supercompilation [Tur86] have the ability to propagate negative binding constraints. However, our technique allows the constraint handling to represent more complex properties, depending on the constraint domain(s) of the partial evaluator. In this way, we endeavour to obtain the degree of information propagation of generalized partial computation, where an automated theorem prover evaluates general conditions of conditional statements in the program [FN88]. We have not yet been able to obtain the degree of specialisation for the 91-function example as described in [FN88]; it is ongoing research to determine whether this can be obtained by partial evaluation with constraint solving.

10   Conclusions and Further Work

We have presented an algorithm for the partial evaluation of rewriting-based functional logic programs which uses constraint-based information propagation to obtain more precision during specialisation. The algorithm incorporates techniques from the partial evaluation of logic programs with techniques developed for positive supercompilation in order to guarantee termination of the algorithm. The results of the implementation of the algorithm in Escher show that the partial evaluator generates KMP pattern matching programs, thus passing the KMP test. This is the first use of constraint-based partial evaluation for functional logic languages. Future work will include extending the constraint domain to Boolean, Herbrand, linear, and non-linear constraint domains in order to explore the possible increased specialisation for some programs.

Acknowledgements

The first author is supported under a National Science Foundation Graduate Fellowship. The authors would like to thank John Lloyd, Kerstin Eder, and Antony Bowers for many discussions about Escher, and the referees for helpful comments.

References

[AFJV97] M. Alpuente, M. Falschi, P. Julián, and G. Vidal. Specialization of Lazy Functional Logic Programs. In *Partial Evaluation and Semantics-Based Program Manipulation, Amsterdam, The Netherlands, June 1997*, pages 151–162. New York: ACM, 1997.

[AFV96] M. Alpuente, M. Falaschi, and G. Vidal. Narrowing-driven Partial Evaluation of Functional Logic Programs. In H. R. Nielson, editor, *Proc. of European Symp. on Programming Languages, ESOP'96*, pages 45–61. Springer LNCS 1058, 1996.

[CC77] P. Cousot and R. Cousot. Abstract interpretation: A unified lattice model for static analysis of programs by construction or approximation of fixpoints. In *Proceedings of the 4th ACM Symposium on Principles of Programming Languages, Los Angeles*, pages 238–252. 1977.

[CK96] W.-N. Chin and S.-C. Khoo. Better Consumers for Program Specializations. *Journal of Functional and Logic Programming*, (4), 1996.

[FN88] Y. Futamura and K. Nogi. Generalized partial computation. In A.P. Ershov D. Bjørner and N.D. Jones, editors, *Partial Evaluation and Mixed Computation*, page 133. North Holland, 1988.

[Frü94] T. Frühwirth. Constraint Handling Rules. In A. Podelski, editor, *Constraint Programming: Basics and Trends*, volume 910 of *Lecture Notes in Computer Science*, pages 90–107. Springer, 1994.

[GJMS96] R. Glück, J. Jørgensen, B. Martens, and M. H. Sørensen. Controlling conjunctive partial deduction. In H. Kuchen and D. S. Swierstra, editors, *Programming Languages: Implementations, Logics and Programs*, Lecture Notes in Computer Science, pages 137–151. Springer-Verlag, 1996.

[GK93] R. Glück and A. V. Klimov. Occam's razor in metacomputation: the notion of a perfect process tree. In G. Filè P.Cousot, M.Falaschi and A. Rauzy, editors, *Static Analysis. Proceedings*, volume 724 of *Lecture Notes in Computer Science*, pages 112–123. Springer-Verlag, 1993.

[GS94] R. Glück and M. H. Sørensen. Partial deduction and driving are equivalent. In M. Hermenegildo and J. Penjam, editors, *Programming Language Implementation and Logic Programming*, volume 844 of *Lecture Notes in Computer Science*, pages 165–181. Springer-Verlag, 1994.

[GS96] R. Glück and M.H. Sørensen. A Roadmap to Metacomputation by Supercompilation. In O. Danvy, R. Glück, and P. Thiemann, editors, *Partial Evaluation*, volume 1110 of *LNCS*, Dagstuhl Castle, Germany, 1996. Springer.

[Han97]   M. Hanus. A unified computation model for functional and logic programming. In *Proc. 24st ACM Symposium on Principles of Programming Languages (POPL'97)*, pages 80–93, 1997.

[JGS93]   N. D. Jones, C. Gomard, and P. Sestoft. *Partial Evaluation and Automatic Program Generation*. Prentice Hall International, International Series in Computer Science, June 1993. Series editor C. A. R. Hoare.

[Leu97]   M. Leuschel. Extending Homeomorphic Embedding in the Contex of Logic Programming. Technical Report CW 252, Department of Computer Science, Katholieke Universiteit Leuven, June 1997 1997.

[Llo95]   J.W. Lloyd. Declarative Programming in Escher. Technical Report CSTR-95-013, Department of Computer Science, University of Bristol, June 1995.

[LS91]   J. W. Lloyd and J. C. Shepherdson. Partial Evaluation in Logic Programming. *Journal of Logic Programming*, 11(3&4):217–242, October 1991.

[LS95]   M. Leuschel and D. De Schreye. An Almost Perfect Abstraction Operation for Partial Deduction Using Characteristic Trees. Technical Report CW 215, Departement Computerwetenschappen, K.U. Leuven, Belgium, October 1995. Accepted for Publication in *New Generation Computing*.

[LS97]   M. Leuschel and D. De Schreye. Constrained Partial Deduction and the Preservation of Characteristic Trees. Technical report, Department of Computer Science, Katholieke Universiteit Leuven, June 1997. Accepted for publication in New Generation Computing.

[LSdW96]   M. Leuschel, D. De Schreye, and A. de Waal. A Conceptual Embedding of Folding into Partial Deduction; Towards a Maximal Integration. In M. Maher, editor, *Proceedings of the Joint International Conference and Symposium on Logic Programming JICSLP'96*, pages 319–332, Bonn, Germany, September 1996. MIT Press.

[Mar96]   S.D. Marlow. *Deforestation for Higher-Order Functional Languages*. PhD thesis, University of Glasgow, 1996.

[MG95]   B. Martens and J. Gallagher. Ensuring global termination of partial deduction while allowing flexible polyvariance. In L. Stirling, editor, *International Conference on Logic Programming*, pages 597–613. MIT Press, 1995.

[SG95]   M.H. Sørensen and R. Glück. An algorithm of generalization in positive supercompilation. In J. W. Lloyd, editor, *Logic Programming: Proceedings of the 1995 International Symposium*, pages 465–479. MIT Press, 1995.

[SGJ94]   M.H. Sørensen, R. Glück, and N. D. Jones. Towards unifying partial evaluation, deforestation, supercompilation, and GPC. In *ESOP*. Springer-Verlag, 1994.

[SGJ96]   M.H. Sørensen, R. Glück, and N.D. Jones. A Positive Supercompiler. *Journal of Functional Programming*, 6(6):811–838, 1996.

[Sør]   M.H. Sørensen. Convergence of Program Transformers in the Metric Space of Trees With a Reflection on the Set of Reals. Unpublished manuscript.

[TNT82]   V. F. Turchin, R.M. Nirenberg, and D. V. Turchin. Experiments with a supercompiler. In *Conference Record of the 1982 ACM Symposium on Lisp and Functional Programming*, pages 47–55. ACM, ACM, August 1982.

[Tur86]   V.F. Turchin. The concept of a supercompiler. *ACM Transactions on Programming Languages and Systems*, 8(3):292–325, July 1986.

[Wad90]   P. Wadler. Deforestation: Transforming Programs to Eliminate Trees. *Theoretical Computer Science*, 73:231–248, 1990.

Preserving Termination of Tabled Logic Programs While Unfolding

(Extended Abstract)

Michael Leuschel, Bern Martens, and Konstantinos Sagonas

Department of Computer Science
Katholieke Universiteit Leuven
Celestijnenlaan 200A, B-3001 Heverlee, Belgium
{michael,bern,kostis}@cs.kuleuven.ac.be

Abstract. We provide a first investigation of the specialisation and transformation of tabled logic programs through unfolding. We show that — surprisingly — unfolding, even determinate, can worsen the termination behaviour in the context of tabling. We therefore establish two criteria which ensure that such mishaps are avoided. We also briefly discuss the influence of some other transformation techniques on the termination and efficiency of tabled logic programs.

1 Introduction

The use of tabling in logic programming is beginning to emerge as a powerful evaluation technique, since it allows bottom-up evaluation to be incorporated within a top-down framework, combining the advantages of both. Although the concept of tabled execution of logic programs has been around for more than a decade (see [27]), practical systems based on tabling are only beginning to appear. Early experience with these systems suggests that they are indeed practically viable. In particular the XSB system [24], based on SLG-resolution [3], computes in-memory queries about an order of magnitude faster than current semi-naive methods, and evaluates Prolog queries with little reduction in performance when compared to well-known commercial Prolog systems.

At a high level, top-down tabling systems evaluate programs by recording subgoals (referred to as *calls*) and their provable instances (referred to as *answers*) in a table. Predicates are designated *a priori* as either *tabled* or *nontabled*. Clause resolution, which is the basic mechanism for program evaluation, proceeds as follows. For nontabled predicates the call is resolved against program clauses. For tabled predicates, if the call is new to the evaluation, it is entered in the table and Prolog-style program clause resolution is used to compute its answers which are also recorded in the table. If, on the other hand, a variant[1] of the call is

---

[1] Tabling evaluation methods can be based either on variant checks, as SLG-resolution is, or on subsumption checks. Throughout this paper, unless otherwise specified, we assume tabling based on variance, and we refer the reader to [3] Section 7.1 for a discussion on some of the issues that are involved in this choice.

Norbert E. Fuchs (Ed.): LOPSTR'97, LNCS 1463, pp. 189–205, 1998.

already present in the table, then it is resolved against its recorded answers. By using answer tables for resolving subsequent invocations of the same call, tabled evaluation strategies prevent many cases of infinite looping which normally occur in Prolog-style SLD evaluation. As a result, termination characteristics of tabling-based logic programming systems are better than those of Prolog [3].

Given the relative novelty of tabling-based implementations, many promising avenues for substantially improving the performance of tabled programs remain to be explored. Research in this topic has mainly addressed issues related to finding efficient data structures for tabling [22], or suggesting low-level modifications of the SLG-WAM [23]. In this paper we deviate from this path and investigate issues related to the optimisation of tabled programs using more portable techniques such as specialisation through unfolding or similar program transformations.

Program transformation is by now a widely accepted technique for the systematic development of correct and efficient programs. Given a program, the aim of program transformation is to produce a more efficient program which solves the same problem, that is, which is equivalent in meaning to the original one under a semantics of choice. Various systems for program transformation have been developed, usually based on the use of the fold/unfold framework. This framework dates back to at least [2], has been introduced to the logic programming community in a seminal paper of Tamaki and Sato [26], has since been the subject of considerable research (see e.g. the references in [18]), and has been successfully used in many partial evaluators for Prolog-style execution [19, 20, 25, 8]. Unfortunately, no methodology for the transformation or specialisation of tabled logic programs exists. All techniques stay within the context of untabled execution. Initially, one may expect that results established in the "classic" (S)LD setting more or less carry over. This, however, turns out to be far from obviously true as the differences between the execution models are significant.

In this paper, we mainly concentrate on issues related to the safety of unfolding in tabled logic programs. We do so because in the context of program specialisation, unfolding is the most important ingredient. For instance, partial deduction [17] basically only employs unfolding. In untabled execution of logic programs unfolding is not problematic. For example, it preserves both the least Herbrand model and set of computed answer substitutions semantics and — even in the context of the unfair Prolog selection rule — it *cannot* worsen the (universal) termination behaviour of a program [21]. Under tabled execution, however, unfolding — even determinate — may transform a terminating program into a non-terminating one ! Naturally, this is a situation that better be avoided.

To reason about unfolding of tabled logic programs, we describe a framework that captures their termination (under the left-to-right selection rule) and define applicability conditions that ensure the intended equivalence property between the original program and the transformed one. Using this framework we prove that certain non-trivial and commonly used in practice types of unfolding are safe with respect to termination.

In summary, our results regarding unfolding in the context of tabled execution are as follows:

- We prove that left-most unfolding or unfolding without any left-propagation of bindings preserves termination of tabled logic programs.
- We show that even though left-propagation of bindings through unfolding can worsen the termination characteristics of a tabled programs, left-propagation of grounding substitutions is safe wrt termination.

The rest of the paper is organised as follows. In the next section we introduce some preliminaries and in Section 3 we show through an example how unfolding endangers termination of tabled programs. To reason about preservation of termination by unfolding, in Section 4 we introduce the notion of *quasi-termination* of tabled programs, and based on this notion in Section 5 we prove the above results. We end with an extended discussion of the effect that some other commonly used transformation techniques have on the termination and efficiency of tabled programs.

2   Preliminaries

We denote by B_P^E the non-ground extended Herbrand base[2] (i.e. the set of atoms modulo the variant equivalence relation $\approx$ as defined in [7]). We also define the following notations: the set of variables occurring inside an expression F is denoted by $vars(F)$, the *domain* of a substitution θ is defined as $dom(\theta) = \{X \mid X/t \in \theta\}$ and the *range* of θ is defined as $ran(\theta) = \{Y \mid X/t \in \theta \wedge Y \in vars(t)\}$. Finally, we also define $vars(\theta) = dom(\theta) \cup ran(\theta)$ as well as the restriction $\theta|_V$ of a substitution θ to a set of variables V by $\theta|_V = \{X/t \mid X/t \in \theta \wedge X \in V\}$. By $mgu(A, B)$ we denote a substitution θ which is an idempotent (i.e. $\theta\theta = \theta$) and relevant (i.e. $vars(\theta) \subseteq vars(A) \cup vars(B)$) most general unifier of two expressions A and B. In the remainder of this paper we will use the notations $hd(C), bd(C)$ to refer to the head and the body of a clause C respectively.

A program transformation process starting from an initial program P_0 is a sequence of programs $P_0, \ldots, P_n$, called a *transformation sequence*, such that program P_{k+1}, with $0 \leq k < n$, is obtained from P_k by the application of a *transformation rule*, which may depend on $P_0, \ldots, P_k$. Let us now formally define unfolding, slightly adapted from [18, (R1)].

Definition 1.   (Unfolding rule) *Let P_k contain the (renamed apart) clause $C = H \leftarrow F, A, G$, where A is a positive literal and where F and G are (possibly empty) conjunctions of literals. Suppose that:*

---

[2] In some given language, usually inferred from the program and queries under consideration. The superscipt E is used to prevent confusion with the standard definition of the Herbrand base.

1. $\{D_1, \ldots, D_n\}$, with $n \geq 0$, [3] *are all the clauses in a program* P_j, *with* $0 \leq j \leq k$, *such that* A *is unifiable with* $hd(D_1), \ldots, hd(D_n)$, *with most general unifiers* $\theta_1, \ldots, \theta_n$, *and*
2. C_i *is the clause* $(H \leftarrow F, bd(D_i), G)\theta_i$, *for* $i = 1, \ldots, n$.

Each binding in $\theta_i|_{vars(F) \cup vars(H)}$ *is called a* left-propagated binding.
If we unfold C *wrt* A *(using* $D_1, \ldots, D_n$*) in* P_j, *we derive the clauses* $C_1, \ldots, C_n$ *and we get the new program* $P_{k+1} = (P_k \setminus \{C\}) \cup \{C_1, \ldots, C_n\}$. *When* $n = 1$, *i.e., there is exactly one clause whose head is unifiable with* A, *the unfolding is called* determinate. *Finally,* left-most unfolding *unfolds the first literal in* $bd(C)$ *(i.e. F is empty).*[4]

For example, given $P_0 = \{p \leftarrow q \wedge r, q \leftarrow r\}$, we can unfold $p \leftarrow q \wedge r$ wrt q using P_0, deriving the clause $p \leftarrow r \wedge r$ and we get $P_1 = \{p \leftarrow r \wedge r, q \leftarrow r\}$.

Note that, in contrast to [18], we treat programs as *sets* of clauses and not as sequences of clauses. For pure tabled programs, the order (and multiplicity) of clauses makes no difference for the termination properties we are (primarily) interested in preserving (the order of clauses and the order of solutions has no incidence on *universal* — i.e. wrt the entire computation process — termination; it might however affect their *existential* termination, as discussed in Section 6.4).

3   Unfolding Endangers Termination

In the context of program specialisation, unfolding is the most important transformation rule. For instance, partial deduction [17] basically only employs unfolding (although a limited form of implicit folding is obtained by the Lloyd and Shepherdson closedness condition, see e.g. [14]). So in order to study specialisation and transformation of tabled logic programs we will first concentrate on the behaviour of unfolding.

In logic programs — with or without negation — executed under SLD(NF) (or variants thereof) any unfolding is totally correct and does not modify the termination behaviour of the program (see e.g. [18]). In the context of a fixed, unfair selection rule, like Prolog's left-to-right rule, unfolding can even improve termination (cf. [21]), but never worsen it. In the Prolog setting (i.e. if we take clause order, depth-first strategy into account), unrestricted unfolding can only affect the *existential* termination of programs, because unfolding can change the order of solutions. Moreover, *determinate unfolding does not modify the backtracking behaviour* [9] and can thus only be beneficial for efficiency (leading to smaller SLD(NF)-trees).

However, while unfolding is not problematic in the ordinary setting, its influence on efficiency and termination becomes rather involved in the context of

---

[3] [18, (R1)] actually stipulates that $n > 0$ and thus does not allow the selection of an atom which unifies with no clause. However, the "deletion of clauses with finitely failed body" rule [18, (R12)] can be used in those circumstances instead. We can thus effectively allow the case $n = 0$ as well.

[4] Note that left-most unfolding is allowed to instantiate the head, while unfolding without left-propagation is not.

tabled execution. On the one hand, contrary to Prolog-style execution, any unfolding of Datalog (or propositional) programs is safe wrt termination, as SLG
terminates on such programs [3]. On the other hand however, as soon as function symbols are introduced, unfolding, even determinate, can ruin termination.
We suppose from now on, for simplicity of the presentation, that all predicates
are tabled. We also suppose that the predicate $= /2$ is defined by the clause
$= (X, X) \leftarrow$.

Example 1. Let P be the following program.

$$p(X) \leftarrow p(Y), Y = f(X)$$

Under a left-to-right selection rule, this program fails finitely (the selected atom
is a variant of a call for which no answers can be produced) and thus terminates
for e.g. the query $\leftarrow p(X)$. The following program, P', obtained by (determi-
nately) unfolding the atom $Y = f(X)$ does not (see Fig. 1):

$$p(X) \leftarrow p(f(X))$$

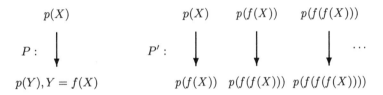

Fig. 1. SLG-forests for the query $\leftarrow p(X)$ before and after unfolding Example 1.

This "infinite slowdown" is of course highly undesirable. In the remainder
of this paper we develop criteria which ensure that termination is preserved by
unfolding.

4   Quasi-Termination

We start out with a formalisation of termination (under a left-to-right selection
rule) in the setting of tabled execution of logic programs.

Definition 2. (call graph) *Given a program P, the* call graph *of P is the
graph whose nodes are the elements of B_P^E and which contains a directed edge
from A to B, denoted by $A \rightarrow_P B$ (or more precisely $A \rightarrow_{P,C,i} B$), iff there
exists a (renamed apart) clause $C = H \leftarrow B_1, \ldots, B_n$ in P such that*
- *A and H unify via an mgu θ and*
- *$B \approx B_i \theta \theta_1 \ldots \theta_{i-1}$ where θ_j is a computed answer substitution (c.a.s.) for
$P \cup \{\leftarrow B_j \theta \theta_1 \ldots \theta_{j-1}\}$.*

By $\to_P^*$ we denote the transitive and reflexive closure of $\to_P$. Given an atom $A \in B_P^E$, we also define $A_P^* = \{B \in B_P^E \mid A \to_P^* B\}$. A subset S of B_P^E is said to be closed iff $A \to_P B$, for some $A \in S$, implies that $B \in S$.

Example 2. Let P be the following program.

$p(a) \leftarrow$
$p(X) \leftarrow q(X), p(X)$
$q(a) \leftarrow$
$q(b) \leftarrow$

We have that e.g. $p(a) \to_P q(a)$, $p(a) \to_P p(a)$ and $p(a)^* = \{p(a), q(a)\}$. The full call graph is depicted in Fig. 2.

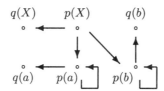

Fig. 2. Call graph of P for Example 2

We now define the notion of quasi-termination of tabled logic programs (a term borrowed from [12], defining a similar notion in the context of termination of off-line partial evaluation of functional programs).

Definition 3.   (quasi-termination) *Let P be a program and S a subset of B_P^E. P is said to be* quasi-terminating wrt S *iff for every $A \in S$ the set A_P^* is finite. Also, P is* quasi-terminating *iff it is quasi-terminating wrt B_P^E.*

E.g. the program P from Example 2 is quasi-terminating wrt the entire B_P^E.

The above definition in essence means that, starting from S, evaluation produces only a finite number of different calls. Equivalently, every LD-tree (i.e. an SLD-tree using the left-to-right selection rule) for $P \cup \{\leftarrow A\}$, $A \in S$, contains only a finite number of selected atoms modulo variable renaming. It is also equivalent to stating that every SLG-forest using the left-to-right selection rule for $P \cup \{\leftarrow A\}$, $A \in S$, contains only finitely many SLG-trees. This means that non-termination can only occur if a call produces an infinite number of computed answers. Hence, *universal* termination holds iff we have quasi-termination and there are only finitely many c.a.s. for the selected atoms (for a more thorough discussion on termination issues in tabled execution see [6]) Thus, if a transformation sequence preserves the set of c.a.s. — something which holds for all the transformations we are interested in — then *preserving quasi-termination is equivalent to preserving universal termination.*

5   Preserving Quasi-Termination While Unfolding

In the problematic Example 1 we have, by unfolding, left-propagated the binding $Y/f(X)$ on the atom $p(Y)$. Without left-propagation the sequence of c.a.s. under untabled LD-resolution is not changed (see e.g. [21]) and even the behaviour of problematic non-logical built-in's like $var/1$ is preserved (see e.g. [19, 25]). We first prove that such restricted unfolding is also safe wrt quasi-termination of tabled logic programs.

Theorem 1. *Let $S \subseteq B_P^E$, and let P' be obtained from P by a sequence of left-most unfolding steps and unfolding steps without left-propagated bindings.*
If P is quasi-terminating wrt S then so is P'.

Proof. In Appendix A.   □

We will now explore extensions of this basic result, as the left-propagation of bindings can often be highly beneficial and, as it allows the evaluation to focus on only the relevant data, can lead to a dramatic pruning of the search space (see e.g. [13]).

However, considerable care has to be taken when performing instantiations in the context of tabled logic programs. We have already illustrated the danger of unfolding with left-propagation of bindings. Note, however, that if we just instantiate the query $\leftarrow p(X)$ to $\leftarrow p(f(X))$, but leave the clause in program P of Example 1 unmodified, quasi-termination is not destroyed. So, one might hope that instantiating a query and leaving the program unmodified should be safe wrt quasi-termination. Alas, there is another more subtle reason why left-propagation of bindings can endanger termination. Termination of ordinary SLD(NF)-resolution has the following property.

Definition 4. *The termination of an evaluation strategy $\mathcal{E}$ is* closed under substitution *iff whenever in a program P a query $\leftarrow Q$ terminates under $\mathcal{E}$, then so does every instance $\leftarrow Q\theta$ of it.*

Surprisingly, this is not a property that carries over to tabled evaluation! We show that *termination (and quasi-termination) of SLG-resolution is not closed under substitution* with the following counterexample.

Example 3. Let $p/2$ be a tabled predicate defined by the following clause:
$$p(f(X), Y) \leftarrow p(X, Y)$$
Then (as shown in Fig. 3), *both* under variant- and subsumption-based tabling, the query $\leftarrow p(X, Y)$ terminates while $\leftarrow p(X, X)$ does not!

As a side-comment, note that, because termination of tabled execution is not closed under substitution, tabling systems based on *(forward) subsumption* have unpredictable termination characteristics in general (termination of queries depends on the chronological order of encountering tabled calls). At least from a purely practical perspective, this is can be seen as an advantage of tabling systems based on variance over those based on subsumption.

$$p(X,Y) \qquad\qquad p(X,X) \qquad p(X,f(X)) \qquad p(X,f(f(X)))$$

$$X = f(X') \Big\downarrow \qquad\qquad X = f(X') \Big\downarrow \qquad X = f(X') \Big\downarrow \qquad X = f(X') \Big\downarrow \cdots$$

$$p(X',Y) \qquad\qquad p(X',f(X')) \quad p(X',f(f(X'))) \quad p(X',f(f(f(X'))))$$

Fig. 3. SLG-forests for the queries $\leftarrow p(X,Y)$ and $\leftarrow p(X,X)$.

Example 3 can be adapted to show that *even left-propagation of bindings which do not introduce any new structure can be dangerous*: $t \leftarrow p(X,Y), X = Y$ terminates while a program containing $t \leftarrow p(X,X)$ does not. Moreover, a variant of the same example shows that *even left-propagation of bindings to variables that appear only in the head can ruin termination* as can be seen by the unfolding of the atom $Z = f(X)$ in the following clause:

$$p(Z,Y) \leftarrow p(X,Y), Z = f(X)$$

So, although left-propagation and instantiation in the context of tabled execution of logic programs seems like a hopeless endeavour, we will now formally establish that a non-trivial class of substitutions can actually be safely left-propagated.

Definition 5. *A substitution γ is called a* grounding substitution *iff for all $X/t \in \gamma$ we have that t is a ground term.*
We say that γ is structurally simpler *than another grounding substitution σ, denoted by $\gamma \trianglelefteq \sigma$, iff for every $X/s \in \gamma$ there exists a $Y/t \in \sigma$ such that s is a subterm of t.*

Note that any term is considered a subterm of itself.

Example 4. Let $\sigma = \{X/f(a), Y/b\}$ be a grounding substitution. Then σ itself as well as e.g. $\{Z/a, X/b\}$ and $\{X/f(a), Y/f(a), Z/b, V/a\}$ are structurally simpler than σ (it would be possible to disallow the last case by a more refined definition, but it is not required for our purposes). However, neither $\{Z/f(f(a))\}$ nor $\{X/c\}$ are structurally simpler than σ.

The interest of the relation $\trianglelefteq$, in the context of quasi-termination, derives from the following proposition.

Lemma 1. *Let σ be a grounding substitution and let A be an atom. Then the set $\{A'\gamma \mid A' \approx A \text{ and } \gamma \trianglelefteq \sigma\}$ is finite up to variable renaming.*

Proof. Let $vars(A') = \{X_1, \ldots, X_n\}$ and let $\gamma \trianglelefteq \sigma$. Then we either have $X_i\gamma = X_i$ or we have that $X_i\gamma = t_i$ where t_i is a subterm of some s_i with $Y/s_i \in \sigma$. Now, as there are only finitely many bindings Y/s in σ and as for each such s there are only finitely many subterms, we can only construct finitely many different atoms $A'\gamma$ up to variable renaming. □

Next, we prove the following lemma, capturing an interesting property of grounding substitutions. Together with Lemma 1, this will enable us to show that left-propagation of grounding substitutions is safe wrt quasi-termination.

Lemma 2. *Let γ be a grounding substitution and let $\leftarrow Q\gamma$ have a derivation leading to $\leftarrow RQ'$. Then $\leftarrow Q$ has a corresponding derivation leading to $\leftarrow RQ$ such that for some grounding substitution $\gamma' \trianglelefteq \gamma$, $RQ' \approx RQ\gamma'$.*

Proof. In Appendix B.   □

We will now put the above lemmas to use.

Theorem 2. *Let P be a program, A an atom and let σ be a grounding substitution. If A_P^* is finite then so is $A\sigma_P^*$.*

Proof. By Lemma 2 we know that for every $A \to_P^* B$ we can only have $A\sigma \to_P^* B\gamma$ for grounding substitutions $\gamma \trianglelefteq \sigma$. This means that $\mathcal{A} = \{B'\gamma \mid B \in A^* \wedge B' \approx B$ and $\gamma \trianglelefteq \sigma\}$ is a safe approximation (i.e. a superset) of $A\sigma_P^*$. We can apply Lemma 1 to deduce that $\mathcal{A}$ is finite whenever A^* is.   □

Theorem 3. *Let $\mathcal{S} \subseteq B_P^E$, and let P' be obtained from P by left-most unfolding steps and unfolding steps such that each left-propagated binding is a grounding substitution. If P is quasi-terminating wrt $\mathcal{S}$ then P' is quasi-terminating wrt $\mathcal{S}$.*

Proof Sketch. The full proof is obtained by adapting the proof of Theorem 1 to make use of Theorem 2 for the left-propagated grounding substitutions. The only tricky aspect is that, when instantiating a body atom B of a clause C to $B\gamma$, Theorem 2 only tells us that if B was terminating in P then $B\gamma$ is also terminating in P. To actually infer that $B\gamma$ also terminates in $P' = P\setminus C\cup\{C_1,\ldots,C_n\}$ we have to take into account that γ might be *repeatedly* applied, i.e. whenever a derivation of B uses the clause C. This is no problem, however, because $\gamma' \trianglelefteq \gamma \Rightarrow \gamma'\gamma \trianglelefteq \gamma$, meaning that Lemma 2 (and thus also Theorem 2) also holds when the grounding substitution is repeatedly applied.   □

A similar result does not hold when using tabling based on subsumption rather than variance as shown by the following example.

Example 5. The following program is quasi-terminating wrt $\{q\}$ when using subsumption checks (but not when using variant checks).

$$p(X) \leftarrow p(f(X))$$
$$q \leftarrow p(X), X = a$$

Unfolding $X = a$ in the last clause will result in the left-propagation of the grounding substitution $\{X/a\}$ and produce the clause $q \leftarrow p(a)$. The resulting program is no longer quasi-terminating wrt $\{q\}$ when using subsumption checks only (term-depth abstraction in the spirit of OLDT-resolution is then also required to ensure termination).

6   Extensions and Efficiency Considerations

6.1   Mixing Tabled and Prolog-Style Execution

So far we have assumed that all predicates are tabled. When not all predicates are tabled, then one can safely left-propagate any substitution on nontabled predicates *if* they do not call tabled predicates themselves (otherwise a problem similar to Example 3 can arise; e.g. through left-propagation of X/Y on the nontabled call $q(X, Y)$, where $q/2$ is defined by $q(X, Y) \leftarrow p(X, Y)$).

One also has to ensure that unfolding does not replace a tabled predicate by a nontabled one. Otherwise, the termination might be affected as the following example shows.

Example 6. In program P of Figure 4 where only $t/1$ is tabled all queries finitely fail; so the program is terminating. However, by determinate unfolding of the first clause wrt to $t(X)$, we end up with the program P' on the right side of the same figure for which the query $\leftarrow p(X)$ is non-terminating.

$$
P : \boxed{\begin{array}{l} p(X) \leftarrow t(X) \\[4pt] t(X) \leftarrow p(X) \end{array}} \qquad\qquad P' : \boxed{\begin{array}{l} p(X) \leftarrow p(X) \\[4pt] t(X) \leftarrow p(X) \end{array}}
$$

Fig. 4. P' is obtained from P by unfolding wrt $t(X)$.

6.2   Polyvariance and Renaming

Most partial evaluators and deducers use a technique called *renaming* (see e.g. [10, 1]) to remove redundant structure from the specialised program but also to ensure the independence condition of [17] (thus avoiding the use of abstraction instead), thereby allowing unlimited polyvariance. In the context of SLD(NF)-execution, such additional polyvariance might increase the code size but is always beneficial in terms of the size of the (run-time) SLD(NF)-trees. The following example shows that, again, in the context of tabled execution, appropriate care has to be taken.

Example 7. Let P be the following program, containing some arbitrary definition of the predicate $p/2$.

$$q(X, Y) \leftarrow p(a, Y), p(X, b)$$

After specialising one might obtain the following program along with definitions for $p_a/1$ and $p_b/1$.

$$q(X, Y) \leftarrow p_a(Y), p_b(X)$$

For the query $\leftarrow q(a, b)$ the call $p(a, b)$ will only be executed once against program clauses in the original program while in the specialised program both $p_a(b)$ *and* $p_b(a)$ will be executed. The specialised program might thus actually be less efficient than the original one !

A conservative, but safe, approach is to apply renaming only when the atoms are independent — it should just be used to remove superfluous structure from the specialised program while the independence condition should be ensured via abstraction.

Similar difficulties can arise when performing conjunctive partial deduction [14, 11] (as well as tupling or deforestation), which specialises entire conjunctions and renames them into new atoms. Indeed, renaming a conjunction into a new atom might diminish the possibility for tabling, i.e. the possibility of reusing earlier computed results. If e.g. we rename the conjunction $p(X, Y) \wedge q(X, Z)$ into $pq(X, Y, Z)$ then the query $\leftarrow p(a, b) \wedge q(a, c)$ can reuse part of the results computed for $\leftarrow p(a, b) \wedge q(a, d)$, while the renamed query $\leftarrow pq(a, b, c)$ cannot reuse results computed for $\leftarrow pq(a, b, d)$.

6.3 A Note on the Efficiency of Unfolding with Left-Propagation

In untabled execution the left-propagation of substitutions usually prunes the search space, and thus can only be beneficial for the efficiency of query evaluation. In tabled execution, as some program clause resolution is substituted by resolution against answers that are materialised in tables and can be retrieved without recomputation, the left-propagation of (even grounding) substitutions may sometimes worsen performance (of course it can also vastly improve it).

For example, in many tabled-based program analysers, it is usual practice to employ what is known as the *most-general call optimisation* [4]; i.e., compute analysis information for the most general form of each predicate and then retrieve this information from the tables, appropriately filtering it by explicit equality constraints. The basic idea of the approach can be illustrated by two simple abstract interpreters from [5] shown in Figure 5. The definition of the $fact/1$ predicate (which can be the only tabled predicate) is the same for both interpreters and assumes that each program clause $H \leftarrow G_1, \ldots, G_n$ is represented as a fact of the form $pc(H, [G_1, \ldots, G_n]) \leftarrow$. A top-level query $\leftarrow fact(X)$ trig-

$fact(Head) \leftarrow$ 　　$pc(Head, Body), prove(Body)$ $prove([]) \leftarrow$ $prove([G\|Gs]) \leftarrow$ 　　$fact(G), prove(Gs)$	$fact(Head) \leftarrow$ 　　$pc(Head, Body), prove(Body)$ $prove([]) \leftarrow$ $prove([G\|Gs]) \leftarrow$ 　　$fact(GenG), GenG = G, prove(Gs)$

Fig. 5. Two abstract meta-interpreters for concrete evaluation.

gers the computation of the program's non-ground minimal S-model that gets recorded in the tables. Only one such table is created when using the interpreter with the most-general call optimisation (shown on the right side of the figure). However, using the interpreter on the left side of the figure the number of tables depends on the number of distinct (up to variance) instantiation patterns for calls to $fact/1$. Besides the overhead in space, this has an associated performance cost especially in complicated abstract domains (see e.g. [4, 5] for more information and experimental evaluation of this technique over a variety of domains).

6.4   Taking Program Clause Order into Account

In existing implementations of tabling, program clause resolution is performed in a style similar to Prolog's; i.e. visiting clauses according to their textual order. Consequently, in tabled programs which are not quasi-terminating, non-determinate unfolding (even without left-propagation) can worsen their existential termination. This, in turn, might affect their behaviour under optimisations which involve pruning, such as *existential negation* (c.f. [24]). We illustrate the problem by the following example, which extends a similar example given in [21].

Example 8. Assuming a scheduling strategy that returns answers to calls as soon as these are generated, program P of Figure 6 produces the answer $X = 0$ for the query $\leftarrow p(X)$, and then loops, while program P' loops without producing any answers.

$$
P : \quad
\begin{array}{|l|}
\hline
p(X) \leftarrow q(X), r \\[4pt]
q(0) \leftarrow \\
q(X) \leftarrow q(s(X)) \\[4pt]
r \leftarrow fail \\
r \\
\hline
\end{array}
\qquad
P' : \quad
\begin{array}{|l|}
\hline
p(X) \leftarrow q(X), fail \\
p(X) \leftarrow q(X) \\[4pt]
q(0) \leftarrow \\
q(X) \leftarrow q(s(X)) \\[4pt]
r \leftarrow fail \\
r \\
\hline
\end{array}
$$

Fig. 6. P' is obtained from P by unfolding wrt r.

7   Discussion

We conclude with a brief discussion of a possible application of this work, namely optimising integrity checking upon updates in *recursive* databases, by specialising meta-interpreters. For hierarchical databases successful results have already been achieved in [13]. Unfortunately, moving to recursive databases has proven to be difficult, because the loop check — which is necessary for termination — requires the use of the ground representation when using SLD(NF)-execution. This imposes a large initial overhead and leads to further difficulties in terms of specialisation [15, 16]. However, by writing the integrity checker in a tabled environment we can use the non-ground representation and together with the techniques explored in this paper, one might obtain effective specialised update procedures even for recursive databases. Note that in the setting of deductive databases left-propagation of grounding substitutions corresponds to the well-known optimisation principle of making selections first, and thus occurs very naturally.

Acknowledgements

Michael Leuschel and Konstantinos Sagonas are post-doctoral fellows of the Fund for Scientific Research - Flanders Belgium (FWO). Michael Leuschel was also partially supported by the Belgian GOA "Non-Standard Applications of Abstract Interpretation". Bern Martens is a post-doctoral fellow of the K.U.Leuven Research Council. We thank Danny De Schreye and Stefaan Decorte for interesting discussions, ideas and comments.

References

[1] K. Benkerimi and P. M. Hill. Supporting Transformations for the Partial Evaluation of Logic Programs. *Journal of Logic and Computation*, 3(5):469–486, October 1993.

[2] R. M. Burstall and J. Darlington. A Transformation System for Developing Recursive Programs. *Journal of the ACM*, 24(1):44–67, January 1977.

[3] W. Chen and D. S. Warren. Tabled Evaluation with Delaying for General Logic Programs. *Journal of the ACM*, 43(1):20–74, January 1996.

[4] M. Codish, M. Bruynooghe, M. García de la Banda, and M. Hermenegildo. Exploiting Goal Independence in the Analysis of Logic Programs. *Journal of Logic Programming*, 32(3):247–262, September 1997.

[5] M. Codish, B. Demoen, and K. Sagonas. Semantic-Based Program Analysis for Logic-Based Languages using XSB. K.U. Leuven Technical Report CW 245. December 1996.

[6] S. Decorte, D. De Schreye, M. Leuschel, B. Martens, and K. Sagonas. Termination Analysis for Tabled Logic Programming. In N. Fuchs, editor, *Proceedings of LOP-STR'97: Logic Program Synthesis and Transformation*, LNCS, Leuven, Belgium, July 1997. Springer-Verlag.

[7] M. Falaschi, G. Levi, C. Palamidessi, and M. Martelli. Declarative Modeling of the Operational Behavior of Logic Languages. *Theoretical Comput. Sci.*, 69(3):289–318, 1989.

[8] J. Gallagher. A System for Specialising Logic Programs. Technical Report TR-91-32, University of Bristol, November 1991.

[9] J. Gallagher. Tutorial on Specialisation of Logic Programs. In *ACM SIGPLAN Symposium on Partial Evaluation and Semantics-Based Program Manipulation*, pages 88–98, Copenhagen, Denmark, June 1993. ACM Press.

[10] J. Gallagher and M. Bruynooghe. Some Low-Level Source Transformations for Logic Programs. In M. Bruynooghe, editor, *Proceedings of the Second Workshop on Meta-programming in Logic*, pages 229–244, Leuven, Belgium, April 1990.

[11] R. Glück, J. Jørgensen, B. Martens, and M. H. Sørensen. Controlling Conjunctive Partial Deduction of Definite Logic Programs. In H. Kuchen and S. Swierstra, editors, *Proceedings of the International Symposium on Programming Languages, Implementations, Logics and Programs (PLILP'96)*, number

1140 in LNCS, pages 152–166, Aachen, Germany, September 1996. Springer-Verlag. Extended version as Technical Report CW 226, K.U. Leuven. Accessible via http://www.cs.kuleuven.ac.be/~lpai.

[12] C. K. Holst. Finiteness Analysis. In J. Hughes, editor, *Proceedings of the 5th ACM Conference on Functional Programming Languages and Computer Architecture (FPCA)*, number 523 in LNCS, pages 473–495. Springer-Verlag, August 1991.

[13] M. Leuschel and D. De Schreye. Towards creating specialised integrity checks through partial evaluation of meta-interpreters. In *Proceedings of PEPM'95, the ACM Sigplan Symposium on Partial Evaluation and Semantics-Based Program Manipulation*, pages 253–263, La Jolla, California, June 1995. ACM Press.

[14] M. Leuschel, D. De Schreye, and A. de Waal. A conceptual embedding of folding into partial deduction: Towards a maximal integration. In M. Maher, editor, *Proceedings of the Joint International Conference and Symposium on Logic Programming JICSLP'96*, pages 319–332, Bonn, Germany, September 1996. MIT Press. Extended version as Technical Report CW 225, K.U. Leuven. Accessible via http://www.cs.kuleuven.ac.be/~lpai.

[15] M. Leuschel and B. Martens. Partial deduction of the ground representation and its application to integrity checking. In J. W. Lloyd, editor, *Proceedings of ILPS'95, the International Logic Programming Symposium*, pages 495–509, Portland, USA, December 1995. MIT Press. Extended version as Technical Report CW 210, K.U. Leuven. Accessible via http://www.cs.kuleuven.ac.be/~lpai.

[16] M. Leuschel and D. Schreye. Logic program specialisation: How to be more specific. In H. Kuchen and S. Swierstra, editors, *Proceedings of the International Symposium on Programming Languages, Implementations, Logics and Programs (PLILP'96)*, number 1140 in LNCS, pages 137–151, Aachen, Germany, September 1996. Springer-Verlag. Extended version as Technical Report CW 232, K.U. Leuven. Accessible via http://www.cs.kuleuven.ac.be/~lpai.

[17] J. W. Lloyd and J. C. Shepherdson. Partial Evaluation in Logic Programming. *Journal of Logic Programming*, 11(3 & 4):217–242, October/November 1991.

[18] A. Pettorossi and M. Proietti. Transformation of Logic Programs: Foundations and Techniques. *Journal of Logic Programming*, 19 & 20:261–320, May/July 1994.

[19] S. Prestwich. An Unfold Rule for Full Prolog. In K.-K. Lau and T. Clement, editors, *Logic Program Synthesis and Transformation: Proceedings of LOPSTR'92*, Workshops in Computing, Manchester, U.K., 1992. Springer-Verlag.

[20] S. Prestwich. The PADDY Partial Deduction System. Technical Report ECRC-92-6, ECRC, Munich, Germany, 1992.

[21] M. Proietti and A. Pettorossi. Semantics Preserving Transformation Rules for Prolog. In *Proceedings of the Symposium on Partial Evaluation and Semantics-Based Program Manipulation*, pages 274–284, Yale University, New Haven, Connecticut, U.S.A., June 1991. ACM Press.

[22] I. V. Ramakrishnan, P. Rao, K. Sagonas, T. Swift, and D. S. Warren. Efficient Tabling Mechanisms for Logic Programs. In L. Sterling, editor, *Proceedings of the 12th International Conference on Logic Programming*, pages 687–711, Tokyo, Japan, June 1995. The MIT Press.

[23] K. Sagonas. *The SLG-WAM: A Search-Efficient Engine for Well-Founded Evaluation of Normal Logic Programs*. PhD thesis, Department of Computer Science, SUNY at Stony Brook, August 1996.

[24] K. Sagonas, T. Swift, and D. S. Warren. XSB as an Efficient Deductive Database Engine. In *Proceedings of the ACM SIGMOD International Conference on the Management of Data*, pages 442–453, Minneapolis, Minnesota, May 1994. ACM Press.

[25] D. Sahlin. Mixtus: An Automatic Partial Evaluator for Full Prolog. *New Generation Computing*, 12(1):7–51, 1993.

[26] H. Tamaki and T. Sato. Unfold/Fold Transformations of Logic Programs. In S.-Å. Tärnlund, editor, *Proceedings of the Second International Conference on Logic Programming*, pages 127–138, Uppsala, Sweden, July 1984.

[27] H. Tamaki and T. Sato. OLD Resolution with Tabulation. In E. Shapiro, editor, *Proceedings of the Third International Conference on Logic Programming*, number 225 in LNCS, pages 84–98, London, July 1986. Springer-Verlag.

A   Proof of Theorem 1

Theorem 1. Let $S \subseteq B_P^E$, and let P' be obtained from P by a sequence of left-most unfolding steps and unfolding steps without left-propagated bindings. If P is quasi-terminating wrt S then so is P'.

Proof. Let $P = P_0, P_1, \ldots, P_r = P'$ be the transformation sequence used to obtain P'. We will prove by induction on the number of unfolding steps that in each intermediate program P_i the transitive closure of $\to_{P_i}$ will be smaller or in the worst case equal to the transitive closure of $\to_P$. This ensures that quasi-termination is indeed preserved. Let P_{i+1} be obtained from unfolding the clause $C = H \leftarrow F, A, G$ in P_i wrt A using $D_1, \ldots, D_n$ in P_j. Let $B \to_{P_i, C', k} B'$. If $C' \neq C$ then we trivially have that this part of the call graph is not modified in P_{i+1} and we have $B \to_{P_{i+1}, C', k} B'$. If on the other hand $C = C'$ then we do not have $B \to_{P_{i+1}, C, k} B'$ as C has been removed and has been replaced by the clauses $\{C_1, \ldots, C_n\}$ of Definition 1. Let $C = H \leftarrow B_1, \ldots, B_r$ with $F = B_1, \ldots, B_{q-1}$, $A = B_q$ and $G = B_{q+1}, \ldots, B_r$. There are now three possibilities:

1. $k < q$. This implies that we have applied unfolding without left-propagation (for left-most unfolding no atoms can be to the left of the unfolded atom B_k). We know that $B \to_{P_{i+1}, C'', k} B'$ for every $C'' \in \{C_1, \ldots, C_n\}$ and as no bindings are left-propagated, $C'' = H \leftarrow F \wedge Rest$. So, if $n > 0$ we have $B \to_{P_{i+1}} B'$ and the relation $\to_{P_{j+1}}$ is the same as $\to_{P_i}$. If $n = 0$ then the unfolding has possibly (there could be other ways to establish $B \to_{P_i} B'$) removed an arrow by going from $\to_{P_i}$ to $\to_{P_{i+1}}$ (if it is actually removed then termination might be improved by pruning a non-terminating computation).

2. $k > q$. In that case we have $B \to_{P_{i+1}} B'$ as unfolding preserves the set of computed answers. More precisely, by Definition 2, we know that $B' = B_k \hat{\theta}$ where $\hat{\theta} = \theta \theta_1 \ldots \theta_{k-1}$. Let us consider the following auxiliary clause $Aux = aux(\bar{X}) \leftarrow (B_1, \ldots, B_q, \ldots, B_{k-1})\theta$ where $\bar{X}$ are the variables in the body of Aux. We know that if we unfold Aux wrt B_q then the set of computed answers of e.g. the query $\leftarrow Aux$ are preserved for any selection rule (so also the left-to-right one). This means that if $\leftarrow (B_1, \ldots, B_q, \ldots, B_{k-1})\theta$ had the computed answer $\hat{\theta}$, then there must be a similar computed answer in the unfolded program and thus we also have $B \to_{P_{i+1}} B_k \hat{\theta}$.

3. $k = q$. In that case we do not have $B \to_{P_{i+1}} B'$ — unless there was another way to establish $B \to_{P_i} B'$ — but it is replaced by several (possibly) new arrows. Let $B' = B_k \hat{\theta}$ where $\hat{\theta} = \theta \theta_1 \ldots \theta_{k-1}$. Let us first consider the case that unfolding without left-propagation has been performed, i.e. let $C_s = H \leftarrow F, bd(D_s)\theta_s, G\theta_s$ be an unfolded clause where $\theta_s = mgu(B_q, hd(D_s))$. If $B \to_{P_{i+1}, C_s, q+k'} B''$ for $0 \leq k' < l$ where l is the number of atoms in $bd(D_s)$ (i.e. we have a new arrow) then we must have $B' \to_{P_j, D_s, k'} B''$:

Take the clause $D_s = hd(D_s) \leftarrow bd(D_s)$. Then the clause $D'_s = B_q\theta_s \leftarrow bd(D_s)\theta_s$ is actually the resultant of a simple derivation of length 1 for $\leftarrow B_q$. Hence we can use e.g. Lemma 4.12 from [17] to deduce that the computed answers of an instance $\leftarrow B'$ of $\leftarrow B_q$ are the same when resolving with D_s as when resolving with D'_s.

By the induction hypothesis we know that both $B \rightarrow_{P_i} B'$ and $B' \rightarrow_{P_j} B''$ were already in the transitive closure of $\rightarrow_P$ and thus the (possibly) new arrow $B \rightarrow_{P_{i+1}} B''$ was also already in the transitive closure of $\rightarrow_P$. Now, in the case that left-most unfolding has been performed then F is empty and we have that $C_s = H\theta_s \leftarrow bd(D_s)\theta_s, G\theta_s$ with $\theta_s = mgu(B_q, hd(D_s))$. Note that in contrast to unfolding without left-propagation the head of C_s is not necessarily equal to H. However, by a similar application of Lemma 4.12 from [17] we can deduce that this has no influence and we can apply the same reasoning as above.

So, the only new arrows which are added were already in the transitive closure of $\rightarrow_P$ and the new transitive closure will thus be smaller (as some arrows might be removed) or equal than the one of $\rightarrow_P$. □

B   Proof of Lemma 2

Lemma 3. *Let A and H be atoms with $vars(A) \cap vars(H) = \emptyset$. Let $\sigma = \{X/t\}$ be a grounding substitution with $X \notin vars(H)$ and $\theta = mgu(A, H)$ and $\theta' = mgu(A\sigma, H)$.*

1. *If $X \notin dom(\theta)$ then $H\theta' \approx H\theta\sigma$.*
2. *If $X \in dom(\theta)$ then there exists a substitution $\gamma \trianglelefteq \sigma$ such that $H\theta' \approx H\theta\gamma$.*

Proof. **Point 1.** If $X \notin vars(A)$ then the property is trivial, as A and $A\sigma$ are identical and X cannot be in $ran(\theta)$ by idempotence of θ.

Now let $X \in vars(A)$. Because $X \notin dom(\theta)$ and t is ground, we have, by definition of composition of substitutions, that $\theta\sigma = \sigma\theta\sigma$.[5] Hence, $(A\sigma)\theta\sigma = A\theta\sigma = H\theta\sigma$ and $\theta\sigma$ is a unifier of $A\sigma$ and H. Thus, as θ' is a most general unifier there must exist a substitution γ' such that $\theta'\gamma' = \theta\sigma$ and thus $H\theta\sigma$ is an instance of $H\theta'$.

We now establish that $H\theta'$ is in turn an instance of $H\theta\sigma$, and thus prove that $H\theta' \approx H\theta\sigma$.

Let $\sigma' = \sigma\theta'$. This substitution is a unifier of A and H: $H\sigma' = H\theta'$ (because $X \notin vars(H)$) and $A\sigma' = A\sigma\theta' = H\theta'$. So there must exist a substitution γ such that $\theta\gamma = \sigma'$ (because θ is an mgu). This means, as $X \notin dom(\theta)$, that $X/t \in \gamma$, i.e. $\gamma = \sigma\hat{\gamma}$ for some $\hat{\gamma}$ because t is ground. Now, $H\theta' = H\sigma' = H\theta\gamma = H\theta\sigma\hat{\gamma}$ and we have established that $H\theta'$ is an instance of $H\theta\sigma$.

Point 2. We have that $X/s \in \theta$ for some term s. We must have that, for some γ, $s\gamma = t$. Indeed, $\sigma\theta'$ is a unifier of A and H (see proof of Point 1.) and therefore for some substitution $\hat{\gamma}$ we have $\theta\hat{\gamma} = \sigma\theta'$. Now, because $X/t \in \sigma\theta'$ (as t is ground) we have that $s\hat{\gamma} = t$. Let $\gamma = \hat{\gamma}|_{vars(s)} = \{X_1/t_1, \ldots, X_n/t_n\}$. We have that all t_i are subterms of t and, unless $n = 1$ and $s = X_1$, the t_i must also be strict subterms. In other words, $\gamma \trianglelefteq \sigma$. We now prove that $H\theta' \approx H\theta\gamma$. First, we have that $X/t \in \theta\gamma$, by definition of

---

[5] This also holds if σ is not a grounding substitution but if we have $ran(\sigma) \cap vars(A) = \emptyset$ instead.

γ, and we can thus find some substitution $\hat{\theta}$ such that $\theta\gamma = \sigma\hat{\theta}$ (because t is ground). Thus $\theta\gamma$ is a unifier of H and $A\sigma$: $(A\sigma)\theta\gamma = A\sigma\sigma\hat{\theta} = $ (because t is ground) $A\sigma\hat{\theta} = A\theta\gamma = H\theta\gamma$. Thus $\theta\gamma$ is an instance of the mgu θ' and $H\theta\gamma$ and $A\theta\gamma$ is an instance of $H\theta'$. Secondly, as already mentioned above, $\theta\hat{\gamma} = \sigma\theta'$. Now, because $X \notin vars(H)$, $H\theta' = H\sigma\theta'$ and thus we have: $H\theta' = H\sigma\theta' = H\theta\hat{\gamma} = H\theta\gamma\gamma''$ for some γ'' (because the t_i are ground) and $H\theta'$ is in turn an instance of $H\theta\gamma$.   □

The following lemma follows immediately from Definition 5.

Lemma 4. *Let* $\gamma_1, \gamma_2, \sigma_1, \sigma_2$ *be grounding substitutions such that* $dom(\sigma_1) \cap dom(\sigma_2) = \emptyset$. *If* $\gamma_1 \trianglelefteq \sigma_1$ *and* $\gamma_2 \trianglelefteq \sigma_2$ *then* $\gamma_1\gamma_2 \trianglelefteq \sigma_1\sigma_2$.

Lemma 5. *Let* A *and* H *be atoms with* $vars(A) \cap vars(H) = \emptyset$. *Let* σ *be a grounding substitution with* $dom(\sigma) \cap vars(H) = \emptyset$ *and* $\theta = mgu(A, H)$ *and* $\theta' = mgu(A\sigma, H)$. *There exists a substitution* $\gamma \trianglelefteq \sigma$ *such that* $H\theta' \approx H\theta\gamma$.

Proof. By induction on the number of elements in σ, using Lemma 3 and Lemma 4.
                                                                                                  □

The following lemma again follows immediately from Definition 5.

Lemma 6. *If* $\gamma_1 \trianglelefteq \gamma_2$ *and* $\gamma_2 \trianglelefteq \gamma_3$ *then* $\gamma_1 \trianglelefteq \gamma_3$

We can finally prove Lemma 2.

Proof of Lemma 2. By induction on the length of the derivation, using Lemma 5 for each derivation step (and the fact that unifiers are relevant and the head of clauses renamed apart meaning that $H\theta' \approx H\theta\gamma$ implies $Body\theta' \approx Body\theta\gamma$ and thus also implies, together with $A\theta' = H\theta'$ and $A\theta\gamma = A\theta\gamma$, that $RQ' \approx RQ\gamma$) and using Lemma 6.   □

Unfolding the Mystery of *Mergesort*[*]

N. Lindenstrauss, Y. Sagiv, and A. Serebrenik

Dept. of Computer Science
Hebrew University
Jerusalem, Israel
{naomil,sagiv,alicser}@cs.huji.ac.il

Abstract. This paper outlines a fully automatic transformation for proving termination of queries to a class of logic programs, for which existing methods do not work directly. The transformation consists of creating adorned clauses and unfolding. In general, the transformation may improve termination behavior by pruning infinite branches from the LD-tree. Conditions are given under which the transformation preserves termination behavior. The work presented here has been done in the framework of the *TermiLog* system, and it complements the algorithms described in [12].

1 Introduction

This paper outlines a fully automatic method for proving termination for a certain class of logic programs for which the existing approaches (e.g., [2,15,19]) do not work directly, but require some preliminary transformations. The work presented here has been done in the framework of the *TermiLog* system, and is an addition to the algorithms described in [12].

We assume that we are given a program P and a query pattern κ. By *query pattern* we mean an atom whose predicate appears in the program and whose arguments are b or f. An atom A in the extended Herbrand base B_P^E (for this notion see [9,21]) is said to be an *instance* of a query pattern κ if it has the predicate of κ and the arguments at the positions of the b's in the pattern are ground. By *termination* of a query pattern κ relative to the program, we mean that for each atom A that is an instance of κ, the LD-tree of $P \cup \{\leftarrow A\}$ is finite. (Recall that the LD-tree is the SLD-tree with the leftmost selection rule.) In the next section, we will see that it is possible to have weaker requirements than groundness for positions of b's in the query pattern, depending on the norm used for proving termination. For more details on termination analysis of logic programs see [1,8,21,15,12].

To motivate our approach, consider the following example of the *mergesort* program, which is a common example in papers dealing with termination of logic programs (e.g., [2,15,19]).

---

[*] This research has been supported by grants from the Israel Science Foundation

Norbert E. Fuchs (Ed.): LOPSTR'97, LNCS 1463, pp. 206–225, 1998.
© Springer-Verlag Berlin Heidelberg 1998

Example 1. The following program sorts a list if we give a query with the pattern *mergesort*(*b*, *f*).

$$
\begin{aligned}
&\texttt{mergesort}([\,],[\,]).\\
&\texttt{mergesort}([\texttt{X}],[\texttt{X}]).\\
&\texttt{mergesort}([\texttt{X},\texttt{Y}|\texttt{Xs}],\texttt{Ys}) :- \texttt{split}([\texttt{X},\texttt{Y}|\texttt{Xs}],\texttt{X1s},\texttt{X2s}),\\
&\qquad\qquad\qquad\qquad\qquad \texttt{mergesort}(\texttt{X1s},\texttt{Y1s}),\\
&\qquad\qquad\qquad\qquad\qquad \texttt{mergesort}(\texttt{X2s},\texttt{Y2s}),\\
&\qquad\qquad\qquad\qquad\qquad \texttt{merge}(\texttt{Y1s},\texttt{Y2s},\texttt{Ys}).\\
&\texttt{split}([\,],[\,],[\,]).\\
&\texttt{split}([\texttt{X}|\texttt{Xs}],[\texttt{X}|\texttt{Ys}],\texttt{Zs}) :- \texttt{split}(\texttt{Xs},\texttt{Zs},\texttt{Ys}).\\
&\texttt{merge}([\,],\texttt{Xs},\texttt{Xs}).\\
&\texttt{merge}(\texttt{Xs},[\,],\texttt{Xs}).\\
&\texttt{merge}([\texttt{X}|\texttt{Xs}],[\texttt{Y}|\texttt{Ys}],[\texttt{X}|\texttt{Zs}]) :- \texttt{X} =< \texttt{Y}, \texttt{merge}(\texttt{Xs},[\texttt{Y}|\texttt{Ys}],\texttt{Zs}).\\
&\texttt{merge}([\texttt{X}|\texttt{Xs}],[\texttt{Y}|\texttt{Ys}],[\texttt{Y}|\texttt{Zs}]) :- \texttt{X} > \texttt{Y}, \texttt{merge}([\texttt{X}|\texttt{Xs}],\texttt{Ys},\texttt{Zs}).
\end{aligned}
$$

However, showing termination for the above program is not easy, and the usual approach is to transform the program before showing termination. For example, Plümer [15]) applies iterated unfolding to replace the recursive clause of *mergesort* with the following clause.

$$
\begin{aligned}
&\texttt{mergesort}([\texttt{X},\texttt{Y}|\texttt{Xs}],\texttt{Ys}) :- \texttt{split}(\texttt{Xs},\texttt{X1s},\texttt{X2s}),\\
&\qquad\qquad\qquad\qquad\qquad \texttt{mergesort}([\texttt{X}|\texttt{X1s}],\texttt{Y1s}),\\
&\qquad\qquad\qquad\qquad\qquad \texttt{mergesort}([\texttt{Y}|\texttt{X2s}],\texttt{Y2s}),\\
&\qquad\qquad\qquad\qquad\qquad \texttt{merge}(\texttt{Y1s},\texttt{Y2s},\texttt{Ys}).
\end{aligned}
$$

Ullman and Van Gelder [19] introduce two auxiliary predicates. Apt and Pedreschi [2] introduce an additional argument that forces termination of the program. For all these transformations, it is not clear how they could be generalized or incorporated in an automatic system for checking termination.

In this paper, we show how to transform programs (for the purpose of showing termination) in a completely automatic way. The work reported here was done in the context of the *TermiLog* system [12,14] for automatic termination analysis of logic programs. The transformation we present is triggered by a failure of the *TermiLog* system to show termination. The rough idea is to identify nonrecursive subcases of a problematic predicate, and separate those cases from the general recursive case. For example, in the case of the *mergesort* program, the problematic predicate is split, and the nonrecursive cases that should be handled separately are those of applying split to either an empty list or a list with just one element.

The transformation we present is based on constraint inference, creation of adorned clauses and unfolding. As in the case of unfolding, our transformation can improve termination in the sense that it may prune infinite branches of the LD-tree. However, we also provide conditions guaranteeing that the transformation preserves termination behavior, in the sense that the transformation neither prunes existing infinite branches nor adds new infinite branches. Therefore, the transformation makes it possible to reason about the termination of the original program.

2   Inference of Monotonicity and Equality Constraints

Automatic termination analysis relies on constraints among argument sizes. We use the following definition (cf. [12]).

Definition 1. *() A linear symbolic norm for the terms created from an alphabet having a finite set of constants and function symbols, and a denumerably infinite set of variable symbols, is defined as follows. If the term is of the form $f(T_1, \ldots T_n)$, for a suitable functor f of arity n and terms $T_1, \ldots T_n$, we define*

$$\|f(T_1, \ldots T_n)\| = c + \sum_{i=1}^{n} a_i \|T_i\| \tag{1}$$

where c and $a_1, \ldots a_n$ are non-negative integers that depend only on f/n. This also defines the norm of constants if we consider them as function symbols with arity 0. If the term is a variable, for example X, we define

$$\|X\| = X$$

that is, with each logical variable, we associate an integer variable to represent its norm. The same name is used for both the logical and integer variables, but the appropriate meaning will be clear from the context.

From the definition, it follows that the linear symbolic norm of a term is a linear expression in its variables.

Definition 2. *() A term is instantiated enough with respect to a linear symbolic norm if the expression giving its linear symbolic norm is an integer.*

For simplicity, we use in this paper the term-size norm (cf. [20]) for measuring sizes of arguments. The term-size norm is defined by setting, in (1), each a_i to 1 and c to n. A term is instantiated enough according to the term-size norm if it is ground. However, our method applies to any linear symbolic norm. (See [12] for details—note that in general, an argument b in a query pattern does not necessarily denote a ground argument, but just an argument that is instantiated enough with respect to the given symbolic norm. So, for example, showing that the query pattern $mergesort(b, f)$ terminates with respect to the list-size norm means that all queries with predicate $mergesort$ and first argument instantiated to a list with finite length terminate. Such an argument need not be ground.

Note, by the way, that if a term is ground, it is instantiated enough with respect to any linear symbolic norm.)

Methods for constraint inference are described in [5,7,20,3]. We use monotonicity and equality constraints [5], which are relatively simple to infer. A *monotonicity constraint* $l(i,j)$ for a predicate p means that the size of the ith argument of p is less than the size of the jth argument of p. Similarly, an *equality constraint* $eq(i,j)$ for a predicate p means that the ith and jth arguments of p have equal sizes.

A *conjunctive constraint* for a predicate is a conjunction of monotonicity and equality constraints for the arguments of that predicate. A *disjunctive constraint* for a predicate is a disjunction of conjunctive constraints for that predicate.

We will represent a conjunction of constraints as a pair of the form (*name, list*), where *name* is the predicate name and *list* is the list of constraints in the conjunction.

For a predicate p, there is a finite number of monotonicity and equality constraints that may hold among its arguments. The inference process may be viewed as an abstract interpretation with a finite domain, and therefore, is guaranteed to terminate. A single inference step consists of substituting already inferred constraints for the subgoals of a clause r, and inferring the constraints for the head. Note that the body of the clause may be empty—we call a clause with empty body *a fact* and a clause with non-empty body *a rule*. In what follows we'll use *rule* in the cases we want to stress that the body of a clause is non-empty.

In [12], a single inference step is done by means of the *weighted rule graph*. Alternatively, a constraint solver can be used for that [6]. Note that we infer a *conjunctive constraint* for the head, although one may get more exact descriptions by using disjunctive constraints. Thus, for the clause $append([],Y,Y)$, we will only infer $eq(2,3)$, and not the more exact disjunctive constraint

$$eq(1,2) \wedge eq(2,3) \vee eq(2,3) \wedge l(1,2)$$

The crucial point is to use some sound method to infer, from conjunctive constraints for the body subgoals, a conjunctive constraint for the head.

Given a predicate p, there may be several possibilities for choosing a clause with this predicate in its head and for substituting constraints for its body subgoals. Hence applying single inference steps for a predicate p may lead to different constraints for p, say $C1$ and $C2$. A usual approach is to find a constraint C, such that $C1 \vee C2 \models C$. For example, when $C1$ and $C2$ are conjunctions of linear constraints, C could be the convex hull of $C1$ and $C2$. We use a different approach and simply keep both $C1$ and $C2$ (i.e., we infer the disjunction $C1 \vee C2$). In other words, a single inference step infers a conjunction, but several such steps can infer a disjunction of conjunctions. The inference of disjunctions terminates, since the underlying abstract domain (describing monotonicity and equality constraints) is finite. The result is a disjunction of conjunctions of constraints for each predicate.

The inference process starts with an empty disjunction for each predicate and is done bottom-up. For each clause r, we choose for each subgoal S one conjunction from the current disjunction for the predicate of S (if the disjunction is empty, then clause r cannot be used in the current bottom-up step). For each choice, we infer a conjunction of constraints for the head predicate of r. Note that all possible choices are considered, thus giving different conjunctions for the head predicate of r. In each single inference step we combine the monotonicity and equality constraints substituted for the subgoals with exact norm computations for the terms that appear in clause r, and hence, the inferred constraints are more precise than those that would be inferred if only monotonicity and equality constraints were taken into account (as in [5]). Also note that the inference may yield inconsistency, meaning that nothing is inferred for the head, so nothing is added to the disjunction of the predicate of the head. For the details see [12,11].

Example 2. Consider the following clauses for `split`.

$$\texttt{split}([], [], []).$$
$$\texttt{split}([\texttt{X}|\texttt{Xs}], [\texttt{X}|\texttt{Ys}], \texttt{Zs}) :- \texttt{split}(\texttt{Xs}, \texttt{Zs}, \texttt{Ys}).$$

From the first clause above, we get the following conjunction.

$$(split, [eq(1,2), eq(1,3), eq(2,3)])$$

Note that in this case there are no body subgoals, so the choice of constraints for them is performed vacuously.

When we substitute this conjunction in the body of the second clause, it means that the following equalities are assumed to hold among the norms of arguments.

$$\|Xs\| = \|Ys\| = \|Zs\|$$

According to the definition of the term-size norm, the following equalities also hold.

$$\|[X|Xs]\| = 2 + \|X\| + \|Xs\|$$
$$\|[X|Ys]\| = 2 + \|X\| + \|Ys\|$$

From all of the above equalities, we can infer the following.

$$\|[X|Xs]\| = \|[X|Ys]\|$$
$$\|[X|Xs]\| > \|Zs\|$$
$$\|[X|Ys]\| > \|Zs\|$$

Hence, the following conjunction is inferred for the head.

$$(split, [eq(1,2), l(3,1), l(3,2)])$$

When the above conjunction is substituted in the body of the second clause, we infer the following conjunction.

$$(split, [l(2,1), l(3,1)])$$

No new conjunctions can be inferred after that. Thus, the constraint inferred for split is the disjunction $C1 \lor C2 \lor C3$, where:

$$C1 = (split, [eq(1,2), eq(1,3), eq(2,3)])$$
$$C2 = (split, [eq(1,2), l(3,1), l(3,2)])$$
$$C3 = (split, [l(2,1), l(3,1)])$$

Note that an inference process working with a single conjunction of pairwise constraints (by replacing a disjunction with a convex hull) would infer the following conjunction for split

$$C4 = (split, [le(2,1), le(3,1)])$$

where le means "less than or equal to."

The constraint inference outlined above is, in the worst case, exponential in the maximal arity of any predicate and the maximal number of subgoals in any clause. Experimental results of using this inference process in practice are given in [13].

The conjunction $C4$ is not sufficient for showing termination of mergesort. Specifically, in the clause

$$\text{mergesort}([X, Y|Xs], Ys) :- \text{split}([X, Y|Xs], X1s, X2s),$$
$$\text{mergesort}(X1s, Y1s),$$
$$\text{mergesort}(X2s, Y2s),$$
$$\text{merge}(Y1s, Y2s, Ys).$$

it is impossible to show, given the constraint $C4$ for split, that in both subgoals of mergesort, the first argument is smaller than the one in the head. Therefore, papers dealing with termination of mergesort were forced to use some special transformation of mergesort. Our approach is to show that neither $C1$ nor $C2$ can hold among the arguments of split in the above clause, and to use $C3$ (which is stronger than $C4$) for showing termination. This approach is completely automatic and is explained in the following sections.

This is the place to point out that we use the constraint inference for a further purpose. The constraint inference is done by a semi-naive bottom-up inference. We mark for each conjunction of constraints whether it is derived in (at least) two different iterations of the semi-naive bottom-up inference. This is easily implemented, since in each iteration of a semi-naive bottom-up inference, we have to determine, in any case, which constraints were obtained for the first time. We say that a conjunction of constraints is *pseudo-recursive* if it is derived in more than one iteration of a semi-naive bottom-up inference. In what follows, we will say that a predicate is a *candidate* for adornment if it has (at least) two conjunctions of constraints, such that one is pseudo-recursive and one is not. If termination cannot be shown, then we will choose some candidate predicate (as will be explained later) and apply to it the transformations of adornment and unfolding described in the following two sections.

3 Creating Adorned Clauses

We will first illustrate how the clauses for split are transformed into clauses that are adorned by the inferred conjunctions $C1$, $C2$ and $C3$, and then we will describe the method in general. Adorned clauses in the context of the magic-set transformation are discussed in [18], and constructing adorned clauses based on inferred constraints is described in [10].

Transforming the clauses for split into adorned clauses is done as follows. First, the adorned predicates are split^{C1}, split^{C2} and split^{C3}. Second, in each one of the original clauses for split, we substitute one of the adorned predicates for each occurrence of split in the body. In general, there is more than one combination of substituting adorned predicates, and consequently, several different clauses may be created from each original clause. After substituting in the body, we infer the adornment of the head as follows. For each adorned subgoal in the body, we substitute the conjunction of constraints specified by its adornment (e.g., $C1$ is substituted for split^{C1}). The adornment for the head is computed from the constraints substituted in the body, as was done in the bottom-up inference of constraints (i.e., using a weighted rule graph or a constraint solver). Note that the adornment for the head must be one of the inferred conjunctions for split, since the inference of the head adornment is the same as in a single step of the bottom-up inference of constraints. Special consideration should be given to the case in which the conjunctions of constraints substituted in the body yield inconsistency. In this case, the adorned clause is eliminated, because it describes a situation that cannot happen (for example, we will never be able to prove a goal in which the norm of the first argument is both smaller and bigger than the norm of the second argument).

Example 3. Consider the original clauses for split.

$$\mathrm{split}([\,], [\,], [\,]).$$
$$\mathrm{split}([X|Xs], [X|Ys], Zs) :- \mathrm{split}(Xs, Zs, Ys).$$

In the first clause, no substitutions are done in the body, since it is empty. The adornment inferred for the head is $C1$. Thus, only one adorned clause is obtained:

$$\mathrm{split}^{C1}([\,], [\,], [\,]).$$

In the second original clause for split, either split^{C1}, split^{C2} or split^{C3} can be substituted for the occurrence of split in the body. The resulting clauses are as follows.

$$\mathrm{split}^{C2}([X|Xs], [X|Ys], Zs) :- \mathrm{split}^{C1}(Xs, Zs, Ys).$$
$$\mathrm{split}^{C3}([X|Xs], [X|Ys], Zs) :- \mathrm{split}^{C2}(Xs, Zs, Ys).$$
$$\mathrm{split}^{C3}([X|Xs], [X|Ys], Zs) :- \mathrm{split}^{C3}(Xs, Zs, Ys).$$

In general, adorning a predicate s is done as follows. If the inferred constraint for s is a single conjunction C, then all occurrences of s are adorned with C, and the adorned predicate is denoted as s^C. Now, suppose that predicate s has the disjunctive constraint

$$C1 \vee \ldots \vee Cn$$

where $n \geq 2$. The adorned versions of s are

$$s^{C1}, \ldots, s^{Cn}$$

The idea is that after replacing s with its adorned versions, the inferred constraint for each s^{Ci} is the single conjunction Ci. The adornment process is done as follows. For each clause $H \leftarrow B_1, \ldots, B_k$ of the program that has an occurrence of s either in the head or in the body, we consider all combinations of

- replacing each occurrence of s in the body with one of $s^{C1}, \ldots, s^{Cn}$, and
- assigning to each subgoal in the body one of the conjunctions of the disjunctive constraint inferred for the predicate of that subgoal (the disjunctive constraint may consist of a single conjunction). Note that for each s^{Ci}, the assigned constraint is Ci.

Next, we infer the constraint for the head of the clause $H \leftarrow B_1, \ldots, B_k$. Note that this inference step is identical to some single step of the bottom-up inference, since the constraints assigned to the subgoals in the body are just conjunctions that were inferred for the predicates of those subgoals. If the inference yields inconsistency, then the adorned clause is discarded. If the predicate of the head is s and the constraint C is inferred for the head, then C becomes the adornment of the head. The following remarks should be noted. First, C must be one of $C1, \ldots, Cn$, since the inference of C is just a repetition of a single step of the bottom-up inference. Second, applying constraint inference to the new program will yield for each s^{Ci} the constraint Ci. Third, in the case of a clause for s that has an empty body, we only need to infer the adornment of the head. Fourth, the adornment process we have described can be used to adorn predicate s without adorning (some or all) the predicates on which s depends.

Discarding clauses (in process of adorning a predicate) may transform a non-terminating program into a terminating one, as shown by the next example.

Example 4. Consider the following clauses.

$$\text{p}(\text{X}, \text{Y}) :- \text{le}(\text{X}, \text{Y}).$$
$$\text{le}(\text{X}, \text{X}).$$
$$\text{le}(\text{X}, \text{s}(\text{Y})) :- \text{le}(\text{X}, \text{Y}).$$
$$\text{le}(\text{s}(\text{X}), \text{s}(\text{Y})) :- \text{le}(\text{X}, \text{Y}).$$
$$\text{le}(\text{s}(\text{X}), \text{X}) :- \text{le}(\text{s}(\text{X}), \text{X}).$$

Two conjunctions of constraints are inferred for le, namely $(le, [eq(1, 2)])$ and $(le, [l(1, 2)])$. We transform le into two adorned predicates, denoted $\text{le}^{[eq(1,2)]}$ and $\text{le}^{[l(1,2)]}$, and obtain the following adorned clauses.

$$p(X, Y) :- le^{[eq(1,2)]}(X, Y).$$
$$p(X, Y) :- le^{[l(1,2)]}(X, Y).$$
$$le^{[eq(1,2)]}(X, X).$$
$$le^{[l(1,2)]}(X, s(Y)) :- le^{[eq(1,2)]}(X, Y).$$
$$le^{[l(1,2)]}(X, s(Y)) :- le^{[l(1,2)]}(X, Y).$$
$$le^{[eq(1,2)]}(s(X), s(Y)) :- le^{[eq(1,2)]}(X, Y).$$
$$le^{[l(1,2)]}(s(X), s(Y)) :- le^{[l(1,2)]}(X, Y).$$

Note that the two adorned versions of the last clause of the original program were discarded, because the constraint among the argument sizes in that clause (i.e., the term size of $s(X)$ is greater than the term size of X) and the constraints substituted for the adorned predicates are inconsistent. As a result of the elimination of that clause, queries having the pattern $p(b, b)$ terminate with respect to the transformed program, although queries of the pattern $p(b, b)$ may be non-terminating with respect to the original program.

It should be noted that the transformation of creating adorned clauses preserves the computed answer substitutions (c.a.s) of the program; however, it may prune infinite branches in the LD-tree. Therefore, we can view it as a transformation for improving the behavior of a program with respect to termination. As illustrated in Example 4, the transformation is capable of converting a nonterminating program into a terminating one.

4   Nonrecursive Unfolding

The *predicate dependency graph* for a program is defined (cf. [15]) as a graph that has a node for each predicate and an edge from p to q if there is a rule with predicate p in the head and predicate q in the body. A predicate p is *recursive* if there is a cycle in the predicate dependency graph that goes through p. A predicate p is *nonrecursive* if there is no such cycle, and p is *strongly nonrecursive* if it is nonrecursive and does not depend, directly or indirectly, on any recursive predicate. A rule is (strongly) nonrecursive if all predicates in its body are (strongly) nonrecursive.

Rules for strongly nonrecursive predicates can be completely unfolded into facts. The adorned clauses in Example 3 involve three predicates, $split^{C1}$, $split^{C2}$ and $split^{C3}$, the first two being strongly nonrecursive and the third one—recursive. Thus, both $split^{C1}$ and $split^{C2}$ can be unfolded. A complete unfolding of the rule for $split^{C2}$ yields the following fact.

$$split^{C2}([X], [X], []).$$

Similarly, a strongly nonrecursive rule, such as the following rule

$$split^{C3}([X|Xs], [X|Ys], Zs) :- split^{C2}(Xs, Zs, Ys).$$

can also be replaced with facts. For example, the above rule can be replaced with the following fact.

$$\text{split}^{C3}([X, Y], [X], [Y]).$$

Thus, the four adorned clauses for split from Example 3 can be replaced with the following clauses.

$$\text{split}^{C1}([], [], []).$$
$$\text{split}^{C2}([X], [X], []).$$
$$\text{split}^{C3}([X, Y], [X], [Y]).$$
$$\text{split}^{C3}([X|Xs], [X|Ys], Zs) :- \text{split}^{C3}(Xs, Zs, Ys).$$

After having used unfolding for the adorned clauses for split, we now consider the rule for mergesort that involves split.

$$
\begin{aligned}
\text{mergesort}([X, Y|Xs], Ys) :- & \text{split}([X, Y|Xs], X1s, X2s), \\
& \text{mergesort}(X1s, Y1s), \\
& \text{mergesort}(X2s, Y2s), \\
& \text{merge}(Y1s, Y2s, Ys).
\end{aligned}
$$

According to our method, this rule should be replaced with three rules, where each one of those rules is obtained by replacing split with either split^{C1}, split^{C2} or split^{C3}. In the new rules, the strongly nonrecursive predicates, split^{C1} and split^{C2}, can be completely unfolded. When doing so, $[X, Y|Xs]$ cannot be unified with either $[]$ or $[X]$, and so, two of the new rules disappear and only the following one remains.

$$
\begin{aligned}
\text{mergesort}([X, Y|Xs], Ys) :- & \text{split}^{C3}([X, Y|Xs], X1s, X2s), \\
& \text{mergesort}(X1s, Y1s), \\
& \text{mergesort}(X2s, Y2s), \\
& \text{merge}(Y1s, Y2s, Ys).
\end{aligned}
$$

In general, there are two stages of unfolding—first in the clauses for the adorned predicate, and then in the other clauses.

What we did here can be generalized to predicates that are not strongly nonrecursive, but just nonrecursive. Given the predicate dependency graph, it can be partitioned into strongly connected components (SCC), which can be sorted topologically. The predicates of each SCC depend only on predicates of lower SCCs. Each subgoal of a nonrecursive adorned predicate (that appears in the right-hand side of an adorned rule) can be unfolded into subgoals of predicates in lower SCCs.

5 Reasoning About Termination

Thus far, we have described the two transformations of adorning a predicate and performing nonrecursive unfolding of an adorned predicate, and applied them to the `mergesort` program. Both transformations preserve the computed answer substitutions. However, as the example at the end of Section 3 and Example 1 in [4] show, these transformations may, in general, turn a non-terminating goal into a terminating one. The theorems in this section show that under conditions that are satisfied by the `mergesort` program this will not happen, so the transformed program will have the same termination behavior as the original program.

The first transformation is *adorning* a predicate s. For simplicity, we assume that s is not mutually recursive with any other predicate (otherwise, we have to create simultaneously adorned versions for all predicates that are mutually recursive with s). The steps of the transformation are as follows.

- Infer constraints for predicate s and for the predicates on which s depends. Note that for predicates that are already adorned, the inferred constraints are identical to the adornments.
- Adorn predicate s, as described in Section 3.

In general, the above transformation preserves the c.a.s. semantics of the program (that is, it preserves the computed answer substitutions of all derivations), but it may improve the termination of the program. The following theorem shows that under certain conditions, the above transformation also preserves termination behavior. We need the following definitions.

Definition 3. *() Given a program P and a query pattern κ, we define $calls(\kappa)$ as a set of call patterns that satisfies the following condition. For all queries Q with the pattern κ and for all nodes v in the LD-tree of Q with respect to P, the first subgoal in v must be an instance of some $\sigma \in calls(\kappa)$.*

Note that $calls(\kappa)$ is not uniquely defined. Ideally, we would like $calls(\kappa)$ to be the set of all call patterns generated by κ, but in practice, $calls(\kappa)$ is computed by some abstract interpretation that may only provide an approximation. In the case of *mergesort*, one may have

$$calls(mergesort(b, f)) =$$

$$\{b =< b, \; b > b, \; mergesort(b, f), \; merge(b, b, f), \; split(b, f, f)\}$$

Definition 4. *() Let P be a program, s a predicate in P, and κ a query pattern for a predicate that depends on s. We say that predicate s is terminating with respect to κ and P if all query patterns of s in $calls(\kappa)$ are terminating with respect to P.*

Note that s can be terminating with respect to κ even if κ is not terminating.

Theorem 1. *Let P be a program, s a predicate in P and κ a query pattern, whose predicate belongs to a higher level of the predicate dependency graph of P than s. Suppose that s is terminating with respect to κ and P. Let P^a be obtained from P by creating adorned rules for predicate s as described above. Let Q be a query with pattern κ. The LD-tree of Q with respect to P is finite if and only if the LD-tree of Q with respect to P^a is finite.*

Proof. Note that each clause r^a of P^a has a corresponding clause r of P that is obtained from r^a by deleting the adornments of those predicates that are not adorned in P. Consider a query Q with the pattern κ, and suppose that the LD-tree of Q with respect to P^a has an infinite branch. By deleting the adornments of s from that infinite branch, we get an infinite branch of the LD-tree of Q with respect to P.

To prove the other direction, suppose that there is an infinite branch of the LD-tree of Q with respect to P. Since we assumed that predicate s is terminating with respect to κ and P, refutations of subgoals of s, along that infinite branch, are finite. We will show how to replace each partial branch of the form

$$\leftarrow s(\ldots), g_1(\ldots), \ldots, g_k(\ldots)$$

$$\vdots$$

$$\leftarrow g_1(\ldots), \ldots, g_k(\ldots)$$

(which corresponds to a refutation of $\leftarrow s(\ldots)$ with respect to P) with a partial branch of P^a having the same c.a.s.

Going bottom up along the above partial branch, we will tag predicates in a process that is similar to creating adorned clauses. Suppose that the node

$$\leftarrow H, C, \ldots$$

has the child

$$\leftarrow B_1, \ldots, B_n, C\theta, \ldots$$

that was obtained by using a clause instance $H\theta \leftarrow B_1, \ldots, B_n$ of the clause $H' \leftarrow B'_1, \ldots, B'_n$ (note that $n = 0$ is possible). Inductively, we assume that $B_1, \ldots, B_n$ were already tagged. The tag of each B_i is essentially a conjunctive constraint, and we assign those constraints to $B'_1, \ldots, B'_n$, respectively. The tag for the head H' is just the conjunction of constraints inferred for H'. The tag generated for H' is given to the occurrence of H in the node

$$\leftarrow H, C, \ldots$$

as well as to occurrences of H in ancestors of that node. Note that essentially we have here a bottom-up inference of constraints that starts with instantiated facts of the program. We use the original clause $H' \leftarrow B'_1, \ldots, B'_n$, rather than the instance $H\theta \leftarrow B_1, \ldots, B_n$, in order to guarantee that the inferred constraints are the same as in the original program (if the clause instance had been used, it might have been possible to infer tighter constraints that do not coincide with the adornments of P^a).

The predicates involved in this inference are just s and predicates on which s depends. Some of those predicates may already be adorned in P, and in this case, the tags coincide with the existing adornments. It may also be the case that a predicate is tagged although it is not adorned in P^a. In this case, we simply delete the tags of that predicate at the end of the process. For occurrences of predicate s, the tags become the adornments for s. Thus, we have shown how to transform the infinite branch of the LD-tree of Q with respect to P into an infinite branch of the LD-tree of Q with respect to P^a.   □

If in Theorem 1 we do not make the assumption that s is terminating with respect to κ and P, then only one direction of the theorem holds; that is, if the LD-tree of Q with respect to P is finite then so is the LD-tree of Q with respect to P^a. The converse is not necessarily true, as was shown in Example 4. However, both LD-trees still generate the same c.a.s.

The second transformation is unfolding of adorned versions of s. We apply this transformation in two stages. First, we unfold adorned versions of s in bodies of rules for adorned versions of s. Second, we unfold adorned versions of s in bodies of rules for predicates other than adorned versions of s. In general unfolding may improve termination, as shown by the next theorem [4].

Theorem 2. *Let P be a program and κ a query pattern. Let P' be the program obtained from P by unfolding. Let Q be a query with pattern κ. If the LD-tree of Q with respect to P is finite, so is the LD-tree of Q with respect to P'. Moreover, Q has the same computed answer substitutions with respect to both programs.*

Our goal is not just to show that Q terminates with respect to the transformed program, but also that it terminates with respect to the original program. The following two theorems state conditions for preserving termination behavior under the unfolding transformation. The first theorem deals with unfolding of adorned versions of s in rules for adorned versions of s, and the second theorem deals with a similar unfolding in rules for predicates other than adorned versions of s.

Theorem 3. *Consider a program P and a query pattern κ, and let s be a predicate of P. Let P^a and P^{au} be defined as follows.*

- *Program P^a is obtained from P by the transformation of adorning predicate s.*
- *Program P^{au} is obtained from P^a by unfolding adorned versions of s in bodies of rules of P^a, where the heads of those rules are also adorned versions of s.*

If s is terminating with respect to P and κ, and Q is a query with pattern κ, then the following holds. The LD-tree of P^a with respect to Q is finite if and only if the LD-tree of P^{au} with respect to Q is finite.

Proof. One direction follows from Theorem 2. For the other direction, suppose that the LD-tree of P^a with respect to Q has an infinite branch. Since s is terminating with respect to P and κ, refutations of subgoals of s along the infinite branch are finite. We can replace each refutation of a subgoals of s with a refutation that uses clauses of P^{au}, and the result is an infinite branch of the LD-tree of P^{au} with respect to Q.   □

The above theorem states that any adorned version of s can be unfolded in rules for s while preserving the termination behavior of κ. In practice, however, we would unfold just the nonrecursive adorned versions of s.

Theorem 4. *Consider a program P and a query pattern κ, and let s be a predicate of P. Let P^a, P^{au} and P^{auu} be defined as follows.*

- *Program P^a and P^{au} are obtained as defined in Theorem 3.*
- *Suppose that the adorned versions of predicate s are partitioned into two nonempty subsets A_1 and A_2. Program P^{auu} is obtained from P^{au} by unfolding adorned versions of A_1 in bodies of rules of P^{au} for predicates other than s.*

If s is terminating with respect to P and κ, then the following holds. The LD-tree of P^a with respect to a query Q with pattern κ is finite if and only if the LD-tree of P^{auu} with respect to Q is finite.

Proof. By Theorems 2 and 3 it is enough to prove that it cannot happen that the LD-tree for P^{au} and Q is infinite, while the LD-tree for P^{auu} and Q is not. The main difference between P^{au} and P^{auu} is that in the transition from the first to the second some rules of the form

$$H \; : - \; \ldots, s_i(\ldots), \ldots$$

got eliminated after unfolding because they could only create failing derivations. If such a transformation changes Q from non-terminating to terminating this must be caused by the subgoals preceding s_i in the rule. However since P^{au} contains all the rules

$$H \; : - \; \ldots, s_1(\ldots), \ldots$$
$$H \; : - \; \ldots, s_2(\ldots), \ldots$$
$$\vdots$$
$$H \; : - \; \ldots, s_k(\ldots), \ldots$$

and there is at least one s_i for which we do not perform unfolding, some copies of the subgoals that cause non-termination remain in P^{auu}.   □

The above theorem assumes that the adorned versions of predicate s are partitioned into two nonempty subsets A_1 and A_2, and only adorned versions of A_1 are unfolded. In practice, A_1 would be a set of nonrecursive adorned versions of s, and those adorned versions would be completely unfolded if they are strongly nonrecursive, or just unfolded into predicates from lower SCCs if they are merely nonrecursive.

Now, consider again the *mergesort* program. First, *TermiLog* can show that predicate split is terminating with respect to the original *mergesort* program and a query of the pattern $mergesort(b, f)$. Thus, the transformation of creating adorned rules for split (which is described in Section 3) is termination-behavior preserving by Theorem 1. Secondly, the unfolding applied to the adorned rules of split (which is described in Section 4) is termination-behavior preserving by Theorem 3. Thirdly, the unfolding of the adorned subgoals of split in the rules for mergesort (which is described in Section 4) is termination-behavior preserving by Theorem 4 (in this particular case, it follows that the unfolding is termination-behavior preserving also because the unfolded subgoal is always the leftmost subgoal).

The new program for mergesort, after all the transformations described thus far, is the following one.

$$mergesort([], []).$$
$$mergesort([X], [X]).$$
$$mergesort([X, Y|Xs], Ys) :- split^{C3}([X, Y|Xs], X1s, X2s),$$
$$mergesort(X1s, Y1s),$$
$$mergesort(X2s, Y2s),$$
$$merge(Y1s, Y2s, Ys).$$
$$split^{C1}([], [], []).$$
$$split^{C2}([X], [X], []).$$
$$split^{C3}([X, Y], [X], [Y]).$$
$$split^{C3}([X|Xs], [X|Ys], Zs) :- split^{C3}(Xs, Zs, Ys).$$
$$merge([], Xs, Xs).$$
$$merge(Xs, [], Xs).$$
$$merge([X|Xs], [Y|Ys], [X|Zs]) :- X =< Y, merge(Xs, [Y|Ys], Zs).$$
$$merge([X|Xs], [Y|Ys], [Y|Zs]) :- X > Y, merge([X|Xs], Ys, Zs).$$

Termination of the new program for mergesort can be easily shown by the *TermiLog* system [12,14]. Since the transformations are all termination-behavior preserving, it follows that the original *mergesort* program also terminates.

6   The General Method

In this section, we describe a heuristic for deciding which predicates should be adorned in order to prove termination. In principle, it is possible to find all predicates to which our transformation can be applied, but it may not be practical to do so. Suppose that κ is a query pattern for a program P, and termination of κ cannot be shown, say with *TermiLog*. The purpose of the following steps is to find a predicate s, and apply to s the transformations of creating adorned clauses and unfolding nonrecursive adorned versions of s, in order to show termination.

1. Perform constraint inference for P.
2. Compute $calls(\kappa)$ (see [16] for details).
3. Find a σ in $calls(\kappa)$, such that termination of σ cannot be shown, but all calls of σ to predicates from lower SCCs can be shown to terminate, and σ depends on a predicate from a lower SCC, say s, for which some but not all the constraints are pseudo-recursive. If there is no such σ, then stop.
4. Create adorned clauses for s and compute P^{auu} (see Theorem 4). Note that the unfolding is done with respect to those adornments of s that are not pseudo-recursive, since those adornments yield nonrecursive adorned versions of s. A complete unfolding is performed for strongly nonrecursive predicates, while nonrecursive predicates are unfolded into predicates from lower SCCs.

If, after performing the above transformations for s, termination of σ cannot be shown, then the method is not powerful enough to show termination. If termination of σ can be shown, but termination of κ still cannot be shown, then we repeat the process for κ and P^{auu}. Since each choice of s reduces the number of candidate predicates by 1, the steps cannot be repeated forever.

In the program for mergesort, there was exactly one candidate predicate, namely split. As another example, consider the following program for finding the greatest common divisor, where the query is of the pattern $gcd(b, b, f)$.

Example 5.

$$\text{less}(0, s(X)).$$
$$\text{less}(s(X), s(Y)) :- \text{less}(X, Y).$$
$$\text{less}(X, s(Y)) :- \text{less}(X, Y).$$
$$\text{add}(0, L, L).$$
$$\text{add}(s(X), Y, s(Z)) :- \text{add}(X, Y, Z).$$
$$\text{mod}(s(X), s(X), 0).$$
$$\text{mod}(X, s(Y), X) :- \text{less}(X, s(Y)).$$
$$\text{mod}(X, s(Y), M) :- \text{less}(s(Y), X), \text{add}(s(Y), Y1, X), \text{mod}(Y1, s(Y), M).$$
$$\text{gcd}(s(X), 0, s(X)).$$
$$\text{gcd}(X, s(Y), M) :- \text{mod}(X, s(Y), M1), \text{gcd}(s(Y), M1, M).$$

In this example, there are 4 recursive predicates, and it turns out that all, except less, are candidate predicates. Each predicate of the above program is in a strongly connected component by itself. The predicates less and add are in the lowest layer, followed by mod and then by gcd. The *TermiLog* system can show termination of less and add, but fails to show termination of mod. Our heuristic is to choose a candidate predicate s, such that s appears as a subgoal in some rule of mod and s is from a lower SCC than mod, and to replace s with its adorned versions. In our example, add is the only candidate predicate that appears as a subgoal in some rule for mod, and hence, add is a candidate for applying the transformation into adorned clauses. The following two conjunctions of constraints are inferred for add.

$$A1 = (add, [eq(2,3)])$$
$$A2 = (add, [l(2,3)])$$

Thus, we transform add into the adorned predicates add^{A1} and add^{A2}, where the first one is strongly nonrecursive. After creating adorned clauses and unfolding strongly nonrecursive predicates, we get the following program.

```
less(0, s(X)).
less(s(X), s(Y)) :− less(X, Y).
less(X, s(Y)) :− less(X, Y).
add^A1(0, L, L).
add^A2(s(0), Y, s(Y)).
add^A2(s(X), Y, s(Z)) :− add^A2(X, Y, Z).
mod(s(X), s(X), 0).
mod(X, s(Y), X) :− less(X, s(Y)).
mod(X, s(Y), M) :− less(s(Y), X), add^A2(s(Y), Y1, X), mod(Y1, s(Y), M).
gcd(s(X), 0, s(X)).
gcd(X, s(Y), M) :− mod(X, s(Y), M1), gcd(s(Y), M1, M).
```

Now *TermiLog* can show termination. The theorems of the previous section imply that there also is termination for the original program.

In the following example the transformation has to be performed several times.

Example 6.

```
a(L, L).
a(L, [H|K]) :− a(L, K).
level_0([], []).
level_0([X, X|L], [X|M]) :− a(U, L),
                           level_0(U, M).
level_1([], []).
level_1([X|L], Y) :− level_0([X|L], Z),
                    level_1(Z, Y).
level_2([], []).
level_2([X|L], Y) :− level_1([X|L], Z),
                    level_2(Z, Y).
```

In this case all the predicates are recursive. The predicate a is in the lowest SCC of the predicate dependency graph and is followed by the SCC's of $level\_0, level\_1, level\_2$ in this order. The constraints are

$$(level\_0, [eq(1,2)], nonrec)$$

$$(level\_0, [l(2,1)], rec)$$

$$(level\_1, [eq(1,2)], rec)$$

$$(level\_1, [l(2,1)], rec)$$

$$(level\_2, [eq(1,2)], rec)$$

$$(level\_2, [l(2,1)], rec)$$

and *TermiLog* can prove termination of $level\_0(b, f)$ but not of $level\_1(b, f)$ and $level\_2(b, f)$. So the candidate for adorning and unfolding is $level\_0$. After the transformations we get the program

```
a(L, L).
a(L, [H|K]) :- a(L, K).
level_0^[eq(1,2)]([], []).
level_0^[1(2,1)]([X, X|L], [X]) :- a([], L).
level_0^[1(2,1)]([X, X|L], [X|M]) :- a(U, L),
                                     level_0^[1(2,1)](U, M).
level_1([], []).
level_1([X|L], Y) :- level_0^[1(2,1)]([X|L], Z),
                     level_1(Z, Y).
level_2([], []).
level_2([X|L], Y) :- level_1([X|L], Z),
                     level_2(Z, Y).
```

Now *TermiLog* can prove the termination of $level\_1(b, f)$ but not of $level\_2(b, f)$, and $level\_1$ has the non-pseudo-recursive constraint $[eq(1,2)]$ and the pseudo-recursive constraint $[l(2,1)]$. So we do the adorning and unfolding for $level\_1$, getting the program

```
a(L, L).
a(L, [H|K]) :- a(L, K).
level_0^[eq(1,2)]([], []).
level_0^[1(2,1)]([X, X|L], [X]) :- a([], L).
level_0^[1(2,1)]([X, X|L], [X|M]) :- a(U, L),
                                     level_0^[1(2,1)](U, M).
level_1^[eq(1,2)]([], []).
```

$$\texttt{level\_1}^{[1(2,1)]}([\texttt{X}|\texttt{L}],[]) :- \texttt{level\_0}^{[1(2,1)]}([\texttt{X}|\texttt{L}],[]).$$
$$\texttt{level\_1}^{[1(2,1)]}([\texttt{X}|\texttt{L}],\texttt{Y}) :- \texttt{level\_0}^{[1(2,1)]}([\texttt{X}|\texttt{L}],\texttt{Z}),$$
$$\texttt{level\_1}^{[1(2,1)]}(\texttt{Z},\texttt{Y}).$$
$$\texttt{level\_2}([],[]).$$
$$\texttt{level\_2}([\texttt{X}|\texttt{L}],\texttt{Y}) :- \texttt{level\_1}^{[1(2,1)]}([\texttt{X}|\texttt{L}],\texttt{Z}),$$
$$\texttt{level\_2}(\texttt{Z},\texttt{Y}).$$

Now *TermiLog* can prove termination of *level_2*(b, f) and from the theorems in Section 5 it follows that it also terminates for the original program (Example 6).

The definitions of *level_1* and *level_2* in Example 6 are symmetric. If we added similarly defined functions up to *level_n*, *TermiLog* could prove the termination of *level_n*(b, f) after n transformations.

7   Conclusion

We have presented a transformation that preserves the c.a.s. semantics of logic programs and improves their termination behavior (i.e., infinite branches in the LD-tree may be pruned). We have also provided conditions for preserving termination behavior under that transformation. The transformation is automated and implemented in SICStus Prolog (cf. [17]), and is useful in the context of a system for automatic termination analysis, such as *TermiLog*. The basic idea is, in cases in which we cannot prove termination but there is a predicate with pseudo-recursive and non-pseudo-recursive constraints, to adorn this predicate. Separating the predicate into different adorned predicates may result in a program for which termination can be shown automatically. The success of this transformation underscores the importance of inferring disjunctions of conjunctions of constraints, rather than just a single conjunction (which is the common approach).

We are grateful to the referees for their careful reading and helpful comments.

References

1. K. R. Apt. *From Logic Programming to Prolog.* Prentice Hall, 1997.
2. K. R. Apt and D. Pedreschi. Modular Termination Proofs for Logic and Pure Prolog Programs. In *Advances in Logic Programming Theory*, 183-229. Oxford University Press, 1994.
3. F. Benoy and A. King. Inferring Argument Size Relationships with CLP(R). *LOPSTR'96.* Springer Lecture Notes in Computer Science.
4. A. Bossi and N. Cocco. Preserving Universal Termination Through Unfold/Fold. *ALP'94*, 269-286. Springer Lecture Notes in Computer Science 850, 1994.
5. A. Brodsky and Y. Sagiv. Inference of Monotonicity Constraints in Datalog Programs. *Proceedings of the Eighth ACM SIGACT-SIGART-SIGMOD Symposium on Principles of Database Systems*, 1989, 190-199.

6. M. Codish and C. Taboch. A Semantic Basis for Termination Analysis of Logic Programs. ALP'97.

7. P. Cousot and R. Cousot. Abstract Interpretation and Application to Logic Programs. *J. Logic Programming*, 13:103-179, 1992.

8. D. De Schreye and S. Decorte. Termination of Logic Programs: the Never-Ending Story. *J. Logic Programming*, 19-20:199-260, 1994.

9. M. Falaschi, G. Levi, M. Martelli and C. Palamidessi. Declarative Modeling of the Operational Behaviour of Logic Programs. *Theoretical Computer Science*, 69(3):289-318, 1989.

10. A. Levy and Y. Sagiv. Constraints and Redundancy in Datalog. *PODS'92*, 67-80. ACM, 1992.

11. N. Lindenstrauss and Y. Sagiv. Checking Termination of Queries to Logic Programs. Available at http://www.cs.huji.ac.il/~naomil/

12. N. Lindenstrauss and Y. Sagiv. Automatic Termination Analysis of Logic Programs. *ICLP'97*. MIT Press, 1997.

13. N. Lindenstrauss and Y. Sagiv. Automatic Termination Analysis of Logic Programs (with Detailed Experimental Results). Available at http://www.cs.huji.ac.il/~naomil/

14. N. Lindenstrauss, Y. Sagiv, A. Serebrenik. TermiLog: A System for Checking Termination of Queries to Logic Programs. *CAV'97*. Springer Lecture Notes in Computer Science, 1997.

15. L. Plümer. *Termination Proofs for Logic Programs*. Springer Verlag, LNAI 446, 1990.

16. Y. Sagiv. A termination test for logic programs. In *International Logic Programming Symposium*. MIT Press, 1991.

17. *SICStus Prolog User's Manual, Release 3 # 3*. Swedish Institute of Computer Science, 1995.

18. J. D. Ullman. *Principles of Database and Knowledge-Base Systems*, Vol. II. Computer Science Press, 1989.

19. J. D. Ullman and A. Van Gelder. Efficient Tests for Top-Down Termination of Logical Rules. Journal of the ACM, 35, 1988, 345-373.

20. A. Van Gelder. Deriving Constraints among Argument Sizes in Logic Programs. *Annals of Mathematics and Artificial Intelligence*, 3:361-392, 1991.

21. K. Verschaetse, S. Decorte and D. De Schreye. Automatic Termination Analysis. *LOPSTR 92*, ed. K. K. Lau and T. Clement. Workshops in Computing Series, Springer, 1992.

Towards a Logic for Reasoning About Logic Programs Transformation

Alberto Momigliano[*1] and Mario Ornaghi[2]

[1] Department of Philosophy, Carnegie Mellon University,
15213 Pittsburgh PA, USA, `mobile@cs.cmu.edu`
[2] Dipartimento di Scienze dell'Informazione, Universita' degli studi di Milano,
Via Comelico 39/41, Milano, Italy, `ornaghi@dsi.unimi.it`

Abstract. We give a proof-theoretic analysis of logic programs transformations, viewed as operations on proof trees in the sense of [3,4,9,10]. We present a logic for reasoning about (equivalence preserving) transformations of logic programs. Our main tool is the usage of inference rules; the target program may be obtained as a set of clause introduction proofs with axioms from the source program. The rules are *admissible*, that is every proof according to the latter can be translated back in a derivation of the same consequence built from the source program *without* those rules. In this formal setting, we give a general schema for program transformation analysis, which can be applied to any transformation system based on admissible rules. As examples, we treat Partial Deduction and Unfold/Fold transformations. Furthermore, the proof-theoretic framework allows a uniform generalization of the basic results to other logic programming languages satisfying the simple requirement of *regularity*. Our perspective and overall aim is to develop the proof-theory of (logic) program transformation.

1 Introduction

We give a proof-theoretic analysis of logic programs transformations, viewed as operations on proof trees in the sense of [3,4,9,10]. We present a logic for reasoning about (equivalence preserving) transformations of logic programs. Our framework is natural deduction à la Prawitz [12], although a totally analogous presentation can be given in terms of sequent calculi with definitional reflection [14]. We are not going to fully detail in this paper the systems we are using, though we have shown elsewhere [9] (and it is beginning to be common knowledge, see [3,4]) that, w.r.t. the language of definite clauses, the interpretation of ': −' and ',' as implication and conjunction yields a fragment of positive intuitionistic, (i.e. minimal) logic. Our basic system, let us call it L_0, contains only the assumption rule and a rule for applying clauses (ca), similar to the rule of modus ponens.

---

[*] This work was mostly completed during a visit by the first author to the Dipartimento di Scienze dell'Informazione, Universita' degli studi di Milano.

Norbert E. Fuchs (Ed.): LOPSTR'97, LNCS 1463, pp. 226–244, 1998.
© Springer-Verlag Berlin Heidelberg 1998

We shall follow this path:

1. We achieve the transformation via the usage of inference rules; thus, the target program may be obtained as a set $\mathcal{Q}$ of *clause introduction proofs* with axioms from the source program $\mathcal{P}$ of the form:

$$\mathcal{Q} = \frac{\Pi_1}{C_1 \leftarrow \mathcal{B}_1} r_1, \dots, \frac{\Pi_n}{C_n \leftarrow \mathcal{B}_n} r_n$$

2. We show the rules to be (weakly) admissible, that is every proof Π with consequence A which uses those rules can be translated in a proof $\tau(\Pi)$ of the same proposition *without* them in the basic system with axioms from $\mathcal{P}$. As the proofs in L_0 correspond to *SLD*-derivations, this means that every derivation from $\mathcal{Q}$ is translated into a *SLD*-derivation of $\mathcal{P} \cup \{\leftarrow A\}$.
3. We will look for some adequacy results. Namely, verifying that the success set is preserved requires certain completeness conditions on $\Pi_1, \dots, \Pi_n$; for finite failure we need furthermore the *strict* monotonicity of the translation function.

We pursue two applications: Partial Deduction and Unfold/Fold transformations. Our perspective and future aim is the introduction of a general calculus tailored to the proof-theory of the transformation of (logic) programs.

The paper is organized as follows: in Section 2 we review the basic notions of our framework [9,10] and we relate it to *SLD*-resolution w.r.t. success and failure. Section 3 presents the general transformation schema. The next Section (4) depicts the proof-theoretical reconstruction of Partial Deduction. Section 5 targets Unfold/Fold transformations. Finally, a brief Conclusion winds up the paper.

2   Background on Proof Trees

First we recall some basic definitions: we assume some familiarity with standard notions of natural deduction [12] and logic programming [1].

We use a variant of the Axiom Application Rules introduced in [9]. We consider the *Clause Application Rule* ca, for applying axioms of the form $B \leftarrow A_1, \dots, A_n$. Using the formalism of natural deduction, ca can be expressed as follows:

$$\frac{A_1\theta \; \cdots \; A_n\,\theta \qquad B \leftarrow A_1, \dots, A_n}{B\theta}\,\text{ca}$$

where the applied clause is the *major premise*, $A_1\theta, \dots, A_n\theta$ is the (possibly empty, for $n = 0$) sequence of *minor premises* and $B\theta$ is the consequence. Next, we inductively introduce the notion of *proof tree* (pt).

Definition 1 ((Proof Tree)). *An atom A is a (trivial) proof tree. If $\Pi_1 ::$ $A_1\theta,.., \Pi_n :: A_n\theta$ [1] are proof trees and C is a clause of the form $B \leftarrow A_1, \dots, A_n$, then the following is also a* proof tree:

---

[1] Where $\Pi :: A$ is the linear notation for a proof tree Π with root A

$$\frac{\begin{array}{ccc} \Pi_1 & & \Pi_n \\ A_1\theta & \cdots & A_n\theta \end{array} \quad \mathcal{C}}{B\theta}\,\mathsf{ca}$$

We say that, for non-trivial trees, a formula is an assumption *of a proof tree if it is a minor premise in some leaf. We write this as*

$$\frac{\ldots H \ldots}{\Pi}$$

The clauses *of a proof tree are the ones appearing as major premises. The* root *of a proof tree is called its* consequence. *A proof tree is a* proof *of B from a set $\mathcal{P}$ of clauses iff B is its consequence, its clauses belong to $\mathcal{P}$ and it has no assumption.*

Major premises (i.e. clauses) will be considered modulo variable renaming; equality and substitutions on proof trees are instead defined as follows.

Definition 2 ((Proof Trees Equality)). $\Pi_1 = \Pi_2$ *if their clauses occurrences are equivalent up to renaming, while the other formulæ occurrences are identical.*

Definition 3 ((Proof Trees Substitution)). $\Pi\theta$ *is the tree obtained by simultaneously applying a substitution θ to the root and to all the minor premises. The major premises are left untouched.*

The class of proof trees is closed under substitution w.r.t. the rule ca. The subsumption ordering on expressions is then lifted to proof trees as follows.

Definition 4 ((Subsumption Ordering)). Π_1 *is* less general *than Π_2, written $\Pi_1 \leq \Pi_2$, if there is a substitution σ such that $\Pi_1 = \Pi_2\sigma$. We also say that Π_2* subsumes Π_1. *Moreover, two trees are* equivalent *when one subsumes the other and vice-versa.*

One can easily see that equivalence is equivalence on proof trees up to renaming.

Now we introduce the notions of similarity and of most general proof tree. This will allow us to abstract away from many details of *SLD*-derivations. For example, we do not need a switching lemma or the condition of fairness; analogously we avoid some fastidious standardizing apart.

In [9] similarity was defined via the concept of axiom/rule-occurrences. For the more restricted class of proof trees considered here, we can give a more intuitive characterization, by means of the notion of a proof skeleton:

Definition 5 ((Skeleton)). *The* Skeleton $sk(\Pi)$ *of a proof tree Π is defined recursively as follows:*

1. *Basis:* $sk(A) = []$
2. *Step:*

$$sk \left(\frac{\Pi_1 \ldots \Pi_n \quad C}{B} \mathsf{ca} \right) = \frac{sk(\Pi_1) \ldots sk(\Pi_n) \quad C}{[]} \mathsf{ca}$$

That is, the skeleton of a tree is obtained by systematically replacing the root and minor premises with *holes*: the (equivalence classes of) major premises are unchanged.

Definition 6 ((Similarity)). *Two proof trees* Π_1, Π_2 *are said to be* similar, *written* $\Pi_1 \sim \Pi_2$, *whenever* $sk(\Pi_1) = sk(\Pi_2)$.

One can easily see that ' $\sim$' is an equivalence relation. Most general proof trees are introduced as follows.

Definition 7 ((Most General Proof Tree)). Π *is a* most general proof tree *(mgpt) if it is* maximal *among similar trees.*

As shown in [9], the system L_0 is *regular*, i.e. for any two similar proof trees there is a similar proof tree subsuming them. In regular systems, each similarity class contains a mgpt, which is unique up to renaming. Regularity is a property also of similarity classes of continuations of Π, i.e. similarity classes containing only continuations of Π, where the latter are thusly defined:

Definition 8 ((Continuation)). *Let* $B \leftarrow A_1, \ldots, A_n$ *be a clause* C *and let*

$$\frac{\ldots H \ldots}{\Pi}$$

be a proof tree with an assumption H *such that* $B\theta = H\theta$, *for some substitution* θ. *The* one-step continuation *of* Π *selecting* H *and applying* C *w.r.t.* θ *is the proof tree:*

$$\frac{A_1\theta \cdots A_n\theta \quad B \leftarrow A_1, \ldots, A_n}{\ldots H\theta \ldots} \mathsf{ca}$$
$$\Pi\theta$$

Π_2 *is a* continuation *of* Π_1, *written* $\Pi_1 \preceq \Pi_2$, *if* Π_2 *can be obtained from* Π_1 *by a sequence of one-step continuations.*

Note that substitutions in continuation steps do not need to be most general unifiers. One can easily see that:

Proposition 1. $\Pi_1 \preceq \Pi_2$ *if and only if there is a substitution* σ *such that* $\Pi_1\sigma$ *is an initial subtree of* Π_2.

Definition 9 ((Most General Continuations)). *A continuation is* most general *(mgc) if it is maximal in its similarity class. A continuation is* canonical *iff it is a one-step mgc.*

Since similarity classes of continuations are regular [9], every mgc of a pt is unique up to renaming. One can also see that canonical continuations are the one-step continuations that use most general unifiers.

Definition 10 ((Height)). *The* height *of a proof tree, written* $h(\Pi)$, *is defined here as the length of its* minimum *branch.*

Definition 11 ((Forests)). *A* forest *is a finite sequence of proof-trees. A one-step continuation of a forest selecting H and applying a clause C w.r.t. θ is defined as follows: H is an assumption of a proof tree Π of the forest, Π is substituted by its one-step continuation selecting H and applying C w.r.t. θ, and the substitution θ is applied to the proof trees in the sequence that share variables with Π.*

All the properties of continuations of proof trees extend to continuations of forests. In particular:

Theorem 1 ((Forest Continuation)). $\Pi_1, \ldots, \Pi_n \preceq \Pi_1', \ldots, \Pi_n'$ *if and only if there is a substitution σ such that $\Pi_k \sigma$ is an initial subtree of Π_k', for $1 \leq k \leq n$.*

2.1 Proof Trees and SLD-Resolution

Proof trees have been designed to give an exact proof-theoretical rendering of *SLD*-resolution: for example, let us consider the program *SUM*, built out of the following clauses:

$$
\begin{aligned}
C_0: & \quad sum(X, 0, X) \leftarrow \\
C_1: & \quad sum(X, s(Y), s(Z)) \leftarrow sum(X, Y, Z)
\end{aligned}
$$

An *SLD*-derivation for a goal $\langle \leftarrow A, \theta \rangle$ can be seen as a stepwise construction of a pt $\Pi :: A\theta$. Below, we show the continuations corresponding to the *SLD*-derivation for $\leftarrow sum(ss0, s0, A)$:

$$
\begin{aligned}
& \leftarrow sum(ss0, s0, A) \ \theta_1 = [X/ss0, Y/0, A/s(Z)] \\
& \leftarrow sum(ss0, 0, Z) \ \ \theta_2 = [X_1/ss0, Z/ss0] \\
& \leftarrow \square
\end{aligned}
$$

Notice that the formulæ in the current goal correspond to the assumptions of the relative pt.

$$
sum(ss0, s0, A) \ \preceq \ \frac{sum(ss0, 0, Z) \ \ C_1}{sum(ss0, s0, s(Z))}\text{ca} \ \preceq \ \frac{\dfrac{C_0}{sum(ss0, 0, ss0)}\text{ca} \ \ C_1}{sum(ss0, s0, sss0)}\text{ca}
$$

In this way every *SLD*-derivation can be translated into a pt and this yields the proof-theoretical equivalence between the two systems (see [9]). More formally:

Definition 12. *An* SLD-*derivation is* incomplete *if at any point no literal is selected and the derivation is thusly terminated. It is* relaxed *if mgu's are not necessarily used. If idempotent mgu's are used, then it is* canonical.

Definition 13 ((Resultant)). *Let* $\mathcal{P}$ *be a definite program,* $\leftarrow G$ *a goal and* $\leftarrow G, \leftarrow G_1, \ldots, \leftarrow G_m$ *an incomplete relaxed* SLD-*derivation for* $\mathcal{P} \cup \{\leftarrow G\}$ *with substitutions* $\theta_1, \ldots, \theta_m$. *Let* θ *be the restriction of* $\theta_1 \cdots \theta_m$ *to the variables of* G. *We say that the derivation has* resultant $(G\theta \leftarrow G_m)$.

In a resultant, G_m may be empty, i.e. we consider complete derivations as a limiting case of the incomplete ones.

Theorem 2. *Let* $\mathcal{P}$ *be a definite program and* A *an atom:*

1. *If there is an incomplete relaxed SLD-derivation for* $\mathcal{P} \cup \{\leftarrow A\}$ *with resultant* $(A\delta \leftarrow G_m)$, *then there is a proof-tree* $\Pi :: A\delta$ *in* L_0, *using only axioms from* $\mathcal{P}$, *with assumptions* G_m. *If the SLD-derivation is canonical, then* $\Pi :: A\delta$ *is a most general continuation of* A.
2. *If there is a proof-tree* $\Pi :: A\delta$ *in the system* L_0 *with axioms from* $\mathcal{P}$ *and assumptions* G_m, *then there is an incomplete relaxed SLD-derivation of* $\mathcal{P} \cup \{\leftarrow A\}$ *with resultant* $(A\delta \leftarrow G_m)$. *If* $\Pi :: A\delta$ *is a most general continuation of* A, *then the SLD-derivation is canonical.*

Proof. We give the proof for $G_0 = A$.
1. Let $A = G_0, G_1, \ldots, G_m$ (with clauses $C_1, \ldots, C_m$ and substitutions $\theta_1, \ldots, \theta_m$) be a relaxed incomplete derivation. For $0 \le i \le m$, let δ_i be the composition of the $\theta_1, \ldots, \theta_i$ and $A_{i_1}, \ldots, A_{i_{h_i}}$ be the atoms in the goal G_i; starting with $i = 0$, we associate to $G_0, \ldots, G_i$ a proof tree $\Pi_i :: A\delta_i$ with assumptions $A_{i_1}, \ldots, A_{i_{h_i}}$ as follows:

Step 0. Associate A to G_0.

Step i+1. Let $\Pi :: A\delta_i$ be the proof tree associated to $G_0, \ldots, G_i$ at *step i* and let G_{i+1} be obtained applying C_{i+1} to the selected atom A_{i_n} $(1 \le n \le h_i)$ with *unifier* θ_{i+1}; build the one-step continuation of $\Pi_i :: A\delta_i$ selecting A_{i_n} and applying C_{i+1} w.r.t. θ_{i+1}. If at each step in $G_0, \ldots, G_n$ we apply only mgu's, the corresponding one-step continuations are canonical and we obtain a mgpt.
2. $\Pi :: A\delta$ can be obtained by at least one sequence $A = \Pi_0 \preceq \Pi_1 \preceq \ldots \preceq \Pi_n = \Pi$ of one step continuations; the corresponding SLD-derivation is $G_0, \ldots, G_n$, where G_i are the assumptions of Π_i, for $0 \le i \le n$. If $\Pi :: A\delta$ is a most general continuation of A, then the continuations must be canonical and therefore the derivation $G_0, \ldots, G_n$ is canonical. $\qquad\square$

Similarly, SLD-derivations starting with goals $\leftarrow G$, where G is a sequence of atoms, correspond to stepwise constructions of forests continuing G.

Finally, there is a natural proof-theoretic characterization of finite failure.

Definition 14 ((Failed Assumption)). *In a proof-tree* Π, *an assumption* A *is* failed *w.r.t.* $\mathcal{P}$ *iff there is no continuation of* Π *with selected atom* A *and clauses from* $\mathcal{P}$. *An* ended tree *w.r.t.* $\mathcal{P}$ *is either a proof or a proof tree with at least one failed assumption.*

Definition 15 ((Failure)). *An atom A is* failed w.r.t. $\mathcal{P}$ *if and only if every ended tree (w.r.t. $\mathcal{P}$) $\Pi :: A\sigma$ has at least one failed assumption.*

Definition 16 ((Finite Failure)). *An atom A is* finitely failed w.r.t. $\mathcal{P}$ *if and only if it is failed w.r.t. $\mathcal{P}$ and there exists a k such that every proof-tree $\Pi :: A\sigma$ with axioms from $\mathcal{P}$ has height less or equal to k.*

You can check that this definition of finite failure is equivalent to the usual one in terms of SLD-trees and fairness. The equivalence holds because height is defined as the length of the minimum branch. 'Infinite' failure is non-finite failure, i.e. there is an infinite sequence of continuations $A \preceq \Pi_1 \preceq \cdots \preceq \Pi_k \preceq \cdots$ with increasing height. An *infinite pt $\Pi :: A$* can be seen as the 'limit' of this sequence.

3   The General Framework

In our approach, a transformation system for Horn logic, or more in general, for regular AAR-systems [9] is characterized by a set of rules, called *clause introduction rules*. In this way, we always deal with two inference systems: the basic calculus L_0, containing only the ca rule, and a super-calculus L_1, containing ca and the clause introduction rules. We will write

$$\Pi :: \mathcal{P}, \Gamma \vdash_{L_i} C$$

to indicate that the proof tree Π with clauses from a program $\mathcal{P}$, assumptions Γ and consequence C applies rules of L_i (where $i = 0$ or $i = 1$). If Π is a proof (i.e. Γ is empty) we will write $\Pi :: \mathcal{P} \vdash_{L_i} C$.

The calculus L_1 allows to prove new clauses starting from the ones of a program $\mathcal{P}$. It is used to transform a *source* program $\mathcal{P}$ into a *derived* program:

$$\mathcal{Q} = \frac{\Pi_1}{C_1 \leftarrow \mathcal{B}_1} r_1, \ldots, \frac{\Pi_n}{C_n \leftarrow \mathcal{B}_n} r_n$$

The derived clauses can be used as program clauses.

Definition 17 ((Use of a derived Program)). *A proof tree using a derived program $\mathcal{Q}$ is a proof tree that applies clauses of $\mathcal{Q}$ by means of ca in the basic calculus.*

Thus any proof tree Π using $\mathcal{Q}$ has a double interpretation. On one hand, Π is a proof tree $\Pi :: \mathcal{P}, \Gamma \vdash_{L_1} C$ only using rules of L_1 and axioms of the source program $\mathcal{P}$. On the other hand, if we hide in Π the proofs of the applied clauses, it is apparent that we obtain a proof tree in L_0 with clauses $C_1 \leftarrow \mathcal{B}_1, \ldots, C_n \leftarrow \mathcal{B}_n$. That is, we can consider $\mathcal{Q}$ as a (transformed) program. In this case, we write $\Pi :: \mathcal{Q}, \Gamma \vdash_{L_0} C$.

This double interpretation allows to study the properties of the derived $\mathcal{Q}$ in terms of the properties of the system L_1 and those of the source program $\mathcal{P}$. In this section we will introduce the notions of *weak admissibility* of introduction rules, *strict monotonicity* of the translation function w.r.t. the system L_1 and *completeness* of $\mathcal{Q}$ with respect to success and to infinite trees of $\mathcal{P}$ (to be defined below). Then we set up a general schema to study the correctness of transformation systems, based on the following results: weak admissibility entails partial correctness, completeness with respect to success guarantees that the success set is preserved and, to *preserve the finite failure set*, strict monotonicity and completeness with respect to infinite trees are needed.

3.1 Weak Admissibility and Soundness

Consider a source program $\mathcal{P}$ and a derived program $\mathcal{Q}$, as before.

Definition 18 ((Soundness)). $\mathcal{Q}$ *is* sound with respect to $\mathcal{P}$ *if, for every proof* $\Pi :: \mathcal{Q} \vdash_{L_0} A$, *there is a proof* $\Pi' :: \mathcal{P} \vdash_{L_0} A$.

Soundness is a property of the derived program $\mathcal{Q}$. It is entailed by the weak admissibility of the clause introduction rules of L_1.

Definition 19 ((Weak Admissibility)). *The clause introduction rules of* L_1 *are* weakly admissible *in* L_0 *if there is a translation* τ *that maps every proof* $\Pi :: \mathcal{P} \vdash_{L_1} A$ *into a proof* $\tau(\Pi) :: \mathcal{P} \vdash_{L_0} A$.

Weak admissibility means that τ is a *partial function* from proof trees of L_1 to proof trees of L_0. It must be defined for all the proofs (without assumptions) with atomic consequence. When τ is total, we have the usual notion of admissibility (see e.g. [12]). We have:

Theorem 3. *Weak admissibility entails soundness.*

Proof. This follows from the fact that if $\Pi :: \mathcal{Q} \vdash_{L_0} A$, then $\Pi :: \mathcal{P} \vdash_{L_1} A$ (see the double interpretation of proof-trees using $\mathcal{Q}$). Weak admissibility yields $\Pi :: \mathcal{P} \vdash_{L_0} A$ □

3.2 Strict Monotonicity

Let $\mathcal{P}$ and $\mathcal{Q}$ be as before. We state the following strict monotonicity properties of τ w.r.t. $\mathcal{Q}$:

1. Let Π_1, Π_2 be two pt *using* $\mathcal{Q}$. If $\Pi_1 \preceq \Pi_2$, $h(\Pi_1) < h(\Pi_2)$ and $\tau(\Pi_1)$ and $\tau(\Pi_2)$ are defined, then $h(\tau(\Pi_1)) < h(\tau(\Pi_2))$
2. For every pt Π using $\mathcal{Q}$ with arbitrarily high continuations, there is a continuation Π' of Π using $\mathcal{Q}$ such that $\tau(\Pi')$ is defined.

3.3   Completeness with Respect to Success

Notation. Let G be a finite set of atoms. By $[G]$ we intend the closure under substitution induced by the language of the source program $\mathcal{P}$.

Definition 20 ((Closure)). *We say that a set of atoms is G-closed if it is contained in $[G]$. We say that a clause is G-closed if so is the set of its atoms.*

Now, let $\mathcal{P}$ be a source program,

$$Q = \frac{\Pi_1}{C_1 \leftarrow \mathcal{B}_1} r_1, \ldots, \frac{\Pi_n}{C_n \leftarrow \mathcal{B}_n} r_n$$

be a derived program, and G be a finite set of atoms. We say that $\mathcal{Q}$ is *G-complete w.r.t. success of $\mathcal{P}$* iff

1. For every $A \in [G]$ and proof $\Pi :: \mathcal{P} \vdash_{L_0} A$, there are strict subproofs $\Pi_1 :: A_1, \ldots, \Pi_n :: A_n$ of Π, a derived clause $C_j \leftarrow \mathcal{B}_j$ of $\mathcal{Q}$ and a substitution σ such that:
   (a) $A = C_j\sigma$ and
   (b) $\mathcal{B}_j$ can be continued into a forest $\Pi^* :: \mathcal{Q}, A_1, \ldots, A_n \vdash_{L_0} \mathcal{B}_j\sigma$.
2. $A_i \leftarrow \mathcal{B}_i$ is G-closed, for $1 \leq i \leq n$.

3.4   Completeness with Respect to Infinite Trees

Let $\mathcal{P}, \mathcal{Q}$ be as in Sect. 3.3. We say that $\mathcal{Q}$ is *G-complete w.r.t. infinite trees of $\mathcal{P}$* iff

1. There is a k such that, for every $A \in [G]$, every proof tree $\Pi :: \mathcal{P}, \Gamma \vdash_{L_0} A$ with height $h(\Pi) > k$ has a continuation that satisfies item 1. of Sect. 3.3.
2. $A_i \leftarrow \mathcal{B}_i$ is G-closed, for $1 \leq i \leq n$.

3.5   Main Result

To summarize, we may have the following cases:

1. The rules of L_1 are (weakly) admissible in L_0
2. $\mathcal{Q}$ is G-complete w.r.t. success of $\mathcal{P}$
3. $\mathcal{Q}$ is G-complete w.r.t. infinite pt's of $\mathcal{P}$
4. τ is strictly monotonic w.r.t. $\mathcal{Q}$.

Notation. For a program $\mathcal{P}$, let $SS_{\mathcal{P}}$ be the success set and $Infpt_{\mathcal{P}}$ the set of atoms with infinite proof trees of $\mathcal{P}$.

We can prove the following general results.

Theorem 4. *Given $\mathcal{P}$ and $\mathcal{Q}$ as above:*

1. *entails $SS_{\mathcal{Q}} \subseteq SS_{\mathcal{P}}$*
2. *entails $(SS_{\mathcal{P}} \cap [G]) \subseteq SS_{\mathcal{Q}}$*

3. entails $(Infpt_{\mathcal{P}} \cap [G]) \subseteq Infpt_{\mathcal{Q}}$
4. entails $Infpt_{\mathcal{Q}} \subseteq Infpt_{\mathcal{P}}$.

Proof.

1. By Th. 3.
2. Let us consider a proof $\Pi :: \mathcal{P} \vdash_{L_0} A$, for $A \in [G]$. It is sufficient to prove that there is $\Pi' :: \mathcal{Q} \vdash_{L_0} A$. By G-completeness, there are strict subproofs $\Pi_1 :: A_1, \ldots, \Pi_n :: A_n$ of Π, a derived clause $C_j \leftarrow \mathcal{B}_j$ of $\mathcal{Q}$ and a substitution σ such that $A = C_j\sigma$ and $\mathcal{B}_j$ can be continued into a forest $\Pi^* :: \mathcal{Q}, A_1, \ldots, A_n \vdash_{L_0} \mathcal{B}_j\sigma$. We can build Π' as follows. Consider:

$$\Pi_0 = \frac{\overset{\Pi^*}{\mathcal{B}_j\sigma} \quad \overset{\Pi_j}{C_j \leftarrow \mathcal{B}_j}}{H} \mathsf{ca}$$

Note that $\Pi_0 :: \mathcal{Q}, A_1, \ldots, A_n \vdash_{L_0} A$. Iterate the same procedure to translate $\Pi_1 :: A_1, \ldots, \Pi_n :: A_n$ into proofs using $\mathcal{Q}$. Use the latter proofs to complete Π_0 into a proof Π'. Note that the iteration can be always applied by G-closure and it comes to a halt, as we always consider strict subproofs.
3. Proceed as is the previous case, with the following difference: once you get to the proof tree Π_0, recall that since Π may be continued ad libitum, so does the sequence $\Pi_1 :: A_1, \ldots, \Pi_n :: A_n$. This means that this procedure may be indefinitely iterated, continuing thusly a proof tree using $\mathcal{Q}$ to an arbitrary height.
4. Let $\Pi_0 \preceq \ldots \preceq \Pi_k \preceq \ldots$ be an infinite sequence of continuations (using $\mathcal{Q}$) with increasing height. By strict monotonicity w.r.t. $\mathcal{Q}$, each Π_k can be continued into a proof tree that has a translation. Therefore we can assume without loss of generality that the proof trees in our sequence have translations. Build the infinite sequence $\tau(\Pi_0) \preceq \ldots \preceq \tau(\Pi_k) \preceq \ldots$ It has increasing heights by strict monotonicity. $\quad\square$

Corollary 1.

1. (1. and 2.) entail that success is preserved over G
2. (1.2.3. and 4.) entail that success and finite failure is preserved over G

Proof. The former part 1. is trivial. The latter (2.) follows from the fact that finite failure is the complement of the union of success and atoms with infinite trees. $\quad\square$

4 Partial Deduction

We are now in the position of giving an abstract and very high-level view of *Partial Deduction* (PD) [5,6,7,8], thanks to our framework. Note that we shall not be concerned with the pragmatics of PD [13,11,2] like unfolding rules, loop detection *et cetera*: those issues can be dealt with as usual.

We will express PD be via the converse of the clause application rule, called clause introduction and indicated by ci. The rule discharges the (u-th occurrence(s) of the set of) assumption(s) $\mathcal{B}$.

$$\frac{\overline{\mathcal{B}}^{u} \atop {\Pi \atop C}}{C \leftarrow \mathcal{B}} ci^{u}$$

The latter allows the derivation of resultants. For instance, from the following program EO

$$\begin{array}{ll} c_0 : & e(0) \leftarrow \\ c_1 : & e(s(X)) \leftarrow o(X) \\ c_2 : & o(s(X)) \leftarrow e(X) \end{array}$$

we can derive the resultant $\Pi_0 :: EO \vdash_{L_1} e(ssX) \leftarrow e(X)$:

$$\cfrac{\cfrac{\cfrac{\overline{e(X)}^{0} \quad c_2}{o(sX)} ca \quad c_1}{e(ssX)} ca}{e(ssX) \leftarrow e(X)} ci^0$$

As we said in the beginning of this Section, if we hide the proofs of the derived clauses, we can use them (by the ca rule) just as program clauses. This is shown below.

$$\cfrac{\cfrac{\cfrac{\cfrac{c_0}{e(0)} ca \quad c_2}{o(s0)} ca \quad c_1}{e(ss0)} ca \quad \Pi_0 :: e(ssX) \leftarrow e(X)}{e(ssss0)} ca$$

Therefore we formalize Partial Deduction in the super-calculus L_1 containing the rules ca and ci:

A Partial Deduction of a source program $\mathcal{P}$ with respect to a set G of atoms is a derivation in L_1 of a program $\mathcal{Q} = \{\Pi_i :: C_i \leftarrow \mathcal{B}_i\}, 0 \leq 1 \leq n$, where the C_i are instances of formulæ of G.

We now address the problem of correctness of PD, following the guidelines established by Th. 4, i.e. considering admissibility (and soundness), strict monotonicity and completeness with respect to success and infinite trees.

4.1 Admissibility and Soundness

We have a process analogous to the local $\supset$-reduction step of normalization in natural deduction calculi, yet simpler, due to the restricted syntax of definite programs.

Theorem 5 ((Normalization)). *There is a translation τ such that, for every atom B and proof tree $\Pi :: \mathcal{P}, \Gamma \vdash_{L_1} B$, $\tau(\Pi) :: \mathcal{P}, \Gamma \vdash_{L_0} B$.*

Proof. The mapping τ is defined by induction on Π, as follows:

1. $\tau(B) = B$
2. The applied clause is the program clause $\mathcal{C}$:

$$\tau\left(\cfrac{\cfrac{\Pi_1 \quad \cdots \quad \Pi_n}{A_1\theta \qquad A_n\theta} \quad \mathcal{C}}{B\theta}\text{ca}\right) = \cfrac{\cfrac{\tau(\Pi_1) \quad \cdots \quad \tau(\Pi_n)}{A_1\theta \qquad A_n\theta;} \quad \mathcal{C}}{B\theta}\text{ca}$$

3. The applied clause has been introduced by ci:

$$\tau\left(\cfrac{\cfrac{\Pi_1 \quad \cdots \quad \Pi_n}{A_1\sigma; \qquad A_n\sigma;} \quad \cfrac{\cfrac{\overline{A_1}\ldots\overline{A_n}}{\Pi_0}}{B \leftarrow A_1 \ldots A_n}\text{ci}}{B\sigma}\text{ca}\right) = \begin{array}{c} \tau(\Pi_1)\ldots\tau(\Pi_n) \\ \hline A_1\sigma\ldots A_n\sigma \\ \tau(\Pi_0)\sigma \\ \hline B\sigma \end{array}$$

$\square$

The partial function τ is essentially a normalization operator which eliminates every vicious circle of an introduction immediately followed by an elimination with the same major premise. The mapping is total for proofs in L_1 of atomic consequences, otherwise the translation is undefined for proofs whose last step is ci.

Theorem 5 proves (weak) admissibility of ci in L_0. From Th. 4, this yields soundness.

4.2 Strict Monotonicity

One can easily see that condition 1. of strict monotonicity w.r.t. $\mathcal{Q}$ holds. Condition 2. is obvious, since τ is defined for every proof tree using $\mathcal{Q}$.

4.3 Completeness with Respect to Success

Let $\mathcal{P}$ be the source program. G-completeness with respect to success can be characterized trough G-complete sets of proof trees.

Definition 21 ((G-complete Sets w.r.t. Success)). *Let G be a set of atoms and $\{\Pi_1, \ldots, \Pi_n\}$ be a set of proof trees of L_0 with program $\mathcal{P}$. $\{\Pi_1, \ldots, \Pi_n\}$ is G-complete with respect to success of $\mathcal{P}$ iff, for every $A \in G$ and proof $\Pi :: \mathcal{P} \vdash_{L_0} A\sigma$, Π is a continuation of Π_k, for some k, $1 \leq k \leq n$.*

Now, let

$$\mathcal{Q} = \frac{\Pi_1 :: \mathcal{P}, \mathcal{B}_1 \vdash_{L_1} C_1}{C_1 \leftarrow \mathcal{B}_1} \mathsf{ci}, \ldots, \frac{\Pi_n :: \mathcal{P}, \mathcal{B}_n \vdash_{L_1} C_n}{C_n \leftarrow \mathcal{B}_n} \mathsf{ci}$$

be the derived program.

Theorem 6. *Let G be a set of atoms. $\mathcal{Q}$ is G-complete with respect to success of $\mathcal{P}$ if $\{\tau(\Pi_1), \ldots, \tau(\Pi_n)\}$ is a G-complete set w.r.t. success of $\mathcal{P}$ and each derived clause $C_k \leftarrow \mathcal{B}_k$ $(1 \leq k \leq n)$ is G-closed.*

Proof. Consider $H \in [G]$, and a proof $\Pi :: \mathcal{P} \vdash_{L_0} H$. By G-completeness of $\{\tau(\Pi_1), \ldots, \tau(\Pi_n)\}$, there is $\tau(\Pi_k) \preceq \Pi$. Therefore Π can be decomposed into an initial subtree $\tau(\Pi_k)\sigma$ with root $H = C_k\sigma$ and a forest proving $\mathcal{B}_k\sigma$. In this case the required continuation of $\mathcal{B}_k\sigma$ is (trivially) $\mathcal{B}_k\sigma$ itself. G-closure is required by hypothesis.

4.4 Completeness with Respect to Infinite Trees

Definition 22 ((G-complete Sets w.r.t. Infinite Trees)). *Let $\{\Pi_1, \ldots, \Pi_n\}$ be a set of proof trees of L_0 with program $\mathcal{P}$. $\{\Pi_1, \ldots, \Pi_n\}$ is G-complete with respect to infinite trees of $\mathcal{P}$ iff there is a k such that, for every $A \in G$ and proof tree $\Pi :: \mathcal{P}, \Gamma \vdash_{L_0} A\sigma$ with height greater than k, Π is a continuation of Π_k, for some $k, 1 \leq k \leq n$.*

Now, let $\mathcal{Q}$ be as before.

Theorem 7. *$\mathcal{Q}$ is G-complete with respect to infinite trees of $\mathcal{P}$ if $\{\tau(\Pi_1), \ldots, \tau(\Pi_n)\}$ is G-complete w.r.t. infinite trees of $\mathcal{P}$ and each derived clause $C_k \leftarrow \mathcal{B}_k$ $(1 \leq k \leq n)$ is G-closed.*

We omit the proof, which is similar to the previous one.

4.5 Correctness of Partial Deduction

One can derive sets of G-complete continuations in the usual way, by incomplete SLD-trees with starting goal $\leftarrow G$. Each path of the incomplete SLD-tree is an incomplete SLD-derivation and we can translate it into a forest. The set of non-failed proof trees of all those forests is G-complete both with respect to success and to infinite trees. By the main results of the previous Section, both success and finite failure are preserved.

We can separate success from finite failure by requesting only completeness with respect to the former. In this case, it may be the case that some proof trees required only to preserve infinite trees can be omitted.

5 Unfolding and Folding

Let us now turn to analyzing unfolding and folding ([11,15,16,17], to name just a few).

5.1 Unfolding

Unfolding needs the admissible rule ci, for which we have already given the translation function τ. Admissibility of ci and strict monotonicity of τ have been shown, too.

Since we are interested in all the possible goals, we look for G-completeness, where G contains the predicates $r_1(x_1), \ldots, r_m(x_m)$ of $\mathcal{P}$.

In this way we can inherit the results of the previous section.

Example 1. Referring back to the program EO of Sect. 4, the following unfolded program $\mathcal{Q}$ (which brings back the usual and more efficient definition of even and odd) preserves success and finite failure:

$$
\mathcal{Q} = \left\{
\begin{array}{c}
\dfrac{c_0}{e(0)}\,\text{ca} \\[2pt]
\dfrac{}{e(0) \leftarrow}\,\text{ci}
\end{array}
\quad
\dfrac{\dfrac{\dfrac{\overline{e(X)}^0 \quad c_2}{o(sX)\quad c_1}\,\text{ca}}{e(ssX)}\,\text{ca}}{e(ssX) \leftarrow e(X)}\,\text{ci}^0
\quad
\dfrac{\dfrac{\dfrac{c_0}{e(0)}\,\text{ca} \quad c_2}{o(s0)}\,\text{ca}}{o(s0) \leftarrow}\,\text{ci}
\quad
\dfrac{\dfrac{\dfrac{\overline{o(X)}^0 \quad c_1}{e(sX)\quad c_2}\,\text{ca}}{o(ssX)}\,\text{ca}}{o(ssX) \leftarrow o(X)}\,\text{ci}^0
\right\}
$$

Usually [17,11], an unfolding transformation is seen as a sequence of programs, obtained thorough a sequence of single unfolding steps, where each step preserves completeness. Thus one obtains a final program that preserves success and finite failure. In our case we can define completeness directly on the final derived program $\mathcal{Q}$, since it explicitly contains the proofs of its clauses, starting from the ones of the source program.

5.2 Folding

The folding rule refers to a folding set

$$
\mathcal{F} = \left\{
\dfrac{\mathcal{B}_1\sigma_1}{\dfrac{\Pi_1}{A\sigma_1}}, \ldots, \dfrac{\mathcal{B}_k\sigma_k}{\dfrac{\Pi_k}{A\sigma_k}}
\right\}
$$

of proof trees with clauses from $\mathcal{P}$, such that $\mathcal{F}$ is A-complete w.r.t. success of $\mathcal{P}$.

For such a $\mathcal{F}$, we have the following rules:

$$
\dfrac{H \leftarrow \Gamma, \mathcal{B}_1\sigma_1 \quad \cdots \quad H \leftarrow \Gamma, \mathcal{B}_n\sigma_n}{H \leftarrow \Gamma, A}\,fold(\mathcal{F})
$$

$$\frac{(H \leftarrow \Gamma, \mathcal{B}_1)\sigma_1 \quad \cdots \quad (H \leftarrow \Gamma, \mathcal{B}_n)\sigma_n}{H \leftarrow \Gamma, A} fold^\omega(\mathcal{F})$$

In *fold*, $vars(v\sigma_h) \cap vars(\Gamma, H, A) = \emptyset$ must be satisfied for $1 \le h \le n$ and every $v \in vars(\mathcal{B}_h) \backslash vars(A)$. The rule *fold* allows to treat, for example, Tamaki&Sato's [17] and Shepherdson's [16] folding. The rule $fold^\omega$ does not have restrictions on σ. It allows to treat general folding [11] (R2, p. 268). Indeed, $fold^\omega$ is more general than *fold*. We distinguish the two rules because they have different logical explanations, as briefly remarked in the conclusions.

We can formalize unfold/fold transformations as derivations in the super-calculus L_2 containing the rules ca, ci, $fold(\mathcal{F})$ and $fold^\omega(\mathcal{F})$ (for every folding set $\mathcal{F}$).

Example 2. Given the following program `minmax` to determine the minimum and maximum of a list, where the definition of `sup` and `inf` are left open:

$$
\begin{array}{ll}
m_0 : min([X], X) & \leftarrow \\
m_1 : min([X|XS], Y) & \leftarrow min(XS, Z), inf(X, Z, Y). \\
m_2 : max([X], X) & \leftarrow \\
m_3 : max([X|XS], Y) & \leftarrow max(XS, Z), sup(X, Z, Y). \\
m_4 : minmax(XS, Min, Max) & \leftarrow min(XS, Min), max(XS, Max).
\end{array}
$$

and this folding set:

$$\mathcal{F} = \left\{ \frac{min(XS, Min) \quad max(XS, Max) \quad m_4}{minmax(XS, Min, Max)} ca \right\}$$

The two following trees sum up the transformation process in a very compact way, where each transformation step corresponds and is justified by an inference in the tree.

$$\frac{\dfrac{m_0}{min([X], X)} ca \quad \dfrac{m_2}{max([X], X)} ca \quad m_4}{\dfrac{minmax([X], X, X)}{minmax([X], X, X) \leftarrow} ci} ca$$

$$\frac{\dfrac{\overline{min(XS, Y)} \; \overline{inf(X, Y, Min)} \; m_1}{min([X|XS], Min)} ca \quad \dfrac{\overline{max(XS, Z)} \; \overline{sup(X, Z, Max)} \; m_3}{max([X|XS], Max)} ca \quad m_4}{\dfrac{minmax([X|XS], Min, Max)}{\begin{array}{l} minmax([X|XS], Min, Max) \leftarrow min(XS, Y), max(XS, Z), \\ \qquad\qquad\qquad\qquad\qquad inf(X, Y, Min), sup(X, Z, Max) \end{array}} ci} ca$$

$$\frac{}{\begin{array}{l} minmax([X|XS], Min, Max) \leftarrow minmax(XS, Y, Z), \\ \qquad\qquad\qquad\qquad\qquad inf(X, Y, Min), sup(X, Z, Max) \end{array}} fold(\mathcal{F})$$

We thus obtain by folding the new recursive definition of `minmax`

$$
\begin{array}{ll}
m_5 : minmax([X], X, X) & \leftarrow \\
m_6 : minmax([X|XS], Min, Man) & \leftarrow minmax(XS, Y, Z), \\
& \qquad\qquad inf(X, Y, Min), sup(X, Z, Max)
\end{array}
$$

Weak admissibility holds, i.e. every proof $\Pi :: \mathcal{P} \vdash_{L_2} A$ (where A is an atom) can be translated into a proof $\tau(\Pi) :: \mathcal{P} \vdash_{L_0} A$. Due to the fold rule, translatability is not guaranteed for proof trees $\Pi :: \mathcal{P}, \Gamma \vdash_{L_2} A$ with assumptions.

The partial function τ is recursively defined as follows:

1. The base and the recursive cases for source clauses and clauses introduced by ci are as in Sect. 4.1.
2. If the applied clause is introduced by $fold$, we have the following recursion, where Π^*, Π'^* are forests:

$$\tau\left(\cfrac{\cfrac{\Pi^*}{\Gamma\delta}\quad\cfrac{\Pi_0}{A\delta}\quad\cfrac{\left\{\cfrac{\Delta_i}{H \leftarrow \Gamma, \mathcal{B}_i\sigma_i}\right\}}{H \leftarrow \Gamma, A}fold(\mathcal{F})}{H\delta}ca\right) = \tau\left(\cfrac{\cfrac{\Pi^*}{\Gamma\delta'}\quad\cfrac{\Pi'^*}{\mathcal{B}_h\sigma_h\delta'}\quad\cfrac{\Delta_h}{H \leftarrow \Gamma, \mathcal{B}_h\sigma_h}}{H\delta'}ca\right)$$

provided that $\tau(\Pi_0)$ is a continuation of a proof $\Pi_h \in \mathcal{F}$. Since the latter has consequence $A\sigma_h$ and assumptions $\mathcal{B}_h\sigma_h$, $\tau(\Pi_0)$ has the form of an initial subproof $\Pi_h\delta'$, continued at the top by a forest Π'^* with consequences $\mathcal{B}_h\sigma_h\delta'$ (by the applicability condition, δ and δ' coincide over Γ, H). If $\tau(\Pi_0)$ is not sufficiently high to be a continuation of any proof tree of $\mathcal{F}$, we cannot find the sequence Π'^*, and we halt the translation with an undefined result.

3. If the applied clause is introduced by $fold^\omega$, the translation is defined in a way similar to $fold$ (omitted here for conciseness).

Proposition 2 ((Weak Admissibility)). *If Π is a proof, then $\tau(\Pi)$ successfully halts, i.e. every proof using clauses derived in L_2 can be translated into a proof using only L_0 and clauses from $\mathcal{P}$.*

The proof easily follows from the fact that, in every translation step related to the fold rules, $\tau(\Pi_0)$ is a proof of δA and hence a continuation of some proof of the A-complete set $\mathcal{F}$. □

Now let us consider completeness. As for unfolding, we are interested in all the possible goals, i.e. we look for G-completeness, where G contains the predicates $r_1(x_1), \ldots, r_m(x_m)$ of $\mathcal{P}$.

A useful sufficient condition for $r_1(x_1), \ldots, r_m(x_m)$-completeness is fold completeness:

Definition 23 ((Fold Completeness with respect to Success)). *Let $\mathcal{P}$ be a source program and $\mathcal{Q} = \{\Pi_i :: C_i \leftarrow \mathcal{B}_i\}$, $1 \le i \le n$ be a program derived from $\mathcal{P}$ in L_2. We say that $\mathcal{Q}$ is fold-complete with respect to success of $\mathcal{P}$ if every proof tree*

$$\cfrac{\mathcal{B}\quad\cfrac{\Pi_i}{C_i \leftarrow \mathcal{B}_i}}{C_i}ca$$

has continuations that can be successfully translated and the set of all the translations is $r_1(x_1), \ldots, r_m(x_m)$*-complete w.r.t. success of* $\mathcal{P}$.

Theorem 8 ((Completeness with respect to Success)). *Fold completeness with respect to success of* $\mathcal{P}$ *entails* $r_1(x_1), \ldots, r_m(x_m)$*-completeness with respect to success of* $\mathcal{P}$.

Proof. Consider a proof $\Pi :: \mathcal{P} \vdash_{L_0} H$. By fold completeness, there is $\Pi' ::$ $\mathcal{Q}, A_1, \ldots, A_n \vdash_{L_0} H$ such that: $\tau(\Pi') \preceq \Pi$ and Π' applies (at the root) a derived rule, say $C_i \leftarrow \mathcal{B}_i$. Therefore Π' contains the required forest proving $\mathcal{B}_i \sigma$, and Π contains the required strict subproofs. G-closure is required by hypothesis. $\square$

Fold Completeness with respect to infinite trees is obtained if, in Def. 23, we replace *success* by *infinite trees*.

By the last theorem and our general results, fold completeness with respect to success of $\mathcal{P}$ guarantees that the success set is preserved. Note that there are cases of folding that are incomplete. Appealing to that, we can explain the well-known problems related to self-folding. Consider the source program $\mathcal{P}$:

$$p \leftarrow r$$
$$r \leftarrow$$

A p-complete $\mathcal{F}$ is

$$\mathcal{F} = \left\{ \frac{r \quad p \leftarrow r}{p} \mathsf{ca} \right\}$$

and the transformed program is

$$\mathcal{Q} = \left\{ \begin{array}{l} \dfrac{p \leftarrow r}{p \leftarrow p} \mathrm{fold}(\mathcal{F}) \\[2ex] r \leftarrow \end{array} \right\}$$

$\mathcal{Q}$ is incomplete since for every continuation in $\mathcal{Q}$ of the proof tree below

$$\frac{p \quad \dfrac{p \leftarrow r}{p \leftarrow p} \mathrm{fold}(\mathcal{F})}{p} \mathsf{ca}$$

the translation fails. On the other hand, the program $\mathcal{Q}_1$

$$\mathcal{Q}_1 = \left\{ \begin{array}{l} \dfrac{p \leftarrow r}{p \leftarrow p} \mathrm{fold}(\mathcal{F}) \\[2ex] p \leftarrow r \\ r \leftarrow \end{array} \right\}$$

is fold-complete. Indeed the continuation

$$\frac{\dfrac{r \quad p \leftarrow r}{p} \mathsf{ca} \quad \dfrac{p \leftarrow r}{p \leftarrow p} \mathrm{fold}(\mathcal{F})}{p} \mathsf{ca}$$

is translated into

$$\frac{r \quad p \leftarrow r}{p}\mathsf{ca}$$

Finally, as an immediate consequence of the general results, we have also the following theorem:

Theorem 9. *If Q is fold-compete with respect to success and infinite trees and τ is strictly monotone w.r.t. Q, then finite failure is preserved.*

6   Conclusions and Perspectives

We have given a proof-theoretic analysis of some well known transformation rules. We have omitted for conciseness the treatment of the preservation of open answers. This can be done in our general framework by using the notion of most general proof trees.

Our analysis shows that one can use a very general schema, based on the notions of admissibility, completeness with respect to the source program and properties of the translation function, like strict monotonicity. Moreover, our formalism and general results nicely generalize to other logic programming languages: in fact it is possible to apply our general schema to logic programming languages that can be formulated as *Axiom Application Systems* [9,10], say for example normal or disjunctive programs.

This paper presents work in progress. A further main step is the study of a set of basic logical inference rules and non-logical principles, that allow to derive all the admissible rules corresponding to the kind of transformations known in the literature. In other words, we are looking for a calculus to infer program transformation rules. In this way we achieve two main advantages:

1. We can study and classify the rules from a logical point of view. For example, one can prove that the two folding rules have different logical justifications. In fact, *fold* can be derived from the completion of $\mathcal{P}$, by using only the logical rules. To derive $fold^\omega$, we need also an ω-rule, as the one given in [14] in the context of Partial Inductive Definitions. Moreover derivations can be embedded in the context of a specific theory, for example in the axiomatization of a data type. In this way transformations can be guided by the knowledge of a specific problem domain.
2. By using a set of basic rules, we can, in principle, derive new transformation rules. Of course, their usefulness is a question of experimental work.

A final point that we want to exploit is the use of proof-schemas. For example, one could try to detect regularities in a schema: this information could suggest the definition of suitable new eureka predicates, to be used in transformation. Up to now we have tried only some experiments in this direction, using examples like the Fibonacci numbers, or the 'average' program considered in [11].

Acknowledgments. We would like to thanks Frank Pfenning and one anonymous referee for having carefully read and suggested useful modifications to the previous version of the paper.

References

1. Apt, K.A.: Logic Programming. In: Leuween J. (ed.): Handbook of Theoretical Computer Science. Elsevier (1990)
2. Danvy, O., Gluck, R., Thiemann, P., (eds.): Partial Evaluation. International Seminar. Dagstuhl Castle, Germany, February 12-16. Selected Papers. LNCS 1110. Springer Verlag (1996)
3. Hallnäs, L., Schroeder-Heister, P.: A Proof-theoretic Approach to Logic Programming: Clauses as Rules. Journal of Logic and Computation **1:2** (1990) 261-283
4. Hodges, W.: Logical Features of Horn Clauses. In: Gabbay, D.M., Hogger, C.J, Robinson, J.A., (eds.): Handbook of Logic in Artificial Intelligence and Logic Programming. Volume 1: Logical Foundations. Oxford University Press (1993) 449–503
5. Komorowski, J.: A Prolegomenon to Partial Deduction. Fundamenta Informaticae. Annales Societatis Mathematicae Polonae **8** (1993) 41–63
6. Komorowski, J. (Guest Editor): Special Issue on Partial Deduction. Journal of Logic Programming **14** (1993)
7. Jones, N.D.: An Introduction to Partial Evaluation. Acm Computing Surveys **28:3** (1996) 480–531
8. Lloyd, J.W., Shepherdson, J.: Partial Evaluation in Logic Programming. Journal of Logic Programming **11** (1991) 217-242
9. Momigliano, A., Ornaghi, M.: Regular Search Spaces as a Foundation of Logic Programming. In: Dyckhoff R. (ed.): Extensions of Logic Programming. LNAI 798. Springer Verlag (1994) 222–254
10. Momigliano, A., Ornaghi, M.: Regular Search Spaces and Constructive Negation. Journal of Logic and Computation **7:3** (1997) 367–403
11. Pettorossi, A., Proietti, M.: Transformation of Logic Programs: Foundations and Techniques. Journal of Logic Programming **19–20** (1994) 261–321
12. Prawitz, D.: Natural deduction. A Proof-Theoretical Study. Almquist Wiksell (1965)
13. Sahlin, D.: An Automatic Partial Evaluator for Full Prolog. Report TRITA-TCS **91:01** (1991)
14. Schroeder-Heister, P.: Rules of definitional reflection. In: Proceedings of the IEEE Symposium on Logic in Computer Science. (1993) 222–232
15. Seki, H.: Unfold/Fold Transformation of Stratified Programs. Theoretical Computer Science **86** (1991) 107–139
16. Sheperdson, J.C.: Unfold/Fold Transformations of Logic Programs. Math. Structure Comp. Science **2** (1992) 143–157
17. Tamaki, H , Sato, T.: Unfold/Fold Transformation of Logic Programs. In: S-A Tärlund (Ed.): Proceedings of ICLP84. Uppsala. (1984) 127–138

A Higher Order Reconstruction of Stepwise Enhancement

Lee Naish and Leon Sterling

Department of Computer Science
University of Melbourne,
Parkville, Vic. 3052, Australia
{lee,leon}@cs.mu.oz.au

Abstract. This paper presents two views of stepwise enhancement, one a pragmatic syntax-based approach and the other a semantic approach based on higher order functions and relating to shape and polytypism. The approaches are outlined, and the perhaps surprisingly close relationship between the two described. By combining the advantages of both approaches, it is shown how more code in both functional and logic programming languages can be constructed in a systematic and partially automated way.

1 Motivation

In the last couple of years, there has been renewed interest in systematic methods for the construction of Prolog programs, for example (Gegg-Harrison, 1995), (Power and Sterling, 1990), (Kirschenbaum et al., 1996), (Sterling and Yalçinalp, 1996), and (Vasconcelos and Fuchs, 1995). This paper loosely characterises the progression of approaches that have been offered for systematic construction of logic (usually Prolog) programs. There is a trade-off between what is accessible for practical programmers and what is clearly explained in theory.

We claim that both audiences can be addressed through stepwise enhancement. The method can be explained directly in term of programming techniques applied to simple programs, and also given a more theoretical basis in terms of higher order functions. We review stepwise enhancement, sketch how to capture an enhancement as a higher order function adapted from `foldr`, and then sketch how individual enhancements are specialisations of the particular foldr predicate. We show how this is closely related to the new ideas on shape and polytypism being discussed in the functional programming community (Jay and Cockett, 1994), (Jay, 1995), (Bellé et al., 1996) (Jeuring and Jansson, 1996), (Jansson and Jeuring, 1997). We go on to generalise this work in several ways, utilising key features of logic programming such as nondeterminism and flexible modes, and show how `foldl` can also be adapted.

2 Approaches to Developing Prolog Programs

1. The early approach, characterised by 'Programming in Prolog' (Clocksin and Mellish, 1981) and 'Prolog by Example' (Coelho et al., 1988) was completely

Norbert E. Fuchs (Ed.): LOPSTR'97, LNCS 1463, pp. 245–262, 1998.
© Springer-Verlag Berlin Heidelberg 1998

ad hoc. Prolog was a declarative language and it was easier/fun/exciting for many researchers to code in a declarative style. The approach did not lead to systematic Prolog training nor encourage high productivity.

2. Another approach is based on structural induction. Anyone who programs in a logic language notices that code manipulating lists typically has a similar, recursive structure. It is well known that recursion in programming languages is related to proofs by induction in mathematics. This observation can lead to a systematic approach where logic programs are developed along with structural induction proofs of correctness. A coherent account of structural induction as the basis for systematic logic program construction is given in (Deville, 1990). It is not clear how well Deville's approach scales nor how easy it is for the non-mathematically inclined to master.

3. An approach advocated for teaching Prolog has been to use templates or schemas. Students are invited to 'fill in the blanks'. The blanks can be thought of as parameters which are predicates. Advocates of schemas are O'Keefe (1990) and Gegg-Harrison (1991). Schemas have not been widely adapted, due partly to the fact that those who grasped Prolog programming didn't need them, and those that didn't had an extra level of complexity to learn, the language that the schemas were expressed in.

4. The recent work by Fuchs and colleagues (Fuchs and Fromherz, 1991), (Vasconcelos and Fuchs, 1995) attempts to combine the previous two approaches. A logical specification is (somehow) arrived at, and then schemas are used to guide the transformation of the specification to a program.

5. Stepwise enhancement (Lakhotia, 1989), (Sterling and Kirschenbaum, 1993), and (Sterling and Shapiro, 1994) was introduced by Sterling and colleagues in an attempt to simplify the teaching of complicated Prolog programs. Rather than have to explain higher order concepts, programmers and novices were taught programming techniques which at all times manipulated concrete Prolog programs.

6. Naish (1996) advocated a higher order style of programming, very similar to that used in functional programming languages. It was shown how some operations of stepwise enhancement, such as applying a technique to a skeleton and composition, could be elegantly reproduced in a higher order framework.

This paper continues the discussion between the authors on how best to characterise stepwise enhancement. The current work was sparked by the challenge to use the higher order approach to explain a 'complicated' program, the rule interpreter described in Section 17.4 of the second edition of *The Art of Prolog* (Sterling and Shapiro, 1994). In explaining the program, a new method was formulated: the final program is built around an output type rather than an input type. In this paper we give another example of this technique, using a different interpreter.

What has emerged is a better understanding of how types can drive program development, and how Naish and Sterling's views of systematic program construction via stepwise enhancement are complementary. The work relates to recent, exciting work in the functional programming community concerning shape, which sets our views on program development in a broader context and also suggests that logic program development is more general. This paper presents the dual view of stepwise enhancement.

3   Stepwise Enhancement for Program Construction

The method of stepwise enhancement (Lakhotia, 1989) was originally conceived as an adaptation of stepwise refinement to Prolog. It was advocated as a way to systematically construct Prolog programs which exploits Prolog's high-level features. The key idea underlying stepwise enhancement is to visualise a program or solution in terms of its central control flow, or skeleton, and techniques which perform computations while the control flow of the skeleton is followed. Techniques can be developed independently and combined automatically using the method of composition.

The most common data structure for logic programs is the list, and many programs are based on skeletons for traversing lists. A tutorial example of using stepwise enhancement to develop a simple program is given in Chapter 13 of (Sterling and Shapiro, 1994). In this section we give the basic list processing program as Program 1 for reference, and a (slightly) more elaborate example with binary trees.

```
is_list([]).
is_list([X|Xs]) :- is_list(Xs).
```

Program 1: A skeleton for list traversal (or definition of lists)

Programs 2a and 2b are skeleton programs for traversing binary trees with values only at leaf nodes. Program 2a, the left-hand program, does a complete traversal of the tree, while Program 2b, the right-hand program, traverses a single branch of the tree. Note that Program 2a can be viewed as a type definition of trees.

```
is_tree(leaf(X)).                 branch(leaf(X)).
is_tree(tree(L,R)) :-             branch(tree(L,R)) :- branch(L).
    is_tree(L),                   branch(tree(L,R)) :- branch(R).
    is_tree(R).
```

Programs 2a, 2b: Skeletons for traversing a tree

Techniques capture basic Prolog programming practices, such as building a data structure or performing calculations in recursive code. Informally, a programming technique interleaves some additional computation around the control flow of a skeleton program. The additional computation might calculate a value or produce a side effect such as screen output. Syntactically, techniques may rename predicates, add arguments to predicates, add goals to clauses, and/or add clauses to programs. Unlike skeletons, techniques are not programs but can be conceived as a family of operations that can be applied to a program to produce a program.

A technique applied to a skeleton yields an *enhancement*. An enhancement which preserves the computational behaviour of the skeleton is called an *extension*.

We give examples of techniques. The two most commonly used techniques are the calculate and build techniques. They both compute something, a value or a data structure, while following the control flow of the skeleton. An extra argument is added to the defining predicate in the skeleton, and an extra goal is added to the body of each recursive clause. In the case of the calculate technique, the added goal is an arithmetic calculation; in the case of the build technique, the added goal builds a data structure. In both cases, the added goal relates the extra argument in the head of the clause to the extra argument(s) in the body of the clause.

Two typical examples of the application of the calculate technique are given as Programs 3a and 3b. Both are extensions of Program 2a which traverses a binary tree with values at its leaves. The left-hand program (3a) computes the product of the value of the leaves of the trees. The extra argument in the base case is the value of the leaf node. In the recursive case, the extra goal says that the product of a tree is the product of its left subtree and its right subtree. The predicate `is_tree` has been renamed to `prod_leaves`. The right-hand program (3b), which computes the sum of the leaves, is very similar, the only difference being choice of names and the extra goal.

```
prod_leaves(leaf(X),X).              sum_leaves(leaf(X),X).
prod_leaves(tree(L,R),Prod) :-       sum_leaves(tree(L,R),Sum) :-
    prod_leaves(L,LProd),                sum_leaves(L,LSum),
    prod_leaves(R,RProd),                sum_leaves(R,RSum),
    Prod is LProd*RProd.                 Sum is LSum+RSum.
```

Programs 3a, 3b: Extensions of Program 2a using calculate

Two enhancements of the same skeleton share computational behaviour. They can be combined into a single program which combines the functionality of each separate enhancement. Techniques can be developed independently and subsequently combined automatically. The (syntactic) operation for combining enhancements is called *composition*. This is similar in intent to function composition where the functionality of separate functions are combined into a single function. Program 4 is the result of the composition of Programs 3a and 3b.

```
prod_sum_leaves(leaf(X),X,X).
prod_sum_leaves(tree(L,R),Prod,Sum) :-
    prod_sum_leaves(L,LProd,LSum),
    prod_sum_leaves(R,RProd,RSum),
    Prod is LProd*RProd,
    Sum is LSum+RSum.
```

Program 4: The composition of two extensions

A different programming technique uses accumulators. The accumulator-calculate technique adds two arguments to the defining predicate in the skeleton. The first argument is used to record the current value of the variable in question and the second contains the final result of the computation. The base case relates the input and output arguments, usually via unification. One difference between calculate and accumulate-calculate is in the need to add an auxiliary predicate. Another is that goals and initial values need to be placed differently.

Program 5 shows the result of applying the accumulate-calculate technique to the tree traversal program, Program 2a. It computes the sum of the leaves of a binary tree and is comparable to Program 3b. In general, programs written with accumulator techniques will run more efficiently than the equivalent program written with calculate and build techniques, due to the way tail recursion is implemented in Prolog.

```
sum_leaves(Tree,Sum) :- accum_sum_leaves(Tree,0,Sum).

accum_sum_leaves(leaf(X),Accum,Sum) :-
    Sum is Accum + X.
accum_sum_leaves(tree(L,R),Accum,Sum) :-
    accum_sum_leaves(L,Accum,Accum1),
    accum_sum_leaves(R,Accum1,Sum).
```

Program 5: Extension of Program 2a using accumulate-calculate

Program 6 is an example of the application of the accumulate-build technique, also applied to Program 2a. It builds an inorder traversal of the leaves of the tree. There is no explicit arithmetic calculation, rather lists built by unification in the base clause. There is one trick here. Accumulators build structures in reverse order and hence the right subtree is traversed before the left subtree in order to have the final list in the correct order.

```
traversal(Tree,Xs) :- accum_leaves(Tree,[],Sum).
```

```
accum_leaves(leaf(X),Accum,[X|Accum]).
accum_leaves(tree(L,R),Accum,Xs) :-
    accum_leaves(R,Accum,Accum1),
    accum_leaves(L,Accum1,Sum),
```

Program 6: Extension of Program 2a using accumulate-build

The skeletons and techniques presented in this paper are all taken from Prolog, but stepwise enhancement is equally applicable to other logic programming languages, as discussed in Kirschenbaum, Michaylov and Sterling (1996). They claim that skeletons and techniques should be identified when a language is first used, in order to encourage systematic, effective program development. This learning approach should be stressed during teaching. They show that the skeletons and techniques for Prolog can be extended to constraint logic programming languages, notably CLP(R), concurrent logic programming languages such as Flat Concurrent Prolog and Strand, and higher order logic program languages, in particular Lambda-Prolog (Nadathur and Miller, 1988).

4   A Higher Order View of Programming Techniques

Naish (1996) argued for a higher order approach to programming in Prolog, based on similar techniques which are widely used in functional programming. One of the key steps in this approach is to develop suitable higher order predicates which can be used for a whole class of computations over a particular data structure. Modern functional languages have certain data types and higher order functions built in. For example, the polymorphic type list(T) and higher order function foldr which generalises the common simple recursion used to compute a value from a list. Program 7 demonstrates the use of foldr using Prolog syntax in the style of (Naish, 1996).

```
:- type list(T) ---> [] ; [T|list(T)].

foldr(F, B, [], B).
foldr(F, B, [A|As], R) :-
    foldr(F, B, As, R1),
    call(F, A, R1, R).

sum(As, S) :- foldr(plus, 0, As, S).
product(As, P) :- foldr(times, 1, As, P).
length(As, L) :- foldr(add1, 0, As, L).
add1(_, TailLen, Len) :- Len is TailLen + 1.
```

Program 7: Using foldr

In addition to the input list and result, `foldr` has two other arguments. One is the base case: what to return when the end of the list is reached. The other is a function — a predicate in the Prolog context. The predicate takes the head of a list and the result of folding the tail of a list to give the result of folding the whole list. The `call/N` predicates are available as builtins or library predicates in several Prolog systems. The first argument (a predicate) is called with the additional arguments added. For example, `call(plus(A),R1,R)` is equivalent to `plus(A,R1,R)`, which is true if A+R1=R. In (Naish, 1996) an alternative higher order primitive, `apply/3`, is recommended due to its greater flexibility. In this paper we simply use `call/N` as it is more widely known.

Examples in (Naish, 1996) show how `foldr` can be used to compute both the sum and product in a single pass by using a pair of numbers for the base case, intermediate results and final answer. These higher order definitions can be optimised very effectively using a partial evaluator such as Mixtus (Sahlin, 1993). Further examples are given to show how predicates which are analogous to `foldr` can be constructed.

5   Incorporating Shape

Recent work on shape (Jay and Cockett, 1994), (Jay, 1995), (Bellé et al., 1996) and polytypism (Jeuring and Jansson, 1996), (Jansson and Jeuring, 1996) has formalised how many data types have certain higher order functions naturally associated with them. For example, `map` takes a list and produces another list of the same length. The shape of the output, the list structure, is the same as the shape of the input and the elements of the lists are related by the function `map` applies. The idea of `map` can be applied to any algebraic type such as lists and trees, and also arrays and matrices. A generic version of `map` applied to a binary tree will produce a binary tree of the same shape where the elements of the trees are related by the function `map` applies.

Similarly, `foldr` can be generalised to any algebraic type. For lists, a call to `foldr` specifies two things: what should be returned for the empty list, and what should be returned for a non-empty list, given the head and the result of folding the tail. For a general algebraic type we need to specify what should be returned for each constructor in the type, given the arguments of the constructor corresponding to type parameters and the result of folding the arguments which correspond to a concrete type (generally the type being defined recursively).

Consider the `prod_leaves` example given earlier as Program 3a. The overall operation is to fold a tree into a single number. We need to define the results of folding terms of the form `leaf(X)` and `tree(L,R)`, given the folded versions of L and R.

Reconstructing the predicate `is_tree` as a definition of the type `bt(T)` and using the approach of (Naish, 1996) we arrive at Program 8: the definition of `foldr` for this tree type, and corresponding definitions of `prod_leaves` and `sum_leaves`. In (Naish, 1996) it was assumed that `foldrbt` would be written by

a programmer who has the required degree of insight. It is now clear that this predicate can be generated *automatically* from a definition of the type.

```
:- type bt(T) ---> leaf(T) ; tree(bt(T),bt(T)).

foldrbt(TreeP, LeafP, leaf(X), Folded) :-
    call(LeafP, X, Folded).
foldrbt(TreeP, LeafP, tree(L, R), Folded) :-
    foldrbt(TreeP, LeafP, L, FoldedL),
    foldrbt(TreeP, LeafP, R, FoldedR),
    call(TreeP, FoldedL, FoldedR, Folded).

prod_leaves(T, P) :- foldrbt(times, =, T, P).
sum_leaves(T, P) :- foldrbt(plus, =, T, P).
```

Program 8: Extensions of Program 2a using foldr

6   You'll Take the High Road and I'll Take the Low Road

The previous work of the authors sketched above can be seen as taking two different roads for program development starting from the same place (a type definition) and arriving at the same destination (the enhanced program), as shown in Figure 1.

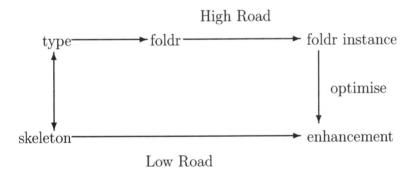

Fig. 1. Two roads to enhancement

Sterling suggested the low road in Figure 1, going from the type to the enhancement via the skeleton. To explain how to travel the low road is simple and does not require very abstract thinking or complex software tools. Such an approach to systematic program construction may be favoured by many programmers.

Naish suggested the high road in Figure 1, writing a version of `foldr` for the given type, using an instance of this `foldr` (a particular call to it) and then optimising, for example using a partial evaluator. The additional abstraction and concentration on semantics rather than syntax may be favoured by more experienced programmers using more advanced programming environments. The work on shape allows us to automatically obtain the `foldr` definition from the definition of the type.

There is a very simple mapping between algebraic types and a class of logic programs called RUL programs (Yardeni and Shapiro, 1990). RUL programs only have unary predicates. The argument of each clause head has the top level functor instantiated but all sub-terms are unique variables. Clause heads are mutually non-unifiable (thus predicates are deterministic when their arguments are instantiated). The arguments of all calls are variables which occur in the head and nowhere else in the body. Examples of RUL programs are `is_list` (Program 1) and `is_tree` (Program 2a).

The high road taken by functional programmers is equivalent to starting with a skeleton which is a RUL program and enhancing it with predicates which behave as functions, that is, they are deterministic and always succeed. The theory of functional programming can be used to prove results concerning composition of enhancements, for example, and generally give a theoretical justification for the idea of enhancement.

7   Generalising Both Approaches

Having found a class of programs for which the high and low roads are equivalent, we can see several ways to generalise both. The low road can have improved handling of non-recursive clauses and more flexible skeletons. The high road can be made more flexible by eliminating the type, mode and determinism restrictions inherited from functional programming.

7.1   Goals in Base Cases

The first (very simple) observation is that enhancements should allow general goals to be added to the base cases of enhancements. For pedagogical reasons, the original presentation classified enhancements into different categories according to the kind of goal added to recursive clauses and only allowed additional unifications to be added to facts. The limited abstraction simplifies learning but also restricts the scope of enhancements. For example, to find the sum of the squares of the leaves of a tree using `foldrbt` we could use `foldrbt(plus, square, Tree, SumXX)`, where `square` takes a number and returns its square. The optimised program (or enhanced skeleton) would have a call to `square` in the base case.

7.2   Non-deterministic Skeletons

Algebraic types correspond to RUL programs, in which are predicates are deterministic and only have single arguments. The stepwise enhancement paradigm has no such restriction: nondeterministic skeletons such as branch (Program 2b) and connected (Program 9) can be used.

```
connected(A, A).
connected(A0, A) :-
    edge(A0, A1),
    connected(A1, A).
```

Program 9: Transitive closure of the edge/2 relation

As noted in (Naish, 1996), higher order logic programs can also be nondeterministic and nondeterministic analogues of foldr can be constructed. A version of foldr for paths in a graph was written (using considerable intellectual effort) based on the simple transitive closure procedure connected, above. The close relationship between 'shape' and stepwise enhancement we have uncovered can be used to generalise the transformation from algebraic types (or RUL programs) to foldr functions. From an arbitrary skeleton (not necessarily a RUL program), we can generate an appropriate version of foldr as follows.

A procedure with A arguments and C clauses leads to a higher order procedure with $C+A+1$ arguments. It has C 'higher order' arguments and one additional 'result' argument. The recursive calls in the clause bodies have the same higher order arguments as the head and new variables for their results. Each clause also has an additional call/N with the higher order argument for that clause, the variables in the head which did not appear in any recursive body calls, result arguments of the body calls and the result argument of the head. If this call has only two arguments then call/2 is replaced by =/2 (the higher order argument is simply a term which is returned for the base case). Mutual recursion can be treated in the same way (read recursive as mutually recursive), where C is the number of clauses in the set of mutually recursive procedures.

For list/1 and tree/1 the results are the foldr/4 and foldrbt/4 definitions given in programs 7 and 8. For branch and connected the results are in Program 10. The foldrcon procedure here is actually more general than the manually constructed version (which had a base case of V=FB instead of call/3) and can be used in the applications described in (Naish, 1996).

```
foldrb(FL, FR, FB, leaf(X), V) :-
    call(FB, X, V).
foldrb(FL, FR, FB, t(L,R), V) :-
    foldrb(FL, FR, FB, L, V1),
    call(FL, R, V1, V).
foldrb(FL, FR, FB, t(L,R), V) :-
    foldrb(FL, FR, FB, R, V2),
    call(FR, L, V2, V).
```

```
foldrcon(FE, FB, A, A, V) :-
    call(FB, A, V).
foldrcon(FE, FB, A0, A, V) :-
    edge(A0, A1),
    foldrcon(FE, FB, A1, A, V1),
    call(FE, A0, V1, V).
```

Program 10: Nondeterministic foldr for branch and connected

7.3   Polymorphic Types and Higher Order Skeletons

Monomorphic types such as *list* correspond to first order skeletons (RUL programs, as we have seen). The work on shape and polytypism uses polymorphic types such as *list(T)*, where T is a type parameter. Polymorphic types correspond to higher order skeletons with additional arguments. A type $t(T1, T2)$ can be mapped to a predicate t(T1,T2,X) which succeeds if X is of type $t(T1,T2)$. If the definition of type t contains the constructor $c(E1,E2)$ (where $E1$ and $E2$ are type expressions) then t/3 will have the clause
t(T1, T2, c(X, Y)) :- call($E1$, X), call($E2$, Y).

Instances of call/N can be specialised if their first argument is a nonvariable. For example, the type *list(T)* leads to the predicate list/2 in Program 11. The type *rtree(T)*, an M-way tree consisting of a term $rt(X, Y)$ where X is of type T and Y is of type *list(rtree(T))* can be defined using the predicate rtree/2.

```
list(T, []).
list(T, [X|Xs]) :-
    call(T, X), list(T, Xs).

rtree(T, rt(X, RTs)) :-
    call(T, X), list(rtree(T), RTs).
```

Program 11: Higher order skeletons for list(T) and rtree(T)

Higher order skeletons go against the spirit of simplicity embodied in stepwise enhancement and the control flow of the program above (mutual recursion through call/N) would certainly be confusing for a novice programmer. The advantage is that it saves having multiple copies of similar code. Rather than have a separate skeletons for simple lists, lists of lists, lists of rtrees et cetera, a single higher order definition can be given. A specialised definition of a type such as *rtree(any)* can be obtained by partial evaluation (eliminating all instances of call/N) and a version of foldr can be derived as described above. For rtree, the result is Program 12.

```
rtree_any(rt(X, RTs)) :-
    list_rtree_any(RTs).
```

```
list_rtree_any([]).
list_rtree_any([RT|RTs]) :-
    rtree_any(RT),
    list_rtree_any(RTs).

foldrrt(FR, FC, B, rt(X, RTs), V) :-
    foldrlrt(FR, FC, B, RTs, V1),
    call(FR, X, V1, V).

foldrlrt(FR, FC, B, [], V) :-
    B = V.
foldrlrt(FR, FC, B, [RT|RTs], V) :-
    foldrrt(FR, FC, B, RT, V1),
    foldrlrt(FR, FC, B, RTs, V2),
    call(FC, V1, V2, V).
```

Program 12: Specialised skeleton and version of foldr for rtree

7.4   Flexible Modes

As well as allowing flexibility with types and nondeterminism, logic programs allow flexibility with modes. Rather than having fixed inputs and one output, as in functional programs, logic programs can potentially be run backwards — computing what would normally be considered the input from a given output. This flexibility can extend to higher order predicates, including those generated automatically from skeletons.

As an example, we will construct a meta interpreter for Prolog by using foldrrt backwards. A Prolog proof tree can be represented by an rtree, where each node contains (the representation of) a Prolog atom which succeeded. The foldrrt procedure can be used to check that an rtree of atoms is a valid proof tree for a particular program and goal. A proof tree is valid if the atom in the root is the goal and for each node in the tree containing atom A and children $B1,B2,...,$ there is a program clause instance $A:-B1,B2,....$ The proof_of procedure in Program 13 represents clauses as a head plus a list of body atoms (procedure lclause) and can check that an rtree is a valid proof tree and return the atom which has been proved.

```
% Checks Proof is a valid proof tree and returns proved Atom;
% run backwards its a meta interpreter returning a proof tree
proof_of(Proof, Atom) :-
    foldrrt(lclause2, cons, [], Proof, Atom).

% checks H :- B is a clause instance; returns H
lclause2(H, B, H) :- lclause(H, B).
```

```
% clause/2 where clause bodies are lists
lclause(append([],A,A), []).
lclause(append([A|B],C,[A|D]), [append(B,C,D)]).
lclause(append3(A,B,C,D), [append(A,B,E),append(E,C,D)]).
...

cons(H, T, [H|T]).
```

Program 13: Interpreter constructed using rtree

With a suitable evaluation order, the code can also be run backwards. Given an atom, `foldrrt` acts as a meta interpreter, (nondeterministically) returning a proof tree for (a computed instance of) the atom. This is an example of constructing a program based on the type of its output, as discussed earlier. By utilising the natural association between a type and `foldr` and the flexible modes of logic programming, much of the process can be automated.

7.5 Foldl

In many cases, the higher order function `foldl` is preferable to `foldr` since it is tail recursive rather than left recursive (thus more efficient, at least for strict evaluation). It is not immediately obvious how to adapt `foldl` to general tree types rather than just lists. One possibility, suggested by Barry Jay is to perform a breadth first traversal (`foldr` uses a depth first traversal). This can be coded in a tail recursive fashion and is a familiar programming technique.

Another possibility, which we pursued initially and is used in (Belleannie et al 1997), is to use `foldr` with more complex data flow, using logic variables. The result argument of `foldr` can be a pair of terms, one of which can be used as an input, and the accumulator style of programming can be used. If the accumulator is a list, we can think of `foldr` returning a difference list (Sterling and Shapiro, 1994) instead of a list. With this style of programming, the data dependencies are such that the instances of `call/N` in the `foldr` definitions can be executed before the recursive call(s), allowing tail recursion.

However, we believe the most elegant and natural generalisation of `foldl` is evident in the stepwise enhancement paradigm. We adapted stepwise enhancement to produce higher order `foldr` procedures using a generalisation of the calculate and build techniques. By using *accumulator techniques* we can produce a `foldl` procedure for any skeleton. Accumulators are used much more widely than breadth first traversals and the code produced has simple data flow and can be translated into a functional language if the initial skeleton corresponds to an algebraic type.

The transformation is similar to the one described for `foldr`. The same number of higher order arguments are used and there is one output argument, as before, but there is also an extra accumulator argument. The `call/N` is the leftmost atom in the body and the accumulator and output arguments are 'threaded' through this and the recursive calls in the clause body in the familiar way (Sterling and Shapiro, 1994). The accumulator and output arguments can be made implicit by using the standard Definite Clause Grammar notation. The resulting version of foldl for lists is as follows.

```
% Explicit accumulator version
foldl(FC, FB, [], A0, A) :-
    call(FB, A0, A).
foldl(FC, FB, [X|Xs], A0, A) :-
    call(FC, X, A0, A1),
    foldl(FC, FB, Xs, A1, A).

% DCG (implicit accumulator) version
foldl(FC, FB, []) -->
    call(FB).
foldl(FC, FB, [X|Xs]) -->
    call(FC, X),
    foldl(FC, FB, Xs).
```

Program 14: Automatically derived foldl for lists

There are two differences between this version of foldl and the standard foldl for lists. The first is the argument order for the call to the FC 'function' is swapped. This is not essential but allows the accumulator and output arguments to be implicit using the DCG notation. It is also consistent with foldr. The second difference is the use of a function called in the base case. The standard version of foldl simply returns the accumulator when the end of the list is reached. This is equivalent to our version of foldl with the identity function (=/2 in Prolog) as the function for the base case.

For 'linear' data structure such as lists, calling a function when the base case is reached adds no real power. The function can always be called at the top level after foldl has returned, with the same effect. However, for tree structures, a function application at the base case is often essential. Below are the versions of foldl for the bt type and connected procedure. Note prod_leaves (sum_leaves) has the multiplication (addition) at the leaves, as in Program 5.

```
foldlbt(F, B, leaf(X)) -->
    call(B, X).
foldlbt(F, B, t(L,R)) -->
    call(F),
    foldlbt(F, B, L),
    foldlbt(F, B, R).

prod_leaves(T, P) :-
    foldlbt(=, times, T, 1, P).
```

```
sum_leaves(T, P) :-
    foldlbt(=, plus, T, 0, P).

rev_traverse(Tree, Xs) :-
    foldlbt(=, cons, Tree, [], Xs).

foldlcon(F, B, A, A) -->
    call(B, A).
foldlcon(F, B, A0, A) -->
    call(F, A0),
    {edge(A0, A1)},
    foldlcon(F, B, A1, A).

% non-looping connected; returns path
con_no_loop(A0, A, As) :-
    foldlcon(cons_nm, cons, A0, A, [], As).

cons_nm(A0, As, [A0|As]) :-
    not member(A0, As).
```

Program 15: Versions of foldl for is_tree and connected

For foldlcon, the call to edge is not recursive, so accumulator arguments
are not added (braces are used to indicate this in the DCG notation). From
foldlcon it is simple to code con_no_loop which finds connected nodes but
avoids cycles. The accumulator is the list of nodes visited so far, in reverse
order. The procedure which adds a new node to the accumulator, cons_nm, fails
if the node is already on the path. The path is also be returned at the top level.

Since the skeleton is_tree is a RUL program and hence equivalent to an
algebraic type, foldlbt is deterministic and behaves as a higher order function
over that type. The threading of the accumulator and result arguments in the
body of a clause is equivalent to nesting of functional expressions. For completeness, we give the equivalent Haskell code in Program 16.

```
>data Bt a = Leaf a | Tree (Bt a) (Bt a)
>foldlbt :: (a->a)->(b->a->a)->(Bt b)->a->a
>foldlbt f b (Leaf x) a = b x a
>foldlbt f b (Tree l r) a =
>    foldlbt f b r (foldlbt f b l (f a))

>sum_leaves t = foldlbt (id) (+) t 0
```

Program 16: Haskell version of foldl for is_tree/type bt

There are actually two possible versions of foldlbt, depending on the order
in which the two subtrees are visited. By swapping the two recursive calls in

the DCG version, the argument threading is also changed, leading to a logically different procedure. The procedure `rev_traverse` in Program 15 returns the reverse of the traversal returned by Program 6. Using the other version of `foldlbt` would result in the same traversal order. The choice of traversal orders and additional argument in `foldl` are consistent with the intuition that programming with accumulators or `foldl` is more complicated than using simple recursion or `foldr`.

8   Further Work

A category theoretic reconstruction of our method for deriving versions of `foldl` (restricted to RUL programs) may produce some deeper insights and should extend the understanding of shape and polytypism for functional languages. A more theoretical treatment of the higher order logic programs we derive may also be worthwhile. For example, our approach can be adapted to logic programming languages such as Lambda-Prolog (Nadathur and Miller, 1988) which have higher order constructs with well defined semantics.

Further generalisations of `foldr` and `foldl` could also be devised (Belleannie et al 1997). For example, we could add higher order calls to the start *and* end of each clause body, or even between each call as well. Other 'shapely' operations such as `zip2` (which takes two lists and returns a list of pairs) could also be generalised, as suggested by (Jay, 1995). We note that more expressive higher order predicates are not necessarily better in practice. There is no benefit in using a generalised `foldr` which is applicable in five percent more situations if each use is ten percent more complicated than `foldr`. The ideal situation is to have a collection of higher order predicates or functions with a good tradeoff between applicability and complexity. Such sets can be developed over time, based on coding patterns which occur in practice.

9   Conclusions

Research into systematic program construction has the important aim of elevating coding from the realm of arts and entertainment to science and engineering. In this paper we have built a bridge between the pragmatic syntax-based approach of stepwise enhancement and the very theoretical semantic approach of shape and polytypism. Despite the gulf between the research methodologies behind these two approaches, there is a very close relationship between them. This is pleasing in itself but also allows us to see ways in which both approaches can be generalised.

From the work on shape and polytypism in functional languages we have the generality of arbitrary functions as parameters, polymorphic types and the automatic synthesis of certain higher order functions from algebraic types. From the work on stepwise enhancement in logic programming, we have the generality of nondeterminism, additional arguments, flexible modes and use of accumulators. By combining the advantages of both approaches, we have shown how more code in both functional and logic programming languages can be constructed in a systematic and partially automated way.

References

Belleannie, C., Brisset, P., Ridoux O., A Pragmatic Reconstruction of Lambda-Prolog, Publication Interne IRISA no. 877, October 1994 (revised 1997)

Bellé, G., Jay, C. B. and Moggi, E., Functorial ML, *Proc. PLILP '96*, Springer LNCS 1140, pp. 32-46, 1996

Clocksin, W. and Mellish, C. *Programming in Prolog*, Springer-Verlag, 1981

Coelho, H., Cotta, J. and Pereira, L.M. *Prolog by Example*, Springer-Verlag, New York, 1988

Deville, Y. Logic Programming: *Systematic Program Development*, Addison Wesley, 1990

Fuchs, N. and Fromherz, M. Schema-based Transformations of Logic Programs, *Proc. 5th International Workshop on Logic Program Synthesis and Transformation*, Proietti, M. (ed.), pp. 111-125, Springer-Verlag, 1991.

Gegg-Harrison, T. Learning Prolog in a Schema-Based Environment, *Instructional Science*, 20:173-192, 1991.

Gegg-Harrison, T. Representing Logic Program Schemata in Lambda-Prolog, *Proc. 12th International Logic Programming Conference* (ed. L. Sterling), pp. 467-481, MIT Press, 1995

Jansson, P. and Jeuring, J. PolyP — a polytypic programming language extension. *In Conference Record of POPL '97: The 24th ACM SIGPLAN-SIGACT Symposium on Principles of Programming Languages*, pp. 470–482, 1997

Jay, C.B., A semantics for shape, *Science of Computer Programming*, 25, pp. 251-283, 1995

Jay, C.B. and Cockett, J.R.B. Shapely Types and Shape Polymorphism, *Proc. Programming Languages and Systems — ESOP '94: 5th European Symposium on Programming*, (ed. D. Sannella), Springer LNCS, pp. 302-316, Edinburgh, U.K., April 1994

Jeuring, J. and Jansson, P. Polytypic programming. In J. Launchbury, E. Meijer and T. Sheard *Advanced Functional Programming*, LNCS 1129, pp. 68–114, Springer-Verlag, 1996.

Kirschenbaum, M., Michaylov, S. and Sterling, L.S. Skeletons and Techniques as a Normative Approach to Program Development in Logic-Based Languages, *Proc. ACSC'96, Australian Computer Science Communications*, 18(1), pp. 516-524, 1996

Lakhotia, A. A Workbench for Developing Logic Programs by Stepwise Enhancement, Ph.D. Thesis, Case Western Reserve University, 1989.

Nadathur, G., Miller D., An Overview of Lambda-Prolog, *Proceedings of JICSLP* (eds. Bowen, K. and Kowlaski, R.), pp. 810-827, MIT Press, 1988

Naish, L. Higher Order Logic Programming in Prolog, Proc. Workshop on Multi-Paradigm Logic Programming, JICSLP'96, Bonn, 1996 (Also available as Tech. Report 96/2, Dept. Computer Science, University of Melbourne, 1996.)

O'Keefe, R. *The Craft of Prolog*, MIT Press, 1990

Power, A.J. and Sterling, L.S. A Notion of Map between Logic Programs. *Proceedings of 7th ICLP* (eds. Warren and Szeredi), pp. 390-404, MIT Press, 1990

Sahlin, D. Mixtus: An Automatic Partial Evaluator for Full Prolog, *New Generation Computing*, 12(1), pp. 7-51, 1993

Sterling, L.S. and Kirschenbaum, M. Applying Techniques to Skeletons, in *Constructing Logic Programs*, (ed. J.M. Jacquet), pp. 127-140, Wiley, 1993.

Sterling, L.S. and Shapiro, E.Y. *The Art of Prolog, 2nd edition*, MIT Press, 1994.

Sterling, L.S. and Yalçinalp, U. Logic Programming and Software Engineering — Implications for Software Design, *Knowledge Engineering Review*, 11(4), pp. 333-345, 1996

Vasconcelos, W. and Fuchs, N.E. An Opportunistic Approach for Logic Program Analysis and Optimisation using Enhanced Schema-based Transformations, *Proc. LOPSTR'95*, (ed. M. Proietti), Springer LNCS, pp. 174-188, 1995

Yardeni, E. and Shapiro E.Y., A Type System for Logic Programs, *Journal of Logic Programming*, 10(2), pp. 125-154, 1990

Development of Correct Transformation Schemata for Prolog Programs

Julian Richardson[1]* and Norbert Fuchs[2]

[1] Department of Artificial Intelligence, Edinburgh University, 80 South Bridge,
Edinburgh EH1 1HN, Scotland
`julianr@dai.ed.ac.uk`
[2] Department of Computer Science, University of Zurich, CH-8057 Zurich,
Switzerland
`fuchs@ifi.unizh.ch`

Abstract. Schema-based program transformation [8] has been proposed as an effective technique for the optimisation of logic programs. Schemata are applied to a logic program, mapping inefficient constructs to more efficient ones. One challenging aspect of the technique is that of proving that the schemata are correct.

This paper addresses the issue of correctness. We define operations for developing correct schemata by construction. The schema development operations are higher order equivalents of the classic program transformations of fold/unfold [6]. We consider a transformation schema to be correct if its application yields a target program which is equivalent to the source program under the *pure Prolog semantics*.

The work described in this paper makes three contributions: a methodology for the development of provably correct program transformation schemata, abstraction of program transformation operations to transformation operations on schemata, and a higher-order unification algorithm which forms the basis of the schema transformation operations.

1 Schema-Based Transformations

A program transformation technique based on transformation *schemata* is described in [8]. Transformation schemata are defined using patterns — higher-order terms which can be instantiated to program fragments. A transformation schema is applied to a program by scanning the program for a piece of code which matches the source pattern, and replacing it with the instantiated target pattern.

---

* The first author is supported by EPSRC Grant GR/L11724. Most of the work described was performed while the first author was a visiting research fellow at the University of Zurich, supported by HCM-Network "Logic Program Synthesis and Transformation", contract no. CHRX-CT93-0414, Project BBW 93.0268.

Norbert E. Fuchs (Ed.): LOPSTR'97, LNCS 1463, pp. 263–281, 1998.
© Springer-Verlag Berlin Heidelberg 1998

A program transformation schema is defined in [8] as a 4-tuple, which specifies that a conjunction of goals $G_1, ..., G_n$ with corresponding predicate definitions $S_1, ..., S_n$ can be transformed into a conjunction of goals $H_1, ..., H_n$ with corresponding predicate definitions $T_1, ..., T_n$:

$$\langle \langle G_1, ..., G_n \rangle, \langle S_1, ..., S_n \rangle, \langle H_1, ..., H_n \rangle, \langle T_1, ..., T_n \rangle \rangle \tag{1}$$

Such schemata can encode a wide range of useful transformations, e.g. loop fusion, accumulator introduction and goal reordering.

This paper addresses the issue of proving the correctness of transformation schemata. There are two basic design decisions we must make when considering the correctness of program transformation schemata:

1. Do we seek to prove the correctness of existing schemata, or do we instead only provide tools for constructing new schemata which are guaranteed to be correct? We have decided to take the latter approach.
2. How do we define the correctness of a program transformation? This question is discussed in the next section.

The paper is organised as follows. First we discuss related work in §2. We define equivalence of programs in §3 relative to the pure Prolog semantics, then outline in §4 how correct transformation schemata can be constructed incrementally by the application of abstract transformation operations, which are the equivalents on program patterns of the classic fold/unfold transformations on programs. We define a language for expressing program patterns and transformation schemata in §5, and outline a unification algorithm for program patterns in §6. The abstract transformation operations are described in §7, concentrating on the development of a correct unfold operation. We discuss the representation of transformation correctness conditions (§8) and the progress of our implementation (§9), before outlining how predicate termination information could be used (§10). Finally, we discuss further work (§12) and draw our conclusions (§13). Appendix A presents the unification algorithm, and appendix B goes through an example schema development using schema folding and unfolding operations.

2   Related Work

Research on schemata is a very active field. Of the many papers that have been published in the last years we will focus on three that describe recent developments.

After discussing the advantages and disadvantages of various schema languages, [4] introduce a new language to represent program schemata based on a subset of second-order logic, enhanced with specific schema features, and with global and local constraints. Their language is a variant of the language proposed by [8], though with the essential difference that constraints are not part of the schemata but are made explicit in a first-order language. The introduction of explicit constraints not only increases the expressiveness of the language but also guides the matching of the schema with a program through the successive application of rewriting and reduction rules. Starting with a schema S, a set of initial constraints C, and a program P, the pair $\langle S = P, C \rangle$ is successively rewritten and reduced to $\langle \emptyset, C' \rangle$. All occurring constraint sets are consistent. Then there is a substitution $\theta \in C'$ so that $S\theta = P$ and θ satisfies the initial constraint set C.

While most researchers — including [4] and ourselves — represent schemata purely syntactically as first- or second-order expressions, [5] express schemata as full first-order theories called specification frameworks. A specification framework axiomatises an application domain. It contains an open — i.e. only partially defined — program that represents the schema itself. The authors state that the main advantage of their approach is that it simplifies the semantics of schemata since the specification framework can be given a model-theoretic semantics in the form of reachable isoinitial models. Based on this semantics the authors define a notion of correctness for schemata. Correct schemata are expressed as parametric specification frameworks that contain steadfast open programs, where steadfast means that the programs are always correct provided their open relations are computed correctly. Based on the notion of correct program schemata one can synthesise steadfast open programs which are not only correct but also reusable.

The authors of [3] base their work on the concepts of specification-frameworks and steadfastness suggested by [5]. To extend these concepts to be used for program transformations they introduce the additional concept of the equivalence of the open — i.e. partially defined — programs computing the same relation. Then they define a transformation schema as a 5-tuple $\langle S_1, S_2, A, O_{12}, O_{21} \rangle$ where S_1 and S_2 are program schemata, i.e. specification frameworks, A an applicability condition ensuring the equivalence of the open programs within S_1 and S_2 with respect to the top-level relation computed, and O_{12} (resp. O_{21}) a set of optimisability conditions which ensure the optimisability of S_2 (resp. S_1). The authors present some concrete transformation schemata that they have implemented: divide-and-conquer, tupling generalisation, descending generalisation, and duality laws. The authors evaluate these transformation schemata with a small number of performance tests. The results show that the transformations cannot be used blindly thus necessitating the above mentioned optimisability conditions.

3   Choice of Semantics

A transformation is defined to be totally correct if the source and target programs are equivalent under the chosen semantics. We must choose which semantics to use.

The correctness of transformations of Prolog programs under a variety of semantics is discussed in [6]. Much of the existing work on the transformation of Prolog programs only considers the simplest semantics, the Herbrand semantics. This permits many powerful and interesting transformations. Unfortunately, if these transformations were let loose on a real Prolog program, they would wreak havoc, because the Herbrand semantics does not capture the intended meaning of

Prolog programs as they are written in practice. Schema-based transformations have, from the outset, been intended as a practical tool for program transformation, so we have decided to use a realistic semantics, the so-called *pure Prolog semantics* so that the resulting transformations can be applied to real programs. The pure Prolog semantics accurately reflects the semantics of Prolog programs when executed under the standard SLD resolution strategy. Programs must be cut-free and negation-free, and it is assumed that Prolog unification includes an occurs check.

4   Correctness by Construction

Many of the program transformations which are correct under the Herbrand semantics, e.g. unfold, are only correct under the pure Prolog semantics if certain conditions hold. For example, a literal (other than the first one) can only be unfolded in a clause if it is "non-left propagating". Generally, conditions such as this can only be established when the transformation schema is applied to a concrete program. We therefore modify the presentation of schemata given in [8] (as the authors of [8] suggest) by extending schemata with correctness conditions. The goal conjunctions $G_1, ...G_n$ and $H_1, ..., H_n$ which provide the transformation context in (1) can be provided by adding a predicate with body $G_1, ..., G_n$ to the source program, so we omit them in this presentation.

The state of development of a schema transformation is represented by a tuple (2), where *Schema* is a list of labeled clauses as described in §5, *Op* is the schema transformation operation which was applied to bring us to this state, Φ is a set of conditions which must be satisfied when the schema is applied to a Prolog program to ensure correctness of the resulting transformation, and *PreviousHistory* is another history structure.

$$history(Schema, Op, \Phi, PreviousHistory). \tag{2}$$

Correct schemata are developed by successive application of the available transformation operations, which are defined in such a way that when the resulting schema is applied to a program, there is a correspondence between the abstract operations which were used to develop that schema, and transformation operations on the source program yielding the target program.

The top line of figure 1 depicts a complete schema development. The figure as a whole illustrates how matching a schema pattern to a program fragment induces a matching process from the transformation operations and correctness conditions on schema patterns to corresponding transformation operations and correctness conditions on programs. The correctness conditions, Φ_i are accumulated during the development process, so that $\Phi_{k+1} \rightarrow \Phi_1 \wedge ... \wedge \Phi_k$. Once development has been completed, the intermediate stages can be stripped away, leaving just $Schema_0$, Φ_n and $Schema_n$. In principle, such a development could perform the transformation of a number of predicates. If the predicates which are transformed have heads $P_1, ..., P_k$ in $Schema_0$, and $P'_1, ..., P'_k$ in $Schema_n$,

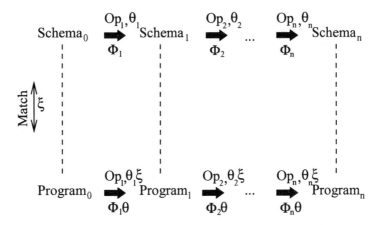

Fig. 1. A schema development. Each horizontal arrow is labeled with an operation together with its associated substitution and correctness conditions.

then we could express the resulting transformation schema in the language of Fuchs and Vasconcelos [8] as a tuple:

$$\langle \langle P_1, ..., P_k \rangle, Schema_0, \langle P'_1, ..., P'_k \rangle, Schema_n, \Phi_n \rangle$$

Note that some of the schema development operations $Schema_k \overset{Op}{\Rightarrow} Schema_{k+1}$ may modify $Schema_k$ in addition to $Schema_{k+1}$. If such an operation is applied, then we can only define a transformation schema from $Schema_k$ to $Schema_n$, and we say that the source pattern has been reset.

5   The Schema Language

The starting point for a schema development is a list of clauses. Each clause is represented internally as a term $label : clause(Head, Tail)$, which is portrayed as: $label : Head \leftarrow Tail$. We distinguish the following kinds of term:

1. Object-level variables $var(Name)$, portrayed form "Name".
2. Vector variables $vec(Type, Length, Name)$. $Type$ is the atom 'G' to indicate that this is a vector of goals, or 'A' to indicate that it is a vector of arguments. $Length$ is either a positive integer or zero or a Prolog variable. $Name$ is either an atom or an integer. The portrayed form is TypeName:Length, so for example $vec('G', \_, x)$ is portrayed as "Gx:_".
3. Predicates $pred(P, Args)$, where P is an atom or a variable $var(Name)$ and $Args$ is a list of arguments. The portrayed form is "P(Args)".
4. Function applications $apply(F, Args)$, where F is an atom or a variable $var(Name)$ and $Args$ is a list of arguments. The portrayed form is "F(Args)".

5. Lists of arguments or goals. The elements of the list can either be predicates or function applications, as appropriate for the type of the list, or vectors of the appropriate type.

6. Clauses $Head \leftarrow Tail$. $Head$ must be a single goal $pred(Name, Args)$. $Tail$ is a (possibly empty) list of goals or goal vectors.
7. Sequences of clauses $\overline{\chi}$.

The language defined above is close to that defined in [8], except that we do not require the notation $x\#n$ (used in [8] to mean that x occurs as the nth argument of a predicate or function). The facility to specify the lengths of vectors can be used to perform the same function, e.g. $f(\overline{L}, X\#n, \overline{R})$ is replaced by $f(vec('A', n-1, L), X, vec('A', \_, R))$. In addition, we define a notation $(\overline{\chi})$ for representing sequences of clauses, which allows us to refer during schema development to the context of the predicates to be transformed.

6   Unification of Schemata

Unification is the essential component of the Prolog execution strategy. A higher-order matching algorithm is also an essential component of the application of schemata to programs, during which patterns in the schema must be matched to parts of the Prolog program which are to be transformed. When we are constructing correct transformation schemata, unification is again essential, to allow us to apply abstract versions of the familiar program transformation steps of fold, unfold etc. This unification is an extension of the matching used when applying schemata to programs.

In the next section, we outline a higher-order unification algorithm for program patterns. The generality of this algorithm allows us to define very powerful equivalents on program patterns of the fold and unfold program transformations, but this generality also means that we have to be quite careful how we define them.

6.1   There Is No Single Most General Unifier

The principal problem is of how to unify two terms which consist of a mixture of goal (or argument) vectors and predicates (or functions). If we consider vectors of goals to be lists, and single goals to be singleton lists, then the separating comma can be considered as the list append operation. Unification of goal patterns then involves unification of lists modulo the associative append operation. Associative unification is discussed in [1, p309]. A decision procedure exists to determine whether two terms are unifiable, but there may be an infinite number of most general unifiers (mgus). For example, $p(\overline{X}), q(\overline{X}, a)$ and $p(\overline{Y}), q(a, \overline{Y})$ unify producing an infinite sequence of substitutions:[1]

$$\{a/\overline{X}, a/\overline{Y}\}, \{(a,a)/\overline{X}, (a,a)/\overline{Y}\}, ..., \{a^n/\overline{X}, a^n/\overline{Y}\}, ...$$

Usually, however, we expect only a finite set of most general unifiers, and may raise an error condition if there are too many unifiers to process. Often, we only

---

[1] Substitutions are oriented such that applying a substitution $\{X/Y\}$ to Y yields X.

need the first unifier which is returned by the algorithm, and need not consider other possible unifiers. When this is not the case, we may be able to rank the unifiers according to some measure and only use the best one. We will come back to the problem of multiple unifiers later.

6.2 The Unification Algorithm

Unification proceeds left-to-right. We allow terms in which function and predicate symbols may be variables. We have implemented such a unification algorithm, which is presented in appendix A. As an example, consider the problem of unifying $\overline{G}_2, Q(X), \overline{G}_3$ with $\overline{H}_2, Q(Y), \overline{H}_3$, given the substitution σ. There are four possible distinct ways to partition the goals and vectors between the two terms:

1. $\overline{H}_2 = \overline{G}_2$. Add the substitution $\{\overline{G}_2/\overline{H}_2\}$ to σ, and try to unify $Q(X), \overline{G}_3$ with $Q(Y), \overline{H}_3$.
2. $\overline{H}_2 = \overline{G}_2, \overline{D}_2$ where $\overline{D}_2$ is nonempty. Add the substitution $\{(\overline{G}_2, \overline{D}_2)/\overline{H}_2\}$ to σ, and try to unify $Q(X), \overline{G}_3$ with $\overline{D}_2, Q(Y), \overline{H}_3$.
3. $\overline{G}_2 = \overline{H}_2, \overline{D}_2$ where $\overline{D}_2$ is nonempty. $\{(\overline{H}_2, \overline{D}_2)/\overline{G}_2\}$ to σ, and try to unify $\overline{D}_2, Q(X), \overline{G}_3$ with $Q(Y), \overline{H}_3$.
4. Otherwise. The two terms do not unify. This branch of unification fails, and the algorithm backtracks.

In the example above, there are 5 unifiers: $(\overline{H}_2, Q(Y), \overline{H}_3)$, $(\overline{H}_2, Q(Y), Q(X), \overline{G}_3)$, $(\overline{H}_2, Q(Y), \overline{D}_3, Q(X), \overline{G}_3)$, $(\overline{G}_2, Q(X), Q(Y), \overline{H}_3)$ and $(\overline{G}_2, Q(X), \overline{D}_3, Q(Y), \overline{H}_3)$.

7 Transformation Operations on Program Patterns

Theorem 14 of [6] describes how the transformation rules of leftmost unfolding, deterministic non-left propagating unfolding, Tamaki-Sato folding, Tamaki-Sato definition and definition elimination can be used correctly to transform a definite-clause program under the pure Prolog semantics. In this section we show how to define versions of these operations on program schemata. We concentrate on the fold and unfold, only outlining the case for the other transformations. The example of appendix B uses these operations to develop an example transformation schema.

7.1 Schema Initialisation, Clause Addition, Specialisation

Schema development starts with a completely blank program pattern. Three operations are provided whose main purpose is to introduce sufficient structure into the program pattern to give the operations of folding and unfolding something to work with. These operations are: initialisation, clause addition, and specialisation. *Initialisation* throws away any current schema development and starts again from the blank pattern. *Clause addition* appends a new clause pattern $H \leftarrow \overline{T}$ to the program pattern. There are two types of *clause specialisation*:

pattern instantiation unifies a chosen subterm of a clause pattern with a user-specified pattern term, and division splits a chosen argument or goal vector in a clause into two.

Although each of these operations can be applied at any time during development, applying one of them to a program pattern P to give a new program pattern P' resets the source program pattern to P'. It is therefore preferable to apply them only at the beginning of a schema development.

7.2   Abstract Unfold

Care Is Needed with Unification

We would like the abstract unfold operation on program patterns to mirror the concrete unfold operation on programs, as described in [6, p.284]. At first sight, we can say that to apply an abstract unfold operation to an atom A in an abstract clause, $c : H \leftarrow \overline{L}, A, \overline{R}$ using abstract clauses $u_1 : H_1 \leftarrow \overline{T}_1, ..., u_n : H_n \leftarrow \overline{T}_n$, we replace c by n clauses $c_1, ..., c_n$ defined by $c_i : H\theta_i \leftarrow (\overline{L}, \overline{T}_i, \overline{R})\theta_i$ where for each c_i, θ_i is a most general unifier such that $A\theta_i = H_i\theta_i$, plus abstract versions of the concrete unfold correctness conditions, in particular that the unfold be *non-left propagating*.[2] This means that the atoms to the left of the $\overline{T}_i$ in the new clauses c_i must be variants of (i.e. identical up to renaming) the atoms to the left of A in c.

Unfortunately, the definition above has several problems. As noted in §6.1, there may be more than one mgu for each unification problem. Each such mgu makes certain commitments in the transformed program. We cannot use *all* the mgus, since they are not in general disjoint, and so doing would introduce repeated solutions. Therefore we must pick one mgu for each unification.

Picking one unifier (and hence one set of commitments) from several possibilities means that the resulting transformation schema may be a program *specialisation*, not an equivalence. In order to prevent specialisation of the transformed program, we must apply the unifier to both the source and the target pattern. How can we do this when there are multiple clauses with which to unfold? The choice of unifier we make when unfolding with each of the clauses will generally be incompatible. For example, when unfolding an atom $p(\overline{A}, K, \overline{B})$ using a clause with head $p(\overline{W}, cons(H, T), \overline{Z})$ we are faced with a choice of unifiers like those in §6.2.

The solution we adopt here to ensure that we do not pick incompatible unifiers for the unfolding clauses is to generalise the heads of the unfolding clauses u_i so that they are identical, and insert appropriate equality atoms explicitly into the bodies of the clauses. This allows us to pick a single unifier for all the u_i.

---

[2] As the example of [6][Example 14] shows, left-propagating unfolds can change the order of the returned answer substitutions, so we must disallow them.

The Abstract Unfold Operation

For an example of the application of the unfold operation defined in this section, see appendix B. To resolve the problems outlined above, we unfold a clause $c : P \leftarrow \overline{L}, A, \overline{R}$ using clauses $u_1 : H_1 \leftarrow \overline{T}_1, ..., u_n : H_n \leftarrow \overline{T}_n$, in the following steps:

1. Generalise the H_i to $\mathcal{H}$ such that the arguments of $\mathcal{H}$ are variables or vectors. Let θ_i be an assignment of values to these arguments so that $\mathcal{H}\theta_i = H_i$. In order to ensure that each θ_i is unique, the unification is made deterministic by disabling rules (4) and (5) of Appendix A, which disallows substitutions of the form $\{()/vector\}$ or $\{(vector, vector)/vector\}$. Each substitution θ_i is expressed as a list of equations[3] $X_j^i = E_j^i$.
2. Find an mgu Θ such that $A\Theta = \mathcal{H}\Theta$. This is the only point in the unfold step at which we must make a choice of unifier, and making this choice necessitates the next step.
3. In the source, replace clause c with $c' : P\Theta \leftarrow \overline{L}\Theta, A\Theta, \overline{R}\Theta$. In certain special cases, this may not be necessary. See the explanatory note in the paragraph at the end of this section.
4. In the target, replace clause c with n clauses:

$$c_i : P\Theta \leftarrow (X_1^i = E_1^i, ..., X_{k_i}^i = E_{k_i}^i)\Theta, \overline{L}\Theta, \overline{T}_i\Theta, \overline{R}\Theta$$

5. For each c_i, eliminate any intermediate variables and vectors which were introduced by the unification algorithm, i.e. were not present in c or $u_1, ..., u_n$.

In accordance with [6, p.284], we require the following conditions to hold:

1. $u_1, ..., u_n$ constitute one entire predicate definition — the program to be transformed contains no clauses apart from $u_1, ..., u_n$ which define the same predicate, and these are all the clauses which define the predicate.
2. In addition, either:
   (a) $\overline{L} = ()$ — the unfold is a leftmost unfold, or
   (b) the unfold is non-left propagating. This condition can only be checked when the pattern has been instantiated by matching with a program fragment, so for each c_i, a term $non\_left\_propagating(c,A,c_i)$ is added to the set Φ of transformation conditions.

By applying the unifier Θ to the source pattern as well as to the target, we ensure that the resulting schema does not specialise the program to which it is applied. This disturbs the development history, and means that we must essentially start a new development with the new source pattern as the initial pattern.

---

[3] Note that each of the unifying substitutions θ_i must be converted to a list of equations. The equations are unoriented, and this allows us to compose the θ_i with the mgu θ, since applying θ to an equation $X = Y$ yields a new equation (which is later solved by unification in step (5) above) $X\theta = Y\theta$, whereas applying θ to a substitution $\{X/Y\}$ may not yield a valid substitution, e.g. when $\theta = \{f(a)/Y\}$.

However, in the special case where Θ is only a renaming of c, no modification of the source pattern is necessary, allowing the development history to be retained. In the case that there is more than one possible unifier Θ, it is preferable to choose one which is a renaming where this is possible — this can be achieved by modifying the pattern unification algorithm to return renamings before other unifiers. In order to encourage the existence of renaming unifiers, it is important to try to develop enough structure in the pattern using the clause addition and specialisation operations before applying unfolding.

7.3   Abstract Fold

With folding, as with unfolding, we must take care not to specialise the transformed program. An example of the development of a transformation schema for loop fusion using folding and unfolding is contained in appendix B.

The abstract fold definition mirrors that of Tamaki-Sato folding (definition R3 of [6]). There are a number of conditions which need to be checked to ensure that the fold is a correctness-preserving transformation:

1. The folding atoms must be fold-allowing as described in Theorem 14 and Definition 7 of [6]. In order to keep track of which atoms are fold-allowing and which are not we must allow vectors to be marked with their fold-allowing status (*true* or *false*), and ensure that any unification which splits a vector into a number of vectors or atoms marks them with the same fold-allowing status as their parent.
2. As stated in [6], there is also a restriction on the substitution which unifies the body of the folding predicate with the folded atoms; suppose we are folding a number of atoms $\overline{E}$ in the body of a clause $H \leftarrow \overline{L}, \overline{E}, \overline{R}$ using the body of a clause $H' \leftarrow \overline{G}$. If θ is the unifying substitution, i.e. $\overline{E}\theta = \overline{G}\theta$, then θ restricted to the set $vars(\overline{G}) - vars(H')$ is a variable renaming whose image has an empty intersection with the set $vars(H, \overline{L}, H'\theta, \overline{R})$. In general, it is not possible to decide this until the schema is matched with a program, but there is a significant special case when $vars(\overline{G}) - vars(H') = \{\}$ which arises when all the vectors and object-level variables of the folding predicate's body, $\overline{G}$, also occur in the folding predicate's head, H'. In this special case, the condition is trivially satisfied (clause $c6$ of Appendix B falls into this special case, for example).
3. Folding generally requires that some states in the schema development will simultaneously contain both old and new predicates, and the two types of clause must be carefully distinguished to ensure correctness is guaranteed.

7.4   Definition Introduction

In order to develop powerful transformations such as loop fusion, it is necessary to be able to apply the *definition introduction* rule. We use the Tamaki-Sato definition rule described in [6, R15], which allows a new clause to be introduced as long as its head is a predicate which does not already occur in the program, and the literals in its body are made from predicates which are already in the program.

8   Transformation Correctness Conditions

Application of a schema development operation entails checking certain correctness conditions. These conditions can be partially checked while the schema development is taking place, but there is always a residual condition which can only be checked when the schema is applied to a program. For example, suppose we need to ensure that a certain clause is not recursive. This means checking that there is no goal in the body of the predicate with the same predicate (and arity) as the head of the predicate. For the following clause, it is easy to verify that this condition does not hold:

$$P(X) \leftarrow \overline{G}, P(Y), \overline{H}$$

If, however, we replace $P(Y)$ in the body by $Q(Y)$, we cannot be certain. We cannot say immediately that the condition does not hold, but there is a residual which must be checked whenever the resulting transformation schema is applied to a program, namely that P is not equal to Q, and that P does not appear in $\overline{G}$ or $\overline{H}$.

The way in which the correctness conditions are expressed will be an important factor in ensuring the correctness of a schema development system. For example, for each schema development operation there could be a corresponding Prolog predicate. This simplifies the implementation of the correctness conditions (they are just pieces of Prolog code), but is unsatisfactory for several reasons:

1. ensuring the correctness of the schema development system is then made difficult, because it depends on the correctness of these checking predicates, and
2. it is difficult to perform reasoning about Prolog predicates.

The preferable alternative is to express these conditions using logical formulae containing a small number of primitives such as $subterm(X, T)$ — X is a subterm of T, $vars(T, V)$ — V is the set of variables in term T etc., connected by logical connectives (universal and existential quantifiers, conjunction and negation). This not only permits a high degree of confidence in the correctness conditions, but the finer grain and logical nature of such a language also makes it possible to perform some reasoning with the conditions.

9   Implementation

The unification algorithm, and simplified versions of the fold and unfold operations have been implemented in Sicstus Prolog. Some correctness conditions are enforced, but many more need to be added. A text-based user interface allows the user to apply the abstract schema development operations discussed in this paper, and allows schema developments to be loaded and saved. Output of pattern terms is easily achieved with suitable definitions of the `portray/1` predicate. Input is more tricky, since we would like to be able to input higher-order terms in a natural way. For example, the term $P(\overline{L}, A, \overline{R})$ is represented internally as `pred(var(p),[vec('A',_,1),var(a),vec('A',_,r)])`, and both portrayed and input as `P(Al:_,A,Ar:_)`. This is achieved by reading input into a string, which is then parsed by a DCG. Vector lengths are represented by Prolog variables, and Prolog handles their unification.

10   Exploiting Predicate Termination Information

One of the problems we encounter when constructing transformations which are correct under the pure Prolog semantics is that we must take care to preserve the termination behaviour of predicates. This means that we cannot simply prune a clause such as (3), because if G_1 or G_2 does not terminate, then nor will c, whereas the pruned version (in which the entire body is replaced by "fail") fails finitely.

$$c : Head \leftarrow G_1, G_2, 1 = 2, G_3. \qquad (3)$$

This can be overcome either by allowing the transformation of infinite to finite failure, or by exploiting the termination properties of predicates when the transformation schema is applied. It is expected that many useful transformation schemata will require information on the termination properties of the predicates to which they are applied.

The termination properties of some predicates are already known, for example arithmetic goals, unification and test predicates. More generally, determining termination properties of predicates is a problem which has already been addressed by several researchers. For example termination properties are heavily used in the Mercury system [7]. The simplest approach is to allow the user to annotate predicate definitions to indicate termination properties. Termination may be established only for certain modes of a predicate. Modal inference and annotation would therefore be another useful extension.

11   Laws

The application of laws is essential to many transformation techniques. For example, the associativity of append is necessary for the transformation of naïve reverse into the tail-recursive version. Laws can be represented using program patterns. For example, associativity can be represented as below, and declaring a predicate to be associative corresponds to a particular instantiation of P:

$$P(A, B, T), P(T, C, E) \equiv P(B, C, V), P(A, V, E).$$

12 Further Work

There are many directions for further work. First and foremost, it is necessary to prove the correctness of the abstracted unfold operation, fully define and prove correctness conditions for the abstracted fold operation, define a flexible mechanism for applying laws, and extend the implementation accordingly. Following this, further schema transformation operations can be developed, for example a pruning operation, as described in §10.

Vector lengths can be used very effectively to reduce the number of solutions returned when two patterns are unified. Currently only equality relationships between vector lengths can be expressed. In particular, if a vector $\overline{V}:L_1$ is unified with a pattern $\overline{X}_1:M_1, \overline{X}_2:M_2$, we cannot express the fact that $L_1 = M_1 + M_2$. In [4], vector lengths can be constrained using $=, =<$ inequalities, but in the light of the above example, we could go further and extend the system to represent and solve such constraints, which are problems in Presburger arithmetic and therefore decidable.

It may be useful to introduce some automatic guidance into a schema development system, which may suggest strategies such as generalisation or tupling when appropriate. Proof plans [2] may be suitable for this. Indeed, we can view the schema development operations as tactics, in which case it is natural that proof plans should provide the meta-level.

It is also important to study the expressiveness of the resulting transformation schemata. The lack of induction in schema development operations is likely to be one source of these restrictions.

13 Conclusions

In this document we have proposed a technique for developing correct transformation schemata for Prolog programs. Correct transformation schemata are constructed by applying a sequence of development operations. A transformation is correct if when it is applied to a program, it yields a new program which is equivalent to the original one under the pure Prolog semantics. This means the program must be negation and cut-free.

The system is based on a higher-order unification algorithm for schema terms. The schema development operations, which are abstract equivalents of the classical fold/unfold etc. transformation operations, are defined in terms of this unification, and conditions are defined to ensure their correctness. These conditions can be partially checked during schema development, but generally leave a residual which can only be checked when the schema is applied to a program.

We have implemented the higher-order unification algorithm, and a simplified version of some of the transformations.

14 Acknowledgements

We would like to thank the respective funding bodies for their support, and the members of the IFI for their generous hospitality to the first author, in particular

Norbert Fuchs, Rolf Schwitter, Raja Dravid and Alex Riegler. We are grateful to the referees for their comments.

References

1. Alan Bundy. *The Computer Modelling of Mathematical Reasoning.* Academic Press, 1983. Second Edition.
2. Alan Bundy. The use of explicit plans to guide inductive proofs. In R. Lusk and R. Overbeek, editors, *9th Conference on Automated Deduction*, pages 111–120. Springer-Verlag, 1988. Longer version available from Edinburgh as DAI Research Paper No. 349.
3. H. Büyükyıldız and P. Flener. Generalized logic program transformation schemas. In N. E. Fuchs, editor, *LOPSTR '97: Proceedings of the Seventh International Workshop on Logic Program Synthesis and Transformation, Leuven, Belgium, July 10-12 1997 (this volume)*. Lecture Notes in Computer Science, Springer Verlag, forthcoming, 1998.
4. E. Chasseur and Y. Deville. Logic program schemas, constraints and semi-unification. In N. E. Fuchs, editor, *LOPSTR '97: Proceedings of the Seventh International Workshop on Logic Program Synthesis and Transformation, Leuven, Belgium, July 10-12 1997 (this volume)*. Lecture Notes in Computer Science, Springer Verlag, forthcoming, 1998.
5. P. Flener, K.-K. Lau, and M. Ornaghi. On correct program schemas. In N. E. Fuchs, editor, *LOPSTR '97: Proceedings of the Seventh International Workshop on Logic Program Synthesis and Transformation, Leuven, Belgium, July 10-12 1997 (this volume)*. Lecture Notes in Computer Science, Springer Verlag, forthcoming, 1998.
6. A. Pettorossi and M. Proietti. Transformation of logic programs: Foundations and techniques. *Journal of Logic Programming*, 19/20:261–320, 1994.
7. Zoltan Somogyi, Fergus Henderson, and Thomas Conway. The execution algorithm of Mercury: an efficient purely declarative logic programming language. *Journal of Logic Programming*, 29(1):17–64, October 1996.
8. W. W. Vasconcelos and N.E. Fuchs. An opportunistic approach for logic program analysis and optimisation using enhanced schema-based transformations. In *Proceedings of LoPSTr'95, Fifth International Workshop on Logic Program Synthesis and Transformation, Utrecht, Netherlands*, volume 1048 of *Lecture Notes in Computer Science*, pages 175–188. Springer Verlag, 1996.

A   The Schema Unification Algorithm

In the following presentation, Var denotes an object-level variable, $\overline{V}{:}l$ represents a vector with length l, $Atom$ denotes an atom, $P(\overline{A})$ represents a function or predicate with head P and arguments $\overline{A}$. For brevity, it is assumed in this presentation that atoms, predicates, functions or object-level variables can be freely converted to vectors of length 1.

$$\frac{B =_\sigma A}{A =_\sigma B}$$

$$\frac{P =_{\sigma_1} Q,\ \overline{A}_1\sigma_1 =_\sigma \overline{A}_2\sigma_2}{P(\overline{A}_1) =_{\sigma_1 \circ \sigma} Q(\overline{A}_2)} \qquad \frac{Var \notin P(\overline{A}_1)}{P(\overline{A}_1) =_{\{P(\overline{A}_1)/Var\}} Var}$$

$$\frac{}{Atom =_{\{\}} Atom} \qquad \frac{}{Atom =_{\{Atom/Var\}} Var}$$

$$\frac{}{\overline{V}{:}l =_{\{Atom/\overline{V},\, l=1\}} Atom} \qquad \frac{}{\overline{V}{:}l =_{\{Var/\overline{V},\, l=1\}} Var}$$

$$\frac{\overline{V}{:}l \notin P(\overline{A})}{P(\overline{A}) =_{\{P(\overline{A})/\overline{V},\, l=1\}} \overline{V}{:}l} \qquad \frac{}{Var_1 =_{\{Var_1/Var_2\}} Var_2}$$

$$\frac{}{\overline{V}_1{:}l_1 =_{\{V_1/V_2,\, l_1=l_2\}} \overline{V}_2{:}l_2} \qquad \frac{l_j = 1,\ l_{i\,(i \neq j)} = 0,\ \overline{V}_j{:}1 =_\sigma P(\overline{A})}{(\overline{V}_1{:}l_1, ..., \overline{V}_k{:}l_k) =_\sigma P(\overline{A})}$$

$$\frac{l_j = 1,\ l_{i\,(i \neq j)} = 0,\ \overline{V}_j{:}1 =_\sigma Var}{(\overline{V}_1{:}l_1, ..., \overline{V}_k{:}l_k) =_\sigma Var}$$

$$\frac{\sum_{i=1}^k l_i = n}{(\overline{V}_1{:}l_1, ..., \overline{V}_k{:}l_k) =_{\{(\overline{V}_1{:}l_1,...,\overline{V}_k{:}l_k)/\overline{V}{:}n\}} \overline{V}{:}n}$$

$$\frac{\exists \overline{X}, n \,.\, (\overline{X}{:}n, \overline{V}_2{:}l_2, ..., \overline{V}_k{:}l_k) =_\sigma (\overline{W}_2{:}m_2, ..., \overline{W}_j{:}m_j),\ m_1 + n = l_1}{(\overline{V}_1{:}l_1, ...; \overline{V}_k{:}l_k) =_{\{(\overline{W},\overline{X})/\overline{V}_1\} \circ \sigma} (\overline{W}_1{:}m_1, ..., \overline{W}_j{:}m_j)} \tag{4}$$

$$\frac{(\overline{V}_2{:}l_2, ..., \overline{V}_k{:}l_k) =_\sigma (\overline{W}_1{:}m_1, ..., \overline{W}_j{:}m_j)\quad l_1 = 0}{(\overline{V}_1{:}l_1, ..., \overline{V}_k{:}l_k) =_{\{()/\overline{V}_1\} \circ \sigma} (\overline{W}_1{:}m_1, ..., \overline{W}_j{:}m_j)} \tag{5}$$

B   Fold/Unfold Example

We now present a modified version of the tupling example from §2 of [6]. Vectors and atoms which are not fold-allowing are underlined.

B.1   Initial Program Schema

We start with a program *Program* with clauses as follows:

$$\overline{X}_1$$
$$c1 : P(\overline{X}_1) \leftarrow P_1(\overline{Y}_1, L, \overline{Y}_2), P_2(\overline{Z}_1, L, \overline{Z}_2), \overline{R}.$$
$$c2 : P_1(\overline{A}_1, nil, \overline{A}_2) \leftarrow .$$
$$c3 : P_1(\overline{A}_3, cons(H_1, T_1), \overline{A}_4) \leftarrow P_1(\overline{A}_5, T_1, \overline{A}_6).$$
$$c4 : P_2(\overline{A}_7, nil, \overline{A}_8) \leftarrow .$$
$$c5 : P_2(\overline{A}_9, cons(H_2, T_2), \overline{A}_{10}) \leftarrow P_2(\overline{A}_{11}, T_2, \overline{A}_{12}), F(\overline{A}_{13}).$$
$$\overline{X}_2$$

Note that when a schema pattern is finally matched to a fragment of Prolog program, different instances of the same schema variable name must match with Prolog-unifiable pieces of the program, so we must be careful to ensure that schema variable names are different where we do not wish this to be the case.

B.2   Schema Development

Define a new predicate with the first two atoms from the body of $c1$. The new predicate should have the same arguments as the atoms in its body, although we are free to reorder them and remove repeated occurrences as we see fit. The new predicate name must not already be in use, so $\Phi_0 = \{New \notin \{\overline{X}_1, c1, c2, c3, c4, c5, \overline{X}_2\}\}$. The new predicate name is instantiated when the schema is applied to a program.

$$c6 : New(L, \overline{Y}_1, \overline{Y}_2, \overline{Z}_1, \overline{Z}_2) \leftarrow \underline{P_1(\overline{Y}_1, L, \overline{Y}_2), P_2(\overline{Z}_1, L, \overline{Z}_2)}.$$

Fold the first two atoms of the body of $c1$ using $c6$. Since $c6$ is a new predicate, and $c1$ is old, the fold is allowed. The unifier is trivial so there is no specialisation.

$$c7 : P(\overline{X}_1) \leftarrow New(L, \overline{Y}_1, \overline{Y}_2, \overline{Z}_1, \overline{Z}_2), \overline{R}.$$

Unfold the first literal of $c6$ using $c2$ and $c3$. Since this is a leftmost unfold, it is correct as long as we follow the five unfolding steps defined in §2:

1. Generalise the heads of the unfolding clauses $(c2, c3)$:

$$\mathcal{H} = P_1(\overline{B}_1, M, \overline{B}_2) \quad \theta_1 = \{nil/M, \overline{A}_1/\overline{B}_1, \overline{A}_2/\overline{B}_2\}$$
$$A = P_1(\overline{Y}_1, L, \overline{Y}_2) \quad \theta_2 = \{L/M, \overline{Y}_1/\overline{B}_1, \overline{Y}_2/\overline{B}_2\}$$

2. Find Θ such that $A\Theta = \mathcal{H}\Theta$. Here, we can choose $\Theta = \{\overline{B}_1 = \overline{Y}_1, M = L, \overline{B}_2 = \overline{Y}_2\}$. Other possible unifiers correspond to cases where the list L appears more than once in the head of P_1 or in the first literal of $c6$.
3. Apply Θ to the source predicate $c6$. Since Θ is a renaming, this step is trivial and the development history is undisturbed.
4. Produce the new clauses, $(c8, c9)$:

$$c8 : New(L, \overline{Y}_1, \overline{Y}_2, \overline{Z}_1, \overline{Z}_2) \leftarrow (M = nil, \overline{A}_1 = \overline{B}_1, \overline{A}_2 = \overline{B}_2),$$
$$\underline{P_2(\overline{Z}_1, L, \overline{Z}_2)}.\{M = L, \overline{B}_1 = \overline{Y}_1, \overline{B}_2 = \overline{Y}_2\}$$
$$c9 : New(L, \overline{Y}_1, \overline{Y}_2, \overline{Z}_1, \overline{Z}_2) \leftarrow (M = cons(H_1, T_1), \overline{A}_3 = \overline{B}_1, \overline{A}_4 = \overline{B}_2),$$
$$P_1(\overline{A}_3, T, \overline{A}_4), \underline{P_2(\overline{Z}_1, M, \overline{Z}_2)}.\{M = L, \overline{B}_1 = \overline{Y}_1, \overline{B}_2 = \overline{Y}_2\}$$

5. Solve the introduced equations. This gives:

$$c8' : New(nil, \overline{Y}_1, \overline{Y}_2, \overline{Z}_1, \overline{Z}_2) \leftarrow \overline{A}_1 = \overline{Y}_1, \overline{A}_2 = \overline{Y}_2, \underline{P_2(\overline{Z}_1, nil, \overline{Z}_2)}.$$
$$c9' : New(cons(H_1, T_1), \overline{Y}_1, \overline{Y}_2, \overline{Z}_1, \overline{Z}_2) \leftarrow \overline{A}_3 = \overline{Y}_1, \overline{A}_4 = \overline{Y}_2,$$
$$P_1(\overline{A}_5, T, \overline{A}_6), \underline{P_2(\overline{Z}_1, cons(H_1, T_1), \overline{Z}_2)}.$$

Now we unfold the newly introduced clauses $(c8', c9')$ using $(c4, c5)$.
First unfold $c8'$ using $(c4, c5)$:

$$\mathcal{H} = P_2(\overline{C}_1, N, \overline{C}_2) \quad \theta_1 = \{\overline{A}_7/\overline{C}_1, nil/N, \overline{A}_8/\overline{C}_2\}$$
$$A = P_2(\overline{Z}_1, nil, \overline{Z}_2) \quad \theta_2 = \{\overline{A}_9/\overline{C}_1, cons(H_2, T_2)/N, \overline{A}_{10}/\overline{C}_2\}$$

Find Θ such that $A\Theta = \mathcal{H}\Theta$. One possible unifier is $\{\overline{Z}_1/\overline{C}_1, nil/N, \overline{Z}_2/\overline{C}_2\}$. This is a renaming of the unfolding atom, so no program modification is necessary.

Apply Θ to $c8'$ and produce the two new clauses:

$$c10 : New(nil, \overline{Y}_1, \overline{Y}_2, \overline{Z}_1, \overline{Z}_2) \leftarrow (\overline{A}_7 = \overline{C}_1, \overline{A}_8 = \overline{C}_2, N = nil), \overline{A}_1 = \overline{Y}_1,$$
$$\overline{A}_2 = \overline{Y}_2, \{\overline{Z}_1 = \overline{C}_1, nil = N, \overline{Z}_2 = \overline{C}_2\}.$$
$$c11 : New(nil, \overline{Y}_1, \overline{Y}_2, \overline{Z}_1, \overline{Z}_2) \leftarrow (\overline{A}_9 = \overline{C}_1, cons(H_2, T_2) = N, \overline{A}_{10} = \overline{C}_2),$$
$$\overline{A}_1 = \overline{Y}_1, \overline{A}_2 = \overline{Y}_2, \{\overline{Z}_1 = \overline{C}_1, nil = N, \overline{Z}_2 = \overline{C}_2,\}$$

Clearly the body of $c11$ contains an inconsistent substitution and so is finitely failing and can be omitted from the final program.

Since $\overline{C}_1$, $\overline{C}_2$ and N do not appear in the original program schema — they were only introduced during the pattern unification process — we can eliminate them from $c10$ above to give:

$$c10' : New(nil, \overline{Y}_1, \overline{Y}_2, \overline{Z}_1, \overline{Z}_2) \leftarrow \overline{Z}_1 = \overline{A}_7, \overline{Z}_2 = \overline{A}_8, \overline{A}_1 = \overline{Y}_1, \overline{A}_2 = \overline{Y}_2.$$

Next, unfold $c9'$:

$$\mathcal{H} = P_2(\overline{C}_1, N, \overline{C}_2) \qquad \theta_1 = \{\overline{A}_7/\overline{C}_1, nil/N, \overline{A}_8/\overline{C}_2\}$$
$$A = P_2(\overline{Z}_1, cons(H_1, T_1), \overline{Z}_2) \quad \theta_2 = \{\overline{A}_9/\overline{C}_1, cons(H_2, T_2)/N, \overline{A}_{10}/\overline{C}_2\}$$

Find Θ such that $A\Theta = \mathcal{H}\Theta$. One unifier is $\{\overline{Z}_1/\overline{C}_1, cons(H_1,T_1)/N, \overline{Z}_2/\overline{C}_2\}$. This is a renaming of the unfolding atom, so no program modification is necessary.

Apply Θ to $c9'$ and produce the two new clauses:

$$c12 : New(cons(H_1,T_1),\overline{Y}_1,\overline{Y}_2,\overline{Z}_1,\overline{Z}_2) \leftarrow (\overline{A}_7 = \overline{C}_1, nil = N,$$
$$\overline{A}_8 = \overline{C}_2), \overline{A}_3 = \overline{Y}_1, \overline{A}_4 = \overline{Y}_2, P_1(\overline{A}_5,T_1,\overline{A}_6), \{\overline{Z}_1 = \overline{C}_1,$$
$$N = cons(H_1,T_1), \overline{Z}_2 = \overline{C}_2\}.$$
$$c13 : New(cons(H_1,T_1),\overline{Y}_1,\overline{Y}_2,\overline{Z}_1,\overline{Z}_2) \leftarrow (\overline{A}_9 = \overline{C}_1, cons(H_2,T_2) = N,$$
$$\overline{A}_{10} = \overline{C}_2), \overline{A}_3 = \overline{Y}_1, \overline{A}_4 = \overline{Y}_2, P_1(\overline{A}_5,T_1,\overline{A}_6), P_2(\overline{A}_{11},T_2,\overline{A}_{12}),$$
$$F(\overline{A}_{13}), \{\overline{Z}_1 = \overline{C}_1, N = cons(H_1,T_1), \overline{Z}_2 = \overline{C}_2\}.$$

Clearly the body of $c12$ contains an inconsistent substitution and so is finitely failing and can be omitted from the final program.

As before, we can eliminate the variables $\overline{C}_1$, $\overline{C}_2$, and N which were introduced during the pattern unification process.

$$c13' : New(cons(H_1,T_1),\overline{Y}_1,\overline{Y}_2,\overline{Z}_1,\overline{Z}_2) \leftarrow \overline{Z}_1 = \overline{A}_9, H_1 = H_2, T_1 = T_2,$$
$$\overline{Z}_2 = \overline{A}_{10}, \overline{A}_3 = \overline{Y}_1, \overline{A}_4 = \overline{Y}_2, P_1(\overline{A}_5,T_1,\overline{A}_6), P_2(\overline{A}_{11},T_1,\overline{A}_{12}), F(\overline{A}_{13}).$$

Now we fold $c13'$ using $c6'$. As noted in the second item of §7.3, we must check the unifying substitution. In general this condition can only be checked when the schema is instantiated with a Prolog program, but in this case we can easily see that $vars(bd(c6)) - vars(hd(c6)) = \{\}$. We produce the new clause:

$$c14 : New(cons(H_1,T_1),\overline{Y}_1,\overline{Y}_2,\overline{Z}_1,\overline{Z}_2) \leftarrow \overline{Z}_1 = \overline{A}_9, H_1 = H_2, T_1 = T_2,$$
$$\overline{Z}_2 = \overline{A}_{10}, \overline{A}_3 = \overline{Y}_1, \overline{A}_4 = \overline{Y}_2, New(T_1,\overline{A}_5,\overline{A}_6,\overline{A}_{11},\overline{A}_{12}), F(\overline{A}_{13}).$$

The final program is made up from clauses $c7$, $c10'$, $c14$, $c2$, $c3$, $c4$, $c5$. By tracing through the substitutions we can eliminate the intermediate variables introduced in the presentation above to produce an equivalent list of clauses using variable names from the original schema:

$$c7 : P(\overline{X}_1) \leftarrow New(L,\overline{Y}_1,\overline{Y}_2,\overline{Z}_1,\overline{Z}_2), \overline{R}.$$
$$c10' : New(nil,\overline{Y}_1,\overline{Y}_2,\overline{Z}_1,\overline{Z}_2) \leftarrow \overline{Z}_1 = \overline{A}_7, \overline{Z}_2 = \overline{A}_8, \overline{A}_1 = \overline{Y}_1, \overline{A}_2 = \overline{Y}_2.$$
$$c14 : New(cons(H_1,T_1),\overline{Y}_1,\overline{Y}_2,\overline{Z}_1,\overline{Z}_2) \leftarrow \overline{Z}_1 = \overline{A}_9, H_1 = H_2, T_1 = T_2,$$
$$\overline{Z}_2 = \overline{A}_{10}, \overline{A}_3 = \overline{Y}_1, \overline{A}_4 = \overline{Y}_2, New(T_1,\overline{A}_5,\overline{A}_6,\overline{A}_{11},\overline{A}_{12}), F(\overline{A}_{13}).$$
$$c2 : P_1(\overline{A}_1, nil, \overline{A}_2) \leftarrow .$$
$$c3 : P_1(\overline{A}_3, cons(H_1,T_1), \overline{A}_4) \leftarrow P_1(\overline{A}_5,T_1,\overline{A}_6).$$
$$c4 : P_2(\overline{A}_7, nil, \overline{A}_8) \leftarrow .$$
$$c5 : P_2(\overline{A}_9, cons(H_2,T_2), \overline{A}_{10}) \leftarrow P_2(\overline{A}_{11},T_2,\overline{A}_{12}), F(\overline{A}_{13}).$$

The transformation schema is made up of the initial and final schema patterns. Note that the schema we have derived has some generality. For example, the use of vectors in the heads of P_1 and P_2 means that we do not require the list argument to be in any particular position.

B.3   Application of the Schema to a Program: An Example

Consider the program from [6][p.264]:

$c1 : average(L, A) \leftarrow length(L, N), sumlist(L, S), div(S, N, A).$
$c2 : length(nil, 0) \leftarrow .$
$c3 : length(cons(H1, T1), s(N1)) \leftarrow length(T1, N1).$
$c4 : sumlist(nil, 0) \leftarrow .$
$c5 : sumlist(cons(H2, T2), S1) \leftarrow sumlist(T2, S2), sum(H2, S2, S1).$

Matching the input schema with the program above gives:

$P = average$	$P_1 = length$	$P_2 = sumlist$	$\overline{A}_1 = ()$
$\overline{A}_2 = 0$	$\overline{A}_3 = ()$	$\overline{A}_4 = s(N1)$	$\overline{A}_5 = ()$
$\overline{A}_6 = N1$	$\overline{A}_7 = ()$	$\overline{A}_8 = 0$	$\overline{A}_9 = ()$
$\overline{A}_{10} = S1$	$\overline{A}_{11} = ()$	$\overline{A}_{12} = S2$	$\overline{A}_{13} = (H2, S2, S1)$
$\overline{R} = div(S, N, A)$	$\overline{X}_1 = (L, A)$	$\overline{Y}_1 = ()$	$\overline{Y}_2 = N$
$\overline{Z}_1 = ()$	$\overline{Z}_2 = S$	$L = L$	$H_1 = H1$
$H_2 = H2$	$T_1 = T1$	$T_2 = T2$	

Applying this substitution (omitting trivial variable assignments) to the final program schema gives the following program, as expected:

$c7 : average(L, A) \leftarrow new(L, N, S), div(S, N, A).$
$c10 : new(nil, N, S) \leftarrow S = 0, N = 0.$
$c14 : new(cons(H1, T1), N, S) \leftarrow H1 = H2, T1 = T2, s(N1) = N, S = S1,$
$\qquad\qquad\qquad\qquad\qquad new(T1, N1, S2), sum(H2, S2, S1).$
$c2 : length(nil, 0) \leftarrow .$
$c3 : length(cons(H1, T1), s(N1)) \leftarrow length(T1, N1).$
$c4 : sumlist(nil, 0) \leftarrow .$
$c5 : sumlist(cons(H2, T2), S1) \leftarrow sumlist(T2, S2), sum(H2, S2, S1).$

Constrained Regular Approximation of Logic Programs

Hüseyin Sağlam[1] and John P. Gallagher[1]

[1] Department of Computer Science, University of Bristol,
The Merchant Venturers Building, Woodland Road, Bristol BS8 1UB, U.K.
{saglam,john}@compsci.bristol.ac.uk

Abstract. Regular approximation is a well-known and useful analysis technique for conventional logic programming. Given the existence of constraint solving techniques, one may wish to obtain more precise approximations of programs while retaining the decidable properties of the approximation. Greater precision could increase the effectiveness of applications that make use of regular approximation, such as the detection of useless clauses and type analysis. In this paper, we introduce arithmetic constraints, based on convex polyhedra, into regular approximation. In addition, Herbrand constraints can be introduced to capture dependencies among arguments.

Keywords: regular approximation, linear constraints, convex polyhedra.

1   Introduction

Regular approximation is a program analysis technique sometimes identified with "type inference". *Type inference* is the process of determining the type of program units. Type systems are designed to allow the programmer to describe the set of intended values that an argument can take.

Regular approximations are not true types, but rather syntactic descriptions of the success set of programs. Thus the word "type inference" is not strictly correct although for definite logic programs the concept of "type" and success set of predicates coincide quite closely for practical purposes. The practical usefulness of regular approximation is to provide a decidable description of the set of terms that can appear in each argument position in correct answers. In previous work on regular approximations, or the closely related concepts of (rigid) type graphs, sets of terms are given by recursive descriptions which are essentially deterministic finite automata. Certain built-in sets such as numbers can be included in the descriptions. It is possible to improve on the precision of regular type description, departing from strictly regular description, without losing decidability. One such method will be explored in this paper, namely, the addition of constraints to regular descriptions.

Norbert E. Fuchs (Ed.): LOPSTR'97, LNCS 1463, pp. 282–299, 1998.

The class of regular unary logic (RUL) programs was defined by Yardeni and Shapiro [21]. They define a class of types called regular types, and show the equivalence between regular types and RUL programs. They represent regular types by Deterministic Finite Automata (DFA) and use tuple distributive closure for types as defined by Mishra [11]. Their formalism for describing sets of terms is adopted in [6], and also followed in [15] and [16] as extensions of [6]. In [6] Gallagher and de Waal define an efficient regular approximation framework. All procedures they define such as upper bound and intersection, handle programs whose clauses are in a special, restricted form (RUL clause). This form is given in the following definition.

Definition 1. *A* (canonical) regular unary (RUL) clause *is a clause of the form*

$$t_0(f(x_1, \ldots, x_n)) \leftarrow t_1(x_1), \ldots, t_n(x_n) \quad n \geq 0$$

where $x_1, \ldots, x_n$ *are distinct variables.*

By relaxing Definition 1 we make an extension to the notion of regular approximation, by allowing arithmetic and Herbrand constraints in the bodies of regular clauses. This permits us to capture dependencies between the arguments of terms, and also, in certain cases, to capture dependencies between arguments at different levels of a term. For example, we can capture dependencies between successive elements of a list, or every other element of a list by imposing a suitable depth bound.

2   Constrained Regular Approximation

In order to achieve the aforementioned extension, the general form of a constrained regular unary clause can be given as follows.

Definition 2. *A* constrained regular unary (CRUL) clause *is a clause of the form*

$$t_0(f(x_1, \ldots, x_n)) \leftarrow \mathcal{C}, t_1(x_1), \ldots, t_n(x_n) \quad n \geq 0$$

where $x_1, \ldots, x_n$ *are distinct variables and* $\mathcal{C}$ *is a conjunction of constraints projected onto* $x_1, \ldots, x_n$.

Note that we usually use sets to deal with conjunctions; in the definitions below, a set of some syntactic objects, if any, stands for a conjunction of the syntactic objects.

Example 1. The following clause is a constrained regular unary clause.

$$sorted([X|Y]) \leftarrow Y = [Z|W], X \leq Z, sorted(Y).$$

Note that the constraints contain local variables Z and W. There is also an implicit unary atom $any(X)$ in the body to fit the defined form, where $any(X)$ is true for all X.

Some definitions are next given to define the main operations and relations on CRUL clauses.

Definition 3. *Let t be a term and C a conjunction of constraints. A pair (t, C) is called a* constrained term. *Two constrained terms (t_1, C_1) and (t_2, C_2)* overlap *if there is a substitution θ such that both*

1. *$t_1\theta = t_2\theta$, and*
2. *$C_1\theta$ and $C_2\theta$ are satisfiable.*

We say that two CRUL clauses $p(u_1) \leftarrow C_1, t_1(x_1), \ldots, t_n(x_n)$ and $q(u_2) \leftarrow C_2, s_1(x_1), \ldots, s_n(x_n)$ overlap if the constrained terms (u_1, C_1) and (u_2, C_2) overlap.

Definition 4. *CRUL program*

A constrained regular unary logic *(CRUL) program is a finite set of constrained regular unary clauses in which no two (standardised apart) clauses overlap.*

Definition 5. *Let P be a definite program and P' a CRUL program containing a special unary predicate $approx/1$. Assuming a fixed interpretation of constraint predicates and functions and Herbrand interpretations of the other predicates and functions, let $M(P)$ be the least model of P. Then P' is a* constrained regular approximation *of P if $M(P)$ is contained in the set $\{ A \mid approx(A) \in M(P') \}$.*

Note that, as in [6], in using $approx/1$ we abuse notation by confusing predicate and function symbols. Using the $approx$ predicate allows us to restrict attention to CRUL programs. Often it is omitted and a clause $approx(p(x_1, \ldots, x_n)) \leftarrow C, p_1(x_1), \ldots, p_n(x_n)$ is written as $p(x_1, \ldots, x_n) \leftarrow C, p_1(x_1), \ldots, p_n(x_n)$.

Definition 6. *Let p be a predicate. Then, in the context of some program P, $proc(p)$ is the set of all the clauses in P whose head contains p.*

Definition 7. *Let p be a predicate. Then, in the context of some program P, $def(p)$ is the set of all the clauses in P defining p, including subsidiary definitions. Formally,*

$$def(p) = proc(p) \cup \bigcup \{ def(q) \mid q \text{ occurs in } proc(p) \}.$$

2.1 Operations on Constraints and CRUL Programs

We approximate arithmetic constraints using convex polyhedra since it seems to be the most interesting approach for general use, although there are other approaches such as affine sub-spaces, intervals, and signed inequalities [20],[9], [19],[10].

A convex polyhedron is characterised by a system of linear constraints. The set of solutions to a finite system of loose linear inequalities can be interpreted geometrically as a *closed convex polyhedron* of $\mathbb{R}^n$. The least polyhedron containing this set is called its *convex hull*. There is no loss of generality in considering only loose linear inequalities since strict inequalities can be handled by adding an auxiliary variable ϵ, $0 \leq \epsilon \leq 1$ as shown in [7].

Least upper bound and widening operations over polyhedra are defined in [3]. De Backer and Beringer introduced "linear relaxation" in [4] where explicit computation of the constraints defining the convex hull is not needed. The expression is obtained by only adding new variables to the initial problem. Although it looks potentially expensive, it is easy to implement for computing the least upper bound of convex polyhedra [1].

A predicate can be given a constrained regular definition. The clauses of the predicate require some form that allows operations to be efficiently performed. Moreover terms in constraints having unbounded depth increase the difficulty of defining a terminating fixpoint computation (see Section 2.3). A depth bound is needed to put an upper bound on the size of CRUL programs. This helps to ensure termination of the approximation procedure.

Definition 8. *constrained regular definition of a predicate*

Let p be a unary predicate. A constrained regular definition *of p for some depth k is a constrained regular unary program whose clause heads all have predicate p, and where the maximum depth of terms in the constraints is k.*

Intersection of regular unary predicates is required in order to produce CRUL clauses. Let $t_1(x), t_2(x)$ be a conjunction. We compute a new predicate $r = t_1 \bigcap t_2$ such that $\forall x (t_1(x) \land t_2(x) \leftrightarrow r(x))$.

To simplify the presentation, let us assume that the CRUL clauses contain only Herbrand and linear arithmetic constraints in their constraint parts. That is, each CRUL clause is of the form $p(f(x_1, \ldots, x_n)) \leftarrow H, A, p_1(x_1), \ldots, p_n(x_n)$ where H and A are conjunctions of Herbrand and arithmetic constraints respectively. We assume that H is of the form $\{v_1 = t_1, \ldots, v_k = t_k\}$ where no v_j occurs in $t_1, \ldots, t_k$.

Definition 9. *intersection of constrained regular unary predicates*

Let p and q be unary predicates with constrained regular definitions proc(p) and proc(q) respectively. Then their intersection $p \bigcap q$ *is defined by a predicate r with constrained regular definition given as follows.*

$$
\left\{
\begin{array}{l}
r(t) \leftarrow mgu(H_p, H_q), \\
\quad A_p \wedge A_q, \\
\quad r_1(x_1), \\
\quad \vdots \\
\quad r_n(x_n)
\end{array}
\right|
\begin{array}{l}
\textit{for each } t \textit{ such that} \\
p(t) \leftarrow H_p, A_p, p_1(x_1), \ldots, p_n(x_n) \textit{ and} \\
q(t) \leftarrow H_q, A_q, q_1(x_1), \ldots, q_n(x_n) \\
\textit{occur in proc(p) and proc(q) respectively,} \\
A_p \wedge A_q \textit{ is satisfiable and} \\
(t, H_p), (t, H_q) \textit{ overlap.}
\end{array}
\left.
\right\}
$$

where $r_i = p_i \cap q_i$, and H_p, H_q are sets of Herbrand constraints, A_p, A_q are sets of arithmetic constraints, and $mgu(H_p, H_q)$ is the set of equations in the solved form of $H_p \cup H_q$.

An upper bound operation for CRUL predicates will be defined to reduce the number of clauses in the definition of a predicate by merging overlapping ones. To form the upper bound of two CRUL predicates, definitions for both predicates including the definitions of the subsidiary predicates in the bodies of the clauses defining the predicates are needed. We can separate the construction of upper bound of predicates into two parts. One of them is the construction of the constraint part and the other one is the construction of the regular part. Let us first give some definitions to define the upper bound of the constraint parts.

Definition 10. *generalisation of terms*
    Let t_1 and t_2 be two terms. Then a term t is a generalisation of the terms t_1 and t_2 if there exist two substitutions θ_1 and θ_2 such that $t\theta_1 = t_1$ and $t\theta_2 = t_2$.

Definition 11. *most specific generalisation of terms*
    Let t be a generalisation of the terms t_1 and t_2. Then t is the most specific generalisation of t_1 and t_2, denoted $msg(t_1, t_2)$, if for any generalisation t' of t_1 and t_2, there exists a substitution θ' such that $t'\theta' = t$ [13], [12].

Definition 12. *most specific generalisation of set of equations*
    Let $H_1 = \{x_1 = t_1, \ldots, x_n = t_n\}$ and $H_2 = \{y_1 = s_1, \ldots, y_m = s_m\}$. Let $z_1, \ldots, z_k$ be the variables that occur on the left hand side of equations in both H_1 and H_2, say $z_1 = \bar{t}_1, \ldots, z_k = \bar{t}_k$ in H_1 and $z_1 = \bar{s}_1, \ldots, z_k = \bar{s}_k$ in H_2. Then $msg(H_1, H_2)$ is the set of equations $\{z_1 = r_1, \ldots, z_k = r_k\}$ where $\langle r_1, \ldots, r_k \rangle = msg(\langle \bar{t}_1, \ldots, \bar{t}_k \rangle, \langle \bar{s}_1, \ldots, \bar{s}_k \rangle)$.

Note that we usually use sets to deal with conjunctions; in the above definition a set of some syntactic objects stands for a conjunction of the syntactic objects.

Definition 13. *upper bound of constraints*
    Let (H_1, A_1) and (H_2, A_2) be conjunctions of Herbrand and arithmetic constraints. Then an upper bound (H, A) denoted $(H_1, A_1) \bigsqcup (H_2, A_2)$ is computed as follows.

begin
$\quad H := msg(H_1, H_2)$
$\quad \theta_1 := mgu(H, H_1)$
$\quad \theta_2 := mgu(H, H_2)$
$\qquad$ **while** $\exists y_i/v, y_k/v \in \theta_1, i \neq k, v \text{ occurs in } A_1$
$\qquad\quad \theta_1 := \theta_1 - \{y_k/v\}$
$\qquad\quad A_1 := A_1 \cup \{y_i = y_k\}$
$\qquad$ **end**
$\qquad$ **while** $\exists y_j/w, y_l/w \in \theta_2, j \neq l, w \text{ occurs in } A_2$
$\qquad\quad \theta_2 := \theta_2 - \{y_l/w\}$
$\qquad\quad A_2 := A_2 \cup \{y_j = y_l\}$
$\qquad$ **end**
$\quad \rho_1 := \{v/y_i | y_i/v \in \theta_1, v \text{ is a variable}\}$
$\quad \rho_2 := \{w/y_j | y_j/w \in \theta_2, w \text{ is a variable}\}$
$\quad A := CH(A_1\rho_1, A_2\rho_2)$
end

where $CH(A_1\rho_1, A_2\rho_2)$ is the convex hull computed from the conjunctions of arithmetic constraints $A_1\rho_1$ and $A_2\rho_2$.

The purpose of this construction is to compute the most specific generalisation (msg) of the Herbrand constraints, and then derive suitable renamings for the arithmetic constraints to make them compatible with the variables in the msg. During this process, aliasing among arithmetic variables which is lost in the msg is recovered, and added as arithmetic equalities. Finally the convex hull of the renamed arithmetic constraints is computed.

Example 2. Let (H_1, A_1) be $X = f(Y, Y), Y > 0$ and
$\quad$ let (H_2, A_2) be $Z = f(U, V), -U = V$.
$\quad$ Then

$$msg(H_1, H_2) = (Z_1 = f(Z_2, Z_3)),$$
$$\theta_1 = \{Z_1/X, Z_2/Y, Z_3/Y\},$$
$$\theta_2 = \{Z_1/Z, Z_2/U, Z_3/V\}.$$

At the end of the **while** loops,

$$\rho_1 = \{X/Z_1, Y/Z_2\},$$
$$\rho_2 = \{Z/Z_1, U/Z_2, V/Z_3\}, A_1 = \{Y > 0, Z_2 = Z_3\}$$
$$A_2 = \{-U = V\}.$$

Hence after applying the convex hull procedure $CH(A_1\rho_1, A_2\rho_2)$, the result
is

$$(H, A) = (Z_1 = f(Z_2, Z_3), -Z_2 \leq Z_3).$$

Lemma 1. *Let $C_1 = (H_1, A_1)$ and $C_2 = (H_2, A_2)$ be conjunctions of constraints. Let their upper bound $C = C_1 \bigsqcup C_2$ be $(H, A) = (H_1, A_1) \bigsqcup (H_2, A_2)$. Assume H_1 and H_2 are of the form $x_1 = t_1, \ldots, x_n = t_n$ and $x_1 = s_1, \ldots, x_n = s_n$ respectively, which implies we can assume that H is of the form $x_1 = r_1, \ldots, x_n = r_n$.*

Then $\forall x_1, \ldots, x_n \ \forall (C_1 \to C \land C_2 \to C)$.

Proof. Outline. Let the upper bound $C = C_1 \bigsqcup C_2$ be $(H, A) = (H_1, A_1) \bigsqcup (H_2, A_2)$, where $H = msg(H_1, H_2)$ and $A = CH(A_1\rho_1, A_2\rho_2)$, ρ_1 and ρ_2 being variable renamings as constructed in Definition 13.

Then, $\forall((H_1, A_1) \to H)$ since $H = msg(H_1, H_2)$ is the most specific generalisation of the conjunction of Herbrand constraints H_1 and H_2 where the variables in H_1, H_2 and H are renamed to be the same.

$\forall((H_1, A_1) \to A_1\rho_1)$ holds since the renaming ρ_1 only introduces fresh variables.

$\forall(A_1\rho_1 \to CH(A_1\rho_1, A_2\rho_2))$ because $CH(A_1\rho_1, A_2\rho_2)$ describes a polyhedron containing both $A_1\rho_1$ and $A_2\rho_2$. Hence $\forall((H_1, A_1) \to A)$.

Then, since H and A are true independent of the truth of each other, $\forall((H_1, A_1) \to (H, A))$ holds. Similarly, for (H_2, A_2), $\forall((H_2, A_2) \to (H, A))$ holds.

Let us now define the upper bound of two CRUL clauses before defining the upper bound of two predicates. We denote the upper bound of two predicates t and s by $t \bigsqcup_p s$, which will be defined in Definition 18.

Definition 14. *upper bound of two constrained regular unary clauses*
Let $p(u) \leftarrow H_1, A_1, t_1(x_1), \ldots, t_n(x_n)$ and $p(u) \leftarrow H_2, A_2, s_1(x_1), \ldots, s_n(x_n)$ be two overlapping clauses, with variables renamed so that the heads are identical. Then their upper bound is

$$p(u) \leftarrow H, A, r_1(x_1), \ldots, r_n(x_n)$$

where $r_i = t_i \bigsqcup_p s_i$ and $(H, A) = (H_1, A_1) \bigsqcup (H_2, A_2)$.

Next we show how to assign unique names to the upper bounds of predicates. This is done in order to ensure termination of the upper bound procedure.

Let $\mathsf{Pred} = \{p_1, \ldots, p_n\}$ be a set of unary predicates. Define $\mathsf{Pred}^{\bigsqcup}$ to be a set of $2^n - 1$ unary predicates, including $p_1, \ldots, p_n$. Identify each element q of $\mathsf{Pred}^{\bigsqcup}$ with a unique non-empty subset of Pred, denoted $Name(q)$.

The function $Name$ is extended to upper bounds of predicates in $\mathsf{Pred}^{\bigsqcup}$, such that

$$Name(q_1 \bigsqcup_p q_2) = Name(q_1) \cup Name(q_2).$$

Thus for all $q_1, q_2 \in \mathsf{Pred}^{\bigsqcup}$, $q_1 \bigsqcup_p q_2$ is associated with a unique element of $\mathsf{Pred}^{\bigsqcup}$, say q_3 where $Name(q_3) = Name(q_1) \cup Name(q_2)$.

Intuitively, a set of predicates uniquely determines their upper bound, and so $\mathsf{Pred}^{\sqcup}$ contains sufficient predicates to name each upper bound of predicates in Pred.

We next define an operation that converts a set of CRUL clauses into a CRUL program, by successively removing overlapping clauses. First we define some simple operations.

Definition 15. *Let* Pred *be a set of unary predicates. Let* r *and* t *be predicates* $\in \mathsf{Pred}^{\sqcup}$. *Let* s *be the predicate such that* $Name(s) = Name(r \bigsqcup_p t)$. *Then* $merge(r,t)$ *is the set of clauses obtained from* $proc(r) \cup proc(t)$ *by replacing the predicates in the heads by* s.

Definition 16. *Let* r *and* t *be predicates and* R *a set of clauses.* $merge_R(r,t)$ *is defined to be:*

- $\emptyset$, *if* R *contains the predicate* s *such that* $Name(s) = Name(r) \cup Name(t)$;
- $merge(r,t)$, *otherwise.*

Definition 17. *normalisation of a set of CRUL clauses*
  Let R *be a set of CRUL clauses. Define* $norm(R)$ *as follows:*

- $norm(R) = R$ *if* R *has no overlapping clauses;*
- $norm(R) = norm(R - \{C_1, C_2\} \cup \{C\} \cup merge_R(t_1, s_1) \cup \ldots \cup merge_R(t_n, s_n))$, *where* $C_1 = A_1 \leftarrow D_1, t_1(x_1), \ldots, t_n(x_n)$ *and* $C_2 = A_2 \leftarrow D_2, r_1(x_1), \ldots, r_n(x_n)$ *are overlapping clauses in* R, *and* $C = C_1 \bigsqcup_c C_2$.

Informally, the *norm* operation removes a pair of overlapping clauses, and replaces them by their upper bound. This may introduce new clauses since the upper bound can contain new predicates; the operation is repeated until no overlapping clauses remain.

Note that the use of the operation $merge_R$ in the definition of *norm* is necessary to ensure termination of normalisation, since it prevents the addition of clauses for predicates already in the program. Without this operation it would be possible to reintroduce overlapping clauses that had previously been removed.

Proposition 1. *The operation* $norm(P)$ *terminates.*

Proof. Let Pred be the set of predicates in P. We define a mapping from CRUL programs onto a well-founded set. Then we show that in the recursive equation in the definition of *norm*, the argument of the call to *norm* on the right is strictly less (with respect to the associated ordering on the well-founded set) than the argument of the call on the left.

The well-founded set consists of pairs $\langle N, V \rangle$, where N, V are natural numbers. The ordering is the lexicographical ordering, that is,

$$\langle N_1, V_1 \rangle < \langle N_2, V_2 \rangle \text{ iff } N_1 < N_2, \text{ or } N_1 = N_2 \text{ and } V_1 < V_2$$

Let $P = P_0$; the computation of $norm(P)$ gives rise to a sequence of calls $norm(P_0)$, $norm(P_1)$, $norm(P_2)$, ... Define $\langle N_j, V_j \rangle$ as follows. N_j is the number of predicates in $\mathsf{Pred}^{\sqcup}$ that do not appear in P_j, and V_j is the number of clauses in P_j.

Consider the relationship between P_{j+1} and P_j, which is given by the left and right hand sides of the recursive equation for $norm$. Either

1. the number of unused predicates is decreased (in the case that some new predicates are introduced into P_{j+1}, by the $merge_{P_i}$ components); or
2. the number of clauses in P_{j+1} is one less than the number in P_j (in the case that no new predicates are introduced).

In both cases $\langle N_{j+1}, V_{j+1} \rangle < \langle N_j, V_j \rangle$. Since the relation $<$ is a well-founded order, the sequence of calls to $norm$ is finite. Note that the number of clauses can increase during the procedure, but only in the case when the number of unused predicates symbols simultaneously decreases.

We can now use the $norm$ operation to define the upper bound of two predicates.

Definition 18. *Let r and t be two unary predicates. Then the upper bound of r and t is given by the predicate $r \sqcup_p t$ such that $Name(r \sqcup_p t) = Name(r) \cup Name(t)$ defined by the clauses $norm(R)$, where*

$$R = def(r) \cup def(t) - proc(r) - proc(t) \cup merge(r, t)$$

Also using the $norm$ operation, we define the upper bound of two CRUL programs.

Definition 19. *The upper bound of two CRUL programs, P and Q, denoted $P \sqcup_{Prog} Q$, is defined to be $norm(P \cup Q)$.*

Example 3. The following program is used to give some idea of the operations defined.

```
p([X1|X2]) :- X2=[X3|X4],  X1>=0, X1>=X3, t1(X2).
p([X1|X2]) :- X2=[X3|X4],  X1>=3, X1=<2*X3, s1(X2).

t1([X1|X2]) :- X1=<2, t2(X2).
t2([]).
s1([X1|X2]) :- X1=<10, s2(X2).
s2([]).
```

The two clauses defining p/1 overlap. The upper bound t13 of predicates t1 and s1 is computed to compute the upper bound of the clauses for predicate p. The resulting program is given below.

```
p(X1)  :- X1=[X2,X3], X3=<10, X2-0.3*X3>=0, X2>=0, t29(X1).
t29([X1|X2]) :- X2=[X3|X4], X3=<10, X1-0.3*X3>=0, X1>=0, t13(X2).
t13([X1|X2]) :- X2=[], X1=<10, t14(X2).
t14([]) :- true.
```

An essential operation when computing a fixpoint is to check inclusion of one constrained regular unary predicate in another.

Definition 20. *inclusion of constrained regular unary predicates*
    Let p and q be defined in a CRUL program. Then the inclusion *of the predicates p and q is checked as follows.*

$$p \subseteq q \quad \text{iff for all clauses } (p(t_i) \leftarrow H_{p_i}, A_{p_i}, p_{i_1}(x_1), \ldots, p_{i_n}(x_n)),$$
$$\text{there exists a clause } (q(t_j) \leftarrow H_{q_j}, A_{q_j}, q_{j_1}(x_1), \ldots, q_{j_n}(x_n))$$
$$\text{and there is a substitution } \theta \text{ such that}$$

$$1. \ (t_i, H_{p_i}) = (t_j, H_{q_j})\theta, \text{and } A_{p_i} \Rightarrow A_{q_j}\theta,$$
$$2. \ p_{i_1} \subseteq q_{j_1}, \ldots, p_{i_n} \subseteq q_{j_n}.$$

Definition 21. *depth-k abstraction of a CRUL clause*
    Let $p(t) \leftarrow H, A, p_1(x_1), \ldots, p_n(x_n)$ be a CRUL clause. Then the depth-k *abstraction of the clause is $p(t) \leftarrow H_k, A_k, p_1(x_1), \ldots, p_n(x_n)$ where H_k is depth-bounded version of H and A_k is A projected onto the variables occurring in H_k and t.*

Depth-k abstraction is performed just after the intersection operation and the depth of terms does not have to be taken into account during the intersection, upper-bound, or widening operations. The depth-2 abstraction of the clause
    `p([X1|X2]) :- X2=[X3,X5|X6]],X1>X3,X3>X5,q(X1),r(X2)`
is
    `p([X1|X2]):- X2=[X3|X4],X1>X3, q(X1), r(X2).`
Depth-3 abstraction makes no change in this case. Using depth-2 is a good compromise since it allows inferring dependencies between one level and the next, and since dependencies between terms at widely separated levels within a term do not occur frequently.

2.2   Computation of a Constrained Regular Approximation

A semantic function is defined similarly to the one in [17]. The approximation of a program P is computed by an iterative fixpoint computation with widening.

A sequence of constrained regular approximations $P_0, P_1, P_2, \ldots$ is computed as follows.

$$P_0 = \emptyset$$
$$P_{i+1} = P_i \bigtriangledown_{Prog} T(P_i) \quad (i \geq 0)$$

where

$$T(P_i) = P_i \bigsqcup_{Prog} (\bigcup \{\text{solve}(C, P_i) \mid C \in P\}).$$

$\text{solve}(C, P_i)$ takes a clause C and a CRUL program P_i and returns a constrained regular definition of the predicate in the head of C. The operations intersection and depth-k are included in solve. The body of C is solved in the current approximation P_i which involves unfolding the body and intersecting the predicates with the same argument.

The limit of the sequence $P_0, P_1, P_2, \ldots$ is the constrained regular approximation of P.

The operators $\bigtriangledown_{Prog}$ and $\bigsqcup_{Prog}$ (see Definition 18) are *widening* and *upper bound* operators on programs respectively. The only requirement on these operations is that they should be safe with respect to the underlying order of the approximations.

2.3   Termination of Fixpoint Computation

There are two different fixpoint computations, taking place at the same time, to be terminated. One is for the arithmetic approximation, and the other one is for the regular approximation.

For the fixpoint computation of arithmetic constraints we have existing tools for applying various different upper bound and widening operators with different trade-offs of precision and efficiency and an optional narrowing operator. The operators were suggested in [3] and [2]. We use simplified and efficient versions of them [18].

Effective abstract interpretation procedures for computing a regular approximation of a program (using RUL programs or some equivalent notation) have been defined in [8] and [6]. Several other works contain other solutions to the problem. For the termination of regular approximation we adopted the "shortening" defined in [6]. A "widening" [8] operator could also be chosen.

Definition 22. *shortening of CRUL predicates*
   Let P be a CRUL program containing predicates t and s $(t \neq s)$. Let an occurrence of predicate t depend on predicate s, and let t and s have the same function symbols in their clause heads. Then the occurrence of s is replaced by t, if s is included in t.

The shortening operation defined in [6] is less precise, but sometimes faster. In the shortening there, a recursive approximation is introduced whenever predicate t depends on predicate s, and t and s have the same function symbols in their clause heads, without checking the inclusion. We can further improve precision comparing to [6] by taking into account the Herbrand constraints as well as the head functions.

3 Examples

A number of simple examples are given in this section to illustrate the approximation.

Example 4. List of sorted numbers
    Let us consider the constrained regular approximation of the following simple program.

```
sorted([]).
sorted([X]) :- X >= 0.
sorted([X,Y|Z]) :- X >= Y, sorted([Y|Z]).
```

The limit of the successive approximations of the program gives the following result.

```
sorted(X1) :-t1(X1).
t1([]) :-true.
t1([X1|X2]) :-X2=[],X1>=0,any(X1),t2(X2).
t1([X1|X2]) :-X2=[X3|X4],X1>=0,X1-X3>=0,any(X1),t1(X2).
t2([]) :-true.
```

Example 5. List of uniform elements
    We can capture other dependencies, not necessarily arithmetic, between different levels as in the following program.

```
uniform([]).
uniform([X]).
uniform([X,X|Y]) :- uniform([X|Y]).
```

The following CRUL program is generated as the limit of the successive approximations of the above program.

```
uniform(X1) :-t1(X1).
t1([]) :-true.
t1([X1|X2]) :-X2=[],any(X1),t2(X2).
t1([X1|X2]) :-X2=[X1|X3],any(X1),t1(X2).
t2([]) :-true.
```

The redundant atoms in the clauses of above programs, such as any(X1) are not removed for the sake of implementation ease and for conforming to the definitions on CRUL clauses.

Example 6. Let us show the intersection and upper bound of the above programs, to clarify the operations.

```
sorted_and_uniform(X) :- sorted(X),
                         uniform(X).

sorted_or_uniform(X) :- sorted(X).
sorted_or_uniform(X) :- uniform(X).
```

The analysis gives the following CRUL program.

```
sorted_and_uniform(X1) :-t1(X1).
t1([]) :-true.
t1([X1|X2]) :-X2=[],X1>=0,any(X1),t2(X2).
t1([X1|X2]) :-X2=[X1|X3],X1>=0,any(X1),t1(X2).
t2([]) :-true.

sorted_or_uniform(X1) :- t3(X1).
t3([]) :-true.
t3([X1|X2]) :-X2=[],any(X1),t4(X2).
t3([X1|X2]) :-X2=[X3|X4],any(X1),t3(X2).
t4([]) :-true.
```

Example 7. For a comparison, let us now consider the regular approximation and the constrained regular approximation of the following predicate taken from an alpha-beta procedure for the game of kalah.

```
initialize(kalah,board(a,0,a,0),opponent).
initialize(kalah,toto(b,1,b,1),computer).
initialize(kalah,board(c,2,c,2),computer).
initialize(kalah,board(a,0,a,0),computer).
initialize(kalah,board(c,2,c,2),opponent).
```

Regular Approximation Program:

```
initialize(X1,X2,X3) :-t349(X1),t378(X2),t374(X3).
t349(kalah) :-true.
t378(board(X1,X2,X3,X4)) :-t380(X1),t381(X2),t382(X3),t383(X4).
t378(toto(X1,X2,X3,X4)) :-t343(X1),t344(X2),t345(X3),t346(X4).
t374(opponent) :-true.
t374(computer) :-true.
t380(a) :-true.
t380(c) :-true.
t381(0) :-true.
```

```
t381(2) :-true.
t382(a) :-true.
t382(c) :-true.
t383(0) :-true.
t383(2) :-true.
t343(b) :-true.
t344(1) :-true.
t345(b) :-true.
t346(1) :-true.
```

Constrained Regular Approximation Program:

```
initialize(X1,X2,X3) :-t326(X1),t349(X2),t345(X3).
t326(kalah) :-true.
t349(board(X1,X2,X3,X4)) :-X1=c,X3=c,X2=2.0,X4=2.0,t328(X1),
                          any(X2),t329(X3),any(X4).
t349(toto(X1,X2,X3,X4)) :-X1=b,X3=b,X2=1.0,X4=1.0,t322(X1),
                          any(X2),t323(X3),any(X4).
t349(board(X1,X2,X3,X4) ) :-X1=a,X3=a,X2=0.0,X4=0.0,t316(X1),
                          any(X2),t317(X3),any(X4).
t345(opponent) :-true.
t345(computer) :-true.
t328(c) :-true.
t329(c) :-true.
t322(b) :-true.
t323(b) :-true.
t316(a) :-true.
t317(a) :-true.
```

Example 8. For greater precision, we introduce some type information into the approximation, thus avoiding the overapproximation of some arguments. In the following example, numeric is such a type that describes any number. numeric(X) can be viewed as an arithmetic constraint that is true for all numbers X, i.e. like X =:= X which would normally be removed by the constraint simplification.

```
disjunct([]).
disjunct([[A,B,C,D]|R]):-
    disj(A,B,C,D),
    disjunct(R).

disj(Aa,Ad,Ba,Bd):-
    gteqc(Ba,Aa,Ad).
disj(Aa,Ad,Ba,Bd):-
    gteqc(Aa,Ba,Bd).
gteqc(X,Y,C) :-
    X >= Y + C.
```

Regular Approximation Program:

```
gteqc(X1,X2,X3) :-any(X1),any(X2),any(X3).
disj(X1,X2,X3,X4) :-any(X1),any(X2),any(X3),any(X4).
disjunct(X1) :-t38(X1).
t38([]) :-true.
t38([X1|X2]) :-t32(X1),t38(X2).
t32([X1|X2]) :-any(X1),t33(X2).
t33([X1|X2]) :-any(X1),t34(X2).
t34([X1|X2]) :-any(X1),t35(X2).
t35([X1|X2]) :-any(X1),t36(X2).
t36([]) :-true.
```

Constrained Regular Approximation Program:

```
gteqc(X1,X2,X3) :-X1-X2-X3>=0.0.
disj(X1,X2,X3,X4) :-numeric(X1),numeric(X3),any(X2),any(X4).
disjunct(X1) :-t39(X1).
t39([]) :-true.
t39([X1|X2]) :-t33(X1),t39(X2).
t33([X1|X2]) :-X2=[X3|X4],numeric(X1),t34(X2).
t34([X1|X2]) :-X2=[X3|X4],any(X1),t35(X2).
t35([X1|X2]) :-X2=[X3|X4],numeric(X1),t36(X2).
t36([X1|X2]) :-X2=[],any(X1),t37(X2).
t37([]) :-true.
```

4   Limitations

There are some dependencies that our method cannot capture. Consider the following partition predicate taken from a quicksort program.

Example 9. Partitioning a list of numbers

```
partition(_,[],[],[]).
partition(X,[Y|Ys],L,[Y|G]) :- X =< Y,
       partition(X,Ys,L,G).
partition(X,[Y|Ys],[Y|L],G) :- Y < X,
       partition(X,Ys,L,G).
```

The analysis gives no precise result.

```
partition(X1,X2,X3,X4) :-any(X1),t1(X2),t2(X3),t3(X4).
```

where t1, t2 and t3 define lists of any elements. Ideally we would like to capture the information that there is a dependency between t2 and t3.

If the first argument of `partition` can be fixed, for example in a goal directed analysis of `partition(3,X2,X3,X4)` the dependency between the subarguments of the third and fourth arguments, that is all the elements of the third argument are strictly less than all the elements of the fourth argument, of `partition` can be captured. Without knowing the value of the first argument, CRUL clauses are not expressive enough to capture the dependency.

5   Implementation and Related Work

The implementation of the regular approximation procedure defined in [6] is the basis for the implementation of this work.

Recent studies on approximation of arithmetic constraints have been done in a CLP framework by Benoy and King [1] and Sağlam and Gallagher [18]. The method defined in this paper includes arithmetic approximations such as those discussed in [1], [18] as a special case, where all predicates are arithmetic. For example, the list length analysis of the well known *append* predicate gives the result $append(X, Y, Z) \leftarrow Z = X + Y, X \geq 0, Y \geq 0, any(X), any(Y), any(Z)$.

The combination of Herbrand and arithmetic constraints, called "mixed disjunctive constraints", was studied in [17] which is based on the framework set out in [5] and uses abstract compilation, where constraint logic programs are used to define pre-interpretations as in [14]. It handles predicate arguments containing both Herbrand and arithmetic subterms. Termination is not guaranteed if the Herbrand terms are of unbounded depth. Procedures from [17] are used for the implementation of this work.

6   Conclusion and Future Work

We have demonstrated a method that extends regular approximations to capture additional decidable properties of a program. We capture dependencies between the arguments of terms, and also, dependencies between arguments at different levels of a term.

In our implementation, we provide a number of choices on upper bound and widening operators, such as coarse and upper bounds, and simple and precise widenings on arithmetic constraints, tuple-distributive upper bound and most specific generalisations, and simple and precise widenings on term constraints, to obtain substantially different approximations of programs. Constrained regular approximation becomes much more efficient (and less precise) if we employ depth-1 for the arguments of *approx*/1, and depth-2 for the arguments of the other functions, since it disregards the Herbrand dependencies between the arguments of predicates, while the top level dependencies within each argument are still preserved. Leaving aside the arithmetic constraints, the result of employing a depth bound of 1 throughout gives the same result as regular approximation.

The ability that the method defined in this paper lacks is the handling of dependencies among variable arguments of some predicates. In Example 9 one can expect an approximation that captures the information that one argument

is a list of numbers which are all greater than or equal to the numbers in the
other list, which is the other argument. To capture this kind of properties a
parameterised regular clause definition could be appropriate, analogous to the
addition of polymorphism in types. This is a possible extension of the method.
Before that this work needs to be experimented on. The stage at which depth-k
abstraction is performed might change the precision and/or efficiency. Currently
we perform depth-k abstraction after the intersection operation. It could well be
a part of widening in the approximation. The performance results and complexity
analysis compared with standard regular approximation are subjects of current
investigation.

Integrating Boolean constraints will give a greater precision and flexibility
and it appears to be a natural extension of the method.

References

[1] F. Benoy and A. King. Inferring argument size relations with CLP(R). In *Proceedings of the 6th International Workshop on Logic Program Synthesis and Transformation (LOPSTR-96); Sweden*. Springer-Verlag, 1996.
[2] P. Cousot and R. Cousot. Comparing the Galois connection and widening/narrowing approaches to abstract interpretation. In *Proceedings of the 4th International Symposium on Programming Language Implementation and Logic Programming, PLILP'92, Leuven, Belgium*, volume 631 of *lncs*, pages 269–295. Springer-Verlag, 1992.
[3] P. Cousot and N. Halbwachs. Automatic discovery of linear restraints among variables of a program. In *Proceedings of the 5th Annual ACM Symposium on Principles of Programming Languages*, pages 84–96, 1978.
[4] B. De Backer and H. Beringer. A CLP language handling disjunctions of linear constraints. In *Proceedings of the International Conference on Logic Programming (ICLP'93)*, pages 550–563. MIT Press, 1993.
[5] J. Gallagher, D. Boulanger, and H. Sağlam. Practical model-based static analysis for definite logic programs. In J. W. Lloyd, editor, *Proc. of International Logic Programming Symposium*, pages 351–365. MIT Press, 1995.
[6] J. Gallagher and D. A. de Waal. Fast and precise regular approximation of logic programs. In P. Van Hentenryck, editor, *Proceedings of the International Conference on Logic Programming (ICLP'94), Santa Margherita Ligure, Italy*, pages 599–613. MIT Press, 1994.
[7] N. Halbwachs, Y. E. Proy, and P. Raymond. Verification of linear hybrid systems by means of convex approximations. In *Proceedings of the First Symposium on Static Analysis*, volume 864 of *lncs*, pages 223–237. Springer-Verlag, September 1994.
[8] P. Van Hentenryck, A. Cortesi, and B. Le Charlier. Type analysis of Prolog using type graphs. *Journal of Logic Programming*, 22(3):179–210, 1994.
[9] G. Janssens, M. Bruynooghe, and V. Englebert. Abstracting numerical values in CLP(H,N). Technical Report CW189, K.U. Leuven, Belgium, 1994.
[10] K. Marriott and P.J. Stuckey. The 3 R's of optimizing constraint logic programs: Refinement, removal and reordering. In *Proceedings of the 20th Annual ACM SIGPLAN-SIGACT Symposium on Principles of Programming Languages; Charleston, South Carolina*, pages 334 – 344, January 1993.

[11] P. Mishra. Towards a theory of types in prolog. In *Proceedings of the IEEE International Symposium on Logic Programming*, 1984.

[12] G. Plotkin. A note on inductive generalisation. In B. Meltzer and D. Michie, editors, *Machine Intelligence*, Vol.5. Edinburgh University Press, 1974.

[13] J. C. Reynolds. Transformational systems and the algebraic structure of atomic formulas. In B. Meltzer and D. Michie, editors, *Machine Intelligence*, Vol.5. Edinburgh University Press, 1974.

[14] H. Sağlam. Static analysis of logic programs by abstract compilation into CLP. In *Proceedings of the Eighth European Summer School on Logic, Language and Information, ESSLLI'96 Student Session*. Czech Technical University, Prague, Czech Republic, 1996.

[15] H. Sağlam and J. Gallagher. Approximating logic programs using types and regular descriptions. Technical Report CSTR-94-19, University of Bristol, Department of Computer Science, 1994.

[16] H. Sağlam and J. Gallagher. Approximating constraint logic programs using polymorphic types and regular descriptions. In *Proceedings of the 7th International Symposium on Programming Languages, Implementations, Logics and Programs, PLILP'95 (poster abstract), Utrecht, Holland; (full version is Technical Report CSTR-95-016, Department of Computer Science, University of Bristol)*, 1995.

[17] H. Sağlam and J. Gallagher. Proving properties of terms using abstract compilation into CLP. In *Proceedings of JICSLP'96 post conference Workshop on Meta Programming and Metareasoning in Logic, META'96*. Uppsala University, Uppsala, Sweden, 1996.

[18] H. Sağlam and J. Gallagher. Static analysis of logic programs using CLP as a meta-language. Technical Report CSTR-96-003, University of Bristol, Department of Computer Science, 1996.

[19] A. van Gelder. Deriving constraints among argument sizes in logic programs. In *Principles of Database Systems; Nashville, Tennessee*, pages 47–60, 1990.

[20] K. Verschaetse and D. De Schreye. Derivation of linear size relations by abstract interpretation. In *Proceedings of the 4th International Symposium on Programming Language Implementation and Logic Programming, PLILP'92, Leuven, Belgium*, volume 631 of *lncs*, pages 296–310. Springer-Verlag, 1992.

[21] E. Yardeni and E.Y. Shapiro. A type system for logic programs. *Journal of Logic Programming*, 10(2):125–154, 1990.

A Logic Framework for the Incremental Inductive Synthesis of Datalog Theories

Giovanni Semeraro, Floriana Esposito, Donato Malerba, Nicola Fanizzi, and
Stefano Ferilli

Dipartimento di Informatica, Universitá degli Studi di Bari
Via E. Orabona 4, 70126 Bari, Italy
{semeraro, esposito, malerba}@di.uniba.it
{fanizzi, ferilli}@lacam.di.uniba.it

Abstract. This paper presents a logic framework for the incremental inductive synthesis of Datalog theories. It allows us to cast the problem as a process of abstract diagnosis and debugging of an incorrect theory. This process involves a search in a space, whose algebraic structure (conferred by the notion of *object identity*) makes easy the definition of algorithms that meet several properties which are deemed as desirable from the point of view of the theoretical computer science. Such algorithms embody two *ideal* refinement operators, one for generalizing *incomplete* clauses, and the other one for specializing *inconsistent* clauses.

These algorithms have been implemented in INCR/H, an incremental learning system whose main characteristic consists of the capability of extending autonomously the search to the space of $Datalog^\neg$ clauses, when no correct theories exist in the space of $Datalog$ clauses. Experimental results show that INCR/H is able to cope effectively and efficiently with the real-world task of document understanding.

1 Introduction

A logical theory can be viewed as a set of conditions, expressed in a logic language, that are necessary and sufficient to explain a number of observations in a given environment. In addition to the capability of explaining past events, the usefulness of a theory relies on its ability of predicting future situations in the same environment.

If we assume that the only source of knowledge available is represented by a set of previously classified observations and no prior knowledge can be exploited, the process of formulating a new theory is bound to be progressive. Starting from contingent observations, it is not possible to infer concept definitions that are universally regarded as correct. The validity of the theory itself extends to the available knowledge. Conversely, new observations can point out the inadequacies in the current formulation of the concepts. In such a case, the theory is incorrect and a suitable process of theory revision should be activated.

A theory may be incorrect because, given a new observation, one of the following cases occurs: This observation is erroneously explained by the theory, thus

Norbert E. Fuchs (Ed.): LOPSTR'97, LNCS 1463, pp. 300–321, 1998.

the theory is too general and needs to be specialized; this observation is erroneously not explained by the theory, thus the theory is too specific and needs to be generalized. In this paper, we address these problems in a logic framework. The solutions that we propose require to perform a process of abstract diagnosis and debugging of the theory in order to restore its correctness. Specifically, the debugging of the theory is cast as a search for either a specialization (*downward refinement*) or a generalization (*upward refinement*) of that part of the theory detected as source of incorrectness by the diagnosis step. This search aims at finding a *minimal* refinement of a theory [24]. Indeed, in a logic-constrained belief revision approach, a contraction of a belief set with respect to (wrt) a new fact consists of a peculiar belief change, which requires the retraction of the information causing the violation of consistency, when this property is regarded as an integrity constraint.

Formulating logical theories from facts is the ultimate objective of concept learning. In this area, a *theory* consists of a set of hypotheses, a *hypothesis* is a concept definition and observations are called *examples*. An example that should be explained by a hypothesis is called *positive*, an example that should be refuted is called *negative*.

Initially, the research efforts in this area centred on the analysis and development of inductive systems that synthesize a logical theory in a *batch* way. These systems start from an empty theory and stop the inductive process when the current set of hypotheses is able to explain all the available examples. When new evidence contradicts the synthesized theory, the whole process must be repeated, taking no advantage of the previous version of the hypotheses. This is not true for incremental inductive systems. These systems are able to revise and refine a theory in an *incremental* way, thus the previously generated hypotheses are not completely rejected, but they are taken as the starting point of a search process whose goal consists of a new theory that explains both old and new observations. Incremental synthesis of theories is necessary in several cases, like changing world, sloppy modeling and selection bias [25], even though problems might arise with recursive theories.

This paper addresses the problem of incremental synthesis of theories in a logic framework, that allows us to cast this problem as a search in a space whose algebraic structure is now thoroughly understood [16], and that makes easy the definition of search algorithms which meet many properties that are deemed as desirable from the point of view of the mathematical theory of computation (e.g., non-termination) [16], as well as from that of the theory of the computational complexity [5] [18].

The plan of the paper is as follows. In the next section, the logic language adopted to represent both the synthesized theory and the examples is briefly introduced. Section 3 recalls the logic framework, based on the notion of *object identity*, within which the problem of *debugging* an incorrect theory is addressed. Section 4 introduces the basic notions regarding incremental inductive synthesis of logical theories, while Sections 5 and 6 present the refinement operators that have been developed and implemented in a new version of INCR/H [17], an incremental system that can inductively synthesize and correct logical theories. The results of the application of INCR/H to the real-world problem of document understanding are shown in Section 7.

2   The Representation Language

Henceforth, we refer to [11] for what concerns the basic definitions of a *substitution*, *positive* and *negative literal*, *clause*, *definite* and *program clause*, and *normal program*. We will indifferently use the set notation and the Prolog notation for clauses. Given a first-order clause C, $vars(C)$, $consts(C)$ and $\mid C \mid$ denote respectively the set of the variables, the set of the constants and the number of literals occurring in C.

By *logical theory* we mean a set of hypotheses; by *hypothesis* we mean a set of program clauses with the same head. In the paper, we are concerned exclusively with logical theories expressed as *hierarchical programs*, that is, as (non-recursive) programs for which it is possible to find a *level mapping* [11] such that, in every program clause $P(t_1, t_2, \ldots, t_n) \leftarrow L_1, L_2, \ldots, L_m$, the level of every predicate symbol occurring in the body is less than the level of P.

Another constraint on the representation language is that, whenever we write about clauses, we mean *Datalog linked* clauses. Here, we refer to [1] [9] for the basic notions about Datalog and its extensions $Datalog^{\neq}$ and $Datalog^{\neg}$. A definition of linked clause is the following [7]. A Horn clause is *linked* if all of its literals are; a positive literal is linked if at least one of its arguments is; an argument of a literal is linked if either the literal is the head of the clause or another argument in the same literal is linked. An instance of a linked clause is $C- = \{P(x), \neg Q(x, y), \neg Q(y, z)\}$. Conversely, the clauses $D = C\{\neg Q(x, y)\}$ and $F = C \cup \{\neg R(v, w)\}$ are not linked. Indeed, the literal $\neg Q(y, z)$ is not linked in D, whereas $\neg R(v, w)$ is not linked in F.

The differences existing between examples and hypotheses are the following: Each example is represented by one ground clause with a unique literal in the head; each hypothesis is a set of program clauses with the same head.

An *example E* is *positive* for a hypothesis H if its head has the same predicate letter and sign as the head of the clauses in H. The example E is *negative* for H if its head has the same predicate, but opposite sign. An instance of a positive example is: *Uncle(Sam, Bob) ← Parent(Tim, Bob), Brother(Sam, Tim).*
An instance of a negative example is:
¬ *Uncle(Mary, Bob) ← Parent(Tim, Bob), Female(Mary).*
Furthermore, no predicate invention is performed.

3   Object Identity and θ_{OI}-Subsumption

Here, we introduce a logic language, called $Datalog^{OI}$, which is an instance of constraint logic programming [8]. The basic notion of $Datalog^{OI}$ is that of *object identity*. We recall the definition of object identity, previously given in [4]

[16] for a first order logic that is both function-free and constant-free, and later generalized to a full first order logic [5] [18].

Definition 1 (Object Identity). *Within a clause, terms denoted with different symbols must be distinct.*

This notion is the basis for the definition of both an equational theory for Datalog clauses and a quasi-ordering upon them. In Datalog, the adoption of the object identity assumption can be viewed as a method for building an equational theory into the ordering as well as into the inference rules of the calculus (resolution, factorization and paramodulation) [14]. Such equational theory is very simple, since it consists of just one rewrite rule (in bold-face), in addition to the set of the axioms of Clark's Equality Theory (CET) [11]:
$t \neq s \in body(C)$ for each clause C in $\mathcal{L}$ and
for all pairs t, s of distinct terms that occur in C   **(OI)**
where $\mathcal{L}$ denotes the language that consists of all the possible Datalog clauses built from a finite number of predicates.

The (OI) rewrite rule can be viewed as an extension of both Reiter's *unique-names* assumption [15] and axioms (7), (8) and (9) of CET [11] to the variables of the language. Under object identity assumption, the Datalog clause

$$C = P(x) : -Q(x, x), Q(y, a)$$

is an abbreviation for the Datalog^{OI} clause

$$C_{OI} = P(x) : -Q(x, x), Q(y, a) \parallel [x \neq y], [x \neq a], [y \neq a]$$

where P, Q denote predicate letters, x, y variables, a is a constant and the inequations attached to the clause can be seen as constraints on its terms. These constraints are generated in a systematic way by the (OI) rewrite rule. In addition, they can be dealt with in the same way as the other literals in the clause. Therefore, under object identity, any Datalog clause C generates a new Datalog$^{\neq}$ clause C_{OI} consisting of two components, called $core(C_{OI})$ and $constraints(C_{OI})$, where $core(C_{OI}) = C$ and $constraints(C_{OI})$ is the set of the inequalities generated by the (OI) rewrite rule, that is to say,
$constraints(C_{OI}) = \{t \neq s \mid t, s \in terms(C), t, s \text{ distinct}\}$
Therefore, Datalog^{OI} is a sublanguage of Datalog$^{\neq}$. Formally, a Datalog^{OI} program is made up of a set of Datalog$^{\neq}$ clauses of the form

$$Q(x_1, x_2, \ldots, x_n) : -\varphi \parallel I$$

where Q and φ are as in Datalog, I is the set of inequations generated by the (OI) rule and $n \geq 0$. The symbol "$\parallel$" means *and* just like ",", but is used for the sake of readability, in order to separate the predicates coming from the (OI) rewrite rule from the rest of the clause. Nevertheless, Datalog^{OI} has the same expressive power as Datalog. Indeed, it is possible to prove the following results.

Proposition 2. $\forall C \in Datalog \ \exists C' = \{C_1, C_2, \ldots, C_n\} \subseteq Datalog^{OI}$:
$T_C \uparrow \omega = T_{C'} \uparrow \omega$

that is, for each Datalog clause we can find a set of $Datalog^{OI}$ clauses equivalent
to it.

Proof. The difference between a Datalog clause and a $Datalog^{OI}$ clause is that, in
the former case, it is interpreted without any constraint on the variables appearing in it, while, in the latter, additional literals expressing the OI-constraints
are implicitly assumed. If we progressively eliminate from the clause all the
possible combinations of inequations and introduce new clauses reflecting their
unification, every possible substitution we can think of will involve one of the
combinations already considered (maybe the empty one), so we can refer to
the corresponding clause which we introduced and which eliminated the *noisy*
constraints. These observations lead to the following algorithm, that, given a
Datalog clause C, computes the set of $Datalog^{OI}$ clauses $C' = \{C_1, C_2, \ldots, C_n\}$
such that $T_C \uparrow \omega = T_{C'} \uparrow \omega$.

function GenerateDatalogOIClauses (C : DatalogClause) : DatalogOIClauses
begin
$C' := \{\}$;
for $k = 0, 1, \ldots, | \, vars(C) \, |$ do
   foreach combination of k variables out of $| \, vars(C) \, |$ do
     begin
     Define some ordering between the k variables;
     foreach permutation with replacement of k constants out of $|consts(C)|$ do
       for $h = 1, 2, \ldots, | \, vars(C) \, | - k$ do
         begin
         $C'_h := \{\}$;
         foreach partition $(V_i)_{i=1,2,\ldots,h}$ of the remaining variables s.t.
         $\forall i, j = 1, 2, \ldots, h, i < j : | \, V_i \, | = r_i, r_i \leq r_j$ do
           begin
           $C'_h := \{\}$;
           Build a clause D by replacing the l-th ($l = 1, 2, \ldots, k$) variable
           of the combination with the l-th constant of the permutation
           and $\forall i = 1, 2, \ldots, h$ all the r_i variables belonging to V_i with
           one new variable;
           if $\forall i, j = 1, 2, \ldots, k, i \neq j : r_i \neq r_j$ then Insert D in C'_h
           elsif there exists no renaming of D in C'_h then Insert D in C'_h
         end;
         $C' := C' \cup C'_h$
         end;
     end;
   return C'
end;

By definition, the T_P operator acts only on the ground instances of the clauses of the program it is applied to. As a consequence, proving the thesis is equivalent to demonstrating that the following sets A and B are equal.

$A = \text{ground}(C)$ $\hspace{6cm}$ $B = \{ground(D) \mid D \in C'\}$

where $ground(E)$ denotes the set of the ground instances of the clause E.

As the clauses in C' have been obtained from C by simply unifying variables (among them or with a constant), their *structure* is surely equal to that of C. But then, when comparing an element of ground(C) with one of ground(C'), it suffices to consider ground terms, which will be constants (since we work in Datalog and Datalog^{OI}). After this introduction, let us prove the thesis.

$(A \subseteq B)$ Any ground instance of C is obtained by substituting all the variables in C with constants.

  i) If all these constants are already in C, then the algorithm generates (in the last step of the loop) all the possible combinations of substitutions of variables in C with constants in C;

 ii) If none of these constants is already in C, then we will have a partition of $vars(C)$, $(V_i)_{i=1,2,...,k}$ $(1 \leq k \leq \mid vars(C) \mid)$, s.t. $\forall i = 1, 2, \ldots, k$ all variables in V_i are associated to the same constant a_i $(a_i \neq a_j \forall i \neq j)$. But then the algorithm generates (in the first step of the loop) a clause which unifies among them all the variables in each V_i, to which we can apply the same substitution, since the *noisy* OI-constraint has been removed;

iii) If some of these constants are already in C and others are not, the algorithm applies the same substitutions on the constants which are already present, and unifies the remaining variables according to the partition introduced by the remaining constants (see ii), thus generating a clause to which it is possible to apply the same substitution.

Note that i) and ii) can be seen as particular cases of iii).

$(B \subseteq A)$ On the other hand, given any ground instance of a clause $C_i \in C'$, it can be obtained immediately from C by substituting every variable with the constant which appears in the same position in that ground instance of C_i, because in C we do not have the OI-constraint. Indeed, the algorithm generates C' from C by leaving untouched all the constants, and at most by unifying some variables. $\hspace{2cm}$ □

Corollary 3. $\forall P \subseteq Datalog \ \exists P' \subseteq Datalog^{OI} : T_P \uparrow \omega = T_{P'} \uparrow \omega.$

that is, for any Datalog program we can find a Datalog^{OI} program equivalent to it.

Proof. Even for this result, the proof is constructive. It suffices applying the algorithm in the proof of Proposition 2 to every clause in P, and taking as P' the set of all the clauses generated by the following algorithm:

function GenerateDatalogOIProgram $(P.$ DatalogProgram): DatalogOIProgram
begin
$P' := \{\};$
foreach clause $C \in P$ do
    begin
    $C' :=$ GenerateDatalogOIClauses $(C);$
    $P' := P' \cup C'$
    end;
return P'
end;

Again, the semantic equivalence is cast (by definition of T_P) to proving the equality of the following sets:

A = $\{ground(D) \mid D \in P\}$ B = $\{ground(D) \mid D \in P'\}$

$(A \subseteq B)$ Given a ground instance of a clause $C \in P$, C has been surely considered in some step of this last algorithm, thus it generates a set of clauses $C' \subseteq P'$. But then, the proof of $(A \subseteq B)$ in Proposition 2 holds for the (unique) ground instance of C and for the set of ground instances of clauses in C'.

$(B \subseteq A)$ Given a ground instance of a clause $C'_i \in P'$, C'_i has been generated by this last algorithm in correspondence of a clause $C \in P$. But then, the proof of $(B \subseteq A)$ in Proposition 2 holds for the ground instance of C'_i and for the set of ground instances of C.   □

Now, we can recall the ordering relation defined by the notion of θ-subsumption under object identity – $\theta_{OI} - subsumption$ – upon the set of Datalog clauses [5] [18]. The following definition extends to Datalog the definition given in [4] [16] for constant-free (other than function-free) logic languages.

Definition 4 (θ_{OI}-subsumption ordering). *Let C, D be two Datalog clauses. We say that D θ-subsumes C under object identity (D θ_{OI}-subsumes C) if and only if (iff) there exists a substitution σ such that (s.t.) $D_{OI}.\sigma \subseteq C_{OI}$.*
In such a case, we say that D is more general than or equivalent to C (D is an upward refinement of C and C is a downward refinement of D) under object identity and we write $C \leq_{OI} D$. We write $C <_{OI} D$ when $C \leq_{OI} D$ and not($D \leq_{OI} C$) and we say that D is more general than C (D is a proper upward refinement of C) or C is more specific than D (C is a proper downward refinement of D) or D properly θ_{OI}-subsumes C. We write $C \sim_{OI} D$, and we say that C and D are equivalent clauses under object identity, when $C \leq_{OI} D$ and $D \leq_{OI} C$.

Like θ-subsumption, θ_{OI}-subsumption induces a quasi-ordering upon the space of the Datalog clauses, as stated by the following result.

Proposition 5. *Let C, D, E be Datalog clauses. Then:*
a) $C \leq_{OI} C$ *b) $C \leq_{OI} D$ and $D \leq_{OI} E \Rightarrow C \leq_{OI} E$*

Proof. a) $C \subseteq C$ implies $C_{OI}.\{\} \subseteq C_{OI}$, thus $C \leq_{OI} C$.
b) If $C \leq_{OI} D$ and $D \leq_{OI} E$ then there exist the substitutions σ and θ s.t. $D_{OI}.\sigma \subseteq C_{OI}$ and $E_{OI}.\theta \subseteq D_{OI}$. Thus, it holds $E_{OI}.\theta\sigma \subseteq D_{OI}.\sigma \subseteq C_{OI}$, where $\theta\sigma$ denotes the composite of the substitutions θ and σ. This proves $C \leq_{OI} E$. □

A characterization of the notion of θ_{OI}-subsumption is:

Proposition 6. *Let C, D be two Datalog clauses, $C \leq_{OI} D \Leftrightarrow$*
$\exists \sigma s.t. core(D_{OI}).\sigma \subseteq core(C_{OI})$ *and* $constraints(D_{OI}).\sigma \subseteq constraints(C_{OI})$

Proof. ' $\Rightarrow$ ': From Definition 4, $C \leq_{OI} D$ means that there exists a substitution σ s.t. $D_{OI}.\sigma \subseteq C_{OI} \Leftrightarrow$
$(core(D_{OI}) \cup constraints(D_{OI})).\sigma \subseteq core(C_{OI}) \cup constraints(C_{OI}) \Leftrightarrow$
$(core(D_{OI}).\sigma \cup constraints(D_{OI}).\sigma) \subseteq core(C_{OI}) \cup constraints(C_{OI})$.
But inequalitites cannot occur in a Datalog clause, thus it yields:
$core(D_{OI}).\sigma \cap constraints(D_{OI}).\sigma = \emptyset$
$core(C_{OI}) \cap constraints(C_{OI}) = \emptyset$
$core(D_{OI}).\sigma \cap constraints(C_{OI}) = \emptyset$
$constraints(D_{OI}).\sigma \cap core(C_{OI}) = \emptyset$
By simple algebraic manipulations, it is possible to obtain:
$core(D_{OI}).\sigma \subseteq core(C_{OI})$ and $constraints(D_{OI}).\sigma \subseteq constraints(C_{OI})$.
' $\Leftarrow$ ': Trivial. □

4 Incremental Inductive Synthesis Basics

Generally, the canonical inductive paradigm requires the fulfilment of the properties of completeness and consistency for the synthesized theory. Formally, we introduce the following definitions, strictly valid for hierarchical theories, where E^- and E^+ denote the sets of all the negative and positive examples, respectively.

Definition 7 (Inconsistency). *A theory T is inconsistent iff $\exists H \in T$, $\exists N \in E$: H is inconsistent wrt N. A hypothesis H is inconsistent wrt N iff $\exists C \in H$: C is inconsistent wrt N. A clause C is inconsistent wrt N iff $\exists \sigma$:*

> 1. $body(C).\sigma \subseteq body(N)$ 2. $\neg head(C).\sigma = head(N)$
> 3. $constraints(C_{OI}).\sigma \subseteq constraints(N_{OI})$

where $body(\varphi)$ and $head(\varphi)$ denote the body and the head of a clause φ, respectively. Note that, in this definition, we cannot use the $\leq_{OI}$ notation, since we need to find a unique σ that satisfies conditions 1), 2) and 3). If at least one of the three conditions above is not met, we say that C is consistent wrt N.

Definition 8 (Incompleteness). *A theory T is incomplete iff $\exists H \in T$, $\exists P \in E^+$: H is incomplete wrt P. A hypothesis H is incomplete wrt P iff $\forall C \in H$: not($P \leq_{OI} C$). Otherwise it is complete wrt P.*

Now, we can formally define the notions of commission and omission error.

Definition 9 (Commission/Omission error). *Given a theory T and an example E: T makes a commission error iff $\exists H \in T$, $\exists C \in H$: C is inconsistent wrt E; T makes an omission error iff $\exists H \in T$: H is incomplete wrt E.*

Whenever a commission error occurs, it becomes necessary to specialize all the inconsistent clauses C so that each new clause C' restores the consistency property of the theory. When an omission error occurs, it becomes necessary to generalize the incomplete hypothesis H so that the new hypothesis H' restores the completeness property of the theory. This points out that the process of abstract diagnosis of an incorrect theory is performed at different levels of granularity, according to the type of error found. Specifically, if a commission error occurs, the diagnosis can be carried as far as the level of a single inconsistent clause, which is the only cause of the commission error, while if an omission error occurs, we are compelled to limit the scope of the diagnosis process to the coarser level of hypotheses, that is to say, the cause of an omission error is a single hypothesis. As to the debugging process, commission errors can be solved by exploiting properly a downward refinement operator, while, dually, upward refinement operators can cope with omission errors.

As we pointed out in [18], in a logic framework for the inductive synthesis of Datalog theories from facts, a fundamental problem is the definition of *locally finite*, *proper* and *complete* (*ideal*) refinement operators. Indeed, when the aim is to develop incrementally a logic program, that should be *correct* with respect to its *intended model* at the end of the development process, it becomes relevant to define operators that allow a stepwise (incremental) refinement of *too weak* or *too strong* programs [10]. The *ideality* of the refinement operators plays a key role when the efficiency and the effectiveness of the design process is an unnegligible requirement. Unfortunately, when full Horn clause logic is chosen as representation language and either *θ-subsumption* or *implication* is adopted as generalization model, there exist no ideal refinement operators [20] [21] [22]. On the contrary, they do exist under the weaker, but more mechanizable and manageable, ordering induced by θ_{OI}-*subsumption*, as proved in [5] [18].

5   Upward Refinement

The upward refinement operator is inspired from the Interference Matching proposed by Hayes-Roth and McDermott [6]. Differently from the original operator, our algorithm works on clauses rather than on Parameterized Structural Representations (PSR's). Therefore, it extends the notion of *maximal abstraction* to the concept of *least general generalizations* (lgg) under θ_{OI}-subsumption.

Definition 10 (lgg_{OI}). *A least general generalization under θ_{OI}-subsumption of two clauses is a generalization which is not more general than any other such generalization, that is, it is either more specific than or not comparable to any other such generalization.*

Formally, given two Datalog clauses C_1 and C_2, C is a lgg under θ_{OI}-subsumption of C_1 and C_2 iff:

1. $C_i \leq_{OI} C$, $i=1,2$ 2. $\forall D$ s.t. $C_i \leq_{OI} D$, $i=1,2$: $not(D <_{OI} C)$
$lgg_{OI}(C_1, C_2) = \{C \mid C_i \leq_{OI} C, i = 1,2$ and $\forall D$ s.t. $C_i \leq_{OI} D, i = 1,2$: $not(D <_{OI} C)\}$

In the following, we describe an algorithm that computes the set of the least general generalizations under θ_{OI}-subsumption of two any Datalog^{OI} clauses (the lgg is no longer unique under θ_{OI}-$subsumption$ [16]). Such an algorithm is a straightforward extension to Datalog^{OI} of a similar algorithm given by Plotkin (1970). This extension is necessary since the space of Datalog clauses is not a lattice when ordered by θ_{OI}-subsumption [16], while it is a lattice when ordered by θ-subsumption [13].
Preliminarily, we extend the definition of *selection* in [13] to Datalog^{OI} clauses.

Definition 11 (Selection under object identity). *Let C_1 and C_2 be two Datalog^{OI} clauses. A selection under object identity of C_1 and C_2 is a pair of literals $< c_i, d_j >$, where $c_i \in core(C_{1_{OI}})$, $d_j \in core(C_{2_{OI}})$, s.t. c_i and d_j have the same predicate symbol, sign, and arity.*

Algorithm *(lgg$_{OI}$ computation)* Let C_1 and C_2 be two variable disjoint Datalog^{OI} clauses. The set of the least general generalizations under θ_{OI}-subsumption of C_1 and C_2, denoted with lgg$_{OI}(C_1, C_2)$, is a set of clauses where each clause G_{OI} is defined as follows.

$$G_{OI} = G_{core} \cup G_{constraints}$$

where

- $G_{core} = \{g \mid g = lgg(c_i , d_j), < c_i, d_j >$ selection under object identity of C_1 and C_2 and $\varphi_k(x) \neq \varphi_k(y)$, $k = 1, 2\}$ $lgg(c_i, d_j)$ denotes the least general generalization of c_i and d_j computed with the algorithm given by Plotkin (1970). The functions φ_k, $k = 1, 2$, are the substitutions s.t. $G_{core} \cdot \varphi_k \subseteq core(C_k)$, $k = 1, 2$. More precisely, if we call ϕ the function

$$\phi: terms(C_1) \times terms(C_2) \longrightarrow nvars \cup (consts(C_1) \cap const(C_2)) \text{ s.t.}$$
$$\phi(t_i, s_i) = \begin{cases} t_i \text{ if } t_i = s_i \\ X \text{ otherwise} \end{cases}$$

  where $< c_j, d_w >$ is a selection under object identity of C_1 and C_2, $c_j = P(t_1, t_2, \ldots, t_n)$, $d_w = P(s_1, s_2, \ldots, s_n)$, $nvars$ denotes a set of *new* variables and X is in $nvars$, then φ_1 and φ_2 are the projections of the inverse function of ϕ onto $terms(C_1)$ and $terms(C_2)$, respectively.
- $G_{constraints} = \{x \neq y \mid \varphi_k(x) \neq \varphi_k(y), k = 1, 2\}$

The only difference of this algorithm with respect to Plotkin's (1970) lies in the fact that it takes into account the (OI) rule in order to determine a partition of the literals in G_{core}. This allows the algorithm to find the set of all the possible lgg's under object identity rather than the unique lgg under θ-subsumption.

6 Downward Refinement

Differently from the upward refinement operator, the downward refinement operator proposed in this paper is completely novel. Essentially, it relies on the addition of a non-redundant literal to a clause that turns out to be inconsistent wrt a negative example, in order to restore the consistency property of the clause. The space in which such a literal should be searched for is potentially infinite and, in any case, its size is so large that an exhaustive search is unfeasible.

We can formally define the search space as the partially ordered set (*poset*) $(\mathcal{L}/\sim_{OI}, \leq_{OI})$, where $\mathcal{L}/\sim_{OI}$ is the quotient set of the Datalog linked clauses and $\leq_{OI}$ is the quasi ordering relation defined in Section 3, which can be straightforwardly extended to equivalence classes under $\sim_{OI}$ [16]. Henceforth, we will always work on the quotient set $\mathcal{L}/\sim_{OI}$ and, when convenient, we will denote with the name of a clause the equivalence class it belongs to.

The novelty of the operator consists in focusing the search into the portion of the space that contains the solution of the *diagnosed* commission error. This is the result of an analysis of the algebraic structure of the search space.

The search is firstly performed in the space of positive literals. This space contains information coming from the positive examples used to synthesize the current theory, but not yet exploited by it. When the search in this space fails, the algorithm autonomously performs a *representation change*, that allows it to extend the search to the space of the *program* clauses rather than the definite ones. Thus, the search is performed into a space of negative literals, built by taking into account the negative example that caused the commission error. First of all, given a hypothesis H which is inconsistent wrt a negative example N, the process of abstract diagnosis detects all the clauses of H that caused the inconsistency. Let us suppose that the subset of the positive examples θ_{OI} -subsumed by an inconsistent clause C is $\{P_1, P_2, \ldots, P_n\}$. The search process aims at finding one of the *most general downward refinements under object identity* of C against N given $P_1, P_2, \ldots, P_n$, denoted with $mgdr_{OI}(C, N \mid P_1, P_2, \ldots, P_n)$:

$$mgdr_{OI}(C, N | P_1, P_2, \ldots, P_n) = \{M \in mgdr_{OI}(C, N) \mid P_j \leq_{OI} M,$$
$$j = 1, 2, \ldots, n\}$$

where the superset of the *most general downward refinements under object identity* of C against a negative example N, denoted by $mgdr_{OI}(C, N)$, is:

$$mgdr_{OI}(C, N) = \{M \mid M \leq_{OI} C, M consistent wrt N, \forall D : D \leq_{OI}$$
$$C, D consistent wrt N : not(M <_{OI} D)\}$$

Throughout this section, we shall denote with C a clause that needs to be specialized, since it is inconsistent wrt an example N. More precisely, the body of C needs to be subjected to a suitable process of downward refinement in order to restore the consistency property.

Let us consider the problem of finding one of the clauses in the set $mgdr_{OI}(C, N \mid P_1, P_2, \ldots, P_n)$. Since the downward refinements we are looking for must satisfy the property of maximal generality, it may happen that the specializations of the clause C are overly general, even after some refinement steps. This suggests us the possibility of further exploiting the positive examples in order to specialize C. Specifically, if there exists a literal that, when added to the body of C, is able to discriminate from the negative example N that caused the inconsistency of C, then the downward refinement operator should be able to find it. The resulting specialization should restore the consistency of the clause C, by refining it into a clause C' which still θ_{OI}-subsumes the positive examples P_i, $i = 1, 2, \ldots, n$. The process of refining a clause by means of positive literals can be described as follows. For each P_i, $i = 1, 2, \ldots, n$, let us suppose that there exist n_i distinct substitutions such that $C\,\theta_{OI}$-subsumes P_i. Then, let us consider all the possible n-tuples of substitutions obtained by picking one of such substitutions for every positive example. Each of these substitutions is used to produce a distinct *residual*, consisting of all the literals in the positive example that are not involved in the θ_{OI}-subsumption test, after having properly turned their constants into variables. Formally, a residual can be defined as follows.

Definition 12 (Residual). *Let C be a clause, E an example, and σ_j a substitution s.t. $body(C).\sigma_j \subseteq body(E)$ and $constraints(C_{OI}).\sigma_j \subseteq constraints(E_{OI})$. A residual of E wrt C under the mapping σ_j, denoted by $\Delta_j(E, C)$, is:*

$$\Delta_j(E, C) = body(E).\underline{\sigma}_j^{-1} - body(C)$$

where $\underline{\sigma}_j^{-1}$ is the *extended antisubstitution* (or *inductive substitution*) obtained by inverting the corresponding substitution σ_j. Indeed, an antisubstitution is a mapping from terms and *addresses* into variables. When a clause $C\,\theta_{OI}$-subsumes an example E through a substitution σ, then it is possible to define a corresponding antisubstitution, σ^{-1}, which is exactly the inverse function of σ. Then, σ^{-1} maps some constants in E to variables in C. Not all constants in E have a corresponding variable according to σ^{-1}. Therefore, in Definition 12, we introduce the extension of σ^{-1}, denoted with $\underline{\sigma}^{-1}$, that is defined on the whole set of constants occurring in E, $consts(E)$, and takes values in the set of the variables of the language:

$$\underline{\sigma}^{-1}(c_n) = \begin{cases} \sigma^{-1}(c_n) \ if c_n \in vars(C).\sigma \\ \_ \qquad otherwise \end{cases}$$

Henceforth, variables denoted by _ will be called *new* variables and managed as in Prolog. The residuals obtained from the positive examples P_i, $i = 1, 2, \ldots, n$, can be exploited to build a *space of complete positive downward refinements*, denoted with **P**, and formally defined as follows.

$$\mathbf{P} = \bigcup_{\substack{i=1,2,\ldots,n \\ j_i=1,2,\ldots,n_i}} \bigcap_{k=1,2,\ldots,n} \Delta_{j_k}(P_k, C)$$

where $\Delta_{j_k}(P_k, C)$ denotes one of the n_k residuals of P_k wrt C and $\cap_{k=1,2,\ldots,n}\Delta_{j_k}(P_k, C)$, when j_k takes one of the values in $\{1, 2, \ldots, n_k\}$, is the set of the literals common to an n-tuple of residuals (one residual for each positive example P_k, $k = 1, 2, \ldots, n$). Moreover, denoted with θ_j, $j = 1, 2, \ldots, m$, all the substitutions which make C inconsistent wrt N, let us define a new space:

$$\mathbf{S} = \bigcup_{j=1,2,\ldots,m} \Delta_j(N,C)$$

Then, the following proposition holds.

Proposition 13. *Given a clause C, that θ_{OI}-subsumes the positive examples $P_1, P_2, \ldots, P_n$ and is inconsistent wrt the negative example N, then any linked clause $C' = C \cup \{l\}$, with $l \in \mathbf{P} - \mathbf{S}$, is in $mgdr_{OI}(C,N|P_1,P_2,\ldots,P_n)$. Formally:$\{C' \mid C' = C \cup \{l\}, l \in \mathbf{P} - \mathbf{S}\} \subseteq mgdr_{OI}(C,N|P_1,P_2,\ldots,P_n)$.*

Note that l is an element of $body(C')$.

Proof. In order to prove $C' <_{OI} C$, let us observe that in the space $(\mathcal{L}/\sim_{OI}, \leq_{OI})$ the set of all constant-free upward refinements of a clause C' corresponds to the set $2^{C'}$, thus each proper upward refinement of C' has a number of literals less than the number of literals of C' [23]. Therefore $C \subset C' \Rightarrow C' <_{OI} C$, i.e. C' is a proper downward refinement of C under θ_{OI}-subsumption.

Let us show now that C' is consistent wrt N. First of all, observe that $\forall j = 1,2,\ldots,m : \neg head(C').\theta_j = \neg head(C).\theta_j = head(N)$.

Moreover, $\forall j = 1,2,\ldots,m : body(C').\theta_j = body(C').\underline{\theta}_j = (body(C) \cup \{l\}).\underline{\theta}_j =$

$$body(C).\underline{\theta}_j \cup \{l\}.\underline{\theta}_j \tag{1}$$

$l \in \mathbf{P} - \mathbf{S} \Rightarrow l \notin \mathbf{S} = \bigcup_{j=1,2,\ldots,m} \Delta_j(N,C) \Rightarrow \forall j = 1,2,\ldots,m : l \notin \Delta_j(N,C)$. By definition of $\mathbf{P}$,

$$l \in \mathbf{P} \Rightarrow l \notin C, \text{ then } \forall j = 1,2,\ldots,m : l \notin body(N).\theta_j^{-1} \Rightarrow l.\underline{\theta}_j \notin body(N)$$
$$\Rightarrow \{l\}.\underline{\theta}_j \not\subset body(N).$$

Then, looking back at (1), we can conclude that:

$$\forall j = 1,2,\ldots,m : body(C').\theta_j \not\subset body(N).$$

This proves that C' is consistent wrt N. Indeed, any other substitution causing the inconsistency of C' would be a superset of a θ_j ($j = 1,2,\ldots,m$) because of our assumption that they were the only possible substitutions under object identity s.t. $body(C).\theta_j \subseteq body(N)$ and we have just proved that each of them makes C' consistent wrt N.

Now suppose that $\exists F$ which is consistent wrt N and s.t. $C' <_{OI} F \leq_{OI} C$
$\Rightarrow |C'| = |C| + 1 > |F| \geq |C| \Rightarrow |F| = |C|$
But F is a specialization of C, then it can be inferred that $F \sim_{OI} C$. Thus F is inconsistent wrt N, just as C.

According to the hypotheses of the proposition:
$\forall k = 1,2,\ldots,n: head(C).\sigma_{j_k} = head(P_k)$ and $body(C).\sigma_{j_k} \subseteq body(P_k)$ (σ_{j_k} are the substitutions that appear in the definition of $\mathbf{P}$).
$l \in \mathbf{P} \Rightarrow l \in \bigcap_{k=1,2,\ldots,n} \Delta_{j_k}(P_k,C) \Rightarrow \forall k = 1,2,\ldots,n : l \in body(P_k)$.
$\underline{\sigma}_{j_k}^{-1} \Rightarrow \forall k = 1,2,\ldots,n : l.\underline{\sigma}_{j_k} \in body(P_k)$. Then, $body(C').\underline{\sigma}_{j_k} = body(C).\underline{\sigma}_{j_k} \cup \{l\}.\underline{\sigma}_{j_k} \subseteq body(P_k), \forall k = 1,2,\ldots,n$. Then, $P_k \leq_{OI} C'$. $\square$

Proposition 13 states that every downward refinement built by adding a literal in **P** – **S** to the inconsistent clause C restores the properties of consistency and completeness of the original hypothesis. Moreover, it is one of the most general downward refinements of C against N.

When the space **P** – **S** does not contain any solution to the problem of specializing an inconsistent clause, the search is automatically extended to the space of negative literals. Specifically, let us suppose that the operator did not succeed in refining a clause wrt a negative example N in a complete and consistent way. In such a case, a change of representation must be performed in order to search for literals in another space, corresponding to the quotient set of the Datalog$^\neg$ linked clauses. Therefore, it is necessary to define a new target space, called the *space of negative downward refinements*. Given a clause C, an example N and the set of all substitutions θ_j, $j = 1, 2, \ldots, m$, such that C is inconsistent wrt N, the *space of negative downward refinements*, denoted with $\mathbf{S}_n$, is:

$$\mathbf{S}_n = \text{neg}(\mathbf{S}) = \text{neg}(\cup_{j=1,2,\ldots,m}\Delta_j(N, C))$$

where, given a set of literals $\varphi = \{l_1, l_2, \ldots, l_n\}$, $n \geq 1$, $neg(\varphi)$ denotes the set of literals $\{\neg l_1, \neg l_2, \ldots, \neg l_n\}$.

As for the process of downward refinement by positive literals, we are interested in a specific subset of $\mathbf{S}_n$, because of the properties satisfied by its elements. Such a subset, called *space of consistent negative downward refinements*, is denoted with $\mathbf{S}_c$ and is defined as follows.

$$\mathbf{S}_c = \text{neg}(\cap_{j=1,2,\ldots,m}\Delta_j(N, C))$$

The reason why the operator focuses onto the subset $\mathbf{S}_c$, rather than onto the whole set $\mathbf{S}_n$, lies in the following result:

Proposition 14. *Given a clause C, an example N and the set of all substitutions θ_j, $j = 1, 2, \ldots, m$, such that C is inconsistent wrt N, then any linked program clause $C' = C \cup \{l\}$, with $l \in \mathbf{S}_c$, is in $mgdr_{OI}(C, N)$.*
Formally:$\{C' \mid C' = C \cup \{l\}, l \in \mathbf{S}_c\} \subseteq mgdr_{OI}(C, N)$

Note that l is a negated literal occurring in the body of C', thus $C' \in Datalog^\neg$.

Proof. As to the proof that C' is a proper downward refinement of C under θ_{OI}-subsumption, refer to the proof of Proposition 12.

Given a linked program clause $C' = C \cup \{l\}$, with $l \in \mathbf{S}_c$, in order to prove that C' is consistent wrt N, let us suppose (reductio ad absurdum) there exists a substitution σ_1 s.t. C' is inconsistent wrt N. Then, from Definition 7:

1. $\text{body}(C').\sigma_1 \subseteq \text{body}(N)$ 2. $\neg\, \text{head}(C').\sigma_1 = \text{head}(N)$
3. $\text{constraints}(C'_{OI}).\sigma_1 \subseteq \text{constraints}(N_{OI})$

As a consequence, σ_1 is also one of the k substitutions that make C inconsistent wrt N. We also have from the hypotheses of the proposition:
$\text{body}(C').\sigma_1 = \text{body}(C').\underline{\sigma}_1 = (\text{body}(C)\cup \{l\}).\underline{\sigma}_1 = \text{body}(C).\underline{\sigma}_1 \cup \{l\}.\underline{\sigma}_1$
with $l \in \mathbf{S}_c = \text{neg}(\cap_{j=1,2,\ldots,m}\Delta_j(N, C))$. But:

$\{l\}.\underline{\sigma}_1 \subseteq \mathbf{S}_c.\underline{\sigma}_1 \subseteq neg(\Delta_1(N,C)).\underline{\sigma}_1 = neg(body(N).\underline{\sigma}_1^{-1} - body(C)).\underline{\sigma}_1 = neg(body(N).\underline{\sigma}_1^{-1}.\underline{\sigma}_1 - body(C).\underline{\sigma}_1) =$
$neg(body(N) - body(C).\underline{\sigma}_1) \subseteq neg(body(N))$ and
$\{l\}.\underline{\sigma}_1 \subseteq body(C').\underline{\sigma}_1 = body(C').\sigma_1 \subseteq body(N)$, according to 1.
But this is impossible since $body(N) \cap neg(body(N)) = \emptyset$.
In order to prove that C' is in $mgdr_{OI}(C,N)$, it remains to demonstrate that:
$\forall D, D \leq_{OI} C$, D consistent wrt N: $not(C' <_{OI} D)$.
Suppose (ad absurdum) that $\exists D$ s.t. $D \leq_{OI} C$, D consistent wrt N and $C' <_{OI}$
D. Then:

$$C' <_{OI} D \Rightarrow |D| < |C'| = |C| + 1 \Rightarrow |D| \leq |C| \qquad (2)$$

$$D \leq_{OI} C \Rightarrow |D| \geq |C| \qquad (3)$$

Therefore, from (2) and (3), it results: $|D| = |C|$.
By hypothesis, C is a generalization of D, but the only constant-free upward refinement of D having the same number of literals of D is D itself. Thus, $C = D$ and this is a contradiction because C is inconsistent wrt N, whilst D is consistent wrt N by hypothesis.   □

Proposition 14 easily extends to any linked literal l which introduces new variables, due to negation-as-failure rule. Generally speaking, we can say that, given a clause C and an example N such that C is inconsistent wrt N due to some substitutions θ_j, $j = 1, 2, \ldots, k$, the search for a complete and consistent hypothesis can be viewed as a two-stage process: the former stage searches into the space $\mathbf{P} - \mathbf{S}$, the latter into $\mathbf{S}_c$. By means of Propositions 13 and 14, we are now able to formally define our novel downward refinement operator on the space of constant-free Datalog linked program clauses, denoted with ρ_{OI}^{cons}.

Definition 15 (ρ_{OI}^{cons}). $\rho_{OI}^{cons} : \mathcal{L} \to 2^{\mathcal{L}}$, $\forall C \in \mathcal{L} : \rho_{OI}^{cons}(C) = \{C' \mid C' = C \cup \{l\}, l \in (\mathbf{P} - \mathbf{S}) \cup \mathbf{S}_c\}$

Proposition 16. *The downward refinement operator ρ_{OI}^{cons} is ideal.*

Proof.
(properness)
ρ_{OI}^{cons} is proper as a consequence of the definition of $mgdr_{OI}(C,N)$ and of Propositions 12 and 13. Indeed, $\rho_{OI}^{cons}(C) \subseteq mgdr_{OI}(C,N)$.
(local finiteness)
The choice of l in ρ_{OI}^{cons} is related to the construction of the sets $\mathbf{P}$, $\mathbf{S}$ and $\mathbf{S}_c$. Note that the number of substitutions s.t. a clause C θ_{OI}-subsumes a clause D is finite and equal to

$$|vars(D)| \times (|vars(D)| - 1) \times \ldots \times (|vars(D)| - |vars(C)| + 1).$$

It is worthwhile to note that $\mathbf{S}_c$ is an intersection of a finite number of residuals, by definition. This number depends on the (finite) number of substitutions between the clause C to be refined and the example N which causes the problem of inconsistency. In turn, each residual is a finite difference-set of literals between

two clauses. Thus, S_c is finite and computable. P is also an intersection of a finite number of difference-sets between two clauses. This number depends on the number of substitutions between C and the positive examples already processed. Finally, the set S is the union of a finite number of difference-sets between two clauses. This number depends on the number of substitutions between C and N. Since these sets are both finite and computable, ρ_{OI}^{cons} is locally finite.
(completeness)
Let C, D be two clauses s.t. $D <_{OI} C$ $(C, D \in \mathcal{L})$. In this case, there exist some substitutions σ_j, $j = 1, 2, \ldots, s$ s.t. $| \Delta_j(D,C) | = r$.
For a given $j \in \{1, 2, \ldots, s\}$, let us consider the literals in $\Delta_j(D, C)$. Then, we may write D as follows:

$$D = C.\sigma_j \cup \{l_1, l_2, \ldots, l_r\}, \text{ where } l_k.\underline{\sigma}_j^{-1} \in \Delta_j(D, C), \; k = 1, 2, \ldots, r.$$

We can build the following set of clauses:

$$\{F_h\}_{h=0,1,\ldots,r}, \text{ where } F_h = C.\sigma_j \cup \{l_1, l_2, \ldots, l_h\}, \text{ for } h = 0, 1, \ldots, r.$$

Note that: $F_0 = C.\sigma_j$ and $F_r = D$.
In order to demonstrate the completeness property, it is to be proven that:

$$\forall k = 0, 1, \ldots, r - 1 : F_{k+1} \in \rho_{OI}^{cons}(F_k).$$

For a given $k \in \{0, 1, \ldots, r-1\}$, let us consider $F_{k+1} = C.\sigma_j \cup \{l_1, l_2, \ldots, l_{k+1}\} = F_k \cup \{l_{k+1}\}$.
Let us suppose now, without loss of generality, that the database of the available positive examples is made up of the set $\{P_1, P_2, \ldots, P_n\}$ and that N_k is the negative example which calls for the downward refinement operator ρ_{OI}^{cons}.
If l_{k+1} is a positive literal in the body of F_{k+1}, then, by looking back at the definition of ρ_{OI}^{cons}, we note that we are able to build the sets P and S s.t. $l_{k+1} \in P - S$, and then $F_{k+1} = F_k \cup \{l_{k+1}\} \in \rho_{OI}^{cons}(F_k)$. In fact, the set P depends on the positive examples $\{P_1, P_2, \ldots, P_n\}$, and the set S depends on N_k, which can be chosen in such a way that $l_{k+1} \notin \Delta_m(N_k, F_k)$ for each substitution γ_m between N_k and F_k causing F_k to be inconsistent wrt N_k.
If l_{k+1} is a negative literal in the body of F_{k+1}, then by definition of ρ_{OI}^{cons}, we are able to build the set S_c, which in turn depends on N_k and F_k, in such a way that $l_{k+1} \in neg(\Delta_m(N_k, F_k))$ for each substitution γ_m above.   □

The ideality of the refinement operator ρ_{OI}^{cons} is owed to the peculiar structure of the search space when ordered by the relation $\leq_{OI}$. In the same search space ordered by θ-subsumption, an ideal refinement operator does not exist [21].

7 Application to Document Understanding

We implemented the operators described in Sections 5 and 6 in an incremental system, called INCR/H, in order to compare the performance of Datalog theories synthesized incrementally to those synthesized in batch mode. Experimental results obtained by running the learning system FOCL are available in [2].

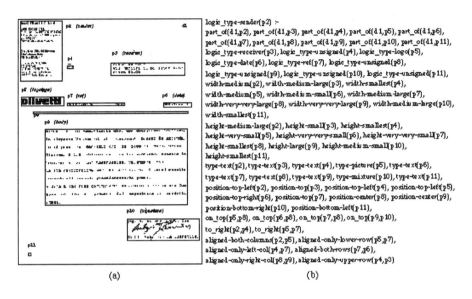

Fig. 1. (a) A single-page A4 Olivetti letter. (b) A positive example of *sender*

Several experiments were carried out in the area of *electronic document understanding*. For all the experiments, we considered a database of 30 single-page A4 documents (Olivetti letters), in each of which we labelled the layout components with the corresponding logical meaning (*logotype, signature, body, reference number, sender, date, receiver*) in order to obtain the clauses representing the examples. Each labelled object is a positive example for the component it is associated to and, at the same time, is a negative example for all the other components. Thus, each document generates a set of examples. A positive example of *sender*, generated by the document in Fig. 1a, is shown in Fig. 1b. An example of a Datalog theory made up of just one hypothesis for the concept *receiver* is:
$logic\_type - receiver(X)$:- $height - very - small(X), type - text(X)$.
$logic\_type - receiver(X)$:- $to\_right(Y, X), aligned - only - middle - column(Y, Z)$.
The experiments have been replicated 10 times, by randomly splitting the database into two subsets, namely a *learning* set (with size 20) and a *test* set (with size 10). In turn, the learning set has been subdivided into *training* set and *tuning* set, with size 5 and 15, respectively, and has been exploited in two distinct ways, according to the mode – batch or incremental – adopted to synthesize the Datalog theories. In the former case, this set has been entirely given to the batch system INDUBI/H [3] as its input. In the latter case, only the training set has been used by INDUBI/H in order to produce the set of hypotheses representing the first version of the theory; then, the tuning set has been exploited to correct incrementally both omission and commission errors, if any, through the refinement process described in Sections 5 and 6. The test set has been exploited to evaluate the error rate of the inferred theories on unclassified components.

	Learning set (batch) #pos+#neg	Training set (incr.) #pos+#neg	Tuning set #pos+ #neg	Test set #pos+ #neg
logotype	20+220	5+55	15+165	10+110
signature	19+221	4+56	15+165	10+110
body	20+220	5+55	15+165	10+110
ref	31+209	8+52	23+157	15+105
sender	23+217	6+54	17+163	12+108
date	24+216	6+54	18+162	12+108
receiver	24+216	6+54	18+162	12+108

Table 1. Sizes of the example sets in the experimentations concerning the problem of document understanding

Table 1 reports the information concerning the experimental setup, i.e. the mean number of positive and negative examples used by the different phases. Note that many documents generated two or more instances of the concept *ref*, thus it has 31 positive examples rather than 20 (the number of documents used for the learning set). Fig. 2 shows the results of the comparison between the theory synthesized in batch mode and that obtained incrementally, as concerns the error rate on the test set and the computational time taken by the system to produce the theories. Specifically, the *batch time* refers to the training set for the batch mode, while the *incremental time* is computed as the sum of the computational time concerning the training set for the incremental mode plus the time concerning the tuning set. Values concerning the error rate are percentages, while those concerning the time are expressed in seconds. All the reported figures refer to the average on the ten replications. Table 2 illustrates the results of two statistical methods exploited to evaluate the significance of the observed differences as to the error rate and time for each type of logical label, namely the paired t test (parametric) and the Wilcoxon test (non parametric). For a thorough explanation of the two statistical tests, refer to [12]. The t test has been performed as two-sided test at a 0.01 level of significance, while the Wilcoxon test both at 0.05 and at 0.01 level. Each entry in the table contains the t value and the corresponding significance value for the t test, the W value and the corresponding critical value, along with the sample sizes, for the Wilcoxon test.

It is well-known that the t test requires that the population data be normally distributed, when used with small sample sizes (less than 30). Conversely, the Wilcoxon test does not make any assumption on the distribution of the population data. In our setting, the sample size is 10, i.e. the number of replications, thus the t test might seem to be unsuitable. However, we performed preventively a normality test in order to establish whether the population data are normally distributed. Such a test allows us to state that the population is normally distributed at a 0.01 level of significance.

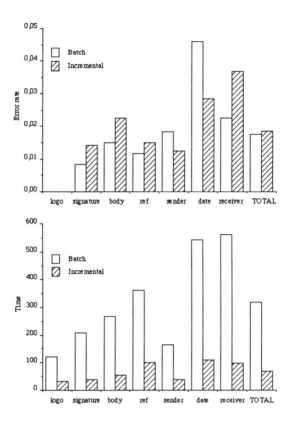

Fig. 2. Experimental results obtained with INCR/H

Fig. 2 shows that the batch theories outperform the incremental ones for all the classes, with the exception of *sender* and *date*, as regards the error rate; on the contrary, as to the computational times the incremental system outperforms the batch one in all cases. However, the t test reveals no statistically significant difference between the error rates (clear boxes in Table 2), but a great difference in the case of computational time (shaded boxes). According to the Wilcoxon test the results are the same.

8   Conclusions and Future Work

In this paper, we presented a logic framework for the incremental inductive synthesis of Datalog theories. It allows us to define algorithms for abstract diagnosis and debugging of incorrect theories, which strongly rely on effective and efficient (*ideal*) refinement operators. These algorithms have been implemented in a new version of an incremental system for inductive synthesis of Datalog theories, called INCR/H, whose performance has been successfully tested on the real-world problem of electronic document understanding.

Document understanding	t test				Wilcoxon test								
	batch vs. incremental				batch vs. incremental								
	Error rate		Time		Error rate				Time				
	t value	sign. value	t value	sign. value	W value	crit. value =0.05	crit. value =0.01	sample size	W value	crit. value =0.05	crit. value =0.01	sample size
logo	-	-	33.242	.0001	-	-	-	10	55	39	45	10
signature	1.3	.2259	13.322	.0001	16	24	28	7	55	39	45	10
body	1.353	.2091	9.948	.0001	22	33	39	9	55	39	45	10
ref	.318	.7577	8.297	.0001	2	24	28	7	55	39	45	10
sender	2.333	.0445	8.002	.0001	-22	24	28	7	55	39	45	10
date	-1.849	.0975	9.879	.0001	-20	24	28	7	55	39	45	10
receiver	1.769	.1108	14.141	.0001	15	19	21	6	55	39	45	10

Table 2. Statistical results

Future work will aim at integrating INCR/H in the *learning server* component of a prototypical intelligent digital library service, called IDL. In IDL, document classification and understanding play a key role in the process of information capture and semantic indexing of the stored documents [19].

Another extension of INCR/H concerns the possibility of dealing with stratified theories (with recursion).

References

1. Ceri, S., Gottlob, G., and Tanca, L.: Logic Programming and Databases. Springer-Verlag, Berlin Heidelberg New York (1990)
2. Esposito, F., Malerba, D., and Semeraro, G.: Automated Acquisition of Rules for Document Understanding. Proceedings of the 2nd International Conference on Document Analysis and Recognition ICDAR93. IEEE Computer Society Press, Los Alamitos, CA (1993) 650-654
3. Esposito, F., Malerba, D., and Semeraro, G.: Multistrategy Learning for Document Recognition. Applied Artificial Intelligence: An Int. J. **8** (1994) 33-84
4. Esposito, F., Malerba, D., Semeraro, G., Brunk, C., and Pazzani, M.: Traps and Pitfalls when Learning Logical Definitions from Relations. In: Ras, Z.W., Zemankova, M. (eds.): Methodologies for Intelligent Systems. Lecture Notes in Artificial Intelligence, Vol. 869. Springer-Verlag, Berlin Heidelberg New York (1994) 376-385
5. Esposito, F., Laterza, A., Malerba, D., and Semeraro, G.: Locally Finite, Proper and Complete Operators for Refining Datalog Programs. In: Ras, Z.W., Michalewicz, M. (eds.): Foundations of Intelligent Systems. Lecture Notes in Artificial Intelligence, Vol. 1079. Springer-Verlag, Berlin Heidelberg New York (1996) 468-478
6. Hayes-Roth, F., and McDermott, J.: Knowledge acquisition from structural descriptions. Proceed. of the 5th International Joint Conference on AI. Cambridge, MA (1977) 356-362

7. Helft, N.: Inductive Generalization: A Logical Framework. In: Bratko, I., Lavrac, N. (eds.): Progress in Machine Learning. Sigma Press, Wilmslow (1987) 149-157

8. Jaffar, J., and Maher, M.J.: Constraint Logic Programming: a Survey. J. Logic Programming **19** (1994) 503-581

9. Kanellakis, P.C.: Elements of Relational Database Theory. In: Van Leeuwen, J. (ed.): Handbook of Theoretical Computer Science, Volume B, Formal Models and Semantics. Elsevier Science Publishers (1990) 1073-1156

10. Komorowski, J., and Trcek, S.: Towards Refinement of Definite Logic Programs. In: Ras, Z.W., Zemankova, M. (eds.): Methodologies for Intelligent Systems. Lecture Notes in Artificial Intelligence, Vol. 869. Springer-Verlag, Berlin Heidelberg New York (1994) 315-325

11. Lloyd, J.W.: Foundations of Logic Programming. 2nd edn. Springer-Verlag, Berlin Heidelberg New York (1987)

12. Orkin, M., and Drogin, R.: Vital Statistics. McGraw-Hill, New York (1990)

13. Plotkin, G.D.: A Note on Inductive Generalization. In: Meltzer, B., Michie, D. (eds.): Machine Intelligence 5. Edinburgh University Press (1970) 153-163

14. Plotkin, G.D.: Building-in Equational Theories. In: Meltzer, B., Michie, D. (eds.): Machine Intelligence 7. Edinburgh University Press (1972) 73-90

15. Reiter, R.: Equality and domain closure in first order databases. J. ACM **27** (1980) 235-249

16. Semeraro, G., Esposito, F., Malerba, D., Brunk, C., and Pazzani, M.: Avoiding Non-Termination when Learning Logic Programs: A Case Study with FOIL and FOCL. In: Fribourg, L., Turini, F. (eds.): Logic Program Synthesis and Transformation - Meta-Programming in Logic. Lecture Notes in Computer Science, Vol. 883. Springer-Verlag, Berlin Heidelberg New York (1994) 183-198

17. Semeraro, G., Esposito, F., Fanizzi, N., and Malerba, D.: Revision of Logical Theories. In: Gori, M., Soda, G. (eds.): Topics in Artificial Intelligence. Lecture Notes in Artificial Intelligence, Vol. 992. Springer-Verlag, Berlin Heidelberg New York (1995) 365-376

18. Semeraro, G., Esposito, F., and Malerba, D.: Ideal Refinement of Datalog Programs. In: Proietti, M. (ed.): Logic Program Synthesis and Transformation. Lecture Notes in Computer Science, Vol. 1048. Springer-Verlag, Berlin Heidelberg New York (1996) 120-136

19. Semeraro, G., Esposito, F., Malerba, D., Fanizzi, N., and Ferilli, S.: Machine Learning + On-line Libraries = IDL. In: Peters, C., Thanos, C. (eds.): Research and Advanced Technology for Digital Libraries. Lecture Notes in Computer Science, Vol. 1324. Springer-Verlag, Berlin Heidelberg New York (1997) 195-214

20. van der Laag, P.R.J., and Nienhuys-Cheng, S.-H.: A Note on Ideal Refinement Operators in Inductive Logic Programming. In: Wrobel, S. (ed.): Proceedings of the Fourth International Workshop on Inductive Logic Programming ILP-94. GMD-Studien Nr. 237 (1994) 247-260

21. van der Laag, P.R.J., and Nienhuys-Cheng, S.-H.: Existence and Nonexistence of Complete Refinement Operators. In: Bergadano, F., De Raedt, L. (eds.): Machine Learning: ECML-94 - Proceedings of the European Conference on Machine Learning. Lecture Notes in Artificial Intelligence, Vol. 784. Springer-Verlag, Berlin Heidelberg New York (1994) 307-322

22. van der Laag, P.R.J.: An Analysis of Refinement Operators in Inductive Logic Programming. Ph.D. dissertation, Tinbergen Institute Research Series (1995)

23. VanLehn, K.: Efficient Specialization of Relational Concepts. Machine Learning **4** (1989) 99-106

24. Wrobel, S.: On the proper definition of minimality in specialization and theory revision. In: Brazdil, P.B. (ed.): Machine Learning: ECML-93 - Proceedings of the European Conference on Machine Learning. Lecture Notes in Artificial Intelligence, Vol. 667. Springer-Verlag, Berlin Heidelberg New York (1993) 65-82
25. Wrobel, S.: Concept Formation and Knowledge Revision. Kluwer Academic Publishers, Dordrecht Boston London (1994)

To Parse or Not To Parse

Wim Vanhoof * and Bern Martens **

Department of Computer Science, Katholieke Universiteit Leuven,
Celestijnenlaan 200A, B-3001, Heverlee, Belgium.
{wimvh,bern}@cs.kuleuven.ac.be

Abstract. In this paper, we reconsider the problem of specialising the
vanilla meta interpreter through fully automatic and completely general
partial deduction techniques. In particular, we study how the homeomorphic embedding relation guides specialisation of the interpreter. We
focus on the so-called *parsing* problem, i.e. removing all parsing overhead
from the program, and demonstrate that further refinements in the control of general partial deduction are necessary to properly deal with it. In
particular, we modify *local* control on the basis of information imported
from the *global* level. The resulting control strategy, while remaining fully
general, leads to excellent specialisation of vanilla like meta programs.
Parsing is always specialised, but – appropriately, as we will show – not
always completely removed. As a concrete application, we subject an extended vanilla meta interpreter capable of dealing with compositions of
programs to our techniques, showing we equal or surpass results obtained
through a more ad hoc approach.

1 Introduction

Writing meta interpreters is a well-known technique to enhance the expressive
power of logic programs (see e.g. [32, 1, 12]). However, the resulting interpretation overhead considerably slows down program execution [2].

A natural approach to solving this efficiency problem consists in specialising
the interpreter with respect to a given object program [9, 33, 28], thus removing
the overhead by performing all interpretation of the object program (in essence
parsing the object program) during specialisation. Fully achieving the latter goal
however, turns out to be a non trivial task [15, 27, 2, 23]. Satisfying results could
often only be obtained at the cost of using not fully automatic and/or ad hoc
techniques [16]. In a recent paper [5], Brogi and Contiero address specialisation
of a non-ground *vanilla*-like meta interpreter [31, 13, 32, 24], extended in order to
deal with program compositions [6, 7, 3, 5]. Again, the interpretion overhead is
removed by an ad hoc specialiser, specifically constructed to handle the extended
interpreter.

---

* Supported by a specialisation grant of the Flemish Institute for the Promotion of
Scientific-Technological Research in Industry (IWT), Belgium.
** Postdoctoral Fellow of the K.U.Leuven Research Council, Belgium. Also partially
supported by the Belgian GOA "Non-Standard Applications of Abstract Interpretation".

Norbert E. Fuchs (Ed.): LOPSTR'97, LNCS 1463, pp. 322–342, 1998.
© Springer-Verlag Berlin Heidelberg 1998

On the other hand, research on partial deduction of logic programs meanwhile resulted in *fully automatic and completely general* specialisation techniques, not requiring any specific a priori knowledge about the kind of programs to be specialised, nor any help from the programmer (e.g. [10, 8, 18]).

The key idea in automatic (on-line) partial deduction consists of building a number of different SLD-trees that together cover the complete computation of an atomic[1] goal G in a program P: To that extent, the control of on-line partial deduction is conceptually divided into two levels [10, 26]: the first one, often referred to as the *local* control level, deals with constructing a finite, possibly incomplete SLD-tree for a certain atom. Specialised clauses are produced from such a tree, one per branch, taking the root as head and the leaves as body. The *global* control level, on the other hand, concerns the set of atoms for which an SLD-tree is built. It decides on the amount of polyvariance: how many different specialised versions will be produced for a given predicate definition? The global set must be kept finite, precise and correct (i.e. satisfying the conditions in [22]).

In this paper, we pinpoint a remaining shortcoming of this control scheme when specialising vanilla like meta interpreters. We show that the problem can be solved by modifying the *local* control level such that it takes information from the *global* level into account, and we present a concrete refinement of the local control that is capable of achieving excellent results when specialising this sort of interpreters.

The outline of the paper is as follows. In Section 2, we recapitulate the crucial aspects of the automatic partial deduction strategy we use. Section 3 considers specialisation of the vanilla meta interpreter and constitutes the main body of this paper. Subsequently, in Section 4, specialisation of the program composition interpreter in [5] is addressed. We conclude with a discussion of our results and the ensuing plans for further research in Section 5. Throughout this paper, we only consider definite logic programs.

2   Automatic Partial Deduction

In this section, we briefly describe the essential ingredients of the partial deduction method we use in this paper. Experiments were conducted using the ECCE automatic partial deduction system [21]. Further details on correctness and control of (on-line) partial deduction can be found in [22] and e.g. [10, 8, 19] respectively.

2.1   Local Control

Local control essentially consists of an unfolding rule, through which an SLD-tree is built for a certain atom. As a starting point for local control, we use the one proposed in Section 4.2 of [11], adapted from [30, 18]. The following definitions are taken from [11].

---

[1] G can be supposed atomic without loss of generality: If $G = \leftarrow A_1, \ldots, A_n$, one enhances the program with a clause $A \leftarrow A_1, \ldots, A_n$.

Definition 1. Given an SLD-tree τ. Let $G = \leftarrow A_1 \wedge \ldots \wedge A_n$ be a goal in τ, A_m the selected atom in G, $A \leftarrow A'_1 \wedge \ldots \wedge A'_k$ a clause of P such that θ is an mgu of A_m and A. Then in $\leftarrow (A_1 \wedge \ldots \wedge A'_1 \wedge \ldots \wedge A'_k \wedge \ldots \wedge A_n)\theta$, for each $i \in \{1, \ldots, k\}$, $A'_i\theta$ *descends from* A_m, and for each $i \in \{1, \ldots, n\}\backslash\{m\}$, $A_i\theta$ descends from A_i. If A' descends from A, and A'' descends from A', then A'' also descends from A, i.e. the relation is transitive.

We define the *homeomorphic embedding relation* $\trianglelefteq$ as follows. As usual, $e_1 \prec e_2$ denotes that e_2 is a strict instance of e_1.

Definition 2. Let X, Y range over variables, f over functors, and p over predicates. Define $\trianglelefteq$ on terms and atoms:

$$X \trianglelefteq Y$$
$$s \trianglelefteq f(t_1, \ldots, t_n) \qquad \Leftarrow s \trianglelefteq t_i \text{ for some } i$$
$$f(s_1, \ldots, s_n) \trianglelefteq f(t_1, \ldots, t_n) \Leftarrow s_i \trianglelefteq t_i \text{ for all } i$$
$$p(s_1, \ldots, s_n) \trianglelefteq p(t_1, \ldots, t_n) \Leftarrow s_i \trianglelefteq t_i \text{ for all } i \text{ and } p(t_1, \ldots, t_n) \not\prec p(s_1, \ldots, s_n)$$

For atoms A,B: $A \triangleleft B$ iff $A \trianglelefteq B$ and $A \not\approx B$ (where $A \approx B$ denotes that A and B are variants). The extra condition in the fourth line was first introduced in [18] (Definition 15). It enables a more refined treatment of variables: Since $p(X, Y) \prec p(X, X)$, $p(X, X) \not\trianglelefteq p(X, Y)$ whereas $p(X, Y) \trianglelefteq p(X, X)$ (since obviously $p(X, Y)$ is *not* a (strict) instance of $p(X, X)$: $p(X, X) \not\prec p(X, Y)$).

Definition 3. An atom A in a goal at the leaf of an SLD-tree is *selectable* unless it descends from a selected atom A', with $A' \trianglelefteq A$.

Definition 4. The *unfolding rule* $U_{\trianglelefteq}$ unfolds the left-most selectable atom in each goal G of the SLD-tree under construction. If no atom is selectable, no further unfolding is performed.

The intuition behind $U_{\trianglelefteq}$ is that every atom in a goal of the SLD-tree under construction will be unfolded (in left to right order), unless it descends from an atom which it embeds. The use of the $\trianglelefteq$-relation guarantees termination [11, 19]. Independently of whether it is selectable according to definition 3, often we will denote the selected atom (under any unfolding rule) in a goal G by $s(G)$, leaving the unfolding rule implicit. For a program P and a goal G, $\tau_U(P, G)$ will denote the SLD-tree built by unfolding rule U for G in P, often simply written as $\tau_U(G)$ or τ_G. Given an SLD-tree τ, $AL(\tau)$ denotes the set of atoms in its leaves.

2.2   Global Control

At the global level, we start out with the atom in the goal G. For that atom, an SLD-tree is constructed according to $U_{\trianglelefteq}$. To ensure correctness [22] while producing a maximally precise partial deduction, for atoms appearing in the leaf of a constructed SLD-tree, a fresh such tree needs to be built when there is not yet one with (a variant of) the given atom as its root. In this way, a set of partially deduced atoms and associated SLD-trees is produced. Without further measures, this set will often expand infinitely. Therefore, it is necessary to apply appropriate generalisations, replacing two or more atoms by their most specific generalisation (msg). This process can be made maximally precise through organising the set in a global tree structure, denoted by $\mathcal{G}(P, G)$. Before explaining how exactly this tree is constructed, we need the following notions which we here only describe informally:

- A *characteristic tree* $\overline{\tau}$ is an abstraction of an SLD-tree τ, that registers which atoms have been selected for unfolding and which clauses were used for resolution when building τ.
- A *characteristic atom* is a couple $(A, \overline{\tau}_A)$ consisting of an atom A and the characteristic tree of its associated SLD-tree τ_A.

Next, we extend the embedding relation $\trianglelefteq$ to characteristic atoms. This can be achieved by defining a term representation of a characteristic tree and subsequently using $\trianglelefteq$ with this term representation [18]: To that extent, a total mapping, denoted by $\lceil . \rceil$ from characteristic trees to terms (expressible in some finite alphabet) can be defined such that $\lceil . \rceil$ is strictly monotonic and $msg(\overline{\tau}_{A_1}, \overline{\tau}_{A_2})$ is defined when $\lceil \overline{\tau}_{A_1} \rceil \trianglelefteq \lceil \overline{\tau}_{A_2} \rceil$. Informally, $\lceil \overline{\tau}_{A_1} \rceil \trianglelefteq \lceil \overline{\tau}_{A_2} \rceil$ means that $\overline{\tau}_{A_1}$ can be obtained from $\overline{\tau}_{A_2}$ by "wiping out" some sub-branches of $\overline{\tau}_{A_2}$ and $msg(\overline{\tau}_{A_1}, \overline{\tau}_{A_2})$ is the common initial subtree of $\overline{\tau}_{A_1}$ and $\overline{\tau}_{A_2}$. For more precise definitions of the above concepts, see [20, 19].

Definition 5. *Let* $(A_1, \overline{\tau}_{A_1})$, $(A_2, \overline{\tau}_{A_2})$ *be characteristic atoms. We say that* $(A_2, \overline{\tau}_{A_2})$ *embeds* $(A_1, \overline{\tau}_{A_1})$, *if and only if* $A_1 \trianglelefteq A_2$ *and* $\lceil \overline{\tau}_{A_1} \rceil \trianglelefteq \lceil \overline{\tau}_{A_2} \rceil$.

Initially, $\mathcal{G}(P, G)$ consists of one node: the root node G. Now, for an atom A in a leaf node of $\mathcal{G}(P, G)$, an SLD-tree τ_A is built according to the specific local control strategy used. For each atom $B \in AL(\tau_A)$, a new node in $\mathcal{G}(P, G)$ is created as a child of the node A unless there is already a variant of B present in the part of $\mathcal{G}(P, G)$ constructed so far. However, to ensure termination, if B has an ancestor B' in $\mathcal{G}(P, G)$ such that $(B, \overline{\tau}_B)$ embeds $(B', \overline{\tau}_{B'})$, the subtree with root B' in $\mathcal{G}(P, G)$ is replaced by the single node $(msg(B', B), msg(\overline{\tau}_{B'}, \overline{\tau}_B))$.[2]

By using embedding on characteristic atoms, the decision when to generalise is based not only on the syntactic structure (the atoms), but also on their specialisation behaviour (the characteristic trees), which ensures a much better control of polyvariance [20, 18, 19].

Below, we will often refer to a node G in a global tree while we actually intend to name the atom in such a node. The intention will always be clear from the context, and, as a result, notation will be more simple.

---

[2] Actually, instead of just inserting the new node in the tree, one reiterates the process, first checking for variants and embedded ancestors.

2.3   Code Generation

Consider a program P, a goal G and the global tree $\mathcal{G}(P, G)$ as a result of the partial deduction of P w.r.t. G. Then consider a node $G_0 \in \mathcal{G}(P, G)$ with the associated SLD-tree τ_{G_0}. For each leaf L of τ_{G_0}, consisting of the atoms $A_1, \ldots, A_n$ a resultant clause is generated having the following form: $G_0\theta \leftarrow A_1, \ldots, A_n$ where θ is the substitution built along the branch $G_0 \ldots \leftarrow A_1, \ldots A_n$.

With each node $G_0 \in \mathcal{G}(P, G)$ a renaming $p_{G_0}(\overline{X})$ is associated, where p_{G_0} is a unique predicate name, and $\overline{X}$ is the vector of free variables of G_0. Then each resultant clause C, defined as $G_0\theta \leftarrow A_1, \ldots, A_n$ is renamed to $p_{G_0}\theta \leftarrow p_{G_1}\phi_1, \ldots, p_{G_n}\phi_n$ where $\forall i \in \{1 \ldots n\}$: $A_i \approx G_i\phi_i$ for a substitution ϕ_i such that $\nexists G' \in \mathcal{G}(P, G) : A_i \approx G'\phi'$ for a substitution ϕ' and $G_i \prec G'$.

With $PD(P, G)$ we denote the collection of renamed resultant clauses constituting the final partial deduction of P w.r.t. G using the techniques as introduced above.

3   Behaviour of $U_\lhd$ when Unfolding Meta Interpreters

In this section, we investigate automatic partial deduction of non-ground, vanilla meta programs, using the general technique presented in Section 2. Let us first repeat the definition of the well-known vanilla meta interpreter [31, 13, 32, 24].

Definition 6. *The* vanilla meta interpreter V:
   (1) $solve(true)$.
   (2) $solve((A, B)) \leftarrow solve(A), solve(B)$.
   (3) $solve(H) \leftarrow pclause(H, B), solve(B)$.

As usual, an object program will be represented as a database of *pclause*-facts. Omitting the formal definition, we just include an example.

Example 1. Consider as object program P, *reverse* with an accumulating parameter, where a type check on the accumulator is added [18], and its meta representation $C(P)$.

$reverse(L, R) \leftarrow rev(L, [], R)$.
$rev([], L, L)$. $ls([])$.
$rev([X|X_s], L, R) \leftarrow ls(L), rev(X_s, [X|L], R)$. $ls([X|X_s]) \leftarrow ls(X_s)$.

$pclause(reverse(L, R), rev(L, [], R))$.
$pclause(rev([], L, L), true)$.
$pclause(rev([X|X_s], L, R), (ls(L), rev(X_s, [X|L], R)))$.
$pclause(ls([]), true)$.
$pclause(ls([X|X_s]), ls(X_s))$.

The combination of the interpreter, V, and the "encoded" object program, $C(P)$, will be denoted by V_P.

3.1   Removing Interpretation Overhead

For an object program P, we call *meta structure* all program structure in V_P that can never appear in arguments in P.[3] In concrete terms, this means the constant *true*, the functor , /2, and all functors representing object level predicates.

A crucial aspect in the specialisation of meta interpreters is removing the handling of meta structure from the program, by performing all parsing operations (the operations that explicitly deal with this structure) at specialisation time. The problem of achieving this is often referred to as the *parsing problem* [16, 23].

Definition 7. *For any program P and goal G, the residual program, $PD(V_P, G)$ is called* meta structure free *if for each renamed resultant clause*

$$p_{G_0}\theta \leftarrow p_{G_1}\phi_1, \ldots, p_{G_n}\phi_n \in PD(V_P, G)$$

$\theta, \phi_1, \ldots, \phi_n$ *contains no meta structure.*

We will show that by extending our unfolding rule, it can be proven that for any program P and goal $G = \leftarrow solve(p(\overline{X}))$ where p denotes a predicate in P and $\overline{X}$ a sufficient number of distinct variables filling up its argument positions, $PD(V_P, G)$ is meta structure free.[4]

The following results are fairly obvious:

Proposition 1. *For any V_P, atoms with pclause as predicate are always unfolded by $U_{\unlhd}$.*

Corollary 1. *For any P and G, $\mathcal{G}(V_P, G)$ contains only solve atoms.*

Obviously, in case no generalisations occur while constructing $\mathcal{G}(V_P, G)$, for all $G_0 \in \mathcal{G}(V_P, G)$ and for all $A \in AL(\tau_{G_0})$ there exists a $G' \in \mathcal{G}(V_P, G)$ such that $A \approx G'$. Since the same holds for the atom in G, and $solve(X)$ will not appear in any SLD-tree, code generation will produce a meta structure free residual program.

Moreover, suppose $G_1, G_2 \in \mathcal{G}(P, G)$ are generalised such that $G_1 = msg(G_1, G_2)\theta_1$, $G_2 = msg(G_1, G_2)\theta_2$ and neither θ_1 nor θ_2 contains meta structure. Since during code generation the only atoms A that are mapped on $msg(G_1, G_2)$ are variants of G_1, G_2 or their msg, the residual program will again be meta structure free. We illustrate this with the partial deduction of Example 1.

Example 2. P and $C(P)$ are as in Example 1. $PD(V_P, solve(reverse(L, R)))$ then looks as follows:

---

[3]   For more formal details, see [24].

[4]   If $G = \leftarrow solve(X)$, the definition of the predicate, created from this root, will contain meta structure, in order to parse the top level goal. Although we do not consider this top level parsing to be a problem, we restrict the form of G in order to simplify the formulation of the theory and shorten the examples. Note however, that this restriction does not diminish the generality of our technique.

$d_1([],[]) \leftarrow$
$d_1([X_1|X_2], X_3) \leftarrow d_2([], X_2, X_1, X_3).$
$d_2([],[], X_1, [X_1]) \leftarrow$
$d_2([], [X_1|X_2], X_3, X_4) \leftarrow d_2([X_3], X_2, X_1, X_4).$
$d_2([X_1|X_2], [], X_3, [X_3, X_1|X_2]) \leftarrow d_3(X_2).$
$d_2([X_1|X_2], [X_3|X_4], X_5, X_6) \leftarrow d_3(X_2), d_2([X_5, X_1|X_2], X_4, X_3, X_6).$

$d_3([]) \leftarrow$
$d_3([X_1|X_2]) \leftarrow d_3(X_2).$

3.2 In Case Generalisations Take Place

$U_\lhd$ (and similar unfolding rules [25]) performs well when predicate arguments
either shrink or grow throughout the unfolding process. Unfolding is allowed as
long as information is consumed and appropriately halted when such is no longer
the case.

Problems however arise for predicates handling *fluctuating* structure(s): structures that can grow, but also shrink between successive recursive calls. Most
natural logic programs do not contain such predicates, but meta interpreters do.
This is one of the main reasons why it is notoriously difficult to handle them
well in automatic, general partial deduction.

Consider a clause of the following form:
$$p([X|X_s], A) \leftarrow a(X), p(X_s, [X|A])$$
If somewhere during the process, $solve(p(X, A))$ in the global tree gives rise to
$solve((a(X'), p(X_s, [X'|A])))$, homeomorphic embedding will be detected between the two atoms. We obtain $solve(X)$ after generalisation of $solve(p(X, A))$
and $solve((a(X'), p(X_s, [X'|A])))$. The problem is that the p-functor and all
structure surrounding the embedded term are lost in the generalisation. Since
for this generalised atom, a new SLD-tree will be built, this would result in a
residual predicate handling (parsing) this meta structure.

Now, if $solve((a(X'), p(X_s, [X'|A])))$ was unfolded (locally) by $U_\lhd$ one step
further, the atoms $solve(a(X'))$ and $solve(p(X_s, [X'|A]))$ would be brought onto
the global level, and the generalisation would occur between $solve(p(X, A))$ and
$solve(p(X_s, [X'|A]))$, leading to $solve(p(Y, Z))$ and leaving $solve(a(X'))$ as it
is. In this case, a generalisation still occurs, but less structure (and no meta
structure) is lost by it. So, when unfolding the call $solve((a(X'), p(X_s, [X'|A])))$
(the clause unifying with it only performs parsing: it splits the conjunction), the
SLD-tree ends in a leaf of which the atoms are better suited to be put on the
global level from a viewpoint of creating a meta-structure free residual program.

In [16], it was noticed that *always* unfolding such parsing calls seems a good
idea, although no indication was given how to incorporate this idea in a general,
automatic partial deduction technique. In subsection 3.3, we argue that, if we
aim at obtaining a high degree of specialisation, it is often a better idea *not*
to unfold parsing calls, at the cost of obtaining what we will call *specialised*
parsing. We will therefore aim at further unfolding parsing calls only if they lead
to generalisation. To that end, we *modify our unfolding rule such that it takes
global information into account* and tries to avoid generalisation (or minimise
the structure lost by it) when this can be safely achieved through some extra
unfolding.

First, we introduce an unfolding rule that will unfold an atomic goal $G =\leftarrow A_G$ only if it can deterministically be unfolded into a set of atoms $\mathcal{A}$ such that for every atom $A \in \mathcal{A} : A \lhd A_G$. If this is the case, it means that an atom (predicate call) can be unfolded into several new calls to the same predicate, each with less structure in them.

Definition 8. *The unfolding rule U_{ext} is applied to an atomic goal G_0 as follows: If through (left-to-right) deterministic[5] unfolding of G_0, a derivation $G_0 \ldots G_n$ can be constructed such that $\not\exists i,j \in \{0 \ldots n\}, i < j: s(G_j)$ descends from $s(G_i)$, $s(G_i) \unlhd s(G_j)$ and $G_n =\leftarrow A_1, \ldots, A_m$ where $\forall i \in \{1 \ldots m\}: A_i \lhd G_0$, then $U_{ext}(G_0) = G_0 \ldots G_n$, where G_n is the first such goal found, else $U_{ext}(G_0) = G_0$.*

We will try to take fluctuating structure into account by merging $U_\lhd$ and U_{ext}: an SLD-tree, τ, is built as usual, using $U_\unlhd$, but when an atom $A \in \overline{AL}(\tau)$ would cause a generalisation if introduced onto the global level and if $U_{ext}(A) \neq A$, τ is extended with the path $U_{ext}(A)$.

Before presenting our extended unfolding rule, $U_\unlhd^+$, we introduce some extra notation: $V_{ext}(G_0)$ denotes the set of variables of G_0, denoted by $Vars(G_0)$, that are instantiated by U_{ext} in case $U_{ext}(G_0) \neq G_0$.

Algorithm
Input: a program P, goal G, a global tree $\mathcal{G}(P,G)$ with A a leaf of $\mathcal{G}(P,G)$.
Output: SLD-tree $\tau_{U_\unlhd^+}(A)$.
Init: $i \leftarrow 0$, $\tau_0 \leftarrow \emptyset$, $\tau_1 \leftarrow \tau_{U_\unlhd}(A)$, Let $Anc(A)$ be the ancestors of A
   (A included) in $\mathcal{G}(P,G)$.
while $\tau_{i+1} \neq \tau_i$ **do**
   $i \leftarrow i+1$
   If $\exists$ a leaf $L =\leftarrow C,B,C'$ of τ_i with B an atom and C, C' (possibly empty)
      conjunctions of atoms such that $\exists B' \in Anc(A)$ **where**
      $B' \unlhd B$, $U_{ext}(B) \neq B$ **and** $V_{ext}(B) \cap (Vars(C) \cup Vars(C')) = \emptyset$.[6] (*)
   then $\tau_{i+1} \leftarrow \tau_i \uplus_L U_{ext}(B)$
   else $\tau_{i+1} \leftarrow \tau_i$
end while
$\tau_{U_\unlhd^+}(A) \leftarrow \tau_i$
where $\tau(A) \uplus_L \leftarrow G_0 \ldots \leftarrow G_n$ is defined as extending the derivation
$$\leftarrow A \ldots \leftarrow L =\leftarrow C, G_0, C' \text{ in } \tau(A) \text{ into}$$
$$\leftarrow A \ldots \leftarrow L =\leftarrow C, G_0, C' \ \ldots \ \leftarrow C, G_n, C'.$$

Theorem 1. *The algorithm terminates and $\tau_{U_\unlhd^+}(A)$ is an SLD-tree for A.*

Now, we can formulate an important result:

Theorem 2. *For any program P, goal $G =\leftarrow solve(p(\overline{X}))$ with p a predicate in P, using the global control techniques described in Section 2 and the enhanced unfolding rule $U_\unlhd^+$, $PD(V_P, G)$ is meta structure free.*

---

[5] using a look-ahead

[6] This condition is necessary for the present proof of Theorem 1 (see Appendix A). We are currently investigating to what extent it can be relaxed.

3.3 Specialised Parsing

Opposite to observations in [16], where it is argued that (parsing) calls should always be unfolded, $U_\lhd$ as well as $U_\lhd^+$ will often stop unfolding at such calls: $solve(C)$ where C is a meta representation of an object level conjunction. During code generation, a new predicate will be made from $\tau_{solve(C)}$, carrying all the (object) information of the conjunction. Consider the following example:

Example 3. P: $p([]) \leftarrow$
$\qquad p([X|X_s]) \leftarrow q(X), p(X_s).$ $\qquad\qquad\qquad q(X) \leftarrow q(X).$
$\quad$ Figure 1 shows the most interesting branches of the SLD-trees generated during derivation of $PD(V_P, solve(p(X)))$. If code is generated, by renaming $G1$

$$
\begin{array}{ll}
G1: \Leftarrow solve(p(X)) & G2: \Leftarrow solve((q(X), p(Xs))) \\
\quad | \ X=[X1|Xs1] & \quad | \\
\Leftarrow solve((q(X1),p(Xs1))) & \Leftarrow solve(q(X)), solve(p(Xs)) \\
& \quad | \\
& \Leftarrow solve(q(X)), solve(p(Xs)) \\
& \quad | \ Xs=[X2|Xs2] \\
& \Leftarrow solve(q(X)), solve((q(X2),p(Xs2)))
\end{array}
$$

Fig. 1. Branches of the first two SLD-trees constructed during generation of $PD(V_P, solve(p(X)))$

to d_1, $G2$ to d_2 and d_3 is the specialised predicate for $solve(q(X))$, we get the following program:

$d_1([]) \leftarrow$ $\qquad\qquad\qquad\qquad d_2(X, []) \leftarrow d_3(X).$
$d_1([X|X_s]) \leftarrow d_2(X, X_s).$ $\qquad\quad d_2(X, [Y|Y_s]) \leftarrow d_3(X), d_2(Y, Y_s).$
$d_3(X) \leftarrow d_3(X).$

$\quad$ Note how d_2 carries out "specialised", i.e. meta structure-less, parsing. If we unfold $G1$ one step further, using V's parsing clause (2), we get the following program (renaming stays the same, although we have no predicate d_2 now).

$d_1([]) \leftarrow$ $\qquad\qquad\qquad\qquad d_3(X) \leftarrow d_3(X)$
$d_1([X|X_s]) \leftarrow d_3(X), d_1(X_s)$

$\quad$ This gives an indication that always unfolding parsing calls might be necessary to obtain a program that is fully equivalent to the original object program. On the other hand, if we aim at obtaining a large degree of specialisation, it might be worthwhile to stop unfolding at a parsing call, especially when information propagation in the atoms of the object conjunction is involved. Consider the following program P:

Example 4. $a(mammal) \leftarrow$ $\qquad\qquad\qquad b(cat, mammal) \leftarrow$
$\qquad\qquad a(X) \leftarrow b(X, Y), a(Y).$ $\qquad\quad b(dog, mammal) \leftarrow$
$\qquad\qquad p([X|X_s]) \leftarrow a(X), p(X_s)$ $\qquad\quad b(eagle, bird) \leftarrow$

Using $U_\lhd^+$, partial deduction of $solve(p(X))$ returns the following program P_1:

$d_1([X|X_s]) \leftarrow d_2(X), d_1(X_s).$
$d_2(mammal) \leftarrow \qquad\qquad d_2(cat) \leftarrow \qquad\qquad d_2(dog) \leftarrow$

which is considerably more specialised than P. Always unfolding the parsing calls during specialisation of V_P, on the other hand, would yield a program essentially equal to P. However, if V_P is specialised using $U_\lhd$ without the extension U_{ext}, due to a generalisation, a less specialised program is obtained.

$d_1(p([X|X_s]) \leftarrow d_3(X, X_s) \qquad\qquad d_2(cat) \leftarrow$
$d_1(a(X)) \leftarrow d_2(X, Y) \qquad\qquad\quad d_2(dog) \leftarrow$
$d_1(a(mammal)) \leftarrow \qquad\qquad\quad d_3(mammal, [X|X_s]) \leftarrow d_3(X, X_s)$
$d_1(b(cat, mammal)) \leftarrow \qquad\qquad d_3(X, [Y|Y_s]) \leftarrow d_2(X), d_3(Y, Y_s)$
$d_1(b(dog, mammal)) \leftarrow$
$d_1(b(eagle, bird)) \leftarrow$

So, contrary to what is generally believed, unfolding parsing calls during partial deduction does not always lead to optimal results. Unfolding some of the parsing calls, however, seems appropriate. This leaves us with several open issues, to which we will briefly return in Section 5.

4   Specialising an Extended Vanilla Meta Interpreter

In [5, 4], Brogi and Contiero discuss specialisation of the following extended vanilla meta interpreter, adapted here to our notation:

$demo(E, true) \leftarrow$
$demo(E, (A, B)) \leftarrow demo(E, A), demo(E, B).$
$demo(E, H) \leftarrow clause(E, H, B), demo(E, B).$
$clause(union(E_1, E_2), H, B) \leftarrow clause(E_1, H, B).$
$clause(union(E_1, E_2), H, B) \leftarrow clause(E_2, H, B).$
$clause(inters(E_1, E_2), H, B) \leftarrow clause(E_1, H, B), clause(E_2, H, B).$
$clause(enc(E), H, true) \leftarrow demo(E, H).$
$clause(pr(P), H, B) \leftarrow statement(P, H, B).$

The *clause* predicate implements operations needed for program composition: *union, intersection and encapsulation*. Single object programs are represented by $statement(P, H, B)$ facts, where P is the program name, H the clause head and B the clause body. An elaborated discussion of these composition operators can be found in [6, 7, 3, 5].

In the following, D will denote the extended vanilla interpreter above. The combination of D and a fully instantiated composition of object programs e will be denoted by D_e.

In [5], a specific program specialisation technique is developed in order to deal with these program compositions. A thorough discussion of the specialisation method is outside the scope of this paper, but it is noteworthy that the method relies heavily on knowledge about D. In case no *enc* operation is present in e, specialisation of D_e will lead to a program where all manipulations of e are removed. It is also pointed out that this program *can* be transformed into an equivalent object program. No indication, however, is given how to automate this transformation, possibly also relying on information about D. In case e contains an *enc* operation, the method of [5] removes all explicit handling of e, but the resulting program is, in essence, a set of different *solve* vanilla meta interpreters, each with an associated *pclause* database. Thus no overhead due to the interpretation of a single program is removed. Also, since the object level goal is not taken into account during specialisation, no specialisation at the object level can be achieved.

An interesting question is how our general, automatic, partial deduction technique handles specialisation of D_e. Instead of giving a full formal comparison, we present some important observations. Concrete examples and experimental results can be found in Appendix B. As these examples show, our method is capable of achieving object specialisation as well.

Theorem 3. *For any program composition e, $PD(D_e, demo(e, X))$ contains no meta structure concerning e.*

Theorem 4. *For any program composition e not containing an enc operation, $PD(D_e, demo(e, p(\overline{X})))$ with p a predicate in e, contains no meta structure.*

5   Discussion and Further Work

Although in this paper, we did not elaborate all details of the partial deduction method used, we would like to stress some important facts. The partial deduction method presented in this paper is a very general one, not specifically tuned to specialisation of V. The combination of $U_\lhd$ with the global control techniques gave satisfying results in previous contexts (see e.g. [14]). If removal of structure is an important goal, it is necessary not to weaken the variant check on the global level: It should e.g. not be replaced by an (otherwise correct) instance check. Also, the use of $\lhd$ on *atoms* instead of *characteristic* atoms, is too weak. In some examples (e.g. Example 4), the use of characteristic atoms was a key factor in obtaining object specialisation. On the other hand, experiments indicated that the way in which a characteristic tree is imposed upon a generalisation [18, 19] should be refined through further unfolding the greatest common initial subtree. Always simply imposing the latter gives rise to unwanted *clause* atoms in the global tree.

In [27] it is argued that if partial evaluation (PE) has to be able to specialise meta interpreters as effectively as specialisation by hand, numerous enhancements should be incorporated into a basic PE system. Among these are automatic control of termination and the ability to handle more transformations (such as folding). The most vital feature of a PE system [27] however seems to be its flexibility in deciding where to apply which particular transformation. In this paper, we made automatic partial deduction more "flexible" in this sense, by basing decisions it must take on more information.

Other approaches to specialising this kind of meta interpreters rely on additional information about which atoms should be unfolded [16, 31]. Since this information has to be provided by the programmer, automation of the proposed techniques is problematic. In [23], automatic specialisation of meta interpreters is investigated, based on the notion of well-founded unfolding. Although good results are obtained on several examples, some issues in making it a generally applicable technique are still open.

The loop prevention mechanism used in the partial evaluator Mixtus [29] is based on comparing terms by comparing their outermost functors up to a certain (ad hoc) depth and subsequently using the *termsize* function to determine whether there is a danger of looping. While this mechanism performs well on most simple examples, setting the system variables like *max_depth* may be non trivial in the case of specialising more complex meta interpreters.

The effect of always unfolding parsing calls, as described in [16], can be achieved by altering $U_{\unlhd}^{+}$: instead of only using U_{ext} on atoms that would cause a generalisation when brought in the global tree, U_{ext} could be applied to *every* atom that is brought in the global tree. On the other hand, we demonstrated that keeping the object atoms together in one *solve* atom can cause more specialisation to be achieved. In the near future, we will investigate to what extent similar effects can be obtained through conjunctive partial deduction [17, 11]. Keeping the object atoms together in one *solve* atom often results in what we called *specialised* parsing. The question whether this is good or bad is not easily answered, since besides 'parsing', unifications on different head arguments are often involved, indicating that the performance of the specialised program can be system dependent.

As several experiments showed, generalising $solve(C)$ with C a meta representation of an object conjunction, and further processing the generalised atom often does result in a node G on which $solve(C)$ can be mapped during code generation without loss of meta structure. This indicates that $U_{\unlhd}^{+}$ is perhaps too rash, splitting *solve* atoms when it is not necessary and suggests that the decision for which atoms residual code will be generated, should be based on even more information, including information from the global level. This may require to (partially) redo some local unfoldings when more information gets available. However, this is a topic of further research.

U_{ext} and $U_{\unlhd}^{+}$ as introduced in this paper are general rules, not requiring any information about what precisely is "meta" structure. The resulting partial deduction method nevertheless deals very well with V and is, to the best of our knowledge, the first fully automatic, non ad hoc method to do so. In further work, we will investigate its performance in other contexts, including the specialisation of other, more involved meta interpreters.

Acknowledgements

We thank Michael Leuschel for stimulating discussions, and for patiently explaining to us some of the inner workings of his ECCE partial deduction system.

334 Wim Vanhoof and Bern Martens

We also thank Danny De Schreye and Karel De Vlaminck for their interest and support. Finally, we are grateful to anonymous referees for providing valuable feedback which helped to improve the paper.

References

[1] J. Barklund. Metaprogramming in logic. In A. Kent and J.G. Williams, editors, *Encyclopedia of Computer Science and Technology, Vol. 33*, pages 205–227. Marcell Dekker, Inc., New York, 1995.

[2] A. F. Bowers and C. A. Gurr. Towards fast and declarative meta-programming. In K. R. Apt and F. Turini, editors, *Meta-logics and Logic Programming*, pages 137–166. MIT Press, 1995.

[3] A. Brogi and S. Contiero. Gödel as a meta language for composing logic programs. In A. Turini, editor, *Proceedings Meta'94*, pages 377–394. University of Pisa, 1994.

[4] A. Brogi and S. Contiero. A program specialiser for meta-level compositions of logic programs. Technical Report TR-96-20, Dipartimento di Informatica, Università di Pisa, Pisa, Italy, May 1996.

[5] A. Brogi and S. Contiero. Specialising meta-level compositions of logic programs. In J. Gallagher, editor, *Proceedings LOPSTR'96*, pages 275–294, Stockholm, 1997. Springer-Verlag, LNCS 1207.

[6] A. Brogi, P. Mancarella, D. Pedreschi, and F. Turini. Composition operators for logic theories. In J. W. Lloyd, editor, *Proceedings of the Esprit Symposium on Computational Logic*, pages 117–134. Springer-Verlag, November 1990.

[7] A. Brogi, P. Mancarella, D. Pedreschi, and F. Turini. Meta for modularising logic programming. In A. Pettorossi, editor, *Proceedings Meta'92*, pages 105–119. Springer-Verlag, LNCS 649, 1992.

[8] D. De Schreye, M. Leuschel, and B. Martens. Tutorial on program specialisation (abstract). In J.W. Lloyd, editor, *Proceedings ILPS'95*, pages 615–616, Portland, Oregon, December 1995. MIT Press.

[9] J. Gallagher. Transforming logic programs by specialising interpreters. In *Proceedings ECAI'86*, pages 109–122, 1986.

[10] J. Gallagher. Specialisation of logic programs: A tutorial. In *Proceedings PEPM'93, ACM SIGPLAN Symposium on Partial Evaluation and Semantics-Based Program Manipulation*, pages 88–98, Copenhagen, June 1993. ACM Press.

[11] R. Glück, J. Jørgensen, B. Martens, and M. H. Sørensen. Controlling conjunctive partial deduction of definite logic programs. In H. Kuchen and S.D. Swierstra, editors, *Proceedings PLILP'96*, pages 152–166, Aachen, Germany, September 1996. Springer-Verlag, LNCS 1140.

[12] P. M. Hill and J. Gallagher. Meta-programming in logic programming. Technical Report 94.22, School of Computer Studies, University of Leeds, U.K., August 1994. To appear in Volume V of the Handbook of Logic in Artificial Intelligence and Logic Programming, Oxford University Press.

[13] P. M. Hill and J. W. Lloyd. Analysis of meta-programs. In H. D. Abramson and M. H. Rogers, editors, *Proceedings Meta'88*, pages 23–51. MIT Press, 1989.

[14] J. Jørgensen, M. Leuschel, and B. Martens. Conjunctive partial deduction in practice. In J. Gallagher, editor, *Proceedings LOPSTR'96*, pages 59–82, Stockholm, August 1997. Springer-Verlag, LNCS 1207. Shorter and preliminary version in Proceedings of Benelog'96.

[15] A. Lakhotia. To PE or not to PE. In M. Bruynooghe, editor, *Proceedings Meta'90*, pages 218–228, Leuven, April 1990.

[16] A. Lakhotia and L. Sterling. How to control unfolding when specializing interpreters. *New Generation Computing*, 8(1):61–70, 1990.

[17] M. Leuschel, D. De Schreye, and A. de Waal. A conceptual embedding of folding into partial deduction: Towards a maximal integration. In M. Maher, editor, *Proceedings JICSLP'96*, pages 319–332, Bonn, Germany, September 1996. MIT Press.

[18] M. Leuschel and B. Martens. Global control for partial deduction through characteristic atoms and global trees. In O. Danvy, R. Glück, and P. Thiemann, editors, *Proceedings Dagstuhl Seminar on Partial Evaluation*, pages 263–283, Schloss Dagstuhl, Germany, 1996. Springer-Verlag, LNCS 1110.

[19] M. Leuschel, B. Martens, and D. De Schreye. Controlling generalisation and polyvariance in partial deduction of normal logic programs. *ACM Transactions on Programming Languages and Systems*. To Appear. Preliminary version as Technical Report CW248, Departement Computerwetenschappen, K.U.Leuven, February 1997, Belgium. See `http://www.cs.kuleuven.ac.be/publicaties/rapporten/CW1997.html`.

[20] Michael Leuschel. Ecological partial deduction: Preserving characteristic trees without constraints. In Maurizio Proietti, editor, Logic Program Synthesis and Transformation. *Proceedings of LOPSTR'95*, LNCS 1048, pages 1–16, Utrecht, The Netherlands, September 1995. Springer-Verlag.

[21] Michael Leuschel. The ECCE partial deduction system and the DPPD library of benchmarks. Obtainable via `http://www.cs.kuleuven.ac.be/~lpai`, 1996.

[22] J. W. Lloyd and J. C. Shepherdson. Partial evaluation in logic programming. *Journal of Logic Programming*, 11(3&4):217–242, 1991.

[23] B. Martens. *On the Semantics of Meta-Programming and the Control of Partial Deduction in Logic Programming*. PhD thesis, Departement Computerwetenschappen, K.U.Leuven, Belgium, February 1994.

[24] B. Martens and D. De Schreye. Why untyped non-ground meta-programming is not (much of) a problem. *Journal of Logic Programming*, 22(1):47–99, 1995.

[25] B. Martens and D. De Schreye. Automatic finite unfolding using well-founded measures. *Journal of Logic Programming*, 28(2):89–146, 1996.

[26] B. Martens and J. Gallagher. Ensuring global termination of partial deduction while allowing flexible polyvariance. In L. Sterling, editor, *Proceedings ICLP'95*, pages 597–611, Shonan Village Center, Kanagawa, Japan, June 1995. MIT Press.

[27] S. Owen. Issues in the partial evaluation of meta-interpreters. In H. D. Abramson and M. H. Rogers, editors, *Proceedings Meta'88*, pages 319–339. MIT Press, 1989.

[28] S. Safra and E. Shapiro. Meta interpreters for real. In H.-J. Kugler, editor, *Information Processing 86*, pages 271–278, 1986.

[29] D. Sahlin. Mixtus: An automatic partial evaluator for full Prolog. *New Generation Computing*, 12(1):7–51, 1993.

[30] M. H. Sørensen and R. Glück. An algorithm of generalization in positive supercompilation. In J.W. Lloyd, editor, *Proceedings ILPS'95*, pages 465–479, Portland, Oregon, December 1995. MIT Press.

[31] L. Sterling and R. D. Beer. Meta interpreters for expert system construction. *Journal of Logic Programming*, 6(1&2):163–178, 1989.

[32] L. Sterling and E. Shapiro. *The Art of Prolog*. MIT Press, 1986.

[33] A. Takeuchi and K. Furukawa. Partial evaluation of Prolog programs and its application to metaprogramming. In H.-J. Kugler, editor, *Information Processing 86*, pages 415–420, 1986.

A   Proofs

We first introduce some notation: For any program P, we denote by $\mathcal{L}_P$ the language underlying P. If e denotes a program composition, consisting of programs $P_1, \ldots, P_n$, then $\mathcal{L}_e$ denotes the language of e, i.e. $\mathcal{L}_e = \mathcal{L}_{P_1} \cup \ldots \cup \mathcal{L}_{P_n}$.

The proof of Proposition 1 and Corollary 1 is straightforward, since $pclause$ is non recursive. Moreover, Proposition 1 and Corollary 1 also hold when using $U_{\unlhd}^+$.

Lemma 1. *For any program P. Let A be an atom in $\mathcal{L}_P$. Let C be a meta representation of a conjunction of atoms in $\mathcal{L}_P$; $C = (A_1, (A_2, \ldots, (A_{n-1}, A_n)))$. Then $U_{ext}(\leftarrow solve((A, C))) = \leftarrow solve((A, C)), \leftarrow solve(A), solve(C)$.*

Proof. $solve((A, C))$ can be deterministically[7] unfolded by using clause (2) of V, resulting in $solve(A), solve(C)$. Since during this unfolding no instantiations are made in A nor C, $solve(A) \unlhd solve((A, C))$ and $solve(C) \unlhd solve((A, C))$ by Definition 2. Moreover, since only one unfolding was performed, the set $\{solve(A), solve(C)\}$ is the first set $\{p_1, \ldots, p_n\}$ found such that $\forall i \in \{1 \ldots n\}$: $solve(p_i) \unlhd solve((A, C))$. So, by Definition 8, $U_{ext}(\leftarrow solve((A, C))) = \leftarrow solve((A, C)), \leftarrow solve(A), solve(C)$.   □

The following two lemma's imply that every atom in $\mathcal{G}(V_P, G)$ for a program P and goal $G = \leftarrow solve(p(\overline{X}))$ with p a predicate in P, is of the form $solve(A)$ with A an atom in $\mathcal{L}_P$.

Lemma 2. *For any program P, goal G, $\forall G_0 \in \mathcal{G}(V_P, G)$: If $G_0 = \leftarrow solve((A, C))$ with A an atom in $\mathcal{L}_P$ and C an atom or a meta representation of a conjunction of atoms in $\mathcal{L}_P$, then, using $U_{\unlhd}^+$ and global control as defined in Section 2, $\nexists G_a \in Anc(G_0)$ such that $G_a \unlhd solve((A, C))$, where $Anc(G_0)$ denotes the set of ancestors of G_0 in $\mathcal{G}(V_P, G)$.*

Proof. Suppose there exist $G_0, G_a \in \mathcal{G}(V_P, G)$ with $G_a \in Anc(G_0)$ and $G_0 = \leftarrow solve((A, C))$ such that $G_a \unlhd solve((A, C))$. By Algorithm 3.2, $U_{ext}(G_0) = G_0$. Since $G_0 = \leftarrow solve((A, C))$, this contradicts Lemma 1.   □

Lemma 3. *For any program P, goal $G = \leftarrow solve(p(\overline{X}))$ with p a predicate in P, let $\mathcal{G}(V_P, G)$ be the global tree built by $U_{\unlhd}^+$ and the global control as defined in Section 2. Then $solve(true) \notin \mathcal{G}(V_P, G)$.*

Proof. $solve(true)$ is not the root of $\mathcal{G}(V_P, G)$ and since $U_{\unlhd}$ will always unfold $solve(true)$, it cannot occur in a local leaf, and therefore not in $\mathcal{G}(V_P, G)$.   □

The following lemma states that if two atoms in some $\mathcal{G}(V_P, G)$ are generalised, the structure lost by the generalisation will not contain any meta structure.

---
[7]   using a look-ahead.

Lemma 4. *For any program P, goal G, let $\mathcal{G}(V_P, G)$ be the global tree built by $U_{\lhd}^+$ and the global control as defined in Section 2. For any $G_0, G' \in \mathcal{G}(V_P, G)$: If $G_0 \unlhd G'$ such that G_0 is generalised to $G_{gen} = msg(G_0, G')$, then $G_0 = G_{gen}\theta$ where θ is a substitution not containing any meta structure.*

Proof. From Corollary 1, Lemma's 2 and Lemma 3, $G_0 = solve(p(t_1, \ldots, t_n))$ with $p(t_1, \ldots, t_n)$ an atom in $\mathcal{L}_P$. Since $G_0 \unlhd G'$, $G' = solve(p(s_1, \ldots, s_n))$ with $p(s_1, \ldots, s_n)$ an atom in $\mathcal{L}_P$. By the definition of msg, $msg(G_0, G') = solve(p(g_1, \ldots, g_n))$, where $\forall i \in \{1 \ldots n\}$: $g_i = msg(t_i, s_i)$, where t_i and g_i are terms in $\mathcal{L}_P$. From this, the result follows. □

From Lemma 4, the proof of Theorem 2 is straightforward.

Lemma 5. *For any D_e, atoms with clause or statement as predicate are always unfolded by $U_{\lhd}$.*

Proof. Atoms with a *statement* predicate are always unfolded by $U_{\lhd}$ since the definition of *statement* is non recursive. *clause* predicates are recursive, but the first argument of either *clause* or *demo* is fully instantiated and, as can be seen from the definition of D, never growing between successive *clause* or *demo* calls. It even always shrinks in size between successive clause calls. Therefore, in an SLD-tree, no atom $clause(e_1, t_1)$ can have an ancestor $clause(e_2, t_2)$ such that $clause(e_2, t_2) \unlhd clause(e_1, t_1)$. □

Corollary 2. *For any program composition e and goal G, $\mathcal{G}(D_e, G)$ contains only demo atoms if $\mathcal{G}(D_e, G)$ is built using the techniques of Section 2 and $U_{\lhd}$ (or $U_{\lhd}^+$).*

Lemma 6. *Consider two atoms $demo(e_1, t_1)$, $demo(e_2, t_2)$: $demo(e_1, t_1)$ ancestor of $demo(e_2, t_2)$ in $\mathcal{G}(D_e, G)$. If $demo(e_1, t_1) \unlhd demo(e_2, t_2)$, then $e_1 = e_2$.*

Proof. Suppose $e_1 \neq e_2$; since $e_1 \unlhd e_2$, e_2 should be strictly greater than e_1. But then, by the definition of D, $demo(e_2, t_2)$ cannot descend from $demo(e_1, t_1)$. □

Lemma 7. *For a program composition e and atoms t_1, t_2 in $\mathcal{L}_e$: $msg(demo(e, t_1), demo(e, t_2)) = demo(e, msg(t_1, t_2))$.*

Proof. Follows from the definition of msg. □

Proof of Theorem 3

Proof. Since all atoms in $\mathcal{G}(D_e, demo(e, X))$ have *demo* as predicate (Lemma 5), all we must prove is that, when the new predicates are generated, the program composition is filtered away during code generation. The only reason why it would not be filtered away, is because of a generalisation. But by Lemmas 6 and 7, $\forall G \in \mathcal{G}(D_e, demo(e, X))$, $G = demo(e', t)$, e' will not be generalised. □

Proof of Theorem 4

Proof. If e contains no enc operation, $\forall G \in \mathcal{G}(D_e, demo(e, p(\overline{X})))$, $G = demo(e, t)$. Since every atom in $\mathcal{G}(D_e, demo(e, p(\overline{X})))$ contains the same e, and since this e does not influence the generalisations made (see Lemmas 6 and 7), this first argument from all nodes G can be deleted, and the building of $\mathcal{G}(D_e, demo(e, p(\overline{X})))$ can be seen as equivalent to the building of $\mathcal{G}(V_P, solve(p(\overline{X})))$ for some program P, and the proof of Theorem 2 can be used.   □

Proof of Theorem 1

Proof. First, we will prove termination of the algorithm: Since $\tau_{U_\lhd}(A)$ is a finite, possibly incomplete SLD-tree, it has a finite amount of leaves. Therefore, we only need to concentrate on one such leaf. For every branch β in an SLD-tree τ, ending in a leaf L, extending this leaf, by repeatedly performing U_{ext}, will result in the branch β being lengthened a number of times into β'. The set of nodes $\{G_0, \ldots, G_n\} \in \beta'$ is defined as follows: $G_0 = L$, $\forall i \in \{1 \ldots n\}$: $G_i = Leaf(U_{ext}(G_{i-1}))$, where $Leaf(D)$ denotes the end point of the derivation D. No other branches are created in τ since U_{ext} only performs deterministic unfolding. Now, we will proof that β' has a finite number of nodes.

- $U_{ext}(A)$ creates a finite derivation $A = K_0 \ldots K_m$, where $\forall i \in \{0 \ldots m\}$, K_i denotes a goal in the derivation. This follows from using $\lhd$ in Definition 8.
- Consider the nodes $\{G_0 \ldots G_n\}$. This set is finite. Otherwise $\exists i, j$ with $i < j$: $s(G_i) \lhd s(G_j)$. But, by Definition 8, condition (*) and transitivity of $\lhd$, $s(G_j) \lhd s(G_i)$, and we have a contradiction.

The second part of Theorem 1 states that the result of the algorithm is an SLD-tree. By Definition 8, if $U_{ext}(A) = G_0 \ldots G_m$, then $G_0 \ldots G_m$ is an SLD-derivation. The result now follows from Definition 8 and the construction in the $\uplus_L$-algorithm.   □

B   Examples

In this appendix, we show some examples from [4]. Without giving an in depth comparison of the method of [4, 5] with our automatic method, we do present the obtained results.

Consider the following example, adapted from [4]. The example consists of 3 program modules: *path*, *train* and *ic*.

```
statement(path, path(_C1, _C2), train(_C1, _C2, _T)).
statement(path, path(_C1, _C2), (train(_C1, _C3, _T), path(_C3, _C2))).
statement(train, train(florence, pisa, reg), true).
statement(train, train(florence, rome, int), true).
statement(train, train(pisa, genova, nat), true).
statement(train, train(pisa, rome, nat), true).
statement(train, train(milan, florence, int), true).
statement(train, train(milan, pisa, nat), true).
statement(ic, train(_X, _Y, int), true).
```

B.1   Without an *enc* Operation

Example 5. $PD(D_e, demo(union(pr(path), inters(pr(train), pr(ic))), X1))$,
where e denotes $union(pr(path), inters(pr(train), pr(ic)))$.

```
demo(union(pr(path),inters(pr(train),pr(ic))),X1)  :-
    demo__1(X1).
demo__1(true).
demo__1(',' (X1,X2))  :-
    demo__1(X1),
    demo__1(X2).
demo__1(path(X1,X2))  :-
    demo__2(X1,X2).
demo__1(path(X1,X2))  :-
    demo__3(X1,X2).
demo__1(train(florence,rome,int)).
demo__1(train(milan,florence,int)).
demo__2(florence,rome).
demo__2(milan,florence).
demo__3(milan,rome).
```

Notice how demo__1 performs top level parsing, which is unavoidable, since we started with an object goal that is unknown at specialisation time. Besides this top level parsing, all meta structure has vanished from the program. Notice how our automatic technique has performed some specialisation, unrelated to the handling of the program compositions, by precomputing all possible paths (demo__2 and demo__3).

In order to avoid this top level parsing, let us partially deduce the same example, but now w.r.t. a top level predicate path(X,Y):
$PD(D_e, demo(union(pr(path), inters(pr(train), pr(ic))), path(X,Y)))$:

```
demo(union(pr(path),inters(pr(train),pr(ic))),path(X1,X2))  :-
    demo__1(X1,X2).
demo__1(florence,rome).
demo__1(milan,florence).
demo__1(X1,X2):-
    demo__2(X1,X3), demo__1(X3,X2).
demo__2(florence,rome).
demo__2(milan,florence).
```

Notice how the threat of generalisation causes $U_{\trianglelefteq}^+$ to split

$$demo(e, (train(X,Z), path(Z,Y)))$$

into $demo(e, train(X,Z))$ and $demo(e, path(Z,Y))$, thereby loosing the information propagation.[8] In order to avoid this generalisation, let us partially evaluate the same example, but now w.r.t. a new top level predicate p.

---

[8]   Using $U_{\trianglelefteq}$ instead of $U_{\trianglelefteq}^+$ leads to generalisation and a program similar to the one containing top level parsing.

```
statement(path,p(X,Y),path(X,Y)).
```

$PD(D_e, demo(union(pr(path), inters(pr(train), pr(ic))), p(X,Y)))$:[9]

```
demo(union(pr(path),inters(pr(train),pr(ic))),p(X1,X2))  :-
    demo__1(X1,X2).
demo__1(florence,rome).
demo__1(milan,florence).
demo__1(X1,X2)  :-
    demo__2(X1,X2).
demo__2(milan,rome).
```

For comparison, the method of [4] yields the following program:

```
path(X,Y):-train(X,Y,T).
path(X,Y):-train(X,Z,T), path(Z,Y).
train(florence, rome, int).
train(milan, florence, int).
```

B.2   With an *enc* Operation

Example 6. $PD(D_e, demo(union(pr(path), enc(inters(pr(train), pr(ic)))), X1))$, where e denotes $union(pr(path), enc(inters(pr(train), pr(ic))))$:

```
demo__1(true).
demo__1(','(X1,X2))  :-
    demo__1(X1),
    demo__1(X2).
demo__1(path(X1,X2))  :-
    demo__2(X1,X2,X3).
demo__1(path(X1,X2))  :-
    demo__3(X1,X3,X4,X2).
demo__1(','(X1,X2))  :-
    demo__4(X1),
    demo__4(X2).
demo__1(train(florence,rome,int)).
demo__1(train(milan,florence,int)).
demo__2(florence,rome,int).
demo__2(milan,florence,int).
demo__3(milan,florence,int,rome).
demo__4(true).
demo__4(','(X1,X2))  :-
    demo__4(X1),
    demo__4(X2).
demo__4(train(florence,rome,int)).
demo__4(train(milan,florence,int)).
```

In this example, surrounding the intersection between *train* and *ic* with an encapsulation operation does not change the obtained degree of specialisation:

---

[9]   After deterministic post-unfolding, a new demo__1(milan,rome) fact replaces the demo__2 predicate.

besides the necessary top level parsing, no meta structure is present: all manipulations concerning the program compositions have been specialised away, as well as all manipulations concerning parsing of the single object programs. Moreover, all possible paths have once again been precomputed during the specialisation.[10]

Compare this result with the obtained result of the specific technique, as reported in [4]:

```
demo(union(pr(path), enc(inters(pr(train),pr(ic)))), X):- demo_0(X).
demo_0(_E, true).
demo_0(_E, (_H,_T)):-demo_0(_E, _H),demo_0(_E,_T).
demo_0(_E, _H):-clause_0(_E, _H, _B), demo_0(_E, _B).
clause_0(path(_C1, _C2), train(_C1, _C2, _T)).
clause_0(path(_C1, _C2), (train(_C1, _C3,_T), path(_C3, _C2, _T))).
clause_0(X, true):- demo_1(X).
demo_1(_E, true).
demo_1(_E, (_H,_T)):-demo_1(_E, _H),demo_1(_E,_T).
demo_1(_E, _H):-clause_1(_E, _H, _B), demo_1(_E, _B).
clause_1(train(florence, rome, int), true).
clause_1(train(milan, florence, int), true).
```

This example illustrates well the fact that, using the technique of [4, 5], all overhead due to the handling of the program compositions has vanished, but none of the overhead due to the handling (interpretation) of single object programs has.

B.3   Object Specialisation

We conclude with an example showing that extra information in the object goal can be used to obtain specialisation of the object program:

Example 7. $PD(D_e, demo(union(pr(train), pr(path)), path(X, rome)))$, where e denotes $union(pr(train), pr(path))$:

```
demo(union(pr(path),pr(train)),path(X1,rome)) :-
     demo__1(X1).
demo__1(florence).
demo__1(pisa).
demo__1(X1):-
     demo__2(X1,X2),demo__1(X2).
demo__2(florence,pisa).
demo__2(florence,rome).
demo__2(pisa,genova).
demo__2(pisa,rome).
demo__2(milan,florence).
demo__2(milan,pisa).
```

---

[10]   The duplication of the parsing clause demo(','(A,B)) is due to some strange behaviour of the *enc* composition operator: the goal demo(enc(e),(A,B)) will unify with the second clause of D (and a derivation will be started for demo(enc(e),A), demo(enc(e),B)) as well as with the third clause of D (starting a derivation for demo(e,(A,B)), such that the object atoms A and B are evaluated once more. Of course, this behaviour is reflected in the specialised program.

The same remark as in Example 5 can be made. Specialisation w.r.t. p(X,rome) yields (after deterministic post-unfolding and removing duplicate clauses):

```
demo(union(pr(path),pr(train)),p(X1,rome)) :-
    demo__1(X1).
demo__1(florence).
demo__1(pisa).
demo__1(milan).
```

Author Index

Lecture Notes in Computer Science

For information about Vols. 1–1415

please contact your bookseller or Springer-Verlag